RACE, CLASS, AND GENDER IN THE UNITED STATES

An Integrated Study

In this painting I continue to explore our pedestrian world from an overhead perspective. I'm most interested in the spontaneity, gesture, and motion I can experience and witness from above as opposed to composed and controlled movement should my presence be known or the movement prechoreographed; at least for right now. Family and groups have captured my attention and ponderings lately, so I addressed them in this composition.

Leslie Lusardi

RACE, CLASS, AND GENDER IN THE UNITED STATES

An Integrated Study

EIGHTH EDITION

Paula S. Rothenberg
Senior Fellow, The Murphy Institute, CUNY

Worth Publishers

Publisher: Catherine Woods
Acquisitions Editor: Erik Gilg
Marketing Manager: Amy Shefferd
Senior Media Editor: Andrea Musick
Art Director: Babs Reingold
Cover Designer: Kevin Kall
Text Designer: Paul Lacy
Cover Researcher: Bianca Moscatelli
Cover Art: Leslie Lusardi, *4 of 9, Museum,* © 2005
Associate Managing Editor: Tracey Kuehn
Project Editor: Kerry O'Shaughnessy
Production Manager: Barbara Anne Seixas
Composition: Matrix Publishing Services
Printing and Binding: RR Donnelley

Library of Congress Control Number: 2009931820

ISBN-13: 978-1-4292-1788-0
ISBN-10: 1-4292-1788-X

Printed in the United States of America

First printing

Worth Publishers
41 Madison Avenue
New York, NY 10010
www.worthpublishers.com

CONTENTS

Part IV **DISCRIMINATION IN EVERYDAY LIFE** 239

| Part VI | **MANY VOICES, MANY LIVES: SOME CONSEQUENCES OF RACE, CLASS, AND GENDER INEQUALITY** | 373 |

Part VII | **HOW IT HAPPENED:**
RACE AND GENDER ISSUES IN U.S. LAW   491

Part VIII | **MAINTAINING RACE, CLASS, AND GENDER HIERARCHIES: REPRODUCING "REALITY"**   567

Part VIII | SOCIAL CHANGE: REVISIONING THE FUTURE
AND MAKING A DIFFERENCE   **659**

PREFACE

This new edition of *Race, Class, and Gender in the United States* comes at a time of crisis and change for the United States. We hope that both these realities are reflected in the new edition and that the new articles included in it are helpful to its readers as they try to navigate this challenging course. Like its predecessors, this edition undertakes the study of race, gender, and sexuality within the context of class. The book's opening section introduces these issues by simultaneously examining the ways in which each has been socially constructed and by examining the social construction of difference or hierarchy itself, which underlies all of them. Part II takes an in-depth look at racism, sexism, heterosexism, and class privilege and introduces the concepts of patriarchy and white privilege. Designed to both focus on the similarities and differences between and among these forms of oppression and to emphasize the ways in which they intersect, the structure of this book continually explores the interlocking nature of these systems as they work in combination, impacting on virtually every aspect of life in U.S. society today.

New to the last edition was a section entitled "Beyond Black and White: Complicating Issues of Race and Ethnicity." Now, in the eighth edition, it is titled "Race in the 21st Century." It moves beyond the standard Black/white paradigm for race and racism that is operative in this country to encourage a richer and more nuanced understanding of how issues of race and ethnicity play out for a broad spectrum of racial/ethnic groups in this country. The challenge for those of us who think and write about such topics is to do justice to the complexity of the multicultural diversity that increasingly characterizes the United States, and at the same time to not lose sight of the uniquely important defining role that Black/white relations and the history of those relations continues to play in shaping the categories of race and the practice of racism.

One of the most formidable impediments to teaching this material to college-age students is the belief held by some that discrimination based on race, gender, sexual orientation, or class is a thing of the past. A surprising number are convinced that unfair treatment, if it ever existed, has largely been eliminated. Others believe that if unfair treatment exists, it is white people, specifically white men, who are currently disadvantaged. Part IV of this text, "Discrimination in Everyday Life," speaks directly to this misconception. Using newspaper accounts of individual and institutional discrimination, this section reveals the ongoing unfair and unequal treatment that occurs daily in this society based on people's race/ethnicity, class, gender, sexual orientation, or some combination of them. This section is guaranteed to produce some lively classroom discussion.

There are many new articles in this book as well as articles from previous editions that have been reinstated, and some articles from the last edition have been updated by the authors especially for this one. The new articles include "White Like Me" by *New York Times* columnist Frank Rich, Sam Roberts's "A Nation of None and All of the Above," "Race and Extreme Inequality" by Dedrick Muhammad, "Post-Racial? Not Yet" by Fred McKissack Jr., "Forty Acres and a Gap in Wealth" by Henry Louis Gates Jr., "Women Losing Ground" by Ruth Conniff, "Beach Blanket Baja" by Helena María Viramontes, "Her College Experience Is Not His" by Linda Sax, "Gay Marriage Is a Question of Love" by Keith Olbermann, "Upload Real Change" by Roberto Lovato, and "Eight Is Enough" by Patricia J. Williams. Among those specially revised and updated for this edition are Gregory Mantsios' piece on class in America, Holly Sklar's "Imagine a Country—2009," and Paula Ettelbrick's piece on issues of sexuality. This means that, once again, the statistics in this text are as up to date as humanly possible.

New articles and essays consider the ways in which changing U.S. demographics and recent immigration history have complicated both racial and ethnic categories as well as the relationships between and among groups within those categories. Several readings compare the successes and failures of various racial and ethnic groups and the causes for the same. By broadening the consideration of issues of ethnicity and race, this edition reflects some of the ways in which this discourse is changing during the first part of this new century. Additional attention is also paid to examining both white skin privilege and class privilege and making them more visible to readers who are sometimes reluctant to recognize that the flip side of discrimination is privilege.

Throughout this book, issues of gender are framed in inclusive terms so as to include attention to the socialization of men and boys as well as that of women and girls. Attention is paid to some of the ways in which male socialization is related to misogyny and homophobia, and a number of articles make clear that male privilege has its price. On the other hand, a number of articles go beyond victimology to present positive accounts of the experiences of individuals and groups as they claim identities that were previously viewed by many as problematic. Additionally, the Obama administration brings reason for optimism in the changes it has already enacted, for example, President Obama's almost immediate signing of the Lilly Ledbetter Fair Pay Act into law (see "Lilly's Big Day" in Part V).

Part VIII, "Maintaining Race, Class, and Gender Hierarchies: Reproducing 'Reality,'" is particularly strong. Back by popular demand is Mark Snyder's "Self-Fulfilling Stereotypes," and essays by Sut Jhally and Michael Parenti provide hard-hitting and specific criticisms of the way our economic system is organized and whose interests that organization and those priorities serve. In addition, Jonathan Kozol's important article takes a hard look at how education in the United States reproduces race and class hierarchy, while William Chafe explains the role played by violence in maintaining social control.

Finally, Part IX, "Social Change: Revisioning the Future and Making a Difference," brings back several pieces from previous editions that encourage us to redefine difference and to think in broad terms about the kind of society we wish to live in and the kinds of relationships we wish to have with others. These essays by Audre Lorde, bell hooks, and Cooper Thompson serve as a prelude to other articles that focus concretely on the ways in which people who care about issues of inequality, privilege, and injustice can and are making a difference in the world. I think faculty using this book will find that this section allows them to end their courses in a very positive way. This is important because students who study social problems often end up feeling overwhelmed by the extent and severity of these issues. The articles in the last section leave students with an understanding that ordinary people acting on their principles really can make a difference!

Organization and Structure

Individual instructors may wish to modify the order of presentation of readings to conform to their own vision of how this complex and challenging material is best presented. The articles included in the eighth edition provide considerable flexibility in this respect. For example, the Mantsios article on class that appears in Part II could easily be used early in Part V to frame the discussion of the economics of race, class, and gender in the United States. The piece by Evelyn Alsutany, "Los Intersticios," in Part III might well be used in conjunction with essays in Parts I and II to illustrate the ways in which identity is constructed and contextualized, as could Jewelle Gomez's essay in Part VI. Carrie Ching's article "Personal Voices: Facing Up to Race" ends Part III, but it too could be used earlier. Douglas Baynton's essay "Disability and the Justification of Inequality in American History" can be combined with selections 25 and 26 in Part VI to provide a focus on disability issues. Articles that focus on male socialization and men's experience might be grouped together for a special section on the social construction of masculinity. These include the Kimmel essay in Part I, the Johnson piece in Part II, the Sabo, Zirin, Avicollo, Jordan, and Copeland pieces in Part VI, Berger's "White Lies" in Part VIII, and "A New Vision of Masculinity" by Cooper Thompson in Part IX.

I continue to place the historical materials in Part VI, fairly late in the book, because I continue to believe that students are more likely to read and digest this material after their interest has been captured by the more contemporary readings. To my mind, this ordering helps students see that history holds answers to perplexing contemporary questions rather than simply providing background for them. Other instructors will undoubtedly prefer to use the historical material earlier. Countless other reorderings will emerge from the contents, depending on each instructor's own vision for the course being taught. I think this flexibility is one of the strong points of a collection that is genuinely interdisciplinary and inclusive.

In this new edition, I have tried to continue to enlarge the scope of vision and deepen the analysis that prompted this book in the first place. I have been helped by conversations with faculty and students throughout the country who have shared their experiences in using this text with me. The fact that so many have found this book useful confirms my own belief that these topics are an essential part of a liberal education. To me, it is unthinkable that students graduating from college in the twenty-first century would fail to grapple with issues of diversity, difference, and inequality in the course of their studies. This book is intended to facilitate that conversation.

Acknowledgments

Many people contributed to this book. First, I owe a profound debt to the old 12th Street study group, with whom I first studied black history and first came to understand the centrality of the issue of race. I am also indebted to the group's members, who provided me with a lasting example of what it means to commit one's life to the struggle for equality and justice for all people.

Next, I owe an equally profound debt to my friends and colleagues in the New Jersey Project on Inclusive Scholarship, Curriculum, and Teaching, and to friends, colleagues, and students at William Paterson University who have been involved in the various race and gender projects we have carried out over the years. I have learned a great deal from all of them. And, of course, Kelly Mayhew and I have worked on this book for a while now—each time to its betterment, I hope.

I continue to be grateful to Arlene Hirschfelder and Dennis White of the Association of American Indian Affairs and Marion Saviola of the Center for Independence of the Disabled, New York City, for their help. I would also like to thank the faculty and students, too numerous to name, at the many colleges and universities where I have lectured over the years. They have included Berea College, St. Louis Community College, Spellman College, Seton Hall University, Eastern Oregon University, Northern Illinois University, Prescott College, University of South Florida, University of California-Chico, Elmhurst College, New Jersey City University, Jackson State University, The College of New Jersey, and University of Nevada-Las Vegas, to name a few. Their generous sharing of bibliographies, articles, insights, and questions, their thoughtful comments, and the breadth of their perspectives have enriched this book immeasurably. The same is true of the e-mails I have received from faculty and students around the country who have shared with me their responses to this text. I welcome such communications and can be reached at rothenbergp@wpunj.edu.

Over the years, both Judy Baker and Helena Farrell, formerly of The New Jersey Project, made many contributions to the preparation of this book. I thank them still.

The eighth edition has benefited greatly from the professional contributions of many people at Worth Publishers, all of whom set the standard for excellence in the industry. My thanks go to Worth's President, Liz Widdicombe, its Publisher, Catherine Woods, and my superlative editor and friend, Erik E. Gilg. My thanks also go to Assistant Editor Jaclyn Castaldo. Over the years I have worked with a terrific team of professionals at Worth which includes Babs Reingold, Art Director; Kevin Kall, Designer; Katrina Washington, who secured permissions; Tracey Kuehn, Associate Managing Editor; Barbara Seixas, Production Manager; Kerry O'Shaughnessy, Project Editor; Andrea Musick, Senior Media Editor; and Marketing Manager Amy Shefferd.

Finally, I want to thank my partner, Greg Mantsios, and our now-grown children, Alexi Mantsios and Andrea Mantsios, for never giving up and making sure that I didn't either. You mean the world!

Paula Rothenberg

ABOUT THE AUTHOR

Paula Rothenberg writes, lectures, and consults on a variety of topics, including multicultural curriculum transformation, issues of inequality, equity, and privilege, globalizing the curriculum, and white privilege. From 1989 to 2006, she served as Director of The New Jersey Project on Inclusive Scholarship, Curriculum, and Teaching, and Professor of Philosophy and Women's Studies at The William Paterson University of New Jersey. She is the author of *Invisible Privilege: A Memoir about Race, Class and Gender* (University Press of Kansas), and her anthology *White Privilege: Readings on the Other Side of Racism* is now in its third edition. *Beyond Borders: Thinking Critically about Global Issues* was published by Worth in 2005, and her newest anthology, *What's the Problem? A Brief Guide to Critical Thinking*, will be out in 2009. Paula Rothenberg is also co-editor of a number of other anthologies, including *Creating an Inclusive College Curriculum: A Teaching Sourcebook from the New Jersey Project* and *Feminist Frameworks: Alternative Theoretical Accounts of the Relations between Women and Men*. Her articles and essays appear in journals and anthologies across the disciplines and many have been widely reprinted.

RACE, CLASS, AND GENDER IN THE UNITED STATES

An Integrated Study

Introduction

It is impossible to make sense out of either the past or the present without using race, class, gender, and sexuality as central categories of description and analysis. Ironically, many of us are the products of an educational system that has taught us *not* to use these categories and hence, taught us *not* to see the differences in power and privilege that surround us. As a result, things that some people identify as clear examples of sexism or racism appear to others to be simply "the way things are." Understandably, this often makes conversation difficult and frustrating. A basic premise of this book is that much of what passes for a neutral perspective across the disciplines and in cultural life already "smuggles in" elements of class, race, and gender bias and distortion. Because the so-called "neutral" point of view is so pervasive, it is often difficult to identify. One of the goals of this text is to help the reader learn to recognize some of the ways in which issues of race, class, and gender are embedded in ordinary discourse and daily life. Learning to identify and employ race, class, and gender as fundamental categories of description and analysis is essential if we wish to understand our own lives and the lives of others.

Beginning the Study

Beginning our study together makes apparent some immediate differences from other academic enterprises. Whereas students and faculty in an introductory literature or chemistry class rarely begin the semester with deeply felt and firmly entrenched attitudes toward the subject, almost every student in a course that deals with issues of race, class, gender, and sexuality enters the room on the first day with strong feelings, and almost every faculty member does so as well. This can have either very good or very bad consequences. Under the best conditions, and if we acknowledge them head on, these feelings can provide the basis for a passionate and personal study of the topics and can make this course something out of the ordinary, one that has real long-term meaning for both students and teachers. But if we fail to find a way to channel these feelings positively, they are likely to function as obstacles that prevent the study from ever beginning in earnest. For this reason, it is important to acknowledge the existence of these feelings and devise some ground rules for classroom interactions, rules that help create an atmosphere that encourages candid and respectful dialogue.

Approaching this material presents many challenges. Racism, sexism, hetero-sexism, and class privilege are each a system of oppression with its own particular history and its own intrinsic logic (or, illogic); for this reason, it is important to explore each of these systems in its own right. At the same time, these systems operate in conjunction with each other to form an enormously complex set of interlocking and self-perpetuating relations of domination and subordination. It is essential that we understand the ways in which these systems overlap and intersect and play off each other. For purposes of analysis it may be necessary to talk as if it were possible to abstract race or sexuality from, say, gender and class, and subject it to exclusive scrutiny for a time, even though such distinctions are never possible in reality. When we engage in this kind of abstraction, we should never lose sight of the fact that any particular woman or man has an ethnic background, class location, age, sexual orientation, religious orientation, gender, and so forth, and all these characteristics are inseparable from the person and from each other. Always, the particular combination of these identities shapes the individual and locates him or her in society.

It is also true that in talking about racism, sexism, and heterosexism within the context of class, we may have to make generalizations about the experience of different groups of people, even as we affirm that each individual is unique. For example, in order to highlight similarities in the experiences of some individuals, this book often talks about "people of color" or "women of color," even though these terms are somewhat problematic. When I refer to "women" in this book instead of "white women" or "women of color," it is usually in order to focus on the particular experiences or the legal status of women qua women. In doing so, I use language in much the same way that one might write a guide to "the anatomy of the cat." There is no such thing as "the cat" any more than there is "a woman" or there are "people of color." Yet for the purposes of discussion and analysis, it is often necessary to make artificial distinctions in order to focus on particular aspects of experience that may not be separable in reality. Language both mirrors reality and helps to structure it. No wonder, then, that it is so difficult to use our language in ways that adequately address our topics.

Structure of the Book

This book begins with an examination of the ways in which race, class, gender, and sexuality have been socially constructed in the United States as "difference" in the form of hierarchy. Part I treats the idea of difference itself as a social construct, one that underlies and grounds racism, sexism, class privilege, and homophobia. Each of the authors included would agree that while some of these differences may appear to be "natural" or given in nature, they are in fact socially constructed and the meanings and values associated with these differences create a hierarchy of power and privilege that, precisely because it does appear to be "natural," is used to rationalize inequality. Part II introduces the concept of "oppression" in order to examine racism, sexism, heterosexism, and class privilege as interlocking systems of oppression that insure advantages for some and diminished opportunities for others. Part III moves us beyond a black/white paradigm for thinking about issues of race and examines some of the complexities of doing justice to the experiences and the challenges that arise from living in a genuinely diverse, multicultural society in which white privilege continues to play a major role in shaping economic, political, and social life.

Part IV provides us with concrete examples of how the systems of oppression operate in contemporary society. Through the use of newspaper stories and other materials we get a firsthand look at the kinds of discrimination that are faced by members of groups subject to unequal and discriminatory treatment.

What exactly does it mean to claim that someone or some group of people is "different"? What kind of evidence might be offered to support this claim? What does it mean to construct differences? And how does society treat people who are categorized in this way? The readings in Parts I, II, III, and IV of this book are intended to initiate a dialogue about the ways in which U.S. society constructs difference and the social, political, and personal consequences that flow from that construction. These readings encourage us to think about the meaning of racism, sexism, heterosexism, and class privilege and how these systems intersect.

Defining racism and sexism is always a volatile undertaking. Most of us have fairly strong feelings about race and gender relations and have a stake in the way those relations are portrayed and analyzed. Definitions, after all, are powerful. They can focus attention on certain aspects of reality and make others disappear. They may even end up assigning blame or responsibility for the phenomena under consideration. Parts I–IV are intended to initiate this process of definition. The readings allow us to discuss the ways in which we have been taught to think about race, class, and gender differences and to examine how these differences manifest themselves in daily life. The purpose of this entire volume is to carry this enterprise further, deepening our understanding of these phenomena, their manifestations, and their intersections.

Part V provides statistics and analyses that demonstrate the impact of race, class, and gender difference on people's lives. Whereas previous selections depended primarily on narrative to define, describe, and illustrate discrimination and oppression, the material in Part V presents current data, much of it drawn from U.S. government sources, that document the ways in which socially constructed differences mean real differences in opportunity, expectations, and treatment. These differences are brought to life in the articles, poems, and stories in Part VI, which offer a glimpse into the lives of women and men of different ethnic and class backgrounds, expressing their sexuality and culture in a variety of ways. Although many selections are highly personal, each points beyond the individual's experience to social policy or practice or culturally conditioned attitudes.

When people first begin to recognize the enormous toll that racism, sexism, heterosexism, and class privilege takes on our lives, they often are overwhelmed. How can we reconcile our belief that the United States extends liberty and justice and equal opportunity for all with the reality presented in these pages? How did it happen? At this point we must turn to history.

Part VII highlights important aspects of the history of subordinated groups in the United States by focusing on historical documents that address race and gender issues in U.S. law since the beginning of the Republic. When these documents are read in the context of the earlier material describing race, gender, and class differences in contemporary society, history becomes a way of using the past to make sense of the present. Focusing on the legal status of women of all colors and men of color allows us to telescope hundreds of years of history into manageable size, while still providing the historical information needed to make sense of contemporary society.

Our survey of racism and sexism in the United States, past and present, has shown that these phenomena can assume different forms in different contexts. For some, the experiences that Richard Wright describes in "The Ethics of Living Jim Crow" (Part I) are still all too real today; but for others they reflect a crude, blatant racism that seems incompatible with contemporary life. How then are racism, sexism, homophobia, and class privilege perpetuated in contemporary society? Why do these divisions and the accompanying differences in opportunity and achievement continue? How are they reproduced? Why is it so difficult to recognize the reality that lies behind a rhetoric of equality of opportunity and justice for all? Part VIII offers some suggestions.

A classic essay on sex-role conditioning draws an important distinction between discrimination (which frustrates choices already made) and the force of a largely unconscious gender-role ideology (which compromises one's ability to choose).* In Part VIII our discussion of stereotypes, violence, ideology, and social control is concerned with analyzing how the way we conceive of others—and, equally important, the way we come to conceive of ourselves—helps perpetuate racism, sexism, heterosexism, and class privilege. The discussion moves beyond the specificity of stereotypes; it analyzes how modes of conceptualizing reality itself are conditioned by forces that are not always obvious. Racism, sexism, and classism are not only systems of oppression that provide advantages and privileges to some, not simply identifiable attitudes, policies, and practices that affect individuals lives—racism, sexism, heterosexism, and classism operate on a basic level to structure what we come to think of as "reality." In this way, they limit our possibilities and personhood. They cause us to internalize beliefs that distort our perspective and expectations and make it more difficult to identify the origins of unequal and unjust distribution of resources. This hierarchy of privilege and disadvantage has been institutionalized throughout our society and in this way it has been rationalized and normalized. We grow up being taught that the prevailing hierarchy in society is natural and inevitable, perhaps even desirable, and so we fail to identity the unequal distribution itself as a problem.

*Sandra L. Bem and Daryl J. Bem. "Homogenizing the American Woman," in *Beliefs, Attitudes, and Human Affairs* by D. J. Bem (Monterey, Calif.: Brooks/Cole Publishing, 1970), pp. 89–99.

Finally, Part IX offers some suggestions for moving beyond racism, sexism, and classism. The selections are intended to stimulate discussion about the kinds of change we might wish to explore in order to transform society. Some of the articles offer ideas about the causes of and cures for the pervasive social and economic inequality and injustice that are documented in this volume and suggest ways of revisioning our society and our social relationships. Others move from theory to practice by offering very specific suggestions about, and concrete examples of, how to interrupt the cycle of oppression and bring about social change. Some of these articles suggest things that individuals can do in the course of their everyday life in order to make a difference and others provide examples of people working together to bring about social change. But the basic message that comes through all the pieces in this part is summed up in the title of the final essay: "Here. Now. Do Something." The task is enormous, time is short, and our collective future is at stake.

PART I

The Social Construction of Difference: Race, Class, Gender, and Sexuality

Every society grapples with the question of how to distribute its wealth, power, resources, and opportunity. In some cases the distribution is relatively egalitarian and in others it is dramatically unequal. Those societies that tend toward a less egalitarian distribution have adopted various ways to apportion privilege; some have used age, others have used ancestry. United States society, like many others, places a priority on sex, race, and class. To this end, race and gender difference have been portrayed as unbridgeable and immutable. Men and women have been portrayed as polar opposites with innately different abilities and capacities. The very personality traits that were considered positive in a man were seen as signs of dysfunction in a woman, and the qualities that were praised in women were often ridiculed in men. In fact, until very recently, introductory psychology textbooks provided a description of neurosis in a woman that was virtually identical with their description of a healthy male personality.

Race difference has been similarly portrayed. White-skinned people of European origins have viewed themselves as innately superior in intelligence and ability to people with darker skin or different physical characteristics. As both the South Carolina Slave Code of 1712 and the Dred Scott Decision in Part VII make clear, "Negroes" were believed to be members of a different and lesser race. Their enslavement, like the genocide carried out against Native Americans, was justified based on this assumed difference. In the Southwest, Anglo landowners claimed that "Orientals" and Mexicans were naturally suited to perform certain kinds of brutal, sometimes crippling, farm labor to which whites were "physically unable to adapt."[1] Women from various Asian populations have been said to be naturally suited to the tedious and precise labor required in the electronics industry (an appeal to supposedly innate race and gender difference).

Class status, too, has been correlated with supposed differences in innate ability and moral worth. Property qualifications for voting have been used not only to prevent African Americans from exercising the right to vote, but to exclude poor whites as well. From the beginnings of U.S. society, being a person of property was considered an indication of superior intelligence and character. The most dramatic expression of this belief is found in Calvinism, which taught that success in business was a sign of being in God's grace and, similarly, that being poor was a punishment inflicted by the Almighty.

In Part I we begin with a different premise. All the readings in this section argue that, far from reflecting natural and innate differences among people, the categories of gender, race, and class are themselves socially constructed. Rather than being "given" in nature, they reflect culturally constructed differences that maintain the prevailing distribution of power and privilege in a society, and they change in relation to changes in social, political, and economic life.

At first this may seem to be a strange claim. On the face of it, whether a person is male or female or a member of a particular race seems to be a straightforward question of biology. But like most differences that are alleged to be "natural" and "immutable," or unchangeable, the categories of race and gender are far more complex than they might seem. While it is true that most (though, as Judith Lorber points out in Selection 5, not all) of us are born unambiguously "male" or "female" as defined by our chromosomes or genitalia, the meaning of being a man or a woman differs from culture to culture and within each society. It is this difference in connotation or meaning that theorists point to when they claim that gender is socially constructed.

Social scientists distinguish between "sex," which is, in fact, a biologically based category, and "gender," which refers to the particular set of socially constructed meanings that are associated with each sex. These are seen to vary over time and place so that what is understood as "naturally" masculine or feminine behavior in one society may be the exact opposite of what is considered "natural" for women or men in another culture. Furthermore, while it is true that most societies have sex-role stereotypes that identify certain jobs or activities as appropriate for women and others for men, and claim that these divisions reflect "natural" differences in ability and/or interest, there is little consistency in what kinds of tasks have been so categorized. Whereas in many cultures strenuous physical activity is considered to be more appropriate to men than to women, in one society where women are responsible for such labor the heaviest loads are described as being "so heavy only a woman can lift it." In some societies it is women who are responsible for agricultural labor, and in others it is men. Even within cultures that claim that women are unsuited for heavy manual labor, some women (usually women of color and poor, white working women) have always been expected and required to perform backbreaking physical work—on plantations, in factories, on farms, in commercial laundries, and in their homes. The actual lives of real women and real men throughout history stand in sharp contrast to the images of masculinity and femininity that have been constructed by society and then rationalized as reflecting innate differences between the sexes.

In addition to pointing out the enormous differences in how societies have defined what is "naturally" feminine or masculine, and using these disparities to challenge the notion of an innate masculine or feminine nature, some theorists, such as Ruth Hubbard, Judith Lorber, and Michael Kimmel talk about the social construction of gender to make an even more profoundly challenging claim. They argue that the notion of difference itself is constructed and suggest that the claim that women and men are naturally and profoundly different reflects a political and social decision rather than a distinction given in nature. Anthropologist Gayle Rubin explains it this way:

> Gender is a socially imposed division of the sexes. . . . Men and women are, of course, different. But they are not as different as day and night, earth and sky, yin and yang, life and death. In fact from the standpoint of nature, men and women are closer to each other than either is to anything else—for instance mountains, kangaroos, or coconut palms. The idea that men and women are more different from one another than either is from anything else must come from somewhere other than nature.[2]

In fact, we might go on to argue, along with Rubin, that "far from being an expression of natural differences, exclusive gender identity is the suppression of natural similarities."[3] Boys and girls, women and men are under enormous pressure from the earliest ages to conform to sex-role stereotypes that divide basic human attributes between the two sexes. In Selection 5, Judith Lorber argues that differences between women and men are never merely differences but are constructed hierarchically so that women are always portrayed as different in the sense of being deviant and deficient. Central to this construction of difference is the social construction of sexuality, a process Ruth Hubbard, Jonathan Ned Katz, and Michael Kimmel analyze in Selections 6, 7, and 8. If they are correct, in a society where parents thought of their job as raising "human beings" instead of "boys" and "girls," we would likely find all people sharing a wide range of human attributes. In such a society, the belief that men and women naturally occupy two mutually exclusive categories would not structure social, political, and economic life.

The idea of race has been socially constructed in similar ways. The claim that race is a social construction takes issue with the once popular belief that people were born into different races with innate, biologically based differences in intellect, temperament, and character. The idea of ethnicity, in contrast to race, focuses on the shared social/cultural experiences and heritages of various groups and divides or categorizes them according to these shared experiences and traits. The important difference here is that those who talk of race and racial identity believe that they are dividing people according to biological or genetic similarities and differences, whereas those who talk of ethnicity simply point to commonalities that are understood as social, not biological, in origin.

Contemporary historian Ronald Takaki suggests that in the United States, "race . . . has been a social construction that has historically set apart racial minorities from European immigrant groups."[4] Michael Omi and Howard Winant, authors of Selection 1, would agree. They maintain that race is more a political categorization than a biological or scientific category. They point to the relatively arbitrary way in which the category has been constructed and suggest that changes in the meaning and use of racial distinctions can be correlated with economic and political changes in U.S. society. Dark-skinned men and women from Spain were once classified as "white" along with fair-skinned immigrants from England and Ireland, whereas early Greek immigrants were often classified as "Orientals" and subjected to the same discrimination that Chinese and Japanese immigrants experienced under the laws of California and other western states. In South Africa, Japanese immigrants were categorized as "white," not "black" or "colored," presumably because the South African economy depended on trade with Japan. In contemporary U.S. society, dark-skinned Latin people are often categorized as "black" by individuals who continue to equate something called "race" with skin color. In Selection 3, Pem Davidson Buck argues that whiteness and white privilege were constructed historically along with race difference in order to divide working people from each other and in this way protect the wealth and power of a small, privileged elite. In Selection 4, entitled "How Jews Became White Folks," Karen Brodkin provides a detailed account of the specific ways in which the status and classifications of one group, Jewish immigrants to the United States, changed over time as a result of and in relation to economic, political, and social changes in our society.

The claim that race is a social construction is not meant to deny the obvious differences in skin color and physical characteristics that people manifest. It simply sees these differences on a continuum of diversity rather than as reflecting innate genetic differences among peoples. Scientists have long argued that all human beings are descended from a common stock. Some years ago, New York's Museum of Modern Art presented a photography exhibition called *The Family of Man.* It included numerous photographs of people from all over the world and challenged readers to survey the enormous diversity among the people depicted and point out where one race ended and the other began. Of course, it was impossible to do so. The photographs did not reflect sharply distinguished races but simply diversity on one and the same continuum.

The opening line of the autobiographical account by Richard Wright (Selection 2) provides another opportunity to think about the ways in which race is socially constructed. Wright begins his account by announcing, "My first lesson in how to live as a Negro came when I was quite small." Although it is true that Wright was born with dark skin, an unambiguous physical characteristic, it was for others to define the meaning of being black. As Wright's selection makes clear, in the South during the early 1900s it was primarily whites who defined what it meant to be a "Negro." They did so by making clear what behavior would be acceptable and what behavior would provoke violence, perhaps even death. In Part VIII of this book, William Chafe draws an analogy between the way in which (white) women and black men have been socialized in this country under the threat of violence to conform to rigid race and gender roles. The irony is that when this socialization is successful, its results are used to support the claim that sex and race stereotypes are valid and reflect innate differences.

Writing about racism, Algerian-born French philosopher Albert Memmi once explained that racism consists of stressing a difference between individuals or populations. The difference can be real or imagined and in itself doesn't entail racism (or, by analogy, sexism). It is not difference itself that leads to subordination, but the interpretation of difference. It is the assigning of a value to a particular difference in a way that discredits an individual or group to the advantage of another that transforms mere difference into deficiency.[5] In this country, both race and gender difference have been carefully constructed as hierarchy. This means that in the United States, women are not merely described as different than men, but also that difference is understood to leave them deficient. The same is true of race. People of color are not merely described as different from white people, but that difference too is understood as deviance from an acceptable norm—even as pathology—and in both cases difference is used to rationalize racism and sexism.

In Selection 8, Michael Kimmel argues that homophobia is "intimately interwoven with both sexism and racism." According to Kimmel, the ideal of masculinity that prevails in U.S. society today is one that reflects the needs and interests of capitalism. It effectively defines "women, nonwhite men, nonnative-born men, homosexual men" as "other" and deficient, and in this way renders members of all these groups as well as large numbers of white working-class and middle-class men powerless in contemporary society. Our understanding of the ways in which race and gender difference has been constructed is further enriched by Douglas Baynton's analysis in Selection 9. Baynton argues that the idea of disability has functioned historically to justify unequal treatment for women and minority groups as well as justifying inequality for disabled people themselves. In his essay, he explores the ways in which the *concept* of disability has been used at different moments in history to disenfranchise various groups in U.S. society and to justify discrimination against them.

The social construction of class is analogous but not identical to that of race and gender. Differences between rich and poor, which result from particular ways of structuring the economy, are socially constructed as innate differences among people. They are then used to rationalize or justify the unequal distribution of wealth and power that results from economic decisions made to perpetuate privilege. In addition, straightforward numerical differences in earnings are rarely the basis for conferring class status. For example, school teachers and college professors are usually considered to have a higher status than plumbers and electricians even though the latters' earnings are often significantly higher. Where people are presumed to fit into the class hierarchy has less to do with clear-cut numerical categories than it does with the socially constructed superiority of those who perform mental labor (i.e., work with their heads) over those who perform manual labor (i.e., work with their hands). In addition, the status of various occupations and the class position they imply often changes depending on whether the occupation is predominately female or male and according to its racial composition as well.

Equally significant, differences in wealth and family income have been overladen with value judgments and stereotypes to the extent that identifying someone as a member of the middle class, working class, or underclass carries implicit statements about his or her moral character and ability. As Herbert Gans suggests in Selection

10, various ways of classifying and portraying poor people in this country have been used to imply that their poverty reflected a personal failure rather than a social problem for which society as a whole might be held responsible. In the nineteenth century, proponents of Calvinism and social Darwinism maintained that being poor in itself indicated that an individual was morally flawed and thus deserved his or her poverty—again relieving society of any responsibility for social ills.

Finally, class difference can be said to be socially constructed in a way that parallels the construction of race and gender as difference. In this respect, U.S. society is organized in such a way as to make hierarchy or class itself appear natural and inevitable. We grade and rank children from their earliest ages and claim to be sorting them according to something called natural ability. The tracking that permeates our system of education both reflects and creates the expectation that there are A people, B people, C people, and so forth. Well before high school, children come to define themselves and others in just this way and accept this kind of classification as natural. Consequently, quite apart from accepting the particular mythology or ideology of class difference prevailing at any given moment (i.e., "the poor are lazy and worthless" versus "the poor are meek and humble and will inherit the earth"), we come to think it natural and inevitable that there should be class differences in the first place. In the final essay in Part I, Jean Baker Miller asks and answers the question "What do people do to people who are different from them and why?"

NOTES

1. Ronald Takaki, *A Different Mirror: Multicultural American History* (Boston: Little, Brown, 1993), p. 321.

2. Gayle Rubin, "The Traffic in Women," in *Toward an Anthropology of Women*, Rayna R. Reiter, ed. (New York: Monthly Review Press, 1975), p. 179.

3. *Ibid.*, p. 180.

4. Takaki, *Different Mirror.*

5. Albert Memmi, *Dominated Man* (Boston: Beacon Press, 1968).

1

RACIAL FORMATIONS

Michael Omi and Howard Winant

In 1982–83, Susie Guillory Phipps unsuccessfully sued the Louisiana Bureau of Vital Records to change her racial classification from black to white. The descendant of an eighteenth-century white planter and a black slave, Phipps was designated "black" in her birth certificate in accordance with a 1970 state law which declared anyone with at least one-thirty-second "Negro blood" to be black. The legal battle raised intriguing questions about the concept of race, its meaning in contemporary society, and its use (and abuse) in public policy. Assistant Attorney General Ron Davis defended the law by pointing out that some type of racial classification was necessary to comply with federal record-keeping requirements and to facilitate programs for the prevention of genetic diseases. Phipps's attorney, Brian Begue, argued that the assignment of racial categories on birth certificates was unconstitutional and that the one-thirty-second designation was inaccurate. He called on a retired Tulane University professor who cited research indicating that most whites have one-twentieth "Negro" ancestry. In the end, Phipps lost. The court upheld a state law which quantified racial identity, and in so doing affirmed the legality of assigning individuals to specific racial groupings.[1]

The Phipps case illustrates the continuing dilemma of defining race and establishing its meaning in institutional life. Today, to assert that variations in human physiognomy are racially based is to enter a constant and intense debate. *Scientific* interpretations of race have not been alone in sparking heated controversy; *religious* perspectives have done so as well.[2] Most centrally, of course, race has been a matter of *political* contention. This has been particularly true in the United States, where the concept of race has varied enormously over time without ever leaving the center stage of US history.

What Is Race?

Race consciousness, and its articulation in theories of race, is largely a modern phenomenon. When European explorers in the New World "discovered" people who looked different than themselves, these "natives" challenged then existing conceptions of the origins of the human species, and raised disturbing questions as to whether *all* could be considered in the same "family of man."[3] Religious debates flared over the attempt to reconcile the Bible with the existence of "racially distinct" people. Arguments took place over creation itself, as theories of polygenesis questioned whether God had made only one species of humanity ("monogenesis"). Europeans wondered if the natives of the New World were indeed human beings with redeemable souls. At stake were not only the prospects for conversion, but the types of treatment to be accorded them. The expropriation of property, the denial of political rights, the introduction of slavery and other forms of coercive labor, as well as outright extermination, all presupposed a worldview which distinguished Europeans—children of God, human beings, etc.—from "others." Such a worldview was needed to explain why some should be "free" and others enslaved, why some had rights to land and property while others did not. Race, and the interpretation of racial differences, was a central factor in that worldview.

In the colonial epoch science was no less a field of controversy than religion in attempts to comprehend the concept of race and its meaning. Spurred on by the classificatory scheme of living organisms devised by Linnaeus in *Systema Naturae*, many scholars in the eighteenth and nineteenth centuries dedicated themselves to the identification and ranking of variations in humankind. Race was thought of as a *biological* concept, yet its precise definition was the subject of debates which, as we have noted, continue to rage today. Despite efforts ranging from Dr. Samuel Morton's studies of cranial capacity[4] to contemporary attempts to base racial classification on shared gene pools,[5] the concept of race has defied biological definition. . . .

Attempts to discern the *scientific meaning* of race continue to the present day. Although most physical anthropologists and biologists have abandoned the quest for a scientific basis to determine racial categories, controversies have recently flared in the area of genetics and educational psychology. For instance, an essay by Arthur Jensen which argued that hereditary factors shape intelligence not only revived the "nature or nurture" controversy, but raised highly volatile questions about racial equality itself.[6] Clearly the attempt to establish a *biological* basis of race has not been swept into the dustbin of history, but is being resurrected in various scientific arenas. All such attempts seek to remove the concept of race from fundamental social, political, or economic determination. They suggest instead that the truth of race lies in the terrain of innate characteristics, of which skin color and other physical attributes provide only the most obvious, and in some respects most superficial, indicators.

Race as a Social Concept

The social sciences have come to reject biologistic notions of race in favor of an approach which regards race as a *social* concept. Beginning in the eighteenth century, this trend has been slow and uneven, but its direction clear. In the nineteenth century Max Weber discounted biological explanations for racial conflict and instead highlighted the social and political factors which engendered such conflict.[7] The work of pioneering cultural anthropologist Franz Boas was crucial in refuting the scientific racism of the early twentieth century by rejecting the connection between race and culture, and the assumption of a continuum of "higher" and "lower" cultural groups. Within the contemporary social science literature, race is assumed to be a variable which is shaped by broader societal forces.

Race is indeed a pre-eminently *sociohistorical* concept. Racial categories and the meaning of race are given concrete expression by the specific social relations and historical context in which they are embedded. Racial meanings have varied tremendously over time and between different societies.

In the United States, the black/white color line has historically been rigidly defined and enforced. White is seen as a "pure" category. Any racial intermixture makes one "nonwhite." In the movie *Raintree County*, Elizabeth Taylor describes the worst of fates to befall whites as "havin' a little Negra blood in ya' — just one little teeny drop and a person's all Negra."[8] This thinking flows from what Marvin Harris has characterized as the principle of *hypo-descent*:

> By what ingenious computation is the genetic tracery of a million years of evolution unraveled and each man [*sic*] assigned his proper social box? In the United States, the mechanism employed is the rule of hypo-descent. This descent rule requires Americans to believe that anyone who is known to have had a Negro ancestor is a Negro. We admit nothing in between. . . . "Hypo-descent" means affiliation with the subordinate rather than the superordinate group in order to avoid the ambiguity of intermediate identity. . . . The rule of hypo-descent is, therefore, an invention, which we in the United States have made in order to keep biological facts from intruding into our collective racist fantasies.[9]

The Susie Guillory Phipps case merely represents the contemporary expression of this racial logic.

By contrast, a striking feature of race relations in the lowland areas of Latin America since the abolition of slavery has been the relative absence of sharply defined racial groupings. No such rigid descent rule characterizes racial identity in many Latin American societies. Brazil, for example, has historically had less rigid conceptions of race, and thus a variety of "intermediate" racial categories exists. Indeed, as Harris notes, "One of the most striking consequences of the Brazilian system of racial identification is that parents and children and even brothers and sisters are frequently accepted as representatives of quite opposite racial types."[10] Such a possibility is incomprehensible within the logic of racial categories in the US.

To suggest another example: the notion of "passing" takes on new meaning if we compare various American cultures' means of assigning racial identity. In the United States, individuals who are actually "black" by the logic of hypo-descent have attempted to skirt the discriminatory barriers imposed by law and custom by attempting to "pass" for white.[11] Ironically, these same individuals would not be able to pass for "black" in many Latin American societies.

Consideration of the term "black" illustrates the diversity of racial meanings which can be found among different societies and historically within a given society. In contemporary British politics the term "black" is used to refer to all non-whites. Interestingly this designation has not arisen through the racist discourse of groups such as the National Front. Rather, in political and cultural movements, Asian as well as Afro-Caribbean youth are adopting the term as an expression of self-identity.[12] The wide-ranging meanings of "black" illustrate the manner in which racial categories are shaped politically.[13]

The meaning of race is defined and contested throughout society, in both collective action and personal practice. In the process, racial categories themselves are formed, transformed, destroyed and re-formed. We use the term *racial formation* to refer to the process by which social, economic and political forces determine the content and importance of racial categories, and by which they are in turn shaped by racial meanings. Crucial to this formulation is the treatment of race as a *central axis* of social relations which cannot be subsumed under or reduced to some broader category or conception.

Racial Ideology and Racial Identity

The seemingly obvious, "natural" and "common sense" qualities which the existing racial order exhibits themselves testify to the effectiveness of the racial formation process in constructing racial meanings and racial identities.

One of the first things we notice about people when we meet them (along with their sex) is their race. We utilize race to provide clues about *who* a person is. This fact is made painfully obvious when we encounter someone whom we cannot conveniently racially categorize—someone who is, for example, racially "mixed" or of an ethnic/racial group with which we are not familiar. Such an encounter becomes a source of discomfort and momentarily a crisis of racial meaning. Without a racial identity, one is in danger of having no identity.

Our compass for navigating race relations depends on preconceived notions of what each specific racial group looks like. Comments such as, "Funny, you don't look black," betray an underlying image of what black should be. We also become disoriented when people do not act "black," "Latino," or indeed "white." The content of such stereotypes reveals a series of unsubstantiated beliefs about who these groups are and what "they" are like.[14]

In US society, then, a kind of "racial etiquette" exists, a set of interpretative codes and racial meanings which operate in the interactions of daily life. Rules shaped by our perception of race in a comprehensively racial society determine the "presentation of self,"[15] distinctions of status, and appropriate modes of conduct.

"Etiquette" is not mere universal adherence to the dominant group's rules, but a more dynamic combination of these rules with the values and beliefs of subordinated groupings. This racial "subjection" is quintessentially ideological. Everybody learns some combination, some version, of the rules of racial classification, and of their own racial identity, often without obvious teaching or conscious inculcation. Race becomes "common sense"—a way of comprehending, explaining and acting in the world.

Racial beliefs operate as an "amateur biology," a way of explaining the variations in "human nature."[16] Differences in skin color and other obvious physical characteristics supposedly provide visible clues to differences lurking underneath. Temperament, sexuality, intelligence, athletic ability, aesthetic preferences and so on are presumed to be fixed and discernible from the palpable mark of race. Such diverse questions as our confidence and trust in others (for example, clerks or salespeople, media figures, neighbors), our sexual preferences and romantic images, our tastes in music, films, dance, or sports, and our very ways of talking, walking, eating and dreaming are ineluctably shaped by notions of race. Skin color "differences" are thought to explain perceived differences in intellectual, physical and artistic temperaments, and to justify distinct treatment of racially identified individuals and groups.

The continuing persistence of racial ideology suggests that these racial myths and stereotypes cannot be exposed as such in the popular imagination. They are, we think, too essential, too integral, to the maintenance of the US social order. Of course, particular meanings, stereotypes and myths can change, but the presence of a *system* of racial meanings and stereotypes, of racial ideology, seems to be a permanent feature of US culture.

Film and television, for example, have been notorious in disseminating images of racial minorities which establish for audiences what people from these groups look like, how they behave, and "who they are."[17] The power of the media lies not only in their ability to reflect the dominant racial ideology, but in their capacity to shape that ideology in the first place. D. W. Griffith's epic *Birth of a Nation*, a sympathetic treatment of the rise of the Ku Klux Klan during Reconstruction, helped to generate, consolidate and "nationalize" images of blacks which had been more disparate (more regionally specific, for example) prior to the film's appearance.[18] In US television, the necessity to define characters in the briefest and most condensed manner has led to the perpetuation of racial caricatures, as racial stereotypes serve as shorthand for scriptwriters, directors and actors, in commercials, etc. Television's tendency to address the "lowest common denominator" in order to render programs "familiar" to an enormous and diverse audience leads it regularly to assign and reassign racial characteristics to particular groups, both minority and majority.

These and innumerable other examples show that we tend to view race as something fixed and immutable—something rooted in "nature." Thus we mask the historical construction of racial categories, the shifting meaning of race, and the crucial role of politics and ideology in shaping race relations. Races do not emerge full-blown. They are the results of diverse historical practices and are continually subject to challenge over their definition and meaning.

Racialization: The Historical Development of Race

In the United States, the racial category of "black" evolved with the consolidation of racial slavery. By the end of the seventeenth century, Africans whose specific identity was Ibo, Yoruba, Fulani, etc. were rendered "black" by an ideology of exploitation based on racial logic—the establishment and maintenance of a "color line." This of course did not occur overnight. A period of indentured servitude which was not rooted in racial logic preceded the consolidation of racial slavery. With slavery, however, a racially based understanding of society was set in motion which resulted in the shaping of a specific *racial* identity not only for the slaves but for the European settlers as well. Winthrop Jordan has observed: "From the initially common term *Christian*, at mid-century there was a marked shift toward the terms *English* and *free*. After about 1680, taking the colonies as a whole, a new term of self-identification appeared—*white*."[19]

We employ the term *racialization* to signify the extension of racial meaning to a previously racially unclassified relationship, social practice or group. Racialization is an ideological process, an historically specific one. Racial ideology is constructed from pre-existing conceptual (or, if one prefers, "discursive") elements and emerges from the struggles of competing political projects and ideas seeking to articulate similar elements differently. An account of racialization processes that avoids the pitfalls of US ethnic history[20] remains to be written.

Particularly during the nineteenth century, the category of "white" was subject to challenges brought about by the influx of diverse groups who were not of the same Anglo-Saxon stock as the founding immigrants. In the nineteenth century, political and ideological struggles emerged over the classification of Southern Europeans, the Irish and Jews, among other "non-white" categories.[21] Nativism was only effectively curbed by the institutionalization of a racial order that drew the color line *around*, rather than *within*, Europe.

By stopping short of racializing immigrants from Europe after the Civil War, and by subsequently allowing their assimilation, the American racial order was reconsolidated in the wake of the tremendous challenge placed before it by the abolition of racial slavery.[22] With the end of Reconstruction in 1877, an effective program for limiting the emergent class struggles of the later nineteenth century was forged: the definition of the working class *in racial terms*—as "white." This was not accomplished by any legislative decree or capitalist maneuvering to divide the working class, but rather by white workers themselves. Many of them were recent immigrants, who organized on racial lines as much as on traditionally defined class lines.[23] The Irish on the West Coast, for example, engaged in vicious anti-Chinese race-baiting and committed many pogrom-type assaults on Chinese in the course of consolidating the trade union movement in California.

Thus the very political organization of the working class was in important ways a racial project. The legacy of racial conflicts and arrangements shaped the definition of interests and in turn led to the consolidation of institutional patterns (e.g., segregated unions, dual labor markets, exclusionary legislation) which perpetuated the color line *within* the working class. Selig Perlman, whose study of the development of the labor movement is fairly sympathetic to this process, notes that:

> The political issue after 1877 was racial, not financial, and the weapon was not merely the ballot, but also "direct action"—violence. The anti-Chinese agitation in California, culminating as it did in the Exclusion Law passed by Congress in 1882, was doubtless the most important single factor in the history of American labor, for without it the entire country might have been overrun by Mongolian [sic] labor and *the labor movement might have become a conflict of races instead of one of classes.*[24]

More recent economic transformations in the US have also altered interpretations of racial identities and meanings. The automation of southern agriculture and the augmented labor demand of the postwar boom transformed blacks from a largely rural, impoverished labor force to a largely urban, working-class group by 1970.[25] When boom became bust and liberal welfare statism moved rightwards, the majority of blacks came to be seen, increasingly, as part of the "underclass," as state "dependents." Thus the particularly deleterious effects on blacks of global and national economic shifts (generally rising unemployment rates, changes in the employment structure away from reliance on labor intensive work, etc.) were explained once again in the late 1970s and 1980s (as they had been in the 1940s and mid-1960s) as the result of defective black cultural norms, of familial disorganization, etc.[26] In this way new racial attributions, new racial myths, are affixed to "blacks."[27] Similar changes in racial identity are presently affecting Asians and Latinos, as such economic forces as increasing Third World impoverishment and indebtedness fuel immigration and high interest rates, Japanese competition spurs resentments, and US jobs seem to fly away to Korea and Singapore.[28] . . .

Once we understand that race overflows the boundaries of skin color, super-exploitation, social stratification, discrimination and prejudice, cultural domination and cultural resistance, state policy (or of any other particular social relationship we list), once we recognize the racial dimension present to some degree in *every* identity, institution and social practice in the United States—once we have done this, it becomes possible to speak of *racial formation*. This recognition is hard-won; there is a continuous temptation to think of race as an *essence*, as something fixed, concrete and objective, as (for example) one of the categories just enumerated. And there is also an opposite temptation: to see it as a mere illusion, which an ideal social order would eliminate.

In our view it is crucial to break with these habits of thought. The effort must be made to understand race as *an unstable and "decentered" complex of social meanings constantly being transformed by political struggle*. . . .

NOTES

1. *San Francisco Chronicle*, 14 September 1982, 19 May 1983. Ironically, the 1970 Louisiana law was enacted to supersede an old Jim Crow statute which relied on the idea of "common report" in determining an infant's race. Following Phipps's unsuccessful attempt to change her classification and have the law declared unconstitutional, a legislative effort arose which culminated in the repeal of the law. See *San Francisco Chronicle*, 23 June 1983.

2. The Mormon church, for example, has been heavily criticized for its doctrine of black inferiority.

3. Thomas F. Gossett notes:

> Race theory . . . had up until fairly modern times no firm hold on European thought. On the other hand, race theory and race prejudice were by no means unknown at the time when the English colonists came to North America. Undoubtedly, the age of exploration led many to speculate on race differences at a period when neither Europeans nor Englishmen were prepared to make allowances for vast cultural diversities. Even though race theories had not then secured wide acceptance or even sophisticated formulation, the first contacts of the Spanish with the Indians in the Americas can now be recognized as the beginning of a struggle between conceptions of the nature of primitive peoples which has not yet been wholly settled. (Thomas F. Gossett, *Race: The History of an Idea in America* [New York: Schocken Books, 1965], p. 16).

Winthrop Jordan provides a detailed account of early European colonialists' attitudes about color and race in *White Over Black: American Attitudes Toward the Negro, 1550–1812* (New York: Norton, 1977 [1968]), pp. 3–43.

4. Pro-slavery physician Samuel George Morton (1799–1851) compiled a collection of 800 crania from all parts of the world which formed the sample for his studies of race. Assuming that the larger the size of the cranium translated into greater intelligence, Morton established a relationship between race and skull capacity. Gossett reports that:

> In 1849, one of his studies included the following results: The English skulls in his collection proved to be the largest, with an average cranial capacity of 96 cubic inches. The Americans and Germans were rather poor seconds, both with cranial capacities of 90 cubic inches. At the bottom of the list were the Negroes with 83 cubic inches, the Chinese with 82, and the Indians with 79. (Ibid., p. 74).

On Morton's methods, see Stephen J. Gould, "The Finagle Factor," *Human Nature* (July 1978).

5. Definitions of race founded upon a common pool of genes have not held up when confronted by scientific research which suggests that the differences *within* a given human population are greater than those *between* populations. See L. L. Cavalli-Sforza, "The Genetics of Human Populations," *Scientific American* (September 1974), pp. 81–9.

6. Arthur Jensen, "How Much Can We Boost IQ and Scholastic Achievement?" *Harvard Educational Review*, vol. 39 (1969), pp. 1–123.

7. Ernst Moritz Manasse, "Max Weber on Race," *Social Research*, vol. 14 (1947), pp. 191–221.

8. Quoted in Edward D. C. Campbell, Jr., *The Celluloid South: Hollywood and the Southern Myth* (Knoxville: University of Tennessee Press, 1981), pp. 168–70.

9. Marvin Harris, *Patterns of Race in the Americas* (New York: Norton, 1964), p. 56.

10. Ibid., p. 57.

11. After James Meredith had been admitted as the first black student at the University of Mississippi, Harry S. Murphy announced that he, and not Meredith, was the first black student to attend "Ole Miss." Murphy described himself as black but was able to pass for white and spent nine months at the institution without attracting any notice (ibid., p. 56).

12. A. Sivanandan, "From Resistance to Rebellion: Asian and Afro-Caribbean Struggles in Britain," *Race and Class*, vol. 23, nos. 2–3 (Autumn–Winter 1981).

13. Consider the contradictions in racial status which abound in the country with the most rigidly defined racial categories—South Africa. There a race classification agency is employed to adjudicate claims for upgrading of official racial identity. This is particularly necessary for the "coloured" category. The apartheid system considers Chinese as "Asians" while the Japanese are accorded the status of "honorary whites." This logic nearly detaches race from any grounding in skin color and other physical attributes and nakedly exposes race as a juridical category subject to economic, social and political influences. (We are indebted to Steve Talbot for clarification of some of these points.)

14. Gordon W. Allport, *The Nature of Prejudice* (Garden City, New York: Doubleday, 1958), pp. 184–200.

15. We wish to use this phrase loosely, without committing ourselves to a particular position on such social psychological approaches as symbolic interactionism, which are outside the scope of this study. An interesting study on this subject is S. M. Lyman and W. A. Douglass, "Ethnicity: Strategies of Individual and Collective Impression Management," *Social Research*, vol. 40, no. 2 (1973).

16. Michael Billig, "Patterns of Racism: Interviews with National Front Members," *Race and Class*, vol. 20, no. 2 (Autumn 1978), pp. 161–79.

17. "Miss San Antonio USA Lisa Fernandez and other Hispanics auditioning for a role in a television soap opera did not fit the Hollywood image of real Mexicans and had to darken their faces before filming." Model Aurora Garza said that their faces were bronzed with powder because they looked too white. "'I'm a real Mexican [Garza said] and very dark anyway. I'm even darker right now because I have a tan. But they kept wanting me to make my face darker and darker'" (*San Francisco Chronicle*, 21 September 1984). A similar dilemma faces Asian American actors who feel that Asian character lead roles inevitably go to white actors who make themselves up to be Asian. Scores of Charlie Chan films, for example, have been made with white leads (the last one was the 1981 *Charlie Chan and the Curse of the Dragon Queen*). Roland Winters, who played in six Chan features, was asked by playwright Frank Chin to explain the logic of casting a white man in the role of Charlie Chan: "'The only thing I can think of is, if you want to cast a homosexual in a show, and you get a homosexual, it'll be awful. It won't be funny . . . and maybe there's something there . . .'" (Frank Chin, "Confessions of the Chinatown Cowboy," *Bulletin of Concerned Asian Scholars*, vol. 4, no. 3 [Fall 1972]).

18. Melanie Martindale-Sikes, "Nationalizing 'Nigger' Imagery Through 'Birth of a Nation'," paper prepared for the 73rd Annual Meeting of the American Sociological Association, 4–8 September 1978, in San Francisco.

19. Winthrop D. Jordan, op. cit., p. 95; emphasis added.

20. Historical focus has been placed either on particular racially defined groups or on immigration and the "incorporation" of ethnic groups. In the former case the characteristic ethnicity theory pitfalls and apologetics such as functionalism and cultural pluralism may be avoided, but only by sacrificing much of the focus on race. In the latter case, race is considered a manifestation of ethnicity.

21. The degree of antipathy for these groups should not be minimized. A northern commentator observed in the 1850s: "An Irish Catholic seldom attempts to rise to a higher condition than that in which he is placed, while the Negro often makes the attempt with success." Quoted in Gossett, op. cit., p. 288.

22. This analysis, as will perhaps be obvious, is essentially DuBoisian. Its main source will be found in the monumental (and still largely unappreciated) *Black Reconstruction in the United States, 1860–1880* (New York: Atheneum, 1977 [1935]).

23. Alexander Saxton argues that:

North Americans of European background have experienced three great racial confrontations: with the Indian, with the African, and with the Oriental. Central to each transaction has been a totally one-sided preponderance of power, exerted for the exploitation of nonwhites by the dominant white society. In each case (but especially in the two that began with systems of enforced labor), white workingmen have played a crucial, yet ambivalent, role. They have been both exploited and exploiters. On the one hand, thrown into competition with nonwhites as enslaved or "cheap" labor, they suffered economically; on the other hand, being white, they benefited by that very exploitation which was compelling the nonwhites to work for low wages or for nothing. Ideologically they were drawn in opposite directions. *Racial identification cut at right angles to class consciousness.* (Alexander Saxton, *The Indispensable Enemy: Labor and the Anti-Chinese Movement in California* (Berkeley and Los Angeles: University of California Press, 1971), p. 1; emphasis added.)

24. Selig Perlman, *The History of Trade Unionism in the United States* (New York: Augustus Kelley, 1950), p. 52; emphasis added.

25. Whether southern blacks were "peasants" or rural workers is unimportant in this context. Sometime during the 1960s blacks attained a higher degree of urbanization than whites. Before World War II most blacks had been rural dwellers and nearly 80 percent lived in the South.

26. See George Gilder, *Wealth and Poverty* (New York: Basic Books, 1981); Charles Murray, *Losing Ground* (New York: Basic Books, 1984).

27. A brilliant study of the racialization process in Britain, focused on the rise of "mugging" as a popular fear in the 1970s, in Stuart Hall *et al.*, *Policing the Crisis* (London: Macmillan, 1978).

28. The case of Vincent Chin, a Chinese American man beaten to death in 1982 by a laid-off Detroit auto worker and his stepson who mistook him for Japanese and blamed him for the loss of their jobs, has been widely publicized in Asian American communities. On immigration conflicts and pressures, see Michael Omi, "New Wave Dread: Immigration and Intra–Third World Conflict," *Socialist Review*, no. 60 (November–December 1981).

2

THE ETHICS OF LIVING JIM CROW
An Autobiographical Sketch

Richard Wright

I

My first lesson in how to live as a Negro came when I was quite small. We were living in Arkansas. Our house stood behind the railroad tracks. Its skimpy yard was paved with black cinders. Nothing green ever grew in that yard. The only touch of green we could see was far away, beyond the tracks, over where the white folks lived. But cinders were good enough for me and I never missed the green growing things. And anyhow cinders were fine weapons. You could always have a nice hot war with huge black cinders. All you had to do was crouch behind the brick pillars of a house with your hands full of gritty ammunition. And the first woolly black head you saw pop out from behind another row of pillars was your target. You tried your very best to knock it off. It was great fun.

I never fully realized the appalling disadvantages of a cinder environment till one day the gang to which I belonged found itself engaged in a war with the white boys who lived beyond the tracks. As usual we laid down our cinder barrage, thinking that this would wipe the white boys out. But they replied with a steady bombardment of broken bottles. We doubled our cinder barrage, but they hid behind trees, hedges, and the sloping embankments of their lawns. Having no such fortifications, we retreated to the brick pillars of our homes. During the retreat a broken milk bottle caught me behind the ear, opening a deep gash which bled profusely. The sight of blood pouring over my face completely demoralized our ranks. My fellow-combatants left me standing paralyzed in the center of the yard, and scurried for their homes. A kind neighbor saw me and rushed me to a doctor, who took three stitches in my neck.

I sat brooding on my front steps, nursing my wound and waiting for my mother to come from work. I felt that a grave injustice had been done me. It was all right to throw cinders. The greatest harm a cinder could do was leave a bruise. But broken bottles were dangerous; they left you cut, bleeding, and helpless.

When night fell, my mother came from the white folks' kitchen. I raced down the street to meet her. I could just feel in my bones that she would understand. I knew she would tell me exactly what to do next time. I grabbed her hand and babbled out the whole story. She examined my wound, then slapped me.

"How come yuh didn't hide?" she asked me. "How come yuh awways fightin'?"

I was outraged, and bawled. Between sobs I told her that I didn't have any trees or hedges to hide behind. There wasn't a thing I could have used as a trench. And you couldn't throw very far when you were hiding behind the brick pillars of a house. She grabbed a barrel stave, dragged me home, stripped me naked, and beat me till I had a fever of one hundred and two. She would smack my rump with the stave, and, while the skin was still smarting, impart to me gems of Jim Crow wisdom. I was never to throw cinders any more. I was never to fight any more wars. I was never, never, under any conditions, to fight *white* folks again. And they were absolutely right in clouting me with the broken milk bottle. Didn't I know she was working hard every day in the hot kitchens of the white folks to make money to take care of me? When was I ever going to learn to be a good boy? She couldn't be bothered with my fights. She finished by telling me that I ought to be thankful to God as long as I lived that they didn't kill me.

All that night I was delirious and could not sleep. Each time I closed my eyes I saw monstrous white faces suspended from the ceiling, leering at me.

From that time on, the charm of my cinder yard was gone. The green trees, the trimmed hedges, the cropped lawns grew very meaningful, became a symbol. Even today when I think of white folks, the hard, sharp outlines of white houses surrounded by trees, lawns, and hedges are present somewhere in the background of my mind. Through the years they grew into an overreaching symbol of fear.

It was a long time before I came in close contact with white folks again. We moved from Arkansas to Mississippi. Here we had the good fortune not to live behind the railroad tracks, or close to white neighborhoods. We lived in the very heart of the local Black Belt. There were black churches and black preachers; there were black schools and black teachers; black groceries and black clerks. In fact, everything was so solidly black that for a long time I did not even think of white folks, save in remote and vague terms. But this could not last forever. As one grows older one eats more. One's clothing costs more. When I finished grammar school I had to go to work. My mother could no longer feed and clothe me on her cooking job.

There is but one place where a black boy who knows no trade can get a job, and that's where the houses and faces are white, where the trees, lawns, and hedges are green. My first job was with an optical company in Jackson, Mississippi. The morning I applied I stood straight and neat before the boss, answering all his questions with sharp yessirs and nosirs. I was very careful to pronounce my *sirs* distinctly, in order that he might know that I was polite, that I knew where I was, and that I knew he was a *white* man. I wanted that job badly.

He looked me over as though he were examining a prize poodle. He questioned me closely about my schooling, being particularly insistent about how much mathematics I had had. He seemed very pleased when I told him I had had two years of algebra.

"Boy, how would you like to try to learn something around here?" he asked me.

"I'd like it fine, sir," I said, happy. I had visions of "working my way up." Even Negroes have those visions.

"All right," he said. "Come on."

I followed him to the small factory.

"Pease," he said to a white man of about thirty-five, "this is Richard. He's going to work for us."

Pease looked at me and nodded.

I was then taken to a white boy of about seventeen.

"Morrie, this is Richard, who's going to work for us."

"Whut yuh sayin' there, boy!" Morrie boomed at me.

"Fine!" I answered.

The boss instructed these two to help me, teach me, give me jobs to do, and let me learn what I could in my spare time.

My wages were five dollars a week.

I worked hard, trying to please. For the first month I got along O.K. Both Pease and Morrie seemed to like me. But one thing was missing. And I kept thinking about it. I was not learning anything and nobody was volunteering to help me. Thinking they had forgotten that I was to learn something about the mechanics of grinding lenses, I asked Morrie one day to tell me about the work. He grew red.

"Whut yuh tryin' t' do, nigger, get smart?" he asked.

"Naw; I ain' tryin' t' git smart," I said.

"Well, don't, if yuh know whut's good for yuh!"

I was puzzled. Maybe he just doesn't want to help me, I thought. I went to Pease.

"Say, are yuh crazy, you black bastard?" Pease asked me, his gray eyes growing hard.

I spoke out, reminding him that the boss had said I was to be given a chance to learn something.

"Nigger, you think you're white, don't you?"

"Naw, sir!"

"Well, you're acting mighty like it!"

"But, Mr. Pease, the boss said . . ."

Pease shook his fist in my face.

"This is a *white* man's work around here, and you better watch yourself!"

From then on they changed toward me. They said good-morning no more. When I was just a bit slow in performing some duty, I was called a lazy black son-of-a-bitch.

Once I thought of reporting all this to the boss. But the mere idea of what would happen to me if Pease and Morrie should learn that I had "snitched" stopped me. And after all the boss was a white man, too. What was the use?

The climax came at noon one summer day. Pease called me to his workbench. To get to him I had to go between two narrow benches and stand with my back against a wall.

"Yes, sir," I said.

"Richard, I want to ask you something," Pease began pleasantly, not looking up from his work.

"Yes, sir," I said again.

Morrie came over, blocking the narrow passage between the benches. He folded his arms, staring at me solemnly.

I looked from one to the other, sensing that something was coming.

"Yes, sir," I said for the third time.

Pease looked up and spoke very slowly.

"Richard, Mr. Morrie here tells me you called me *Pease*."

I stiffened. A void seemed to open up in me. I knew this was the show-down.

He meant that I had failed to call him Mr. Pease. I looked at Morrie. He was gripping a steel bar in his hands. I opened my mouth to speak, to protest, to assure Pease that I had never called him simply *Pease*, and that I had never had any intentions of doing so, when Morrie grabbed me by the collar, ramming my head against the wall.

"Now, be careful, nigger!" snarled Morrie, baring his teeth. "*I* heard yuh call 'im *Pease!* 'N' if yuh say yuh didn't, yuh're callin' me a *lie*, see?" He waved the steel bar threateningly.

If I had said: No, sir, Mr. Pease, I never called you *Pease*, I would have been automatically calling Morrie a liar. And if I had said: Yes, sir, Mr. Pease, I called you *Pease*, I would have been pleading guilty to having uttered the worst insult that a Negro can utter to a southern white man. I stood hesitating, trying to frame a neutral reply.

"Richard, I asked you a question!" said Pease. Anger was creeping into his voice.

"I don't remember calling you *Pease*, Mr. Pease," I said cautiously. "And if I did, I sure didn't mean . . ."

"You black son-of-a-bitch! You called me *Pease*, then!" he spat, slapping me till I bent sideways over a bench. Morrie was on top of me, demanding:

"Didn't yuh call 'im *Pease?* If yuh say yuh didn't, I'll rip yo' gut string loose with this bar, yuh black granny dodger! Yuh can't call a white man a lie 'n' git erway with it, you black son-of-a-bitch!"

I wilted. I begged them not to bother me. I knew what they wanted. They wanted me to leave.

"I'll leave," I promised. "I'll leave right *now*."

They gave me a minute to get out of the factory. I was warned not to show up again, or tell the boss.

I went.

When I told the folks at home what had happened, they called me a fool. They told me that I must never again attempt to exceed my boundaries. When you are working for white folks, they said, you got to "stay in your place" if you want to keep working.

II

My Jim Crow education continued on my next job, which was portering in a clothing store. One morning, while polishing brass out front, the boss and his twenty-year-old son got out of their car and half dragged and half kicked a Negro woman into the store. A policeman standing at the corner looked on, twirling his nightstick. I watched out of the corner of my eye, never slackening the strokes of my chamois upon the brass. After a few minutes, I heard shrill screams coming from the rear of the store. Later the woman stumbled out, bleeding, crying, and holding her stomach. When she reached the end of the block, the policeman grabbed her and accused her of being drunk. Silently, I watched him throw her into a patrol wagon.

When I went to the rear of the store, the boss and his son were washing their hands at the sink. They were chuckling. The floor was bloody and strewn with wisps of hair and clothing. No doubt I must have appeared pretty shocked, for the boss slapped me reassuringly on the back.

"Boy, that's what we do to niggers when they don't want to pay their bills," he said, laughing.

His son looked at me and grinned.

"Here, hava cigarette," he said.

Not knowing what to do, I took it. He lit his and held the match for me. This was a gesture of kindness, indicating that even if they had beaten the poor old woman, they would not beat me if I knew enough to keep my mouth shut.

"Yes, sir," I said, and asked no questions.

After they had gone, I sat on the edge of a packing box and stared at the bloody floor till the cigarette went out.

That day at noon, while eating in a hamburger joint, I told my fellow Negro porters what had happened. No one seemed surprised. One fellow, after swallowing a huge bite, turned to me and asked:

"Huh! Is tha' all they did t' her?"

"Yeah. Wasn't tha' enough?" I asked.

"Shucks! Man, she's a lucky bitch!" he said, burying his lips deep into a juicy hamburger. "Hell, it's a wonder they didn't lay her when they got through."

III

I was learning fast, but not quite fast enough. One day, while I was delivering packages in the suburbs, my bicycle tire was punctured. I walked along the hot, dusty road, sweating and leading my bicycle by the handle-bars.

A car slowed at my side.

"What's the matter, boy?" a white man called.

I told him my bicycle was broken and I was walking back to town.

"That's too bad," he said, "Hop on the running board."

He stopped the car. I clutched hard at my bicycle with one hand and clung to the side of the car with the other.

"All set?"

"Yes, sir," I answered. The car started.

It was full of young white men. They were drinking. I watched the flask pass from mouth to mouth.

"Wanna drink, boy?" one asked.

I laughed as the wind whipped my face. Instinctively obeying the freshly planted precepts of my mother, I said:

"Oh, no!"

The words were hardly out of my mouth before I felt something hard and cold smash me between the eyes. It was an empty whisky bottle. I saw stars, and fell backwards from the speeding car into the dust of the road, my feet becoming entangled in the steel spokes of my bicycle. The white men piled out and stood over me.

"Nigger, ain' yuh learned no better sense'n tha' yet?" asked the man who hit me. "Ain't yuh learned t' say *sir* t' a white man yet?"

Dazed, I pulled to my feet. My elbows and legs were bleeding. Fists doubled, the white man advanced, kicking my bicycle out of the way.

"Aw, leave the bastard alone. He's got enough," said one.

They stood looking at me. I rubbed my shins, trying to stop the flow of blood. No doubt they felt a sort of contemptuous pity, for one asked:

"Yuh wanna ride t' town now, nigger? Yuh reckon yuh know enough t' ride now?"

"I wanna walk," I said, simply.

Maybe it sounded funny. They laughed.

"Well, walk, yuh black son-of-a-bitch!"

When they left they comforted me with:

"Nigger, yuh sho better be damn glad it wuz us yuh talked t' tha' way. Yuh're a lucky bastard, 'cause if yuh'd said tha' t' somebody else, yuh might've been a dead nigger now."

IV

Negroes who have lived South know the dread of being caught alone upon the streets in white neighborhoods after the sun has set. In such a simple situation as this the plight of the Negro in America is graphically symbolized. While white strangers may be in these neighborhoods trying to get home, they can pass unmolested. But the color of a Negro's skin makes him easily recognizable, makes him suspect, converts him into a defenseless target.

Late one Saturday night I made some deliveries in a white neighborhood. I was pedaling my bicycle back to the store as fast as I could, when a police car, swerving toward me, jammed me into the curbing.

"Get down and put up your hands!" the policemen ordered.

I did. They climbed out of the car, guns drawn, faces set, and advanced slowly.

"Keep still!" they ordered.

I reached my hands higher. They searched my pockets and packages. They seemed dissatisfied when they could find nothing incriminating. Finally, one of them said:

"Boy, tell your boss not to send you out in white neighborhoods after sundown."

As usual, I said:

"Yes, sir."

V

My next job was a hall-boy in a hotel. Here my Jim Crow education broadened and deepened. When the bell-boys were busy, I was often called to assist them. As many of the rooms in the hotel were occupied by prostitutes, I was constantly called to carry them liquor and cigarettes. These women were nude most of the time. They did not bother about clothing, even for bell-boys. When you went into their rooms, you were supposed to take their nakedness for granted, as though it startled you no more than a blue vase or a red rug. Your presence awoke in them no sense of shame, for you were not regarded as human. If they were alone, you could steal sidelong glimpses at them. But if they were receiving men, not a flicker of your eyelids could show. I remember one incident vividly. A new woman, a huge, snowy-skinned blonde, took a room on my floor. I was sent to wait upon her. She was in bed with a thick-set man; both were nude and uncovered. She said she wanted some liquor and slid out of bed and waddled across the floor to get her money from a dresser drawer. I watched her.

"Nigger, what in hell you looking at?" the white man asked me, raising himself upon his elbows.

"Nothing," I answered, looking miles deep into the blank wall of the room.

"Keep your eyes where they belong, if you want to be healthy!" he said.

"Yes, sir."

VI

One of the bell-boys I knew in this hotel was keeping steady company with one of the Negro maids. Out of a clear sky the police descended upon his home and arrested him, accusing him of bastardy. The poor boy swore he had had no intimate relations with the girl. Nevertheless, they forced him to marry her. When the child arrived, it was found to be much lighter in complexion than either of the two supposedly legal parents. The white men around the hotel made a great joke of it.

They spread the rumor that some white cow must have scared the poor girl while she was carrying the baby. If you were in their presence when this explanation was offered, you were supposed to laugh.

VII

One of the bell-boys was caught in bed with a white prostitute. He was castrated and run out of town. Immediately after this all the bell-boys and hall-boys were called together and warned. We were given to understand that the boy who had been castrated was a "mighty, mighty lucky bastard." We were impressed with the fact that next time the management of the hotel would not be responsible for the lives of "trouble-makin' niggers." We were silent.

VIII

One night, just as I was about to go home, I met one of the Negro maids. She lived in my direction, and we fell in to walk part of the way home together. As we passed the white night-watchman, he slapped the maid on her buttock. I turned around, amazed. The watchman looked at me with a long, hard, fixed-under stare. Suddenly he pulled his gun and asked:

"Nigger, don't yuh like it?"

I hesitated.

"I asked yuh don't yuh like it?" he asked again, stepping forward.

"Yes, sir," I mumbled.

"Talk like it, then!"

"Oh, yes sir!" I said with as much heartiness as I could muster.

Outside, I walked ahead of the girl, ashamed to face her. She caught up with me and said:

"Don't be a fool! Yuh couldn't help it!"

This watchman boasted of having killed two Negroes in self-defense.

Yet, in spite of all this, the life of the hotel ran with an amazing smoothness. It would have been impossible for a stranger to detect anything. The maids, the hallboys, and the bell-boys were all smiles. They had to be.

IX

I had learned my Jim Crow lessons so thoroughly that I kept the hotel job till I left Jackson for Memphis. It so happened that while in Memphis I applied for a job at a branch of the optical company. I was hired. And for some reason, as long as I worked there, they never brought my past against me.

Here my Jim Crow education assumed quite a different form. It was no longer brutally cruel, but subtly cruel. Here I learned to lie, to steal, to dissemble. I learned to play that dual role which every Negro must play if he wants to eat and live.

For example, it was almost impossible to get a book to read. It was assumed that after a Negro had imbibed what scanty schooling the state furnished he had no further need for books. I was always borrowing books from men on the job. One day I mustered enough courage to ask one of the men to let me get books from the library in his name. Surprisingly, he consented. I cannot help but think that he consented because he was a Roman Catholic and felt a vague sympathy for Negroes, being himself an object of hatred. Armed with a library card, I obtained books in the following manner: I would write a note to the librarian, saying: "Please let this nigger boy have the following books." I would then sign it with the white man's name.

When I went to the library, I would stand at the desk, hat in hand, looking as unbookish as possible. When I received the books desired I would take them home. If the books listed in the note happened to be out, I would sneak into the lobby and forge a new one. I never took any chances guessing with the white librarian about what the fictitious white man would want to read. No doubt if any of the white patrons had suspected that some of the volumes they enjoyed had been in the home of a Negro, they would not have tolerated it for an instant.

The factory force of the optical company in Memphis was much larger than that in Jackson, and more urbanized. At least they liked to talk, and would engage the Negro help in conversation whenever possible. By this means I found that many subjects were taboo from the white man's point of view. Among the topics they did not like to discuss with Negroes were the following: American white women; the Ku Klux Klan; France, and how Negro soldiers fared while there; French women; Jack Johnson; the entire northern part of the United States; the Civil War; Abraham Lincoln; U. S. Grant; General Sherman; Catholics; the Pope; Jews; the Republican Party; slavery; social equality; Communism; Socialism; the 13th and 14th Amendments to the Constitution; or any topic calling for positive knowledge or manly self-assertion on the part of the Negro. The most accepted topics were sex and religion.

There were many times when I had to exercise a great deal of ingenuity to keep out of trouble. It is a southern custom that all men must take off their hats when they enter an elevator. And especially did this apply to us blacks with rigid force. One day I stepped into an elevator with my arms full of packages. I was forced to ride with my hat on. Two white men stared at me coldly. Then one of them very kindly lifted my hat and placed it upon my armful of packages. Now the most accepted response for a Negro to make under such circumstances is to look at the white man out of the corner of his eye and grin. To have said: "Thank you!" would have made the white man *think* that you *thought* you were receiving from him a personal service. For such an act I have seen Negroes take a blow in the mouth. Finding the first alternative distasteful, and the second dangerous, I hit upon an acceptable course of action which fell safely between these two poles. I immediately—no sooner than my hat was lifted—pretended that my packages were about to spill, and appeared deeply distressed with keeping them in my arms. In this fashion I evaded having to acknowledge his service, and, in spite of adverse circumstances, salvaged a slender shred of personal pride.

How do Negroes feel about the way they have to live? How do they discuss it when alone amongst themselves? I think this question can be answered in a single sentence. A friend of mine who ran an elevator once told me:

"Lawd, man! Ef it wuzn't fer them polices 'n' them ol' lynch-mobs, there wouldn't be nothin' but uproar down here!"

3

CONSTRUCTING RACE, CREATING WHITE PRIVILEGE

Pem Davidson Buck

Constructing Race

Improbable as it now seems, since Americans live in a society where racial characterization and self-definition appear to be parts of nature, in the early days of colonization before slavery was solidified and clearly distinguished from other forms of forced labor, Europeans and Africans seem not to have seen their physical differences in that way.[1] It took until the end of the 1700s for ideas about race to develop until they resembled those we live with today. Before Bacon's Rebellion, African and European indentured servants made love with each other, married each other, ran away with each other, lived as neighbors, liked or disliked each other according to individual personality. Sometimes they died or were punished together for resisting or revolting. And masters had to free both Europeans and Africans if they survived to the end of their indentures. Likewise, Europeans initially did not place all Native Americans in a single racial category. They saw cultural, not biological, differences among Native Americans as distinguishing one tribe from another and from themselves.

Given the tendency of slaves, servants, and landless free Europeans and Africans to cooperate in rebellion, the elite had to "teach Whites the value of whiteness" in order to divide and rule their labor force.[2] After Bacon's Rebellion they utilized their domination of colonial legislatures that made laws and of courts that administered them, gradually building a racial strategy based on the earlier tightening and lengthening of African indenture. Part of this process was tighter control of voting. Free property-owning blacks, mulattos, and Native Americans, all identified as *not* of European ancestry, were denied the vote in 1723.[3]

To keep the racial categories separate, a 1691 law increased the punishment of European women who married African or Indian men; toward the end of the 1600s a white woman could be whipped or enslaved for marrying a Black. Eventually enslavement for white women was abolished because it transgressed the definition of slavery as black. The problem of what to do with white women's "black" children was eventually partially solved by the control of white women's reproduction to prevent the existence of such children. The potentially "white" children of black women were defined out of existence; they were "black" and shifted from serving a thirty-year indenture to being slaves. To facilitate these reproductive distinctions and to discourage the intimacy that can lead to solidarity and revolts, laws were passed requiring separate quarters for black and white laborers. Kathleen Brown points out that the control of women's bodies thus became critical to the maintenance of whiteness and to the production of slaves.[4] At the same time black men were denied the rights of colonial masculinity as property ownership, guns, and access to white women were forbidden. Children were made to inherit their mother's status, freeing European fathers from any vestiges of responsibility for their offspring born to indentured or enslaved African mothers. This legal shift has had a profound effect on the distribution of wealth in the United States ever since; slaveholding fathers were some of the richest men in the country, and their wealth, distributed among *all* their children, would have created a significant wealthy black segment of the population.

At the same time a changing panoply of specific laws molded European behavior into patterns that made slave revolt and cross-race unity more and more difficult.[5] These laws limited, for instance, the European right to teach slaves to read. Europeans couldn't use slaves in skilled jobs, which were reserved for Europeans. Europeans had to administer prescribed punishment for slave "misbehavior" and were expected to participate in patrolling at night. They did not have the legal right to befriend Blacks. A white servant who ran away with a Black was subject to additional punishment beyond that for simply running away. European rights to free their slaves were also curtailed.

Built into all this, rarely mentioned but nevertheless basic to the elite's ability to create and maintain whiteness, slavery, and exploitation, was the use of force against both Blacks and Whites. Fear kept many Whites from challenging, or even questioning, the system. It is worth quoting Lerone Bennett's analysis of how the differentiation between black and white was accomplished:

> The whole system of separation and subordination rested on official state terror. The exigencies of the situation required men to kill some white people to keep them white and to kill many blacks to keep them black. In the North and South, men and women were maimed, tortured, and murdered in a comprehensive campaign of mass conditioning. The severed heads of black and white rebels were impaled on poles along the road as warnings to black people and white people, and opponents of the status quo were starved to death in chains and roasted slowly over open fires. Some rebels were

branded; others were castrated. This exemplary cruelty, which was carried out as a deliberate process of mass education, was an inherent part of the new system.[6]

Creating White Privilege

White privileges were established. The "daily exercise of white personal power over black individuals had become a cherished aspect of Southern culture," a critically important part of getting Whites to "settle for being white."[7] Privilege encouraged Whites to identify with the big slaveholding planters as members of the same "race." They were led to act on the belief that all Whites had an equal interest in the maintenance of whiteness and white privilege, and that it was the elite—those controlling the economic system, the political system, and the judicial system—who ultimately protected the benefits of being white.[8]

More pain could be inflicted on Blacks than on Whites.[9] Whites alone could bear arms; Whites alone had the right of self-defense. White servants could own livestock; Africans couldn't. It became illegal to whip naked Whites. Whites but not Africans had to be given their freedom dues at the end of their indenture. Whites were given the right to beat any Blacks, even those they didn't own, for failing to show proper respect. Only Whites could be hired to force black labor as overseers. White servants and laborers were given lighter tasks and a monopoly, for a time, on skilled jobs. White men were given the right to control "their" women without elite interference; Blacks as slaves were denied the right to family at all, since family would mean that slave husbands, not owners, controlled slave wives. In 1668, all free African women were defined as labor, for whom husbands or employers had to pay a tithe, while white women were defined as keepers of men's homes, not as labor; their husbands paid no tax on them. White women were indirectly given control of black slaves and the right to substitute slave labor for their own labor in the fields.

Despite these privileges, landless Whites, some of them living in "miserable huts," might have rejected white privilege if they saw that in fact it made little *positive* difference in their lives, and instead merely protected them from the worst *negative* effects of elite punishment and interference, such as were inflicted on those of African descent.[10] After all, the right to whip someone doesn't cure your own hunger or landlessness. By the end of the Revolutionary War unrest was in the air. Direct control by the elite was no longer politically or militarily feasible. Rebellions and attempted rebellions had been fairly frequent in the hundred years following Bacon's Rebellion.[11] They indicated the continuing depth of landless European discontent. Baptist ferment against the belief in the inherent superiority of the upper classes simply underscored the danger.[12]

So landless Europeans had to be given some *material* reason to reject those aspects of their lives that made them similar to landless Africans and Native Americans, and to focus instead on their similarity to the landed Europeans—to accept whiteness as their defining characteristic. Landless Europeans' only real similarity to the elite was their European ancestry itself, so that ancestry had to be given real significance: European ancestry was identified with upward mobility and the right to use the labor of the non-eligible in their upward climb. So, since land at that time was the source of upward mobility, land had to be made available, if only to a few.

Meanwhile, Thomas Jefferson advocated the establishment of a solid white Anglo-Saxon yeoman class of small farmers, who, as property owners, would acquire a vested interest in law and order and reject class conflict with the elite. These small farmers would, by upholding "law and order," support and sometimes administer the legal mechanisms—jails, workhouses and poorhouses, and vagrancy laws—that would control other Whites who would remain a landless labor force. They would support the legal and illegal mechanisms controlling Native Americans, Africans, and poor Whites, becoming a buffer class between the elite and those they most exploited, disguising the elite's continuing grip on power and wealth. . . .

The Psychological Wage

The initial construction of whiteness had been based on a material benefit for Whites: land, or the apparently realistic hope of land. By the 1830s and 1840s, most families identified by their European descent had had several generations of believing their whiteness was real. But its material benefit had faded. Many Whites were poor, selling their labor either as farm renters or as industrial workers, and they feared wage slavery, no longer certain they were much freer than slaves.[13] But this time, to control unrest, the elite had no material benefits they were willing to part with. Nor were employers willing to raise wages. Instead, politicians and elites emphasized whiteness as a benefit in itself.

The work of particular white intellectuals, who underscored the already existing belief in white superiority and the worries about white slavery, was funded by elites and published in elite-owned printing houses.[14] These intellectuals provided fodder for newspaper discussions, speeches, scientific analysis, novels, sermons, songs, and blackface minstrel shows in which white superiority was phrased as if whiteness in and of itself was naturally a benefit, despite its lack of material advantage. This sense of superiority allowed struggling northern Whites to look down their noses at free Blacks and at recent immigrants, particularly the Irish. This version of whiteness was supposed to make up for their otherwise difficult situation, providing them with a "psychological wage" instead of cash—a bit like being employee of the month and given a special parking place instead of a raise.

Many Whites bought into the psychological wage, expressing their superiority over non-Whites and defining them, rather than the capitalists, as the enemy. They focused, often with trade union help, on excluding Blacks and immigrants from skilled trades and better-paying jobs. Employers cooperated in confining Blacks and immigrants to manual labor and domestic work, making a clear definition of the work suitable for white men.[15] Native white men began shifting away from defining themselves by their landowning freedom and independence. Instead they accepted their dependence on capitalists and the control employers exercised over their lives, and began to define themselves by their class position as skilled "mechanics" working for better wages under better working conditions than other people. They became proud of their productivity, which grew with the growing efficiency of industrial technology, and began using it to define whiteness—and manhood. The ethnic of individual hard work gained far wider currency. Successful competition in the labor marketplace gradually became a mark of manhood, and "white man's work" became the defining characteristic of whiteness.[16] Freedom was equated with the right to own and sell your own labor, as opposed to slavery, which allowed neither right. Independence was now defined not only by property ownership but also by possession of skill and tools that allowed wage-earning men to acquire status as a head of household controlling dependents.[17]

This redefinition of whiteness was built as much on changing gender as on changing class relationships.[18] Many native white men and women, including workers, journalists, scientists, and politicians, began discouraging married women from working for wages, claiming that true women served only their own families. Despite this claim—the cult of domesticity, or of true womanhood—many wives of working class men actually did work outside the home. They were less likely to do so in those cases where native men were able, through strikes and the exclusion of women, immigrants, and free Blacks, to create an artificial labor shortage. Such shortages gave native working class men the leverage to force employers to pay them enough to afford a non-earning wife. Women in the families of such men frequently did "stay home" and frequently helped to promote the idea that people who couldn't do the same were genetically or racially or culturally inferior.

But native Whites whose wages actually weren't sufficient struggled on in poverty. If a native woman worked for wages, particularly in a factory, the family lost status. Many female factory workers were now immigrants rather than native Whites. Many had no husband or had husbands whose wages, when they could get work, came nowhere near supporting a family.[19] It is no wonder immigrant women weren't particularly "domestic." Such families didn't meet the cultural requirements for white privilege—male "productivity" in "white man's work" and dependent female "domesticity." These supposed white virtues became a bludgeon with which to defend white privilege and to deny it to not-quite-Whites and not-Whites, helping to construct a new working class hierarchy. This new hierarchy reserved managerial and skilled jobs for "productive" native Whites. So, for the price of reserving better jobs for some native Whites, the capitalist class gained native white consent to their own loss of independence and to keeping most of the working class on abysmally low wages.

In the South, where there was less industry, the psychological wage slowly developed an additional role. It was used not only to gain consent to oppressive industrial relations, but also to convince poor farming Whites to support Southern elites in their conflict with Northern elites. Du Bois points out that by the Civil War

> . . . it became the fashion to pat the disenfranchised poor white man on the back and tell him after all he was white and that he and the planters had a common object in keeping the white man superior. This virus increased bitterness and relentless hatred, and after the war it became a chief ingredient in the division of the working class in the Southern States.[20]

REFERENCES

1. My discussion of the construction of race and racial slavery is deeply indebted to Lerone Bennett, *The Shaping of Black America* (New York: Penguin Books, 1993 [1975]), 1–109. See also Theodore Allen, *Invention of the White Race*, vol. II, *The Origin of Racial Oppression in Anglo-America* (New York: Verso, 1997), 75–109; Audrey Smedley, *Race in North America: Origin and Evolution of a Worldview* (Boulder: Westview Press, 1993), 100–1, 109, 142–3, 198; Kathleen Brown, *Good Wives, Nasty Wenches, and Anxious Patriarchs: Gender, Race, and Power in Colonial Virginia* (Chapel Hill: University of North Carolina Press, 1996), 107–244; bell hooks, *Ain't I a Woman: Black Women and Feminism* (Boston: South End Press, 1981), 15–51.

2. Bennett, *Shaping of Black America*, 74–5.

3. Allen, *Invention*, vol. II, 241.

4. Brown, *Good Wives*, pays particular attention to control of women's bodies and status in producing slavery and race (see especially 181, 129–33, 116); also see Allen, *Invention*, vol. II, 128–35, 146–7, 177–88; Bennett, *Shaping of Black America*, 75.

5. For this section see Bennett, *Shaping of Black America*, 72; Edmund Morgan, *American Slavery, American Freedom: The Ordeal of Colonial Virginia* (New York: W. W. Norton and Co, 1975), 311–3; Allen, *Invention*, vol. II, 249–53.

6. Bennett, *Shaping of Black America*, 73–4.

7. The first quote is from Smedley, *Race in North America*, 224; the second is from David Roediger, *The Wages of Whiteness: Race and the Making of the American Working Class* (New York: Verso, 1991), 6.

8. Allen, *Invention*, vol. II, 162, 248–53, emphasizes that elites invented white supremacy to protect their own interests, although working-class Whites did much of the "dirty work" of oppression.

9. Morgan, *American Slavery*, 312–3. On white privileges see Ronald Takaki, *A Different Mirror: A History of Multicultural America* (Boston: Little, Brown, 1993), 67–8; Allen, *Invention*, vol. II, 250–3; Brown, *Good Wives*, 180–3.

10. The quote is from Allen, *Invention*, vol. II, 256, citing a contemporary traveler.

11. Howard Zinn, *A People's History of the United States* (New York: HarperCollins, 1995, 2nd ed.), 58.

12. Smedley, *Race in North America*, 174–5.

13. Bennett, *Shaping of Black America*, 10, 44–5.

14. Allen, *Invention*, vol. I, 109.

15. On runaways see Morgan, *American Slavery, American Freedom*, 217; Smedley, *Race*, 103–5; Bennett, *Shaping of Black America*, 55.

16. On the tendency to make common cause, see Allen, *Invention*, vol. II, 148–58; Bennett, *Shaping of Black America*, 19–22, 74. On increasing anger and landlessness see Allen, *Invention*, vol. II, 208–9, 343 n. 33; Ronald Takaki, *A Different Mirror: A History of Multicultural America* (Boston: Little, Brown, 1993), 62.

17. Berkeley is quoted in Takaki, *Different Mirror*, 63.

18. On Bacon's Rebellion see Takaki, *Different Mirror*, 63–5; Morgan, *American Slavery, American Freedom*, 254–70; Allen, *Invention*, vol. II, 163–5, 208–17, 239; Brown, *Good Wives*, 137–86. Although interpretations of the rebellion vary widely, it does seem clear that the frightening aspect of the rebellion for those who controlled the drainage system was its dramatic demonstration of the power of a united opposition to those who monopolized land, labor, and trade with Native Americans.

19. Allan Kulikoff, *Tobacco and Slaves: The Development of Southern Cultures in the Chesapeake 1680–1800* (Chapel Hill: University of North Carolina Press, 1986), 77, 104–17.

20. Morgan, *American Slavery, American Freedom*, 271–9.

4

HOW JEWS BECAME WHITE FOLKS
And What That Says About Race in America

Karen Brodkin

> The American nation was founded and developed by the Nordic race, but if a few more million members of the Alpine, Mediterranean and Semitic races are poured among us, the result must inevitably be a hybrid race of people as worthless and futile as the good-for-nothing mongrels of Central America and Southeastern Europe.
>
> —KENNETH ROBERTS, "WHY EUROPE LEAVES HOME"

It is clear that Kenneth Roberts did not think of my ancestors as white, like him. The late nineteenth century and early decades of the twentieth saw a steady stream of warnings by scientists, policymakers, and the popular press that "mongrelization" of the Nordic or Anglo-Saxon race—the real Americans—by inferior European races (as well as by inferior non-European ones) was destroying the fabric of the nation.

I continue to be surprised when I read books that indicate that America once regarded its immigrant European workers as something other than white, as biolog-

From *How Jews Became White Folks and What That Says About Race in America* (Rutgers University Press). Reprinted by permission of the author.

ically different. My parents are not surprised; they expect anti-Semitism to be part of the fabric of daily life, much as I expect racism to be part of it. They came of age in the Jewish world of the 1920s and 1930s, at the peak of anti-Semitism in America.[1] They are rightly proud of their upward mobility and think of themselves as pulling themselves up by their own bootstraps. I grew up during the 1950s in the Euro-ethnic New York suburb of Valley Stream, where Jews were simply one kind of white folks and where ethnicity meant little more to my generation than food and family heritage. Part of my ethnic heritage was the belief that Jews were smart and that our success was due to our own efforts and abilities, reinforced by a culture that valued sticking together, hard work, education, and deferred gratification.

I am willing to affirm all those abilities and ideals and their contribution to Jews' upward mobility, but I also argue that they were still far from sufficient to account for Jewish success. I say this because the belief in a Jewish version of Horatio Alger has become a point of entry for some mainstream Jewish organizations to adopt a racist attitude against African Americans especially and to oppose affirmative action for people of color.[2] Instead I want to suggest that Jewish success is a product not only of ability but also of the removal of powerful social barriers to its realization.

It is certainly true that the United States has a history of anti-Semitism and of beliefs that Jews are members of an inferior race. But Jews were hardly alone. American anti-Semitism was part of a broader pattern of late-nineteenth-century racism against all southern and eastern European immigrants, as well as against Asian immigrants, not to mention African Americans, Native Americans, and Mexicans. These views justified all sorts of discriminatory treatment, including closing the doors, between 1882 and 1927, to immigration from Europe and Asia. This picture changed radically after World War II. Suddenly, the same folks who had promoted nativism and xenophobia were eager to believe that the Euro-origin people whom they had deported, reviled as members of inferior races, and prevented from immigrating only a few years earlier, were now model middle-class white suburban citizens.[3]

It was not an educational epiphany that made those in power change their hearts, their minds, and our race. Instead, it was the biggest and best affirmative action program in the history of our nation, and it was for Euromales. That is not how it was billed, but it is the way it worked out in practice. I tell this story to show the institutional nature of racism and the centrality of state policies to creating and changing races. Here, those policies reconfigured the category of whiteness to include European immigrants. There are similarities and differences in the ways each of the European immigrant groups became "whitened." I tell the story in a way that links anti-Semitism to other varieties of anti-European racism because this highlights what Jews shared with other Euro-immigrants.

Euroraces

The U.S. "discovery" that Europe was divided into inferior and superior races began with the racialization of the Irish in the mid-nineteenth century and flowered in response to the great waves of immigration from southern and eastern Europe that began in the late nineteenth century. Before that time, European immigrants—including Jews—had been largely assimilated into the white population. However, the 23 million European immigrants who came to work in U.S. cities in the waves of migration after 1880 were too many and too concentrated to absorb. Since immigrants and their children made up more than 70 percent of the population of most of the country's largest cities, by the 1890s urban America had taken on a distinctly southern and eastern European immigrant flavor. Like the Irish in Boston and New York, their urban concentrations in dilapidated neighborhoods put them cheek by jowl next to the rising elites and the middle class with whom they shared public space and to whom their working-class ethnic communities were particularly visible.

The Red Scare of 1919 clearly linked anti-immigrant with anti-working-class sentiment—to the extent that the Seattle general strike by largely native-born workers was blamed on foreign agitators. The Red Scare was fueled by an economic depression, a massive postwar wave of strikes, the Russian Revolution, and another influx of postwar immigration. . . .

Not surprisingly, the belief in European races took root most deeply among the wealthy, U.S.-born Protestant elite, who feared a hostile and seemingly inassimilable working class. By the end of the nineteenth century, Senator Henry Cabot Lodge pressed Congress to cut off immigration to the United States; Theodore Roosevelt raised the alarm of "race suicide" and took Anglo-Saxon women to task for allowing "native" stock to be outbred by inferior immigrants. In the early twentieth century, these fears gained a great deal of social legitimacy thanks to the efforts of an influential network of aristocrats and scientists who developed theories of eugenics—breeding for a "better" humanity—and scientific racism.

Key to these efforts was Madison Grant's influential *The Passing of the Great Race*, published in 1916. Grant popularized notions developed by William Z. Ripley and Daniel Brinton that there existed three or four major European races, ranging from the superior Nordics of northwestern Europe to the inferior southern and eastern races of the Alpines, Mediterraneans, and worst of all, Jews, who seemed to be everywhere in his native New York City. Grant's nightmare was race-mixing among Europeans. For him, "the cross between any of the three European races and a Jew is a Jew." He didn't have good things to say about Alpine or Mediterranean "races" either. For Grant, race and class were interwoven: the upper class was racially pure Nordic; the lower classes came from the lower races.[4]

Far from being on the fringe, Grant's views were well within the popular mainstream. Here is the *New York Times* describing the Jewish Lower East Side of a century ago:

> The neighborhood where these people live is absolutely impassable for wheeled vehicles other than their pushcarts. If a truck driver tries to get through where

their pushcarts are standing they apply to him all kinds of vile and indecent ep-ithets. The driver is fortunate if he gets out of the street without being hit with a stone or having a putrid fish or piece of meat thrown in his face. This neigh-borhood, peopled almost entirely by the people who claim to have been driven from Poland and Russia, is the eyesore of New York and perhaps the filthiest place on the western continent. It is impossible for a Christian to live there be-cause he will be driven out, either by blows or the dirt and stench. Cleanliness is an unknown quantity to these people. They cannot be lifted up to a higher plane because they do not want to be. If the cholera should ever get among these people, they would scatter its germs as a sower does grain.[5]

Such views were well within the mainstream of the early-twentieth-century sci-entific community.[6] Madison Grant and eugenicist Charles B. Davenport orga-nized the Galton Society in 1918 in order to foster research, promote eugenics, and restrict immigration.[7] . . .

By the 1920s, scientific racism sanctified the notion that real Americans were white and that real whites came from northwest Europe. Racism by white workers in the West fueled laws excluding and expelling the Chinese in 1882. Widespread racism led to closing the immigration door to virtually all Asians and most Euro-peans between 1924 and 1927, and to deportation of Mexicans during the Great Depression.

Racism in general, and anti-Semitism in particular, flourished in higher edu-cation. Jews were the first of the Euro-immigrant groups to enter college in signif-icant numbers, so it was not surprising that they faced the brunt of discrimination there. The Protestant elite complained that Jews were unwashed, uncouth, unre-fined, loud, and pushy. Harvard University President A. Lawrence Lowell, who was also a vice president of the Immigration Restriction League, was open about his opposition to Jews at Harvard. The Seven Sister schools had a reputation for "fla-grant discrimination." . . .

Columbia's quota against Jews was well known in my parents' community. My father is very proud of having beaten it and been admitted to Columbia Dental School on the basis of his skill at carving a soap ball. Although he became a teacher instead because the tuition was too high, he took me to the dentist every week of my childhood and prolonged the agony by discussing the finer points of tooth-filling and dental care. My father also almost failed the speech test required for his teaching license because he didn't speak "standard," i.e., nonimmigrant, nonac-cented English. For my parents and most of their friends, English was the language they had learned when they went to school, since their home and neighborhood language was Yiddish. They saw the speech test as designed to keep all ethnics, not just Jews, out of teaching.

There is an ironic twist to this story. My mother always urged me to speak well, like her friend Ruth Saronson, who was a speech teacher. Ruth remained my model for perfect diction until I went away to college. When I talked to her on one of my visits home, I heard the New York accent of my version of "standard English," compared to the Boston academic version.

My parents believe that Jewish success, like their own, was due to hard work and a high value placed on education. They attended Brooklyn College during the Depression. My mother worked days and went to school at night; my father went during the day. Both their families encouraged them. More accurately, their families expected it. Everyone they knew was in the same boat, and their world was made up of Jews who were advancing just as they were. The picture for New York—where most Jews lived—seems to back them up. In 1920, Jews made up 80 percent of the students at New York's City College, 90 percent of Hunter College, and before World War I, 40 percent of private Columbia University. By 1934, Jews made up almost 24 percent of all law students nationally and 56 percent of those in New York City. Still, more Jews became public school teachers, like my parents and their friends, than doctors or lawyers. Indeed, Ruth Jacknow Markowitz has shown that "my daughter, the teacher" was, for parents, an aspiration equivalent to "my son, the doctor."[8]

How we interpret Jewish social mobility in this milieu depends on whom we compare them to. Compared with other immigrants, Jews were upwardly mobile. But compared with nonimmigrant whites, that mobility was very limited and circumscribed. The existence of anti-immigrant, racist, and anti-Semitic barriers kept the Jewish middle class confined to a small number of occupations. Jews were excluded from mainstream corporate management and corporately employed professions, except in the garment and movie industries, in which they were pioneers. Jews were almost totally excluded from university faculties (the few who made it had powerful patrons). Eastern European Jews were concentrated in small businesses, and in professions where they served a largely Jewish clientele. . . .

My parents' generation believed that Jews overcame anti-Semitic barriers because Jews are special. My answer is that the Jews who were upwardly mobile were special among Jews (and were also well placed to write the story). My generation might well respond to our parents' story of pulling themselves up by their own bootstraps with "But think what you might have been without the racism and with some affirmative action!" And that is precisely what the post-World War II boom, the decline of systematic, public, anti-Euro racism and anti-Semitism, and governmental affirmative action extended to white males let us see.

Whitening Euro-ethnics

By the time I was an adolescent, Jews were just as white as the next white person. Until I was eight, I was a Jew in a world of Jews. Everyone on Avenue Z in Sheepshead Bay was Jewish. I spent my days playing and going to school on three blocks of Avenue Z, and visiting my grandparents in the nearby Jewish neighborhoods of Brighton Beach and Coney Island. There were plenty of Italians in my neighborhood, but they lived around the corner. They were a kind of Jew, but on the margins of my social horizons. Portuguese were even more distant, at the end of the bus ride, at Sheepshead Bay. The *shul*, or temple, was on Avenue Z, and I begged my father to take me like all the other fathers took their kids, but religion wasn't part of my family's Judaism. Just how Jewish my neighborhood was hit me in first grade, when I was one of two kids to go to school on Rosh Hashanah. My teacher was shocked—she was Jewish too—and I was embarrassed to tears when she sent me home. I was never again sent to school on Jewish holidays. We left that world in 1949 when we moved to Valley Stream, Long Island, which was Protestant and Republican and even had farms until Irish, Italian, and Jewish ex-urbanities like us gave it a more suburban and Democratic flavor.

Neither religion nor ethnicity separated us at school or in the neighborhood. Except temporarily. During my elementary school years, I remember a fair number of dirt-bomb (a good suburban weapon) wars on the block. Periodically, one of the Catholic boys would accuse me or my brother of killing his god, to which we'd reply, "Did not," and start lobbing dirt bombs. Sometimes he'd get his friends from Catholic school and I'd get mine from public school kids on the block, some of whom were Catholic. Hostilities didn't last for more than a couple of hours and punctuated an otherwise friendly relationship. They ended by our junior high years, when other things became more important. Jews, Catholics, and Protestants, Italians, Irish, Poles, "English" (I don't remember hearing WASP as a kid), were mixed up on the block and in school. We thought of ourselves as middle class and very enlightened because our ethnic backgrounds seemed so irrelevant to high school culture. We didn't see race (we thought), and racism was not part of our peer consciousness. Nor were the immigrant or working-class histories of our families.

As with most chicken-and-egg problems, it is hard to know which came first. Did Jews and other Euro-ethnics become white because they became middle-class? That is, did money whiten? Or did being incorporated into an expanded version of whiteness open up the economic doors to middle-class status? Clearly, both tendencies were at work.

Some of the changes set in motion during the war against fascism led to a more inclusive version of whiteness. Anti-Semitism and anti-European racism lost respectability. The 1940 Census no longer distinguished native whites of native parentage from those, like my parents, of immigrant parentage, so Euro-immigrants and their children were more securely white by submersion in an expanded notion of whiteness.[9]

Theories of nurture and culture replaced theories of nature and biology. Instead of dirty and dangerous races that would destroy American democracy, immigrants became ethnic groups whose children had successfully assimilated into the mainstream and risen to the middle class. In this new myth, Euro-ethnic suburbs like mine became the measure of American democracy's victory over racism. Jewish mobility became a new Horatio Alger story. In time and with hard work, every ethnic group would get a piece of the pie, and the United States would be a nation with equal opportunity for all its people to become part of a prosperous middle-class majority. And it seemed that Euro-ethnic immigrants and their children were delighted to join middle America.

This is not to say that anti-Semitism disappeared after World War II, only that it fell from fashion and was driven underground. . . .

Although changing views on who was white made it easier for Euro-ethnics to become middle class, economic prosperity also played a very powerful role in the whitening process. The economic mobility of Jews and other Euro-ethnics derived ultimately from America's postwar economic prosperity and its enormously expanded need for professional, technical, and managerial labor, as well as on government assistance in providing it.

The United States emerged from the war with the strongest economy in the world. Real wages rose between 1946 and 1960, increasing buying power a hefty 22 percent and giving most Americans some discretionary income. American manufacturing, banking, and business services were increasingly dominated by large corporations, and these grew into multinational corporations. Their organizational centers lay in big, new urban headquarters that demanded growing numbers of clerical, technical, and managerial workers. The postwar period was a historic moment for real class mobility and for the affluence we have erroneously come to believe was the American norm. It was a time when the old white and the newly white masses became middle class.[10]

The GI Bill of Rights, as the 1944 Serviceman's Readjustment Act was known, is arguably the most massive affirmative action program in American history. It was created to develop needed labor force skills and to provide those who had them with a lifestyle that reflected their value to the economy. The GI benefits that were ultimately extended to 16 million GIs (of the Korean War as well) included priority in jobs—that is, preferential hiring, but no one objected to it then—financial support during the job search, small loans for starting up businesses, and most important, low-interest home loans and educational benefits, which included tuition and living expenses. This legislation was rightly regarded as one of the most revolutionary postwar programs. I call it affirmative action because it was aimed at and disproportionately helped male, Euro-origin GIs.[11] . . .

Education and Occupation

It is important to remember that, prior to the war, a college degree was still very much a "mark of the upper class," that colleges were largely finishing schools for Protestant elites. Before the postwar boom, schools could not begin to accommodate the American masses. Even in New York City before the 1930s, neither the public schools nor City College had room for more than a tiny fraction of potential immigrant students.[12]

Not so after the war. The almost 8 million GIs who took advantage of their educational benefits under the GI Bill caused "the greatest wave of college building in American history." White male GIs were able to take advantage of their educational benefits for college and technical training, so they were particularly well positioned to seize the opportunities provided by the new demands for professional, managerial, and technical labor.

It has been well documented that the GI educational benefits transformed American higher education and raised the educational level of that generation and generations to come. With many provisions for assistance in upgrading their educational attainments, veterans pulled ahead of nonveterans in earning capacity. In the long run it was the nonveterans who had fewer opportunities.[13]

. . . Even more significantly, the postwar boom transformed America's class structure—or at least its status structure—so that the middle class expanded to encompass most of the population. Before the war, most Jews, like most other Americans, were part of the working class, defined in terms of occupation, education, and income. Already upwardly mobile before the war relative to other immigrants, Jews floated high on this rising economic tide, and most of them entered the middle class. The children of other immigrants did too. Still, even the high tide missed some Jews. As late as 1973, some 15 percent of New York's Jews were poor or near poor, and in the 1960s, almost 25 percent of employed Jewish men remained manual workers.[14]

The reason I refer to educational and occupational GI benefits as affirmative action programs for white males is because they were decidedly not extended to African Americans or to women of any race. Theoretically they were available to all veterans; in practice women and black veterans did not get anywhere near their share. Women's Army and Air Force units were initially organized as auxiliaries, hence not part of the military. When that status was changed, in July 1943, only those who reenlisted in the armed forces were eligible for veterans' benefits. Many women thought they were simply being demobilized and returned home. The majority remained and were ultimately eligible for veterans' benefits. But there was little counseling, and a social climate that discouraged women's careers and independence cut down on women's knowledge and sense of entitlement. The Veterans Administration kept no statistics on the number of women who used their GI benefits.[15]

The barriers that almost completely shut African American GIs out of their benefits were even more formidable. In Neil Wynn's portrait, black GIs anticipated starting new lives, just like their white counterparts. Over 43 percent hoped to return to school, and most expected to relocate, to find better jobs in new lines of work. The exodus from the South toward the North and West was particularly large. So it was not a question of any lack of ambition on the part of African American GIs. White male privilege was shaped against the backdrop of wartime racism and postwar sexism.

During and after the war, there was an upsurge in white racist violence against black servicemen, in public schools, and by the Ku Klux Klan. It spread to California and New York. The number of lynchings rose during the war, and in 1943 there were antiblack race riots in several large northern cities. Although there was a wartime labor shortage, black people were discriminated against when it came to well-paid defense industry jobs and housing. In 1946, white riots against African Americans occurred across the South and in Chicago and Philadelphia.

Gains made as a result of the wartime civil rights movement, especially in defense-related employment, were lost with peacetime conversion, as black workers were the first to be fired, often in violation of seniority. White women were also laid off, ostensibly to make room for jobs for demobilized servicemen, and in the long run women lost most of the gains they had made in wartime. We now know that women did not leave the labor force in any significant numbers but, instead, were forced to find inferior jobs, largely nonunion, part-time, and clerical.[16]

The military, the Veterans Administration, the U.S. Employment Services (USES), and the Federal Housing Administration effectively denied African American GIs access to their benefits and to new educational, occupational, and residential opportunities. Black GIs who served in the thoroughly segregated armed forces during World War II served under white officers. African American soldiers were given a disproportionate share of dishonorable discharges, which denied them veterans' rights under the GI Bill. Between August and November 1946, for example, 21 percent of white soldiers and 39 percent of black soldiers were dishonorably discharged. Those who did get an honorable discharge then faced the Veterans Administration and the USES. The latter, which was responsible for job placements, employed very few African Americans, especially in the South. This meant that black veterans did not receive much employment information and that the offers they did receive were for low-paid and menial jobs. "In one survey of 50 cities, the movement of blacks into peacetime employment was found to be lagging far behind that of white veterans: in Arkansas ninety-five percent of the placements made by the USES for Afro-Americans were in service or unskilled jobs."[17] African Americans were also less likely than whites, regardless of GI status, to gain new jobs commensurate with their wartime jobs. For example, in San Francisco, by 1948, black Americans "had dropped back halfway to their prewar employment status."[18]

Black GIs faced discrimination in the educational system as well. Despite the end of restrictions on Jews and other Euro-ethnics, African Americans were not welcome in white colleges. Black colleges were overcrowded, but the combination of segregation and prejudice made for few alternatives. About 20,000 black veterans attended college by 1947, most in black colleges, but almost as many, 15,000, could not gain entry. Predictably, the disproportionately few African Americans who did gain access to their educational benefits were able, like their white counterparts, to become doctors and engineers, and to enter the black middle class.[19]

Suburbanization

In 1949, ensconced in Valley Stream, I watched potato farms turn into Levittown and Idlewild (later Kennedy) airport. This was the major spectator sport in our first years on Long Island. A typical weekend would bring various aunts, uncles, and cousins out from the city. After a huge meal, we'd pile into the car—itself a novelty—to look at the bulldozed acres and comment on the matchbox construction. During the week, my mother and I would look at the houses going up within walking distance.

Bill Levitt built a basic, 900–1,000 square foot, somewhat expandable house for a lower-middle-class and working-class market on Long Island, and later in Pennsylvania and New Jersey. Levittown started out as 2,000 units of rental housing at $60 a month, designed to meet the low-income housing needs of returning war vets, many of whom, like my Aunt Evie and Uncle Julie, were living in Quonset huts. By May 1947, Levitt and Sons had acquired enough land in Hempstead Township on Long Island to build 4,000 houses, and by the next February, he had built 6,000 units and named the development after himself. After 1948, federal financing for the construction of rental housing tightened, and Levitt switched to building houses for sale. By 1951, Levittown was a development of some 15,000 families.[20]

At the beginning of World War II, about one-third of all American families owned their houses. That percentage doubled in twenty years. Most Levittowners looked just like my family. They came from New York City or Long Island; about 17 percent were military, from nearby Mitchell Field; Levittown was their first house, and almost everyone was married. Three-quarters of the 1947 inhabitants were white collar, but by 1950 more blue-collar families had moved in, so that by 1951, "barely half" of the new residents were white collar, and by 1960 their occupational profile was somewhat more working class than for Nassau County as a whole. By this time too, almost one-third of Levittown's people were either foreign-born or, like my parents, first-generation U.S.-born.[21]

The Federal Housing Administration (FHA) was key to buyers and builders alike. Thanks to the FHA, suburbia was open to more than GIs. People like us would never have been in the market for houses without FHA and Veterans Administration (VA) low-down-payment, low-interest, long-term loans to young buyers. . . .

The FHA believed in racial segregation. Throughout its history, it publicly and actively promoted restrictive covenants. Before the war, these forbade sales to Jews and Catholics as well as to African Americans. The deed to my house in Detroit had such a covenant, which theoretically prevented it from being sold to Jews or African Americans. Even after the Supreme Court outlawed restrictive covenants in 1948, the FHA continued to encourage builders to write them in against African Americans. FHA underwriting manuals openly insisted on racially homogeneous neighborhoods, and their loans were made only in white neighborhoods. I bought my Detroit house in 1972, from Jews who were leaving a largely African American neighborhood. By that time, restrictive covenants were a dead letter, but block busting by realtors was replacing it.

With the federal government behind them, virtually all developers refused to sell to African Americans. Palo Alto and Levittown, like most suburbs as late as 1960, were virtually all white. Out of 15,741 houses and 65,276 people, averaging 4.2 people per house, only 220 Levittowners, or 52 households, were "nonwhite."

In 1958, Levitt announced publicly, at a press conference held to open his New Jersey development, that he would not sell to black buyers. This caused a furor because the state of New Jersey (but not the U.S. government) prohibited discrimination in federally subsidized housing. Levitt was sued and fought it. There had been a white riot in his Pennsylvania development when a black family moved in a few years earlier. In New Jersey, he was ultimately persuaded by township ministers to integrate. . . .

The result of these policies was that African Americans were totally shut out of the suburban boom. An article in *Harper's* described the housing available to black GIs.

> On his way to the base each morning, Sergeant Smith passes an attractive air-conditioned, FHA-financed housing project. It was built for service families. Its rents are little more than the Smiths pay for their shack. And there are half-a-dozen vacancies, but none for Negroes.[22]

Where my family felt the seductive pull of suburbia, Marshall Berman's experienced the brutal push of urban renewal. In the Bronx, in the 1950s, Robert Moses's Cross-Bronx Expressway erased "a dozen solid, settled, densely populated neighborhoods like our own. . . . [S]omething like 60,000 working- and lower-middle-class people, mostly Jews, but with many Italians, Irish, and Blacks thrown in, would be thrown out of their homes. . . . For ten years, through the late 1950s and early 1960s, the center of the Bronx was pounded and blasted and smashed."[23]

Urban renewal made postwar cities into bad places to live. At a physical level, urban renewal reshaped them, and federal programs brought private developers and public officials together to create downtown central business districts where there had formerly been a mix of manufacturing, commerce, and working-class neighborhoods. Manufacturing was scattered to the peripheries of the city, which were ringed and bisected by a national system of highways. Some working-class neighborhoods were bulldozed, but others remained. In Los Angeles, as in New York's Bronx, the postwar period saw massive freeway construction right through the heart of old working-class neighborhoods. In East Los Angeles and Santa Monica, Chicana/o and African American communities were divided in half or blasted to smithereens by the highways bringing Angelenos to the new white suburbs, or to make way for civic monuments like Dodger Stadium.[24]

Urban renewal was the other side of the process by which Jewish and other working-class Euro-immigrants became middle class. It was the push to suburbia's seductive pull. The fortunate white survivors of urban renewal headed disproportionately for suburbia, where they could partake of prosperity and the good life. . . .

If the federal stick of urban renewal joined the FHA carrot of cheap mortgages to send masses of Euro-Americans to the suburbs, the FHA had a different kind of one-two punch for African Americans. Segregation kept them out of the suburbs, and redlining made sure they could not buy or repair their homes in the neighborhoods in which they were allowed to live. The FHA practiced systematic redlining. This was a practice developed by its predecessor, the Home Owners Loan Corporation (HOLC), which in the 1930s developed an elaborate neighborhood rating system that placed the highest (green) value on all-white, middle-class neighborhoods, and the lowest (red) on racially nonwhite or mixed and working-class neighborhoods. High ratings meant high property values. The idea was that low property values in redlined neighborhoods made them bad investments. The FHA was, after all, created by and for banks and the housing industry. Redlining warned banks not to lend there, and the FHA would not insure mortgages in such neighborhoods. Redlining created a self-fulfilling prophesy.

> With the assistance of local realtors and banks, it assigned one of the four ratings to every block in every city. The resulting information was then translated into the appropriate color [green, blue, yellow, or red] and duly recorded on secret "Residential Security Maps" in local HOLC offices. The maps themselves were placed in elaborate "City Survey Files," which consisted of reports, questionnaires, and workpapers relating to current and future values of real estate.[25]

The FHA's and VA's refusal to guarantee loans in redlined neighborhoods made it virtually impossible for African Americans to borrow money for home improvement or purchase. Because these maps and surveys were quite secret, it took the civil rights movement to make these practices and their devastating consequences public. As a result, those who fought urban renewal, or who sought to make a home in the urban ruins, found themselves locked out of the middle class. They also faced an ideological assault that labeled their neighborhoods slums and called them slumdwellers.[26]

Conclusion

The record is very clear. Instead of seizing the opportunity to end institutionalized racism, the federal government did its level best to shut and double-seal the postwar window of opportunity in African Americans' faces. It consistently refused to combat segregation in the social institutions that were key to upward mobility in education, housing, and employment. Moreover, federal programs that were themselves designed to assist demobilized GIs and young families systematically discriminated against African Americans. Such programs reinforced white/nonwhite racial distinctions even as intrawhite racialization was falling out of fashion. This other side of the coin, that white men of northwest European ancestry and white men of southeastern European ancestry were treated equally in theory and in practice with regard to the benefits they received, was part of the larger postwar whitening of Jews and other eastern and southern Europeans.

The myth that Jews pulled themselves up by their own bootstraps ignores the fact that it took federal programs to create the conditions whereby the abilities of

Jews and other European immigrants could be recognized and rewarded rather than denigrated and denied. The GI Bill and FHA and VA mortgages, even though they were advertised as open to all, functioned as a set of racial privileges. They were privileges because they were extended to white GIs but not to black GIs. Such privileges were forms of affirmative action that allowed Jews and other Euro-American men to become suburban homeowners and to get the training that allowed them—but much less so women vets or war workers—to become professionals, technicians, salesmen, and managers in a growing economy. Jews and other white ethnics' upward mobility was due to programs that allowed us to float on a rising economic tide. To African Americans, the government offered the cement boots of segregation, redlining, urban renewal, and discrimination.

Those racially skewed gains have been passed across the generations, so that racial inequality seems to maintain itself "naturally," even after legal segregation ended. Today, I own a house in Venice, California, like the one in which I grew up in Valley Stream, and my brother until recently owned a house in Palo Alto much like an Eichler house. Both of us are where we are thanks largely to the postwar benefits our parents received and passed on to us, and to the educational benefits we received in the 1960s as a result of affluence and the social agitation that developed from the black Freedom Movement. I have white, African American, and Asian American colleagues whose parents received fewer or none of America's postwar benefits and who expect never to own a house despite their considerable academic achievements. Some of these colleagues who are a few years younger than I also carry staggering debts for their education, which they expect to have to repay for the rest of their lives.

Conventional wisdom has it that the United States has always been an affluent land of opportunity. But the truth is that affluence has been the exception and that real upward mobility has required massive affirmative action programs. . . .

NOTES

1. Gerber 1986; Dinnerstein 1987, 1994.

2. On the belief in Jewish and Asian versions of Horatio Alger, see Steinberg 1989, chap. 3; Gilman 1996. On Jewish culture, see Gordon 1964; see Sowell 1981 for an updated version.

3. Not all Jews are white or unambiguously white. It has been suggested, for example, that Hasidim lack the privileges of whiteness. Rodriguez (1997, 12, 15) has begun to unpack the claims of white Jewish "amenity migrants" and the different racial meanings of Chicano claims to a crypto-Jewish identity in New Mexico. See also Thomas 1996 on African American Jews.

4. M. Grant 1916; Ripley 1923; see also Patterson 1997; M. Grant, quoted in Higham 1955, 156.

5. *New York Times*, 30 July 1893, "East Side Street Vendors," reprinted in Schoener 1967, 57–58.

6. Gould 1981; Higham 1955; Patterson 1997, 108–115.

7. It was intended, as Davenport wrote to the president of the American Museum of Natural History, Henry Fairfield Osborne, as "an anthropological society . . . with a central governing body, self-elected and self-perpetuating, and very limited in members, and also confined to native Americans [*sic*] who are anthropologically, socially and politically sound, no Bolsheviki need apply" (Barkan 1992, 67–68).

8. Steinberg 1989, 137, 227; Markowitz 1993.

9. This census also explicitly changed the Mexican race to white (U.S. Bureau of the Census 1940, 2:4).

10. Nash et al. 1986, 885–886.

11. On planning for veterans, see F. J. Brown 1946; Hurd 1946; Mosch 1975; "Postwar Jobs for Veterans" 1945; Willenz 1983.

12. Willenz 1983, 165.

13. Nash et al. 1986, 885; Willenz 1983, 165. On mobility among veterans and non veterans, see Havighurst et al. 1951.

14. Steinberg 1989, 89–90.

15. Willenz 1983, 20–28, 94–97. I thank Nancy G. Cattell for calling my attention to the fact that women GIs were ultimately eligible for benefits.

16. Willenz 1983, 168; Dalfiume 1969, 133–134; Wynn 1976, 114–116; Anderson 1981; Milkman 1987.

17. Nalty and MacGregor 1981, 218, 60–61.

18. Wynn 1976, 114, 116.

19. On African Americans in the U.S. military, see Foner 1974; Dalfiume 1969; Johnson 1967; Binkin and Eitelberg 1982; Nalty and MacGregor 1981. On schooling, see Walker 1970, 4–9.

20. Hartman (1975, 141–142) cites massive abuses in the 1940s and 1950s by builders under the Section 608 program in which "the FHA granted extraordinarily liberal concessions to lackadaisically supervised private developers to induce them to produce rental housing rapidly in the postwar period." Eichler (1982) indicates that things were not that different in the subsequent FHA-funded home-building industry.

21. Dobriner 1963, 91, 100.

22. Quoted in Foner 1974, 195.

23. Berman 1982, 292.

24. On urban renewal and housing policies, see Greer 1965; Hartman 1975; Squires 1989. On Los Angeles, see Pardo 1990; Cockroft 1990.

25. Jackson 1985, 197. These ideas from the real estate industry were "codified and legitimated in 1930s work by University of Chicago sociologist Robert Park and real estate professor Homer Hoyt" (Ibid., 198–199).

26. See Gans 1962.

REFERENCES

Anderson, Karen. 1981. *Wartime Women*. Westport, Conn.: Greenwood.

Barkan, Elazar. 1992. *The Retreat of Scientific Racism: Changing Concepts of Race in Britain and the United States Between the World Wars*. New York: Cambridge University Press.

Berman, Marshall. 1982. *All That Is Solid Melts into Air: The Experience of Modernity.* New York: Simon and Schuster.

Binkin, Martin, and Mark J. Eitelberg. 1982. *Blacks and the Military.* Washington, D.C.: Brookings Institution.

Brown, Francis J. 1946. *Educational Opportunities for Veterans.* Washington, D.C.: Public Affairs Press American Council on Public Affairs.

Cockcroft, Eva. 1990. *Signs from the Heart: California Chicano Murals.* Venice, Calif.: Social and Public Art Resource Center.

Dalfiume, Richard M. 1969. *Desegregation of the U.S. Armed Forces: Fighting on Two Fronts, 1939–1953.* Columbia: University of Missouri Press.

Dinnerstein, Leonard, 1987. *Uneasy at Home: Anti-Semitism and the American Jewish Experience.* New York: Columbia University Press.

———. 1994. *Anti-Semitism in America.* New York: Oxford University Press.

Dobriner, William. M. 1963. *Class in Suburbia.* Englewood Cliffs, N.J.: Prentice-Hall.

Eichler, Ned. 1982. *The Merchant Builders.* Cambridge, Mass.: MIT Press.

Foner, Jack. 1974. *Blacks and the Military in American History: A New Perspective.* New York: Praeger Publishers.

Gans, Herbert. 1962. *The Urban Villagers.* New York: Free Press of Glencoe.

Gerber, David, ed. 1986. *Anti-Semitism in American History.* Urbana: University of Illinois Press.

Gilman, Sander. 1996. *Smart Jews: The Construction of the Image of Jewish Superior Intelligence.* Lincoln: University of Nebraska Press.

Gordon, Milton. 1964. *Assimilation in American Life: The Role of Race, Religion and National Origins.* New York: Oxford University Press.

Gould, Stephen J. 1981. *The Mismeasure of Man.* New York: Norton.

Grant, Madison. 1916. *The Passing of the Great Race: Or the Racial Basis of European History.* New York: Charles Scribner.

Greer, Scott. 1965. *Urban Renewal and American Cities.* Indianapolis: Bobbs-Merrill.

Hartman, Chester. 1975. *Housing and Social Policy.* Englewood Cliffs, N.J.: Prentice-Hall.

Havighurst, Robert J., John W. Baughman, Walter H. Eaton, and Ernest W. Burgess. 1951. *The American Veteran Back Home: A Study of Veteran Readjustment.* New York: Longmans, Green and Co.

Higham, John. 1955. *Strangers in the Land.* New Brunswick, N.J.: Rutgers University Press.

Hurd, Charles. 1946. *The Veterans' Program: A Complete Guide to Its Benefits, Rights and Options.* New York: McGraw-Hill Book Company.

Jackson, Kenneth T. 1985. *Crabgrass Frontier: The Suburbanization of the United States.* New York: Oxford University Press.

Johnson, Jesse J. 1967. *Ebony Brass: An Autobiography of Negro Frustration Amid Aspiration.* New York: The William Frederick Press.

Markowitz, Ruth Jacknow. 1993. *My Daughter, the Teacher: Jewish Teachers in the New York City Schools.* New Brunswick, N.J.: Rutgers University Press.

Milkman, Ruth. 1987. *Gender at Work: The Dynamics of Job Segregation by Sex During World War II.* Urbana: University of Illinois Press.

Mosch, Theodore R. 1975. *The GI Bill: A Breakthrough in Educational and Social Policy in the United States.* Hicksville, N.Y.: Exposition Press.

Nalty, Bernard C., and Morris J. MacGregor, eds. 1981. *Blacks in the Military: Essential Documents.* Wilmington, Del.: Scholarly Resources, Inc.

Nash, Gary B., Julie Roy Jeffrey, John R. Howe, Allen F. Davis, Peter J. Frederick, and Allen M. Winkler. 1986. *The American People: Creating a Nation and a Society.* New York: Harper and Row.

Pardo, Mary. 1990. "Mexican-American Women Grassroots Community Activists: 'Mothers of East Los Angeles'." *Frontiers* 11, 1:1–7.

Patterson, Thomas C. 1997. *Inventing Western Civilization.* New York: Monthly Review Press.

"Postwar Jobs for Veterans." 1945. *The Annals of the American Academy of Political and Social Science* 238 (March).

Ripley, William Z. 1923. *The Races of Europe: A Sociological Study.* New York: Appleton.

Rodriguez, Sylvia. 1997. "Tourism, Whiteness, and the Vanishing Anglo." Paper presented at the conference "Seeing and Being Seen: Tourism in the American West." Center for the American West, Boulder, Colorado, 2 May.

Schoener, Allon. 1967. *Portal to America: The Lower East Side 1870–1925.* New York: Holt, Rinehart, and Winston.

Sowell, Thomas. 1981. *Ethnic America: A History.* New York: Basic Books.

Squires, Gregory D., ed. 1989. *Unequal Partnerships: The Political Economy of Urban Redevelopment in Postwar America.* New Brunswick, N.J.: Rutgers University Press.

Steinberg, Stephen. 1989. *The Ethnic Myth: Race, Ethnicity and Class in America.* 2d ed. Boston: Beacon Press.

Thomas, Laurence Mordekhai. 1996. "The Soul of Identity: Jews and Blacks." In *People of the Book,* ed. S. F. Fishkin and J. Rubin-Dorsky. Madison: University of Wisconsin Press, 169–186.

U.S. Bureau of the Census. 1940. *Sixteenth Census of the United States,* V.2. Washington, D.C.: U.S. Government Printing Office.

Walker, Olive. 1970. "The Windsor Hills School Story." *Integrated Education: Race and Schools* 8, 3:4–9.

Willenz, June A. 1983. *Women Veterans: America's Forgotten Heroines.* New York: Continuum.

Wynn, Neil A. 1976. *The Afro-American and the Second World War.* London: Paul Elek.

5

"NIGHT TO HIS DAY"
The Social Construction of Gender

Judith Lorber

Talking about gender for most people is the equivalent of fish talking about water. Gender is so much the routine ground of everyday activities that questioning its taken-for-granted assumptions and presuppositions is like thinking about whether the sun will come up.[1] Gender is so pervasive that in our society we assume it is bred into our genes. Most people find it hard to believe that gender is constantly created and re-created out of human interaction, out of social life, and is the texture and order of that social life. Yet gender, like culture, is a human production that depends on everyone constantly "doing gender" (West and Zimmerman 1987).

And everyone "does gender" without thinking about it. Today, on the subway, I saw a well-dressed man with a year-old child in a stroller. Yesterday, on a bus, I saw a man with a tiny baby in a carrier on his chest. Seeing men taking care of small children in public is increasingly common—at least in New York City. But both men were quite obviously stared at—and smiled at, approvingly. Everyone was doing gender—the men who were changing the role of fathers and the other passengers, who were applauding them silently. But there was more gendering going on that probably fewer people noticed. The baby was wearing a white crocheted cap and white clothes. You couldn't tell if it was a boy or a girl. The child in the stroller was wearing a dark blue T-shirt and dark print pants. As they started to leave the train, the father put a Yankee baseball cap on the child's head. Ah, a boy, I thought. Then I noticed the gleam of tiny earrings in the child's ears, and as they got off, I saw the little flowered sneakers and lace-trimmed socks. Not a boy after all. Gender done.

Gender is such a familiar part of daily life that it usually takes a deliberate disruption of our expectations of how women and men are supposed to act to pay attention to how it is produced. Gender signs and signals are so ubiquitous that we usually fail to note them—unless they are missing or ambiguous. Then we are uncomfortable until we have successfully placed the other person in a gender status; otherwise, we feel socially dislocated. . . .

For the individual, gender construction starts with assignment to a sex category on the basis of what the genitalia look like at birth.[2] Then babies are dressed or adorned in a way that displays the category because parents don't want to be constantly asked whether their baby is a girl or a boy. A sex category becomes a gender status through naming, dress, and the use of other gender markers. Once a child's gender is evident, others treat those in one gender differently from those in the other, and the children respond to the different treatment by feeling different and behaving differently. As soon as they can talk, they start to refer to themselves as members of their gender. Sex doesn't come into play again until puberty, but by that time, sexual feelings and desires and practices have been shaped by gendered norms and expectations. Adolescent boys and girls approach and avoid each other in an elaborately scripted and gendered mating dance. Parenting is gendered, with different expectations for mothers and for fathers, and people of different genders work at different kinds of jobs. The work adults do as mothers and fathers and as low-level workers and high-level bosses, shapes women's and men's life experiences, and these experiences produce different feelings, consciousness, relationships, skills—ways of being that we call feminine or masculine.[3] All of these processes constitute the social construction of gender.

Gendered roles change—today fathers are taking care of little children, girls and boys are wearing unisex clothing and getting the same education, women and men are working at the same jobs. Although many traditional social groups are quite strict about maintaining gender differences, in other social groups they seem to be blurring. Then why the one-year-old's earrings? Why is it still so important to mark a child as a girl or a boy, to make sure she is not taken for a boy or he for a girl? What would happen if they were? They would, quite literally, have changed places in their social world.

To explain why gendering is done from birth, constantly and by everyone, we have to look not only at the way individuals experience gender but at gender as a social institution. As a social institution, gender is one of the major ways that human beings organize their lives. Human society depends on a predictable division of labor, a designated allocation of scarce goods, assigned responsibility for children and others who cannot care for themselves, common values and their systematic transmission to new members, legitimate leadership, music, art, stories, games, and other symbolic productions. One way of choosing people for the different tasks of society is on the basis of their talents, motivations, and competence—their demonstrated achievements. The other way is on the basis of gender, race, ethnicity—ascribed membership in a category of people. Although societies vary in the extent to which they use one or the other of these ways of allocating people to work and to carry out other responsibilities, every society uses gender and age grades. Every society classifies people as "girl and boy children," "girls and boys ready to be married," and "fully adult women and men," constructs similarities among them and differences between them, and assigns them to different roles and responsibilities. Personality characteristics, feelings, motivations, and ambitions flow from these different life experiences so that the members of these different groups become different kinds of people. The process of gendering and its outcome are legitimated by religion, law, science, and the society's entire set of values. . . .

Western society's values legitimate gendering by claiming that it all comes from physiology—female and male procreative differences. But gender and sex are not equivalent, and gender as a social construction does not flow automatically from genitalia and reproductive organs, the main physiological differences of females and males. In the construction of ascribed social statuses, physiological differences such as sex, stage of development, color of skin, and size are crude markers. They are not the source of the social statuses of gender, age grade, and race. Social statuses are carefully constructed through prescribed processes of teaching, learning, emulation, and enforcement. Whatever genes, hormones, and biological evolution contribute to human social institutions is materially as well as qualitatively transformed by social practices. Every social institution has a material base, but culture and social practices transform that base into something with qualitatively different patterns and constraints. The economy is much more than producing food and goods and distributing them to eaters and users; family and kinship are not the equivalent of having sex and procreating; morals and religions cannot be equated with the fears and ecstasies of the brain; language goes far beyond the sounds produced by tongue and larynx. No one eats "money" or "credit"; the concepts of "god" and "angels" are the subjects of theological disquisitions; not only words but objects, such as their flag, "speak" to the citizens of a country.

Similarly, gender cannot be equated with biological and physiological differences between human females and males. The building blocks of gender are *socially constructed statuses*. Western societies have only two genders, "man" and "woman." Some societies have three genders—men, women, and *berdaches* or *hijras* or *xaniths*. Berdaches, hijras, and xaniths are biological males who behave, dress, work, and are treated in most respects as social women; they are therefore not men, nor are they female women; they are, in our language, "male women."[4] There are African and American Indian societies that have a gender status called *manly hearted women*—biological females who work, marry, and parent as men; their social status is "female men" (Amadiume 1987; Blackwood 1984). They do not have to behave or dress as men to have the social responsibilities and prerogatives of husbands and fathers; what makes them men is enough wealth to buy a wife.

Modern Western societies' *transsexuals* and *transvestites* are the nearest equivalent of these crossover genders, but they are not institutionalized as third genders (Bolin 1987). Transsexuals are biological males and females who have sex-change operations to alter their genitalia. They do so in order to bring their physical anatomy in congruence with the way they want to live and with their own sense of gender identity. They do not become a third gender; they change genders. Transvestites are males who live as women and females who live as men but do not intend to have sex-change surgery. Their dress, appearance, and mannerisms fall within the range of what is expected from members of the opposite gender, so that they "pass." They also change genders, sometimes temporarily, some for most of their lives. Transvestite women have fought in wars as men soldiers as recently as the nineteenth century; some married women, and others went back to being women and married men once the war was over.[5] Some were discovered when their wounds were treated; others not until they died. In order to work as a jazz musician, a man's occupation, Billy Tipton, a woman, lived most of her life as a man. She died recently at seventy-four, leaving a wife and three adopted sons for whom she was husband and father, and musicians with whom she had played and traveled, for whom she was "one of the boys" (*New York Times* 1989).[6] There have been many other such occurrences of women passing as men to do more prestigious or lucrative men's work (Matthaei 1982, 192–93).[7]

Genders, therefore, are not attached to a biological substratum. Gender boundaries are breachable, and individual and socially organized shifts from one gender to another call attention to "cultural, social, or aesthetic dissonances" (Garber 1992, 16). These odd or deviant or third genders show us what we ordinarily take for granted—that people have to learn to be women and men. . . .

For Individuals, Gender Means Sameness

Although the possible combinations of genitalia, body shapes, clothing, mannerisms, sexuality, and roles could produce infinite varieties in human beings, the social institution of gender depends on the production and maintenance of a limited number of gender statuses and of making the members of these statuses similar to each other. Individuals are born sexed but not gendered, and they have to be taught to be masculine or feminine.[8] As Simone de Beauvoir said: "One is not born, but rather becomes, a woman . . . ; it is civilization as a whole that produces this creature . . . which is described as feminine" (1953, 267).

Children learn to walk, talk, and gesture the way their social group says girls and boys should. Ray Birdwhistell, in his analysis of body motion as human communication, calls these learned gender displays *tertiary* sex characteristics and argues that they are needed to distinguish genders because humans are a weakly dimorphic species—their only sex markers are genitalia (1970, 39–46). Clothing, paradoxically, often hides the sex but displays the gender.

In early childhood, humans develop gendered personality structures and sexual orientations through their interactions with parents of the same and opposite gender. As adolescents, they conduct their sexual behavior according to gendered scripts. Schools, parents, peers, and the mass media guide young people into gendered work and family roles. As adults, they take on a gendered social status in their society's stratification system. Gender is thus both ascribed and achieved (West and Zimmerman 1987). . . .

Gender norms are inscribed in the way people move, gesture, and even eat. In one African society, men were supposed to eat with their "whole mouth, wholeheartedly, and not, like women, just with the lips, that is halfheartedly, with reservation and restraint" (Bourdieu [1980] 1990, 70). Men and women in this society learned to walk in ways that proclaimed their different positions in the society:

> The manly man . . . stands up straight into the face of the person he approaches, or wishes to welcome. Ever on the alert, because ever threatened, he misses nothing of what happens around him. . . . Conversely, a well brought-up woman . . . is expected to walk with a slight stoop, avoiding every misplaced movement of her body, her head or her arms, looking down, keeping her eyes on the spot where she will next put her foot, especially if she happens to have to walk past the men's assembly. (70)

. . . For human beings there is no essential femaleness or maleness, femininity or masculinity, womanhood or manhood, but once gender is ascribed, the social order constructs and holds individuals to strongly gendered norms and expectations. Individuals may vary on many of the components of gender and may shift genders temporarily or permanently, but they must fit into the limited number of gender statuses their society recognizes. In the process, they re-create their society's version of women and men: "If we do gender appropriately, we simultaneously sustain, reproduce, and render legitimate the institutional arrangements. . . . If we fail to do gender appropriately, we as individuals—not the institutional arrangements— may be called to account (for our character, motives, and predispositions)" (West and Zimmerman 1987, 146).

The gendered practices of everyday life reproduce a society's view of how women and men should act (Bourdieu [1980] 1990). Gendered social arrangements are justified by religion and cultural productions and backed by law, but the most powerful means of sustaining the moral hegemony of the dominant gender ideology is that the process is made invisible; any possible alternatives are virtually unthinkable (Foucault 1972; Gramsci 1971).[9]

For Society, Gender Means Difference

The pervasiveness of gender as a way of structuring social life demands that gender statuses be clearly differentiated. Varied talents, sexual preferences, identities, personalities, interests, and ways of interacting fragment the individual's bodily and social experiences. Nonetheless, these are organized in Western cultures into two and only two socially and legally recognized gender statuses, "man" and "woman."[10] In the social construction of gender, it does not matter what men and women actually do; it does not even matter if they do exactly the same thing. The social institution of gender insists only that what they do is *perceived* as different.

If men and women are doing the same tasks, they are usually spatially segregated to maintain gender separation, and often the tasks are given different job titles as well, such as executive secretary and administrative assistant (Reskin 1988). If the differences between women and men begin to blur, society's "sameness taboo" goes into action (Rubin 1975, 178). At a rock and roll dance at West Point in 1976, the year women were admitted to the prestigious military academy for the first time, the school's administrators "were reportedly perturbed by the sight of mirror-image couples dancing in short hair and dress gray trousers," and a rule was established that women cadets could dance at these events only if they wore skirts (Barkalow and Raab 1990, 53).[11] Women recruits in the U.S. Marine Corps are required to wear makeup—at a minimum, lipstick and eye shadow—and they have to take classes in makeup, hair care, poise, and etiquette. This feminization is part of a deliberate policy of making them clearly distinguishable from men Marines. Christine Williams quotes a twenty-five-year-old woman drill instructor as saying: "A lot of the recruits who come here don't wear makeup; they're tomboyish or athletic. A lot of them have the preconceived idea that going into the military means they can still be a tomboy. They don't realize that you are a *Woman* Marine" (1989, 76–77).[12]

If gender differences were genetic, physiological, or hormonal, gender bending and gender ambiguity would occur only in hermaphrodites, who are born with chromosomes and genitalia that are not clearly female or male. Since gender differences are socially constructed, all men and all women can enact the behavior of the other, because they know the other's social script: " 'Man' and 'woman' are at once empty and overflowing categories. Empty because they have no ultimate, transcendental meaning. Overflowing because even when they appear to be fixed, they still contain within them alternative, denied, or suppressed definitions" (Scott 1988, 49). . . .

For one transsexual man-to-woman, the experience of living as a woman changed his/her whole personality. As James, Morris had been a soldier, foreign correspondent, and mountain climber; as Jan, Morris is a successful travel writer. But socially, James was superior to Jan, and so Jan developed the "learned helplessness" that is supposed to characterize women in Western society:

> We are told that the social gap between the sexes is narrowing, but I can only report that having, in the second half of the twentieth century, experienced life in both roles, there seems to me no aspect of existence, no moment of the day, no contact, no arrangement, no response, which is not different for men and for women. The very tone of voice in which I was now addressed, the very posture of the person next in the queue, the very feel in the air when I entered a room or sat at a restaurant table, constantly emphasized my change of status.

> And if other's responses shifted, so did my own. The more I was treated as woman, the more woman I became. I adapted willy-nilly. If I was assumed to be incompetent at reversing cars, or opening bottles, oddly incompetent I found myself becoming. If a case was thought too heavy for me, inexplicably I found it so myself. . . . Women treated me with a frankness which, while it was one of the happiest discoveries of my metamorphosis, did imply membership of a camp, a faction, or at least a school of thought; so I found myself gravitating always towards the female, whether in sharing a railway compartment or supporting a political cause. Men treated me more and more as junior, . . . and so, addressed every day of my life as an inferior, involuntar-

ily, month by month I accepted the condition. I discovered that even now men prefer women to be less informed, less able, less talkative, and certainly less self-centered than they are themselves; so I generally obliged them. (1975, 165–66)[13]

Gender as Process, Stratification, and Structure

As a social institution, gender is a process of creating distinguishable social statuses for the assignment of rights and responsibilities. As part of a stratification system that ranks these statuses unequally, gender is a major building block in the social structures built on these unequal statuses.

As a *process*, gender creates the social differences that define "woman" and "man." In social interaction throughout their lives, individuals learn what is expected, see what is expected, act and react in expected ways, and thus simultaneously construct and maintain the gender order: "The very injunction to be a given gender takes place through discursive routes: to be a good mother, to be a heterosexually desirable object, to be a fit worker, in sum, to signify a multiplicity of guarantees in response to a variety of different demands all at once" (Butler 1990, 145). Members of a social group neither make up gender as they go along nor exactly replicate in rote fashion what was done before. In almost every encounter, human beings produce gender, behaving in the ways they learned were appropriate for their status, or resisting or rebelling against these norms. Resistance and rebellion have altered gender norms, but so far they have rarely eroded the statuses.

Gendered patterns of interaction acquire additional layers of gendered sexuality, parenting, and work behaviors in childhood, adolescence, and adulthood. Gendered norms and expectations are enforced through informal sanctions of gender-inappropriate behavior by peers and by formal punishment or threat of punishment by those in authority should behavior deviate too far from socially imposed standards for women and men. ⋅ . . .

As part of a *stratification* system, gender ranks men above women of the same race and class. Women and men could be different but equal. In practice, the process of creating difference depends to a great extent on differential evaluation. As Nancy Jay (1981) says: "That which is defined, separated out, isolated from all else is A and pure. Not-A is necessarily impure, a random catchall, to which nothing is external except A and the principle of order that separates it from Not-A" (45). From the individual's point of view, whichever gender is A, the other is Not-A; gender boundaries tell the individual who is like him or her, and all the rest are unlike. From society's point of view, however, one gender is usually the touchstone, the normal, the dominant, and the other is different, deviant, and subordinate. In Western society, "man" is A, "wo-man" is Not-A. (Consider what a society would be like where woman was A and man Not-A.)

The further dichotomization by race and class constructs the gradations of a heterogeneous society's stratification scheme. Thus, in the United States, white is A, African American is Not-A; middle class is A, working class is Not-A, and "African-American women occupy a position whereby the inferior half of a series of these dichotomies converge" (Collins 1990, 70). The dominant categories are the hegemonic ideals, taken so for granted as the way things should be that white is not ordinarily thought of as a race, middle class as a class, or men as a gender. The characteristics of these categories define the Other as that which lacks the valuable qualities the dominants exhibit.

In a gender-stratified society, what men do is usually valued more highly than what women do because men do it, even when their activities are very similar or the same. In different regions of southern India, for example, harvesting rice is men's work, shared work, or women's work: "Wherever a task is done by women it is considered easy, and where it is done by [men] it is considered difficult" (Mencher 1988, 104). A gathering and hunting society's survival usually depends on the nuts, grubs, and small animals brought in by the women's foraging trips, but when the men's hunt is successful, it is the occasion for a celebration. Conversely, because they are the superior group, white men do not have to do the "dirty work," such as housework; the most inferior group does it, usually poor women of color (Palmer 1989). . . .

Societies vary in the extent of the inequality in social status of their women and men members, but where there is inequality, the status "woman" (and its attendant behavior and role allocations) is usually held in lesser esteem than the status "man." Since gender is also intertwined with a society's other constructed statuses of differential evaluation—race, religion, occupation, class, country of origin, and so on—men and women members of the favored groups command more power, more prestige, and more property than the members of the disfavored groups. Within many social groups, however, men are advantaged over women. The more economic resources, such as education and job opportunities, are available to a group, the more they tend to be monopolized by men. In poorer groups that have few resources (such as working-class African Americans in the United States), women and men are more nearly equal, and the women may even outstrip the men in education and occupational status (Almquist 1987).

As a *structure*, gender divides work in the home and in economic production, legitimates those in authority, and organizes sexuality and emotional life (Connell 1987, 91–142). As primary parents, women significantly influence children's psychological development and emotional attachments, in the process reproducing gender. Emergent sexuality is shaped by heterosexual, homosexual, bisexual, and sadomasochistic patterns that are gendered—different for girls and boys, and for women and men—so that sexual statuses reflect gender statuses.

When gender is a major component of structured inequality, the devalued genders have less power, prestige, and economic rewards than the valued genders. In countries that discourage gender discrimination, many major roles are still gendered; women still do most of the domestic labor and child rearing, even while doing full-time paid work; women and men are segregated on the job and each does work considered "appropriate"; women's work is usually paid less than men's work. Men dominate the positions of authority and leadership in government, the military, and the law; cultural productions, religions, and sports reflect men's interests.

In societies that create the greatest gender difference, such as Saudi Arabia, women are kept out of sight behind walls or veils, have no civil rights, and often create a cultural and emotional world of their own (Bernard 1981). But even in societies with less rigid gender boundaries, women and men spend much of their time with people of their own gender because of the way work and family are organized. This spatial separation of women and men reinforces gendered different-ness, identity, and ways of thinking and behaving (Coser 1986).

Gender inequality—the devaluation of "women" and the social domination of "men"—has social functions and a social history. It is not the result of sex, procreation, physiology, anatomy, hormones, or genetic predispositions. It is produced and maintained by identifiable social processes and built into the general social structure and individual identities deliberately and purposefully. The social order as we know it in Western societies is organized around racial ethnic, class, and gender inequality. I contend, therefore, that the continuing purpose of gender as a modern social institution is to construct women as a group to be the subordinates of men as a group. The life of everyone placed in the status "woman" is "night to his day—that has forever been the fantasy. Black to his white. Shut out of his system's space, she is the repressed that ensures the system's functioning" (Cixous and Clément [1975] 1986, 67).

NOTES

1. Gender is, in Erving Goffman's words, an aspect of *Felicity's Condition*: "any arrangement which leads us to judge an individual's . . . acts not to be a manifestation of strangeness. Behind Felicity's Condition is our sense of what it is to be sane" (1983, 27). Also see Bem 1993; Frye 1983, 17–40; Goffman 1977.

2. In cases of ambiguity in countries with modern medicine, surgery is usually performed to make the genitalia more clearly male or female.

3. See Butler 1990 for an analysis of how doing gender *is* gender identity.

4. On the hijras of India, see Nanda 1990; on the xaniths of Oman, Wikan 1982, 168–86; on the American Indian berdaches, W. L. Williams 1986. Other societies that have similar institutionalized third-gender men are the Koniag of Alaska, the Tanala of Madagascar, the Mesakin of Nuba, and the Chukchee of Siberia (Wikan 1982, 170).

5. Durova 1989; Freeman and Bond 1992; Wheelwright 1989.

6. Gender segregation of work in popular music still has not changed very much, according to Groce and Cooper 1990, despite considerable androgyny in some very popular figures. See Garber 1992 on the androgyny. She discusses Tipton on pp. 67–70.

7. In the nineteenth century, not only did these women get men's wages, but they also "had male privileges and could do all manner of things other women could not: open a bank account, write checks, own property, go anywhere unaccompanied, vote in elections" (Faderman 1991, 44).

8. For an account of how a potential man-to-woman transsexual learned to be feminine, see Garfinkel 1967, 116–85, 285–88. For a gloss on this account that points out how, throughout his encounters with Agnes, Garfinkel failed to see how he himself was constructing his own masculinity, see Rogers 1992.

9. The concepts of moral hegemony, the effects of everyday activities (praxis) on thought and personality, and the necessity of consciousness of these processes before political change can occur are all based on Marx's analysis of class relations.

10. Other societies recognize more than two categories, but usually no more than three or four (Jacobs and Roberts 1989).

11. Carol Barkalow's book has a photograph of eleven first-year West Pointers in a math class, who are dressed in regulation pants, shirts, and sweaters, with short haircuts. The caption challenges the reader to locate the only woman in the room.

12. The taboo on males and females looking alike reflects the U.S. military's homophobia (Bérubé 1989). If you can't tell those with a penis from those with a vagina, how are you going to determine whether their sexual interest is heterosexual or homosexual unless you watch them having sexual relations?

13. See Bolin 1988, 149–50, for transsexual men-to-women's discovery of the dangers of rape and sexual harassment. Devor's "gender blenders" went in the opposite direction. Because they found that it was an advantage to be taken for men, they did not deliberately cross-dress, but they did not feminize themselves either (1989, 126–40).

REFERENCES

Almquist, Elizabeth M. 1987. Labor market gendered inequality in minority groups. *Gender & Society* 1:400–14.

Amadiume, Ifi. 1987. *Male daughters, female husbands: Gender and sex in an African society*. London: Zed Books.

Barkalow, Carol, with Andrea Raab. 1990. *In the men's house*. New York: Poseidon Press.

Bem, Sandra Lipsitz. 1993. *The lenses of gender: Transforming the debate on sexual inequality*. New Haven: Yale University Press.

Bernard, Jessie. 1981. *The female world*. New York: Free Press.

Bérubé, Allan. 1989. Marching to a different drummer: Gay and lesbian GIs in World War II. In Duberman, Vicinus, and Chauncey.

Birdwhistell, Ray L. 1970. *Kinesics and context: Essays on body motion communication*. Philadelphia: University of Pennsylvania Press.

Blackwood, Evelyn. 1984. Sexuality and gender in certain Native American tribes: The case of cross-gender females. *Signs: Journal of Women in Culture and Society* 10:27–42.

Bolin, Anne. 1987. Transsexualism and the limits of traditional analysis. *American Behavioral Scientist* 31:41–65.

_____. 1988. *In search of Eve: Transsexual rites of passage*. South Hadley, Mass.: Bergin & Garvey.

Bourdieu, Pierre. [1980] 1990. *The logic of practice*. Stanford, Calif.: Stanford University Press.

Butler, Judith. 1990. *Gender trouble: Feminism and the subversion of identity*. New York and London: Routledge.

Cixous, Hélène, and Catherine Clément. [1975] 1986. *The newly born woman*, translated by Betsy Wing. Minneapolis: University of Minnesota Press.

Collins, Patricia Hill. 1990. *Black feminist thought: Knowledge, consciousness, and the politics of empowerment*. Boston: Unwin Hyman.

Connell, R.[Robert] W. 1987. *Gender and power: Society, the person, and sexual politics*. Stanford, Calif.: Stanford University Press.

Coser, Rose Laub. 1986. Cognitive structure and the use of social space. *Sociological Forum* 1:1–26.

De Beauvoir, Simone. 1953. *The second sex*, translated by H. M. Parshley. New York: Knopf.

Devor, Holly. 1989. *Gender blending: Confronting the limits of duality.* Bloomington: Indiana University Press.

Duberman, Martin Bauml, Martha Vicinus, and George Chauncey, Jr. (eds.). 1989. *Hidden from history: Reclaiming the gay and lesbian past.* New York: New American Library.

Durova, Nadezhda. 1989. *The cavalry maiden: Journals of a Russian officer in the Napoleonic Wars,* translated by Mary Fleming Zirin. Bloomington: Indiana University Press.

Dwyer, Daisy, and Judith Bruce (eds.). 1988. *A home divided: Women and income in the Third World.* Palo Alto, Calif.: Stanford University Press.

Faderman, Lillian. 1991. *Odd girls and twilight lovers: A history of lesbian life in twentieth-century America.* New York: Columbia University Press.

Foucault, Michel. 1972. *The archeology of knowledge and the discourse on language,* translated by A. M. Sheridan Smith. New York: Pantheon.

Freeman, Lucy, and Alma Halbert Bond. 1992. *America's first woman warrior: The courage of Deborah Sampson.* New York: Paragon.

Frye, Marilyn. 1983. *The politics of reality: Essays in feminist theory.* Trumansburg, N.Y.: Crossing Press.

Garber, Marjorie. 1992. *Vested interests: Cross-dressing and cultural anxiety.* New York and London: Routledge.

Garfinkel, Harold. 1967. *Studies in ethnomethodology.* Englewood Cliffs, N.J.: Prentice-Hall.

Goffman, Erving. 1977. The arrangement between the sexes. *Theory and Society* 4:301–33.

_____. 1983. Felicity's condition. *American Journal of Sociology* 89:1–53.

Gramsci, Antonio. 1971. *Selections from the prison notebooks,* translated and edited by Quintin Hoare and Geoffrey Nowell Smith. New York: International Publishers.

Groce, Stephen B., and Margaret Cooper. 1990. Just me and the boys? Women in local-level rock and roll. *Gender & Society* 4:220–29.

Jacobs, Sue-Ellen, and Christine Roberts. 1989. Sex, sexuality, gender, and gender variance. In *Gender and anthropology,* edited by Sandra Morgen. Washington, D.C.: American Anthropological Association.

Jay, Nancy. 1981. Gender and dichotomy. *Feminist Studies* 7:38–56.

Matthaei, Julie A. 1982. *An economic history of women's work in America.* New York: Schocken.

Mencher, Joan. 1988. Women's work and poverty: Women's contribution to household maintenance in South India. In Dwyer and Bruce.

Morris, Jan. 1975. *Conundrum.* New York: Signet.

Nanda, Serena. 1990. *Neither man nor woman: The hijras of India.* Belmont, Calif.: Wadsworth.

New York Times. 1989. Musician's death at 74 reveals he was a woman. 2 February.

Palmer, Phyllis. 1989. *Domesticity and dirt: Housewives and domestic servants in the United States, 1920–1945.* Philadelphia: Temple University Press.

Reskin, Barbara F. 1988. Bringing the men back in: Sex differentiation and the devaluation of women's work. *Gender & Society* 2:58–81.

Rogers, Mary F. 1992. They were all passing: Agnes, Garfinkel, and company. *Gender & Society* 6:169–91.

Rubin, Gayle. 1975. The traffic in women: Notes on the political economy of sex. In *Toward an anthropology of women*, edited by Rayna R[app] Reiter. New York: Monthly Review Press.

Scott, Joan Wallach. 1988. *Gender and the politics of history*. New York: Columbia University Press.

West, Candace, and Don Zimmerman. 1987. Doing gender. *Gender & Society* 1:125–51.

Wheelwright, Julie. 1989. *Amazons and military maids: Women who cross-dressed in pursuit of life, liberty and happiness*. London: Pandora Press.

Wikan, Unni. 1982. *Behind the veil in Arabia: Women in Oman*. Baltimore, Md.: Johns Hopkins University Press.

Williams, Christine L. 1989. *Gender differences at work: Women and men in nontraditional occupations*. Berkeley: University of California Press.

Williams, Walter L. 1986. *The spirit and the flesh: Sexual diversity in American Indian culture*. Boston: Beacon Press.

6

THE SOCIAL CONSTRUCTION OF SEXUALITY

Ruth Hubbard

There is no "natural" human sexuality. This is not to say that our sexual feelings are "unnatural" but that whatever feelings and activities our society interprets as sexual are channeled from birth into socially acceptable forms of expression.

Western thinking about sexuality is based on the Christian equation of sexuality with sin, which must be redeemed through making babies. To fulfill the Christian mandate, sexuality must be intended for procreation, and thus all forms of sexual expression and enjoyment other than heterosexuality are invalidated. Actually, for most Christians nowadays just plain heterosexuality will do, irrespective of whether it is intended to generate offspring.

These ideas about sexuality set up a major contradiction in what we tell children about sex and procreation. We teach them that sex and sexuality are about becoming mommies and daddies and warn them not to explore sex by themselves or with playmates of either sex until they are old enough to have babies. Then, when they reach adolescence and the entire culture pressures them into heterosexual activity, whether they themselves feel ready for it or not, the more "enlightened" among us tell them how to be sexually (meaning heterosexually) active without having babies. Surprise: It doesn't work very well. Teenagers do not act "responsibly"—teenage pregnancies and abortions are on the rise and teenage fathers do not acknowledge and support their partners and babies. Somewhere we forget that we have been telling lies. Sexuality and procreation are not linked in societies like ours. On the contrary, we expect youngsters to be heterosexually active from their teens on but to put off having children until they are economically independent and married, and even then to have only two or, at most, three children.

Other contradictions: This society, on the whole, accepts Freud's assumption that children are sexual beings from birth and that society channels their polymorphously perverse childhood sexuality into the accepted forms. Yet we expect our children to be asexual. We raise girls and boys together more than is done in many societies while insisting that they must not explore their own or each other's sexual parts or feelings.

What if we acknowledged the separation of sexuality from procreation and encouraged our children to express themselves sexually if they were so inclined? What if we, further, encouraged them to explore their own bodies as well as those of friends of the same and the other sex when they felt like it? They might then be able to feel at home with their sexuality, have some sense of their own and other people's sexual needs, and know how to talk about sexuality and procreation with their friends and sexual partners before their ability to procreate becomes an issue for them. In this age of AIDS and other serious sexually transmitted infections, such a course of action seems like essential preventive hygiene. Without the embarrassment of unexplored and unacknowledged sexual needs, contraceptive needs would be much easier to confront when they arise. So, of course, would same-sex love relationships.

Such a more open and accepting approach to sexuality would make life easier for children and adolescents of either sex, but it would be especially advantageous for girls. When a boy discovers his penis as an organ of pleasure, it is the same organ he is taught about as his organ of procreation. A girl exploring her pleasurable sensations finds her clitoris, but when she is taught about making babies, she hears about the functions of the vagina in sex and birthing. Usually, the clitoris goes unmentioned, and she doesn't even learn its name until much later. Therefore for boys there is an obvious link between procreation and their own pleasurable, erotic explorations; for most girls, there isn't.

Individual Sexual Scripts

Each of us writes our own sexual script out of the range of our experiences. None of this script is inborn or biologically given. We construct it out of our diverse life situations, limited by what we are taught or what we can imagine to be permissible and correct. There is no unique female sexual experience, no male sexual experience, no unique heterosexual, lesbian, or gay male experience. We take the experiences of different people and sort and lump them according to socially significant categories. When I hear generalizations about *the* sexual experience of some particular group, exceptions immediately come to mind. Except that I refuse to call them exceptions: They are part of the range of our sexual experiences. Of course, the similar circumstances in which members of a particular group find themselves will give rise to group similarities. But we tend to exaggerate them when we go looking for similarities within groups or differences between them.

This exaggeration is easy to see when we look at the dichotomy between "the heterosexual" and "the homosexual." The concept of "the homosexual," along with many other human typologies, originated toward the end of the nineteenth century. Certain kinds of behavior stopped being attributed to particular persons and came to define them. A person who had sexual relations with someone of the same sex became a certain kind of person, a "homosexual"; a person who had sexual relations with people of the other sex, a different kind, a "heterosexual."

This way of categorizing people obscured the hitherto accepted fact that many people do not have sexual relations exclusively with persons of one or the other sex. (None of us has sex with a kind of person; we have sex with a person.) This categorization created the stereotypes that were popularized by the sex reformers, such as Havelock Ellis and Edward Carpenter, who biologized the "difference." "The homosexual" became a person who is different by nature and therefore should not be made responsible for his or her so-called deviance. This definition served the purpose of the reformers (although the laws have been slow to change), but it turned same-sex love into a medical problem to be treated by doctors rather than punished by judges — an improvement, perhaps, but not acceptance or liberation. . . .

Toward a Nondeterministic Model of Sexuality

. . . Some gay men and lesbians feel that they were born "different" and have always been homosexual. They recall feeling strongly attracted to members of their own sex when they were children and adolescents. But many women who live with men and think of themselves as heterosexual also had strong affective and erotic ties to girls and women while they were growing up. If they were now in loving relationships with women, they might look back on their earlier loves as proof that they were always lesbians. But if they are now involved with men, they may be tempted to devalue their former feelings as "puppy love" or "crushes."

Even within the preferred sex, most of us feel a greater affinity for certain "types" than for others. Not any man or woman will do. No one has seriously suggested that something in our innate makeup makes us light up in the presence of only certain women or men. We would think it absurd to look to hormone levels or any other simplistic biological cause for our preference for a specific "type" within a sex. In fact, scientists rarely bother to ask what in our psychosocial experience shapes these kinds of tastes and preferences. We assume it must have something to do with our relationship to our parents or with other experiences, but we do not probe deeply unless people prefer the "wrong" sex. Then, suddenly, scientists begin to look for specific causes.

Because of our recent history and political experiences, feminists tend to reject simplistic, causal models of how our sexuality develops. Many women who have thought of themselves as heterosexual for much of their life and who have been married and have had children have fallen in love with a woman (or women) when they have had the opportunity to rethink, refeel, and restructure their lives.

The society in which we live channels, guides, and limits our imagination in sexual as well as other matters. Why some of us give ourselves permission to love people of our own sex whereas others cannot even imagine doing so is an interesting question. But I do not think it will be answered by measuring our hormone levels or by trying to unearth our earliest affectional ties. As women begin to speak freely about our sexual experiences, we are getting a varied range of information with which we can reexamine, reevaluate, and change ourselves. Lately, increasing numbers of women have begun to acknowledge their "bisexuality"—the fact that they can love women and men in succession or simultaneously. People fall in love with individuals, not with a sex. Gender need not be a significant factor in our choice, although for some of us it may be.

7

THE INVENTION OF HETEROSEXUALITY

Jonathan Ned Katz

Heterosexuality is old as procreation, ancient as the lust of Eve and Adam. That first lady and gentleman, we assume, perceived themselves, behaved, and felt just like today's heterosexuals. We suppose that heterosexuality is unchanging, universal, essential: ahistorical.

I'm grateful to Lisa Duggan, Judith Levine, Sharon Thompson, Carole S. Vance, and Jeffrey Weeks for comments on a recent version of this manuscript, and to Manfred Herzer and his editor, John DeCecco, for sharing, prepublication, Herzer's most recent research on Kertbeny. I'm also indebted to John Gagnon, Philip Greven, and Catharine R. Stimpson for bravely supporting my (unsuccessful) attempts to fund research for a full-length study of heterosexual history.

From *Socialist Review* 20 (January–March 1990): 7–34. Copyright © 1990. Reprinted by permission of the author.

Contrary to that common sense conjecture, the concept of heterosexuality is only one particular historical way of perceiving, categorizing, and imagining the social relations of the sexes. Not ancient at all, the idea of heterosexuality is a modern invention, dating to the late nineteenth century. The heterosexual belief, with its metaphysical claim to eternity, has a particular, pivotal place in the social universe of the late nineteenth and twentieth centuries that it did not inhabit earlier. This essay traces the historical process by which the heterosexual idea was created as ahistorical and taken-for-granted. . . .

By not studying the heterosexual idea in history, analysts of sex, gay and straight, have continued to privilege the "normal" and "natural" at the expense of the "abnormal" and "unnatural." Such privileging of the norm accedes to its domination, protecting it from questions. By making the normal the object of a thoroughgoing historical study we simultaneously pursue a pure truth and a sex-radical and subversive goal: we upset basic preconceptions. We discover that the heterosexual, the normal, and the natural have a history of changing definitions. Studying the history of the term challenges its power.

Contrary to our usual assumption, past Americans and other peoples named, perceived, and socially organized the bodies, lusts, and intercourse of the sexes in ways radically different from the way we do. If we care to understand this vast past sexual diversity, we need to stop promiscuously projecting our own hetero and homo arrangement. Though lip-service is often paid to the distorting, ethnocentric effect of such conceptual imperialism, the category heterosexuality continues to be applied uncritically as a universal analytical tool. Recognizing the time-bound and culturally-specific character of the heterosexual category can help us begin to work toward a thoroughly historical view of sex. . . .

Before Heterosexuality: Early Victorian True Love, 1820–1860

In the early nineteenth-century United States, from about 1820 to 1860, the heterosexual did not exist. Middle-class white Americans idealized a True Womanhood, True Manhood, and True Love, all characterized by "purity"—the freedom from sensuality.[1] Presented mainly in literary and religious texts, this True Love was a fine romance with no lascivious kisses. This ideal contrasts strikingly with late nineteenth- and twentieth-century American incitements to a hetero sex.*

Early Victorian True Love was only realized within the mode of proper procreation, marriage, the legal organization for producing a new set of correctly gen-

---

*Some historians have recently told us to revise our idea of sexless Victorians: their experience and even their ideology, it is said, were more erotic than we previously thought. Despite the revisionists, I argue that "purity" was indeed the dominant, early Victorian, white middle-class standard. For the debate on Victorian sexuality see John D'Emilio and Estelle Freedman, *Intimate Matters: A History of Sexuality in America* (New York: Harper & Row, 1988), p. xii.

dered women and men. Proper womanhood, manhood, and progeny—not a normal male-female eros—was the main product of this mode of engendering and of human reproduction.

The actors in this sexual economy were identified as manly men and womanly women and as procreators, not specifically as erotic beings or heterosexuals. Eros did not constitute the core of a heterosexual identity that inhered, democratically, in both men and women. True Women were defined by their distance from lust. True Men, though thought to live closer to carnality, and in less control of it, aspired to the same freedom from concupiscence.

Legitimate natural desire was for procreation and a proper manhood or womanhood; no heteroerotic desire was thought to be directed exclusively and naturally toward the other sex; lust in men was roving. The human body was thought of as a means towards procreation and production; penis and vagina were instruments of reproduction, not of pleasure. Human energy, thought of as a closed and severely limited system, was to be used in producing children and in work, not wasted in libidinous pleasures.

The location of all this engendering and procreative labor was the sacred sanctum of early Victorian True Love, the home of the True Woman and True Man—a temple of purity threatened from within by the monster masturbator, an archetypal early Victorian cult figure of illicit lust. The home of True Love was a castle far removed from the erotic exotic ghetto inhabited most notoriously then by the prostitute, another archetypal Victorian erotic monster. . . .

Late Victorian Sex-Love: 1860–1892

"Heterosexuality" and "homosexuality" did not appear out of the blue in the 1890s. These two eroticisms were in the making from the 1860s on. In late Victorian America and in Germany, from about 1860 to 1892, our modern idea of an eroticized universe began to develop, and the experience of a heterolust began to be widely documented and named. . . .

In the late nineteenth-century United States, several social factors converged to cause the eroticizing of consciousness, behavior, emotion, and identity that became typical of the twentieth-century Western middle class. The transformation of the family from producer to consumer unit resulted in a change in family members' relation to their own bodies; from being an instrument primarily of work, the human body was integrated into a new economy, and began more commonly to be perceived as a means of consumption and pleasure. Historical work has recently begun on how the biological human body is differently integrated into changing modes of production, procreation, engendering, and pleasure so as to alter radically the identity, activity, and experience of that body.[2]

The growth of a consumer economy also fostered a new pleasure ethic. This imperative challenged the early Victorian work ethic, finally helping to usher in a major transformation of values. While the early Victorian work ethic had touted the value of economic production, that era's procreation ethic had extolled the virtues of human reproduction. In contrast, the late Victorian economic ethic hawked the pleasures of consuming, while its sex ethic praised an erotic pleasure principle for men and even for women.

In the late nineteenth century, the erotic became the raw material for a new consumer culture. Newspapers, books, plays, and films touching on sex, "normal" and "abnormal," became available for a price. Restaurants, bars, and baths opened, catering to sexual consumers with cash. Late Victorian entrepreneurs of desire incited the proliferation of a new eroticism, a commoditized culture of pleasure.

In these same years, the rise in power and prestige of medical doctors allowed these upwardly mobile professionals to prescribe a healthy new sexuality. Medical men, in the name of science, defined a new ideal of male-female relationships that included, in women as well as men, an essential, necessary, normal eroticism. Doctors, who had earlier named and judged the sex-enjoying woman a "nymphomaniac," now began to label women's *lack* of sexual pleasure a mental disturbance, speaking critically, for example, of female "frigidity" and "anesthesia."*

By the 1880s, the rise of doctors as a professional group fostered the rise of a new medical model of Normal Love, replete with sexuality. The new Normal Woman and Man were endowed with a healthy libido. The new theory of Normal Love was the modern medical alternative to the old Cult of True Love. The doctors prescribed a new sexual ethic as if it were a morally neutral, medical description of health. The creation of the new Normal Sexual had its counterpart in the invention of the late Victorian Sexual Pervert. The attention paid the sexual abnormal created a need to name the sexual normal, the better to distinguish the average him and her from the deviant it.

Heterosexuality: The First Years, 1892–1900

In the periodization of heterosexual American history suggested here, the years 1892 to 1900 represent "The First Years" of the heterosexual epoch, eight key years in which the idea of the heterosexual and homosexual were initially and tentatively formulated by U.S. doctors. The earliest-known American use of the word "heterosexual" occurs in a medical journal article by Dr. James G. Kiernan of Chicago, read before the city's medical society on March 7, 1892, and published that May—portentous dates in sexual history.[3] But Dr. Kiernan's heterosexuals were definitely not exemplars of normality. Heterosexuals, said Kiernan, were defined by a mental condition, "psychical hermaphroditism." Its symptoms were "inclinations to both sexes." These heterodox sexuals also betrayed inclinations "to abnormal meth-

---

*This reference to females reminds us that the invention of heterosexuality had vastly different impacts on the histories of women and men. It also differed in its impact on lesbians and heterosexual women, homosexual and heterosexual men, the middle class and working class, and on different religious, racial, national, and geographic groups.

ods of gratification," that is, techniques to insure pleasure without procreation. Dr. Kiernan's heterogeneous sexuals did demonstrate "traces of the normal sexual appetite" (a touch of procreative desire). Kiernan's normal sexuals were implicitly defined by a monolithic other-sex inclination and procreative aim. Significantly, they still lacked a name.

Dr. Kiernan's article of 1892 also included one of the earliest-known uses of the word "homosexual" in American English. Kiernan defined "Pure homosexuals" as persons whose "general mental state is that of the opposite sex." Kiernan thus defined homosexuals by their deviance from a gender norm. His heterosexuals displayed a double deviance from both gender and procreative norms.

Though Kiernan used the new words heterosexual and homosexual, an old procreative standard and a new gender norm coexisted uneasily in his thought. His word heterosexual defined a mixed person and compound urge, abnormal because they wantonly included procreative and non-procreative objectives, as well as same-sex and different-sex attractions.

That same year, 1892, Dr. Krafft-Ebing's influential *Psychopathia Sexualis* was first translated and published in the United States.[4] But Kiernan and Krafft-Ebing by no means agreed on the definition of the heterosexual. In Krafft-Ebing's book, "hetero-sexual" was used unambiguously in the modern sense to refer to an erotic feeling for a different sex. "Homo-sexual" referred unambiguously to an erotic feeling for a "same sex." In Krafft-Ebing's volume, unlike Kiernan's article, heterosexual and homosexual were clearly distinguished from a third category, a "psycho-sexual hermaphroditism," defined by impulses toward both sexes.

Krafft-Ebing hypothesized an inborn "sexual instinct" for relations with the "opposite sex," the inherent "purpose" of which was to foster procreation. Krafft-Ebing's erotic drive was still a reproductive instinct. But the doctor's clear focus on a different-sex versus same-sex sexuality constituted a historic, epochal move from an absolute procreative standard of normality toward a new norm. His definition of heterosexuality as other-sex attraction provided the basis for a revolutionary, modern break with a centuries-old procreative standard.

It is difficult to overstress the importance of that new way of categorizing. The German's mode of labeling was radical in referring to the biological sex, masculinity or femininity, and the pleasure of actors (along with the procreant purpose of acts). Krafft-Ebing's heterosexual offered the modern world a new norm that came to dominate our idea of the sexual universe, helping to change it from a mode of human reproduction and engendering to a mode of pleasure. The heterosexual category provided the basis for a move from a production-oriented, procreative imperative to a consumerist pleasure principle—an institutionalized pursuit of happiness. . . .

Only gradually did doctors agree that heterosexual referred to a normal, "other-sex" eros. This new standard-model heterosex provided the pivotal term for the modern regularization of eros that paralleled similar attempts to standardize masculinity and femininity, intelligence, and manufacturing.[5] The idea of heterosexuality as the master sex from which all others deviated was (like the idea of the master race) deeply authoritarian. The doctors' normalization of a sex that was hetero proclaimed a new heterosexual separatism—an erotic apartheid that forcefully segregated the sex normals from the sex perverts. The new, strict boundaries made the emerging erotic world less polymorphous—safer for sex normals. However, the idea of such creatures as heterosexuals and homosexuals emerged from the narrow world of medicine to become a commonly accepted notion only in the early twentieth century. In 1901, in the comprehensive *Oxford English Dictionary*, "heterosexual" and "homosexual" had not yet made it.

The Distribution of the Heterosexual Mystique: 1900–1930

In the early years of this heterosexual century the tentative hetero hypothesis was stabilized, fixed, and widely distributed as the ruling sexual orthodoxy: The Heterosexual Mystique. Starting among pleasure-affirming urban working-class youths, southern blacks, and Greenwich-Village bohemians as defensive subculture, heterosex soon triumphed as dominant culture.[6]

In its earliest version, the twentieth-century heterosexual imperative usually continued to associate heterosexuality with a supposed human "need," "drive," or "instinct" for propagation, a procreant urge linked inexorably with carnal lust as it had not been earlier. In the early twentieth century, the falling birth rate, rising divorce rate, and "war of the sexes" of the middle class were matters of increasing public concern. Giving vent to heteroerotic emotions was thus praised as enhancing baby-making capacity, marital intimacy, and family stability. (Only many years later, in the mid-1960s, would heteroeroticism be distinguished completely, in practice and theory, from procreativity and male-female pleasure sex justified in its own name.)

The first part of the new sex norm—hetero—referred to a basic gender divergence. The "oppositeness" of the sexes was alleged to be the basis for a universal, normal, erotic attraction between males and females. The stress on the sexes' "oppositeness," which harked back to the early nineteenth century, by no means simply registered biological differences of females and males. The early twentieth-century focus on physiological and gender dimorphism reflected the deep anxieties of men about the shifting work, social roles, and power of men over women, and about the ideals of womanhood and manhood. That gender anxiety is documented, for example, in 1897, in *The New York Times'* publication of the Reverend Charles Parkhurst's diatribe against female "andromaniacs," the preacher's derogatory, scientific-sounding name for women who tried to "minimize distinctions by which manhood and womanhood are differentiated."[7] The stress on gender difference was a conservative response to the changing social-sexual division of activity and feeling which gave rise to the independent "New Woman" of the 1880s and eroticized "Flapper" of the 1920s.

The second part of the new hetero norm referred positively to sexuality. That novel upbeat focus on the hedonistic possibilities of male-female conjunctions also reflected a social transformation—a revaluing of pleasure and procreation, consumption and work in commercial, capitalist society. The democratic attribution of a normal lust to human females (as well as males) served to authorize women's enjoyment of their own bodies and began to undermine the early Victorian idea of the pure True Woman—a sex-affirmative action still part of women's struggle. The twentieth-century Erotic Woman also undercut nineteenth-century feminist assertion of women's moral superiority, cast suspicions of lust on women's passionate romantic friendships with women, and asserted the presence of a menacing female monster, "the lesbian."[8] . . .

In the perspective of heterosexual history, this early twentieth-century struggle for the more explicit depiction of an "opposite-sex" eros appears in a curious new light. Ironically, we find sex-conservatives, the social purity advocates of censorship and repression, fighting against the depiction not just of sexual perversity but also of the new normal heterosexuality. That a more open depiction of normal sex had to be defended against forces of propriety confirms the claim that heterosexuality's predecessor, Victorian True Love, had included no legitimate eros. . . .

The Heterosexual Steps Out: 1930–1945

In 1930, in *The New York Times,* heterosexuality first became a love that dared to speak its name. On April 30th of that year, the word "heterosexual" is first known to have appeared in *The New York Times Book Review.* There, a critic described the subject of André Gide's *The Immoralist* proceeding "from a heterosexual liaison to a homosexual one." The ability to slip between sexual categories was referred to casually as a rather unremarkable aspect of human possibility. This is also the first known reference by *The Times* to the new hetero/homo duo.[9]

The following month the second reference to the hetero/homo dyad appeared in *The New York Times Book Review,* in a comment on Floyd Dell's *Love in the Machine Age.* This work revealed a prominent antipuritan of the 1930s using the dire threat of homosexuality as his rationale for greater heterosexual freedom. *The Times* quoted Dell's warning that current abnormal social conditions kept the young dependent on their parents, causing "infantilism, prostitution and homosexuality." Also quoted was Dell's attack on the "inculcation of purity" that "breeds distrust of the opposite sex." Young people, Dell said, should be "permitted to develop normally to heterosexual adulthood." "But," *The Times* reviewer emphasized, "such a state already exists, here and now." And so it did. Heterosexuality, a new gender-sex category, had been distributed from the narrow, rarified realm of a few doctors to become a nationally, even internationally, cited aspect of middle-class life.[10] . . .

Heterosexual Hegemony: 1945–1965

The "cult of domesticity" following World War II—the reassociation of women with the home, motherhood, and child-care; men with fatherhood and wage work out-side the home—was a period in which the predominance of the hetero norm went almost unchallenged, an era of heterosexual hegemony. This was an age in which conservative mental-health professionals reasserted the old link between heterosex-uality and procreation. In contrast, sex-liberals of the day strove, ultimately with suc-cess, to expand the heterosexual ideal to include within the boundaries of normality a wider-than-ever range of nonprocreative, premarital, and extramarital behaviors. But sex-liberal reform actually helped to extend and secure the dominance of the heterosexual idea, as we shall see when we get to Kinsey.

The postwar sex-conservative tendency was illustrated in 1947, in Ferdinand Lundberg and Dr. Marnia Farnham's book, *Modern Woman: The Lost Sex*. Im-proper masculinity and femininity were exemplified, the authors decreed, by "en-gagement in heterosexual relations . . . with the complete intent to see to it that they do not eventuate in reproduction."[11] Their procreatively defined heterosex was one expression of a postwar ideology of fecundity that, internalized and enacted duti-fully by a large part of the population, gave rise to the postwar baby boom.

The idea of the feminine female and masculine male as prolific breeders was also reflected in the stress, specific to the late 1940s, on the homosexual as sad sym-bol of "sterility"—that particular loaded term appears incessantly in comments on homosex dating to the fecund forties.

In 1948, in *The New York Times Book Review*, sex liberalism was in ascen-dancy. Dr. Howard A. Rusk declared that Alfred Kinsey's just published report on *Sexual Behavior in the Human Male* had found "wide variations in sex concepts and behavior." This raised the question: "What is 'normal' and 'abnormal'?" In particular, the report had found that "homosexual experience is much more com-mon than previously thought," and "there is often a mixture of both homo and hetero experience."[12]

Kinsey's counting of orgasms indeed stressed the wide range of behaviors and feelings that fell within the boundaries of a quantitative, statistically accounted het-erosexuality. Kinsey's liberal reform of the hetero/homo dualism widened the nar-row, old hetero category to accord better with the varieties of social experience. He thereby contradicted the older idea of a monolithic, qualitatively defined, natural procreative act, experience, and person.[13]

Though Kinsey explicitly questioned "whether the terms 'normal' and 'abnor-mal' belong in a scientific vocabulary," his counting of climaxes was generally un-derstood to define normal sex as majority sex. This quantified norm constituted a final, society-wide break with the old qualitatively defined reproductive standard. Though conceived of as purely scientific, the statistical definition of the normal as the-sex-most-people-are-having substituted a new, quantitative moral standard for the old, qualitative sex ethic—another triumph for the spirit of capitalism.

Kinsey also explicitly contested the idea of an absolute, either/or antithesis between hetero and homo persons. He denied that human beings "represent two discrete populations, heterosexual and homosexual." The world, he ordered, "is not to be divided into sheep and goats." The hetero/homo division was not nature's doing: "Only the human mind invents categories and tries to force facts into separated pigeon-holes. The living world is a continuum."[14]

With a wave of the taxonomist's hand, Kinsey dismissed the social and historical division of people into heteros and homos. His denial of heterosexual and homosexual personhood rejected the social reality and profound subjective force of a historically constructed tradition which, since 1892 in the United States, had cut the sexual population in two and helped to establish the social reality of a heterosexual and homosexual identity.

On the one hand, the social construction of homosexual persons has led to the development of a powerful gay liberation identity politics based on an ethnic group model. This has freed generations of women and men from a deep, painful, socially induced sense of shame, and helped to bring about a society-wide liberalization of attitudes and responses to homosexuals.[15] On the other hand, contesting the notion of homosexual and heterosexual persons was one early, partial resistance to the limits of the hetero/homo construction. Gore Vidal, rebel son of Kinsey, has for years been joyfully proclaiming:

> there is no such thing as a homosexual or a heterosexual person. There are only homo- or heterosexual acts. Most people are a mixture of impulses if not practices, and what anyone does with a willing partner is of no social or cosmic significance.

> So why all the fuss? In order for a ruling class to rule, there must be arbitrary prohibitions. Of all prohibitions, sexual taboo is the most useful because sex involves everyone. . . . we have allowed our governors to divide the population into two teams. One team is good, godly, straight; the other is evil, sick, vicious.[16]

Heterosexuality Questioned: 1965–1982

By the late 1960s, anti-establishment counterculturalists, fledgling feminists, and homosexual-rights activists had begun to produce an unprecedented critique of sexual repression in general, of women's sexual repression in particular, of marriage and the family—and of some forms of heterosexuality. This critique even found its way into *The New York Times*.

In March 1968, in the theater section of that paper, freelancer Rosalyn Regelson cited a scene from a satirical review brought to New York by a San Francisco troupe:

> a heterosexual man wanders inadvertently into a homosexual bar. Before he realizes his mistake, he becomes involved with an aggressive queen who orders a drink for him. Being a broadminded liberal and trying to play it cool until he can back out of the situation gracefully, he asks, "How do you like being a ah homosexual?" To which the queen drawls drily, "How do you like being ah whatever it is you are?"

Regelson continued:

> The Two Cultures in confrontation. The middle-class liberal, challenged today on many fronts, finds his last remaining fixed value, his heterosexuality, called into question. The theater . . . recalls the strategies he uses in dealing with this ultimate threat to his world view.[17]

Heterosexual History: Out of the Shadows

Our brief survey of the heterosexual idea suggests a new hypothesis. Rather than naming a conjunction old as Eve and Adam, heterosexual designates a word and concept, a norm and role, an individual and group identity, a behavior and feeling, and a peculiar sexual-political institution particular to the late nineteenth and twentieth centuries.

Because much stress has been placed here on heterosexuality as word and concept, it seems important to affirm that heterosexuality (and homosexuality) came into existence before it was named and thought about. The formulation of the heterosexual idea did not create a heterosexual experience or behavior; to suggest otherwise would be to ascribe determining power to labels and concepts. But the titling and envisioning of heterosexuality did play an important role in consolidating the construction of the heterosexual's social existence. Before the wide use of the word "heterosexual," I suggest, women and men did not mutually lust with the same profound, sure sense of normalcy that followed the distribution of "heterosexual" as universal sanctifier.

According to this proposal, women and men make their own sexual histories. But they do not produce their sex lives just as they please. They make their sexualities within a particular mode of organization given by the past and altered by their changing desire, their present power and activity, and their vision of a better world. That hypothesis suggests a number of good reasons for the immediate inauguration of research on a historically specific heterosexuality.

The study of the history of the heterosexual experience will forward a great intellectual struggle still in its early stages. This is the fight to pull heterosexuality, homosexuality, and all the sexualities out of the realm of nature and biology [and] into the realm of the social and historical. Feminists have explained to us that anatomy does not determine our gender destinies (our masculinities and femininities). But we've only recently begun to consider that *biology does not settle our erotic fates*. The common notion that biology determines the object of sexual desire, or that physiology and society together cause sexual orientation, are determinisms that deny the break existing between our bodies and situations and our desiring. Just as the biology of our hearing organs will never tell us why we take pleasure in Bach or delight in Dixieland, our female or male anatomies, hormones, and genes will never tell us why we yearn for women, men, both, other, or none. That is because desiring is a self-generated project of individuals within particular historical cultures. Heterosexual history can help us see the place of values and judgments in the construction of our own and others' pleasures, and to see how our erotic tastes—our aesthetics of the flesh—are socially institutionalized through the struggle of individuals and classes.

The study of heterosexuality in time will also help us to recognize the *vast historical diversity of sexual emotions and behaviors*—a variety that challenges the monolithic heterosexual hypothesis. John D'Emilio and Estelle Freedman's *Intimate Matters: A History of Sexuality in America* refers in passing to numerous substantial changes in sexual activity and feeling: for example, the widespread use of contraceptives in the nineteenth century, the twentieth-century incitement of the female orgasm, and the recent sexual conduct changes by gay men in response to the AIDS epidemic. It's now a commonplace of family history that people in particular classes feel and behave in substantially different ways under different historical conditions.[18] Only when we stop assuming an invariable essence of heterosexuality will we begin the research to reveal the full variety of sexual emotions and behaviors.

The historical study of the heterosexual experience can help us *understand the erotic relationships of women and men in terms of their changing modes of social organization.* Such modal analysis actually characterizes a sex history well underway.[19] This suggests that the eros-gender-procreation system (the social ordering of lust, femininity and masculinity, and baby-making) has been linked closely to a society's particular organization of power and production. To understand the subtle history of heterosexuality we need to look carefully at correlations between (1) society's organization of eros and pleasure; (2) its mode of engendering persons as feminine or masculine (its making of women and men); (3) its ordering of human reproduction; and (4) its dominant political economy. This General Theory of Sexual Relativity proposes that substantial historical changes in the social organization of eros, gender, and procreation have basically altered the activity and experience of human beings within those modes.[20]

A historical view locates heterosexuality and homosexuality in time, helping us distance ourselves from them. This distancing can help us formulate new questions that clarify our long-range sexual-political goals: What has been and is the social function of sexual categorizing? Whose interests have been served by the division of the world into heterosexual and homosexual? Do we dare not draw a line between those two erotic species? Is some sexual naming socially necessary? Would human freedom be enhanced if the sex-biology of our partners in lust was of no particular concern, and had no name? In what kind of society could we all more freely explore our desire and our flesh?

As we move [into the year 2000], a new sense of the historical making of the heterosexual and homosexual suggests that these are ways of feeling, acting, and being with each other that we can together unmake and radically remake according to our present desire, power, and our vision of a future political-economy of pleasure.

NOTES

1. Barbara Welter, "The Cult of True Womanhood: 1820–1860," *American Quarterly*, vol. 18 (Summer 1966); Welter's analysis is extended here to include True Men and True Love.

2. See, for example, Catherine Gallagher and Thomas Laqueur, eds., "The Making of the Modern Body: Sexuality and Society in the Nineteenth Century," *Representations*, no. 14 (Spring 1986) (republished, Berkeley: University of California Press, 1987).

3. Dr. James G. Kiernan, "Responsibility in Sexual Perversion," *Chicago Medical Recorder*, vol. 3 (May 1892), pp. 185–210.

4. R. von Krafft-Ebing, *Psychopathia Sexualis, with Especial Reference to Contrary Sexual Instinct: A Medico-Legal Study*, trans. Charles Gilbert Chaddock (Philadelphia: F. A. Davis, 1892), from the 7th and revised German ed. Preface, November 1892.

5. For the standardization of gender see Lewis Terman and C. C. Miles, *Sex and Personality, Studies in Femininity and Masculinity* (New York: McGraw Hill, 1936). For the standardization of intelligence see Lewis Terman, *Stanford-Binet Intelligence Scale* (Boston: Houghton Mifflin, 1916). For the standardization of work, see "scientific management" and "Taylorism" in Harry Braverman, *Labor and Monopoly Capital: The Degradation of Work in the Twentieth Century* (New York: Monthly Review Press, 1974).

6. See D'Emilio and Freedman, *Intimate Matters*, pp. 194–201, 231, 241, 295–96; Ellen Kay Trimberger, "Feminism, Men, and Modern Love: Greenwich Village, 1900–1925," in *Powers of Desire: The Politics of Sexuality*, ed. Ann Snitow, Christine Stansell, Sharon Thompson (New York: Monthly Review Press, 1983), pp. 131–52; Kathy Peiss, "'Charity Girls' and City Pleasures: Historical Notes on Working Class Sexuality, 1880–1920," in *Powers of Desire*, pp. 74–87; and Mary P. Ryan, "The Sexy Saleslady: Psychology, Heterosexuality, and Consumption in the Twentieth Century," in her *Womanhood in America*, 2nd ed. (New York: Franklin Watts, 1979), pp. 151–82.

7. [Rev. Charles Parkhurst], "Woman. Calls Them Andromaniacs. Dr. Parkhurst So Characterizes Certain Women Who Passionately Ape Everything That Is Mannish. Woman Divinely Preferred. Her Supremacy Lies in Her Womanliness, and She Should Make the Most of It—Her Sphere of Best Usefulness the Home," *The New York Times*, May 23, 1897, p. 16:1.

8. See Lisa Duggan, "The Social Enforcement of Heterosexuality and Lesbian Resistance in the 1920s," in *Class, Race, and Sex: The Dynamics of Control*, ed. Amy Swerdlow and Hanah Lessinger (Boston: G. K. Hall, 1983), pp. 75–92; Rayna Rapp and Ellen Ross, "The Twenties Backlash: Compulsory Heterosexuality, the Consumer Family, and the Waning of Feminism," in *Class, Race, and Sex*; Christina Simmons, "Companionate Marriage and the Lesbian Threat," *Frontiers*, vol. 4, no. 3 (Fall 1979), pp. 54–59; and Lillian Faderman, *Surpassing the Love of Men* (New York: William Morrow, 1981).

9. Louis Kronenberger, review of André Gide, *The Immoralist*, *New York Times Book Review*, April 20, 1930, p. 9.

10. Henry James Forman, review of Floyd Dell, *Love in the Machine Age* (New York: Farrar & Rinehart), *New York Times Book Review*, September 14, 1930, p. 9.

11. Ferdinand Lundberg and Dr. Marnia F. Farnham, *Modern Woman: The Lost Sex* (New York: Harper, 1947).

12. Dr. Howard A. Rusk, *New York Times Book Review*, January 4, 1948, p. 3.

13. Alfred Kinsey, Wardell B. Pomeroy, Clyde E. Martin, *Sexual Behavior in the Human Male* (Philadelphia: W. B. Saunders, 1948), pp. 199–200.

14. Kinsey, *Sexual Behavior*, pp. 637, 639.

15. See Steven Epstein, "Gay Politics, Ethnic Identity: The Limits of Social Constructionism," *Socialist Review* 93/93 (1987), pp. 9–54.

16. Gore Vidal, "Someone to Laugh at the Squares With" [Tennessee Williams], *New York Review of Books*, June 13, 1985; reprinted in his *At Home: Essays, 1982–1988* (New York: Random House, 1988), p. 48.

17. Rosalyn Regelson, "Up the Camp Staircase," *The New York Times*, March 3, 1968, Section II, p. 1:5.

18. D'Emilio and Freedman, *Intimate Matters*, pp. 57–63, 268, 356.

19. Ryan, *Womanhood*; John D'Emilio, "Capitalism and Gay Identity," in *Powers of Desire*, pp. 100–13; Jeffrey Weeks, *Coming Out: Homosexual Politics in Britain from the Nineteenth Century to the Present* (London: Quartet Books, 1977); D'Emilio and Freedman, *Intimate Matters*; Katz, "Early Colonial Exploration, Agriculture, and Commerce: The Age of Sodomitical Sin, 1607–1740," *Gay/Lesbian Almanac*, pp. 23–65.

20. This tripartite system is intended as a revision of Gayle Rubin's pioneering work on the social-historical orgainization of eros and gender. See "The Traffic in Women: Notes on the Political-Economy of Sex," in *Toward an Anthropology of Women*, ed. Rayna R. Reiter (New York: Monthly Review Press, 1975), pp. 157–210, and "Thinking Sex: Notes for a Radical Theory of the Politics of Sexuality," in *Pleasure and Danger: Exploring Female Sexuality*, ed. Carole S. Vance (Boston: Routledge & Kegan Paul, 1984), pp. 267–329.

8

MASCULINITY AS HOMOPHOBIA
Fear, Shame, and Silence in the Construction of Gender Identity

Michael S. Kimmel

We think of manhood as eternal, a timeless essence that resides deep in the heart of every man. We think of manhood as a thing, a quality that one either has or doesn't have. We think of manhood as innate, residing in the particular biological

From *Theorizing Masculinities*, Harry Brod and Michael Kaufman, eds., pp. 119–141. Copyright © 1994. Reprinted by permission of Sage Publications, Inc. I am grateful to Tim Beneke, Harry Brod, Michael Kaufman, Iona Mara-Drita, and Lillian Rubin for comments on earlier versions of the chapter.

composition of the human male, the result of androgens or the possession of a penis. We think of manhood as a transcendent tangible property that each man must manifest in the world, the reward presented with great ceremony to a young novice by his elders for having successfully competed an arduous initiation ritual. . . .

In this chapter, I view masculinity as a constantly changing collection of meanings that we construct through our relationships with ourselves, with each other, and with our world. Manhood is neither static nor timeless; it is historical. Manhood is not the manifestation of an inner essence; it is socially constructed. Manhood does not bubble up to consciousness from our biological makeup; it is created in culture. Manhood means different things at different times to different people. We come to know what it means to be a man in our culture by setting our definitions in opposition to a set of "others"—racial minorities, sexual minorities, and, above all, women. . . .

Classical Social Theory as a Hidden Meditation of Manhood

Begin this inquiry by looking at four passages from that set of texts commonly called classical social and political theory. You will, no doubt, recognize them, but I invite you to recall the way they were discussed in your undergraduate or graduate courses in theory:

> The bourgeoisie cannot exist without constantly revolutionizing the instruments of production, and thereby the relations of production, and with them the whole relations of society. Conservation of the old modes of production in unaltered form, was, on the contrary, the first condition of existence for all earlier industrial classes. Constant revolutionizing of production, uninterrupted disturbance of all social conditions, everlasting uncertainty and agitation distinguish the bourgeois epoch from all earlier ones. All fixed, fast-frozen relations, with their train of ancient and venerable prejudices and opinions are swept away, all new-formed ones become antiquated before they can ossify. All that is solid melts into air, all that is holy is profaned, and man is at last compelled to face with sober senses, his real conditions of life, and his relation with his kind. (Marx & Engels, 1848/1964)

> An American will build a house in which to pass his old age and sell it before the roof is on; he will plant a garden and rent it just as the trees are coming into bearing; he will clear a field and leave others to reap the harvest; he will take up a profession and leave it, settle in one place and soon go off elsewhere with his changing desires. . . . At first sight there is something astonishing in this spectacle of so many lucky men restless in the midst of abundance. But it is a spectacle as old as the world; all that is new is to see a whole people performing in it. (Tocqueville, 1835/1967)

> Where the fulfillment of the calling cannot directly be related to the highest spiritual and cultural values, or when, on the other hand, it need not be felt simply as economic compulsion, the individual generally abandons the attempt to justify it at all. In the field of its highest development, in the United States, the pursuit of wealth, stripped of

its religious and ethical meaning, tends to become associated with purely mundane passions, which often actually give it the character of sport. (Weber, 1905/1966)

We are warned by a proverb against serving two masters at the same time. The poor ego has things even worse: it serves three severe masters and does what it can to bring their claims and demands into harmony with one another. These claims are always divergent and often seem incompatible. No wonder that the ego so often fails in its task. Its three tyrannical masters are the external world, the super ego and the id. . . . It feels hemmed in on three sides, threatened by three kinds of danger, to which, if it is hard pressed, it reacts by generating anxiety. . . . Thus the ego, driven by the id, confined by the super ego, repulsed by reality, struggles to master its economic task of bringing about harmony among the forces and influences working in and upon it; and we can understand how it is that so often we cannot suppress a cry: "Life is not easy!" (Freud, "The Dissection of the Psychical Personality," 1933/1966)

If your social science training was anything like mine, these were offered as descriptions of the bourgeoisie under capitalism, of individuals in democratic societies, of the fate of the Protestant work ethic under the ever rationalizing spirit of capitalism, or of the arduous task of the autonomous ego in psychological development. Did anyone ever mention that in all four cases the theorists were describing men? Not just "man" as in generic mankind, but a particular type of masculinity, a definition of manhood that derives its identity from participation in the marketplace, from interaction with other men in that marketplace—in short, a model of masculinity for whom identity is based on homosocial competition? Three years before Tocqueville found Americans "restless in the midst of abundance," Senator Henry Clay had called the United States "a nation of self-made men."

What does it mean to be "self-made"? What are the consequences of self-making for the individual man, for other men, for women? It is this notion of manhood—rooted in the sphere of production, the public arena, a masculinity grounded not in land ownership or in artisanal republican virtue but in successful participation in marketplace competition—this has been the defining notion of American manhood. Masculinity must be proved, and no sooner is it proved than it is again questioned and must be proved again—constant, relentless, unachievable, and ultimately the quest for proof becomes so meaningless that it takes on the characteristic, as Weber said, of a sport. He who has the most toys when he dies wins. . . .

Masculinity as History and the History of Masculinity

The idea of masculinity expressed in the previous extracts is the product of historical shifts in the grounds on which men rooted their sense of themselves as men. To argue that cultural definitions of gender identity are historically specific goes only so far; we have to specify exactly what those models were. In my historical inquiry into the development of these models of manhood[1] I chart the fate of two models for manhood at the turn of the 19th century and the emergence of a third in the first few decades of that century.

In the late 18th and early 19th centuries, two models of manhood prevailed. The *Genteel Patriarch* derived his identity from landownership. Supervising his estate, he was refined, elegant, and given to casual sensuousness. He was a doting and devoted father, who spent much of his time supervising the estate and with his family. Think of George Washington or Thomas Jefferson as examples. By contrast, the *Heroic Artisan* embodied the physical strength and republican virtue that Jefferson observed in the yeoman farmer, independent urban craftsman, or shopkeeper. Also a devoted father, the Heroic Artisan taught his son his craft, bringing him through ritual apprenticeship to status as master craftsman. Economically autonomous, the Heroic Artisan also cherished his democratic community, delighting in the participatory democracy of the town meeting. Think of Paul Revere at his pewter shop, shirtsleeves rolled up, a leather apron—a man who took pride in his work.

Heroic Artisans and Genteel Patriarchs lived in casual accord, in part because their gender ideals were complementary (both supported participatory democracy and individual autonomy, although patriarchs tended to support more powerful state machineries and also supported slavery) and because they rarely saw one another: Artisans were decidedly urban and the Genteel Patriarchs ruled their rural estates. By the 1830s, though, this casual symbiosis was shattered by the emergence of a new vision of masculinity, *Marketplace Manhood*.

Marketplace Man derived his identity entirely from his success in the capitalist marketplace, as he accumulated wealth, power, status. He was the urban entrepreneur, the businessman. Restless, agitated, and anxious, Marketplace Man was an absentee landlord at home and an absent father with his children, devoting himself to his work in an increasingly homosocial environment—a male-only world in which he pits himself against other men. His efforts at self-making transform the political and economic spheres, casting aside the Genteel Patriarch as an anachronistic feminized dandy—sweet, but ineffective and outmoded, and transforming the Heroic Artisan into a dispossessed proletarian, a wage slave.

As Tocqueville would have seen it, the coexistence of the Genteel Patriarch and the Heroic Artisan embodied the fusion of liberty and equality. Genteel Patriarchy was the manhood of the traditional aristocracy, the class that embodied the virtue of liberty. The Heroic Artisan embodied democratic community, the solidarity of the urban shopkeeper or craftsman. Liberty and democracy, the patriarch and the artisan, could, and did, coexist. But Marketplace Man is capitalist man, and he makes both freedom and equality problematic, eliminating the freedom of the aristocracy and proletarianizing the equality of the artisan. In one sense, American history has been an effort to restore, retrieve, or reconstitute the virtues of Genteel Patriarchy and Heroic Artisanate as they were being transformed in the capitalist marketplace.

Marketplace Manhood was a manhood that required proof, and that required the acquisition of tangible goods as evidence of success. It reconstituted itself by the exclusion of "others"—women, nonwhite men, nonnative-born men, homosexual men—and by terrified flight into a pristine mythic homosocial Eden where men could, at last, be real men among other men. The story of the ways in which Marketplace Man becomes American Everyman is a tragic tale, a tale of striving to live up to impossible ideals of success leading to chronic terrors of emasculation, emotional emptiness, and a gendered rage that leave a wide swath of destruction in its wake.

Masculinities as Power Relations

Marketplace Masculinity describes the normative definition of American masculinity. It describes his characteristics—aggression, competition, anxiety—and the arena in which those characteristics are deployed—the public sphere, the marketplace. If the marketplace is the arena in which manhood is tested and proved, it is a gendered arena, in which tensions between women and men and tensions among different groups of men are weighted with meaning. These tensions suggest that cultural definitions of gender are played out in a contested terrain and are themselves power relations.

All masculinities are not created equal; or rather, we are all *created* equal, but any hypothetical equality evaporates quickly because our definitions of masculinity are not equally valued in our society. One definition of manhood continues to remain the standard against which other forms of manhood are measured and evaluated. Within the dominant culture, the masculinity that defines white, middle class, early middle-aged, heterosexual men is the masculinity that sets the standards for other men, against which other men are measured and, more often than not, found wanting. Sociologist Erving Goffman (1963) wrote that in America, there is only "one complete, unblushing male":

> a young, married, white, urban, northern heterosexual, Protestant father of college education, fully employed, of good complexion, weight and height, and a recent record in sports. Every American male tends to look out upon the world from this perspective. . . . Any male who fails to qualify in any one of these ways is likely to view himself . . . as unworthy, incomplete, and inferior. (p. 128)

This is the definition that we will call "hegemonic" masculinity, the image of masculinity of those men who hold power, which has become the standard in psychological evaluations, sociological research, and self-help and advice literature for teaching young men to become "real men" (Connell, 1987). The hegemonic definition of manhood is a man *in* power, a man *with* power, and a man *of* power. We equate manhood with being strong, successful, capable, reliable, in control. The very definitions of manhood we have developed in our culture maintain the power that some men have over other men and that men have over women.

Our culture's definition of masculinity is thus several stories at once. It is about the individual man's quest to accumulate those cultural symbols that denote manhood, signs that he has in fact achieved it. It is about those standards being used against women to prevent their inclusion in public life and their consignment to a devalued private sphere. It is about the differential access that different types of men have to those cultural resources that confer manhood and about how each of these groups then develops their own modifications to preserve and claim their manhood. It is about the power of these definitions themselves to serve to maintain the real-life power that men have over women and that some men have over other men.

This definition of manhood has been summarized cleverly by psychologist Robert Brannon (1976) into four succinct phrases:

1. "No Sissy Stuff!" One may never do anything that even remotely suggests femininity. Masculinity is the relentless repudiation of the feminine.
2. "Be a Big Wheel." Masculinity is measured by power, success, wealth, and status. As the current saying goes, "He who has the most toys when he dies wins."
3. "Be a Sturdy Oak." Masculinity depends on remaining calm and reliable in a crisis, holding emotions in check. In fact, proving you're a man depends on never showing your emotions at all. Boys don't cry.
4. "Give 'em Hell." Exude an aura of manly daring and aggression. Go for it. Take risks.

These rules contain the elements of the definition against which virtually all American men are measured. Failure to embody these rules, to affirm the power of the rules and one's achievement of them is a source of men's confusion and pain. Such a model is, of course, unrealizable for any man. But we keep trying, valiantly and vainly, to measure up. American masculinity is a relentless test.[2] The chief test is contained in the first rule. Whatever the variations by race, class, age, ethnicity, or sexual orientation, being a man means "not being like women." This notion of anti-femininity lies at the heart of contemporary and historical conceptions of manhood, so that masculinity is defined more by what one is not rather than who one is.

Masculinity as the Flight from the Feminine

Historically and developmentally, masculinity has been defined as the flight from women, the repudiation of femininity. . . .

The drive to repudiate the mother as the indication of the acquisition of masculine gender identity has three consequences for the young boy. First, he pushes away his real mother, and with her the traits of nurturance, compassion, and tenderness she may have embodied. Second, he suppresses those traits in himself, because they will reveal his incomplete separation from mother. His life becomes a lifelong project to demonstrate that he possesses none of his mother's traits. Masculine identity is born in the renunciation of the feminine, not in the direct affirmation of the masculine, which leaves masculine gender identity tenuous and fragile.

Third, as if to demonstrate the accomplishment of these first two tasks, the boy also learns to devalue all women in his society, as the living embodiments of those traits in himself he has learned to despise. Whether or not he was aware of it, Freud also described the origins of sexism—the systematic devaluation of women—in the desperate efforts of the boy to separate from mother. We may *want* "a girl just like the girl that married dear old Dad," as the popular song had it, but we certainly don't want to *be like* her.

This chronic uncertainty about gender identity helps us understand several obsessive behaviors. Take, for example, the continuing problem of the school-yard bully. Parents remind us that the bully is the *least* secure about his manhood, and so he is constantly trying to prove it. But he "proves" it by choosing opponents he is absolutely certain he can defeat; thus the standard taunt to a bully is to "pick on someone your own size." He can't, though, and after defeating a smaller and weaker opponent, which he was sure would prove his manhood, he is left with the empty gnawing feeling that he has not proved it after all, and he must find another opponent, again one smaller and weaker, that he can again defeat to prove it to himself.[3] . . .

When does it end? Never. To admit weakness, to admit frailty or fragility, is to be seen as a wimp, a sissy, not a real man. But seen by whom?

Masculinity as a Homosocial Enactment

Other men: We are under the constant careful scrutiny of other men. Other men watch us, rank us, grant our acceptance into the realm of manhood. Manhood is demonstrated for other men's approval. It is other men who evaluate the performance. Literary critic David Leverenz (1991) argues that "ideologies of manhood have functioned primarily in relation to the gaze of male peers and male authority" (p. 769). Think of how men boast to one another of their accomplishments—from their latest sexual conquest to the size of the fish they caught—and how we constantly parade the markers of manhood—wealth, power, status, sexy women—in front of other men, desperate for their approval.

That men prove their manhood in the eyes of other men is both a consequence of sexism and one of its chief props. "Women have, in men's minds, such a low place on the social ladder of this country that it's useless to define yourself in terms of a woman," noted playwright David Mamet. "What men need is men's approval." Women become a kind of currency that men use to improve their ranking on the masculine social scale. (Even those moments of heroic conquest of women carry, I believe, a current of homosocial evaluation.) Masculinity is a *homosocial* enactment. We test ourselves, perform heroic feats, take enormous risks, all because we want other men to grant us our manhood. . . .

Masculinity as Homophobia

. . . That nightmare from which we never seem to awaken is that those other men will see that sense of inadequacy, they will see that in our own eyes we are not who we are pretending to be. What we call masculinity is often a hedge against being revealed as a fraud, an exaggerated set of activities that keep others from seeing through us, and a frenzied effort to keep at bay those fears within ourselves. Our real fear "is not fear of women but of being ashamed or humiliated in front of other men, or being dominated by stronger men" (Leverenz, 1986, p. 451).

This, then, is the great secret of American manhood: *We are afraid of other men.* Homophobia is a central organizing principle of our cultural definition of manhood. Homophobia is more than the irrational fear of gay men, more than the fear that we might be perceived as gay. "The word 'faggot' has nothing to do with homosexual experience or even with fears of homosexuals," writes David Leverenz (1986). "It comes out of the depths of manhood: a label of ultimate contempt for anyone who seems sissy, untough, uncool" (p. 455). Homophobia is the fear that other men will unmask us, emasculate us, reveal to us and the world that we do not measure up, that we are not real men. We are afraid to let other men see that fear. Fear makes us ashamed, because the recognition of fear in ourselves is proof to ourselves that we are not as manly as we pretend, that we are, like the young man in a poem by Yeats, "one that ruffles in a manly pose for all his timid heart." Our fear is the fear of humiliation. We are ashamed to be afraid.

Shame leads to silence—the silences that keep other people believing that we actually approve of the things that are done to women, to minorities, to gays and lesbians in our culture. The frightened silence as we scurry past a woman being hassled by men on the street. That furtive silence when men make sexist or racist jokes in a bar. That clammy-handed silence when guys in the office make gay-bashing jokes. Our fears are the sources of our silences, and men's silence is what keeps the system running. This might help to explain why women often complain that their male friends or partners are often so understanding when they are alone and yet laugh at sexist jokes or even make those jokes themselves when they are out with a group.

The fear of being seen as a sissy dominates the cultural definitions of manhood. It starts so early. "Boys among boys are ashamed to be unmanly," wrote one educator in 1871 (cited in Rotundo, 1993, p. 264). I have a standing bet with a friend that I can walk onto any playground in America where 6-year-old boys are happily playing and by asking one question, I can provoke a fight. That question is simple: "Who's a sissy around here?" Once posed, the challenge is made. One of two things is likely to happen. One boy will accuse another of being a sissy, to which that boy will respond that he is not a sissy, that the first boy is. They may have to fight it out to see who's lying. Or a whole group of boys will surround one boy and all shout "He is! He is!" That boy will either burst into tears and run home crying, disgraced, or he will have to take on several boys at once, to prove that he's not a sissy. (And what will his father or older brothers tell him if he chooses to run home crying?) It will be some time before he regains any sense of self-respect.

Violence is often the single most evident marker of manhood. Rather it is the willingness to fight, the desire to fight. The origin of our expression that one has a chip on one's shoulder lies in the practice of an adolescent boy in the country or small town at the turn of the century, who would literally walk around with a chip of wood balanced on his shoulder—a signal of his readiness to fight with anyone who would take the initiative of knocking the chip off (see Gorer, 1964, p. 38; Mead, 1965).

As adolescents, we learn that our peers are a kind of gender police, constantly threatening to unmask us as feminine, as sissies. One of the favorite tricks when I was an adolescent was to ask a boy to look at his fingernails. If he held his palm toward his face and curled his fingers back to see them, he passed the test. He'd look at his nails "like a man." But if he held the back of his hand away from his face, and looked at his fingernails with arm outstretched, he was immediately ridiculed as sissy.

As young men we are constantly riding those gender boundaries, checking the fences we have constructed on the perimeter, making sure that nothing even remotely feminine might show through. The possibilities of being unmasked are everywhere. Even the most seemingly insignificant thing can pose a threat or activate that haunting terror. On the day the students in my course "Sociology of Men and Masculinities" were scheduled to discuss homophobia and male-male friendships, one student provided a touching illustration. Noting that it was a beautiful day, the first day of spring after a brutal northeast winter, he decided to wear shorts to class. "I had this really nice pair of new Madras shorts," he commented. "But then I thought to myself, these shorts have lavender and pink in them. Today's class topic is homophobia. Maybe today is not the best day to wear these shorts."

Our efforts to maintain a manly front cover everything we do. What we wear. How we talk. How we walk. What we eat. Every mannerism, every movement contains a coded gender language. Think, for example, of how you would answer the question: How do you "know" if a man is homosexual? When I ask this question in classes or workshops, respondents invariably provide a pretty standard list of stereotypically effeminate behaviors. He walks a certain way, talks a certain way, acts a certain way. He's very emotional; he shows his feelings. One woman commented that she "knows" a man is gay if he really cares about her; another said she knows he's gay if he shows no interest in her, if he leaves her alone.

Now alter the question and imagine what heterosexual men do to make sure no one could possibly get the "wrong idea" about them. Responses typically refer to the original stereotypes, this time as a set of negative rules about behavior. Never dress that way. Never talk or walk that way. Never show your feelings or get emotional. Always be prepared to demonstrate sexual interest in women that you meet, so it is impossible for any woman to get the wrong idea about you. In this sense, homophobia, the fear of being perceived as gay, as not a real man, keeps men exaggerating all the traditional rules of masculinity, including sexual predation with women. Homophobia and sexism go hand in hand. . . .

Homophobia as a Cause of Sexism, Heterosexism, and Racism

Homophobia is intimately interwoven with both sexism and racism. The fear—sometimes conscious, sometimes not—that others might perceive us as homosexual propels men to enact all manner of exaggerated masculine behaviors and attitudes to make sure that no one could possibly get the wrong idea about us. One of the centerpieces of that exaggerated masculinity is putting women down, both by excluding them from the public sphere and by the quotidian put-downs in speech and behaviors that organize the daily life of the American man. Women and gay men become the "other" against which heterosexual men project their identities, against whom they stack the decks so as to compete in a situation in which they will always win, so that by suppressing them, men can stake a claim for their own manhood. Women threaten emasculation by representing the home, workplace, and familial responsibility, the negation of fun. Gay men have historically played the role of the consummate sissy in the American popular mind because homosexuality is seen as an inversion of normal gender development. There have been other "others." Through American history, various groups have represented the sissy, the non-men against whom American men played out their definitions of manhood, often with vicious results. In fact, these changing groups provide an interesting lesson in American historical development.

At the turn of the 19th century, it was Europeans and children who provided the contrast for American men. The "true American was vigorous, manly, and direct, not effete and corrupt like the supposed Europeans," writes Rupert Wilkinson (1986). "He was plain rather than ornamented, rugged rather than luxury seeking, a liberty loving common man or natural gentleman rather than an aristocratic oppressor or servile minion" (p. 96). The "real man" of the early 19th century was neither noble nor serf. By the middle of the century, black slaves had replaced the effete nobleman. Slaves were seen as dependent, helpless men, incapable of defending their women and children, and therefore less than manly. Native Americans were cast as foolish and naive children, so they could be infantilized as the "Red Children of the Great White Father" and therefore excluded from full manhood.

By the end of the century, new European immigrants were also added to the list of the unreal men, especially the Irish and Italians, who were seen as too passionate and emotionally volatile to remain controlled sturdy oaks, and Jews, who were seen as too bookishly effete and too physically puny to truly measure up. In the mid-20th century, it was also Asians—first the Japanese during the Second World War, and more recently, the Vietnamese during the Vietnam War—who have served as unmanly templates against which American men have hurled their gendered rage. Asian men were seen as small, soft, and effeminate—hardly men at all.

Such a list of "hyphenated" Americans—Italian-, Jewish-, Irish-, African-, Native-, Asian-, gay—composes the majority of American men. So manhood is only possible for a distinct minority, and the definition has been constructed to prevent the others from achieving it. Interestingly, this emasculation of one's enemies has a flip side—and one that is equally gendered. These very groups that have historically been cast as less than manly were also, often simultaneously, cast as hypermasculine, as sexually aggressive, violent rapacious beasts, against whom "civilized" men must take a decisive stand and thereby rescue civilization. Thus black men were depicted as rampaging sexual beasts, women as carnivorously carnal, gay men as sexually insatiable, southern European men as sexually predatory and voracious, and Asian men as vicious and cruel torturers who were immorally disinterested in life itself, willing to sacrifice their entire people for their whims. But whether one saw these groups as effeminate sissies or as brutal savages, the terms with which they were perceived were gendered. These groups become the "others," the screens against which traditional conceptions of manhood were developed. . . .

Power and Powerlessness in the Lives of Men

I have argued that homophobia, men's fear of other men, is the animating condition of the dominant definition of masculinity in America, that the reigning definition of masculinity is a defensive effort to prevent being emasculated. In our efforts to suppress or overcome those fears, the dominant culture exacts a tremendous price from those deemed less than fully manly: women, gay men, nonnative-born men, men of color. This perspective may help clarify a paradox in men's lives, a paradox in which men have virtually all the power and yet do not feel powerful (see Kaufman, 1993).

Manhood is equated with power—over women, over other men. Everywhere we look, we see the institutional expression of that power—in state and national legislatures, on the boards of directors of every major U.S. corporation or law firm, and in every school and hospital administration. . . .

When confronted with the analysis that men have all the power, many men react incredulously. "What do you mean, men have all the power?" they ask. "What are you talking about? My wife bosses me around. My kids boss me around. My boss bosses me around. I have no power at all! I'm completely powerless!"

Men's feelings are not the feelings of the powerful, but of those who see themselves as powerless. These are the feelings that come inevitably from the discontinuity between the social and the psychological, between the aggregate analysis that reveals how men are in power as a group and the psychological fact that they do not feel powerful as individuals. They are the feelings of men who were raised to believe themselves entitled to feel that power, but do not feel it. No wonder many men are frustrated and angry. . . .

Why, then, do American men feel so powerless? Part of the answer is because we've constructed the rules of manhood so that only the tiniest fraction of men come to believe that they are the biggest of wheels, the sturdiest of oaks, the most virulent repudiators of femininity, the most daring and aggressive. We've managed to disempower the overwhelming majority of American men by other means—such as discriminating on the basis of race, class, ethnicity, age, or sexual preference. . .

Others still rehearse the politics of exclusion, as if by clearing away the playing field of secure gender identity of any that we deem less than manly—women, gay men, nonnative-born men, men of color—middle-class, straight, white men can re-ground their sense of themselves without those haunting fears and that deep shame that they are unmanly and will be exposed by other men. This is the manhood of racism, of sexism, of homophobia. It is the manhood that is so chronically insecure that it trembles at the idea of lifting the ban on gays in the military, that is so threat-ened by women in the workplace that women become the targets of sexual harass-ment, that is so deeply frightened of equality that it must ensure that the playing field of male competition remains stacked against all newcomers to the game.

Exclusion and escape have been the dominant methods American men have used to keep their fears of humiliation at bay. The fear of emasculation by other men, of being humiliated, of being seen as a sissy, is the leitmotif in my reading of the history of American manhood. Masculinity has become a relentless test by which we prove to other men, to women, and ultimately to ourselves, that we have successfully mastered the part. The restlessness that men feel today is nothing new in American history; we have been anxious and restless for almost two centuries. Neither exclusion nor escape has ever brought us the relief we've sought, and there is no reason to think that either will solve our problems now. Peace of mind, re-lief from gender struggle, will come only from a politics of inclusion, not exclu-sion, from standing up for equality and justice, and not by running away.

NOTES

1. Much of this work is elaborated in *Manhood: The American Quest* (in press).

2. Although I am here discussing only American masculinity, I am aware that others have located this chronic instability and efforts to prove manhood in the particular cultural and economic arrangements of Western society. Calvin, after all, inveighed against the dis-grace "for men to become effeminate," and countless other theorists have described the me-chanics of manly proof (see, for example, Seidler, 1994).

3. Such observations also led journalist Heywood Broun to argue that most of the at-tacks against feminism came from men who were shorter than 5 ft. 7 in. "The man who, whatever his physical size, feels secure in his own masculinity and in his own relation to life is rarely resentful of the opposite sex" (cited in Symes, 1930, p. 139).

REFERENCES

Brannon, R. (1976). The male sex role—and what it's done for us lately. In R. Brannon & D. David (Eds.), *The forty-nine percent majority* (pp. 1–40). Reading, MA: Addison-Wesley.

Connell, R. W. (1987). *Gender and power.* Stanford, CA: Stanford University Press.

Freud, S. (1933/1966). *New introductory lectures on psychoanalysis* (L. Strachey, Ed.). New York: Norton.

Goffman, E. (1963). *Stigma*. Englewood Cliffs, NJ: Prentice Hall.

Gorer, G. (1964). *The American people: A study in national character*. New York: Norton.

Kaufman, M. (1993). *Cracking the armour: Power and pain in the lives of men*. Toronto: Viking Canada.

Leverenz, D. (1986). Manhood, humiliation and public life: Some stories. *Southwest Review, 71*, Fall.

Leverenz, D. (1991). The last real man in America: From Natty Bumppo to Batman. *American Literary Review, 3*.

Marx, K., & F. Engels. (1848/1964). The communist manifesto. In R. Tucker (Ed.), *The Marx-Engels reader*. New York: Norton.

Mead, M. (1965). *And keep your powder dry*. New York: William Morrow.

Rotundo, E. A. (1993). *American manhood: Transformations in masculinity from the revolution to the modern era*. New York: Basic Books.

Seidler, V. J. (1994). *Unreasonable men: Masculinity and social theory*. New York: Routledge.

Symes, L. (1930). The new masculinism. *Harper's Monthly, 161*, January.

Tocqueville, A. de. (1835/1967). *Democracy in America*. New York: Anchor.

Weber, M. (1905/1966). *The Protestant ethic and the spirit of capitalism*. New York: Charles Scribner's.

Wilkinson, R. (1986). *American tough: The tough-guy tradition and American character*. New York: Harper & Row.

9

DISABILITY AND THE JUSTIFICATION OF INEQUALITY IN AMERICAN HISTORY

Douglas C. Baynton

Since the social and political revolutions of the eighteenth century, the trend in western political thought has been to refuse to take for granted inequalities between persons or groups. Differential and unequal treatment has continued, of course, but it has been considered incumbent on modern societies to produce a rational explanation for such treatment. In recent decades, historians and other scholars in the humanities have studied intensely and often challenged the osten-

From *The New Disability History*, Paul K. Longmore and Lauri Umansky, eds. Copyright © 2000 NYU Press. Reprinted by permission of the publisher.

sibly rational explanations for inequalities based on identity—in particular, gender, race, and ethnicity. Disability, however, one of the most prevalent justifications for inequality, has rarely been the subject of historical inquiry.

Disability has functioned historically to justify inequality for disabled people themselves, but it has also done so for women and minority groups. That is, not only has it been considered justifiable to treat disabled people unequally, but the *concept* of disability has been used to justify discrimination against other groups by attributing disability to them. Disability was a significant factor in the three great citizenship debates of the nineteenth and early twentieth centuries: women's suffrage, African American freedom and civil rights, and the restriction of immigration. When categories of citizenship were questioned, challenged, and disrupted, disability was called on to clarify and define who deserved, and who was deservedly excluded from, citizenship. Opponents of political and social equality for women cited their supposed physical, intellectual, and psychological flaws, deficits, and deviations from the male norm. These flaws—irrationality, excessive emotionality, physical weakness—are in essence mental, emotional, and physical disabilities, although they are rarely discussed or examined as such. Arguments for racial inequality and immigration restrictions invoked supposed tendencies to feeble-mindedness, mental illness, deafness, blindness, and other disabilities in particular races and ethnic groups. Furthermore, disability figured prominently not just in arguments *for* the inequality of women and minorities but also in arguments *against* those inequalities. Such arguments took the form of vigorous denials that the groups in question actually had these disabilities; they were not disabled, the argument went, and therefore were not proper subjects for discrimination. Rarely have oppressed groups denied that disability is an adequate justification for social and political inequality. Thus, while disabled people can be considered one of the minority groups historically assigned inferior status and subjected to discrimination, disability has functioned for all such groups as a sign of and justification for inferiority. . . .

The metaphor of the natural versus the monstrous was a fundamental way of constructing social reality in Edmund Burke's time. By the late nineteenth and early twentieth centuries, however, the concept of the natural was to a great extent displaced or subsumed by the concept of normality.[1] Since then, normality has been deployed in all aspects of modern life as a means of measuring, categorizing, and managing populations (and resisting such management). Normality is a complex concept, with an etiology that includes the rise of the social sciences, the science of statistics, and industrialization with its need for interchangeable parts and interchangeable workers. It has been used in a remarkable range of contexts and with a bewildering variety of connotations. The natural and the normal both are ways of establishing the universal, unquestionable good and right. Both are also ways of establishing social hierarchies that justify the denial of legitimacy and certain rights to individuals or groups. Both are constituted in large part by being set in opposition to culturally variable notions of disability—just as the natural was meaningful in relation to the monstrous and the deformed, so are the cultural meanings of the normal produced in tandem with disability[2]. . . .

As an evolutionary concept, normality was intimately connected to the western notion of progress. By the mid-nineteenth century, nonwhite races were routinely connected to people with disabilities, both of whom were depicted as evolutionary laggards or throwbacks. As a consequence, the concept of disability, intertwined with the concept of race, was also caught up in ideas of evolutionary progress. Physical or mental abnormalities were commonly depicted as instances of atavism, reversions to earlier stages of evolutionary development. Down's syndrome, for example, was called Mongolism by the doctor who first identified it in 1866 because he believed the syndrome to be the result of a biological reversion by Caucasians to the Mongol racial type. Teachers of the deaf at the end of the century spoke of making deaf children more like "normal" people and less like savages by forbidding them the use of sign language, and they opposed deaf marriages with a rhetoric of evolutionary progress and decline. . . .

Disability arguments were prominent in justifications of slavery in the early to mid-nineteenth century and of other forms of unequal relations between white and black Americans after slavery's demise. The most common disability argument for slavery was simply that African Americans lacked sufficient intelligence to participate or compete on an equal basis in society with white Americans. This alleged deficit was sometimes attributed to physical causes, as when an article on the "diseases and physical peculiarities of the negro race" in the *New Orleans Medical and Surgical Journal* helpfully explained, "It is the defective hematosis, or atmospherization of the blood, conjoined with a deficiency of cerebral matter in the cranium, and an excess of nervous matter distributed to the organs of sensation and assimilation, that is the true cause of that debasement of mind, which has rendered the people of Africa unable to take care of themselves." Diseases of blacks were commonly attributed to "inferior organisms and constitutional weaknesses," which were claimed to be among "the most pronounced race characteristics of the American negro." While the supposedly higher intelligence of "mulattos" compared to "pure" blacks was offered as evidence for the superiority of whites, those who argued against "miscegenation" claimed to the contrary that the products of "race-mixing" were themselves less intelligent and less healthy than members of either race in "pure" form.[3] A medical doctor, John Van Evrie of New York, avowed that the "disease and disorganization" in the "abnormal," "blotched, deformed" offspring of this "monstrous" act "could no more exist beyond a given period than any other physical degeneration, no more than tumors, cancers, or other abnormal growths or physical disease can become permanent." Some claimed greater "corporeal vigor" for "mixed offspring" but a deterioration in "moral and intellectual endowments," while still others saw greater intelligence but "frailty," "less stamina," and "inherent physical weakness."[4]

A second line of disability argument was that African Americans, because of their inherent physical and mental weaknesses, were prone to become disabled under conditions of freedom and equality. A New York medical journal reported that deafness was three times more common and blindness twice as common among free blacks in the North compared to slaves in the South. John C. Calhoun, senator from South

Carolina and one of the most influential spokesmen for the slave states, thought it a powerful argument in defense of slavery that the "number of deaf and dumb, blind, idiots, and insane, of the negroes in the States that have changed the ancient relation between the races" was seven times higher than in the slave states.[5]

While much has been written about the justification of slavery by religious leaders in the South, more needs to be said about similar justifications by medical doctors. Dr. Samuel Cartwright, in 1851, for example, described two types of mental illness to which African Americans were especially subject. The first, Drapetomania, a condition that caused slaves to run away — "as much a disease of the mind as any other species of mental alienation" — was common among slaves whose masters had "made themselves too familiar with them, treating them as equals." The need to submit to a master was built into the very bodies of African Americans, in whom "we see '*genu flexit*' written in the physical structure of his knees, being more flexed or bent, than any other kind of man." The second mental disease peculiar to African Americans, Dysaesthesia Aethiopis — a unique ailment differing "from every other species of mental disease, as it is accompanied with physical signs or lesions of the body" — resulted in a desire to avoid work and generally to cause mischief. It was commonly known to overseers as "rascality." Its cause, similar to that of Drapetomania, was a lack of firm governance, and it was therefore far more common among free blacks than among slaves — indeed, nearly universal among them — although it was a "common occurrence on badly-governed plantations" as well.[6]

Dr. Van Evrie also contributed to this line of thought when he wrote in the 1860s that education of African Americans came "at the expense of the body, shortening the existence" and resulted in bodies "dwarfed or destroyed" by the unnatural exertion. "An 'educated negro,' like a 'free negro,' is a social monstrosity, even more unnatural and repulsive than the latter." He argued further that, since they belonged to a race inferior by nature, *all* blacks were necessarily inferior to (nearly) *all* whites. It occasionally happened that a particular white person might not be superior to all black people because of a condition that "deforms or blights individuals; they may be idiotic, insane, or otherwise incapable." But these unnatural exceptions to the rule were "the result of human vices, crimes, or ignorance, immediate or remote." Only disability might lower a white person in the scale of life to the level of being of a marked race.[7] . . .

Daryl Michael Scott has described how both conservatives and liberals have long used an extensive repertory of "damage imagery" to describe African Americans. Conservatives "operated primarily from within a biological framework and argued for the innate inferiority of people of African descent" in order to justify social and political exclusion. Liberals maintained that social conditions were responsible for black inferiority and used damage imagery to argue for inclusion and rehabilitation; but regardless of their intentions, Scott argues, liberal damage imagery "reinforced the belief system that made whites feel superior in the first place." Both the "contempt and pity" of conservatives and liberals — a phrase that equally well describes historically prevalent attitudes toward disabled people — framed Americans of African descent as defective. Scott cites the example of Charles S. Johnson, chair of the social science department and later president of Fisk University, who told students in a 1928 speech that "the sociologists classify Negroes with cripples, persons with recognized physical handicaps." Like Johnson, Scott is critical of the fact that "African Americans were often lumped with the 'defective,' 'delinquent,' and dependent classes." This is obviously a bad place to be "lumped." Scott does not ask, however, why that might be the case[8] The attribution of disease or disability to racial minorities has a long history. Yet, while many have pointed out the injustice and perniciousness of attributing these qualities to a racial or ethnic group, little has been written about why these attributions are such powerful weapons for inequality, why they were so furiously denied and condemned by their targets, and what this tells us about our attitudes toward disability.

During the long-running debate over women's suffrage in the nineteenth and early twentieth centuries, one of the rhetorical tactics of suffrage opponents was to point to the physical, intellectual, and psychological flaws of women, their frailty, irrationality, and emotional excesses. By the late nineteenth century, these claims were sometimes expressed in terms of evolutionary progress; like racial and ethnic minorities, women were said to be less evolved than white men, their disabilities a result of lesser evolutionary development. Cynthia Eagle Russett has noted that "women and savages, together with idiots, criminals, and pathological monstrosities [those with congenital disabilities] were a constant source of anxiety to male intellectuals in the late nineteenth century."[9] What all shared was an evolutionary inferiority, the result of arrested development or atavism.

Paralleling the arguments made in defense of slavery, two types of disability argument were used in opposition to women's suffrage: that women had disabilities that made them incapable of using the franchise responsibly, and that because of their frailty women would become disabled if exposed to the rigors of political participation. The American anti-suffragist Grace Goodwin, for example, pointed to the "great temperamental disabilities" with which women had to contend: "woman lacks endurance in things mental. . . . She lacks nervous stability. The suffragists who dismay England are nervesick women." The second line of argument, which was not incompatible with the first and often accompanied it, went beyond the claim that women's flaws made them incapable of exercising equal political and social rights with men to warn that if women were given those rights, disability would surely follow. This argument is most closely identified with Edward Clarke, author of *Sex in Education; or, A Fair Chance for Girls*. Clarke's argument chiefly concerned education for women, though it was often applied to suffrage as well. Clarke maintained that overuse of the brain among young women was in large part responsible for the "numberless pale, weak, neuralgic, dyspeptic, hysterical, menorraghic, dysmenorrhoeic girls and women" of America. The result of excessive education in this country was "bloodless female faces, that suggest consumption, scrofula, anemia, and neuralgia." An appropriate education designed for their frail constitutions would ensure "a future secure from neuralgia, uterine disease, hysteria, and other derangements of the nervous system."[10]

Similarly, Dr. William Warren Potter, addressing the Medical Society of New York in 1891, suggested that many a mother was made invalid by inappropriate education: "her reproductive organs were dwarfed, deformed, weakened, and diseased, by artificial causes imposed upon her during their development."[11] Dr. A. Lapthorn Smith asserted in *Popular Science Monthly* that educated women were increasingly "sick and suffering before marriage and are physically disabled from performing physiological functions in a normal manner." Antisuffragists likewise warned that female participation in politics invariably led to "nervous prostration" and "hysteria," while Dr. Almroth E. Wright noted the "fact that there is mixed up with the woman's movement much mental disorder." A prominent late nineteenth-century neurophysiologist, Charles L. Dana, estimated that enfranchising women would result in a 25 percent increase in insanity among them and "throw into the electorate a mass of voters of delicate nervous stability . . . which might do injury to itself without promoting the community's good." The answer for Clarke, Potter, and others of like mind was special education suited to women's special needs. As with disabled people today, women's social position was treated as a medical problem that necessitated separate and special care. Those who wrote with acknowledged authority on the "woman question" were doctors. As Clarke wrote, the answer to the "problem of woman's sphere . . . must be obtained from physiology, not from ethics or metaphysics."[12] . . .

Disability figured not just in arguments *for* the inequality of women and minorities but also in arguments *against* those inequalities. Suffragists rarely challenged the notion that disability justified political inequality and instead disputed the claim that women suffered from these disabilities. Their arguments took three forms: one, women were not disabled and therefore deserved the vote; two, women were being erroneously and slanderously classed with disabled people, with those who were legitimately denied suffrage; and three, women were not naturally or inherently disabled but were *made* disabled by inequality—suffrage would ameliorate or cure these disabilities. . . .

Ethnicity also has been defined by disability. One of the fundamental imperatives in the initial formation of American immigration policy at the end of the nineteenth century was the exclusion of disabled people. Beyond the targeting of disabled people, the concept of disability was instrumental in crafting the image of the undesirable immigrant. The first major federal immigration law, the Act of 1882, prohibited entry to any "lunatic, idiot, or any person unable to take care of himself or herself without becoming a public charge." Those placed in the categories "lunatic" and "idiot" were automatically excluded. The "public charge" provision was intended to encompass people with disabilities more generally and was left to the examining officer's discretion. The criteria for excluding disabled people were steadily tightened as the eugenics movement and popular fears about the decline of the national stock gathered strength. The Act of 1891 replaced the phrase "*unable* to take care of himself or herself without becoming a public charge," with "*likely* to become a public charge." The 1907 law then denied entry to anyone judged "mentally or physically defective, such mental or physical defect being of a nature which *may affect* the ability of such alien to earn a living." These changes considerably lowered the threshold for exclusion and expanded the latitude of immigration officials to deny entry.[13]

The category of persons *automatically* excluded was also steadily expanded. In 1903, people with epilepsy were added and, in addition to those judged insane, "persons who have been insane within five years previous [or] who have had two or more attacks of insanity at any time previously." This was reduced to one "attack" in the 1917 law; the classification of "constitutional psychopathic inferiority" was also added, which inspection regulations described as including "various unstable individuals on the border line between sanity and insanity . . . and persons with abnormal sex instincts."[14] This was the regulation under which, until recently, gays and lesbians were excluded. One of the significant factors in lifting this ban, along with other forms of discrimination against gays and lesbians, was the decision by the American Psychiatric Association in 1973 to remove homosexuality from its list of mental illnesses. That is, once gays and lesbians were declared not to be disabled, discrimination became less justifiable.

Legislation in 1907 added "imbeciles" and "feeble-minded persons" to the list, in addition to "idiots," and regulations for inspectors directed them to exclude persons with "any mental abnormality whatever . . . which justifies the statement that the alien is mentally defective." These changes encompassed a much larger number of people and again granted officials considerably more discretion to judge the fitness of immigrants for American life. Fiorello H. LaGuardia, who worked his way through law school as an interpreter at Ellis Island, later wrote that "over fifty percent of the deportations for alleged mental disease were unjustified," based as they often were on "ignorance on the part of the immigrants or the doctors and the inability of the doctors to understand the particular immigrant's norm, or standard."[15]

The detection of physical disabilities was a major aspect of the immigration inspector's work. The Regulations for the medical inspection of immigrants in 1917 included a long list of diseases and disabilities that could be cause for exclusion, among them arthritis, asthma, bunions, deafness, deformities, flat feet, heart disease, hernia, hysteria, poor eyesight, poor physical development, spinal curvature, vascular disease of the heart, and varicose veins. . . .

In short, the exclusion of disabled people was central to the laws and the work of the immigration service. As the Commissioner General of Immigration reported in 1907, "The exclusion from this country of the morally, mentally, and physically deficient is the principal object to be accomplished by the immigration laws." Once the laws and procedures limiting the entry of disabled people were firmly established and functioning well, attention turned to limiting the entry of undesirable ethnic groups. Discussion on this topic often began by pointing to the general public agreement that the laws excluding disabled people had been a positive, if insufficient, step. In 1896, for example, Francis Walker noted in the *Atlantic Monthly* that the necessity of "straining out" immigrants who were "deaf, dumb, blind, idiotic, insane, pauper, or criminal" was "now conceded by men of all shades of opinion"; indeed there was a widespread "resentment at the attempt of such persons to impose themselves upon us." As one restrictionist wrote, the need to exclude the disabled was "self evident."[16]

For the more controversial business of defining and excluding undesirable ethnic groups, however, restrictionists found the *concept* of disability to be a powerful tool. That is, while people with disabilities constituted a distinct category of persons unwelcome in the United States, the charge that certain ethnic groups were mentally and physically deficient was instrumental in arguing for *their* exclusion. The belief that discriminating on the basis of disability was justifiable in turn helped justify the creation of immigration quotas based on ethnic origin. The 1924 Immigration Act instituted a national quota system that severely limited the numbers of immigrants from southern and eastern Europe, but long before that, disabilities stood in for nationality. Superintendents of institutions, philanthropists, immigration reformers, and politicians had been warning for decades before 1924 that immigrants were disproportionately prone to be mentally defective — up to half the immigrants from southern and eastern Europe were feebleminded, according to expert opinion.[17] Rhetoric about "the slow-witted Slav," the "neurotic condition of our Jewish immigrants," and, in general, the "degenerate and psychopathic types, which are so conspicuous and numerous among the immigrants," was pervasive in the debate over restriction.[18] The laws forbidding entry to the feebleminded were motivated in part by the desire to limit immigration from inferior nations, and conversely, it was assumed that the 1924 act would reduce the number of feebleminded immigrants. The issues of ethnicity and disability were so intertwined in the immigration debate as to be inseparable. . . .

Historians have scrutinized the attribution of mental and physical inferiority based on race and ethnicity, but only to condemn the slander. With their attention confined to ethnic stereotypes, they have largely ignored what the attribution of disability might also tell us about attitudes toward disabled people. Racial and ethnic prejudice is exposed while prejudice against people with disabilities is passed over as insignificant and understandable. As a prominent advocate of restriction wrote in 1930, "The necessity of the exclusion of the crippled, the blind, those who are likely to become public charges, and, of course, those with a criminal record is self evident."[19] The necessity has been treated as self-evident by historians as well, so much so that even the possibility of discrimination against people with disabilities in immigration law has gone unrecognized. In historical accounts, disability is present but rendered invisible or insignificant. While it is certain that immigration restriction rests in good part on a fear of "strangers in the land," in John Higham's phrase, American immigration restriction at the turn of the century was also clearly fueled by a fear of *defectives* in the land.

Still today, women and other groups who face discrimination on the basis of identity respond angrily to accusations that they might be characterized by physical, mental, or emotional disabilities. Rather than challenging the basic assumptions behind the hierarchy, they instead work to remove themselves from the negatively marked categories — that is, to disassociate themselves from those people who "really are" disabled — knowing that such categorization invites discrimination.

For example, a recent proposal in Louisiana to permit pregnant women to use parking spaces reserved for people with mobility impairments was opposed by women's organizations. A lobbyist for the Women's Health Foundation said, "We've spent a long time trying to dispel the myth that pregnancy is a disability, for obvious reasons of discrimination." She added, "I have no problem with it being a courtesy, but not when a legislative mandate provides for pregnancy in the same way as for disabled persons."[20] To be associated with disabled people or with the accommodations accorded disabled people is stigmatizing. . . .

This common strategy for attaining equal rights, which seeks to distance one's own group from imputations of disability and therefore tacitly accepts the idea that disability is a legitimate reason for inequality, is perhaps one of the factors responsible for making discrimination against people with disabilities so persistent and the struggle for disability rights so difficult. . . .

Disability is everywhere in history, once you begin looking for it, but conspicuously absent in the histories we write. When historians do take note of disability, they usually treat it merely as personal tragedy or an insult to be deplored and a label to be denied, rather than as a cultural construct to be questioned and explored. Those of us who specialize in the history of disability, like the early historians of other minority groups, have concentrated on writing histories of disabled people and the institutions and laws associated with disability. This is necessary and exciting work. It is through this work that we are building the case that disability is culturally constructed rather than natural and timeless—that disabled people have a history, and a history worth studying. Disability, however, more than an identity, is a fundamental element in cultural signification and indispensable for *any* historian seeking to make sense of the past. It may well be that all social hierarchies have drawn on culturally constructed and socially sanctioned notions of disability. If this is so, then there is much work to do. It is time to bring disability from the margins to the center of historical inquiry.

NOTES

1. Ian Hacking, *The Taming of Chance* (Cambridge and New York: Cambridge University Press, 1990), 160–66. See also Georges Canguilhem, *The Normal and the Pathological* (New York: Zone Books, 1989); Douglas C. Baynton, *Forbidden Signs: American Culture and the Campaign against Sign Language* (Chicago: University of Chicago Press, 1996), chaps. 5–6.

2. Francois Ewald, "Norms Discipline, and the Law," *Representations* 30 (Spring 1990): 146, 149–150, 154; Lennard Davis, *Enforcing Normalcy: Disability, Deafness, and the Body* (London: Verso, 1995); Baynton, *Forbidden Signs*, chaps. 5 and 6.

3. Samuel A. Cartwright, "Report on the Diseases and Physical Peculiarities of the Negro Race," *New Orleans Medical and Surgical Journal* 7 (May 1851): 693; George M. Fredrickson, *The Black Image in the White Mind* (New York: Harper and Row, 1971), 250–51; J. C. Nott, "The Mulatto a Hybrid," *American Journal of Medical Sciences* (July 1843), quoted in Samuel Forry, "Vital Statistics Furnished by the Sixth Census of the

United States," *New York Journal of Medicine and the Collateral Sciences* 1 (September 1843): 151–53.

4. John H. Van Evrie, *White Supremacy and Negro Subordination, or Negroes a Subordinate Race* (New York: Van Evrie, Horton, & Co., 1868), 153–55; Forry, "Vital Statistics," 159; Paul B. Barringer, *The American Negro: His Past and Future* (Raleigh: Edwards & Broughton, 1900), 10.

5. Cited in Forry, "Vital Statistics," 162–63. John C. Calhoun, "Mr. Calhoun to Mr. Pakenham," in Richard K. Cralle, ed., *The works of John C. Calhoun* (New York: D. Appleton, 1888), 5:337.

6. Cartwright, "Report," 707–10. See also Thomas S. Szasz, "The Sane Slave: A Historical Note on the use of Medical Diagnosis as Justificatory Rhetoric," *American Journal of Psychotherapy* 25 (1971): 228–39.

7. Van Evrie, *White Supremacy,* 121, 181, 221. Van Evrie notes in his preface that the book was completed "about the time of Mr. Lincoln's election" and was therefore originally an argument in favor of the continuation of slavery but presently constituted an argument for its restoration.

8. Daryl Michael Scott, *Contempt and Pity: Social Policy and the Image of the Damaged Black Soul, 1880–1996* (Chapel Hill: University of North Carolina Press, 1997), xi–xvii; 12, 208 n. 52.

9. Cynthia Eagle Russett, *Sexual Science: The Victorian Construction of Womanhood* (Cambridge, Mass.: Harvard University Press, 1989), 63. See also Lois N. Magner, "Darwinism and the Woman Question: The Evolving Views of Charlotte Perkins Gilman," in Joanne Karpinski, ed., *Critical Essays on Charlotte Perkins Gilman* (New York: G. K. Hall, 1992), 119–20.

10. Grace Duffield Goodwin, *Anti-Suffrage: Ten Good Reasons* (New York: Duffield and Co., 1913), 91–92 (in Smithsonian Institution Archives, Collection 60—Warshaw Collection, "Women," Box 3). Edward Clarke, *Sex in Education; or, A Fair Chance for Girls* (1873; reprint, New York: Arno Press, 1972), 18, 22, 62.

11. William Warren Potter, "How Should Girls Be Educated? A Public Health Problem for Mothers, Educators, and Physicians," *Transactions of the Medical Society of the State of New York* (1891): 48, quoted in Martha H. Verbrugge, *Able Bodied Womanhood: Personal Health and Social Change in Nineteenth-Century Boston* (Oxford and New York: Oxford University Press, 1988), 121.

12. A. Lapthorn Smith, "Higher Education of Women and Race Suicide," *Popular Science Monthly* (March 1905), reprinted in Louise Michele Newman, ed., *Men's Ideas/Women's Realities: Popular Science, 1870–1915* (New York: Pergamon Press, 1985), 149; Almroth E. Wright quoted in Mara Mayor, "Fears and Fantasies of the Anti-Suffragists," *Connecticut Review* 7 (April 1974): 67; Charles L. Dana quoted in Jane Jerome Camhi, *Women against Women: American Anti-Suffragism, 1880–1920* (New York: Carlson Publishing Co., 1994), 18; Clarke, *Sex in Education,* 12.

13. *United States Statutes at Large* (Washington, D.C.: Government Printing Office, 1883), 22:214. *United States Statutes at Large* (Washington, D.C.: Government Printing Office, 1891), 26:1084; *United States Statutes at Large* (Washington, D.C.: Government Printing Office, 1907), 34:899. Emphases added.

14. *United States Statutes at Large* (Washington, D.C.: Government Printing Office, 1903), 32:1213; United States Public Health Service, *Regulations Governing the Medical Inspection of Aliens* (Washington, D.C.: Government Printing Office, 1917), 28–29.

15. *Statutes* (1907), 34:899; United States Public Health Service, *Regulations,* 30–31; Fiorello H. LaGuardia, *The Making of an Insurgent: An Autobiography, 1882–1919* (1948; reprint, New York: Capricorn, 1961), 65.

16. U.S. Bureau of Immigration, *Annual Report of the Commissioner of Immigration* (Washington, D.C.: Government Printing Office, 1907), 62; Francis A. Walker, "Restriction of Immigration," *Atlantic Monthly* 77 (June 1896): 822; Ellsworth Eliot, Jr., M.D., "Immigration," in Madison Grant and Charles Steward Davison, eds., *The Alien in Our Midst, or Selling Our Birthright for a Mess of Industrial Pottage* (New York: Galton Publishing Co., 1930), 101.

17. See James W. Trent, Jr., *Inventing the Feeble Mind: A History of Mental Retardation in the United States* (Berkeley: University of California Press, 1994), 166–69.

18. Thomas Wray Grayson, "The Effect of the Modern Immigrant on Our Industrial Centers" in *Medical Problems of Immigration* (Easton, Penn.: American Academy of Medicine, 1913), 103, 107–9.

19. Ellsworth Eliot, Jr., M.D., "Immigration," in Grant and Davison, *Alien in Our Midst,* 101.

20. Heather Salerno, "Mother's Little Dividend: Parking," *Washington Post* (September 16, 1997): A1.

10

DECONSTRUCTING THE UNDERCLASS

Herbert Gans

A Matter of Definition?

Buzzwords for the undeserving poor are hardly new, for in the past the poor have been termed paupers, rabble, white trash, and the dangerous classes. Today, however, Americans do not use such harsh terms in their public discourse, whatever people may say to each other in private. Where possible, euphemisms are employed, and if they are from the academy, so much the better. A string of these became popular in the 1960s; the most famous is Oscar Lewis's anthropological concept *culture of poverty,* a term that became his generation's equivalent of underclass.

From *Journal of the American Planning Association,* 271 (Summer 1990). Reprinted by permission of the *Journal of the American Planning Association.*

When Gunnar Myrdal invented or reinvented the term underclass in his 1962 book *Challenge to Affluence,* he used the word as a purely economic concept, to describe the chronically unemployed, underemployed, and underemployables being created by what we now call the post-industrial economy. He was thinking of people being driven to the margins, or entirely out, of the modern economy, here and elsewhere; but his intellectual and policy concern was with reforming that economy, not with changing or punishing the people who were its victims.

Some other academics, this author included, used the term with Myrdal's definition in the 1960s and 1970s. However, gradually the users shifted from Myrdal's concern with unemployment to poverty, so that by the late 1970s social scientists had begun to identify the underclass with acute or persistent poverty rather than joblessness. Around the same time a very different definition of the underclass also emerged that has become the most widely used, and is also the most dangerous.

That definition has two novel elements. The first is racial, for users of this definition see the underclass as being almost entirely black and Hispanic. Second, it adds a number of behavioral patterns to an economic definition—and almost always these patterns involve behavior thought to be undeserving by the definers.

Different definers concentrate on somewhat different behavior patterns, but most include antisocial or otherwise harmful behavior, such as crime. Many definers also focus on various patterns that are *deviant* or aberrant from what they consider middle class norms, but that in fact are not automatically or always harmful, such as common law marriage. Some definers even measure membership in the underclass by deviant answers to public opinion poll questions. . . .

In the past five years the term's diverse definitions have remained basically unchanged, although the defining attempt itself has occasioned a very lively, often angry, debate among scholars. Many researchers have accepted much or all of the now-dominant behavioral definition; some have argued for a purely economic one, like Myrdal's; and some—this author included—have felt that the term has taken on so many connotations of undeservingness and blameworthiness that it has become hopelessly polluted in meaning, ideological overtone and implications, and should be dropped—with the issues involved studied via other concepts. Basically the debate has involved positions usually associated with the Right and the Left, partisans of the former arguing that the underclass is the product of the unwillingness of the black poor to adhere to the American work ethic, among other cultural deficiencies, and the latter claiming that the underclass is a consequence of the development of the post-industrial economy, which no longer needs the unskilled poor.

The debate has swirled in part around William J. Wilson, the University of Chicago sociologist and author of *The Truly Disadvantaged* (1987), who is arguably the most prominent analyst of the underclass in the 1980s. He focuses entirely on the black underclass and insists that this underclass exists mainly because of large-scale and harmful changes in the labor market, and its resulting spatial concentration as well as the isolation of such areas from the more affluent parts of the black community. One of his early definitions also included a reference to aberrant behavior patterns, although his most recent one, offered in November 1989, centers around the notion of "weak attachment to the labor force," an idea that seems nearly to coincide with Myrdal's, especially since Wilson attributes that weakness to faults in the economy rather than in the jobless.

Wilson's work has inspired a lot of new research, not only about the underclass but about poverty in general, and has made poverty research funding, public and private, available again after a long drought. Meanwhile, various scholars have tried to resolve or reorient the political debate, but without much luck, for eventually the issue always boils down to whether the fault for being poor and the responsibility for change should be assigned more to poor people or more to the economy and the state. At the same time, journalistic use of the so-called behavioral definition of the underclass has increased—and so much so that there is a danger of researchers and policy analysts being carried along by the popularity of this definition of the term in the public discourse. . . .

The Power of Buzzwords and Labels

The behavioral definition of the underclass, which in essence proposes that some very poor people are somehow to be selected for separation from the rest of society and henceforth treated as especially undeserving, harbors many dangers—for their civil liberties and ours, for example, for democracy, and for the integration of society. But the rest of this essay will concentrate on what seem to me to be the major dangers for planners. The *first* danger of the term is its unusual power as a buzzword. It is a handy euphemism; while it seems inoffensively technical on the surface, it hides within it all the moral opprobrium Americans have long felt toward those poor people who have been judged to be undeserving. Even when it is being used by journalists, scholars, and others as a technical term, it carries with it this judgmental baggage. . . .

A *second* and related danger of the term is its use as a racial codeword that subtly hides anti-black and anti-Hispanic feelings. A codeword of this kind fits in with the tolerant public discourse of our time, but it also submerges and may further repress racial—and class—antagonisms that continue to exist, yet are sometimes not expressed until socio-political boiling points are reached. Racial and class codewords—and codewords of any kind—get in the way of planners, however, because the citizenry may read codewords even though planners are writing analytical concepts.

A *third* danger of the term is its flexible character. Given the freedom of definition available in a democracy, anyone can decide, or try to persuade others, that yet additional people should be included in the underclass. For example, it is conceivable that in a city, region, or country with a high unemployment rate, powerless competitors for jobs, such as illegal immigrants or even legal but recently arrived workers, might be added to the list of undeserving people. . . .

The *fourth* danger of the term, a particularly serious one, is that it is a synthesizing notion—or what William Kornblum has more aptly called a lumping one—that covers a number of different people. Like other synthesizing notions that have moved far beyond the researchers' journals, it has also become a stereotype. Stereotypes are lay generalizations that are necessary in a very diversified society, and are useful when they are more or less accurate. When they are not, however, or when they are also judgmental terms, they turn into *labels*, to be used by some people to judge, and usually to stigmatize, other people, often those with less power or prestige. . . .

Insofar as poor people keep up with the labels the rest of society sticks on them, they are aware of the latest one. We do not all know the "street-level" consequences of stigmatizing labels, but they cannot be good. One of the likely, and most dangerous, consequences of labels is that they can become self-fulfilling prophecies. People publicly described as members of the underclass may begin to feel that they *are* members of such a class and are therefore unworthy in a new way. At the least, they now have to fight against yet another threat to their self-respect, not to mention another reason for feeling that society would just as soon have them disappear.

More important perhaps, people included in the underclass are quickly treated accordingly in their relations with the private and public agencies in which, like the rest of us, they are embedded—from workplaces, welfare agencies, and schools to the police and the courts. We know from social research that teachers with negative images of their pupils do not expect them to succeed and thus make sure, often unconsciously, that they do not; likewise, boys from single parent families who are picked up by the police are often thought to be wild and therefore guilty because they are assumed to lack male parental control. We know also that areas associated with the underclass do not get the same level of services as more affluent areas. After all, these populations are not likely to protest. . . .

Social Policy Implications

The remaining dangers are more directly relevant for planners, other policy researchers, and policy makers. The most general one, and the *fifth* on my list, is the term's interference with antipoverty policy and other kinds of planning. This results in part from the fact that underclass is a quite distinctive synthesizing term that lumps together a variety of highly diverse people who need different kinds of help. Categorizing them all with one term, and a buzzword at that, can be disastrous, especially if the political climate should demand that planners formulate a single "underclass policy." Whether one thinks of the poorest of the poor as having problems or as making problems for others, or both, they cannot be planned for with a single policy. For example, educational policies to prevent young people from dropping out of school, especially the few good ones in poor areas, have nothing to do with housing policies for dealing with various kinds of homelessness and the lack of affordable dwellings. Such policies are in turn different from programs to reduce street crime, and from methods of discouraging the very poor from escaping into the addictions of drugs, alcohol, mental illness, or pentecostal religion—which has its own harmful side effects. To be sure, policies relevant to one problem may have positive overlaps for another, but no single policy works for all the problems of the different poverty-stricken populations. Experts who claim one policy can do it all, like education, are simply wrong.

This conclusion applies even to jobs and income grant policies. Although it is certain that all of the problems blamed on the people assigned to the underclass would be helped considerably by policies to reduce sharply persistent joblessness and poverty, *and generally before other programs are implemented,* these policies also have limits. While all poor people need economic help, such help will not alone solve other problems some of them have or make for others. Although the middle class does not mug, neither do *the* poor; only a small number of poor male youngsters and young adults do so. Other causal factors are also involved, and effective antipoverty planning has to be based on some understanding of these factors and how to overcome them. Lumping concepts like the underclass can only hurt this effort.

A related or *sixth* danger stems from the persuasive capacity of concepts or buzzwords. These terms may become so *reified* through their use that people think they represent actual groups or aggregates, and may also begin to believe that being in what is, after all, an imaginary group is a *cause* of the characteristics included in its definition. Sometimes journalists and even scholars—especially those of conservative bent—appear to think that becoming very poor and acting in antisocial or deviant ways is an *effect* of being in the underclass. When the underclass becomes a causal term, however, especially on a widespread basis, planners, as well as politicians and citizens, are in trouble; sooner or later, someone will argue that the only policy solution is to lock up everyone described as an underclass member.

Similar planning problems develop if and when the reification of a term leads to its being assigned *moral* causality. Using notions that blame victims may help the blamers to feel better by blowing off the steam of righteous indignation, but it does not eliminate the problems very poor people have or make. Indeed, those who argue that all people are entirely responsible for what they do sidestep the morally and otherwise crucial issue of determining how much responsibility should be assigned to people who lack resources, who are therefore under unusual stress, and who lack effective choices in many areas of life in which even moderate income people can choose relatively freely. . . .

The *seventh* danger of the term, and one also particularly salient for planners, stems from the way the underclass has been analyzed. As already noted, some researchers have tried to identify underclass neighborhoods. Planners must be especially sensitive to the dangers of the underclass neighborhood notion, because, once statistically defined "neighborhoods," or even sets of adjacent census tracts, are marked with the underclass label, the politicians who make the basic land use decisions in the community may propose a variety of harmful policies, such as moving all of a city's homeless into such areas, or declaring them ripe for urban renewal because of the undeservingness of the population. Recall that this is how much of the federal urban renewal of the 1950s and 1960s was justified. In addition, neighborhood policies generally rest on the assumption that people inside the boundaries of such areas are more homogeneous than they in fact are, and that they remain inside boundaries that are more often nothing but lines on a map. Since very poor people tend to suffer more from public policies than they benefit, and since they have fewer defenses than more affluent people against harmful policies, "neighborhood policies" may hurt more often than they will help.

A related danger—and my *eighth*—stems from William J. Wilson's "concentration and isolation" hypotheses. Wilson argues that the economic difficulties of the very poorest blacks are compounded by the fact that as the better-off blacks move out, the poorest are more and more concentrated, having only other very poor people, and the few institutions that minister to them, as neighbors. This concentration causes social isolation, among other things, Wilson suggests, because the very poor are now isolated from access to the people, job networks, role models, institutions, and other connections that might help them escape poverty.

Wilson's hypotheses, summarized all too briefly here, are now being accepted as dogma by many outside the research community. Fortunately, they are also being tested in a number of places, but until they are shown to be valid, planners should probably go slowly with designing action programs—especially programs to reduce concentration. In the minimal-vacancy housing markets in which virtually all poor people live, such a policy might mean having to find a new, and surely more costly, dwelling unit, or having to double up with relatives, or in some cases being driven into shelters or into the streets. Even if working- and middle-class areas were willing to accept relocatees from deconcentrated areas, a response that seems unlikely, the relocatees could not afford to live in such areas—although many would flourish if they had the money to do so. Meanwhile, the dysfunctions of dispersal may be as bad as those of overconcentration, not because the latter has any virtues, but because, until an effective jobs-and-income-grants program has gone into operation, requiring very poor people to move away from the neighborly support structures they *do* have may deprive them of their only resources.

While it may be risky to attempt deconcentration at this stage, it is worth trying to reduce isolation. One form of isolation, the so-called urban-suburban mismatch between jobless workers residing in cities and available suburban jobs, is already being attacked again, which is all to the good. Perhaps something has been learned from the failures of the 1960s to reduce the mismatch. We must bear in mind, however, that in some or perhaps many cases the physical mismatch is only a cover for class and racial discrimination, and the widespread unwillingness of white suburban employers—and white workers—to have black coworkers. . . .

The *ninth* danger is inherent in the concept of an underclass. While it assumes that the people assigned to the underclass are poor, the term itself sidesteps issues of poverty. It also permits analysts to ignore the dramatic recent increases in certain kinds of poverty, or persisting poverty, and hence the need for resuming effective antipoverty programs. For example, terms like underclass make it easier for

conservative researchers to look at the homeless mainly as mentally ill or the victims of rent control, and frees them of any need to discuss the disappearance of
jobs, SROs [single-room occupancies], and other low income housing.

Indeed, to the extent that the underclass notion is turned into a synonym for
the undeserving poor, the political conditions for reinstituting effective antipoverty
policy are removed. If the underclass is undeserving, then the government's responsibility is limited to beefing up the courts and other punitive agencies and institutions that try to isolate the underclass and protect the rest of society from it.
Conversely, the moral imperative to help the poor through the provision of jobs
and income grants is reduced. Describing the poor as undeserving has long been
an effective if immoral short-term approach to tax reduction. . . .

NOTES

I am grateful to Michael Katz for his helpful comments on an earlier draft of this essay.

Kornblum, William. 1984. Lumping the Poor: What *Is* the Underclass. *Dissent.* September: 295–302.

Lewis, Oscar. 1969. The Culture of Poverty. In *On Understanding Poverty*, edited by
Daniel P. Moynihan. New York: Basic.

Myrdal, Gunnar. 1962. *The Challenge to Affluence.* New York: Pantheon.

Wilson, William J. 1987. *The Truly Disadvantaged: The Inner City, the Underclass, and
Public Policy.* Chicago: University of Chicago Press.

11

DOMINATION AND SUBORDINATION

Jean Baker Miller

What do people do to people who are different from them and why? On the individual level, the child grows only via engagement with people very different from
her/himself. Thus, the most significant difference is between the adult and the child.
At the level of humanity in general, we have seen massive problems around a great variety of differences. But the most basic difference is the one between women and men.

On both levels it is appropriate to pose two questions. When does the engagement of difference stimulate the development and the enhancement of both par-

From Jean Baker Miller, *Toward a New Psychology of Women.* © 1976, 1986 by Jean Baker Miller.
Reprinted by permission of Beacon Press, Boston.

ties to the engagement? And, conversely, when does such a confrontation with difference have negative effects: When does it lead to great difficulty, deterioration, and distortion and to some of the worst forms of degradation, terror, and violence—both for individuals and for groups—that human beings can experience? It is clear that "mankind" in general, especially in our Western tradition but in some others as well, does not have a very glorious record in this regard.

It is not always clear that in most instances of difference there is also a factor of inequality—inequality of many kinds of resources, but fundamentally of status and power. One useful way to examine the often confusing results of these confrontations with difference is to ask: What happens in situations of inequality? What forces are set in motion? While we will be using the terms "dominant" and "subordinate" in the discussion, it is useful to remember that flesh and blood women and men are involved. Speaking in abstractions sometimes permits us to accept what we might not admit to on a personal level.

Temporary Inequality

Two types of inequality are pertinent for present purposes. The first might be called temporary inequality. Here, the lesser party is *socially* defined as unequal. Major examples are the relationships between parents and children, teachers and students, and, possibly, therapists and clients. There are certain assumptions in these relationships which are often not made explicit, nor, in fact, are they carried through. But they are the social structuring of the relationship.

The "superior" party presumably has more of some ability or valuable quality, which she/he is supposed to impart to the "lesser" person. While these abilities vary with the particular relationship, they include emotional maturity, experience in the world, physical skills, a body of knowledge, or the techniques for acquiring certain kinds of knowledge. The superior person is supposed to engage with the lesser in such a way as to bring the lesser member up to full parity; that is, the child is to be helped to become the adult. Such is the overall task of this relationship. The lesser, the child, is to be given to, by the person who presumably has more to give. Although the lesser party often also gives much to the superior, these relationships are *based in service* to the lesser party. That is their *raison d'être*.

It is clear, then, that the paramount goal is to end the relationship; that is, to end the relationship of inequality. The period of disparity is meant to be temporary. People may continue their association as friends, colleagues, or even competitors, but not as "superior" and "lesser." At least this is the goal.

The reality is that we have trouble enough with this sort of relationship. Parents or professional institutions often tip toward serving the needs of the donor instead of those of the lesser party (for example, schools can come to serve teachers or administrators, rather than students). Or the lesser person learns how to be a good "lesser" rather than how to make the journey from lesser to full stature. Overall, we have not found very good ways to carry out the central task: to foster the movement from unequal to equal. In childrearing and education we do not have an adequate theory and practice. Nor do we have concepts that work well in such other unequal so-called "helping" relationships as healing, penology, and rehabilitation. Officially, we say we want to do these things, but we often fail.

We have a great deal of trouble deciding on how many rights "to allow" to the lesser party. We agonize about how much power the lesser party shall have. How much can the lesser person express or act on her or his perceptions when these definitely differ from those of the superior? Above all, there is great difficulty in maintaining the conception of the lesser person *as a person of as much intrinsic worth as the superior.*

A crucial point is that power is a major factor in all of these relationships. But power alone will not suffice. Power exists and it has to be taken into account, not denied. The superiors hold all the real power, but power will not accomplish *the task.* It will not bring the unequal party up to equality.

Our troubles with these relationships may stem from the fact that they exist within the context of a second type of inequality that tends to overwhelm the ways we learn to operate in the first kind. The second type molds the very ways we perceive and conceptualize what we are doing in the first, most basic kind of relationships.

The second type of inequality teaches us how to enforce inequality, but not how to make the journey from unequal to equal. Most importantly, its consequences are kept amazingly obscure—in fact they are usually denied. . . . However, the underlying notion is that this second type has determined, and still determines, the only ways we can think and feel in the first type.

Permanent Inequality

In these relationships, some people or groups of people are defined as unequal by means of what sociologists call ascription; that is, your birth defines you. Criteria may be race, sex, class, nationality, religion, or other characteristics ascribed at birth. Here, the terms of the relationships are very different from those of temporary inequality. There is, for example, no notion that superiors are present primarily to help inferiors, to impart to them their advantages and "desirable" characteristics. There is no assumption that the goal of the unequal relationship is to end the inequality; in fact, quite the reverse. A series of other governing tendencies are in force, and occur with great regularity. . . . While some of these elements may appear obvious, in fact there is a great deal of disagreement and confusion about psychological characteristics brought about by conditions as obvious as these.

Dominants

Once a group is defined as inferior, the superiors tend to label it as defective or substandard in various ways. These labels accrete rapidly. Thus, blacks are described as less intelligent than whites, women are supposed to be ruled by emotion, and so on. In addition, the actions and words of the dominant group tend to be destructive of the subordinates. All historical evidence confirms this tendency. And, although they are much less obvious, there are destructive effects on the dominants as well. The latter are of a different order and are much more difficult to recognize.

Dominant groups usually define one or more acceptable roles for the subordinate. Acceptable roles typically involve providing services that no dominant group wants to perform for itself (for example, cleaning up the dominant's waste products). Functions that a dominant group prefers to perform, on the other hand, are carefully guarded and closed to subordinates. Out of the total range of human possibilities, the activities most highly valued in any particular culture will tend to be enclosed within the domain of the dominant group; less valued functions are relegated to the subordinates.

Subordinates are usually said to be unable to perform the preferred roles. Their incapacities are ascribed to innate defects or deficiencies of mind or body, therefore immutable and impossible of change or development. It becomes difficult for dominants even to imagine that subordinates are capable of performing the preferred activities. More importantly, subordinates themselves can come to find it difficult to believe in their own ability. The myth of their inability to fulfill wider or more valued roles is challenged only when a drastic event disrupts the usual arrangements. Such disruptions usually arise from outside the relationship itself. For instance, in the emergency situation of World War II, "incompetent" women suddenly "manned" the factories with great skill.

It follows that subordinates are described in terms of, and encouraged to develop, personal psychological characteristics that are pleasing to the dominant group. These characteristics form a certain familiar cluster: submissiveness, passivity, docility, dependency, lack of initiative, inability to act, to decide, to think, and the like. In general, this cluster includes qualities more characteristic of children than adults—immaturity, weakness, and helplessness. If subordinates adopt these characteristics they are considered well-adjusted.

However, when subordinates show the potential for, or even more dangerously have developed other characteristics—let us say intelligence, initiative, assertiveness—there is usually no room available within the dominant framework for acknowledgement of these characteristics. Such people will be defined as at least unusual, if not definitely abnormal. There will be no opportunities for the direct application of their abilities within the social arrangements. (How many women have pretended to be dumb!)

Dominant groups usually impede the development of subordinates and block their freedom of expression and action. They also tend to militate against stirrings of greater rationality or greater humanity in their own members. It was not too long ago that "nigger lover" was a common appellation, and even now men who "allow their women" more than the usual scope are subject to ridicule in many circles.

A dominant group, inevitably, has the greatest influence in determining a culture's overall outlook—its philosophy, morality, social theory, and even its science. The dominant group, thus, legitimizes the unequal relationship and incorporates it into society's guiding concepts. The social outlook, then, obscures the true nature of this relationship—that is, the very existence of inequality. The culture explains the events that take place in terms of other premises, premises that are inevitably false, such as racial or sexual inferiority. While in recent years we have learned about many such falsities on the larger social level, a full analysis of the psychological implications still remains to be developed. In the case of women, for example, despite overwhelming evidence to the contrary, the notion persists that women are meant to be passive, submissive, docile, secondary. From this premise, the outcome of therapy and encounters with psychology and other "sciences" are often determined.

Inevitably, the dominant group is the model for "normal human relationships." It then becomes "normal" to treat others destructively and to derogate them, to obscure the truth of what you are doing, by creating false explanations, and to oppose actions toward equality. In short, if one's identification is with the dominant group, it is "normal" to continue in this pattern. Even though most of us do not like to think of ourselves as either believing in, or engaging in, such dominations, it is, in fact, difficult for a member of a dominant group to do otherwise. But to keep on doing these things, one need only behave "normally."

It follows from this that dominant groups generally do not like to be told about or even quietly reminded of the existence of inequality. "Normally" they can avoid awareness because their explanation of the relationship becomes so well integrated *in other terms*; they can even believe that both they and the subordinate group share the same interests and, to some extent, a common experience. If pressed a bit, the familiar rationalizations are offered: the home is "women's natural place," and we know "what's best for them anyhow."

Dominants prefer to avoid conflict—open conflict that might call into question the whole situation. This is particularly and tragically so, when many members of the dominant group are not having an easy time of it themselves. Members of a dominant group, or at least some segments of it, such as white working-class men (who are themselves also subordinates), often feel unsure of their own narrow toehold on the material and psychological bounties they believe they desperately need. What dominant groups usually cannot act on, or even see, is that the situation of inequality in fact deprives them, particularly on the psychological level.

Clearly, inequality has created a state of conflict. Yet dominant groups will tend to suppress conflict. They will see any questioning of the "normal" situation as threatening; activities by subordinates in this direction will be perceived with alarm. Dominants are usually convinced that the way things are is right and good, not only for them but especially for the subordinates. All morality confirms this view, and all social structure sustains it.

It is perhaps unnecessary to add that the dominant group usually holds all of the open power and authority and determines the ways in which power may be acceptably used.

Subordinates

What of the subordinates' part in this? Since dominants determine what is normal for a culture, it is much more difficult to understand subordinates. Initial expressions of dissatisfaction and early actions by subordinates always come as a surprise;

they are usually rejected as atypical. After all, dominants *knew* that all women needed and wanted was a man around whom to organize their lives. Members of the dominant group do not understand why "they"—the first to speak out—are so upset and angry.

The characteristics that typify the subordinates are even more complex. A subordinate group has to concentrate on basic survival. Accordingly, direct, honest reaction to destructive treatment is avoided. Open, self-initiated action in its own self-interest must also be avoided. Such actions can, and still do, literally result in death for some subordinate groups. In our own society, a woman's direct action can result in a combination of economic hardship, social ostracism, and psychological isolation—and even the diagnosis of a personality disorder. Any one of these consequences is bad enough. . . .

It is not surprising then that a subordinate group resorts to disguised and indirect ways of acting and reacting. While these actions are designed to accommodate and please the dominant group, they often, in fact, contain hidden defiance and "put ons." Folk tales, black jokes, and women stories are often based on how the wily peasant or sharecropper outwitted the rich landowner, boss, or husband. The essence of the story rests on the fact that the overlord does not even know that he has been made a fool of.

One important result of this indirect mode of operation is that members of the dominant group are denied an essential part of life—the opportunity to acquire self-understanding through knowing their impact on others. They are thus deprived of "consensual validation," feedback, and a chance to correct their actions and expressions. Put simply, subordinates won't tell. For the same reasons, the dominant group is deprived also of valid knowledge about the subordinates. (It is particularly ironic that the societal "experts" in knowledge about subordinates are usually members of the dominant group.)

Subordinates, then, know much more about the dominants than vice versa. They have to. They become highly attuned to the dominants, able to predict their reactions of pleasure and displeasure. Here, I think, is where the long story of "feminine intuition" and "feminine wiles" begins. It seems clear that these "mysterious" gifts are in fact skills, developed through long practice, in reading many small signals, both verbal and nonverbal.

Another important result is that subordinates often know more about the dominants than they know about themselves. If a large part of your fate depends on accommodating to and pleasing the dominants, you concentrate on them. Indeed, there is little purpose in knowing yourself. Why should you when your knowledge of the dominants determines your life? This tendency is reinforced by many other restrictions. One can know oneself only through action and interaction. To the extent that their range of action or interaction is limited, subordinates will lack a realistic evaluation of their capacities and problems. Unfortunately, this difficulty in gaining self-knowledge is even further compounded.

Tragic confusion arises because subordinates absorb a large part of the untruths created by the dominants; there are a great many blacks who feel inferior to whites, and women who still believe they are less important than men. This internalization of dominant beliefs is more likely to occur if there are few alternative concepts at hand. On the other hand, it is also true that members of the subordinate group have certain experiences and perceptions that accurately reflect the truth about themselves and the injustice of their position. Their own more truthful concepts are bound to come into opposition with the mythology they have absorbed from the dominant group. An inner tension between the two sets of concepts and their derivations is almost inevitable.

From a historical perspective, despite the obstacles, subordinate groups have tended to move toward greater freedom of expression and action, although this progress varies greatly from one circumstance to another. There were always some slaves who revolted; there were some women who sought greater development or self-determination. Most records of these actions are not preserved by the dominant culture, making it difficult for the subordinate group to find a supporting tradition and history.

Within each subordinate group, there are tendencies for some members to imitate the dominants. This imitation can take various forms. Some may try to treat their fellow subordinates as destructively as the dominants treat them. A few may develop enough of the qualities valued by the dominants to be partially accepted into their fellowship. Usually they are not wholly accepted, and even then only if they are willing to forsake their own identification with fellow subordinates. "Uncle Toms" and certain professional women have often been in this position. (There are always a few women who have won the praise presumably embodied in the phrase "she thinks like a man.")

To the extent that subordinates move toward freer expression and action, they will expose the inequality and throw into question the basis for its existence. And they will make the inherent conflict an open conflict. They will then have to bear the burden and take the risks that go with being defined as "troublemakers." Since this role flies in the face of their conditioning, subordinates, especially women, do not come to it with ease.

What is immediately apparent from studying the characteristics of the two groups is that mutually enhancing interaction is not probable between unequals. Indeed, conflict is inevitable. The important questions, then, become: Who defines the conflict? Who sets the terms? When is conflict overt or covert? On what issues is the conflict fought? Can anyone win? Is conflict "bad," by definition? If not, what makes for productive or destructive conflict?

Suggestions for Further Reading

Alba, Richard D. *Ethnic Identity: The Transformation of White American Identity.* New Haven: Yale University Press, 1990.

Berkhofer, Robert F., Jr. *The White Man's Indian: Images of the American Indian from Columbus to the Present.* New York: Vintage, 1978.

Blazina, Chris. *Cultural Myth of Masculinity.* Westport, CT: Praeger Publishers, 2003.

Connell, R. W. *Masculinities,* 2nd ed. Berkeley: University of California Press, 2005.

De Beauvoir, Simone. *The Second Sex.* New York: Alfred A. Knopf, 1952.

Epstein, Cynthia Fuchs. *Deceptive Distinctions: Sex, Gender, and the Social Order.* New Haven: Yale University Press; New York: Russell Sage Foundation, 1988.

Frankenberg, Ruth. *White Women, Race Matters.* Minneapolis: University of Minnesota Press, 1993.

Gould, Stephen. *The Mismeasure of Man.* New York: W. W. Norton, 1984.

Gregory, Steven, and Roger Sanjek, eds. *Race.* New Brunswick, NJ: Rutgers University Press, 1994.

Hubbard, Ruth. *The Politics of Women's Biology.* New Brunswick, NJ: Rutgers University Press, 1990.

Katz, Jonathan Ned. *The Invention of Heterosexuality.* New York: Dutton, 1995.

Kimmel, Michael. *Manhood in America,* 2nd ed. New York: Oxford University Press, 2005.

Kleinman, Sherryl, Martha Copp, and Kent Sandstrom. "Making Sexism Visible: Birdcages, Martians, and Pregnant Men." *Teaching Sociology, 35,* pp. 126–142.

Lopez, Ian F. Haney. *White by Law: The Legal Construction of Race.* New York: New York University Press, 1996.

Lorber, Judith. *Paradoxes of Gender.* New Haven: Yale University Press, 1995.

Lowe, M., and R. Hubbard, eds. *Women's Nature: Rationalizations of Inequality.* New York: Pergamon Press, 1983.

Memmi, Albert. *Dominated Man.* Boston: Beacon Press, 1969.

Montague, M. F. Ashley. *Man's Most Dangerous Myth.* New York: Harper & Row, 1952.

Omi, Michael, and Howard Winant. *Racial Formations in the United States,* 2nd ed. New York: Routledge and Kegan Paul, 1994.

Roediger, David. *Colored White: Transcending the Racial Past.* Berkeley: University of California Press, 2003.

Sanday, Peggy R. *Female Power and Male Dominance: On the Origins of Sexual Inequality.* New York: Cambridge University Press, 1981.

Williams, Gregory Howard. *Life on the Color Line.* New York: Dutton, 1995.

Understanding Racism, Sexism, Heterosexism, and Class Privilege

I n Part II, we spend some time analyzing systems of oppression and examining the relations of dominance and subordination they incorporate almost seamlessly into daily life. Racism, sexism, heterosexism, and class privilege are systems of advantage that provide those with the "right" race, sex, sexual orientation, and class (or some combination of these) with opportunities and rewards that are unavailable to other individuals and groups in society. Sometimes they work in isolation from each other but most often they operate in combination to create a system of advantage and disadvantage that enhances the life chances of some while limiting the life chances of others.

The construction of difference as deviance or deficiency underlies the systems of oppression that determine how power, privilege, wealth, and opportunity are distributed. We are surrounded by differences every day but our society chooses to place a value on only some of them. By valuing the characteristics and lifestyles of certain individuals or groups and devaluing those of others, society constructs some of its members as "other." These "others" are understood to be less deserving, less intelligent, even less human. Once this happens, it is possible to distribute wealth, opportunity, and justice unequally without appearing to be unfair. The social construction of race, class, gender, and sexuality as difference—where being white, male, European, heterosexual, and prosperous is the norm and everyone else is considered less able and less worthy—lies at the heart of racism, sexism, heterosexism, and classism.

Some people are uncomfortable with words like "racism," "sexism," and "oppression," which seem to them highly charged and unnecessarily accusatory. They prefer to talk about "discrimination" and "prejudice." However, those who wish to emphasize the complex, pervasive, and self-perpetuating nature of the system of beliefs, policies, practices, and attitudes that enforce the relations of subordination and domination in our society find the term discrimination too narrow and too limited to do so effectively. Words like racism, sexism, and oppression are more appropriate because they capture the comprehensive nature of the systems being studied. In Selection 5, Marilyn Frye does a good job of explaining the meaning of "oppression" in the course of using that concept to convey the pervasive nature of sexism. Frye uses the metaphor of a birdcage to illustrate how a system of oppression, in this case sexism, imprisons its victims through a set of interlocking impediments to motion. Taken alone, none of the barriers seem very powerful or threatening; taken together they are unyielding. They comprise a cage, which appears light and airy, masking the fact that its occupants are trapped as completely as if they were in a sealed vault.

Racism and sexism are systems of advantage based on race and sex. In the United States, racism perpetuates an interlocking system of institutions, attitudes, privileges, and rewards that work to the benefit of white people just as sexism works to the advantage of men. In Selection 1, Beverly Daniel Tatum elaborates on this definition of racism (originally offered by David Wellman in his book *Portraits of White Racism*), and discusses the resistance some of those of us who are white feel toward acknowledging both the existence of racism and the advantages it bestows on us. As Tatum observes, many prefer to define racism in terms of racial prejudice because by adopting this definition it is possible to say that people of color as well as white people can be racist. For many people in this society, being able to say so seems to satisfy a deep emotional need. Confronted with behavior or speech that is hateful, they wish to use the strongest words they can to condemn and deplore it. Once racism is defined as a system of advantages based on race, it is no longer possible to attribute racism to people of color because clearly they do not systematically benefit from racism; only white people do. This, of course, does not deny that people of all colors are capable of hateful and hurtful behavior, nor does it prevent us from taking them to task for their prejudice. But it does mean that we will reserve the term "racism" to refer specifically to the comprehensive system of advantages that work to the benefit of white people in the United States. For more on this important and provocative distinction, you will want to turn directly to the essay by Tatum.

In Selection 2, Eduardo Bonilla-Silva examines the claim made by many white people in the United States today that racism is a thing of the past and that they personally do not see race or skin color (or, by extension, sex, class, disability, etc.); they just see "human beings." Bonilla-Silva and other sociologists have coined the term "color-blind racism" to refer to this new version of racial ideology. In this essay, actually a written version of a talk he gave at Texas A&M, Bonilla-Silva argues that, contrary to what many would like to believe, it is not racists or bigots who perpetuate the system of racial inequality in this country but the ordinary behavior of well-meaning whites as they simply follow "the racial script of America." In this way, Bonilla-Silva directs our attention to some of the ways in which white supremacy and white privilege are institutionalized by the ordinary operations of society. He spends the majority of time in his essay examining the central frames of color-blind racism that allow many of us who are white and who believe that we are "color-blind" to perpetuate the racial status quo without ever having to take responsibility for society's ongoing racism. In contrast to the older and cruder version of racism, Bonilla-Silva warns us, "today there is a sanitized, color-blind way of calling minorities 'niggers,' 'spics,' or 'chinks.' Today, most whites justify keeping minorities out of the good things in life with the language of liberalism. . . ."

Rita Chaundry Sethi (Selection 4) reminds us how easy it is, in certain parts of the United States, to think of racial conflict in Black and white terms. Sethi rejects this simplistic racial paradigm because it leaves no room for the racism that Asian Americans experience. According to Sethi, white America constructs Asian Americans as a model minority and Asian Americans themselves and for their own reasons tend to minimize anti-Asian discrimination as well. As a result, the racism that Asian Americans experience in the United States is often rendered invisible or trivialized. Sethi's project is to uncover the hidden racism directed against Asians and by doing so to broaden the use of the term. Although she does not argue the point directly, unlike Tatum, Sethi seems willing to use the term "racism" to describe certain behavior and attitudes that occur within and among communities of color.

The term "sexism" refers to the oppression of women by men in a society that is largely patriarchal. As defined by Allan G. Johnson in Selection 6, a patriarchal society is male-dominated, male-identified, and male-centered. In such a society, every institution and aspect of culture contrives to rationalize and perpetuate the dominance of men and the subordination of women. Marilyn Frye's article asks us to look closely at examples of some seemingly innocent but oppressive social rituals that perpetuate these relations of domination. She takes as her paradigm, or model, the "male door-opening ritual" and argues that its meaning and implications go far beyond the conscious intentions of the man who opens the door. The point is that sexism and racism can be perpetuated by people who are just trying to be nice. As you think about her example, remember that Frye is analyzing the implications of a social practice, not looking at any individual's motives for carrying out that ritual.

The use of the term "heterosexism" parallels "racism" and "sexism," and according to Suzanne Pharr in Selection 7, involves the assumption that the world is and must be heterosexual at the same time that it rationalizes the existing distribution of power and privilege that flows from this assumption. In her essay Pharr argues that economics, violence, and homophobia, or fear of lesbians and gays, are the most effective weapons of sexism and makes it clear that homophobia and heterosexism are oppressive of all women, not just those of us who are not exclusively heterosexual. For more current statistics on economic inequality (which continue to support Pharr's claims), take a look at the material in Part I of this book.

Finally, "class privilege" refers to the system of advantages that continues to ensure that wealth, power, opportunity, and privilege go hand in hand. In Selection 9, Greg Mantsios explores some of the myths about class that mislead people about their real-life chances and documents the impact of class position on daily life. While many in the United States are oblivious to the full force of class privilege, the statistics in this article suggest that the class position of one's family, not hard work, intelligence, or determination, is probably the single most significant determinant of future success. This gap between people's beliefs about what it takes to succeed and the tremendous role that class privilege plays in determining who is successful provides a dramatic illustration of the effectiveness of systems of oppression both in terms of perpetuating the current systems of advantage and in rendering their continuing operation invisible to so many. This point will be taken up again in Part VIII.

These are powerful and disturbing claims and they are likely to provoke equally strong reactions from many people reading this introduction. Some will feel angry, others will feel depressed and discouraged, some will feel uncomfortable, others will be skeptical, and some will simply feel confused. This is understandable. If what you have just read is true, then things in the United States are neither as fair nor as equitable as most of us would like them to be. If some people, as these definitions suggest, have more than their share, then others have less than they deserve, and each of us must wonder where we will stand in the final computation. Further, many readers who are white and working class or middle class will be hard pressed to imagine what kind of privilege they exercise. They look at their own lives and the lives of their parents and friends and see people who have worked very hard for everything they have achieved. The idea that they are privileged may seem very foreign to them. The same will be true for other readers as well. Heterosexism, class privilege, male privilege? "What have these abstract and politically charged terms got to do with me?" they ask. "I work hard, try to get ahead, wish others well, and feel more like a victim myself than a victimizer." This understandable response underscores how effectively the systems of oppression we are discussing function in contemporary society to rationalize the hierarchy they create, often making its operation invisible both to those who benefit from it and to those who are shortchanged by it. In addition, it points to the complicated and ambiguous nature of privilege, which means that a single individual can be privileged in some respects at the very same time he or she is disadvantaged in other respects. Let us examine these two points in more detail.

Many people who are privileged fail to realize that this is the case because the systems of oppression we are studying so effectively make the current distribution of privilege and power appear almost "natural." In addition, some of us, including those of us who are disadvantaged, grow up believing things about ourselves and others that make our life choices and opportunities or lack of them seem inevitable or deserved. In many cases, people with privileges have enjoyed them so long that they have simply come to take them for granted. Instead of recognizing them as special benefits that come with, for example, white skin, they just assume that these privileges are things to which they have a right. For more on this topic see Peggy McIntosh's essay, Selection 8, which does an excellent job of examining how white privilege works.

In other cases, privilege may be difficult to identify and acknowledge because the individual is privileged in some respects but not in others. For example, those who are privileged by virtue of their sex or sexual orientation may be disadvantaged in other respects, say by virtue of their race/ethnicity or their class position or both. The disadvantages they experience in some areas may seem so unfair and so egregious that they prevent them from recognizing the privileges they nonetheless enjoy. For example, a poor, white, single mother who receives public assistance and who feels very much at the mercy of an unfair and inhumane system might still be able to call upon her white skin privilege or her heterosexual privilege in certain situations and yet be oblivious to that privilege because she feels so disadvantaged in other respects. A working class or lower middle class white male who has trouble stretching his paycheck to cover all his expenses may be so preoccupied with his financial situation that he doesn't recognize the male privilege and white skin privilege from which he nonetheless benefits—privileges which may not feel at all like privileges to him because he takes them for granted and regards them as "natural" and "normal." And finally, since most people are basically decent and fair, those of us who are privileged are often simply reluctant to acknowledge that we have unfair advantages over others because that would require that we re-evaluate our sense of who we are and what we have accomplished in our lives

As should by now be clear, each of the thinkers whose work is included in Part II shares the belief that the various systems of oppression operate in relation to each other, forming an interlocking system of advantages and disadvantages that rationalize and preserve the prevailing distribution of power and privilege in society. As you read these articles, try to keep an open mind about this claim. If these thinkers are correct, they have something important to tell us about this society and the forces that will be in place as each of us goes about creating our own future. Reading some of this material may make some people temporarily uncomfortable, but failing to grapple with it may leave us all the more vulnerable to the forces that play a compelling role in determining the life chances of the individuals and groups that make up our society.

1

DEFINING RACISM
"Can We Talk?"

Beverly Daniel Tatum

Early in my teaching career, a White student I knew asked me what I would be teaching the following semester. I mentioned that I would be teaching a course on racism. She replied, with some surprise in her voice, "Oh, is there still racism?" I assured her that indeed there was and suggested that she sign up for my course. Fifteen years later, after exhaustive media coverage of events such as the Rodney King beating, the Charles Stuart and Susan Smith cases, the O. J. Simpson trial, the appeal to racial prejudices in electoral politics, and the bitter debates about affirmative action and welfare reform, it seems hard to imagine that anyone would still be unaware of the reality of racism in our society. But in fact, in almost every audience I address, there is someone who will suggest that racism is a thing of the past. There is always someone who hasn't noticed the stereotypical images of people of color in the media, who hasn't observed the housing discrimination in their community, who hasn't read the newspaper articles about documented racial bias in lending practices among well-known banks, who isn't aware of the racial tracking pattern at the local school, who hasn't seen the reports of rising incidents of racially motivated hate crimes in America—in short, someone who hasn't been paying attention to issues of race. But if you are paying attention, the legacy of racism is not hard to see, and we are all affected by it.

The impact of racism begins early. Even in our preschool years, we are exposed to misinformation about people different from ourselves. Many of us grew up in neighborhoods where we had limited opportunities to interact with people different from our own families. When I ask my college students, "How many of you grew up in neighborhoods where most of the people were from the same racial group as your own?" almost every hand goes up. There is still a great deal of social segregation in our communities. Consequently, most of the early information we receive about "others"—people racially, religiously, or socioeconomically different from ourselves—does not come as the result of firsthand experience. The secondhand information we do receive has often been distorted, shaped by cultural stereotypes, and left incomplete.

Some examples will highlight this process. Several years ago one of my students conducted a research project investigating preschoolers' conceptions of Native Americans.[1] Using children at a local day care center as her participants, she asked these three- and four-year-olds to draw a picture of a Native American. Most children were stumped by her request. They didn't know what a Native American was. But when she rephrased the question and asked them to draw a picture of an Indian, they readily complied. Almost every picture included one central feature: feathers. In fact, many of them also included a weapon—a knife or tomahawk—and depicted the person in violent or aggressive terms. Though this group of children, almost all of whom were White, did not live near a large Native American population and probably had had little if any personal interaction with American Indians, they all had internalized an image of what Indians were like. How did they know? Cartoon images, in particular the Disney movie *Peter Pan*, were cited by the children as their number-one source of information. At the age of three, these children already had a set of stereotypes in place. Though I would not describe three-year-olds as prejudiced, the stereotypes to which they have been exposed become the foundation for the adult prejudices so many of us have.

Sometimes the assumptions we make about others come not from what we have been told or what we have seen on television or in books, but rather from what we have *not* been told. The distortion of historical information about people of color leads young people (and older people, too) to make assumptions that may go unchallenged for a long time. Consider this conversation between two White students following a discussion about the cultural transmission of racism:

"Yeah, I just found out that Cleopatra was actually a Black woman."

"What?"

The first student went on to explain her newly learned information. The second student exclaimed in disbelief, "That can't be true. Cleopatra was beautiful!"

What had this young woman learned about who in our society is considered beautiful and who is not? Had she conjured up images of Elizabeth Taylor when she thought of Cleopatra? The new information her classmate had shared and her own deeply ingrained assumptions about who is beautiful and who is not were too incongruous to allow her to assimilate the information at that moment.

Omitted information can have similar effects. For example, another young woman, preparing to be a high school English teacher, expressed her dismay that she had never learned about any Black authors in any of her English courses. How was she to teach about them to her future students when she hadn't learned about them herself? A White male student in the class responded to this discussion with frustration in his response journal, writing "It's not my fault that Blacks don't write books." Had one of his elementary, high school, or college teachers ever told him that there were no Black writers? Probably not. Yet because he had never been exposed to Black authors, he had drawn his own conclusion that there were none.

Stereotypes, omissions, and distortions all contribute to the development of prejudice. *Prejudice* is a preconceived judgment or opinion, usually based on limited information. I assume that we all have prejudices, not because we want them, but simply because we are so continually exposed to misinformation about others. Though I have often heard students or workshop participants describe someone as not having "a prejudiced bone in his body," I usually suggest that they look again. Prejudice is one of the inescapable consequences of living in a racist society. Cultural racism—the cultural images and messages that affirm the assumed superiority of Whites and the assumed inferiority of people of color—is like smog in the air. Sometimes it is so thick it is visible, other times it is less apparent, but always, day in and day out, we are breathing it in. None of us would introduce ourselves as "smog-breathers" (and most of us don't want to be described as prejudiced), but if we live in a smoggy place, how can we avoid breathing the air? If we live in an environment in which we are bombarded with stereotypical images in the media, are frequently exposed to the ethnic jokes of friends and family members, and are rarely informed of the accomplishments of oppressed groups, we will develop the negative categorizations of those groups that form the basis of prejudice.

People of color as well as Whites develop these categorizations. Even a member of the stereotyped group may internalize the stereotypical categories about his or her own group to some degree. In fact, this process happens so frequently that it has a name, *internalized oppression*. Some of the consequences of believing the distorted messages about one's own group will be discussed in subsequent chapters.

Certainly some people are more prejudiced than others, actively embracing and perpetuating negative and hateful images of those who are different from themselves. When we claim to be free of prejudice, perhaps what we are really saying is that we are not hatemongers. But none of us is completely innocent. Prejudice is an integral part of our socialization, and it is not our fault. Just as the preschoolers my student interviewed are not to blame for the negative messages they internalized, we are not at fault for the stereotypes, distortions, and omissions that shaped our thinking as we grew up.

To say that it is not our fault does not relieve us of responsibility, however. We may not have polluted the air, but we need to take responsibility, along with others, for cleaning it up. Each of us needs to look at our own behavior. Am I perpetuating and reinforcing the negative messages so pervasive in our culture, or am I seeking to challenge them? If I have not been exposed to positive images of marginalized groups, am I seeking them out, expanding my own knowledge base for myself and my children? Am I acknowledging and examining my own prejudices, my own rigid categorizations of others, thereby minimizing the adverse impact they might have on my interactions with those I have categorized? Unless we engage in these and other conscious acts of reflection and reeducation, we easily repeat the process with our children. We teach what we were taught. The unexamined prejudices of the parents are passed on to the children. It is not our fault, but it is our responsibility to interrupt this cycle.

Racism: A System of Advantage Based on Race

Many people use the terms *prejudice* and *racism* interchangeably. I do not, and I think it is important to make a distinction. In his book *Portraits of White Racism*, David Wellman argues convincingly that limiting our understanding of racism to prejudice does not offer a sufficient explanation for the persistence of racism. He defines racism as a "system of advantage based on race."[2] In illustrating this definition, he provides example after example of how Whites defend their racial advantage—access to better schools, housing, jobs—even when they do not embrace overtly prejudicial thinking. Racism cannot be fully explained as an expression of prejudice alone.

This definition of racism is useful because it allows us to see that racism, like other forms of oppression, is not only a personal ideology based on racial prejudice, but a *system* involving cultural messages and institutional policies and practices as well as the beliefs and actions of individuals. In the context of the United States, this system clearly operates to the advantage of Whites and to the disadvantage of people of color. Another related definition of racism, commonly used by antiracist educators and consultants, is "prejudice plus power." Racial prejudice when combined with social power—access to social, cultural, and economic resources and decision-making—leads to the institutionalization of racist policies and practices. While I think this definition also captures the idea that racism is more than individual beliefs and attitudes, I prefer Wellman's definition because the idea of systematic advantage and disadvantage is critical to an understanding of how racism operates in American society.

In addition, I find that many of my White students and workshop participants do not feel powerful. Defining racism as prejudice plus power has little personal relevance. For some, their response to this definition is the following: "I'm not really prejudiced, and I have no power, so racism has nothing to do with me." However, most White people, if they are really being honest with themselves, can see that there are advantages to being White in the United States. Despite the current rhetoric about affirmative action and "reverse racism," every social indicator, from salary to life expectancy, reveals the advantages of being White.[3]

The systematic advantages of being White are often referred to as White privilege. In a now well-known article, "White Privilege: Unpacking the Invisible Knapsack," Peggy McIntosh, a White feminist scholar, identified a long list of societal privileges that she received simply because she was White.[4] She did not ask for them, and it is important to note that she hadn't always noticed that she was receiving them. They included major and minor advantages. Of course she enjoyed greater access to jobs and housing. But she also was able to shop in department stores without being followed by suspicious salespeople and could always find appropriate hair care products and makeup in any drugstore. She could send her child to school confident that the teacher would not discriminate against him on the basis of race. She could also be late for meetings, and talk with her mouth full, fairly confident that these behaviors would not be attributed to the fact that she was White. She could express an opinion in a meeting or in print and not have it labeled the "White" viewpoint. In other words, she was more often than not viewed as an individual, rather than as a member of a racial group.

This article rings true for most White readers, many of whom may have never considered the benefits of being White. It's one thing to have enough awareness of racism to describe the ways that people of color are disadvantaged by it. But this new understanding of racism is more elusive. In very concrete terms, it means that if a person of color is the victim of housing discrimination, the apartment that would otherwise have been rented to that person of color is still available for a White person. The White tenant is, knowingly or unknowingly, the beneficiary of racism, a system of advantage based on race. The unsuspecting tenant is not to blame for the prior discrimination, but she benefits from it anyway.

For many Whites, this new awareness of the benefits of a racist system elicits considerable pain, often accompanied by feelings of anger and guilt. These uncomfortable emotions can hinder further discussion. We all like to think that we deserve the good things we have received, and that others, too, get what they deserve. Social psychologists call this tendency a "belief in a just world."[5] Racism directly contradicts such notions of justice.

Understanding racism as a system of advantage based on race is antithetical to traditional notions of an American meritocracy. For those who have internalized this myth, this definition generates considerable discomfort. It is more comfortable simply to think of racism as a particular form of prejudice. Notions of power or privilege do not have to be addressed when our understanding of racism is constructed in that way.

The discomfort generated when a systemic definition of racism is introduced is usually quite visible in the workshops I lead. Someone in the group is usually quick to point out that this is not the definition you will find in most dictionaries. I reply, "Who wrote the dictionary?" I am not being facetious with this response. Whose interests are served by a "prejudice only" definition of racism? It is important to understand that the system of advantage is perpetuated when we do not acknowledge its existence.

Racism: For Whites Only?

Frequently someone will say, "You keep talking about White people. People of color can be racist, too." I once asked a White teacher what it would mean to her if a student or parent of color accused her of being racist. She said she would feel as though she had been punched in the stomach or called a "low-life scum." She is not alone in this feeling. The word *racist* holds a lot of emotional power. For many White people, to be called racist is the ultimate insult. The idea that this term might only be applied to Whites becomes highly problematic for after all, can't people of color be "low-life scum" too?

Of course, people of any racial group can hold hateful attitudes and behave in racially discriminatory and bigoted ways. We can all cite examples of horrible hate crimes which have been perpetrated by people of color as well as Whites. Hateful behavior is hateful behavior no matter who does it. But when I am asked, "Can people of color be racist?" I reply, "The answer depends on your definition of racism." If one defines racism as racial prejudice, the answer is yes. People of color can and do have racial prejudices. However, if one defines racism as a system of advantage based on race, the answer is no. People of color are not racist because they do not systematically benefit from racism. And equally important, there is no systematic cultural and institutional support or sanction for the racial bigotry of people of color. In my view, reserving the term *racist* only for behaviors committed by Whites in the context of a White-dominated society is a way of acknowledging the ever-present power differential afforded Whites by the culture and institutions that make up the system of advantage and continue to reinforce notions of White superiority. (Using the same logic, I reserve the word *sexist* for men. Though women can and do have gender-based prejudices, only men systematically benefit from sexism.)

Despite my best efforts to explain my thinking on this point, there are some who will be troubled, perhaps even incensed, by my response. To call the racially motivated acts of a person of color acts of racial bigotry and to describe similar acts committed by Whites as racist will make no sense to some people, including some people of color. To those, I will respectfully say, "We can agree to disagree." At moments like these, it is not agreement that is essential, but clarity. Even if you don't like the definition of racism I am using, hopefully you are now clear about what it is. If I also understand how you are using the term, our conversation can continue—despite our disagreement.

Another provocative question I'm often asked is "Are you saying all Whites are racist?" When asked this question, I again remember that White teacher's response, and I am conscious that perhaps the question I am really being asked is, "Are you saying all Whites are bad people?" The answer to that question is of course not. However, all White people, intentionally or unintentionally, do benefit from racism. A more relevant question is what are White people as individuals doing to interrupt racism? For many White people, the image of a racist is a hood-wearing Klan member or a name-calling Archie Bunker figure. These images represent what might be called *active racism*, blatant, intentional acts of racial bigotry and discrimination. *Passive racism* is more subtle and can be seen in the collusion of laughing when a racist joke is told, of letting exclusionary hiring practices go unchallenged, of accepting as appropriate the omissions of people of color from the curriculum, and of avoiding difficult race-related issues. Because racism is so ingrained in the fabric of American institutions, it is easily self-perpetuating.[6] All that is required to maintain it is business as usual.

I sometimes visualize the ongoing cycle of racism as a moving walkway at the airport. Active racist behavior is equivalent to walking fast on the conveyor belt.

The person engaged in active racist behavior has identified with the ideology of White supremacy and is moving with it. Passive racist behavior is equivalent to standing still on the walkway. No overt effort is being made, but the conveyor belt moves the bystanders along to the same destination as those who are actively walking. Some of the bystanders may feel the motion of the conveyor belt, see the active racists ahead of them, and choose to turn around, unwilling to go to the same destination as the White supremacists. But unless they are walking actively in the opposite direction at a speed faster than the conveyor belt—unless they are actively antiracist—they will find themselves carried along with the others.

So, not all Whites are actively racist. Many are passively racist. Some, though not enough, are actively antiracist. The relevant question is not whether all Whites are racist, but how we can move more White people from a position of active or passive racism to one of active antiracism. The task of interrupting racism is obviously not the task of Whites alone. But the fact of White privilege means that Whites have greater access to the societal institutions in need of transformation. To whom much is given, much is required.

It is important to acknowledge that while all Whites benefit from racism, they do not all benefit equally. Other factors, such as socioeconomic status, gender, age, religious affiliation, sexual orientation, mental and physical ability, also play a role in our access to social influence and power. A White woman on welfare is not privileged to the same extent as a wealthy White heterosexual man. In her case, the systematic disadvantages of sexism and classism intersect with her White privilege, but the privilege is still there. This point was brought home to me in a 1994 study conducted by a Mount Holyoke graduate student, Phyllis Wentworth.[7] Wentworth interviewed a group of female college students, who were both older than their peers and were the first members of their families to attend college, about the pathways that led them to college. All of the women interviewed were White, from working-class backgrounds, from families where women were expected to graduate from high school and get married or get a job. Several had experienced abusive relationships and other personal difficulties prior to coming to college. Yet their experiences were punctuated by "good luck" stories of apartments obtained without a deposit, good jobs offered without experience or extensive reference checks, and encouragement provided by willing mentors. While the women acknowledged their good fortune, none of them discussed their Whiteness. They had not considered the possibility that being White had worked in their favor and helped give them the benefit of the doubt at critical junctures. This study clearly showed that even under difficult circumstances, White privilege was still operating.

It is also true that not all people of color are equally targeted by racism. We all have multiple identities that shape our experience. I can describe myself as a light-skinned, well-educated, heterosexual, able-bodied, Christian African American woman raised in a middle-class suburb. As an African American woman, I am systematically disadvantaged by race and by gender, but I systematically receive benefits in the other categories, which then mediate my experience of racism and sexism. When one is targeted by multiple isms—racism, sexism, classism, heterosexism, ableism, anti-Semitism, ageism—in whatever combination, the effect is intensified. The particular combination of racism and classism in many communities of color is life-threatening. Nonetheless, when I, the middle-class Black mother of two sons, read another story about a Black man's unlucky encounter with a White police officer's deadly force, I am reminded that racism by itself can kill.

NOTES

1. C. O'Toole, "The effect of the media and multicultural education on children's perceptions of Native Americans" (senior thesis, Department of Psychology and Education, Mount Holyoke College, South Hadley, MA, May 1990).

2. For an extended discussion of this point, see David Wellman, *Portraits of White racism* (Cambridge: Cambridge University Press, 1977), ch. 1.

3. For specific statistical information, see R. Farley, "The common destiny of Blacks and Whites: Observations about the social and economic status of the races," pp. 197–233 in H. Hill and J. E. Jones, Jr. (Eds.), *Race in America: The struggle for equality* (Madison: University of Wisconsin Press, 1993).

4. P. McIntosh, "White privilege: Unpacking the invisible knapsack," *Peace and Freedom* (July/August 1989): 10–12.

5. For further discussion of the concept of "belief in a just world," see M. J. Lerner, "Social psychology of justice and interpersonal attraction," in T. Huston (Ed.), *Foundations of interpersonal attraction* (New York: Academic Press, 1974).

6. For a brief historical overview of the institutionalization of racism and sexism in our legal system, see "Part V: How it happened: Race and gender issues in U.S. law," in P. S. Rothenberg (Ed.), *Race, class, and gender in the United States: An integrated study*, 3d ed. (New York: St. Martin's Press, 1995).

7. P. A. Wentworth, "The identity development of non-traditionally aged first-generation women college students: An exploratory study" (master's thesis, Department of Psychology and Education, Mount Holyoke College, South Hadley, MA, 1994).

2

COLOR-BLIND RACISM

Eduardo Bonilla-Silva

This is an edited version of a talk given on March 7, 2001, at a forum on racism at Texas A&M, sponsored by the Multicultural Leadership Forum and the Department of Multicultural Studies.

For most Americans, talking about racism is talking about white supremacist organizations or Archie Bunkers. I anchor my remarks from a different theoretical shore and one that will make many of you feel quite uncomfortable. I contend that racism is, more than anything else, *a matter of group power; it is about a dominant racial group (whites) striving to maintain its systemic advantages and minorities fighting to subvert the racial status quo.* Hence, although "bigots" are part of America's (and A&M's) racial landscape, they are not the central actors responsible for the reproduction of racial inequality. If bigots are not the cogs propelling America's racial dynamics, who are they? My answer: regular white folks just following the racial script of America. Today most whites assert that they "don't see any color, just people"; that although the ugly face of discrimination is still with us, it is no longer the main factor determining minorities' life chances; and, finally, that they, like Dr. Martin Luther King, aspire to live in a society where "people are judged by the content of their character and not by the color of their skin." More poignantly, and in a curious case of group projection, many whites insist that minorities (especially blacks) are the ones responsible for our "racial problems."

But regardless of whites' "sincere fictions," racial considerations shade almost everything that happens in this country. Blacks—and dark-skinned racial minorities—lag well behind whites in virtually every relevant social indicator. For example, blacks are poorer, earn less, and are significantly less wealthy than whites. They also receive an inferior education than do whites even when they attend integrated settings. Regarding housing, blacks pay more for similar units and, because of discrimination, cannot access the totality of the housing market in any locality. In terms of social interaction, blacks receive impolite and discriminatory treatment in stores, restaurants, attempting to hail taxicabs, driving, and in a host of other commercial and social transactions. In short, blacks are, using the apt metaphor coined by Professor Derrick Bell, "at the bottom of the well."

From the lecture "The Strange Enigma of Racism in Contemporary America," by Eduardo Bonilla-Silva. Reprinted by permission of the author.

How is it possible to have this tremendous level of racial inequality in a country where most people (whites) claim that race is no longer a relevant social factor and that "racists" are a species on the brink of extinction? More significantly, how do whites explain the contradiction between their professed color blindness and America's color-coded inequality? I will attempt to answer both of these questions. My main argument is that whites have developed a new, powerful ideology that justifies contemporary racial inequality and thus help maintain "systemic white privilege." I label this new ideology "color-blind racism" because this term fits quite well the language used by whites to defend the racial status quo. This ideology emerged in the 1960s concurrently with what I have labeled the "New Racism." "New Racism" practices maintain white privilege, and, unlike those typical of Jim Crow, tend to be slippery, institutional, and apparently nonracial. Post civil rights discrimination, for the most part, operates in a "now you see it, now you don't" fashion. For instance, instead of whites relying on housing covenants or on the Jim Crow signs of the past (e.g., "This is a WHITE neighborhood"), today realtors steer blacks into certain neighborhoods, individual whites use "smiling discrimination" to exclude blacks (e.g., studies by HUD and The Urban Institute), and, in some white neighborhoods, sponsorship is the hidden strategy relied upon to keep them white. Similar practices are at work in universities, banks, restaurants, and other venues.

Because the tactics for maintaining systemic white privilege changed in the 1960s, the rationalizations for explaining racial inequality changed, too. Whereas Jim Crow racism explained blacks' social standing as the product of their imputed biological and moral inferiority, color-blind racism explains it as the product of market dynamics, naturally occurring phenomena, and presumed cultural deficiencies. Below, I will highlight the central frames of color-blind racism with interview data from two projects: the 1997 Survey of College Students and the 1998 Detroit Area Study. The four central frames of color-blind racism are (1) *Abstract Liberalism,* (2) *Naturalization,* (3) *Biologization of Culture,* and (4) *Minimization of Racism.* I discuss each frame separately.

Abstract Liberalism

Whereas the principles liberalism and humanism were not extended to nonwhites in the past, they have become the main rhetorical weapons to justify contemporary racial inequality. Whites use these principles in an *abstract* way that allows them to support the racial status quo in an apparently "reasonable" fashion. For example, Eric, a corporate auditor in his forties, opposed reparations by relying on an abstract notion of opportunity. He erupted in anger when asked if he thought reparations were due to blacks for the injuries caused by slavery and Jim Crow.

> Oh tell them to shut up, OK! I had nothing to do with the whole situation. The opportunity is there, there is no reparation involved and let's not dwell on it. I'm very opinionated about that!

After suggesting that Jews and Japanese are the only groups worthy of receiving reparations, he added,

> But something that happened three Goddamned generations ago, what do you want us to do about it now? Give them opportunity, give them scholarships, but reparations . . .

Was Eric just a white man with a "principled opposition" to government intervention? This does not seem to be the case since Eric, like most whites, makes a distinction between government spending on behalf of victims of child abuse, the homeless, and battered women (groups whom he deems as legitimate candidates for assistance) and on behalf of blacks (a group whom he deems as unworthy of assistance).

Another tenet of liberalism that whites use to explain racial matters is the Jeffersonian idea of meritocracy—"the cream rises to the top." And whites seem unconcerned by the fact that the color of the "cream" is usually white. For example, Bob, a student at Southern University, explained his opposition to the idea of providing blacks unique educational opportunities in meritocratic fashion:

> No, I would not. I think, um, I believe that you should be judged on your qualifications, your experience, your education, your background, not on your race.

Accordingly, Bob opposed affirmative action as follows:

> I oppose them mainly because, not because I am a racist, but because I think you should have the best person for the job. . . . If I was a business owner, I would want the best person in there to do the job. If I had two people, and had to choose, had to have one black to meet the quota, I think that's ridiculous.

Bob then added the following clincher: "I think (affirmative action) had a good purpose when it was instilled (sic) because it alleviated a lot of anger maybe . . . minorities felt that they were getting a foot back in the door, but I think times have changed." Bob's argumentative reasonableness is bolstered by his belief that "times have changed" and that as far as discrimination in America [is concerned], "the bigger things are already taken care of."

Another tenet of liberalism that whites employ to state their racial views is the notion of individualism. For example, Beverly, a co-owner of a small business and homemaker in her forties, stated her belief that the government has a duty to see that no one is prevented from moving into neighborhoods because of racial considerations. Yet, when asked whether the government should work to guarantee that residential integration becomes a reality, Beverly said the following:

> (Sighs) It, it, it just isn't that important. Where you decide to live is where you decide to live. If you decided to live in and can afford to live in a very upscale house, great! If you're black and you can afford that, fantastic! I mean, people have choices as to

where they live. If they have the economic background or money to do this with . . . I can't envision . . . 97 percent of the black people saying, "I'm going to live in a white neighborhood 'cause it will make my life better." And I can't imagine 97 percent of the white people saying, "I'm gonna move to a black neighborhood 'cause it will make me feel better." You know, I, I, where you decide to live is your choice.

Carol, a student at SU, invoked the notion of individual choice to justify her taste for whiteness. While reviewing her romantic life in response to a question, Carol said:

Um, there really is hardly any (laughs). My romantic life is kinda dry (laughs). I mean, as far as guys go, I mean, I know you're looking for um, white versus minority and. . . . I am interested in white guys, I mean, I don't want it to look like a prejudice thing or anything.

After stating her preference for "white guys," Carol had to do some major rhetorical work to avoid appearing racist. Thus, she interjected the following odd comment to save face: "if a guy comes along and he's black and like I love him, it's not gonna, I mean, I, it's not, I don't think the white–black issue's gonna make a difference, you know what I mean?"

Naturalization

The word "natural" or the phrase "That's the way it is" is often interjected when whites use this frame to normalize events or actions that could otherwise be interpreted as racially motivated (e.g., residential segregation) or even as racist (e.g., preference for whites as friends and partners). For example, Mark, a student at MU, acknowledged that: "most of my close friends don't . . . (I) also don't have that many close black friends." Mark reacted immediately to his potentially problematic confession (no black friends) by saying,

Um . . . I don't know, I guess that circles are tight. It's not like we exclude, I don't feel like we exclude people. I don't think that we go out of our way to include people either, but it's just kinda like that. It seems like that's just the way it works out almost . . .

Later in the interview, Mark, a business major, revealed that most of the students in the business school are white males. When asked if he thought the way things were set up in the business school was racist, Mark answered the following:

I don't really think it's racist. I just think . . . I don't know if it's a perfect example, I just think it's an example . . . or just things aren't set up in such a way where I wouldn't say it favors whites. That's just the way that happens um . . . in the business school. That's all.

Ray, another student at MU, naturalized the fact that he had no minority associates while growing up because, "they lived in different neighborhoods, they went to different schools" and "It wasn't like people were trying to exclude them

. . . It's just the way things were." Hence, his response to a question about whether blacks self-segregate or are made to feel unwelcome by whites was the following:

> I would say it's a combination of the two factors. Um . . . and I don't think that . . . I don't . . . I think its fair it's, uh . . . it's not necessarily fair to read prejudice into either half of the bargain. Um . . . I think it's just, 'em . . . I think it's like what I was saying earlier, I think people feel comfortable around people that they feel that they can identify with.

After struggling rhetorically with the implications of his argument, Ray stated that: "Ah um . . . I think, yes, things are somewhat segregated, but I think it's more, I think it's more about just people . . . feeling comfortable around each other than it is about active discrimination."

Detroit whites also used this frame widely. For instance, Bill, a manager in a manufacturing firm, explained the limited level of post 1954 school integration as a natural affair.

> Bill: I don't think it's anybody's fault. Because people tend to group with their own people. Whether it's white or black or upper-middle class or lower class or, you know, upper class, you know, Asians. People tend to group with their own. Doesn't mean if a black person moves into your neighborhood, they shouldn't go to your school? They should and you should mix and welcome them and everything else, but you can't force people together. . . . If people want to be together, they should intermix more.

> Int: OK. Hmm, so the lack of mixing is really just kind of an individual lack of desire?

> Bill: Well, yeah individuals, it's just the way it is. You know, people group together for lots of different reasons: social, religious. Just as animals in the wild, you know. Elephants group together, cheetahs group together. You bus a cheetah into an elephant herd because they should mix? You can't force that [laughs].

The Biologization of Culture

Modern racial ideology no longer relies on the claim that blacks are biologically inferior to whites. Instead, it has biologized their presumed cultural practices (i.e., presented them as *fixed* features) and used that as the *rationale* for explaining racial inequality. For instance, Karen, a student at MU, agreed with the premise that blacks are poor because they lack the drive to succeed.

> I think, to some extent, that's true. Just from, like looking at the black people that I've met in my classes and the few that I knew before college that . . . not like they're—I don't want to say waiting for a handout, but to some extent, that's kind of what I'm like hinting at. Like, almost like they feel like they were discriminated against hundreds of years ago, now what are you gonna give me? Ya' know, or maybe even it's just their background, that they've never, like maybe they're first generation to be in college so they feel like just that is enough for them.

Although many white respondents used this frame as crudely as Karen, most used it in a kinder and gentler way. For example, Jay, a student at WU, answered the question on why blacks have a worse overall standing than whites as follows:

> Hmm, I think it's due to lack of education. I think because if they didn't grow up in a household that ahhh, afforded them the time to go to school and they had to go out and get jobs right away, I think it is just a cycle (that) perpetuates things, you know. I mean, some people, I mean, I can't say that blacks can't do it because, obviously, there are many, many of them (that) have succeeded in getting good jobs and all that . . .

Although Jay admitted "exceptional blacks," he immediately went back to the cultural frame to explain blacks' status.

> So it's possible that the cycle seems to perpetuate itself because it, I mean, let's say go out and get jobs and they start, they settle down much earlier than they would normally if they had gone to school and then they have kids at a young age and they—these kids have to go and get jobs and so (on).

Detroit respondents used this cultural frame too, but, in general, used it in a more crude fashion than students. For instance, Ian, a manager of information security in an automobile company in his late fifties, explained blacks' worse status compared to whites as follows:

> The majority of 'em just don't strive to do anything, to make themselves better. Again, I've seen that all the way through. "I do this today, I'm fine, I'm happy with it, I don't need anything better." Never, never, never striving or giving extra to, to make themselves better.

Minimization of Racism

Although whites and blacks believed that discrimination is still a problem in America, they dispute its salience. In general, whites believe that discrimination has all but disappeared whereas blacks believe that discrimination—old- and new-fashioned—is as American as cherry pie. For instance, Kim, a student at SU, answered a question dealing with blacks' claims of discrimination in the following manner:

> Um, I disagree. I think that um, I think that it even more like . . . it's uh . . . I mean, from what I've heard, you pretty much have to hire, you know, you have to (hire) everyone, you know? They have quotas and stuff . . .

When asked if she believes the reason why blacks lag behind whites is because they are lazy, Kim said:

> Yeah, I totally agree with that, think that um, I mean, again, I don't think, you know, they're all like that, but I mean . . . I mean, I mean . . . it's just that . . . I mean, if

it wasn't that way, why would there be so many blacks living in the projects? You know, why would there be so many poor blacks? If, if they worked hard, if, if they just went out and went to college and just worked as hard as they could, they would, I mean, they, they could make it just as high as anyone else.

Detroit whites were even more likely than students to use this frame and to use it in a direct and crude manner. Sandra, a retail salesperson in her early forties, answered the question on discrimination as follows:

I think if you are looking for discrimination, I think it's there to be found. But if you make the best of any situation, and if you don't use it as an excuse I think sometimes it's an excuse because, ah, people felt they deserved a job, ah whatever! I think if things didn't go their way I know a lot of people have a tendency to use . . . prejudice or racism as—whatever—as an excuse. I think in some ways, yes there is . . . umm . . . people who are prejudiced. It's not only blacks, it's about Spanish, or women. In a lot of ways there (is) a lot of reverse discrimination. It's just what you wanna make of it.

The policy implications of adopting this frame are extremely important. Since whites do not believe that discrimination is a normal part of America, they view race-targeted government programs as illegitimate. Thus, Henrietta, a transsexual school teacher in his fifties, answered a question on reparations as follows:

As a person who was once reversed discriminated against, I would have to say no. Because the government does not need those programs if they, if people would be motivated to bring themselves out of the poverty level. Ah, [coughing] when we talk about certain programs, when the Irish came over, when the Italians, the Polish, and the Eastern European Jews, they all were immigrants who lived in terrible conditions too, but they had one thing in common, they all knew that education was the way out of that poverty. And they did it. I'm not saying . . . the blacks were brought over here maybe not willingly, but if they realize education's the key, that's it. And that's based on individuality.

Conclusions

I have illustrated the four central frames of color-blind racism, namely, abstract liberalism, naturalization, biologization of culture, and minimization of racism. These frames are central to *old* and *young* whites alike. They form an impregnable yet elastic ideological wall that *barricades* whites off from America's racial reality. An impregnable wall because they provide whites a safe, color-blind way to state racial views without appearing to be irrational or rabidly racist. And an elastic wall—and, hence, a stronger one—because these frames do not rely on absolutes ("All blacks are . . ." or "Discrimination ended in 1965"). Instead, color-blind racism gives room for exceptions and allows for a variety of ways of using the frames—from crude and direct to kinder and indirect—for whites to state their racial views in an angry tone ("Darned lazy blacks") or as compassionate conservatives ("Poor blacks are trapped in *their* inferior schools in *their* cycle of poverty. What a pity.").

Thus, my answers to the strange enigma of racism without "racists" is the following: America does not depend on Archie Bunkers to defend white supremacy. Modern racial ideology does not thrive on the ugliness of the past, on the language and tropes typical of slavery and Jim Crow. Today there is a sanitized, color-blind way of calling minorities "niggers," "spics," or "chinks." Today most whites justify keeping minorities out of the good things in life with the language of liberalism ("I am all for equal opportunity; that's why I oppose affirmative action!"). And today as yesterday, whites do not feel guilty about minorities' plight. Today they believe that minorities have the opportunities to succeed and that if they don't, it's because they do not try hard. And if minorities dare talk about discrimination, they are rebuked with statements such as "Discrimination ended in the sixties, man" or "You guys are hypersensitive."

3

WHITE LIKE ME

Frank Rich

I cannot testify to what black Americans feel as our nation celebrates the inauguration of our first African-American president. But I can speak for myself, as a white American who grew up in the segregated nation's capital of the 1960s. Barack Obama's day is one that I never thought would come, and one that I still can't quite believe is here.

Last week I joined a group of journalists at an off-the-record conversation with the president-elect, a sort of preview of the administration's coming attractions. But as I walked some desolate downtown blocks to the standard-issue federal office building serving as transition headquarters, ghosts of the past mingled with hopes for the future. The contrast between the unemployed men on Washington's frigid streets and the buzzing executive-branch bees inside was, for me, as old as time.

My particular historical vantage point is a product of my upbringing as that odd duck, a native Washingtonian whose parents were not in government. The first presidential transition of my sentient lifetime, Kennedy's, I remember vividly. Even an 11-year-old could see that the sleepy Southern town of the Eisenhower era was waking up, electrified by youth, glamour and the prospect of change.

But some of that change I didn't then understand. J.F.K.'s arrival coincided with Washington's emergence as the first American city with a black majority. Many whites responded by fleeing to the suburbs. My parents did the opposite, moving our family from the enclave of Montgomery County, Md., into the city as I was about to enter the fifth grade.

Our new neighborhood included the Sidwell Friends School. My mother, a public school teacher, decreed that her children would instead enroll in the public system that had been desegregated a half-dozen years earlier, after Brown v. Board of Education. In reality de facto segregation remained in place. Though a few African-Americans and embassy Africans provided the window dressing of "integration," my mostly white elementary, junior high and high schools had roughly the same diversity as, say, today's G.O.P.

I wish I could say we were all outraged at this apartheid. But we were kids — privileged kids at that — and out of sight was out of mind. Except as household help, black Washington was generally as invisible to us as it was to the tourists who were rigidly segregated from the real Washington while visiting its many ivory marble shrines to democratic ideals.

Gradually we would learn more — from our parents and teachers, from televised incidents of violent racial confrontations far away, and from odd cultural phenomena like the 1961 best seller *Black Like Me*. In that book, a white novelist darkened his skin for undercover travels through deepest Dixie, whose bigotry he then described in morbid firsthand detail to shocked adolescents like me.

Surely such horrific injustices could not occur in our nation's capital.

But as an unintended consequence of Washington's particular brand of Jim Crow, white public school students got a tiny taste of what racially mandated second-class citizenship could mean. In those days, the city didn't even have the bastardized form of "self-government" it has now; it was run as a plantation by Congressional District panels led by racist white Southerners (then Democrats). These overseers didn't want to lavish money on an overwhelmingly black school system, and they didn't. By the early 1960s, per-student spending in Washington was less than that of any state, impoverished West Virginia and Mississippi included.

If Washington's white schools received a larger share of that meager budget, as they no doubt did, it was still obvious that our teachers had far fewer resources than their suburban and private school counterparts. Extracurricular activities could be curtailed by the costs of light and heat. The curriculum was also abridged, lest anyone get too agitated by America's racial inequities. In my history class, the Civil War was downsized to a passing speed bump. In English, we read *Tom Sawyer*, not *Huckleberry Finn*.

Now that we were teenagers, we had both the curiosity and mobility to investigate the strangely undemocratic city that dealt us this hand. In the words of Constance McLaughlin Green, a Pulitzer Prize-winning urban historian, the District's black population had long occupied "a secret city all but unknown to the white world round about." We wanted in on the secrets.

There was so much we didn't know, so much Americans still don't know. Take the Lincoln Memorial, to which the Obama family paid so poignant a nocturnal visit this month. If you look up coverage of the memorial's 1922 dedication ceremonies in *The Times*, you can read of President Harding's forceful oration commemorating the demise of slavery. You also learn that Dr. Robert R. Moton, the president of the Tuskegee Institute, was invited to pay tribute to Lincoln "in the name of 12,000,000 Negroes."

Here's what *The Times* did not report about Moton: "Instead of being placed on the speaker's platform, he was relegated along with other distinguished colored people to an all-Negro section separated by a road from the rest of the audience." So wrote Green in *The Secret City*, her landmark history of race relations in Washington. This was no anomaly. A local Ku Klux Klan had been formed months earlier, with no protests from either Congress or the white press, and the young Harding administration had toughened the exclusion of blacks from the city's public recreation facilities.

The eye-opening *Secret City* recounting this secret history was not published until 1967, some four years after the Lincoln Memorial served as a backdrop for "I Have a Dream." It was also in 1967 that I graduated from Woodrow Wilson High. As a valedictory, a bunch of us on the school paper voted to publish an editorial in favor of home rule for D.C. "Washingtonians have to beg, plead and cajole members of Congress for funds to renovate slums and slum schools," it read. That was putting it mildly; we still had much to learn. But the editorial was enough of an irritant that our principal tried to censor it, which prompted a brief civic kerfuffle ("Student Editorial Banned at Wilson" read the headline in *The Washington Post*) and jump-started a few starry-eyed careers in journalism and political activism.

It was one year later that the Rev. Dr. Martin Luther King Jr. was assassinated and Washington's secret city exploded. The fires and riots came within a block of the building where the Obama transition set up shop.

One would like to say in the aftermath of the 2008 election that everyone lived happily ever after. But the American drama, especially when it involves race, is always more complicated than that.

Looking back at my high school years, I'm struck by how slowly history can move. The great civil rights legislation of the Johnson administration had been accomplished in 1964 and 1965, but by the time of my graduation the impact was minimal — even in the city where the laws were written and passed. Today the nation's capital still has no voting representation in Congress and is still a ward of the federal government, reduced to begging, pleading and cajoling for basic needs. Some 19 percent of the population lives below the poverty line, and that 19 percent remains a secret city to many who work within the Beltway.

Washington is its own special American case, but only up to a point. For all our huge progress, we are not "post-racial," whatever that means. The world doesn't change in a day, and the racial frictions that emerged in both the Democratic primary campaign and the general election didn't end on Nov. 4. As Obama himself said in his great speech on race, liberals couldn't "purchase racial reconciliation on the cheap" simply by voting for him. And conservatives? The so-called party of Lincoln has spent much of the past month in spirited debate about whether a white candidate for the party's chairmanship did the right thing by sending out a "humorous" recording of "Barack the Magic Negro" as a holiday gift.

Next to much of our history, this is small stuff. And yet: Of all the coverage of Obama's victory, the most accurate take may still be the piquant morning-after summation of the satirical newspaper *The Onion*. Under the headline "Black Man Given Nation's Worst Job," it reported that our new president will have "to spend four to eight years cleaning up the messes other people left behind."

Those messes are enormous, bigger than Washington, bigger than race, bigger than anything most of us have ever seen. Nearly three months after Election Day, it remains astonishing that the American people have entrusted the job to a young black man who seemed to come out of nowhere looking for that kind of work just as we most needed him.

"In no other country on earth is my story even possible," Obama is fond of saying. That is true, and that is what the country celebrates this week. But it is all the tragic American stories that came before him, some of them still playing out in chilly streets just blocks from the White House, that throw both his remarkable triumph and the huge challenge ahead of him into such heart-stopping relief.

4

SMELLS LIKE RACISM

Rita Chaudhry Sethi

When I started my first job after college, Steve Riley, an African American activist, asked me: "So, how do you feel being black?" I confessed, "I am not black." "In America," Steve responded, "if you're not white, you're black."

U.S. discourse on racism is generally framed in these simplistic terms: the stark polarity of black/white conflict. As it is propagated, it embraces none of the true complexities of racist behavior. Media sensationalism, political expedience, intellectual laziness, and legal constraints conspire to narrow the scope of cognizable racism. What remains is a pared-down image of racism, one that delimits the definition of its forms, its perpetrators, and, especially, its victims. Divergent

From Karin Aguilar-San Juan, ed., *The State of Asian America*. Copyright © 1994. Reprinted by permission of South End Press.

experiences are only included in the hierarchy of racial crimes when they sufficiently resemble the caricature. Race-based offenses that do not conform to this
model are permitted to exist and fester without remedy by legal recourse, collective retribution, or even moral indignation.

Asians' experiences exist in the penumbra of actionable racial affronts. Our cultural, linguistic, religious, national, and color differences do not, as one might
imagine, form the basis for a modified paradigm of racism; rather, they exist on the
periphery of offensiveness. The racial insults we suffer are usually trivialized; our
reactions are dismissed as hypersensitivity or regarded as a source of amusement.
The response to a scene where a Korean-owned store is being destroyed with a bat
in the 1993 film *Falling Down* (a xenophobic and racist diatribe on urban life)[1]
reflects how mainstream America/American culture responds to the phenomenon
of anti-Asian violence:

> There was, in the theater where I saw the film, a good deal of appreciative laugh-
> ter and a smattering of applause during this scene, which of course flunks the most
> obvious test of comparative racism: imagine a black or an Orthodox Jew, say, in that
> Korean's place and you imagine the theater's screen being ripped from the walls.
> Asians, like Arabs, remain safe targets for the movies' casual racism.[2]

The perpetuation of the caricature of racism is attributable to several complex and symbiotic causes. First, Asians often do not ascribe racist motivation to
the discrimination they suffer, or they have felt that they could suffer the injustice of racial intolerance, in return for being later compensated by the fruits of
economic success. Second, many Asians do not identify with other people of
color. Sucheta Mazumdar posits that South Asians exclude themselves from efforts at political mobilization because of their rigid self-perception as Aryan, not
as people of color.[3]

The final and most determinative factor, however, is the perspective that excludes the experiences of Asians (and other people of color) from the rubric of
racism. Whites would deny us our right to speak out against majority prejudice,
partially because it tarnishes their image of Asians as "model" minorities; other
people of color would deny us the same because of monopolistic sentiments that
they alone endure real racism.

For example, a poll conducted by *The Wall Street Journal* and NBC News
revealed that "most American voters thought that Asian Americans did not suffer discrimination" but in fact received too many "special advantages."[4] Similarly, when crimes against Asians were on the rise in housing projects in San
Francisco, the Housing Authority was loathe to label the crimes as racially motivated, despite the clear racial bias involved.[5] The deputy director of the Oakland Housing Authority's response to the issue was: "There may be some issues
of race in it, but it's largely an issue of people who don't speak English feeling
very isolated and not having a support structure to deal with what's happening
to them."[6]

Other minorities reject Asian claims of racial victimization by pointing to economic privilege or perceived whiteness.[7] Such rejections even occur among different Asian groups. Chinese Americans in San Francisco attempted to classify Indians as white for the purposes of the California Minority Business Enterprise Statute: "If you are a white, male buyer in the City, all else being equal, would you buy from another Caucasian [i.e., Indian] or from a person of the Mongolian race?"[8]

The perspective of some people of color that there is a monopoly on oppression is debilitating to an effort at cross-ethnic coalition building. Our experiences are truly distinct, and our battles will in turn be unique; but if we are to achieve a community, we must begin to educate ourselves about our common denominator as well as our different histories and struggles. Ranking and diminishing relative subjugation and discrimination will only subvert our goal of unity. Naheed Islam expresses this sentiment in part of a poem addressed to African American women:

> Ah Sister! What have they done to us! Separated, segregated, unable to love one another, to cross the color line. I am not trying to cash in on your chains. I have my own. The rape, plunder, pain of dislocation is not yours alone. We have different histories, different voices, different ways of expressing our anger, but they used the same bullets to reach us all.[9]

The combination of white America refusing to acknowledge anti-Asian discrimination, and minority America minimizing anti-Asian discrimination, foists a formidable burden upon Asians: to combat our own internalized racial alienation, and to fight extrinsic racial classifications by both whites and other minority groups. It also renders overly simplistic those suggestions that if South Asians simply became "sufficiently politicized" they could overcome fragmentation in the struggle by people of color.[10]

As activists, a narrow-minded construct of racism impairs our political initiatives to use racism as a banner that unites all people of color in a common struggle.[11] The mainstream use of the word "racism" does not embrace Asian experiences, and we are not able to include ourselves in a definition that minimizes our encounters with racism. Participation in an antiracism campaign, therefore, is necessarily limited to those involved in a battle against racism that fits within the confines of the black/white paradigm, and conversely relegates anti-Asian racism to a lesser realm in terms of both exposure and horribleness.

We need to be more sophisticated in our analysis of racism, and less equivocal in our condemnation. In doing so, we will expand the base of opposition against anti-Asian racism, and forge an alliance against all its myriad forms. The first step in this process is for Asians to apply a racial analysis to our lives. This involves developing a greater understanding of how racism has operated socially and institutionally in this country against ourselves and other people of color, as well as acknowledging our own complicity; and secondly, accepting ourselves as people of color, with a shared history of being targeted as visibly Other. Only then can we act in solidarity with other efforts at ending racism.

Anti-Asian Racism: Fashioning a More Inclusive Paradigm

Racism takes on manifold creative and insidious expressions. Intra-racism, racism among different racial communities, and internalized racism all complicate an easy understanding of the phenomenon. My project here is to uncover shrouded racism perpetrated against Asians, particularly South Asians, in an attempt to broaden the use of the term.

Accent

It is only since 1992 that the Courts have begun to realize the legitimacy of discrimination based upon accent.[12] Immigrants, primarily those not of European descent,[13] suffer heightened racism because of their accents, including job discrimination and perpetual taunting and caricaturization. This is a severe and pervasive form of racism that is often not acknowledged as racist, or even offensive. Even among Asians there is a high degree of denial about the accent discrimination that is attributable to race. In a letter to the *New York Times*, an Asian man blithely encouraged immigrants to maintain their accents, without acknowledging the potential discrimination that we face, though he personally was "linguistically gifted" with an "American accent." The man wrote, "Fellow immigrants, don't worry about the way you speak until Peter Jennings eliminates his Canadian accent."[14]

Accent discrimination is linked directly to American jingoism, and its accompanying virulently anti-immigrant undertones. In the aforementioned movie *Falling Down*, the protagonist has the following exchange with a Korean grocer:

> Mr. Lee: Drink eighty-five cent. You pay or go.
>
> Foster: This "fie," I don't understand a "fie." There's a "v" in the word. It's "fie-vah." You don't got "v's" in China?
>
> Mr. Lee: Not Chinese. I'm Korean.
>
> Foster: Whatever. You come to my country, you take my money, you don't even have the grace to learn my language?[15]

A person's accent is yet another symbol of otherness, but it is one that even U.S.-born minorities do not regard as a target for race-based discrimination. Language is implicitly linked with race, and must be treated as such.

Subversive Stereotyping

The myths that are built based on the commonality of race are meant to depersonalize and simplify people. To many, the Indian persona is that of a greedy, unethical, cheap immigrant. This stereotype is reflected in popular culture, where its appearance gives it credibility, thereby reinforcing the image. In the television comedy *The Simpsons*, a purportedly politically sensitive program, one of the characters is a South Asian owner of a convenience store. In one episode, in an effort to make a sale, he says, "I'll sell you expired baby food for a nickel off." Similarly, in the program *Star Trek: Deep Space Nine*, an alien race called the Firengi (Hindi for foreigner) are proprietors and sleazy entrepreneurs who take advantage of any opportunity for wealth, regardless of the moral cost.[16]

These constructs are reified in everyday life as people respond to Indians as if they have certain inherent qualities. Indian physicians, for example, are perceived as shoddy practitioners, who are greedy and disinterested in the health of their patients. In successful medical malpractice suits, Indian doctors are routinely required to pay higher penalties.[17] Similarly, in the now-famous "East Side Butcher" case, where an Indian doctor was convicted of performing illegal abortions, there was no racial analysis despite the fact that no one had been prosecuted for that crime in New York State since the early 1980s despite the fact that hundreds of illegal abortions are performed annually.[18] Another Indian doctor, less than two weeks later, was found guilty of violations in her mammography practice and fined the largest amount in New York State history in such a case. One can not help but wonder if these convictions were, at least in part, motivated by the stereotype of the Indian immigrant.[19]

The Onus

A white, liberal woman once asked my friend Ritu if she wasn't being overly sensitive for taking offense when people put their feet near her face (a high insult in Indian culture), when she could not fairly expect people to understand her culture. The onus is always on us, as outsiders, to explain and justify our culture while also being expected to know and understand majority culture.[20] Constant cultural slights about cows, bindis, and Gandhi are deemed appropriate by the majority while we are expected to subjugate expression of our culture to an understanding and acceptance of American culture. As another example, the swastika is an extremely common, ancient Hindu symbol. However, Hindus cannot wear or display the swastika in America because of Hitler's appropriation of it, and the expectation that we suppress our cultural symbols in an attempt to understand the affront to Jewish Americans. The assumption that it is our normative responsibility to make our culture secondary is racist because it suggests that one culture should be more free to express itself than another.

Religious Fanaticism

Eastern religions are commonly perceived as fraudulent, cultish, and fanatical; they are rarely perceived as equally legitimate as the spiritual doctrines of the Judeo-Christian tradition. The story of immaculate conception is accepted as plausible, while the multiarmed, multiheaded God is an impossible fantasy. Hinduism is portrayed as Hare Krishnas chanting with shaved heads and orange robes; and Islam is characterized as a rigid, violent, military religion. These hyperbolic characterizations are responsible for the fear of religion that causes local communities to refuse to permit places of worship in their neighborhoods.[21]

Western appropriation of Hindu terms reflects the perception of religion as charlatanical; the words have been reshaped through their use in the English language with an edge of irreverence or disbelief.

	Hindi Meaning	*English Use*
1. Guru	Religious teacher	Purported head; self-designated leader
2. Nirvana	Freedom from endless cycle of rebirth	Psychedelic ecstasy; drug-induced high
3. Pundit	Religious scholar	One with claimed knowledge
4. Mantra	A meditative tool; repetition of word or phrase	Mindless chant

Similarly, during times of political crisis (the 1991 Persian Gulf War; the February 1993 World Trade Center bombing), Islam has been the object of derision as a dangerous and destructive religion. After the suspects from the World Trade Center bombing were identified as Muslims, the media, the FBI, and mainstream America responded with gross anti-Muslim rhetoric. A professor in Virginia pointed out the ignorant conflation of the entire Muslim population into one extremist monolith:

> Not all Islamic revivalists are Islamic fundamentalists, and not all Islamic fundamentalists are political activists, and not all Islamic political activists are radical and prone to violence.[22]

Muslims have linked these characterizations of their religion to racial demonization.[23] The *New York Post* carried a headline entitled "The Face of Hate" with the face of a dark-skinned, bearded man of South Asian or Middle Eastern descent (the accused bomber). Similarly, the *New York Times* described the work of courtroom artists: "the defendant's beakish nose, hollow cheeks, cropped beard and the sideways tilt of his head."[24] In an Op-Ed piece in the *New York Times,* one Muslim responded to this description: "Such racial stereotyping serves nothing except to feed an existing hate and fear."[25]

Class Conflicts/Economic Envy

Racism and economic tension are inextricable because race discrimination against Asians has often been manifested as class competition, and vice versa. Since the early 1800s, when Asians became a source of cheap labor for the railroads, we have been an economic threat. As Asians have more recently been portrayed as the prosperous minority, the favored child of America, there has inevitably been sibling rivalry. When auto workers beat up Vincent Chin, was it Japanese competition in the auto industry or unbridled racism that motivated the murderers? When African Americans targeted Korean-owned stores in the riots in Los Angeles after the Rodney King verdict, was it the economic hardship of the inner city and perceived Asian advantages or was it simply racism? The answer is that race and class are inseparable because of the inherent difficulty in identifying the primary or motivating factor; any racial analysis must consider economic scapegoating as an avenue for racial harassment and racial victimization as an excuse for expressing economic tensions.

Conceptual and Perspective Differences

When an immigrant perspective clashes with a white American perspective, the conflict should be considered a racial one. Values such as individuality, privacy, confrontation, competition, and challenging the status quo are considered positive and healthy; however, these components of the liberal state are not necessarily virtues elsewhere. When Hawaiian children do not respond to competitive models of teaching, but thrive in group activities; and when Punjabi children defer to authority, rather than challenge their teachers out of intellectual "curiosity," they are harmed by their inability to function in an essentially and uniquely "American" world. Identifying the differences in perspective and lifestyle between Asian immigrants and Americans will help in recognizing arenas in which we will be at a cultural/racial disadvantage.[26]

NOTES

1. While the film generated much debate about the possible ironic intent of its stereotyping, the reactions of moviegoers showed that the irony was lost on most audiences.

2. Godfrey Cheshire, complete citation for article not available.

3. Mazumdar, Sucheta, "Race and Racism: South Asians in the United States," *Frontiers of Asian American Studies*.

4. Polner, Murray, "Asian-Americans Say They Are Treated Like Foreigners," *The New York Times*, March 7, 1993, Section B, p. 1.

5. Racial slurs were rampant (including "Go home, Chinaman" and accent harassment) and tension between the Asian and African American community was worsening. The fact that the perpetrators were African American might have contributed to the general reluctance to characterize these crimes as racially motivated. Again, this reflects an inability, or an unwillingness, to intellectually digest racism between non-white races, as it falls outside of the narrow black/white paradigm.

6. Chin, Steven A., "Asians Terrorized in Housing Projects," *San Francisco Examiner*, January 17, 1993, p. B1.

7. Witness this morsel of divisiveness: In Miami, where large Latino and African American populations coexist, a Cuban woman was sworn in as State Attorney General. Many in the African American community were dismayed by this decision, and responded by stripping Cubans of their "rank" as a minority. One black lawyer commented: "Cubans are really 'white people whose native language is Spanish'" and others agreed that Cuban Americans should be "disqualified because they have higher income levels than other minorities." Certainly there is complexity in this conflict; however, the net result is that people who could be in alliance based on race are divided. Rohter, Larry, "Black-Cuban Rift Extends to Florida Law School," *The New York Times*, March 19, 1993, p. B16L.

8. Transcript of San Francisco Board of Supervisors Special Session of Economic and Social Policy Committee, April 30, 1991.

9. Islam, Naheed, "Untitled," from *Smell This*, an official publication of The Center for Racial Education, Berkeley, CA, 1991.

10. Mazumdar, *supra* at p. 36.

11. Here, and throughout this chapter, I am operating within the constructs of our existing political reality. I am not addressing the normative question of whether people of color should be in coalition against racism, but given that it has been our primary organizing principle, how can we be more effective and inclusive?

12. Interestingly, the case was brought by the EEOC while under the tenure of Joy Cherian, a naturalized Indian. The Commission's 1980 guidelines covering this type of discrimination were written by an Indian, and the case was brought by an Indian plaintiff. Is that what it takes to obtain recognition of the racism that we experience?

13. The Executive Assistant for the Commissioner noted: "If an employer has an applicant who speaks with a French accent . . . or with an English accent, they say, 'How cute.' But if he speaks with a Hispanic accent they say, 'What's wrong with this guy?'"

14. Letter to the editor from Yan Hong Krompacky, "Immigrants, Don't Be in Such a Hurry to Shed Your Accents," *The New York Times*, March 4, 1993.

15. Foster then proceeds to demolish Mr. Lee's grocery store with a bat, in much the same way that Japanese cars were hatefully demolished just before Vincent Chin's death.

16. That such stereotypes exist in two programs that are perceived as being among the more progressive on television is itself indicative of the continuing denial that anti-Asian racism exists.

17. According to several medical malpractice attorneys.

18. This was exacerbated further by the fact that Dr. Hayat's sentence was so severe that even the District Attorney's Office had expected less and was "pleasantly surprised." Perez-Pena, Richard, "Prison Term for Doctor Convicted in Abortions," *The New York Times*, June 15, 1993, p. B1.

19. These stereotypes find expression everywhere. I was haggling for a pair of earrings in Times Square, and the vendor asked me if I was Indian. When I replied that I was, he responded, "Oh, I should have guessed. Indians don't want to take anything out of their pockets."

20. In an effort to better integrate into American culture, and mend relations with ethnic groups in New York City, Korean grocers are taking seminars to learn to smile more frequently, supposedly rare in their culture. *The New York Times*, March 22, 1993.

21. "It's the Hindus! Circle the Zoning Laws." Viewpoint by Bob Weiner, *Newsday*, April 26, 1993, p. 40.

22. Steinfeld, Peter, "Many Varieties of Fundamentalism," *The New York Times*, no date. An even better response was: [the World Trade bomber suspect's] "variety of fundamentalism was not any more representative of Islam than the people in Waco are representative of [mainstream] Christianity." *Id.*

23. Op Ed Letter to Editor, "Don't Let Trade Center Blast Ignite Witch Hunt," March 23, 1993.

24. "Surprises in a Crowded Courtroom," Moustafa Bayami, March 5, 1993.

25. *Ibid.*

26. Many Asians find themselves in low-ranking jobs in the corporate world because their skills have little application in the old boy cultural network. This is due in part to different concepts of authority and competition, as much as it is pure racial bigotry. My point is that the two should be viewed together to truly understand the full flourish of racism.

5

OPPRESSION

Marilyn Frye

It is a fundamental claim of feminism that women are oppressed. The word "oppression" is a strong word. It repels and attracts. It is dangerous and dangerously fashionable and endangered. It is much misused, and sometimes not innocently.

The statement that women are oppressed is frequently met with the claim that men are oppressed too. We hear that oppressing is oppressive to those who oppress as well as to those they oppress. Some men cite as evidence of their oppression their much-advertised inability to cry. It is tough, we are told, to be masculine. When the stresses and frustrations of being a man are cited as evidence that oppressors are oppressed by their oppressing, the word "oppression" is being stretched to meaninglessness; it is treated as though its scope includes any and all human experience of limitation or suffering, no matter the cause, degree or consequence. Once such usage has been put over on us, then if ever we deny that any person or group is oppressed, we seem to imply that we think they never suffer and have no feelings. We are accused of insensitivity, even of bigotry. For women, such accusation is particularly intimidating, since sensitivity is one of the few virtues that has been assigned to us. If we are found insensitive, we may fear we have no redeeming traits at all and perhaps are not real women. Thus are we silenced before we begin: the name of our situation drained of meaning and our guilt mechanisms tripped.

But this is nonsense. Human beings can be miserable without being oppressed, and it is perfectly consistent to deny that a person or group is oppressed without denying that they have feelings or that they suffer.

We need to think clearly about oppression, and there is much that mitigates against this. I do not want to undertake to prove that women are oppressed (or that men are not), but I want to make clear what is being said when we say it. We need this word, this concept, and we need it to be sharp and sure.

The root of the word "oppression" is the element "press." *The press of the crowd; pressed into military service; to press a pair of pants; printing press; press the button.* Presses are used to mold things or flatten them or reduce them in bulk, sometimes to reduce them by squeezing out the gases or liquids in them. Something pressed is something caught between or among forces and barriers which are so related to each other that jointly they restrain, restrict or prevent the thing's motion or mobility. Mold. Immobilize. Reduce.

The mundane experience of the oppressed provides another clue. One of the most characteristic and ubiquitous features of the world as experienced by oppressed people is the double bind—situations in which options are reduced to a very few and all of them expose one to penalty, censure or deprivation. For example, it is often a requirement upon oppressed people that we smile and be cheerful. If we comply, we signal our docility and our acquiescence in our situation. We need not, then, be taken note of. We acquiesce in being made invisible, in our occupying no space. We participate in our own erasure. On the other hand, anything but the sunniest countenance exposes us to being perceived as mean, bitter, angry or dangerous. This means, at the least, that we may be found "difficult" or unpleasant to work with, which is enough to cost one one's livelihood; at worst, being seen as mean, bitter, angry or dangerous has been known to result in rape, arrest, beating and murder. One can only choose to risk one's preferred form and rate of annihilation.

Another example: It is common in the United States that women, especially younger women, are in a bind where neither sexual activity nor sexual inactivity is all right. If she is heterosexually active, a woman is open to censure and punishment for being loose, unprincipled or a whore. The "punishment" comes in the form of criticism, snide and embarrassing remarks, being treated as an easy lay by men, scorn from her more restrained female friends. She may have to lie and hide her behavior from her parents. She must juggle the risks of unwanted pregnancy and dangerous contraceptives. On the other hand, if she refrains from heterosexual activity, she is fairly constantly harassed by men who try to persuade her into it and pressure her to "relax" and "let her hair down"; she is threatened with labels like "frigid," "uptight," "man-hater," "bitch" and "cocktease." The same parents who would be disapproving of her sexual activity may be worried by her inactivity because it suggests she is not or will not be popular, or is not sexually normal. She may be charged with lesbianism. If a woman is raped, then if she has been hetero-sexually active she is subject to the presumption that she liked it (since her activ-ity is presumed to show that she likes sex), and if she has not been heterosexually active, she is subject to the presumption that she liked it (since she is supposedly "repressed and frustrated"). Both heterosexual activity and heterosexual nonactiv-ity are likely to be taken as proof that you wanted to be raped, and hence, of course, weren't *really* raped at all. You can't win. You are caught in a bind, caught between systematically related pressures.

Women are caught like this, too, by networks of forces and barriers that expose one to penalty, loss or contempt whether one works outside the home or not, is on welfare or not, bears children or not, raises children or not, marries or not, stays married or not, is heterosexual, lesbian, both or neither. Economic necessity; con-finement to racial and/or sexual job ghettos; sexual harassment; sex discrimination; pressures of competing expectations and judgments about *women*, *wives* and *moth-ers* (in the society at large, in racial and ethnic subcultures and in one's own mind); dependence (full or partial) on husbands, parents or the state; commitment to po-litical ideas; loyalties to racial or ethnic or other "minority" groups; the demands of self-respect and responsibilities to others. Each of these factors exists in complex tension with every other, penalizing or prohibiting all of the apparently available options. And nipping at one's heels, always, is the endless pack of little things. If one dresses one way, one is subject to the assumption that one is advertising one's sexual availability; if one dresses another way, one appears to "not care about one-self" or to be "unfeminine." If one uses "strong language," one invites categoriza-tion as a whore or slut; if one does not, one invites categorization as a "lady"—one too delicately constituted to cope with robust speech or the realities to which it pre-sumably refers.

The experience of oppressed people is that the living of one's life is confined and shaped by forces and barriers which are not accidental or occasional and hence avoidable, but are systematically related to each other in such a way as to catch one between and among them and restrict or penalize motion in any direc-tion. It is the experience of being caged in: all avenues, in every direction, are blocked or booby-trapped.

Cages. Consider a birdcage. If you look very closely at just one wire in the cage, you cannot see the other wires. If your conception of what is before you is deter-mined by this myopic focus, you could look at that one wire, up and down the length of it, and be unable to see why a bird would not just fly around the wire any time it wanted to go somewhere. Furthermore, even if, one day at a time, you myopically inspected each wire, you still could not see why a bird would have trouble going past the wires to get anywhere. There is no physical property of any one wire, *nothing* that the closest scrutiny could discover, that will reveal how a bird could be inhibited or harmed by it except in the most accidental way. It is only when you step back, stop looking at the wires one by one, microscopically, and take a macroscopic view of the whole cage, that you can see why the bird does not go anywhere; and then you will see it in a moment. It will require no great subtlety of mental powers. It is perfectly *obvious* that the bird is surrounded by a network of systematically related barriers, no one of which would be the least hindrance to its flight, but which, by their relations to each other, are as confining as the solid walls of a dungeon.

It is now possible to grasp one of the reasons why oppression can be hard to see and recognize: one can study the elements of an oppressive structure with great care and some good will without seeing the structure as a whole, and hence without seeing or being able to understand that one is looking at a cage and that there are people there who are caged, whose motion and mobility are restricted, whose lives are shaped and reduced.

The arresting of vision at a microscopic level yields such common confusion as that about the male door-opening ritual. This ritual, which is remarkably wide-spread across classes and races, puzzles many people, some of whom do and some of whom do not find it offensive. Look at the scene of the two people approaching a door. The male steps slightly ahead and opens the door. The male holds the door open while the female glides through. Then the male goes through. The door closes after them. "Now how," one innocently asks, "can those crazy womenslibbers say that is oppressive? The guy *removed* a barrier to the lady's smooth and unruffled progress." But each repetition of this ritual has a place in a pattern, in fact in several patterns. One has to shift the level of one's perception in order to see the whole picture.

The door-opening pretends to be a helpful service, but the helpfulness is false. This can be seen by noting that it will be done whether or not it makes any practical sense. Infirm men and men burdened with packages will open doors for able-bodied women who are free of physical burdens. Men will impose themselves awkwardly and jostle everyone in order to get to the door first. The act is not determined by convenience or grace. Furthermore, these very numerous acts of unneeded or even noisome "help" occur in counterpoint to a pattern of men not being helpful in many practical ways in which women might welcome help. What *women* experience is a world in which gallant princes charming commonly make a fuss about being helpful and providing small services when help and services are of little or no use, but in which there are rarely ingenious and adroit princes at hand when substantial assistance is really wanted either in mundane affairs or in situations of threat, assault or terror. There is no help with the (his) laundry; no help typing a report at 4:00 A.M.; no help in mediating disputes among relatives or children. There is nothing but advice that women should stay indoors after dark, be chaperoned by a man, or when it comes down to it, "lie back and enjoy it."

The gallant gestures have no practical meaning. Their meaning is symbolic. The door-opening and similar services provided are services which really are needed by people who are for one reason or another incapacitated—unwell, burdened with parcels, etc. So the message is that women are incapable. The detachment of the acts from the concrete realities of what women need and do not need is a vehicle for the message that women's actual needs and interests are unimportant or irrelevant. Finally, these gestures imitate the behavior of servants toward masters and thus mock women, who are in most respects the servants and caretak-

ers of men. The message of the false helpfulness of male gallantry is female dependence, the invisibility or insignificance of women, and contempt for women.

One cannot see the meanings of these rituals if one's focus is riveted upon the
individual event in all its particularity, including the particularity of the individual
man's present conscious intentions and motives and the individual woman's conscious perception of the event in the moment. It seems sometimes that people take
a deliberately myopic view and fill their eyes with things seen microscopically in
order not to see macroscopically. At any rate, whether it is deliberate or not, people can and do fail to see the oppression of women because they fail to see macroscopically and hence fail to see the various elements of the situation as systematically
related in larger schemes.

As the cageness of the birdcage is a macroscopic phenomenon, the oppressiveness of the situations in which women live our various and different lives is a
macroscopic phenomenon. Neither can be *seen* from a microscopic perspective.
But when you look macroscopically you can see it—a network of forces and barriers which are systematically related and which conspire to the immobilization, reduction and molding of women and the lives we live.

PATRIARCHY

Allan G. Johnson

What is patriarchy? A society is patriarchal to the degree that it is *male-dominated,
male-identified,* and *male-centered.* It also involves as one of its key aspects the oppression of women. Patriarchy is male-dominated in that positions of authority—
political, economic, legal, religious, educational, military, domestic—are generally
reserved for men. Heads of state, corporate CEOs and board members, religious
leaders, school principals, members of legislatures at all levels of government, senior law partners, tenured full professors, generals and admirals, and even those
identified as "head of household" all tend to be male under patriarchy. When a
woman finds her way into such positions, people tend to be struck by the excep-

From *The Gender Knot: Unraveling Our Patriarchal Legacy.* Reprinted by permission of Temple
University Press. © 1997 by Allan G. Johnson. All rights reserved.

tion to the rule, and wonder how she'll measure up against a man in the same position. It's a test we rarely apply to men ("I wonder if he'll be as good a president as a woman would be") except, perhaps, on those rare occasions when men venture into the devalued domestic and other "caring" work most women do. Even then, men's failure to measure up can be interpreted as a sign of superiority, a trained incapacity that actually protects their privileged status ("You change the diaper, I'm no good at that sort of thing").

In the simplest sense, male dominance creates power differences between men and women. It means, for example, that men can claim larger shares of income and wealth. It means they can shape culture in ways that reflect and serve men's collective interests by, for example, controlling the content of films and television shows, passing laws that allow husbands to rape their wives, or adjudicating rape and sexual harassment cases in ways that put the victim rather than the defendant on trial. Male dominance also promotes the idea that men are superior to women. In part this occurs because we don't distinguish between the superiority of *positions* in a hierarchy and the kinds of people who usually occupy them.[1] This means that if superior positions are occupied by men, it's a short leap to the idea that *men* must be superior. If presidents, generals, legislators, priests, popes, and corporate CEOs are all men (with a few token women as exceptions to prove the rule), then men as a group become identified with superiority even though most men aren't powerful in their individual lives. In this sense, *every* man's standing in relation to women is enhanced by the male monopoly over authority in patriarchal societies.

Patriarchal societies are *male-identified* in that core cultural ideas about what is considered good, desirable, preferable, or normal are associated with how we think about men and masculinity. The simplest example of this is the still widespread use of male pronouns and nouns to represent people in general. When we routinely refer to human beings as "man" or to doctors as "he," we construct a symbolic world in which men are in the foreground and women in the background, marginalized as outsiders and exceptions to the rule.[2] (This practice can back people into some embarrassingly ridiculous corners, as in the anthropology text that described man as a "species that breast-feeds his young.") But male identification amounts to much more than this, for it also takes men and men's lives as the standard for defining what is normal. The idea of a career, for example, with its 60-hour weeks, is defined in ways that assume the career-holder has something like a wife at home to perform the vital support work of taking care of children, doing laundry, and making sure there's a safe, clean, comfortable haven for rest and recuperation from the stress of the competitive male-dominated world. Since women generally don't have wives, they find it harder to identify with and prosper within this male-identified model.

Another aspect of male identification is the cultural description of masculinity and the ideal man in terms that closely resemble the core values of society as a whole. These include qualities such as control, strength, efficiency, competitiveness, toughness, coolness under pressure, logic, forcefulness, decisiveness, rationality, autonomy, self-sufficiency, and control over any emotion that interferes with other core values (such as invulnerability).[3] These male-identified qualities are associated with the work valued most in most patriarchal societies—such as business, politics, war, athletics, law, and medicine—because this work has been organized in ways that require such qualities for success. In contrast, qualities such as inefficiency, cooperation, mutuality, equality, sharing, compassion, caring, vulnerability, a readiness to negotiate and compromise, emotional expressiveness, and intuitive and other nonlinear ways of thinking are all devalued *and* culturally associated with femininity and femaleness.

Of course, femaleness isn't devalued entirely. Women are often prized for their beauty as objects of male sexual desire, for example, but as such they are often possessed and controlled in ways that ultimately devalue them. There is also a powerful cultural romanticizing of women in general and mothers in particular, but it is a tightly focused sentimentality (as on Mother's Day or Secretaries' Day) that has little effect on how women are regarded and treated on a day-to-day basis. And, like all sentimentality, it doesn't have much weight when it comes to actually doing something to support women's lives by, for example, providing effective and affordable child day-care facilities for working mothers, or family leave policies that allow working women to attend to the caring functions for which we supposedly value them so highly.

Because patriarchy is male-identified, when most women look out on the world they see themselves reflected as women in a few narrow areas of life such as "caring" occupations (teaching, nursing, child care) and personal relationships. To see herself as a leader, for example, a woman must first get around the fact that leadership itself has been gendered through its identification with maleness and masculinity as part of patriarchal culture. While a man might have to learn to see himself as a manager, a woman has to be able to see herself as a *woman* manager who can succeed in spite of the fact that she isn't a man. As a result, any woman who dares strive for standing in the world beyond the sphere of caring relationships must choose between two very different cultural images of who she is and ought to be. For her to assume real public power—as in politics, corporations, or her church—she must resolve a contradiction between her culturally based identity as a woman, on the one hand, and the male-identified *position* that she occupies on the other. For this reason, the more powerful a woman is under patriarchy, the more "unsexed" she becomes in the eyes of others as her female cultural identity recedes beneath the mantle of male-identified power and the masculine images associated with it. With men the effect is just the opposite: the more powerful they are, the more aware we are of their maleness. Power looks sexy on men but not on women.

But for all the pitfalls and limitations, some women do make it to positions of power. What about Margaret Thatcher, Queen Elizabeth I, Catherine the Great, Indira Gandhi, and Golda Meir? Doesn't their power contradict the idea that patriarchy is male-dominated? The answer is that patriarchy can accommodate a limited number of powerful women so long as the society retains its essential patriarchal character, especially in being male-identified.[4] Although some individual women have wielded great power, it has always been in societies organized on a patriarchal model. Each woman was surrounded by powerful men—generals, cabinet ministers, bishops, and wealthy aristocrats or businessmen—whose collective interests she supported and without whom she could not have ruled as she did. And not one of these women could have achieved and held her position without embracing core patriarchal values. Indeed, part of what makes these women stand out as so exceptional is their ability to embody values culturally defined as masculine: they've been tougher, more decisive, more aggressive, more calculating, and more emotionally controlled than most men around them.[5] These women's power, however, has nothing to do with whether women in general are subordinated under patriarchy. It also doesn't mean that putting more women in positions of authority will by itself do much for women unless we also change the patriarchal character of the systems in which they operate. . . .

Since patriarchy identifies power with men, the vast majority of men who aren't powerful but are instead dominated by other men can still feel some connection with the *idea* of male dominance and with men who *are* powerful. It is far easier, for example, for an unemployed working-class man to identify with male leaders and their displays of patriarchal masculine toughness than it is for women of any class. When upper-class U.S. President George Bush "got tough" with Saddam Hussein, for example, men of all classes could identify with his acting out of basic patriarchal values. In this way, male identification gives even the most lowly placed man a cultural basis for feeling some sense of superiority over the otherwise most highly placed woman (which is why a construction worker can feel within his rights as a man when he sexually harasses a well-dressed professional woman who happens to walk by).[6] . . .

In addition to being male-dominated and male-identified, patriarchy is *male-centered*, which means that the focus of attention is primarily on men and what they do. Pick up any newspaper or go to any movie theater and you'll find stories primarily about men and what they've done or haven't done or what they have to say about either. With rare exceptions, women are portrayed as along for the ride, fussing over their support work of domestic labor and maintaining love relationships, providing something for men to fight over, or being foils that reflect or amplify men's heroic struggle with the human condition. If there's a crisis, what we see is what men did to create it and how men dealt with it.

If you want a story about heroism, moral courage, spiritual transformation, endurance, or any of the struggles that give human life its deepest meaning and significance, men and masculinity are usually the terms in which you must see it. (To see what I mean, make a list of the twenty most important movies you've ever seen and count how many focus on men as the central characters whose experience forms the point of the story.) Male experience is what patriarchal culture offers to represent *human* experience and the enduring themes of life, even when these are most often about women in the actual living of them. . . .

A male center of focus is everywhere. Research makes clear, for example, what most women probably already know: that men dominate conversations by talking more, interrupting more, and controlling content.[7] When women suggest ideas in business meetings, they often go unnoticed until a man makes the same suggestion and receives credit for it (or, as a cartoon caption put it, "Excellent idea Ms. Jones. Perhaps one of the men would like to suggest it"). In classrooms at all levels of schooling, boys and men command center stage and receive the lion's share of attention.[8] Even when women gather together, they must often resist the ongoing assumption that no situation can be complete or even entirely real unless a man is there to take the center position. How else do we understand the experience of groups of women who go out for drinks and conversation and are approached by men who ask, "Are you ladies alone?" . . .

Women and Patriarchy

At the heart of patriarchy is the oppression of women, which takes several forms. Historically, for example, women have been excluded from major institutions such as church, state, universities, and the professions. Even when they've been allowed to participate, it's generally been at subordinate, second-class levels. . . .

Because patriarchy is male-identified and male-centered, women and the work they do tends to be devalued, if not made invisible. In their industrial capitalist form, for example, patriarchal cultures do not define the unpaid domestic work that women do as real work, and if women do something, it tends to be valued less than when men do it. As women's numbers in male-dominated occupations increase, the prestige and income that go with them tend to decline, a pattern found in a variety of occupations, from telephone operator and secretary to psychotherapist.[9] Like many minorities, women are routinely repressed in their development as human beings through neglect and discrimination in schools[10] and in occupational hiring, development, promotion, and rewards. Anyone who doubts that patriarchy is an oppressive system need only spend some time with the growing literature documenting not only economic, political, and other institutionalized sexism, but pervasive violence, from pornography to the everyday realities of wife battering, sexual harassment, and sexual assault.[11] . . .

The power of patriarchy is also reflected in its ability to absorb the pressures of superficial change as a defense against deeper challenges. Every social system has a certain amount of "give" in it that allows some change to occur, and in the process leaves deep structures untouched and even invisible. Indeed, the "give" plays a critical part in maintaining the status quo by fostering illusions of fundamental change and acting as a systemic shock absorber. It keeps us focused on symptoms while root causes go unnoticed and unremarked; and it deflects the power we need to take the risky deeper journey that leads to the heart of patriarchy and our involvement in it. . . .

We'd Rather Not Know

We're as stuck as we are primarily because we can't or won't acknowledge the roots of patriarchy and our involvement in it. We show no enthusiasm for going deeper than a surface obsession with sex and gender. We resist even saying the word "patriarchy" in polite conversation. We act as if patriarchy weren't there, because the realization that it does exist is a door that swings only one way and we can't go back again to not knowing. We're like a family colluding in silence over dark secrets of damage and abuse, or like "good and decent Germans" during the Holocaust who "never knew" anything terrible was being done. We cling to the illusion that everything is basically all right, that bad things don't happen to good people, that good people can't participate in the production of evil, and that if we only leave things alone they'll stay pretty much as they are and, we often like to think, always have been.

Many women, of course, do dare to see and speak the truth, but they are always in danger of being attacked and discredited in order to maintain the silence. Even those who would never call themselves feminists often know there is something terribly wrong with the structures of dominance and control that are so central to life in modern societies and without which we think we cannot survive. The public response to feminism has been ferociously defensive precisely because feminism touches such a deep nerve of truth and the denial that keeps us from it. If feminism were truly ridiculous, it would be ignored. But it isn't ridiculous, and so it provokes a vigorous backlash.

We shouldn't be too hard on ourselves for hanging on to denial and illusions about patriarchy. Letting go is risky business, and patriarchy is full of smoke and mirrors that make it difficult to see what has to be let go of. It's relatively easy to accept the idea of patriarchy as male-dominated and male-identified, for example, and even as male-centered. Many people, however, have a much harder time seeing women as oppressed.[12] This is a huge issue that sparks a lot of arguments, and for that reason it will take several chapters to do it justice. Still, it's worthwhile outlining a basic response here.

The reluctance to see women as oppressed has several sources. The first is that many women enjoy race or class privilege and it's difficult for many to see them as oppressed without, as Sam Keen put it, insulting "truly oppressed" groups such as the lower classes or racial minorities.[13] How, for example, can we count upper-class women among the oppressed and lower-class men among their oppressors?

Although Keen's objection has a certain logic to it, it rests on a confusion between the position of women and men as groups and as individuals. To identify "female" as an oppressed status under patriarchy doesn't mean that every woman suffers its consequences to an equal degree, just as living in a racist society doesn't mean that every person of color suffers equally or that every white person shares equally in the benefits of race privilege. Living in patriarchy does mean, however, that every woman must come to grips with an inferior gender *position* and that whatever she achieves will be *in spite of* that position. With the exception of child care and other domestic work and a few paid occupations related to it, women in almost every field of adult endeavor must labor under the presumption that they are inferior to men, that they are interlopers from the margins of society who must justify their participation. Men may have such experiences because of their race, ethnicity, or other minority standing, but rarely if ever because they're men.

It is in this sense that patriarchies are male-dominated even though most individual men may not *feel* dominant, especially in relation to other men. This is a crucial insight that rests on the fact that when we talk about societies, words like "dominance" and "oppression" describe relations between categories of people such as whites and Hispanics, lower and upper classes, or women and men. How dominance and oppression actually play out among individuals is another issue. Sexism, for example, is an ideology, a set of ideas that promote male privilege in part by portraying women as inferior to men. But depending on other social factors such as race, class, or age, individual men will vary in their ability to take advantage of sexism and the benefits it produces. We can make a similar argument about women and the price they pay for belonging to a subordinate group. Upper-class women, for example, are insulated to some degree from the oppressive effects of being women under patriarchy, such as discrimination in the workplace. Their class privilege, however, exists *in spite of* their subordinate standing as women, which they can never completely overcome, especially in relation to husbands.[14] No woman is immune, for example, to the cultural devaluing of women's bodies as sexual objects to be exploited in public and private life, or the ongoing threat of sexual and domestic violence. To a rapist, the most powerful woman in the land is first and foremost a woman, and this more than anything else culturally marks her as a potential victim.

Along with not seeing women as oppressed, we resist seeing men as a privileged oppressor group. This is especially true of men who are aware of their own suffering, who often argue that men and women are both oppressed because of their gender and that neither oppresses the other. Undoubtedly men do suffer because of their participation in patriarchy, but it isn't because men are oppressed *as men*. For women, gender oppression is linked to a cultural devaluing of femaleness itself. Women are subordinated and treated as inferior because they are culturally defined as inferior *as women*, just as many racial and ethnic minorities are devalued simply because they aren't considered to be white. Men, however, do not suffer because maleness is devalued as an oppressed status in relation to some higher, more powerful one. Instead, to the extent that men suffer as men—and not because they're also poor or a racial or ethnic minority—it's because they belong to the dominant gender group in a system of gender oppression, which both privileges them and exacts a price in return.

A key to understanding this is that a group cannot oppress itself. A group can inflict injury on itself, and its members can suffer from their position in society. But if we say that a group can oppress or persecute *itself* we turn the concept of social oppression into a mere synonym for socially caused suffering, which it isn't.[15] Oppression is a social phenomenon that happens between different groups in a society; it is a system of social inequality through which one group is positioned to dominate and benefit from the exploitation and subordination of another. This means not only that a group cannot oppress itself, but also that it cannot be oppressed *by society*. Oppression is a relation that exists *between groups*, not between groups and society as a whole.

To understand oppression, then, we must distinguish it from suffering that has other social roots. Even the massive suffering inflicted on men through the horrors of war is not an oppression of men *as men*, because there is no system in which a group of non-men enforces and benefits from men's suffering. The systems that control the machinery of war are themselves patriarchal, which makes it impossible for them to oppress men as men. Warfare *does* oppress racial and ethnic minorities and the poor, who are often served up as cannon fodder by privileged classes whose interests war most often serves. Some 80 percent of all U.S. troops who served in Vietnam, for example, were from working- and lower-class backgrounds.[16] But this oppression is based on race and class, not gender. . . . If war made men truly disposable *as men*, we wouldn't find monuments and cemeteries in virtually every city and town in the United States dedicated to fallen soldiers (with no mention of their race or class), or endless retrospectives on the fiftieth anniversary of every milestone in World War II.

Rather than devalue or degrade patriarchal manhood, warfare celebrates and affirms it. As I write this on the fiftieth anniversary of the Normandy invasion, I can't help but feel the power of the honor and solemn mourning accorded the casualties of war, the deep respect opponents often feel for one another, and the countless monuments dedicated to men killed while trying to kill other men whose names, in turn, are inscribed on still more monuments.[17] But these ritual remembrances do more than sanctify sacrifice and tragic loss, they also sanctify war itself and the patriarchal institutions that promote it. Military leaders whose misguided orders, blunders, and egomaniacal schemes brought death to tens of thousands, for example, earn not ridicule, disgust, and scorn but a curious historical immunity framed in images of noble tragedy and heroic masculine endeavor. In stark contrast to massive graveyards of honored dead, the memorials, the annual speeches and parades, there are no monuments to the millions of women and children caught in the slaughter and bombed, burned, starved, raped, and left homeless. An estimated nine out of ten wartime casualties are civilians, not soldiers, and these include a huge proportion of children and women,[18] but there are no great national cemeteries devoted to *them*. War, after all, is a man's thing.

Perhaps one of the deepest reasons for denying the reality of women's oppression is that we don't want to admit that a real basis for conflict exists between men and women. We don't want to admit it because, unlike other groups involved in social oppression, such as whites and blacks, females and males really need each other, if only as parents and children. This can make us reluctant to see how patriarchy puts us at odds regardless of what we want or how we feel about it. Who wants to consider the role of gender oppression in everyday married and family life? Who wants to know how dependent we are on patriarchy as a system, how deeply our thoughts, feelings, and behavior are embedded in it? Men resist seeing the oppression of their mothers, wives, sisters, and daughters because we've participated in it, benefited from it, and developed a vested interest in it. . . .

We can move toward a clearer and more critical awareness of what patriarchy is about, of what gets in the way of working to end it, and new ways for all of us—

men in particular—to participate in its long evolutionary process of turning into something else. Patriarchy is our collective legacy, and there's nothing we can do about that or the condition in which we received it. But we can do a lot about what we pass on to those who follow us.

NOTES

1. See Marilyn French, *Beyond Power: On Men, Women, and Morals* (New York: Summit Books, 1985), 303.

2. There is a lot of research that shows how such uses of language affect people's perceptions. See, for example, Mykol C. Hamilton, "Using Masculine Generics: Does Generic 'He' Increase Male Bias in the User's Imagery?" *Sex Roles* 19, nos. 11/12 (1988): 785–799; Wendy Martyna, "Beyond the 'He/Man' Approach: The Case for Nonsexist Language," *Signs* 5 (1980): 482–493; Casey Miller and Kate Swift, *Words and Women*, updated ed. (New York: HarperCollins, 1991); and Joseph W. Schneider and Sally L. Hacker, "Sex Role Imagery in the Use of the Generic 'Man' in Introductory Texts: A Case in the Sociology of Sociology," *American Sociologist* 8 (1973): 12–18.

3. Note that I'm *not* describing actual men and women here, but cultural *ideas* about men and women under patriarchy. As concepts, masculinity and femininity play a complex role in patriarchal societies.

4. Just as a white-racist society can accommodate a certain number of powerful people of color so long as they do not challenge white privilege and the institutions that support it.

5. See, for example, Carole Levin's *The Heart and Stomach of a King: Elizabeth I and the Politics of Sex and Power* (Philadelphia: University of Pennsylvania Press, 1994).

6. See Carol Brooks Gardner, *Passing By: Gender and Public Harassment* (Berkeley: University of California Press, 1995).

7. For more on gender and interaction, see Robin Lakoff, *Language and Woman's Place* (New York: Harper and Row, 1975) and *Talking Power: The Politics of Language in Our Lives* (New York: Basic Books, 1990). See also Deborah Tannen, *Conversational Style: Analyzing Talk among Friends* (Norwood, N.J.: Ablex, 1984); idem, *You Just Don't Understand: Women and Men in Conversation* (New York: William Morrow, 1990).

8. See American Association of University Women, *How Schools Shortchange Girls* (Washington, D.C.: American Association of University Women, 1992); and Myra Sadker and David M. Sadker, *Failing at Fairness: How America's Schools Cheat Girls* (New York: Charles Scribner's Sons, 1994).

9. See Paula England and D. Dunn, "Evaluating Work and Comparable Worth," *Annual Review of Sociology* 14 (1988): 227–248.

10. See American Association of University Women, *How Schools Shortchange Girls*; and Sadker and Sadker, *Failing at Fairness*.

11. See Susan Brownmiller, *Against Our Will: Men, Women, and Rape* (New York: Simon and Schuster, 1975); Andrea Dworkin, *Woman Hating* (New York: E. P. Dutton, 1974); Susan Faludi, *Backlash: The Undeclared War Against American Women* (New York: Crown Publishers, 1991); Marilyn French, *The War Against Women* (New York: Summit Books, 1992); Gardner, *Passing By*; Diana E. H. Russell, *Rape in Marriage* (New York: Macmillan, 1982); idem, *Sexual Exploitation: Rape, Child Sexual Abuse, and Workplace Harassment* (Beverly Hills, Calif.: Sage Publications, 1984); Medical News and Perspectives, *Journal of the American Medical Association* 264, no. 8 (1990): 939; Laura Lederer, ed., *Take*

Back the Night: Women on Pornography (New York: William Morrow, 1980); Diana E. H. Russell, ed., *Making Violence Sexy: Feminist Views on Pornography* (New York: Teachers College Press, 1993); and Catharine MacKinnon, *Only Words* (Cambridge: Harvard University Press, 1993).

12. For more on this, see Marilyn Frye, *The Politics of Reality: Essays in Feminist Theory* (Freedom, Calif.: Crossing Press, 1983).

13. Sam Keen, *Fire in the Belly: On Being a Man* (New York: Bantam, 1991), 203.

14. See, for example, Susan A. Ostrander, *Women of the Upper Class* (Philadelphia: Temple University Press, 1984).

15. See Frye, *Politics of Reality*, 1–16.

16. Christian G. Appy, *Working-Class War: American Combat Soldiers in Vietnam* (Chapel Hill: University of North Carolina Press, 1993).

17. It is useful to note that in thirteenth-century Europe peasants were not allowed to participate in battle, since the nobility's monopoly over the tools and skills of warfare was its main basis for power and domination over land and peasants. Although knights undoubtedly suffered considerably from their endless wars with one another, one could hardly argue that their obligation to fight rendered them an oppressed group. Whatever price they paid for their dominance, the concept of oppression is not the word to describe it. For a lively history of this era, see Barbara Tuchman, *A Distant Mirror* (New York: Alfred A. Knopf, 1978).

18. Save the Children. Study results reported in *The Boston Globe*, 17 November 1994, 23.

7

HOMOPHOBIA AS A WEAPON OF SEXISM

Suzanne Pharr

Patriarchy—an enforced belief in male dominance and control—is the ideology and sexism the system that holds it in place. The catechism goes like this: Who do gender roles serve? Men and the women who seek power from them. Who suffers from gender roles? Women most completely and men in part. How are gender roles maintained? By the weapons of sexism: economics, violence, homophobia.

Why then don't we ardently pursue ways to eliminate gender roles and there-fore sexism? It is my profound belief that all people have a spark in them that yearns for freedom, and the history of the world's atrocities—from the Nazi concentration camps to white dominance in South Africa to the battering of women—is the story of attempts to snuff out that spark. When that spark doesn't move forward to full flame, it is because the weapons designed to control and destroy have wrought such intense damage over time that the spark has been all but extinguished.

Sexism, that system by which women are kept subordinate to men, is kept in place by three powerful weapons designed to cause or threaten women with pain and loss. . . .

We have to look at economics not only as the root cause of sexism but also as the underlying, driving force that keeps all the oppressions in place. In the United States, our economic system is shaped like a pyramid, with a few people at the top, primarily white males, being supported by large numbers of unpaid or low-paid workers at the bottom. When we look at this pyramid, we begin to understand the major connection between sexism and racism because those groups at the bottom of the pyramid are women and people of color. We then begin to understand why there is such a fervent effort to keep those oppressive sys-tems (racism and sexism and all the ways they are manifested) in place to main-tain the unpaid and low-paid labor.

As in most other countries, in the United States, income is unequally distrib-uted. However, among the industrialized countries of the world, the U.S. has the most unequal distribution of income of all. (See *The State of Working America 2000/2001*, p. 388.) What's more, over the past 30 plus years, income distribution has become even more unequal. In an OpEd piece distributed by Knight/Ridder/Tribune NewsService, Holly Sklar reports that poverty rates in 2001 were higher than in the 1970s and the top 5% of households got richer at the expense of every-one else. According to the U.S. Census bureau, there were 33 million poor in the U.S. in 2001 and median pretax income fell for all households except those in the top 5%. In other words, income inequality increased dramatically. In 1967, the wealthiest 5% of households had 17.5% of the income and by 2001 they had increased their share to 22.4%, while the bottom fifth had to make do with 3.5% of aggregate income, down from 4% in 1967 (September 30, 2002). And wealth is even more unequally distributed than income. According to U.S. government fig-ures for 1997, the wealthiest 10% of U.S. families own more than 72% of the total wealth, with 39% of the total wealth concentrated in the hands of the wealthiest 1%. In contrast, the bottom 40% of the population owns less than 1%.

In order for this top-heavy system of economic inequity to maintain itself, the 90 percent on the bottom must keep supplying cheap labor. A very complex, intri-cate system of institutionalized oppressions is necessary to maintain the status quo so that the vast majority will not demand its fair share of wealth and resources and bring the system down. Every institution—schools, banks, churches, government, courts, media, etc.—as well as individuals must be enlisted in the campaign to maintain such a system of gross inequity.

What would happen if women gained the earning opportunities and power that men have? What would happen if these opportunities were distributed equitably, no matter what sex one was, no matter what race one was born into, and no matter where one lived? What if educational and training opportunities were equal? Would women spend most of our youth preparing for marriage? Would marriage be based on economic survival for women? What would happen to issues of power and control? Would women stay with our batterers? If a woman had economic independence in a society where women had equal opportunities, would she still be thought of as owned by her father or husband?

Economics is the great controller in both sexism and racism. If a person can't acquire food, shelter, and clothing and provide them for children, then that person can be forced to do many things in order to survive. The major tactic, worldwide, is to provide unrecompensed or inadequately recompensed labor for the benefit of those who control wealth. Hence, we see women performing unpaid labor in the home or filling low-paid jobs, and we see people of color in the lowest-paid jobs available.

The method is complex: limit educational and training opportunities for women and for people of color and then withhold adequate paying jobs with the excuse that people of color and women are incapable of filling them. Blame the economic victim and keep the victim's self-esteem low through invisibility and distortion within the media and education. Allow a few people of color and women to succeed among the profitmakers so that blaming those who don't "make it" can be intensified. Encourage those few who succeed in gaining power now to turn against those who remain behind rather than to use their resources to make change for all. Maintain the myth of scarcity—that there are not enough jobs, resources, etc., to go around—among the middle class so that they will not unite with laborers, immigrants, and the unemployed. The method keeps in place a system of control and profit by a few and a constant source of cheap labor to maintain it.

If anyone steps out of line, take her/his job away. Let homelessness and hunger do their work. The economic weapon works. And we end up saying, "I would do this or that—be openly who I am, speak out against injustice, work for civil rights, join a labor union, go to a political march, etc.—if I didn't have this job. I can't afford to lose it." We stay in an abusive situation because we see no other way to survive. . . .

Violence against women is directly related to the condition of women in a society that refuses us equal pay, equal access to resources, and equal status with males. From this condition comes men's confirmation of their sense of ownership of women, power over women, and assumed right to control women for their own means. Men physically and emotionally abuse women because they *can*, because they live in a world that gives them permission. Male violence is fed by their sense of their *right* to dominate and control, and their sense of superiority over a group of people who, because of gender, they consider inferior to them.

It is not just the violence but the threat of violence that controls our lives. Because the burden of responsibility has been placed so often on the potential victim, as women we have curtailed our freedom in order to protect ourselves from violence. Because of the threat of rapists, we stay on alert, being careful not to walk in isolated places, being careful where we park our cars, adding incredible security measures to our homes—massive locks, lights, alarms, if we can afford them—and we avoid places where we will appear vulnerable or unprotected while the abuser walks with freedom. Fear, often now so commonplace that it is unacknowledged, shapes our lives, reducing our freedom. . . .

Part of the way sexism stays in place is the societal promise of survival, false and unfulfilled as it is, that women will not suffer violence if we attach ourselves to a man to protect us. A woman without a man is told she is vulnerable to external violence and, worse, that there is something wrong with her. When the male abuser calls a woman a lesbian, he is not so much labeling her a woman who loves women as he is warning her that by resisting him, she is choosing to be outside society's protection from male institutions and therefore from wide-ranging, unspecified, ever-present violence. When she seeks assistance from woman friends or a battered women's shelter, he recognizes the power in woman bonding and fears loss of her servitude and loyalty: the potential loss of his control. The concern is not affectional/sexual identity: the concern is disloyalty and the threat is violence.

The threat of violence against women who step out of line or who are disloyal is made all the more powerful by the fact that women do not have to do anything—they may be paragons of virtue and subservience—to receive violence against our lives: the violence still comes. It comes because of the woman-hating that exists throughout society. Chance plays a larger part than virtue in keeping women safe. Hence, with violence always a threat to us, women can never feel completely secure and confident. Our sense of safety is always fragile and tenuous.

Many women say that verbal violence causes more harm than physical violence because it damages self-esteem so deeply. Women have not wanted to hear battered women say that the verbal abuse was as hurtful as the physical abuse: to acknowledge that truth would be tantamount to acknowledging that *virtually every woman is a battered woman*. It is difficult to keep strong against accusations of being a bitch, stupid, inferior, etc., etc. It is especially difficult when these individual assaults are backed up by a society that shows women in textbooks, advertising, TV programs, movies, etc. as debased, silly, inferior, and sexually objectified, and a society that gives tacit approval to pornography. When we internalize these messages, we call the result "low self-esteem," a therapeutic individualized term. It seems to me we should use the more political expression: when we internalize these messages, we experience *internalized sexism*, and we experience it in common with all women living in a sexist world. The violence against us is supported by a society in which woman-hating is deeply imbedded.

In "Eyes on the Prize," a 1987 Public Television documentary about the Civil Rights Movement, an older white woman says about her youth in the South that it was difficult to be anything different from what was around her when there was no vision for another way to be. Our society presents images of women that say it is appropriate to commit violence against us. Violence is committed against women because we are seen as inferior in status and in worth. It has been the work of the women's movement to present a vision of another way to be.

Every time a woman gains the strength to resist and leave her abuser, we are given a model of the importance of stepping out of line, of moving toward freedom. And we all gain strength when she says to violence, "Never again!" Thousands of women in the last fifteen years have resisted their abusers to come to this country's 1100 battered women's shelters. There they have sat down with other women to share their stories, to discover that their stories again and again are the same, to develop an analysis that shows that violence is a statement about power and control, and to understand how sexism creates the climate for male violence. Those brave women are now a part of a movement that gives hope for another way to live in equality and peace.

Homophobia works effectively as a weapon of sexism because it is joined with a powerful arm, heterosexism. Heterosexism creates the climate for homophobia with its assumption that the world is and must be heterosexual and its display of power and privilege as the norm. Heterosexism is the systemic display of homophobia in the institutions of society. Heterosexism and homophobia work together to enforce compulsory heterosexuality and that bastion of patriarchal power, the nuclear family. The central focus of the rightwing attack against women's liberation is that women's equality, women's self-determination, women's control of our own bodies and lives will damage what they see as the crucial societal institution, the nuclear family. The attack has been led by fundamentalist ministers across the country. The two areas they have focused on most consistently are abortion and homosexuality, and their passion has led them to bomb women's clinics and to recommend deprogramming for homosexuals and establishing camps to quarantine people with AIDS. To resist marriage and/or heterosexuality is to risk severe punishment and loss.

It is not by chance that when children approach puberty and increased sexual awareness they begin to taunt each other by calling these names: "queer," "faggot," "pervert." It is at puberty that the full force of society's pressure to conform to heterosexuality and prepare for marriage is brought to bear. Children know what we have taught them, and we have given clear messages that those who deviate from standard expectations are to be made to get back in line. The best controlling tactic at puberty is to be treated as an outsider, to be ostracized at a time when it feels most vital to be accepted. Those who are different must be made to suffer loss. It is also at puberty that misogyny begins to be more apparent, and girls are pressured to conform to societal norms that do not permit them to realize their full potential. It is at this time that their academic achievements begin to decrease as they are coerced into compulsory heterosexuality and trained for dependency upon a man, that is, for economic survival.

There was a time when the two most condemning accusations against a woman meant to ostracize and disempower her were "whore" and "lesbian." The sexual revolution and changing attitudes about heterosexual behavior may have led to some lessening of the power of the word *whore*, though it still has strength as a threat to sexual property and prostitutes are stigmatized and abused. However, the word *lesbian* is still fully charged and carries with it the full threat of loss of power and privilege, the threat of being cut asunder, abandoned, and left outside society's protection.

To be a lesbian is to be *perceived* as someone who has stepped out of line, who has moved out of sexual/economic dependence on a male, who is woman-identified. A lesbian is perceived as someone who can live without a man, and who is therefore (however illogically) against men. A lesbian is perceived as being outside the acceptable, routinized order of things. She is seen as someone who has no societal institutions to protect her and who is not privileged to the protection of individual males. Many heterosexual women see her as someone who stands in contradiction to the sacrifices they have made to conform to compulsory heterosexuality. A lesbian is perceived as a threat to the nuclear family, to male dominance and control, to the very heart of sexism.

Gay men are perceived also as a threat to male dominance and control, and the homophobia expressed against them has the same roots in sexism as does homophobia against lesbians. Visible gay men are the objects of extreme hatred and fear by heterosexual men because their breaking ranks with male heterosexual solidarity is seen as a damaging rent in the very fabric of sexism. They are seen as betrayers, as traitors who must be punished and eliminated. In the beating and killing of gay men we see clear evidence of this hatred. When we see the fierce homophobia expressed toward gay men, we can begin to understand the ways sexism also affects males through imposing rigid, dehumanizing gender roles on them. The two circumstances in which it is legitimate for men to be openly physically affectionate with one another are in competitive sports and in the crisis of war. For many men, these two experiences are the highlights of their lives, and they think of them again and again with nostalgia. War and sports offer a cover of all-male safety and dominance to keep away the notion of affectionate openness being identified with homosexuality. When gay men break ranks with male roles through bonding and affection outside the arenas of war and sports, they are perceived as not being "real men," that is, as being identified with women, the weaker sex that must be dominated and that over the centuries has been the object of male hatred and abuse. Misogyny gets transferred to gay men with a vengeance and is increased by the fear that their sexual identity and behavior will bring down the entire system of male dominance and compulsory heterosexuality.

If lesbians are established as threats to the status quo, as outcasts who must be punished, homophobia can wield its power over all women through lesbian baiting. Lesbian baiting is an attempt to control women by labeling us as lesbians because our behavior is not acceptable, that is, when we are being independent, going our own way, living whole lives, fighting for our rights, demanding equal pay, saying no to violence, being self-assertive, bonding with and loving the company of women, assuming the right to our bodies, insisting upon our own authority, making changes that include us in society's decision-making; lesbian baiting occurs when women are called lesbians because we resist male dominance and control. And it has little or nothing to do with one's sexual identity.

To be named as lesbian threatens all women, not just lesbians, with great loss. And any woman who steps out of role risks being called a lesbian. To understand how this is a threat to all women, one must understand that any woman can be called a lesbian and there is no real way she can defend herself: there is no way to credential one's sexuality. ("The Children's Hour," a Lillian Hellman play, makes this point when a student asserts two teachers are lesbians and they have no way to disprove it.) She may be married or divorced, have children, dress in the most feminine manner, have sex with men, be celibate—but there are lesbians who do all those things. *Lesbians look like all women and all women look like lesbians.* There is no guaranteed method of identification, and as we all know, sexual identity can be kept hidden. (The same is true for men. There is no way to prove their sexual identity, though many go to extremes to prove heterosexuality.) Also, women are not necessarily born lesbian. Some seem to be, but others become lesbians later in life after having lived heterosexual lives. Lesbian baiting of heterosexual women would not work if there were a definitive way to identify lesbians (or heterosexuals).

We have yet to understand clearly how sexual identity develops. And this is disturbing to some people, especially those who are determined to discover how lesbian and gay identity is formed so that they will know where to start in eliminating it. (Isn't it odd that there is so little concern about discovering the causes of heterosexuality?) There are many theories: genetic makeup, hormones, socialization, environment, etc. But there is no conclusive evidence that indicates that heterosexuality comes from one process and homosexuality from another.

We do know, however, that sexual identity can be in flux, and we know that sexual identity means more than just the gender of people one is attracted to and has sex with. To be a lesbian has as many ramifications as for a woman to be heterosexual. It is more than sex, more than just the bedroom issue many would like to make it: it is a woman-centered life with all the social interconnections that entails. Some lesbians are in long-term relationships, some in short-term ones, some date, some are celibate, some are married to men, some remain as separate as possible from men, some have children by men, some by alternative insemination, some seem "feminine" by societal standards, some "masculine," some are doctors, lawyers and ministers, some laborers, housewives and writers: what all share in common is a sexual/affectional identity that focuses on women in its attractions and social relationships.

If lesbians are simply women with a particular sexual identity who look and act like all women, then the major difference in living out a lesbian sexual identity as opposed to a heterosexual identity is that as lesbians we live in a homophobic world that threatens and imposes damaging loss on us for *being who we are*, for choosing to live whole lives. Homophobic people often assert that homosexuals have the choice of not being homosexual; that is, we don't have to act out our sexual identity. In that case, I want to hear heterosexuals talk about their willingness not to act out their sexual identity, including not just sexual activity but heterosexual social interconnections and heterosexual privilege. It is a question of wholeness. It is very difficult for one to be denied the life of a sexual being, whether expressed in sex or in physical affection, and to feel complete, whole. For our loving relationships with humans feed the life of the spirit and enable us to overcome our basic isolation and to be interconnected with humankind.

If, then, any woman can be named a lesbian and be threatened with terrible losses, what is it she fears? Are these fears real? Being vulnerable to a homophobic world can lead to these losses:

- *Employment.* The loss of job leads us right back to the economic conection to sexism. This fear of job loss exists for almost every lesbian except perhaps those who are self-employed or in a business that does not require societal approval. Consider how many businesses or organizations you know that will hire and protect people who are openly gay or lesbian.
- *Family.* Their approval, acceptance, love.
- *Children.* Many lesbians and gay men have children, but very, very few gain custody in court challenges, even if the other parent is a known abuser. Other children may be kept away from us as though gays and lesbians are abusers. There are written and unwritten laws prohibiting lesbians and gays from being foster parents or from adopting children. There is an irrational fear that children in contact with lesbians and gays will become homosexual through influence or that they will be sexually abused. Despite our knowing that 95 percent of those who sexually abuse children are heterosexual men, there are no policies keeping heterosexual men from teaching or working with children, yet in almost every school system in America, visible gay men and lesbians are not hired through either written or unwritten law.
- *Heterosexual privilege and protection.* No institutions, other than those created by lesbians and gays—such as the Metropolitan Community Church, some counseling centers, political organizations such as the National Gay and Lesbian Task Force, the National Coalition of Black Lesbians and Gays, the Lambda Legal Defense and Education Fund, etc.—affirm homosexuality and offer protection. Affirmation and protection cannot be gained from the criminal justice system, mainline churches, educational institutions, the government.
- *Safety.* There is nowhere to turn for safety from physical and verbal attacks because the norm presently in this country is that it is acceptable to be overtly homophobic. Gay men are beaten on the streets; lesbians are kidnapped and "deprogrammed." The National Gay and Lesbian Task Force, in an extended study, has documented violence against lesbians and gay men and noted the inadequate response of the criminal justice system. One of the major differences between homophobia/heterosexism and

racism and sexism is that because of the Civil Rights Movement and the women's movement racism and sexism are expressed more covertly (though with great harm); because there has not been a major, visible lesbian and gay movement, it is permissible to be overtly homophobic in any institution or public forum. Churches spew forth homophobia in the same way they did racism prior to the Civil Rights Movement. Few laws are in place to protect lesbians and gay men, and the criminal justice system is wracked with homophobia.

- *Mental health.* An overtly homophobic world in which there is full permission to treat lesbians and gay men with cruelty makes it difficult for lesbians and gay men to maintain a strong sense of well-being and self-esteem. Many lesbians and gay men are beaten, raped, killed, subjected to aversion therapy, or put in mental institutions. The impact of such hatred and negativity can lead one to depression and, in some cases, to suicide. The toll on the gay and lesbian community is devastating.

- *Community.* There is rejection by those who live in homophobic fear, those who are afraid of association with lesbians and gay men. For many in the gay and lesbian community, there is a loss of public acceptance, a loss of allies, a loss of place and belonging.

- *Credibility.* This fear is large for many people: the fear that they will no longer be respected, listened to, honored, believed. They fear they will be social outcasts.

The list goes on and on. But any one of these essential components of a full life is large enough to make one deeply fear its loss. A black woman once said to me in a workshop, "When I fought for Civil Rights, I always had my family and community to fall back on even when they didn't fully understand or accept what I was doing. I don't know if I could have borne losing them. And you people don't have either with you. It takes my breath away."

What does a woman have to do to get called a lesbian? Almost anything, sometimes nothing at all, but certainly anything that threatens the status quo, anything that steps out of role, anything that asserts the rights of women, anything that doesn't indicate submission and subordination. Assertiveness, standing up for oneself, asking for more pay, better working conditions, training for and accepting a non-traditional (you mean a man's?) job, enjoying the company of women, being financially independent, being in control of one's life, depending first and foremost upon oneself, thinking that one can do whatever needs to be done, but above all, working for the rights and equality of women.

In the backlash to the gains of the women's liberation movement, there has been an increased effort to keep definitions man-centered. Therefore, to work on behalf of women must mean to work against men. To love women must mean that one hates men. A very effective attack has been made against the word *feminist* to make it a derogatory word. In current backlash usage, *feminist* equals *man-hater* which equals *lesbian.* This formula is created in the hope that women will be frightened away from their work on behalf of women. Consequently, we now have women who believe in the rights of women and work for those rights while from fear deny that they are feminists, or refuse to use the word because it is so "abrasive."

So what does one do in an effort to keep from being called a lesbian? She steps back into line, into the role that is demanded of her, tries to behave in such a way that doesn't threaten the status of men, and if she works for women's rights, she begins modifying that work. When women's organizations begin doing significant social change work, they inevitably are lesbian-baited; that is, funders or institutions or community members tell us that they can't work with us because of our "man-hating attitudes" or the presence of lesbians. We are called too strident, told we are making enemies, not doing good. . . .

In my view, homophobia has been one of the major causes of the failure of the women's liberation movement to make deep and lasting change. (The other major block has been racism.) We were fierce when we set out but when threatened with the loss of heterosexual privilege, we began putting on brakes. Our best-known nationally distributed women's magazine was reluctant to print articles about lesbians, began putting a man on the cover several times a year, and writing articles about women who succeeded in a man's world. We worried about our image, our being all right, our being "real women" despite our work. Instead of talking about the elimination of sexual gender roles, we stepped back and talked about "sex role stereotyping" as the issue. Change around the edges for middle-class white women began to be talked about as successes. We accepted tokenism and integration, forgetting that equality for all women, for all people—and not just equality of white middle-class women with white men—was the goal that we could never put behind us.

But despite backlash and retreats, change is growing from within. The women's liberation movement is beginning to gain strength again because there are women who are talking about liberation for all women. We are examining sexism, racism, homophobia, classism, anti-Semitism, ageism, ableism, and imperialism, and we see everything as connected. This change in point of view represents the third wave of the women's liberation movement, a new direction that does not get mass media coverage and recognition. It has been initiated by women of color and lesbians who were marginalized or rendered invisible by the white heterosexual leaders of earlier efforts. The first wave was the 19th and early 20th century campaign for the vote; the second, beginning in the 1960s, focused on the Equal Rights Amendment and abortion rights. Consisting of predominantly white middle-class women, both failed in recognizing issues of equality and empowerment for all women. The third wave of the movement, multi-racial and multi-issued, seeks the transformation of the world for us all. We know that we won't get there until everyone gets there; that we must move forward in a great strong line, hand in hand, not just a few at a time.

We know that the arguments about homophobia originating from mental health and Biblical/religious attitudes can be settled when we look at the sexism that permeates religious and psychiatric history. The women of the third wave of the women's liberation movement know that *without the existence of sexism, there would be no homophobia.*

Finally, we know that as long as the word *lesbian* can strike fear in any woman's heart, then work on behalf of women can be stopped; the only successful work against sexism must include work against homophobia.

8

WHITE PRIVILEGE
Unpacking the Invisible Knapsack

Peggy McIntosh

Through work to bring materials from Women's Studies into the rest of the curriculum, I have often noticed men's unwillingness to grant that they are over-privileged, even though they may grant that women are disadvantaged. They may say they will work to improve women's status, in the society, the university, or the curriculum, but they can't or won't support the idea of lessening men's. Denials which amount to taboos surround the subject of advantages which men gain from women's disadvantages. These denials protect male privilege from being fully acknowledged, lessened or ended.

Thinking through unacknowledged male privilege as a phenomenon, I realized that since hierarchies in our society are interlocking, there was most likely a phenomenon of white privilege which was similarly denied and protected. As a white person, I realized I had been taught about racism as something which puts others at a disadvantage, but had been taught not to see one of its corollary aspects, white privilege, which puts me at an advantage.

I think whites are carefully taught not to recognize white privilege, as males are taught not to recognize male privilege. So I have begun in an untutored way to ask what it is like to have white privilege. I have come to see white privilege as an invisible package of unearned assets which I can count on cashing in each day, but about which I was "meant" to remain oblivious. White privilege is like an invisible weightless knapsack of special provisions, maps, passports, codebooks, visas, clothes, tools and blank checks.

Describing white privilege makes one newly accountable. As we in Women's Studies work to reveal male privilege and ask men to give up some of their power, so one who writes about having white privilege must ask, "Having described it, what will I do to lessen or end it?"

After I realized the extent to which men work from a base of unacknowledged privilege, I understood that much of their oppressiveness was unconscious. Then I remembered the frequent charges from women of color that white women whom they encounter are oppressive. I began to understand why we are justly seen as oppressive, even when we don't see ourselves that way. I began to count the ways in which I enjoy unearned skin privilege and have been conditioned into oblivion about its existence.

My schooling gave me no training in seeing myself as an oppressor, as an unfairly advantaged person, or as a participant in a damaged culture. I was taught to see myself as an individual whose moral state depended on her individual moral will. My schooling followed the pattern my colleague Elizabeth Minnich has pointed out: whites are taught to think of their lives as morally neutral, normative, and average, and also ideal, so that when we work to benefit others, this is seen as work which will allow "them" to be more like "us."

I decided to try to work on myself at least by identifying some of the daily effects of white privilege in my life. I have chosen those conditions which I think in my case *attach somewhat more to skin-color privilege* than to class, religion, ethnic status, or geographical location, though of course all these other factors are intricately intertwined. As far as I can see, my African American co-workers, friends and acquaintances with whom I come into daily or frequent contact in this particular time, place, and line of work cannot count on most of these conditions.

1. I can if I wish arrange to be in the company of people of my race most of the time.
2. If I should need to move, I can be pretty sure of renting or purchasing housing in an area which I can afford and in which I would want to live.
3. I can be pretty sure that my neighbors in such a location will be neutral or pleasant to me.
4. I can go shopping alone most of the time, pretty well assured that I will not be followed or harassed.
5. I can turn on the television or open to the front page of the paper and see people of my race widely represented.
6. When I am told about our national heritage or about "civilization," I am shown that people of my color made it what it is.

7. I can be sure that my children will be given curricular materials that testify to the existence of their race.

8. If I want to, I can be pretty sure of finding a publisher for this piece on white privilege.

9. I can go into a music shop and count on finding the music of my race represented, into a supermarket and find the staple foods which fit with my cultural traditions, into a hairdresser's shop and find someone who can cut my hair.

10. Whether I use checks, credit cards, or cash, I can count on my skin color not to work against the appearance of financial reliability.

11. I can arrange to protect my children most of the time from people who might not like them.

12. I can swear, or dress in secondhand clothes, or not answer letters, without having people attribute these choices to the bad morals, the poverty, or the illiteracy of my race.

13. I can speak in public to a powerful male group without putting my race on trial.

14. I can do well in a challenging situation without being called a credit to my race.

15. I am never asked to speak for all the people of my racial group.

16. I can remain oblivious of the language and customs of persons of color who constitute the world's majority without feeling in my culture any penalty for such oblivion.

17. I can criticize our government and talk about how much I fear its policies and behavior without being seen as a cultural outsider.

18. I can be pretty sure that if I ask to talk to "the person in charge," I will be facing a person of my race.

19. If a traffic cop pulls me over or if the IRS audits my tax return, I can be sure I haven't been singled out because of my race.

20. I can easily buy posters, postcards, picture books, greeting cards, dolls, toys, and children's magazines featuring people of my race.

21. I can go home from most meetings of organizations I belong to feeling somewhat tied in, rather than isolated, out-of-place, outnumbered, unheard, held at a distance, or feared.

22. I can take a job with an affirmative action employer without having coworkers on the job suspect that I got it because of my race.

23. I can choose public accommodation without fearing that people of my race cannot get in or will be mistreated in the places I have chosen.

24. I can be sure that if I need legal or medical help, my race will not work against me.

25. If my day, week, or year is going badly, I need not ask of each negative episode or situation whether it has racial overtones.

26. I can choose blemish cover or bandages in "flesh" color and have them more or less match my skin.

I repeatedly forgot each of the realizations on this list until I wrote it down. For me white privilege has turned out to be an elusive and fugitive subject. The pressure to avoid it is great, for in facing it I must give up the myth of meritocracy. If these things are true, this is not such a free country; one's life is not what one makes it; many doors open for certain people through no virtues of their own.

In unpacking this invisible knapsack of white privilege, I have listed conditions of daily experience which I once took for granted. Nor did I think of any of these perquisites as bad for the holder. I now think that we need a more finely differentiated taxonomy of privilege, for some of these varieties are only what one would want for everyone in a just society, and others give license to be ignorant, oblivious, arrogant and destructive.

I see a pattern running through the matrix of white privilege, a pattern of assumptions which were passed on to me as a white person. There was one main piece of cultural turf; it was my own turf, and I was among those who could control the turf. *My skin color was an asset for any move I was educated to want to make.* I could think of myself as belonging in major ways, and of making social systems work for me. I could freely disparage, fear, neglect, or be oblivious to anything outside of the dominant cultural forms. Being of the main culture, I could also criticize it fairly freely.

In proportion as my racial group was being made confident, comfortable, and oblivious, other groups were likely being made inconfident, uncomfortable, and alienated. Whiteness protected me from many kinds of hostility, distress, and violence, which I was being subtly trained to visit in turn upon people of color.

For this reason, the word "privilege" now seems to me misleading. We usually think of privilege as being a favored state, whether earned or conferred by birth or luck. Yet some of the conditions I have described here work to systematically overempower certain groups. Such privilege simply *confers dominance* because of one's race or sex.

I want, then, to distinguish between earned strength and unearned power conferred systemically. Power from unearned privilege can look like strength when it is in fact permission to escape or to dominate. But not all of the privileges on my list are inevitably damaging. Some, like the expectation that neighbors will be decent to you, or that your race will not count against you in court, should be the norm in a just society. Others, like the privilege to ignore less powerful people, distort the humanity of the holders as well as the ignored groups.

We might at least start by distinguishing between positive advantages which we can work to spread, and negative types of advantages which unless rejected will always reinforce our present hierarchies. For example, the feeling that one belongs within the human circle, as Native Americans say, should not be seen as privilege for a few. Ideally it is an *unearned entitlement*. At present, since only a few have it, it is an unearned advantage for them. This paper results from a process of coming to see that some of the power which I originally saw as attendant on being a human being in the U.S. consisted in *unearned advantage* and *conferred dominance*.

I have met very few men who are truly distressed about systemic, unearned male advantage and conferred dominance. And so one question for me and others like me is whether we will be like them, or whether we will get truly distressed, even outraged, about unearned race advantage and conferred dominance and if so, what we will do to lessen them. In any case, we need to do more work in identifying how they actually affect our daily lives. Many, perhaps most, of our white students in the U.S. think that racism doesn't affect them because they are not people of color; they do not see "whiteness" as a racial identity. In addition, since race and sex are not the only advantaging systems at work, we need similarly to examine the daily experience of having age advantage, or ethnic advantage, or physical ability, or advantage related to nationality, religion, or sexual orientation.

Difficulties and dangers surrounding the task of finding parallels are many. Since racism, sexism, and heterosexism are not the same, the advantaging associated with them should not be seen as the same. In addition, it is hard to disentangle aspects of unearned advantage which rest more on social class, economic class, race, religion, sex and ethnic identity than on other factors. Still, all of the oppressions are interlocking, as the Combahee River Collective Statement of 1977 continues to remind us eloquently.

One factor seems clear about all of the interlocking oppressions. They take both active forms which we can see and embedded forms which as a member of the dominant group one is taught not to see. In my class and place, I did not see myself as a racist because I was taught to recognize racism only in individual acts of meanness by members of my group, never in invisible systems conferring unsought racial dominance on my group from birth.

Disapproving of the systems won't be enough to change them. I was taught to think that racism could end if white individuals changed their attitudes. [But] a "white" skin in the United States opens many doors for whites whether or not we approve of the way dominance has been conferred on us. Individual acts can palliate, but cannot end, these problems.

To redesign social systems we need first to acknowledge their colossal unseen dimensions. The silences and denials surrounding privilege are the key political tool here. They keep the thinking about equality or equity incomplete, protecting unearned advantage and conferred dominance by making these taboo subjects. Most talk by whites about equal opportunity seems to me now to be about equal opportunity to try to get into a position of dominance while denying that *systems* of dominance exist.

It seems to me that obliviousness about white advantage, like obliviousness about male advantage, is kept strongly inculturated in the United States so as to maintain the myth of meritocracy, the myth that democratic choice is equally available to all. Keeping most people unaware that freedom of confident action is there for just a small number of people props up those in power, and serves to keep power in the hands of the same groups that have most of it already.

Though systemic change takes many decades, there are pressing questions for me and I imagine for some others like me if we raise our daily consciousness on the perquisites of being light-skinned. What will we do with such knowledge? As we know from watching men, it is an open question whether we will choose to use unearned advantage to weaken hidden systems of advantage, and whether we will use any of our arbitrarily-awarded power to try to reconstruct power systems on a broader base.

9

CLASS IN AMERICA—2009

Gregory Mantsios

People in the United States don't like to talk about class. Or so it would seem. We don't speak about class privileges, or class oppression, or the class nature of society. These terms are not part of our everyday vocabulary, and in most circles they are associated with the language of the rhetorical fringe. Unlike people in most other parts of the world, we shrink from using words that classify along economic lines or that point to class distinctions: phrases like "working class," "upper class," and "ruling class" are rarely uttered by Americans.

For the most part, avoidance of class-laden vocabulary crosses class boundaries. There are few among the poor who speak of themselves as lower class; instead, they refer to their race, ethnic group, or geographic location. Workers are more likely to identify with their employer, industry, or occupational group than with other workers, or with the working class.[1]

Neither are those at the other end of the economic spectrum likely to use the word "class." In her study of thirty-eight wealthy and socially prominent women, Susan Ostrander asked participants if they considered themselves members of the upper class. One participant responded, "I hate to use the word 'class.' We are responsible, fortunate people, old families, the people who have something."

Another said, "I hate [the term] upper class. It is so non-upper class to use it. I just call it 'all of us,' those who are wellborn."[2]

The author wishes to thank Mark Major for his assistance in updating this article. From Gregory Mantsios, *Class in America: Myths and Realities.* Copyright © Gregory Mantsios, 2006. Reprinted by permission of the author.

It is not that Americans, rich or poor, aren't keenly aware of class differences—those quoted above obviously are; it is that class is not in the domain of public discourse. Class is not discussed or debated in public because class identity has been stripped from popular culture. The institutions that shape mass culture and define the parameters of public debate have avoided class issues. In politics, in primary and secondary education, and in the mass media, formulating issues in terms of class is unacceptable, perhaps even un-American. See my paper, "Media Magic: Making Class Invisible," Selection 7 in Part VIII of this volume.

There are, however, two notable exceptions to this phenomenon. First, it is acceptable in the United States to talk about "the middle class." Interestingly enough, such references appear to be acceptable precisely because they mute class differences. References to the middle class by politicians, for example, are designed to encompass and attract the broadest possible constituency. Not only do references to the middle class gloss over differences, but these references also avoid any suggestion of conflict or injustice.

This leads us to the second exception to the class-avoidance phenomenon. We are, on occasion, presented with glimpses of the upper class and the lower class (the language used is "the wealthy" and "the poor"). In the media, these presentations are designed to satisfy some real or imagined voyeuristic need of "the ordinary person." As curiosities, the ground-level view of street life and the inside look at the rich and the famous serve as unique models, one to avoid and one to aspire to. In either case, the two models are presented without causal relation to each other: one is not rich because the other is poor.

Similarly, when social commentators or liberal politicians draw attention to the plight of the poor, they do so in a manner that obscures the class structure and denies any sense of exploitation. Wealth and poverty are viewed as one of several natural and inevitable states of being: differences are only differences. One may even say differences are the American way, a reflection of American social diversity.

We are left with one of two possibilities: either talking about class and recognizing class distinctions are not relevant to U.S. society, or we mistakenly hold a set of beliefs that obscure the reality of class differences and their impact on people's lives.

Let us look at four common, albeit contradictory, beliefs about the United States.

Myth 1: The United States is fundamentally a classless society. Class distinctions are largely irrelevant today, and whatever differences do exist in economic standing, they are—for the most part—insignificant. Rich or poor, we are all equal in the eyes of the law, and such basic needs as health care and education are provided to all regardless of economic standing.

Myth 2: We are, essentially, a middle-class nation. Despite some variations in economic status, most Americans have achieved relative affluence in what is widely recognized as a consumer society.

Myth 3: We are all getting richer. The American public as a whole is steadily moving up the economic ladder, and each generation propels itself to greater economic well-being. Despite some fluctuations, the U.S. position in the global economy has brought previously unknown prosperity to most, if not all, Americans.

Myth 4: Everyone has an equal chance to succeed. Success in the United States requires no more than hard work, sacrifice, and perseverance: "In America, anyone can become a millionaire; it's just a matter of being in the right place at the right time."

In trying to assess the legitimacy of these beliefs, we want to ask several important questions. Are there significant class differences among Americans? If these differences do exist, are they getting bigger or smaller, and do these differences have a significant impact on the way we live? Finally, does everyone in the United States really have an equal opportunity to succeed?

The Economic Spectrum

Let's begin by looking at difference. An examination of available data reveals that variations in economic well-being are, in fact, immense. Consider the following:

- The wealthiest 1 percent of the American population holds 34 percent of the total national wealth. That is, they own over one-third of all the consumer durables (such as houses, cars, and stereos) and financial assets (such as stocks, bonds, property, and savings accounts). The richest 20 percent of Americans hold nearly 85 percent of the total household wealth in the country.[3]
- Approximately 338,761 Americans, or approximately eight-tenths of 1 percent of the adult population, earn more than $1 million **annually.**[4] There are nearly 400 billionaires in the U.S today, more than three dozen of them worth more than $10 billion each. It would take the typical (median) American (earning $49,568 and spending absolutely nothing at all) a total of 20,174 years (or approximately 298 lifetimes) to earn just $1 billion.

Affluence and prosperity are clearly alive and well in certain segments of the U.S. population. However, this abundance is in contrast to the poverty and despair that is also prevalent in the United States. At the other end of the spectrum:

- Approximately 13 percent of the American population—that is, nearly one of every eight people in this country—live below the official poverty line (calculated in 2007 at $10,590 for an individual and $21,203 for a family of four).[5] An estimated 3.5 million people—of whom nearly 1.4 million are children—experience homelessness in any given year.[6]

The contrast between rich and poor is sharp, and with nearly one-third of the American population living at one extreme or the other, it is difficult to argue that we live in a classless society. Big-payoff reality shows, celebrity salaries, and multi-million dollar lotteries notwithstanding, evidence suggests that the level of inequality in the United States is getting higher. Census data show the gap between the rich and the poor to be the widest since the government began collecting information in 1947[7] and that this gap is continuing to grow. In one year alone, from 2003 to 2004, the average after-tax income of the top 1 percent increased by 20 percent to $145,500 per year. This is the largest one-year increase going to the top 1 percent in fifteen years. On average the income of the bottom 80 percent increased only 2.7 percent.[8]

Nor is such a gap between rich and poor representative of the rest of the industrialized world. In fact, the United States has by far the most unequal distribution of household income.[9] The income gap between rich and poor in the United States (measured as the percentage of total income held by the wealthiest 10 percent of the population as compared to the poorest 10 percent) is approximately 5.4 to 1, the highest ratio in the industrialized world.[10]

Reality 1: There are enormous differences in the economic standing of American citizens. A sizable proportion of the U.S. population occupies opposite ends of the economic spectrum. In the middle range of the economic spectrum:

- Sixty percent of the American population holds less than 4 percent of the nation's wealth.[11]
- While the real income of the top 1 percent of U.S. families more than doubled (111 percent) between 1979 and 2003, the income of the middle fifth of the population grew only slightly (9 percent over that same 24-year period) and its share of income (15 percent of the total compared to 48 percent of the total for the wealthiest fifth) actually declined during this period.[12]
- Regressive changes in governmental tax policies and the weakening of labor unions over the last quarter century have led to a significant rise in the level of inequality between the rich and the middle class. Between 1979 and 2005, the gap in household income between the top fifth and middle fifth of the population rose by almost 40 percent.[13] From 1962 to 2004, the wealth held by most Americans (80 percent of the total population) increased from $40,000 to $82,000 (not adjusted for inflation). During that same period, the average wealth of the top 1 percent increased from $5.6 million to $14.8 million.[14] One prominent economist described economic growth in the United States as a "spectator sport for the majority of American families."[15] Economic decline, on the other hand, is much more "inclusive," with layoffs impacting hardest on middle- and lower-income families—those with fewer resources to fall back on.

The level of inequality is sometimes difficult to comprehend fully by looking at dollar figures and percentages. To help his students visualize the distribution of income, the well-known economist Paul Samuelson asked them to picture an income pyramid made of children's blocks, with each layer of blocks representing $1,000. If we were to construct Samuelson's pyramid today, the peak of the pyramid would be much higher than the Eiffel Tower, yet almost all of us would be within six feet of the ground.[16] In other words, the distribution of income is heavily skewed; a small minority of families take the lion's share of national income, and the remaining income is distributed among the vast majority of middle-income and low-income families. Keep in mind that Samuelson's pyramid represents the distribution of income, not wealth. The distribution of wealth is skewed even further.

Reality 2: The middle class in the United States holds a very small share of the nation's wealth and that share is declining steadily. The gap between rich and poor and between rich and the middle class is larger than it has ever been.

American Life-Styles

At last count, nearly 37 million Americans across the nation lived in unrelenting poverty.[17] Yet, as political scientist Michael Harrington once commented, "America has the best dressed poverty the world has ever known."[18] Clothing disguises much of the poverty in the United States, and this may explain, in part, its middle-class image. With increased mass marketing of "designer" clothing and with shifts in the nation's economy from blue-collar (and often better-paying) manufacturing jobs to white-collar and pink-collar jobs in the service sector, it is becoming increasingly difficult to distinguish class differences based on appearance.[19] The dress-down environment prevalent in the high-tech industry (what one author refers to as the "no-collars movement") has reduced superficial distinctions even further.[20]

Beneath the surface, there is another reality. Let's look at some "typical" and not-so-typical life-styles.

American Profile	
Name:	Harold S. Browning
Father:	manufacturer, industrialist
Mother:	prominent social figure in the community
Principal child-rearer:	governess
Primary education:	an exclusive private school on Manhattan's Upper East Side
	Note: a small, well-respected primary school where teachers and administrators have a reputation for nurturing student creativity and for providing the finest educational preparation
	Ambition: "to become President"
Supplemental tutoring:	tutors in French and mathematics
Summer camp:	sleep-away camp in northern Connecticut
	Note: camp provides instruction in the creative arts, athletics, and the natural sciences
Secondary education:	a prestigious preparatory school in

	Westchester County
	Note: classmates included the sons of ambassadors, doctors, attorneys, television personalities, and well-known business leaders
	Supplemental education: private SAT tutor
	After-school activities: private riding lessons
	Ambition: "to take over my father's business"
	High-school graduation gift: BMW
Family activities:	theater, recitals, museums, summer vacations in Europe, occasional winter trips to the Caribbean
	Note: as members of and donors to the local art museum, the Brownings and their children attend private receptions and exhibit openings at the invitation of the museum director
Higher education:	an Ivy League liberal arts college in Massachusetts
	Major: economics and political science
	After-class activities: debating club, college newspaper, swim team
	Ambition: "to become a leader in business"
First full-time job (age 23):	assistant manager of operations, Browning Tool and Die, Inc. (family enterprise)
Subsequent employment:	*3 years*—executive assistant to the president, Browning Tool and Die
	Responsibilities included: purchasing (materials and equipment), personnel, and distribution networks
	4 years—advertising manager, Lackheed Manufacturing (home appliances)
	3 years—director of marketing and sales, Comerex, Inc. (business machines)
Present employment (age 38):	executive vice president, SmithBond and Co. (digital instruments)
	Typical daily activities: review financial reports and computer printouts, dictate memoranda, lunch with clients, initiate conference calls, meet with assistants, plan business trips, meet with associates
	Transportation to and from work: chauffeured company limousine
	Annual salary: $324,000

	Ambition: "to become chief executive officer of the firm, or one like it, within the next five to ten years"
Present residence:	eighteenth-floor condominium on Manhattan's Upper West Side, eleven rooms, including five spacious bedrooms and terrace overlooking river
	Interior: professionally decorated and accented with elegant furnishings, valuable antiques, and expensive artwork
	Note: building management provides doorman and elevator attendant; family employs au pair for children and maid for other domestic chores
Second residence:	farm in northwestern Connecticut, used for weekend retreats and for horse breeding (investment/hobby)
	Note: to maintain the farm and cater to the family when they are there, the Brownings employ a part-time maid, groundskeeper, and horse breeder

Harold Browning was born into a world of nurses, maids, and governesses. His world today is one of airplanes and limousines, five-star restaurants, and luxurious living accommodations. The life and life-style of Harold Browning is in sharp contrast to that of Bob Farrell.

	American Profile
Name:	Bob Farrell
Father:	machinist
Mother:	retail clerk
Principal child-rearer:	mother and sitter
Primary education:	a medium-size public school in Queens, New York, characterized by large class size, outmoded physical facilities, and an educational philosophy emphasizing basic skills and student discipline
	Ambition: "to become President"
Supplemental tutoring:	none
Summer camp:	YMCA day camp
	Note: emphasis on team sports, arts and crafts
Secondary education:	large regional high school in Queens
	Note: classmates included the sons and daughters of carpenters, postal clerks,

	teachers, nurses, shopkeepers, mechanics, bus drivers, police officers, salespersons
	Supplemental education: SAT prep course offered by national chain
	After-school activities: basketball and handball in school park
	Ambition: "to make it through college"
	High-school graduation gift: $500 savings bond
Family activities:	family gatherings around television set, softball, an occasional trip to the movie theater, summer Sundays at the public beach
Higher education:	a two-year community college with a technical orientation
	Major: electrical technology
	After-school activities: employed as a part-time bagger in local supermarket
	Ambition: "to become an electrical engineer"
First full-time job (age 19):	service-station attendant
	Note: continued to take college classes in the evening
Subsequent employment:	mail clerk at large insurance firm; manager trainee, large retail chain
Present employment (age 38):	assistant sales manager, building supply firm
	Typical daily activities: demonstrate products, write up product orders, handle customer complaints, check inventory
	Transportation to and from work: city subway
Annual salary:	$45,261
	Ambition: "to open up my own business"
	Additional income: $6,100 in commissions from evening and weekend work as salesman in local men's clothing store
Present residence:	the Farrells own their own home in a working-class neighborhood in Queens, New York

Bob Farrell and Harold Browning live very differently: the life-style of one is privileged; that of the other is not so privileged. The differences are class differences, and these differences have a profound impact on the way they live. They are differences between playing a game of handball in the park and taking riding lessons at a private stable; watching a movie on television and going to the theater; and taking the subway to work and being driven in a limousine. More important, the difference in class determines where they live, who their friends are, how well they are educated, what they do for a living, and what they come to expect from life.

Yet, as dissimilar as their life-styles are, Harold Browning and Bob Farrell have some things in common; they live in the same city, they work long hours, and they are highly motivated. More important, they are both white males.

Let's look at someone else who works long and hard and is highly motivated. This person, however, is black and female.

American Profile

Name:	Cheryl Mitchell
Father:	janitor
Mother:	waitress
Principal child-rearer:	grandmother
Primary education:	large public school in Ocean Hill-Brownsville, Brooklyn, New York
	Note: rote teaching of basic skills and emphasis on conveying the importance of good attendance, good manners, and good work habits; school patrolled by security guards
	Ambition: "to be a teacher"
Supplemental tutoring:	none
Summer camp:	none
Secondary education:	large public school in Ocean Hill-Brownsville
	Note: classmates included sons and daughters of hairdressers, groundskeepers, painters, dressmakers, dishwashers, domestics
	Supplemental education: none
	After-school activities: domestic chores, part-time employment as babysitter and housekeeper
	Ambition: "to be a social worker"
	High-school graduation gift: corsage
Family activities:	church-sponsored socials
Higher education:	one semester of local community college
	Note: dropped out of school for financial reasons
First full-time job (age 17):	counter clerk, local bakery
Subsequent employment:	file clerk with temporary-service agency, supermarket checker
Present employment (age 38):	nurse's aide at a municipal hospital
	Typical daily activities: make up hospital beds, clean out bedpans, weigh patients and assist them to the bathroom, take temperature readings, pass out and collect

	food trays, feed patients who need help, bathe patients, and change dressings *Annual salary:* $16,850 *Ambition:* "to get out of the ghetto"
Present residence:	three-room apartment in the South Bronx, needs painting, has poor ventilation, is in a high-crime area *Note:* Cheryl Mitchell lives with her four-year-old son and her elderly mother

When we look at the lives of Cheryl Mitchell, Bob Farrell, and Harold Browning, we see life-styles that are very different. We are not looking, however, at economic extremes. Cheryl Mitchell's income as a nurse's aide puts her above the government's official poverty line.[21] Below her on the income pyramid are 37 million poverty-stricken Americans. Far from being poor, Bob Farrell has an annual income as an assistant sales manager that puts him well above the median income level—that is, more than 50 percent of the U.S. population earns less money than Bob Farrell.[22] And while Harold Browning's income puts him in a high-income bracket, he stands only a fraction of the way up Samuelson's income pyramid. Well above him are the 338,761 individuals whose annual salary exceeds $1 million. Yet Harold Browning spends more money on his horses than Cheryl Mitchell earns in a year.

Reality 3: Even ignoring the extreme poles of the economic spectrum, we find enormous class differences in the life-styles among the haves, the have-nots, and the have-littles.

Class affects more than life-style and material well-being. It has a significant impact on our physical and mental well-being as well.

Researchers have found an inverse relationship between social class and health. Lower-class standing is correlated to higher rates of infant mortality, eye and ear disease, arthritis, physical disability, diabetes, nutritional deficiency, respiratory disease, mental illness, and heart disease.[23] In all areas of health, poor people do not share the same life chances as those in the social class above them. Furthermore, lower-class standing is correlated with a lower quality of treatment for illness and disease. The results of poor health and poor treatment are borne out in the life expectancy rates within each class. Researchers have found that the higher your class standing, the higher your life expectancy. Conversely, they have also found that within each age group, the lower one's class standing, the higher the death rate; in some age groups, the figures are as much as two and three times as high.[24]

Reality 4: From cradle to grave, class standing has a significant impact on our chances for survival.

The lower one's class standing, the more difficult it is to secure appropriate housing, the more time is spent on the routine tasks of everyday life, the greater is the percentage of income that goes to pay for food and other basic necessities, and the greater is the likelihood of crime victimization.[25] Class can accurately predict chances for both survival and success.

Class and Educational Attainment

School performance (grades and test scores) and educational attainment (level of schooling completed) also correlate strongly with economic class. Furthermore, despite some efforts to make testing fairer and schooling more accessible, current data suggest that the level of inequity is staying the same or getting worse.

In his study for the Carnegie Council on Children in 1978, Richard De Lone examined the test scores of over half a million students who took the College Board exams (SATs). His findings were consistent with earlier studies that showed a relationship between class and scores on standardized tests; his conclusion: "the higher the student's social status, the higher the probability that he or she will get higher grades."[26] Today, more than thirty years after the release of the Carnegie report, College Board surveys reveal data that are no different: test scores still correlate strongly with family income.

Average Combined Scores by Income (400 to 1600 scale)[27]

Family Income	Median Score
More than $100,000	1113
$80,000 to $100,000	1057
$70,000 to $80,000	1032
$60,000 to $70,000	1020
$50,000 to $60,000	1009
$40,000 to $50,000	994
$30,000 to $40,000	966
$20,000 to $30,000	936
$10,000 to $20,000	910
less than $10,000	886

These figures are based on the test results of 1,465,744 SAT takers in 2006.

In another study conducted thirty years ago, researcher William Sewell showed a positive correlation between class and overall educational achievement. In comparing the top quartile (25 percent) of his sample to the bottom quartile, he found that students from upper-class families were twice as likely to obtain training beyond high school and four times as likely to attain a postgraduate degree. Sewell concluded: "Socioeconomic background . . . operates independently of academic ability at every stage in the process of educational attainment."[28]

Today, the pattern persists. There are, however, two significant changes. On the one hand, the odds of getting into college have improved for the bottom quartile of the population, although they still remain relatively low compared to the top. On the other hand, the chances of completing a college degree have deteriorated markedly for the bottom quartile. Researchers estimate the chances of completing a four-year college degree (by age 24) to be nineteen times as great for the top 25 percent of the population as it is for the bottom 25 percent.[29]

Reality 5: Class standing has a significant impact on chances for educational achievement.

Class standing, and consequently life chances, are largely determined at birth. Although examples of individuals who have gone from rags to riches abound in the mass media, statistics on class mobility show these leaps to be extremely rare. In fact, dramatic advances in class standing are relatively infrequent. One study showed that fewer than one in five men surpass the economic status of their fathers.[30] For those whose annual income is in six figures, economic success is due in large part to the wealth and privileges bestowed on them at birth. Over 66 percent of the consumer units with incomes of $100,000 or more have inherited assets. Of these units, over 86 percent reported that inheritances constituted a substantial portion of their total assets.[31]

Economist Harold Wachtel likens inheritance to a series of Monopoly games in which the winner of the first game refuses to relinquish his or her cash and commercial property for the second game. "After all," argues the winner, "I accumulated my wealth and income by my own wits." With such an arrangement, it is not difficult to predict the outcome of subsequent games.[32]

Reality 6: All Americans do not have an equal opportunity to succeed. Inheritance laws ensure a greater likelihood of success for the offspring of the wealthy.

Spheres of Power and Oppression

When we look at society and try to determine what it is that keeps most people down—what holds them back from realizing their potential as healthy, creative, productive individuals—we find institutional forces that are largely beyond individual control. Class domination is one of these forces. People do not choose to be poor or working class; instead, they are limited and confined by the opportunities afforded or denied them by a social and economic system. The class structure in the United States is a function of its economic system: capitalism, a system that is based on private rather than public ownership and control of commercial enterprises. Under capitalism, these enterprises are governed by the need to produce a profit for the owners, rather than to fulfill societal needs. Class divisions arise from the differences between those who own and control corporate enterprise and those who do not.

Racial and gender domination are other forces that hold people down. Although there are significant differences in the way capitalism, racism, and sexism affect our lives, there are also a multitude of parallels. And although class, race, and gender act independently of each other, they are at the same time very much interrelated.

On the one hand, issues of race and gender cut across class lines. Women experience the effects of sexism whether they are well-paid professionals or poorly paid clerks. As women, they are not only subjected to catcalls and stereotyping, but face discrimination and are denied opportunities and privileges that men have. Similarly, a wealthy black man faces racial oppression, is subjected to racial slurs, and is denied opportunities because of his color. Regardless of their class standing, women and members of minority races are constantly dealing with institutional forces that are holding them down precisely because of their gender, the color of their skin, or both.

On the other hand, the experiences of women and minorities are differentiated along class lines. Although they are in subordinate positions vis-à-vis white men, the particular issues that confront women and people of color may be quite different depending on their position in the class structure.

Power is incremental, and class privileges can accrue to individual women and to individual members of a racial minority. While power is incremental, oppression is cumulative, and those who are poor, black, and female are often subject to all of the forces of class, race, and gender discrimination simultaneously. This cumulative situation is what is meant by the double and triple jeopardy of women and minorities.

Furthermore, oppression in one sphere is related to the likelihood of oppression in another. If you are black and female, for example, you are much more likely to be poor or working class than you would be as a white male. Census figures show that the incidence of poverty varies greatly by race and gender.

Chances of Being Poor in America[33]

White male/ female	White female head*	Hispanic male/ female	Hispanic female head*	Black male/ female	Black female head*
1 in 12	1 in 5	1 in 5	1 in 3	1 in 4	1 in 3

*Persons in families with female householder, no husband present.

In other words, being female and being nonwhite are attributes in our society that increase the chances of poverty and of lower-class standing.

Reality 7: Racism and sexism significantly compound the effects of class in society.

None of this makes for a very pretty picture of our country. Despite what we like to think about ourselves as a nation, the truth is that opportunity for success and life itself are highly circumscribed by our race, our gender, and the class we are born into. As individuals, we feel hurt and anger when someone is treating us unfairly; yet as a society we tolerate unconscionable injustice. A more just society will require a radical redistribution of wealth and power. We can start by reversing the current trends that further polarize us as a people and adapt policies and practices that narrow the gaps in income, wealth, and privilege

NOTES

1. See Jay MacLead, *Ain't No Makin' It: Aspirations and Attainment in a Lower-Income Neighborhood* (Boulder, CO: Westview Press, 1995); Benjamin DeMott, *The Imperial Middle* (New York: Morrow, 1990); Ira Katznelson, *City Trenches: Urban Politics and Patterning of Class in the United States* (New York: Pantheon Books, 1981); Charles W. Tucker, "A Comparative Analysis of Subjective Social Class: 1945–1963," *Social Forces*, no. 46, June 1968, pp. 508–514; Robert Nisbet, "The Decline and Fall of Social Class," *Pacific Sociological Review*, vol. 2, Spring 1959, pp. 11–17; and Oscar Glantz, "Class Consciousness and Political Solidarity," *American Sociological Review*, vol. 23, August 1958, pp. 375–382.

2. Susan Ostander, "Upper-Class Women: Class Consciousness as Conduct and Meaning," in G. William Domhoff, *Power Structure Research* (Beverly Hills, CA: Sage Publications, 1980), pp. 78–79. Also see Stephen Birmingham, *America's Secret Aristocracy* (Boston: Little Brown, 1987).

3. Lawrence Mishel, Jared Bernstein, and Sylvia Allegretto, *State of Working America: 2006/2007* (Ithaca, NY: Cornell University Press, 2007), pp. 251, 253.

4. The number of individuals filing tax returns showing a gross adjusted income of $1 million or more in 2006 was 355,204 (Tax Stats at a Glance, Internal Revenue Service, U.S. Treasury Department, available at http://www.irs.gov/taxstats/article/0,,id=102886,00.html).

5. Carmen DeNavas-Walt, Bernadette D. Proctor, and Jessica C. Smith, U.S. Census Bureau, Current Population Reports, P60–235, *Income, Poverty, and Health Insurance Coverage in the United States: 2007* (Washington, DC: U.S. Government Printing Office, 2008), pp. 12–19, available at http://pubdb3.census.gov/macro/032008/pov/new01_100_01.htm.

6. National Coalition for the Homeless, "How Many People Experience Homelessness?" NCH Fact Sheet #2 (June 2008), available at http://www.nationalhomeless.org/publications/facts/How_Many.html. Also see National Coalition for the Homeless, "How Many People Experience Homelessness?" NCH Fact Sheet #2 (June 2006), citing a 2004 National Law Center on Homelessness and Poverty study, available at http://www.nationalhomeless.org/publications/facts/How_Many.pdf; U.S. Conference of Mayors, *Hunger and Homelessness Survey, 2008: A Survey Report on Homelessness and Hunger in American Cities* (Washington, DC: U.S. Conference of Mayors, 2008), pp. 13–23; Martha Burt, *What Will it Take to End Homelessness?* (Washington, DC: Urban Institute, September 2001); Martha Burt, "Chronic Homelessness: Emergence of a Public Policy," *Fordham Urban Law Journal*, 30, no. 3 (2003), pp. 1267–1279; and Kim Hopper, *Reckoning with Homelessness* (Ithaca, NY: Cornell University Press, 2002).

7. Mishel et al., op. cit., p. 253.

8. Arloc Sherman and Aviva Aron-Dine, "New CBO Data Show Income Inequality Continues to Widen" (Washington, DC: Center on Budget and Policy Priorities, January 2007), p. 3.

9. Based on a comparison of 19 industrialized states: Mishel et al., op. cit., pp. 344–349.

10. Mishel et al., op. cit., p. 345.

11. Derived from Mishel et al., p. 255, Table 5.3.

12. Mishel et al., op. cit., p. 64.

13. *Ibid.*, p. 59.

14. *Ibid.*, p. 255.

15. Alan Blinder, quoted by Paul Krugman, in "Disparity and Despair," *U.S. News and World Report*, March 23, 1992, p. 54.

16. Paul Samuelson, *Economics*, 10th ed. (New York: McGraw-Hill, 1976), p. 84.

17. DeNavas-Walt et al., op. cit., p. 12.

18. Michael Harrington, *The Other America* (New York: Macmillan, 1962), pp. 12–13.

19. Stuart Ewen and Elizabeth Ewen, *Channels of Desire: Mass Images and the Shaping of American Consciousness* (New York: McGraw-Hill, 1982).

20. Andrew Ross, *No-Collar: The Humane Work Place and Its Hidden Costs* (New York: Basic Books, 2002).

21. Based on a poverty threshold for a three-person household in 2007 of $16,650. DeNavas-Walt et al., op. cit., p. 1.

22. The median income in 2007 was $45,113 for men working full time, year round; $35,102 for women; and $50,233 for households. DeNavas-Walt et al., op. cit., p. 6.

23. U. S. Government Accountability Office, *Poverty in America: Economic Research Shows Adverse Impacts on Health Status and Other Social Conditions* (Washington, DC: U. S. Government Accountability Office, 2007), pp. 9–16. Also see E. Pamuk, D. Makuc, K. Heck, C. Reuben, and K. Lochner, *Socioeconomic Status and Health Chartbook, Health, United States, 1998* (Hyattsville, MD: National Center for Health Statistics, 1998), pp. 145–159; Vincente Navarro, "Class, Race, and Health Care in the United States," in Bersh Berberoglu, *Critical Perspectives in Sociology*, 2nd ed. (Dubuque, IA: Kendall/Hunt, 1993), pp. 148–156; Melvin Krasner, *Poverty and Health in New York City* (New York: United Hospital Fund of New York, 1989); U.S. Department of Health and Human Services, *Health Status of Minorities and Low Income Groups, 1985*; and Dan Hughes, Kay Johnson, Sara Rosenbaum, Elizabeth Butler, and Janet Simons, *The Health of America's Children* (The Children's Defense Fund, 1988).

24. E. Pamuk et al., op. cit.; Kenneth Neubeck and Davita Glassberg, *Sociology; A Critical Approach* (New York: McGraw-Hill, 1996), pp. 436–438; Aaron Antonovsky, "Social Class, Life Expectancy, and Overall Mortality," in *The Impact of Social Class* (New York: Thomas Crowell, 1972), pp. 467–491. See also Harriet Duleep, "Measuring the Effect of Income on Adult Mortality Using Longitudinal Administrative Record Data," *Journal of Human Resources*, vol. 21, no. 2, Spring 1986. See also Paul Farmer, *Pathologies of Power: Health, Human Rights, and the New War on the Poor* (Berkeley: University of California Press, 2005).

25. E. Pamuk et al., op. cit., fig. 20; Dennis W. Roncek, "Dangerous Places: Crime and Residential Environment," *Social Forces*, vol. 60, no. 1, September 1981, pp. 74–96. Also see Steven D. Levitt, "The Changing Relationship between Income and Crime Victimization," *Economic Policy Review*, 5, No. 3, September 1999.

26. Richard De Lone, *Small Futures* (New York: Harcourt Brace Jovanovich, 1978), pp. 14–19.

27. Derived from Viji Sathy, Sandra Barbuti, and Krista Mattern, "The New SAT and Trends in Test Performance," *College Board*, 2006, pp. 18–20.

28. William H. Sewell, "Inequality of Opportunity for Higher Education," *American Sociological Review*, vol. 36, no. 5, 1971, pp. 793–809.

29. The Mortenson Report on Public Policy Analysis of Opportunity for Postsecondary Education, "Postsecondary Education Opportunity" (Iowa City, IA: September 1993, no. 16).

30. De Lone, op. cit., pp. 14–19. Also see Daniel McMurrer, Mark Condon, and Isabel Sawhill, "Intergenerational Mobility in the United States" (Washington, DC: Urban Institute, 1997), available at http://www.Urbaninstitute.org/url.cfm?ID=406796; and Bhashkar Mazumder, "Earnings Mobility in the US: A New Look at Intergenerational Inequality" (March 21, 2001), FRB Chicago Working Paper No. 2001–18, available at SSRN: http://ssrn.com/abstract=295559, or DOI: 10.2139/ssrn.295559.

31. Howard Tuchman, *Economics of the Rich* (New York: Random House, 1973), p. 15. Also see Greg Duncan, Ariel Kalil, Susan Mayer, Robin Tepper, and Monique Payne, "The Apple Does not Fall Far from the Tree," in Samuel Bowles, Herbert Gintis, and Melissa Groves, *Unequal Chances: Family Background and Economic Success* (Princeton, NJ: Princeton University Press, 2008), pp. 23–79; Bhashkar Mazumder, "The Apple Falls Even Closer to the Tree than We Thought," in Bowles et. al., pp. 80–99. For more information on inheritance, see Sam Bowles and Herbert Gintis, "The Inheritance of Inequality," *The Journal of Economic Perspectives*, 16, no. 3 (Summer 2002), pp. 2–30, and Tom Hertz, *Understanding Mobility in America*, Center for American Progress, available at http://www.americanprogress.org/kf/hertz_mobility_analysis.pdf.

32. Howard Wachtel, *Labor and the Economy* (Orlando, FL: Academic Press, 1984), pp. 161–162.

33. Derived from U.S. Census Bureau, *Current Population Survey*, Tables POV01 and POV2, available at http://pubdb3.census.gov/macro/032008/pov/toc.htm.

Suggestions for Further Reading

Baird, Robert M., and Stuart E. Rosenbaum, eds. *Bigotry, Prejudice, and Hatred.* Buffalo, NY: Prometheus Press, 1992.

Bonilla-Silva, Eduardo. *Racism without Racists: Colorblind Racism and the Persistence of Racial Inequality in the U.S.* New York: Rowman & Littlefield, 2003.

———. *White Supremacy and Racism in the Post Civil Rights Era.* Boulder CO: Rienner, 2001.

Brandt, Eric, ed. *Dangerous Liaisons: Blacks, Gays and the Struggle for Equality.* New York: New Press; 1999.

Brown, Michael K., et al. *Whitewashing Race in America: The Myth of a Colorblind Society.* Berkeley: University of California Press, 2005.

Cose, Ellis. *The Rage of a Privileged Class.* New York: Collins, 1994.

DeMott, Benjamin. *The Trouble with Friendship: Why Americans Can't Think Straight about Race.* New York: Atlantic Monthly Press, 1995.

Dusky, Lorraine. *Still Unequal: The Shameful Truth about Women and Justice in America.* New York: Crown Books, 1996.

Dyer, Richard. *White.* London and New York: Routledge, 1997.

Faludi, Susan. *Backlash: The Undeclared War against American Women.* New York: Crown Publishers, 1991.

Feagin, Joe R. *Racist America: Roots, Realities, and Future Reparations.* New York: Routledge, 2000.

Harris, Leonard. *Racism.* New York: Humanities Books, 1999.

Kadi, Joanne. *Thinking Class: Sketches from a Cultural Worker.* Boston: South End Press, 1996.

Katznelson, Ira. *When Affirmative Action Was White: An Untold History of Racial Inequality in 20th C. America,* New York: W.W. Norton, 2005.

Kimmel, Michael. *The Gendered Society.* New York: Oxford University Press, 2000.

Lipsitz, George. *The Possessive Investment in Whiteness.* Philadelphia, PA: Temple University Press, 1998.

Perry, Barbara. *In the Name of Hate: Understanding Hate Crimes.* New York and London: Routledge, 2001.

Pharr, Suzanne. *Homophobia as a Weapon of Sexism.* Inverness, CA: Chardon Press, 1988.

Pincus, F. L., and H. J. Erlich. *Race and Ethnic Conflict: Contending Views on Prejudice, Discrimination and Ethnoviolence.* Boulder, CO: Westview, 1994.

Rhode, Deborah L. *Speaking of Sex: The Denial of Gender Inequality.* Cambridge, MA, and London, England: Harvard University Press, 1997.

Ronai, Carol R., et al. *Everyday Sexism in the Third Millenium.* New York and London: Routledge, 1997.

Shipler, David K. *A Country of Strangers: Blacks and Whites in America.* New York: Knopf, 1997.

Wellman, David T. *Portraits of White Racism.* Cambridge: Cambridge University Press, 1977.

Williams, Lena. *It's the Little Things, the Everyday Interactions That Get Under the Skin of Blacks and Whites.* New York: Harcourt, 2000.

PART III

Race in the 21st Century: Complicating Questions of Race and Ethnicity

T he United States has long been a nation of immigrants, but recent waves of immigration bringing more than the expected number of Asians and Hispanics to these shores are dramatically changing the racial/ethnic mix in this country. According to current estimates, by the year 2050 whites will no longer be a majority. And in many parts of the country, whites are already the minority population. Selection 2 provides an overview of U.S. immigration policy since 1965 and a look at the changing picture of U.S. demographics. What are the implications of these changes for the way we think about the categories of race and ethnicity and how we define "minority"? What kinds of racial/ethnic categories are adequate to capture the identities of such a rich mix of peoples and cultures, a mix that is often embodied in the multiethnic heritage that individuals in the United States increasingly want to claim?

The difficulty of coming up with adequate categories and paradigms gained national attention in 2000 when the U.S. Census Bureau set out to survey the U.S. population, as it does every ten years. Until the 2000 census, respondents had been asked to identify with one and only one race when filling out the census questionnaire. Beginning with the 2000 census, respondents were given the option of identifying with up to five different racial groups. Although the new categories and the way in which these data are then interpreted continue to meet with criticism, the change itself reflects the indisputably multicultural nature of the U.S. population and gives an indication of how complex and complicated the project of defining racial/ethnic identity adequately and appropriately has become. This complexity is grappled within an autobiographical piece by Evelyn Alsutany in Selection 3.

While it is common today for many people to identify themselves as "Hispanic," before the category "Hispanics" was created by the U.S. government and used in the census in 1980, very few people in the United States thought of themselves in these terms. This is a good example of the ways in which race/ethnicity is socially constructed. Currently, the census asks respondents to specify a race by choosing one or more racial categories from among five options: American Indian or Alaska Native, Asian, Pacific Islander, Black, and white. In addition, people are given the option of choosing "Hispanic" as their ethnicity. According to this approach to classification, there can be white Hispanics, Black Hispanics, and Asian Hispanics. But what is the basis for assigning or choosing this ethnic identity? By common language? Many but not all Hispanics speak Spanish. By physical characteristics? As several articles in this section point out, people who identify in this way come in every shade of skin color. By shared culture? There is significant cultural diversity among people in this category. National origins? Some point to ancestry in a Spanish-speaking country as the basis for this categorization, but this too is not without complications. Some Mexican-Americans, like authors Sandra Cisneros and Luis Rodriguez, reject the term "Hispanic" and prefer to be identified as Latina or Chicano. They contend, as do many people from the Americas and the Caribbean, that the term "Hispanic" is associated with predominantly white Spain and Portugal whereas "Latino" preserves the connection with the darker skinned indigenous Indian population of the Americas that was conquered by those European nations centuries ago. Selections 3 and 4 explore some of the complexities involved in articulating a Latina/o or Hispanic racial/ethnic identity while Selection 5 looks at the politics of skin color as they relate to that choice.

Because for the most part it is white people and a largely white power structure that has had the ability to create racial/ethnic categories and apply them, people of color from very different ethnic backgrounds have often been lumped together with a total disregard for the important cultural, social, and economic differences associated with their individual ethnic and class backgrounds and their country of origin. People born in Puerto Rico, Mexico, and Spain may all be categorized together by white people as Latinos or Hispanics, but this categorization ignores important differences among them. In the same way, through white eyes, people from Ethiopia, Namibia, and Haiti may all look "Black," but this simplistic categorization leaves out vastly different histories and heritages. In Selection 7, "The Myth of the Model Minority," Noy Thrupkaew deplores the failure of the U.S. government and of many people in the United States to recognize the unique situations and challenges faced by various populations lumped together as "Asian Americans." As does Rita Chaudhry Sethi, writing in Part II, he finds the concept of Asians as a model minority more than problematic. Quoting Frank Wu, whom you will have an opportunity to read in Part VI, Thrupkaew suggests that the model minority myth is kept alive by political conservatives who put it to good use rationalizing and obscuring the unequal distribution of wealth, opportunity, and privilege in this county. By idealizing the success of Asian Americans, conservatives are able to imply that African Americans and Latinos who do not succeed fail to do so because they do not work hard enough. Further, although in reality many Southeast Asians in the United States (largely from Cambodia, Laos, and Vietnam) experience an extremely high rate of poverty, by grouping them within the broad category of "Asians," the government is able to both keep alive the model minority myth and fail to identify and address the particular needs of these specific populations.

The increasingly diverse racial/ethnic mix of the U.S. population brings with it new tensions and the potential for new conflicts. As a result, violent interactions flare up between Blacks and Asians in some communities, Hispanics and African Americans in others. Much of the friction between Blacks and Latinos has an economic basis as Latino immigrants are increasingly perceived as taking jobs away from U.S.-born Blacks. But it is often white employers who pit members of different ethnic groups against each other in order to use intergroup hostility and competition to keep wages down and to keep control of their workforce. By reminding workers that there are others willing and eager to step into their jobs, perhaps even at a lower rate of pay, business owners keep control over their employees and guarantee themselves a higher rate of profit. For more on tensions between Blacks and Hispanics in the workplace, see Selection 7 in Part IV.

While acknowledging the tensions that arise among new immigrants as a result of differences in class and culture as they compete for jobs and opportunities at the same time, in "Is This a White Country, or What?" Lillian Rubin in Selection 8 gives voice to the fear of many who are white working class that they are being displaced by the influx of people of color. And, as we have already seen, this fear, if it is focused on numerical displacement, is well founded. But at the heart of this concern is a feeling of economic vulnerability. In the absence of universal health care and the kinds of safety-net programs that have been eliminated by recent administrations in Washington, working people in the United States feel more vulnerable than ever. As data presented in Part V will show, the gap between rich and poor is growing wider each year, the size of the middle class is shrinking, and working full time for minimum wage is unlikely to raise a family above the poverty line. No wonder then that so many working people feel that they are one job or even one paycheck away from poverty. And while Native-born Blacks, as we have seen, are concerned about being displaced economically by the new immigrants, the feeling of vulnerability for whites is heightened by the fact that that so many of the new immigrants are people of color. In her article, Rubin explores some of the complex feelings that whites, themselves often the children of immigrants, sometimes have toward the new immigrant population, as xenophobia and racism come together in a climate of economic scarcity and uncertainty.

Part III concludes with a personal reflection on race by Carrie Ching, a 2005 graduate of the Graduate School of Journalism at the University of California at Berkeley and a freelance journalist. While the material in this part highlights conflicts and antagonisms within and among various racial/ethnic groups, and might lead some people to believe that such antagonisms are inevitable, Ching brings the conversation back to the one element that remains constant throughout, the persistent privileging of whiteness. Echoing the words of some of the people quoted in the Rubin article, Ching reminds us that "'American' still means white." And in the end, the context in which these antagonisms play out is one that consistently privileges whites and whiteness at the expense of all people of color. Why, she asks, is a person whose long-ago ancestors emigrated from China still called an "Asian American," while a person whose parents emigrated from Germany becomes a "plain old American" in just one generation? (For more on issues of race and the definition of an "American," you might wish to take a look at Jewelle Gomez' essay in Part VI.) While Ching acknowledges that class differences are significant, in contrast to an increasing tendency among many social scientists, she comes down firmly on the side of race as the more significant factor to explain inequality in the United States today. Her essay ends with a plea to all of us, but to white people in particular, to take responsibility for recognizing and eradicating racism in their personal lives and in our social institutions.

A NATION OF NONE AND ALL OF THE ABOVE

Sam Roberts

Deep inside a data dump by the Census Bureau last week was a startling racial projection: By midcentury, the United States will be home to 80 million more white people.

Never mind, for a moment, that the bureau also predicts that Americans who identify themselves as Hispanic, black, Asian, American-Indian, Native Hawaiian and Pacific Islander will constitute a majority of the population by 2042. The number of people who say they are white is projected to rise by about two million every year.

At that rate, even while the Hispanic and Asian populations expand enormously, the proportion of Americans who identify themselves as white will barely shrink, from a little more than 79 percent, to 74 percent.

It's not some new math metric that's responsible. It's the way the government defines race: most people who describe their origin or heritage as Hispanic or Latino also identify themselves as white.

Which raises an impertinent question: Why all the fuss about the nation's impending racial and ethnic transformation?

Not only is the census all about self-identification, anyway, but all those projections, today and historically, have been subject to fungible cultural definitions. Mexicans were counted in a separate racial category in the 1930 census, but 10 years later that classification was dropped and the results were revised to count Mexicans as white. (As recently as the 1960s, there was no Hispanic category in the census at all; Asian Indians were classified as white.)

A century or so ago, the Irish Catholics, Italians, Eastern Europeans and even some Germans who arrived in droves in the United States were not universally considered white. (Much earlier, Benjamin Franklin feared that his fellow white Pennsylvanians would be overwhelmed by swarthy Germans, who "will soon so out number us, that all the advantages we have will not in my opinion be able to preserve our language, and even our government will become precarious").

"In the minds of many Americans of influence and position at the time, the post-1890 immigrants — Jews, Italians, various Slavic groups, Greeks — were probably as foreign as 'Hispanics' are today, and considered, as Hispanics are today, as in some degree 'nonwhite,'" said Nathan Glazer, professor emeritus of sociology at Harvard, who wrote *Beyond the Melting Pot* with Daniel Patrick Moynihan. "I wonder whether, in the course of the fierce debates on immigration in the first quarter of the 20th century, anyone ever tried to calculate when 'new immigrants' and their children would be a majority of the U.S. I am sure someone among the immigration restrictionists must have raised that alarm."

Professor Glazer predicted that in the decades to come, racial and ethnic distinctions would be further blurred by intermarriage (about one in three grandchildren of Hispanic immigrants marry non-Hispanic spouses; by 2050, nearly 1 in 20 Americans are expected to classify themselves as multiracial).

Also, since 2000, the number of babies born to Hispanic mothers in the United States has surpassed the number of new Hispanic immigrants, which means a growing proportion of Hispanic people are being raised as Americans from birth.

"The process of assimilation is such that our views of the degree of difference of newer non-white groups changes rapidly," Professor Glazer said. "So the Jews and Italians, considered very foreign at the time of immigration by Henry Adams and others, were much less foreign by the 30s, hardly foreign at all by the 60s — they were then as white as other whites (for a time, called 'white ethnics')."

Race and ethnicity, says Joel E. Cohen, professor of populations at Rockefeller University, are really about culture, not biology. Categories contrived by bureaucrats and politically correct committees can be confusing and skew the results. "Even the notion of Hispanics ranges in people of European origin in Chile to those of native-America origin in the lowlands of Mexico," Professor Cohen said.

Those categories might be driven by political constituencies with a stake in stressing their distinctiveness or by overwhelming increases in immigrants classified as a single group. Between 1970 and 2050, according to the latest census projections, the Hispanic population will increase 14-fold.

For any number of reasons — including the way the Census Bureau configures and words its questionnaires — most people who report their origin as Hispanic also list their race as white. The government defines whites as descendants of "the original peoples of Europe, North Africa or the Middle East" and Hispanic or Latino people as those "who trace their origin or descent to Mexico, Puerto Rico, Cuba, Spanish-speaking Central and South America countries and other Spanish cultures." Origin is defined as "the heritage, nationality group, lineage or country of the person or the person's parents or ancestors before their arrival in the United States."

While the share of Americans who can trace their roots to immigrants who came directly from Europe has been shrinking, "the edges are getting blurrier," says Jeffrey S. Passel, senior demographer of the Pew Hispanic Center.

Professor Glazer agrees. "I don't think a change such that the census category of 'non-Hispanic white' becomes a minority in 30 years is so momentous," he said. "By then we may not even be using that census category and long before then people will be asking why Asians are still considered a 'minority' of any kind."

2

A NEW CENTURY:
IMMIGRATION AND THE US

MPI Staff, updated by Kevin Jernegan

Immigration, perhaps more than any other social, political, or economic process, has shaped the United States over the past century. As the next decades of the 21st century unfold, the rate of immigrant-driven transformation, which began in earnest in the 1960s, will continue to accelerate. Never before has the Statue of Liberty, long the symbol of America's rich immigrant heritage, lifted her torch over so many foreign-born individuals and families.

In short, America's profound demographic and cultural transformation continues—and the policies that govern who can enter the US, and how, will affect every aspect of American life in the new century. Just how to minimize the challenges confronting this "nation of immigrants" while maximizing the attendant opportunities will continue to animate the US immigration policy discourse in the years to come.

Managing Immigration

The United States has a long history of regulating immigration, dating back to the 1860s. Early legislation, such as the 1945 National Origins Act and the Immigration and Nationality Act of 1952, sought overall limits in immigration, but strongly favored immigrants from Europe over other regions of the world.

It was the Immigration and Nationality Act Amendments of 1965, however, which set in motion a powerful set of forces that are still shaping the United States today. The 1965 Amendments ushered in sweeping changes to immigration policy by abolishing the national origins quota system as the basis for immigration and replacing it with a seven-category preference system for the allocation of immigrant visas.

In addition, numerical limits were increased from 154,000 to 290,000, of which 120,000 were reserved for immigrants from the Western Hemisphere. The 290,000-person limit did not include "immediate family members" of US citizens (spouses, minor children, or parents), who were exempt from numerical limitations.

Originally published on the Migration Information Source, a project of the Migration Policy Institute.

In this period, the United States first began to witness the transformation from predominantly European immigration to Latin American and Asian flows that continue to characterize today's immigration patterns.

The Immigration and Nationality Act, as amended by the Refugee Act of 1980, brought US policy in line with the 1967 Protocol to the 1951 UN Refugee Convention. The protocol, together with the 1969 Organization of African Unity (OAU) Convention, expanded the number of persons considered refugees. Whereas previously the definition of refugee had centered on those affected by World War II, the new framework took into account other global conflicts contributing to the refugee population.

In another change, in response to the growing undocumented population in the US, Congress passed the Immigration Reform and Control Act (IRCA) of 1986. IRCA resulted in large part from the recommendations of the Select Commission on Immigration and Refugee Policy, which was created in 1977 to study illegal aliens and other aspects of immigration and refugee policy. The commission's final report in 1981 included over 100 recommendations.

In an attempt to "close the back door while opening the front door," IRCA granted amnesty to illegal immigrants who had resided in the United States for a certain period of time. That period varied depending on whether or not the immigrant worked in agriculture. At the same time, it attempted to curtail incentives for future undocumented immigration by creating a system of employer sanctions. The system criminalized the facilitation of illegal immigration by placing steep penalties on those who would harbor or hire unauthorized residents. The third components of IRCA—enhanced border control—did not begin in earnest until the mid-1990s.

The Immigration Act of 1990 rounded out this set of legislation by adjusting admissions categories and restructuring employment-based entry categories for both permanent and temporary entries. The goal has been to increase the skills and education levels of these entrants.

The decade of the 1990s was marked by state and federal legislation that limited immigrants' access to a range of social services and benefits. In 1994, California passed Proposition 187, one of the most controversial pieces of state law. Specifically, Proposition 187 denied undocumented immigrants in California access to public schools, medical care, and other social services, and required public employees and law enforcement officials to report suspected undocumented immigrants to the Immigration and Naturalization Service.

In 1996, Congress passed three new federal laws that limited access to public benefits and legal protections for non-citizens. Under the Personal Responsibility and Work Opportunity Reconciliation Act (PRWORA), commonly known as the Welfare Reform Act, legal and undocumented immigrants no longer had access to federal public benefits, such as Medicaid, Supplemental Security Income (SSI), and food stamps.

The Illegal Immigration Reform and Immigrant Responsibility Act (IIRIRA) hastened deportation of illegal immigrants who committed crimes. It also made it more difficult for immigrants to make legal appeals following executive branch decisions.

The last in the three pieces of legislation, the Anti-Terrorism and Effective Death Penalty Act (AEDPA), made it easier to arrest, detain, and deport non-citizens.

By the end of the decade, Congress' attention had shifted to the booming economy's increasing need for highly skilled immigrants who could fill technology jobs. The American Competitiveness in the Twenty-First Century Act, passed in 2000, increased the number of temporary work visas (H-1Bs) available per year from 65,000 to 115,000 in fiscal year 2000, then to 195,000 for FY 2001, 2002 and 2003.

The most far-reaching changes in US immigration may stem from the events of September 11, 2001, and related concerns about the growing undocumented population in the country. These issues are discussed in detail below.

Parting the Waves

Non-citizens entering the United States are divided among three streams: "lawful permanent residents (LPRs)," "non-immigrants," and "undocumented migrants."

Lawful permanent residents are foreign-born individuals who have been admitted to reside permanently in the United States. Such immigrants may enter the US through family-sponsored immigration, employment-based immigration, or through refugee and asylum admissions.

Family-sponsored immigration accounts for more than three-quarters of all regular immigration into the United States. In some cases, permanent residents may be admitted through the diversity visa lottery program, which allots additional immigration visas to countries that are underrepresented in US immigration streams.

According to the Department of Homeland Security (DHS), legal immigration in fiscal year 2003 was 705,827, coming mainly from Mexico (115,864), India (50,379), the Philippines (45,397), China (40,659), El Salvador (28,296), the Dominican Republic (26,205) and Vietnam (22,133). Together, these seven countries accounted for nearly half of all legal immigration.

Overall immigrant admissions and adjustments of status for fiscal year 2003 fell by approximately a third, from 1,063,732 in fiscal year 2002, primarily as a consequence of heightened security precautions introduced after the September 11, 2001, terrorist attacks.

In addition to those non-citizens who arrive to take up permanent residence, some enter lawfully as "non-immigrants"—foreigners who are in the United States temporarily. Totaling more than 27.8 million in fiscal year 2003, this category includes tourists as well as those who enter to help fill the temporary needs of US employers—often on visas that allow stays of greater than a year.

There are dozens of non-immigrant visa classifications, including the F-1 category for students in academic or language programs, the J visa for those who enter for cultural exchange purposes, and the TN category for professionals from Canada or Mexico who enter under North American Free Trade Agreement (NAFTA) regulations.

Work-entitled non-immigrants, such as holders of various types of H and other visas, play an increasing role in the US economy. The H-1B visa category provides for the temporary admission of workers with specialized knowledge and skills. Congress determines the number of H-1B visas available each year.The number of H-1B visas Congress approves has declined substantially in recent years, from a high of 195,000 in 2001–2003 to 65,000 for fiscal year 2005.

For six of the last eight years, the number of H-1B visas authorized each year has fallen short of US employers' demand, with the annual cap typically being filled within the first few months or even weeks of the fiscal year. For fiscal year 2005, the cap of 65,000 H-1B visas was depleted on October 1, 2004, the first day of the fiscal year. Despite the high demand, non-immigrant admissions have declined in recent years with a commensurate reduction in tourism, foreign student enrollments at US universities, cultural and scholarly exchange, and business travel.

"Illegal" or "unauthorized" immigrants enter the US by avoiding official inspection, passing through inspection with fraudulent documents, entering legally but overstaying the terms of their temporary visas, or somehow violating other terms of their visa. Under IRCA in 1986, roughly 2.7 million unauthorized migrants were legalized.

While it is notoriously difficult to measure the undocumented population, the US Census Bureau and most independent analysts estimate the figure to be between 9 and 10 million as of 2003, and growing at a rate between 300,000 and 500,000 each year. Mexico remains the leading country of origin, claiming nearly half of the total, with several Central American and European countries also strongly represented.

Closer Look at New Faces

Since the 1960s, the number of foreign-born people in the US has increased. In terms of absolute numbers, this number is at its highest point in history. According to US Census Bureau 2003 Current Population Survey (CPS) data, 33.5 million foreign born lived in the US, representing about 11.7 percent of the entire population. However, this percentage remains well below the historic highs of almost 15 percent in both 1890 and 1910.

Approximately 53.3 percent of these foreign-born persons originate from Latin America (including Central America, South America and the Caribbean), 25.0 percent from Asia, 13.7 percent from Europe, and 8.0 percent from other regions of the world, such as Africa and Oceania.

Migrants from Central America (including, for data purposes, Mexico) account for nearly one-third of the entire foreign-born population. Mexicans, the largest single group, now compose 27 percent of all foreign born.

Mexicans account for the largest proportion of the illegal immigrant population by far, with El Salvador and Guatemala running a distant second and third place. Hispanics now comprise the largest ethnic minority group in the US, at 12.5 percent.

Spreading Out

Data from the US Census Bureau 2004 Current Population Survey reveal that the foreign-born population is geographically concentrated, with 67 percent residing in only six of the 50 states—29 percent in California alone. The other immigrant-heavy states are New York (11 percent), Texas (9 percent), Florida (9 percent), New Jersey (5 percent), and Illinois (4 percent).

While the six states mentioned above continue to attract and retain the bulk of the foreign-born population, there is a growing trend toward broader dispersal across the United States. Economic conditions, such as cost of living and employment opportunities, are increasingly motivating immigrants to move to states such as Georgia, Nevada, North Carolina, Arizona, Arkansas, and Oregon. These non-traditional receiving states have seen significant growth in their foreign-born populations, ushering in a new era of integration challenges across the country. . . .

At the Borders

The US borders with Mexico and Canada are among the most active in the world. Canada is the United States' largest trading partner, with an average of US$1.2 billion traded every day, according to the US Trade Representative. Mexico claims second place, with an average of US$733 million traded per day. With 132 legal ports of entry along the Canadian border and 25 along the Mexican border, cross-border traffic is bustling.

Ninety percent of Canadians live within 100 miles of the US-Canada border. It is estimated that every day, about 250,000 people arrive in the US from Canada for a variety of reasons.

With Mexicans constituting roughly a quarter of the foreign-born population in the United States—far outnumbering other source countries—the southern border is extremely important for the futures of both the United States and Mexico.

In 2001, according to the US Embassy in Mexico City, the US processed 2,650,912 non-immigrant visa applications in Mexico, an increase of 17.65 percent over the 2,252,594 applications processed in 2000, which represented a 37 percent increase over the 1,635,309 applications in 1999.

These numbers indicate that the US is growing more dependent on Mexican labor, and that the two economies are becoming more integrated.

Becoming American

Of the 33.5 million foreign born residing in the US in 2003, approximately 38 percent have obtained US citizenship through naturalization. Applications for naturalization increased dramatically in the 1990s in response to legislative developments restricting access to public benefits and legal protections for non-citizens, including Proposition 187 in California (1994), the Personal Responsibility and Work Opportunity Act (1996), and the Illegal Immigration Reform and Immigrant Responsibility Act (IIRIRA, 1996).

Between 1994 and 1997, the number of naturalization applications filed nearly tripled, from 543,353 to 1,412,712. Since 1999, there have been, on average, slightly more than half a million applications for naturalization received every year.

Increases in the number of applications filed for benefits such as citizenship and immigrant visas, coupled with increased security precautions following the events of September 11, have resulted in historically high backlogs of pending applications.

By the end of fiscal year 2003, the Department of Homeland Security's (DHS) bureau of Citizenship and Immigration Services (CIS) had a backlog of 6.1 million pending applications. Recent efforts to deal with the backlog have reduced it to 4.1 million pending applications at the close of fiscal year 2004.

The US Citizenship and Immigration Service Office (USCIS) is reviewing citizenship testing procedures to standardize testing criteria, eliminate questions based upon rote memorization, and add more interpretative questions. USCIS is conducting pilot studies and planning to offer the new test in late 2006.

21st Century Challenges

Two challenges are clearly front and center on the immigration horizon: security concerns resulting from the events of September 11, 2001, and comprehensive US immigration reform. The latter involves satisfying security concerns about illegal immigration, preventing future unauthorized immigration to the fullest extent possible, and providing adequate legal means for needed immigrants (close family members and workers) to enter the United States. Both challenges stand to reshape immigrations's impact on the United States in the next two decades.

SOURCES

De Jong, Gordon F. and Quynh-Giang Tran. 2001. "Warm Welcome, Cool Welcome: Mapping Receptivity Toward Immigrants in the US." Population Today (November/ December). Population Reference Bureau. Available online.

Fix, Michael and Jeffrey Passel. 2001. "US Immigration at the Beginning of the 21st Century." Testimony before the Subcommittee on Immigration and Claims Hearing on "The US Population and Immigration." Committee on the Judiciary, US House of Representatives. Available online.

Guzman, Betsy. 2001. "The Hispanic Population." Census 2000 Brief. Available online.

Kramer, Roger. 2001. "Developments in International Migration to the United States: 2001." SOPEMI report (30 November). Paris: OECD.

Lapham, Susan J. September 1993. "We the American Foreign Born." Washington, DC: US Department of Commerce, US Census Bureau.

Lollock, Lisa. 2001. "The Foreign-Born Population in the United States: Population Characteristics." Current Population Reports (January). Washington, DC: US Department of Commerce, US Census Bureau.

National Immigration Forum. 2001. "Fast Facts on Today's Newcomers."

OECD. 2001. Trends in International Migration. SOPEMI report. Paris: OECD.

Papademetriou, Demetrios. 2001. "An Immigration and National Security Grand Bargain with Mexico" (30 November). Available online.

Papademetriou, Demetrios and Deborah Meyers. 2001. "Caught in the Middle: Border Communities in an Era of Globalization." Washington, DC: Carnegie Endowment for International Peace.

Passel, Jeffrey. 2002. "New Estimates of the Undocumented Population in the United States." Migration Information Source. Available online.

Population Reference Bureau. 1999. "Main Region of Origin in US Shifts to Latin America." Available online.

Schmidley, Dianne. 2001. "Profile of the Foreign Born in the United States: 2000." US Census Bureau, Special Studies/Current Population Reports. Available online.

US Bureau of Transportation Statistics. Available online.

US Census Bureau. Current Population Survey. US Census Bureau website.Available online.

US Citizenship and Immigration Services, Department of Homeland Security. "Who Gets In: Four Main Immigration Laws." Available online.

US Citizenship and Immigration Services, Department of Homeland Security. "Eligibility Information: Who May Apply to Change to a New Non-immigrant Status?" Available online.

3

LOS INTERSTICIOS: RECASTING MOVING SELVES

Evelyn Alsultany

> Ethnicity in such a world needs to be recast so that our moving selves can be acknowledged. . . . Who am I? When am I? The questions that are asked in the street, of my identity, mold me. Appearing in the flesh, I am cast afresh, a female of color—skin color, hair texture, clothing, speech, all marking me in ways that I could scarcely have conceived of.
>
> —MEENA ALEXANDER

I'm in a graduate class at the New School in New York City. A white female sits next to me and we begin "friendly" conversation. She asks me where I'm from. I

From *This Bridge We Call Home*, Gloria E. Anzaldúa and AnaLouise Keating, eds. Reproduced by permission of Routledge/Taylor & Francis Group, LLC, 2002.

reply that I was born and raised in New York City and return the question. She tells me she is from Ohio and has lived in New York for several years. She continues her inquiry: "Oh . . . well, how about your parents?" (I feel her trying to map me onto her narrow cartography; New York is not a sufficient answer. She analyzes me according to binary axes of sameness and difference. She detects only difference at first glance, and seeks to pigeonhole me. In her framework, my body is marked, excluded, not from this country. A seemingly "friendly" question turns into a claim to land and belonging.) "My father is Iraqi and my mother Cuban," I answer. "How interesting. Are you a U.S. citizen?"

I am waiting for the NYC subway. A man also waiting asks me if I too am Pakistani. I reply that I'm part Iraqi and part Cuban. He asks if I am Muslim, and I reply that I am Muslim. He asks me if I am married, and I tell him I'm not. In cultural camaraderie he leans over and says that he has cousins in Pakistan available for an arranged marriage if my family so desires. (My Cubanness, as well as my own relationship to my cultural identity, evaporates as he assumes that Arab plus Muslim equals arranged marriage. I can identify: he reminds me of my Iraqi relatives and I know he means well.) I tell him that I'm not interested in marriage but thank him for his kindness. (I accept his framework and respond accordingly, avoiding an awkward situation in which he realizes that I am not who he assumes I am, offering him recognition and validation for his [mis]identification.)

I am in a New York City deli waiting for my bagel to toast. The man behind the counter asks if I'm an Arab Muslim (he too is Arab and Muslim). I reply that yes, I am by part of my father. He asks my name, and I say, "Evelyn." In utter disdain, he tells me that I could not possibly be Muslim; if I were truly Muslim I would have a Muslim name. What was I doing with such a name? I reply (after taking a deep breath and telling myself that it's not worth getting upset over) that my Cuban mother named me and that I honor my mother. He points to the fact that I'm wearing lipstick and have not changed my name, which he finds to be completely inappropriate and despicable, and says that I am a reflection of the decay of the Arab Muslim in America.

I'm on an airplane flying from Miami to New York. I'm sitting next to an Ecuadorian man. He asks me where I'm from. I tell him. He asks me if I'm more Arab, Latina, or American, and I state that I'm all of the above. He says that's impossible. I must be more of one ethnicity than another. He determines that I am not really Arab, that I'm more Latina because of the camaraderie he feels in our speaking Spanish.

I am in Costa Rica. I walk the streets and my brown skin and dark hair blend in with the multiple shades of brown around me. I love this first-time experience of blending in! I walk into a coffee shop for some café con leche, and my fantasy of belonging is shattered when the woman preparing the coffee asks me where I'm from. I tell her that I was born and raised in New York City by a Cuban mother and an Arab father. She replies, "Que eres una gringa."

I am shocked by the contextuality of identity: that my body is marked as gringa in Costa Rica, as Latina in some U.S. contexts, Arab in others, in some times and spaces not adequately Arab, or Latina, or "American," and in other contexts simply as *other*.

My body becomes marked with meaning as I enter public space. My identity fractures as I experience differing dislocations in multiple contexts. Sometimes people otherize me, sometimes they identify with me. Both situations can be equally problematic. Those who otherize me fail to see a shared humanity and those who identify with me fail to see difference; my Arab or Muslim identity negates my Cuban heritage. Identification signifies belonging or home, and I pretend to be that home for the mistaken person. It's my good deed for the day (I know how precious it can be to find a moment of familiarity with a stranger). The bridge becomes my back as I feign belonging, and I become that vehicle for others, which I desire for myself. Although it is illusory, I do identify with the humanity of the situation—the desire to belong in this world, to be understood. But the frameworks used to (mis)read my body, to disconnect me, wear on me. I try to develop a new identity. What should I try to pass for next time? Perhaps I'll just say I'm Cuban to those who appear to be Arab or South Asian. A friend suggests I say I'm an Italian from Brooklyn. I wonder if I could successfully pass for that. Ethnicity needs to be recast so that our moving selves can be acknowledged.

NOTES

I would like to thank Marisol Negrón, Alexandra Lang, María Helena Rueda, Ericka Beckman, Karina Hodoyan, Sara Rondinel, Jessi Aaron, and Cynthia María Paccacerqua for their feedback in our writing seminar at Stanford University with Mary Pratt. I would especially like to thank Mary Pratt for her invaluable feedback, and AnaLouise Keating and Gloria Anzaldúa for their thoughtful editing.

4

GOING BEYOND BLACK AND WHITE, HISPANICS IN CENSUS PICK "OTHER"

Mireya Navarro

Patria Rodriguez, an advertising sales director for a women's magazine in New York, takes after her father. With light brown skin and thick, curly hair, she says she resembles the actress Rosie Perez, but some people have asked her if she is Italian, and others have told her she looks like the singer Sade.

Like many Hispanic Americans, Ms. Rodriguez does not think of herself as black or white. "I acknowledge I have both black and white ancestry in me, but I choose to label myself in nonracial terms: Latina. Hispanic. Puerto Rican. Nuyorican," Ms. Rodriguez, 31, said. "I feel that being Latina implies mixed racial heritage, and I wish more people knew that. Why should I have to choose?"

As the Hispanic population booms, the fluid ways that she and other Latinos view their racial identities are drawing more attention and fueling the national debate over racial classifications—what they mean, what they should be and whether they are needed at all.

Now members of the United States' largest minority group, the nation's 38.8 million Hispanics, nearly half of them immigrants, harbor notions of race that are as varied as their Spanish and that often clash with the more bipolar views of many other Americans.

White? Black? Try "moreno," "trigueno" or "indio," terms that indicate skin shades and ancestry and accommodate several hues.

This heterogeneity has stumped the Census Bureau. In its 2000 count, almost half the Hispanic respondents refused to identify themselves by any of the five standard racial categories on the census forms: white, black, Asian, American Indian or Alaska native and a category that includes natives of Hawaii and the Pacific Islands. The agency has since been surveying Hispanics to find a way to pinpoint them racially.

In the census, respondents can mark their ethnicity as Hispanic, but then they are asked to choose a racial label. In 2000, almost half of the Hispanic respondents, 48 percent, identified themselves as white. Only 2 percent chose black.

But from the light-complexioned to the dark, more than 14 million, or more than 42 percent of all Latino respondents, marked the box labeled "some other race" and wrote in such disparate identities as Mayan, Tejano and mestizo. (An additional 6 percent said they were members of two or more races.)

The category "some other race" was used almost exclusively by Hispanics; of all those who chose it, 97 percent were Latino. Claudette Bennett, chief of the Census Bureau's racial-statistics branch, said follow-up research showed that a large portion of these respondents wanted Hispanic to be considered their race.

A recent study by the Lewis Mumford Center for Comparative Urban and Regional Research at the State University of New York at Albany noted that the popularity of the "some other race" category came at the expense of the "white" category, which was the choice of the majority of Latino respondents in 1980.

"There may have been a sense that being white was part of the process of being assimilated," said John R. Logan, Mumford's director. "There's a trend toward rejecting whiteness as a way of expressing success."

"That's the big change over time. There's a Latino identity that's neither white nor black, and it's a positive identity."

While there are clearly white Hispanics and black Hispanics, many more come from racially mixed stock, with white, black and American Indian or other indigenous strains. Even within one family, one sibling may look black by many Americans' standards, another white, and another in between. And factors as disparate as hair texture, education, income and even nationality matter almost as much as skin color in racial self-image.

Israel Coats, 24, a Dominican who moved to New York when he was 11 and is now studying marketing at Baruch College, is black in physical features and in the way he identifies himself. But in the Dominican Republic, he says, he is called "indio," Indian. That is because even the darkest-skinned Dominican often regards "black" as a synonym for Haitian; the two nations, which share the island of Hispaniola, have a long history of conflict.

Physical appearance is not even a factor in how some Latinos sort themselves into racial categories.

Mario Goderich, 36, a police officer in Miami Beach, Fla., who has light brown hair, green eyes and the white skin of his Puerto Rican mother, identifies himself on the census forms as Hispanic and white. His father, Rene Goderich, 62, also identifies himself as white, even though he describes himself as "jabao," the Cuban term for a light-skinned mulatto.

"Over here there's no 'jabao' or 'mulatto,' so I say white," said the elder Mr. Goderich, who is from Santiago, Cuba, and lives in New Jersey. "We're all mixed."

Ms. Rodriguez, the advertising sales director, said one reason she is uncomfortable picking one race is because the words white and black carry political baggage that she does not feel she shares. "White means most privilege and black means overcoming obstacles, a history of civil rights," she said. "As a Latina, I can't try to claim one of these."

Among people of Mexican descent, who make up more than 65 percent of Hispanics in the United States, the racial background includes a strong indigenous influence. Eva Blanco, 32, a college admissions official in San Jose, Calif., said she wished there were a census box labeled "red."

"In college, a friend would call me a Mayan princess, because I have the nose you see in the pictures of Mayans," she said. "I feel there's nothing that describes my race per se. For the most part, I say I'm Mexican."

Ellis Cose, who examined racial identity in Latin America for his 1997 book, *Color-Blind: Seeing Beyond Race in a Race-Obsessed World*, said these malleable views were quickening the pace of a shift in this country that began in the 1960's, after legal segregation ended and intermarriage became more common.

Growing numbers of interracial unions are also making the color line a moving target. By 2000, the census showed, interracial couples, including those in which one person was of Hispanic origin, made up 7 percent of marriages and 13 percent to 15 percent of households with unmarried partners.

"For the first time, the American construct of race is making room for a large group of folks it never made room for before," said Mr. Cose, who is also a contributing editor for *Newsweek*.

The growing multiracial population has interfered with the government's accounting of people by race and has become one of the top issues of research and debate among scholars. On Labor Day weekend, Harvard University drew more than 1,000 participants to a "color lines" research conference that delved into the implications for a nation where so much depends on racial categorization: antidiscrimination and voting-rights laws, health and educational statistics and social policies like affirmative action.

Joel Perlmann, a senior scholar at the Levy Economics Institute of Bard College who was a co-editor of *The New Race Question,* a 2002 book about how the census counts multiracial people, said the changing demographics were casting doubt on the rationale for the categories themselves.

"Where do these categories come from?" he asked. "What are their justification? It helps delegitimize race."

In California, a movement to shelve racial classifications altogether was behind Proposition 54, the unsuccessful measure on last month's recall ballot that sought to halt the collection of most racial and ethnic data by the state government.

One proponent of the measure was Ward Connerly, the black California businessman who led the winning push for laws in California and Washington State that ban the consideration of race in public university admissions, hiring and government contracting. He argues that racial classifications have become so imprecise as to lose all meaning.

"We ought to be trying to find a better way of detecting discrimination than this crude way," Mr. Connerly said, adding that he planned to bring another version of Proposition 54 to voters.

But many civil rights advocates and government officials counter that racial categories, as imperfect as they may be, are the only way to measure disparities among groups and provide remedies. And they say that the way Hispanics see themselves may ultimately be irrelevant if they are still subject to other people's biases.

Letvia Arza-Goderich, a lawyer in Los Angeles and a cousin of Mr. Goderich, the Miami Beach police officer, said she felt that she was not regarded as white in the United States except among Latinos. Her family left Cuba in the late 1960s, and as a teenager in Wisconsin, Ms. Arza-Goderich said, her white schoolmates regarded her as dark-skinned and used a slur to describe her. It did not matter that she had pale white skin that looked even whiter against her black wavy hair.

"We were Cubans, and that wasn't white," she said. "My answer was, 'Not that it matters, but I'm white just like you because the people I came from were from Spain.' They'd look at you in disbelief.

"If you're Latino, you're not white-white in the eyes of white Americans," Ms. Arza-Goderich said.

Still, white Hispanics are more prosperous than other Latinos, the Mumford Center study found. Hispanics who described themselves as white on the 2000 census had the highest incomes and the lowest rates of unemployment and poverty, and they tended to live closest to non-Latino whites, the study said. Black Hispanics, who live in neighborhoods that have nearly as many African-Americans as Hispanic residents, the study found, had lower incomes and higher rates of poverty and unemployment than other Hispanic groups. In those ways they were similar to non-Hispanic blacks.

Those who identified themselves as neither white nor black, the study said, were less affluent than white Hispanics but considerably better off than black Hispanics.

Race relations among Latinos, however, are informed by starkly different experiences compared with those between other groups in America. Among Hispanics, skin color still counts, because Latin American countries have caste systems that discriminate against the dark-skinned. But Latin America did not have Jim Crow laws, or their legacy of bitterness.

Even in the United States, Hispanics who complain of discrimination by other Latinos do not cite race as a major factor, said a national survey last year by the Pew Hispanic Center and the Kaiser Family Foundation. Among those who said they were the victims of bias, the survey found, 41 percent attributed it to disparities in income and education and 34 percent to differences in country of origin. Only 8 percent said it was because of skin color, the survey said.

Hispanics, of course, are not the only ones bending racial identity. Matt Kelly, founder of the Mavin Foundation, a national organization based in Seattle that advocates for multiracial Americans, noted that in the 2000 census, nearly seven million Americans identified themselves as belonging to two or more races, not counting the Latinos who picked "some other race."

And the culture is offering up role models, like Halle Berry and Tiger Woods, who celebrate their multiracial background.

In Los Angeles, where Hispanics are the largest ethnic group, Ms. Arza-Goderich said she and her husband, who is also Cuban, have never discussed with their three sons "whether they are white, or moreno or what."

"Race takes a back seat to what they listen to on their CD players, what movies they see," she said. "One is into Japanese anime. Another is immersed in rap. Basically it's the ghetto culture, but ghetto doesn't mean poor or deprived, but hip."

Her 16-year-old, Ray, has adopted a hip-hop persona and hangs out with Vietnamese, Indian, Chicano, white and black friends. Ms. Arza-Goderich said most of them had Asian girlfriends.

"They say they're hot," she explained.

5

SHADES OF BELONGING: LATINOS AND RACIAL IDENTITY

Sonya Tafoya

When census takers, pollsters or bureaucrats with application forms ask people to identify their race, most have no problem checking a box that corresponds to one of the five, standard, government-defined racial categories. In the 2000 Census, for example, 90 percent of the U.S. population was counted as either white, black, Asian, American Indian or Pacific Islander. Hispanics are the exception. While a little more than half picked one of the standard categories, some 15 million, 42 percent, of the Hispanic population marked "some other race." This and much other evidence suggests that Hispanics take distinctive views of race, and because their numbers are large and growing fast, these views are likely to change the way the nation manages the fundamental social divide that has characterized American society for 400 years.

According to federal policy and accepted social science, Hispanics do not constitute a separate race and can in fact be of any race. The 2000 [Census] asked respondents first to mark off whether they were "Spanish/Hispanic/Latino" and then in a separate question to specify their race. Among those who identified themselves as Hispanics, nearly half (48 percent) were counted as white. Blacks made up 2 percent. The American Indian, Asian, and Pacific Islander categories each accounted for small fractions. Surprisingly, given the large number of Latinos whose parentage includes combinations of white, African and indigenous ancestries, only 6 percent described themselves as being of two or more races. The only racial identifier, other than white, that captured a major share of the Latino population (42 percent) was the non-identifier, "some other race" (SOR). That is a sizeable category of people, outnumbering the total U.S. population of Asians and American Indians combined.

"Some other race" is not exactly a political slogan or rallying cry. Nor is it a term anyone ordinarily would use in conversation or to describe themselves. So, who are the some-other-race Hispanics? And, what are they trying to tell us with their choice of this label?

In order to explore these questions the Pew Hispanic Center examined microdata from the 2000 Census as well as information from surveys and focus groups conducted by the Center. The numbers show that Latinos who call themselves white and those who say they are some other race have distinctly different characteristics, and survey data show they have different attitudes and opinions on a variety of subjects. Consistently across a broad range of variables, Hispanics who identified themselves as white have higher levels of education and income and greater degrees of civic enfranchisement than those who pick the some other race category. The findings of this report suggest that Hispanics see race as a measure of belonging, and whiteness as a measure of inclusion, or of perceived inclusion.

Given immigration's important role in shaping the Hispanic population, nativity—whether a person was born in the United States or abroad—is a key characteristic. More foreign-born Latinos say they are of some other race (46 percent) than native born (40 percent). Cuban-born immigrants are the exception. More importantly, whiteness is clearly associated with distance from the immigrant experience. Thus, the U.S.-born children of immigrants are more likely to declare themselves white than their foreign-born parents, and the share of whiteness is higher still among the grandchildren of immigrants. In addition, U.S. citizenship is associated with racial identification. Among immigrants from the same country, those who have become U.S. citizens identify themselves as white more often than those who are not U.S. citizens. It seems unlikely that the ability and willingness to become a U.S. citizen are somehow linked to skin color. Thus, it may be that developing deeper civic bonds here can help an immigrant feel white.

The full extent to which race is a measure of belonging for Latinos becomes apparent in examining the native born alone. Immigration status and language do not play a direct role in determining economic or social outcomes for Hispanics born in this country, and their conceptions of race are primarily home grown. Among U.S.-born Latinos whiteness is clearly and consistently associated with higher social status, higher levels of civic participation and a stronger sense of acceptance.

- The share of native-born Latinos without a high school diploma is higher for those who say they are some other race (35 percent) than for those who call themselves white (30 percent).
- Unemployment runs two points higher among native-born Hispanic males who declare themselves some other race compared to those who say they are white and poverty rates are four points higher among adults.
- The share of native-born Latino men earning more than $35,000 a year is a third higher for those who say they are white compared to the some other race group (24.7 percent vs. 18.5 percent).
- Among all Hispanics, those who say they are some other race tend to be younger (median age 24) than those who say they are white (median age 27).
- More of those native-born Hispanics who say they are white (85 percent) are registered voters than those who say they are of some other race (67 percent).

- When asked whether they consider themselves Republicans, Democrats, Independents or something else, more native-born Latinos who say they are white (22 percent) pick Republican compared to those who say they are some other race (13 percent). The same pattern prevailed among the foreign-born.
- When asked to choose between the terms "American" versus "Hispanic or Latino" versus a national origin identifier such as "Mexican," far more native-born Latinos who say they are white (55 percent) pick "American" compared to those who say they are some other race (36 percent).
- About a quarter of native-born Latinos who say they are white complain that discrimination is a major problem for Latinos in the United States compared to a third of those who say they are some other race.

These findings suggest that Latinos' choice to identify as white or not does not exclusively reflect permanent markers such as skin color or hair texture but that race is also related to characteristics that can change such as economic status and perceptions of civic enfranchisement. Also, social context and the nature of race relations in a given place also appear to play a role. Hispanics of Mexican origin, who comprise about two-thirds of the total Hispanic population, are almost evenly divided between those who identify as white and those who pick some other race. However, in Texas many more native-born Latinos of Mexican descent say they are white (63 percent) compared to those who live outside of Texas (45 percent). Again, it seems unlikely that skin color is the determining factor. Instead, one can suppose that the unique and complex history of race relations in Texas is a major influence. This is the only state where a large Latino population was caught up both in Southern-style racial segregation and then the civil rights struggle to undo it.

Understanding Latinos' views of their racial identities involves much more than defining a series of demographic sub-categories. Rather it helps illuminate the ways that race is being lived in the United States today. In the commonplace view, Latinos are an additional "group" that has been added to the American mix of white, black, Asian, etc. And, in particular Latinos are categorized as a minority group that is significantly different from the white majority due to factors including a history of discrimination and persistently lower educational outcomes and incomes on average. The temptation is to racialize this population, to make it fit in the traditional American social paradigm which assigns people to race or at least race-like categories. But, the growing Hispanic population may compel a reassessment of the common view of a racial or ethnic group as a readily identifiable category of people who share a common fate and a common identity.

Categorizing Hispanics, particularly a minority group, becomes much more difficult once you realize this population is almost evenly divided between those who identify with the white majority and those who have trouble seeing themselves in any of the standard racial categories. It is not that some are more Hispanic or Latino than the others because they all have taken on that mantle. Nor are they saying that race does not matter to them. Rather, the message seems to be that Latinos in the United States experience race differently. For them, it is not something that pertains exclusively to skin color, let alone to history and heritage.

For Latinos the concept of race appears to extend beyond biology, ancestral origins or a history of grievance in this country. The differences in characteristics and attitudes between those Hispanics who call themselves white and those who identify as some other race, suggests they experience racial identity as a measure of belonging: Feeling white seems to be a reflection of success and a sense of inclusion. The fact that changeable characteristics such as income help determine racial identification among Latinos, versus permanent markers such as skin color, does not necessarily mean that the color lines in American society are fading. On the contrary, these findings show that color has a broader meaning. The Latino experience demonstrates that whiteness remains an important measure of belonging, stature and acceptance. And, Hispanic views of race also show that half of this ever larger segment of the U.S. population is feeling left out.

ASIAN AMERICAN?

Sonia Shah

I was recently asked to write about Asian American History Month, which, since 1979, has been observed during the month of May.

Despite the fact that I write about Asian American issues on a fairly regular basis, and in many ways consider myself an Asian American, it wasn't easy to figure. The very term, "Asian American History," makes our presence here sound so official, so natural.

Yet the term "Asian American" itself is problematic. Most of the people whom others would characterize as "Asian American" most emphatically don't think of themselves that way. (And many, including most of those in my family, would be almost offended: they are Gujuratis, thank you very much!) Our particular histories, ethnicities, and nationalities are one million times more visceral and meaningful in our lives than pan-Asianness (and what would that be, one wonders: "fusion" cooking?).

The push to unify the disparate peoples and histories of Chinese, Japanese, Vietnamese, Hmong, Pakistanis, Thais, and Indians, among others, comes from both right and left. Of course it would be easier for the U.S. census, but also for

Reprinted by permission of the author. First appeared in *ZNet Commentary* (April 26, 1999).

the radicals who started the "Yellow Power" movement in the 1960s, among others. But unlike other diverse ethnic/racial groups, such as African Americans and Native Americans, Asian Pacific Americans share no common historical trauma like slavery or colonization. We share no "Asian" language or ethnicity or nation or color. What we have in common, most of us would rather forget.

There is an undeniable strategic value in our unity. Americans know so little about Asian cultures, in general, that the stereotypes and fantasies projected upon any one group bleed over onto the next. We have those in common, and it wouldn't do any good to resist some and not the others. As a group, Asians have sometimes been held up as "model minorities" and at other times pilloried as spies and interlopers, but always, it seems, we are held at a distance, no matter how "American" we may become. This is at least partly because our role in American society is largely defined not by our unique contributions per se, but by our assigned roles in the unfolding drama between American labor and capital, and between blacks and whites.

Each wave of Asian immigration to American shores has been triggered by U.S. immigration policy or military interventions in Asia. When American labor has gotten too expensive, due to union organizing victories and the like, immigration laws have strategically shifted to import workers from Asia, whether poor Chinese laborers in the 1800s to build the railroads or professional Asians in the 1960s to service the then-growing welfare state. U.S. military interventions in the Philippines, Korea, Vietnam, and elsewhere likewise resulted in floods of Asian refugees at American gates. Today, the workers, farmers, and small landowners in Asia whose livelihoods have been crushed by the demands of U.S. multinational companies—now freer than ever to do business abroad—are being smuggled illegally into the country.

Predictably, backlashes against these workers have followed in each case. Laws excluding Chinese from becoming citizens, owning property, marrying, or attending public schools with whites were enacted in the mid- to late-1800s. In 1942, the U.S. government stripped 110,000 Japanese Americans of their homes, possessions, and savings and forced them into concentration camps; upon their release—jobless, penniless—the government served as an employment agency, fielding the many requests for servants.

The 1980s economy sparked another wave of anti-Asian violence: in 1982, Chinese American Vincent Chin was beaten to death with a baseball bat by unemployed auto workers who thought he was Japanese (and who served not a single day in jail). In 1987, Navraz Mody was beaten to death by a gang of youths in New Jersey, home of the infamous "dotbusters" (a vicious reference to the Indian bindhi).

Today, many Asian workers serve as a sort of middle-tier wedge between blacks and whites, and between corporate elites and workers—most tragically in Los Angeles during the 1992 riots. Even the much-lauded professional Asians are harrassed and excluded on the basis of their accents, their degrees often devalued and held to higher-than-usual standards. For all the fanfare regarding their success, most of them still make less money than whites with comparable educations. Undocumented Asian workers take the jobs nobody else will tolerate, toiling in sweatshops and factories. In one particularly egregious case, dozens of Thai workers were recently found to have been held against their will in a barbed-wire-enclosed southern California sweatshop between 1990 and 1997.

The model minority myth—consciously encouraged by embattled elites in Asian communities—likewise inserts Asians into the larger drama about blacks and whites. While an education can be had and a living made based on model minority myths (at least for some), it is at the cost of indulging the racist delusion that there can be some "good minorities" in implicit contrast to those other "bad minorities," who have only themselves to blame.

Part of the double-bind of Asian Americans is that retaining our Asian heritages can be almost as difficult as becoming American. The American media continues to be fascinated with Asian misery and senseless oppression. When Americans gain a peek into life in Asia, it is invariably a horror scene: Indonesians eating bark; Chinese women drinking pesticides; Thai prostitutes chained to their beds; dead bodies in rivers, contaminated blood supplies, mudslides, train wrecks, massacres. Non-Asians may be strangely comforted by these tales of distant woe. But what could anyone with ties to those countries feel, beside sorrow, shame, rage, alienation, or: Thank God we're here and not there!

The story of Asian American history, in these ways, is a story of not belonging, of alienation from America and Asia. Yet, despite all this ambivalence and contradiction about our place in U.S. society, Asian Americans have played upon the broader American stage and have made lives and history change as a result.

People such as the human rights advocate Yuri Kochiyama; the feminist activist Anannya Bhattacharjee; the queer activist Urvashi Vaid; the radical poet Janice Mirikitani; the public intellectuals Glenn Omatsu, Peter Kwong; and Mari Matsuda; the filmmakers Richard Fung and Renee Tajima to name just a few, among many others, are building an inspired, radical Asian left to improve all of our lives.

Their legacy—the future of history—are today's vibrant Asian American immigrant worker movements, the growing institution of Asian American Studies in universities, a flourishing Asian American arts community, and more. These people and the institutions they have built, against the odds, are the Asian makers of American history. They have and will continue to force America to reckon with the realities of a diverse, multilingual, yellow and brown, ever-more-vocal Asianized America.

7

THE MYTH OF THE MODEL MINORITY

Noy Thrupkaew

Mali Keo fled Cambodia with her husband and four children in 1992. Several years later, she was still haunted by searing memories of "the killing fields," the forced-labor camps where millions of Cambodians died, victims of Communist despot Pol Pot's quest for a perfect agrarian society. Because of the brutal beatings she suffered at the hands of Pol Pot's Khmer Rouge, she was still wracked with physical pain as well. Traumatized and ailing, uneducated, unskilled, and speaking very little English, Mali Keo (a pseudonym assigned by researchers) could barely support her children after her husband abandoned the family.

And now she may not even have public assistance to fall back on, because the 1996 welfare-reform act cut off most federal benefits to immigrants and subsequent amendments have not entirely restored them. In what was supposed to be the land of her salvation, Mali Keo today is severely impoverished. Living in a hard-pressed neighborhood of Philadelphia, she struggles with only mixed success to keep her children out of trouble and in school.

The Southeast Asia Resource Action Center (SEARAC), an advocacy group in Washington, estimates that more than 2.2 million Southeast Asians now live in the United States. They are the largest group of refugees in the country and the fastest-growing minority. Yet for most policy makers, the plight of the many Mali Keos has been overshadowed by the well-known success of the Asian immigrants who came before and engendered the myth of the "model minority." Indeed, conservatives have exploited this racial stereotype—arguing that Asians fare well in the United States because of their strong "family values" and work ethic. These values, they say, and not government assistance, are what all minorities need in order to get ahead.

Paradoxically, Southeast Asians—supposedly part of the model minority—may be suffering most from the resulting public policies. They have been left in the hands of underfunded community-assistance programs and government agencies that, in one example of well-intentioned incompetence, churn out forms in Khmer and Lao for often illiterate populations. But fueled by outrage over bad services and a fraying social safety-net, Southeast Asian immigrants have started to embrace that most American of activities, political protest—by pushing for research on their communities, advocating for their rights, and harnessing their political power.

The model-minority myth has persisted in large part because political conservatives are so attached to it. "Asian Americans have become the darlings of the right," said Frank Wu, a law professor at Howard University and the author of *Yellow: Race beyond Black and White*. "The model-minority myth and its depiction of Asian-American success tells a reassuring story about our society working."

The flip side is also appealing to the right. Because Asian Americans' success stems from their strong families and their dedication to education and hard work, conservatives say, then the poverty of Latinos and African Americans must be explained by their own "values": They are poor because of their nonmarrying, school-skipping, and generally lazy and irresponsible behavior, which government handouts only encourage.

The model-minority myth's "racist love," as author Frank Chin terms it, took hold at a sensitive point in U.S. history: after the 1965 Watts riots and the immigration reforms of that year, which selectively allowed large numbers of educated immigrants into the United States. Highly skilled South and East Asian nurses, doctors, and engineers from countries like India and China began pouring into the United States just as racial tensions were at a fever pitch.

Shortly thereafter, articles like "Success Story of One Minority in the U.S.," published by *U.S. News & World Report* in 1966, trumpeted: "At a time when it is being proposed that hundreds of billions be spent to uplift Negroes and other minorities, the nation's 300,000 Chinese Americans are moving ahead on their own, with no help from anyone else." *Newsweek* in 1971 had Asian Americans "outwhiting the whites." And *Fortune* in 1986 dubbed them a "superminority." As Wu caricatures the model-minority myth in his book:

> Asian Americans vindicate the American Dream. . . . They are living proof of the power of the free market and the absence of racial discrimination. Their good fortune flows from individual self-reliance and community self-sufficiency, not civil-rights activism or government welfare benefits.

A closer look at the data paints another picture, however. If Asian-American households earn more than whites, statistics suggest, it's not because their individual earnings are higher but because Asian Americans live in larger households, with more working adults. In fact, a recent University of Hawaii study found that "most Asian Americans are overeducated compared to whites for the incomes they earn"—evidence that suggests not "family values" but market discrimination.

What most dramatically skews the data, though, is the fact that about half the population of Asian (or, more precisely, Asian-Pacific Islander) Americans is made up of the highly educated immigrants who began arriving with their families in the 1960s. The plight of refugees from Cambodia, Laos, and Vietnam, who make up less than 14 percent of Asian Americans, gets lost in the averaging. Yet these refugees, who started arriving in the United States after 1975, differ markedly from the professional-class Chinese and Indian immigrants who started coming 10 years earlier. The Southeast Asians were fleeing wartime persecution and had few resources. And those disadvantages have had devastating effects on their lives in the United States. The most recent census data available show that 47 percent of Cambodians, 66 percent of Hmong (an ethnic group that lived in the mountains of Laos), 67 percent of Laotians, and 34 percent of Vietnamese were impoverished in 1990—compared with 10 percent of all Americans and 14 percent of all Asian Americans. Significantly, poverty rates among Southeast Asian Americans were much higher than those of even the "nonmodel" minorities: 21 percent of African Americans and 23 percent of Latinos were poor.

Yet despite the clear inaccuracies created by lumping population together, the federal government still groups Southeast Asian refugees under the overbroad category of "Asian" for research and funding purposes. "We've labored under the shadow of this model myth for so long," said Ka Ying Yang, SEARAC's executive director. "There's so little research on us, or we're lumped in with all other Asians, so people don't know the specific needs and contributions of our communities."

To get a sense of those needs, one has to go back to the beginning of the Southeast Asian refugees' story and the circumstances that forced their migration. In 1975, the fall of Saigon sent shock waves throughout Southeast Asia, as communist insurgents toppled U.S.-supported governments in Vietnam and Cambodia. In Laos, where the CIA had trained and funded the Hmong to fight Laotian and Vietnamese communists as U.S. proxies, the communists who took over vowed to purge the country of ethnic Hmong and punish all others who had worked with the U.S. government.

The first refugees to leave Southeast Asia tended to be the most educated and urban, English-speakers with close connections to the U.S. government. One of them was a man who wishes to be identified by the pseudonym John Askulraskul. He spent two years in a Laotian re-education camp—punishment for his ability to speak English, his having been educated, and, most of all, his status as a former employee of the United States Agency for International Development (USAID).

"They tried to brainwash you, to subdue you psychologically, to work you to death on two bowls of rice a day," Askulraskul told me recently.

After being released, he decided to flee the country. He, his sister, and his eldest daughter, five and a half years old, slipped into the Mekong River with a few others. Clinging to an inflated garbage bag, Askulraskul swam alongside their boat out of fear that his weight would sink it.

After they arrived on the shores of Thailand, Askulraskul and his daughter were placed in a refugee camp, where they waited to be reunited with his wife and his two other daughters.

It was not to be.

"My wife tried to escape with two small children. But my daughters couldn't make it"—he paused, drawing a ragged breath—"because the boat sank."

Askulraskul's wife was swept back to Laos, where she was arrested and placed in jail for a month. She succeeded in her next escape attempt, rejoining her suddenly diminished family.

Eventually, with the help of his former boss at USAID, they moved to Connecticut, where Askulraskul found work helping to resettle other refugees. His wife, who had been an elementary-school teacher, took up teaching English as a second language (ESL) to Laotian refugee children. His daughter adjusted quickly and went to school without incident.

Askulraskul now manages a project that provides services for at-risk Southeast Asian children and their families. "The job I am doing now is not only a job," he said. "It is part of my life and my sacrifice. My daughter is 29 now, and I know raising kids in America is not easy. I cannot save everybody, but there is still something I can do."

Like others among the first wave of refugees, Askulraskul considers himself one of the lucky ones. His education, U.S. ties, and English-language ability—everything that set off the tragic chain of events that culminated in his daughters' deaths—proved enormously helpful once he was in the United States.

But the majority of refugees from Southeast Asia had no such advantages. Subsequent waves frequently hailed from rural areas and lacked both financial resources and formal schooling. Their psychological scars were even deeper than the first group's, from their longer years in squalid refugee camps or the killing fields. The ethnic Chinese who began arriving from Vietnam had faced harsh discrimination as well, and the Amerasians—the children of Vietnamese women and U.S. soldiers—had lived for years as pariahs.

Once here, these refugees often found themselves trapped in poverty, providing low-cost labor, and receiving no health or other benefits, while their lack of schooling made decent jobs almost impossible to come by. In 1990, two-thirds of Cambodian, Laotian, and Hmong adults in America had less than a high-school education—compared with 14 percent of whites, 25 percent of African Americans, 45 percent of Latinos, and 15 percent of the general Asian-American population. Before the welfare-reform law cut many of them off, nearly 30 percent of Southeast Asian Americans were on welfare—the highest participation rate of any ethnic group. And having such meager incomes, they usually lived in the worst neighborhoods, with the attendant crime, gang problems, and poor schools.

But shouldn't the touted Asian dedication to schooling have overcome these disadvantages, lifting the refugees' children out of poverty and keeping them off the streets? Unfortunately, it didn't. "There is still a high number of dropouts for Southeast Asians," Yang said. "And if they do graduate, there is a low number going on to higher education."

Their parents' difficulty in navigating American school systems may contribute to the problem. "The parents' lack of education leads to a lack of role models and guidance. Without those things, youth can turn to delinquent behavior and in some very extreme cases, gangs, instead of devoting themselves to education," said Narin Sihavong, director of SEARAC's Successful New Americans Project, which interviewed Mali Keo. "This underscores the need for Southeast Asian school administrators or counselors who can be role models, ease the cultural barrier, and serve as a bridge to their parents."

"Sometimes families have to choose between education and employment, especially when money is tight," said Porthira Chimm, a former SEARAC project director. "And unfortunately, immediate money concerns often win out."

The picture that emerges—of high welfare participation and dropout rates, low levels of education and income—is startlingly similar to the situation of the poorest members of "nonmodel" minority groups. Southeast Asians, Latinos, and African Americans also have in common significant numbers of single-parent families. Largely as a result of the killing fields, nearly a quarter of Cambodian households are headed by single women. Other Southeast Asian families have similar stories. Sihavong's mother, for example, raised him and his five siblings on her own while his father was imprisoned in a Laotian re-education camp.

No matter how "traditional" Southeast Asians may be, they share the fate of other people of color when they are denied access to good education, safe neighborhoods, and jobs that provide a living wage and benefits. But for the sake of preserving the model-minority myth, conservative policy makers have largely ignored the needs of Southeast Asian communities.

One such need is for psychological care. Wartime trauma and "lack of English proficiency, acculturative stress, prejudice, discrimination, and racial hate crimes" place Southeast Asians "at risk for emotional and behavioral problems," according to the U.S. surgeon general's 2001 report on race and mental health. One random sample of Cambodian adults found that 45 percent had post-traumatic stress disorder and 51 percent suffered from depression.

John Askulraskul's past reflects trauma as well, but his education, English-language ability, and U.S. connections helped level the playing field. Less fortunate refugees need literacy training and language assistance. They also need social supports like welfare and strong community-assistance groups. But misled by the model-minority myth, many government agencies seem to be unaware that Southeast Asians require their services, and officials have done little to find these needy refugees or accommodate them. Considering that nearly two-thirds of Southeast Asians say they do not speak English very well and more than 50 percent live in linguistically isolated ethnic enclaves, the lack of outreach and translators effectively denies them many public services.

The problem extends beyond antipoverty programs, as Mali Keo's story illustrates. After her husband left her, she formed a relationship with another man and had two more children. But he beat the family for years, until she asked an organization that served Cambodian refugees to help her file a restraining order. If she had known that a shelter was available, she told her interviewer, even one without Khmer-speaking counselors, she would have escaped much earlier.

Where the government hasn't turned a blind eye, it has often wielded an iron fist. The welfare-reform law of 1996, which cut off welfare, SSI, and food-stamp benefits for most noncitizens—even those who are legal permanent residents—sent Southeast Asian communities into an uproar. Several elderly Hmong in California committed suicide, fearing that they would become burdens to their families. Meanwhile, the lack of literacy programs prevented (and still does prevent) many refugees from passing the written test that would gain them citizenship and the right to public assistance.

"We achieved welfare reform on the backs of newcomers," Frank Wu said. "People said that 'outsiders' don't have a claim to the body politic, and even liberals say we should care for 'our own' first." Few seemed to ask the question posed by sociologist Donald Hernandez: "What responsibility do we have to ensure a basic standard of living for immigrants who have fled their countries as a result of the American government's economic, military, and political involvement there?"

But welfare reform also had a second effect. "It was such a shocking event, it completely galvanized the Southeast Asian community," said Karen Narasaki, executive director of the National Asian Pacific American Legal Consortium. "In different Asian cultures, you have 'the crab who crawls out of the bucket gets pulled back' [and] 'the nail that sticks out gets pounded down.' But in the United States, 'the squeaky wheel gets the grease,' and people had to learn that."

The learning process has been a difficult one. At first, because of their past negative experiences with the United States and their homeland governments, many Southeast Asians feared political involvement. Many saw themselves as noncitizens and second-class "outsiders" with a precarious standing in the United States. But as they have grown more familiar with this country, even noncitizens have started to think of themselves less as refugees in a temporary home and more as "new Americans" who are entitled to shape their destinies through political engagement.

The energy for this new activism grew out of the mutual-assistance associations (MAAs) that have taken root in various Southeast Asian communities. Primarily staffed by people like Askulraskul—the more successful members of the ethnic groups they serve—MAAs form the backbone of support for Southeast Asians, providing, among many other things, child care, job training, school liaisons, and assistance with navigating government bureaucracies.

But the MAAs are facing problems of their own. The funding they used to get from the federal Office of Refugee Resettlement is dwindling. In 1996 new federal guidelines mandated that these funds go exclusively to organizations serving the most recent refugees. (In response, several Southeast Asian MAAs have tried to stay afloat by offering their services to newer refugees from places like Ethiopia and Iraq.) As for outside funding, only 0.3 percent of all philanthropic aid goes to groups that work specifically with Asian-American populations, according to the 1998 edition of *Foundation Giving*. "A lot of people in philanthropy think [that Asians] are doing so well, they don't need help," Narasaki said.

Despite these problems, MAAs and national advocacy organizations like SEARAC have won limited restorations of benefits and food stamps for immigrants. And a significant victory came in 2000, when legislation sponsored by Minnesota Senator Paul Wellstone was adopted: It will allow Hmong veterans—or their widows—from America's "secret war" in Laos to take the U.S. citizenship test in Hmong, with a translator.

One key to the MAAs' success is their networking with other minority-advocacy groups, says Sandy Dang, executive director of Asian American LEAD, an organization based in Washington, that provides a range of services for Vietnamese Americans, including ESL classes, youth mentoring, and parent-support groups.

When Dang founded the organization, she didn't know how to write grant proposals, so she asked the director of a nearby youth center for Latin Americans to provide guidance. "The Latino organizations have a lot of empathy for people starting out," she said. "They understand the refugee-immigrant experience.

"Disadvantaged people share a lot in common," Dang continued, "and we have to help each other. People who are empowered in this country like to play us off each other, like with the model-minority myth. They need the poor and disadvantaged to fight each other. Because if we unite, we can make it difficult for them."

Southeast Asians are disproving the model-minority myth not just with their difficult lives but with their growing insistence that it takes more than "traditional values" and "personal responsibility" to survive in this country. It takes social supports and participation in the legacy of civil rights activism as well.

The refugees and their children are forging their identities as new Americans and are starting to emerge as a political force. At first, Yang said, "we had no time to think about anything else but our communities—and no one was thinking about us. But now we know that what we were grappling with [affects both] me and my neighbor, who might be poor black, Latino, or Asian. We are no longer refugees, we are Americans. And we know what being 'successful' is: It's being someone who is truly aware of the meaning of freedom to speak out."

8

"Is This a White Country, or What?"

Lillian Rubin

"They're letting all these coloreds come in and soon there won't be any place left for white people," broods Tim Walsh, a thirty-three-year-old white construction worker. "It makes you wonder: Is this a white country, or what?"

It's a question that nags at white America, one perhaps that's articulated most often and most clearly by the men and women of the working class. For it's they who feel most vulnerable, who have suffered the economic contractions of recent decades most keenly, who see the new immigrants most clearly as direct competitors for their jobs.

It's not whites alone who stew about immigrants. Native-born blacks, too, fear the newcomers nearly as much as whites—and for the same economic reasons. But for whites the issue is compounded by race, by the fact that the newcomers are primarily people of color. For them, therefore, their economic anxieties have combined with the changing face of America to create a profound uneasiness about immigration—a theme that was sounded by nearly 90 percent of the whites I met, even by those who are themselves first-generation, albeit well-assimilated, immigrants.

Sometimes they spoke about this in response to my questions; equally often the subject of immigration arose spontaneously as people gave voice to their concerns. But because the new immigrants are dominantly people of color, the discourse was almost always cast in terms of race as well as immigration, with the talk slipping from immigration to race and back again as if these are not two separate phenomena. "If we keep letting all them foreigners in, pretty soon there'll be more of them than us and then what will this country be like?" Tim's wife, Mary Anne, frets. "I mean, this is *our* country, but the way things are going, white people will be the minority in our own country. Now does that make any sense?"

Such fears are not new. Americans have always worried about the strangers who came to our shores, fearing that they would corrupt our society, dilute our culture, debase our values. So I remind Mary Anne, "When your ancestors came here, people also thought we were allowing too many foreigners into the country. Yet those earlier immigrants were successfully integrated into the American society. What's different now?"

"Oh, it's different, all right," she replies without hesitation. "When my people came, the immigrants were all white. That makes a big difference." . . .

Listening to Mary Anne's words I was reminded again how little we Americans look to history for its lessons, how impoverished is our historical memory. For, in fact, being white didn't make "a big difference" for many of those earlier immigrants. The dark-skinned Italians and the eastern European Jews who came in the late nineteenth and early twentieth centuries didn't look very white to the fair-skinned Americans who were here then. Indeed, the same people we now call white—Italians, Jews, Irish—were seen as another race at that time. Not black or Asian, it's true, but an alien other, a race apart, although one that didn't have a clearly defined name. Moreover, the racist fears and fantasies of native-born Americans were far less contained then than they are now, largely because there were few social constraints on their expression.

When, during the nineteenth century, for example, some Italians were taken for blacks and lynched in the South, the incidents passed virtually unnoticed. And if Mary Anne and Tim Walsh, both of Irish ancestry, had come to this country during the great Irish immigration of that period, they would have found themselves defined as an inferior race and described with the same language that was used to characterize blacks: "low-browed and savage, grovelling and bestial, lazy and wild, simian and sensual."[1] Not only during that period but for a long time afterward as well, the U.S. Census Bureau counted the Irish as a distinct and separate group, much as it does today with the category it labels "Hispanic."

But there are two important differences between then and now, differences that can be summed up in a few words: the economy and race. Then, a growing industrial economy meant that there were plenty of jobs for both immigrant and native workers, something that can't be said for the contracting economy in which we live today. True, the arrival of the immigrants, who were more readily exploitable than native workers, put Americans at a disadvantage and created discord between the two groups. Nevertheless, work was available for both.

Then, too, the immigrants—no matter how they were labeled, no matter how reviled they may have been—were ultimately assimilable, if for no other reason than that they were white. As they began to lose their alien ways, it became possible for native Americans to see in the white ethnics of yesteryear a reflection of themselves. Once this shift in perception occurred, it was possible for the nation to incorporate them, to take them in, chew them up, digest them, and spit them out as Americans—with subcultural variations not always to the liking of those who hoped to control the manners and mores of the day, to be sure, but still recognizably white Americans.

Today's immigrants, however, are the racial other in a deep and profound way. . . . And integrating masses of people of color into a society where race consciousness lies at the very heart of our central nervous system raises a whole new set of anxieties and tensions. . . .

The increased visibility of other racial groups has focused whites more self-consciously than ever on their own racial identification. Until the new immigration shifted the complexion of the land so perceptibly, whites didn't think of themselves as white in the same way that Chinese know they're Chinese and African-Americans know they're black. Being white was simply a fact of life, one that didn't require any public statement, since it was the definitive social value against which all others were measured. "It's like everything's changed and I don't know what happened," complains Marianne Bardolino. "All of a sudden you have to be thinking all the time about these race things. I don't remember growing up thinking about being white like I think about it now. I'm not saying I didn't know there were coloreds and whites; it's just that I didn't go along thinking, *Gee, I'm a white person*. I never thought about it at all. But now with all the different colored people around, you have to think about it because they're thinking about it all the time."

"You say you feel pushed now to think about being white, but I'm not sure I understand why. What's changed?" I ask.

"I told you," she replies quickly, a small smile covering her impatience with my question. "It's because they think about what they are, and they want things their way, so now I have to think about what I am and what's good for me and my kids." She pauses briefly to let her thoughts catch up with her tongue, then continues. "I mean, if somebody's always yelling at you about being black or Asian or something, then it makes you think about being white. Like, they want the kids in school to learn about their culture, so then I think about being white and being Italian and say: What about my culture? If they're going to teach about theirs, what about mine?"

To which America's racial minorities respond with bewilderment. "I don't understand what white people want," says Gwen Tomalson. "They say if black kids are going to learn about black culture in school, then white people want their kids to learn about white culture. I don't get it. What do they think kids have been learning about all these years? It's all about white people and how they live and what they accomplished. When I was in school you wouldn't have thought black people existed for all our books ever said about us."

As for the charge that they're "thinking about race all the time," as Marianne Bardolino complains, people of color insist that they're forced into it by a white world that never lets them forget. "If you're Chinese, you can't forget it, even if you want to, because there's always something that reminds you," Carol Kwan's husband, Andrew, remarks tartly. "I mean, if Chinese kids get good grades and get into the university, everybody's worried and you read about it in the papers."

While there's little doubt that racial anxieties are at the center of white concerns, our historic nativism also plays a part in escalating white alarm. The new immigrants bring with them a language and an ethnic culture that's vividly expressed wherever they congregate. And it's this also, the constant reminder of an alien presence from which whites are excluded, that's so troublesome to them.

The nativist impulse isn't, of course, given to the white working class alone. But for those in the upper reaches of the class and status hierarchy—those whose children go to private schools, whose closest contact with public transportation is the taxi cab—the immigrant population supplies a source of cheap labor, whether as nannies for their children, maids in their households, or workers in their businesses. They may grouse and complain that "nobody speaks English anymore," just as working-class people do. But for the people who use immigrant labor, legal or illegal, there's a payoff for the inconvenience—a payoff that doesn't exist for the families in this study but that sometimes costs them dearly. For while it may be true that American workers aren't eager for many of the jobs immigrants are willing to take, it's also true that the presence of a large immigrant population—especially those who come from developing countries where living standards are far below our own—helps to make these jobs undesirable by keeping wages depressed well below what most American workers are willing to accept. . . .

It's not surprising, therefore, that working-class women and men speak so angrily about the recent influx of immigrants. They not only see their jobs and their way of life threatened, they feel bruised and assaulted by an environment that seems suddenly to have turned color and in which they feel like strangers in their own land. So they chafe and complain: "They come here to take advantage of us, but they don't really want to learn our ways," Beverly Sowell, a thirty-three-year-old white electronics assembler, grumbles irritably. "They live different than us; it's like another world how they live. And they're so clannish. They keep to themselves, and they don't even *try* to learn English. You go on the bus these days and you might as well be in a foreign country; everybody's talking some other language, you know, Chinese or Spanish or something. Lots of them have been here a long time, too, but they don't care; they just want to take what they can get."

But their complaints reveal an interesting paradox, an illuminating glimpse into the contradictions that beset native-born Americans in their relations with those who seek refuge here. On the one hand, they scorn the immigrants; on the other, they protest because they "keep to themselves." It's the same contradiction that dominates black-white relations. Whites refuse to integrate blacks but are outraged when they stop knocking at the door, when they move to sustain the separation on their own terms—in black theme houses on campuses, for example, or in the newly developing black middle-class suburbs.

I wondered, as I listened to Beverly Sowell and others like her, why the same people who find the lifeways and languages of our foreign-born population offensive also care whether they "keep to themselves."

"Because like I said, they just shouldn't, that's all," Beverly says stubbornly. "If they're going to come here, they should be willing to learn our ways—you know what I mean, be real Americans. That's what my grandparents did, and that's what they should do."

"But your grandparents probably lived in an immigrant neighborhood when they first came here, too," I remind her.

"It was different," she insists. "I don't know why; it was. They wanted to be Americans; these here people now, I don't think they do. They just want to take advantage of this country. . . .

"Everything's changed, and it doesn't make sense. Maybe you get it, but I don't. We can't take care of our own people and we keep bringing more and more foreigners in. Look at all the homeless. Why do we need more people here when our own people haven't got a place to sleep?"

"Why do we need more people here?"—a question Americans have asked for two centuries now. Historically, efforts to curb immigration have come during economic downturns, which suggests that when times are good, when American workers feel confident about their future, they're likely to be more generous in sharing their good fortune with foreigners. But when the economy falters, as it did in the 1990s and workers worry about having to compete for jobs with people whose standard of living is well below their own, resistance to immigration rises. "Don't get me wrong; I've got nothing against these people," Tim Walsh demurs. "But they don't talk English, and they're used to a lot less, so they can work for less money than guys like me can. I see it all the time; they get hired and some white guy gets left out."

It's this confluence of forces—the racial and cultural diversity of our new immigrant population; the claims on the resources of the nation now being made by those minorities who, for generations, have called America their home; the failure of some of our basic institutions to serve the needs of our people; the contracting economy, which threatens the mobility aspirations of working-class families—all these have come together to leave white workers feeling as if everyone else is getting a piece of the action while they get nothing. "I feel like white people are left out in the cold," protests Diane Johnson, a twenty-eight-year-old white single mother who believes she lost a job as a bus driver to a black woman. "First it's the blacks; now it's all those other colored people, and it's like everything always goes their way. It seems like a white person doesn't have a chance anymore. It's like the squeaky wheel gets the grease, and they've been squeaking and we haven't," she concludes angrily.

Until recently, whites didn't need to think about having to "squeak"—at least not specifically as whites. They have, of course, organized and squeaked at various times in the past—sometimes as ethnic groups, sometimes as workers. But not as whites. As whites they have been the dominant group, the favored ones, the ones who could count on getting the job when people of color could not. Now suddenly there are others—not just individual others but identifiable groups, people who share a history, a language, a culture, even a color—who lay claim to some of the rights and privileges that formerly had been labeled "for whites only." And whites react as if they've been betrayed, as if a sacred promise has been broken. They're white, aren't they? They're *real* Americans, aren't they? This is their country, isn't it?

The answers to these questions used to be relatively unambiguous. But not anymore. Being white no longer automatically assures dominance in the politics of a multiracial society. Ethnic group politics, however, has a long and fruitful history. As whites sought a social and political base on which to stand, therefore, it was natural and logical to reach back to their ethnic past. Then they, too, could be "something"; they also would belong to a group; they would have a name, a history, a culture, and a voice. "Why is it only the blacks or Mexicans or Jews that are 'something'?" asks Tim Walsh. "I'm Irish, isn't that something, too? Why doesn't that count?"

In reclaiming their ethnic roots, whites can recount with pride the tribulations and transcendence of their ancestors and insist that others take their place in the line from which they have only recently come. "My people had a rough time, too. But nobody gave us anything, so why do we owe them something? Let them pull their share like the rest of us had to do," says Al Riccardi, a twenty-nine-year-old white taxi driver.

From there it's only a short step to the conviction that those who don't progress up that line are hampered by nothing more than their own inadequacies or, worse yet, by their unwillingness to take advantage of the opportunities offered them. "Those people, they're hollering all the time about discrimination," Al continues, without defining who "those people" are. "Maybe once a long time ago that was true, but not now. The problem is that a lot of those people are lazy. There's plenty of opportunities, but you've got to be willing to work hard."

He stops a moment, as if listening to his own words, then continues, "Yeah, yeah, I know there's a recession on and lots of people don't have jobs. But it's different with some of those people. They don't really want to work, because if they did, there wouldn't be so many of them selling drugs and getting in all kinds of trouble."

"You keep talking about 'those people' without saying who you mean," I remark.

"Aw c'mon, you know who I'm talking about," he says, his body shifting uneasily in his chair. "It's mostly the black people, but the Spanish ones, too."

In reality, however, it's a no-win situation for America's people of color, whether immigrant or native born. For the industriousness of the Asians comes in for nearly as much criticism as the alleged laziness of other groups. When blacks don't make it, it's because, whites like Al Riccardi insist, their culture doesn't teach respect for family; because they're hedonistic, lazy, stupid, and/or criminally inclined. But when Asians demonstrate their ability to overcome the obstacles of an alien language and culture, when the Asian family seems to be the repository of our most highly regarded traditional values, white hostility doesn't disappear. It just changes its form. Then the accomplishments of Asians, the speed with which they move up the economic ladder, aren't credited to their superior culture, diligence, or intelligence—even when these are granted—but to the fact that they're "single minded," "untrustworthy," "clannish drones," "narrow people" who raise children who are insufficiently "well rounded."[2] . . .

Not surprisingly, as competition increases, the various minority groups often are at war among themselves as they press their own particular claims, fight over turf, and compete for an ever-shrinking piece of the pie. In several African-American communities, where Korean shopkeepers have taken the place once held by Jews, the confrontations have been both wrenching and tragic. A Korean grocer in Los Angeles shoots and kills a fifteen-year-old black girl for allegedly trying to steal some trivial item from the store.[3] From New York City to Berkeley, California, African-Americans boycott Korean shop owners who, they charge, invade their neighborhoods, take their money, and treat them disrespectfully.[4] But painful as these incidents are for those involved, they are only symptoms of a deeper malaise in both communities—the contempt and distrust in which the Koreans hold their African-American neighbors, and the rage of blacks as they watch these new immigrants surpass them.

Latino–black conflict also makes headlines when, in the aftermath of the riots in South Central Los Angeles, the two groups fight over who will get the lion's share of the jobs to rebuild the neighborhood. Blacks, insisting that they're being discriminated against, shut down building projects that don't include them in satisfactory numbers. And indeed, many of the jobs that formerly went to African-Americans are now being taken by Latino workers. In an article entitled "Black vs. Brown," Jack Miles, an editorial writer for the *Los Angeles Times*, reports that "janitorial firms serving downtown Los Angeles have almost entirely replaced their unionized black work force with non-unionized immigrants."[5] . . .

But the disagreements among America's racial minorities are of little interest or concern to most white working-class families. Instead of conflicting groups, they see one large mass of people of color, all of them making claims that endanger their own precarious place in the world. It's this perception that has led some white ethnics to believe that reclaiming their ethnicity alone is not enough, that so long as they remain in their separate and distinct groups, their power will be limited. United, however, they can become a formidable countervailing force, one that can stand fast against the threat posed by minority demands. But to come together solely as whites would diminish their impact and leave them open to the charge that their real purpose is simply to retain the privileges of whiteness. A dilemma that has been resolved, at least for some, by the birth of a new entity in the history of American ethnic groups—the "European-Americans."[6] . . .

At the University of California at Berkeley, for example, white students and their faculty supporters insisted that the recently adopted multicultural curriculum include a unit of study of European-Americans. At Queens College in New York City, where white ethnic groups retain a more distinct presence, Italian-American students launched a successful suit to win recognition as a disadvantaged minority and gain the entitlements accompanying that status, including special units of Italian-American studies.

White high school students, too, talk of feeling isolated and, being less sophisticated and wary than their older sisters and brothers, complain quite openly that there's no acceptable and legitimate way for them to acknowledge a white identity. "There's all these things for all the different ethnicities, you know, like clubs for black kids and Hispanic kids, but there's nothing for me and my friends to join," Lisa Marshall, a sixteen-year-old white high school student, explains with exasperation. "They won't let us have a white club because that's supposed to be racist. So we figured we'd just have to call it something else, you know, some ethnic thing, like Euro-Americans. Why not? They have African-American clubs."

Ethnicity, then, often becomes a cover for "white," not necessarily because these students are racist but because racial identity is now such a prominent feature of the discourse in our social world. In a society where racial consciousness is so high, how else can whites define themselves in ways that connect them to a community and, at the same time, allow them to deny their racial antagonisms?

Ethnicity and race—separate phenomena that are now inextricably entwined. Incorporating newcomers has never been easy, as our history of controversy and violence over immigration tells us.[7] But for the first time, the new immigrants are also people of color, which means that they tap both the nativist and racist impulses that are so deeply a part of American life. As in the past, however, the fear of foreigners, the revulsion against their strange customs and seemingly unruly ways, is only part of the reason for the anti-immigrant attitudes that are increasingly being expressed today. For whatever xenophobic suspicions may arise in modern America, economic issues play a critical role in stirring them up.

NOTES

1. David R. Roediger, *The Wages of Whiteness* (New York: Verso, 1991), p. 133.
2. These were, and often still are, the commonly held stereotypes about Jews. Indeed, the Asian immigrants are often referred to as "the new Jews."
3. Soon Ja Du, the Korean grocer who killed fifteen-year-old Latasha Harlins, was found guilty of voluntary manslaughter, for which she was sentenced to four hundred hours

of community service, a $500 fine, reimbursement of funeral costs to the Harlins family, and five years' probation.

4. The incident in Berkeley didn't happen in the black ghetto, as most of the others did. There, the Korean grocery store is near the University of California campus, and the woman involved in the incident is an African-American university student who was Maced by the grocer after an argument over a penny.

5. Jack Miles, "Blacks vs. Browns," *Atlantic Monthly* (October 1992), pp. 41–68.

6. For an interesting analysis of what he calls "the transformation of ethnicity," see Richard D. Alba, *Ethnic Identity* (New Haven, CT: Yale University Press, 1990).

7. In the past, many of those who agitated for a halt to immigration were immigrants or native-born children of immigrants. The same often is true today. As anti-immigrant sentiment grows, at least some of those joining the fray are relatively recent arrivals. One man in this study, for example—a fifty-two-year-old immigrant from Hungary—is one of the leaders of an anti-immigration group in the city where he lives.

REFERENCES

Alba, Richard D. *Ethnic Identity.* New Haven: Yale University Press, 1990.
Roediger, David R. *The Wages of Whiteness.* New York: Verso, 1991.

9

PERSONAL VOICES: FACING UP TO RACE

Carrie Ching

Abercrombie and Fitch is back on the hotseat—this time for racial discrimination in hiring practices. Last year the company was forced to pull T-shirts sporting slant-eyed Chinese laundrymen and the slogan "Two Wongs can make it white" when Asian-Americans protested. This time the stakes are higher. Nine Latino and Asian plaintiffs are suing Abercrombie for only hiring white people for sales floor jobs and pushing black, Latino and Asian applicants into stockroom jobs to project what the clothing company calls the "classic American look."

Used with permission of AlterNet.org.

Here we go again. The media and American public are shaking their heads at the company, but this is hardly a new phenomenon. The case is simply another manifestation of the prevalent belief that "American" still means white. But instead of pointing fingers at flagrant offenders like Abercrombie, we should instead look in the mirror to examine the ways that we all participate on a daily basis in this racist hierarchy that places whites in the center and pushes those whose backgrounds are more "ethnic" to the margins.

Think about it. When you go to an expensive restaurant, the managers and servers are almost always white, while the busboys and kitchen help are almost always people of color. At most offices the managers are usually white, while people of color appear only among the interns and junior staff. Often when you drive by the carwash you'll see white and light-skinned people fanning themselves in plastic chairs while brown-skinned people are scrubbing tires and windshields. Diversity is great, but only when it happens at the lower levels of an organization so as not to challenge the skewed balance of power. The signs are everywhere: Race still plays a major if unspoken role in the way our society is organized.

Yet there are many people—mostly white—who refuse to believe this is true. Two students in my evening class told me recently that they didn't believe race was an issue anymore in America, or at least, not in the San Francisco Bay Area. The two are both white, liberal, educated, upper middle-class professionals in their 50s, and both live in exclusive neighborhoods in the Bay Area. Their argument: Since race relations are so much better today than they were thirty years ago, what are all these angry people of color complaining about? Besides, one of them argued, isn't inequality in America based much more on class than race?

It's true that race relations must be better than they were thirty years ago—as a biracial person I probably wouldn't even be alive if they weren't. But someone who thinks that race is a dead issue must have their head buried pretty deep in the sand, or more appropriately, pretty deep in a wealthy white neighborhood.

I asked the students why a person whose great-great-grandfather emigrated from China 150 years ago is still called an "Asian-American," while a person whose father emigrated from Germany fifty years ago becomes just a plain old "American" in one generation—not a "German-American" or a "European-American." We're all pretty recent transplants here (unless you're indigenous), so why is it that only people of color are forced to face up to their histories of migration? Why is it that people of color are still treated like visitors in their own home? Because being American is still very much about being white.

I'm so tired of hearing these kinds of things from white people. It's like a skinny person saying that fat people aren't discriminated against, or a man claiming that there's no such thing as gender inequality. Is it so difficult to understand? One of the perks of being in a privileged position is that you don't have to think about it.

Racism is so ingrained in our dominant culture that we don't even recognize it for what it is anymore. And we're so squeamish about talking about race that we avoid it at all costs. So we tell ourselves that the profiling of Arabs and other brown-skinned people as potential terrorists is about weeding out religious fanatics, not about race. And although the low-income housing projects in town are filled almost entirely with black men, women and children who ride the bus, while the neighborhoods of trendy boutiques and overpriced cafes are filled with mostly white professionals who drive brand new SUVs, it has nothing to do with race and historic oppression; it's all about class, work ethic, and levels of education, right?

One of the most common arguments I hear against race-based affirmative action is this whole theory that the race problem has been solved and that inequality today falls much more along the lines of class.

I'm not trying to downplay the role of economic class in creating divisions in our society, but I don't think class and race can be compared side-by-side as equally weighted factors. When we compare the struggles of a working-class white person to a middle-class or affluent black, Asian or Latino person, we forget the fundamental difference between class and race: class is mutable, race is not. So if a working-class white man puts on the right clothes, has the right connections, and gets the right education, he can transcend his class status and slip into a "white-collar" world because his skin color allows him to be somewhat "invisible." But no matter how much money or education an affluent black, Asian, or Latino man or woman acquires, in today's America, they will still be treated like a second-class citizen or an "other" in most elite social and professional circles. Many white parents would be less upset if their kid brought home a girlfriend or boyfriend from a different tax bracket than someone who is Korean, black, Arab or Mexican. Let's not forget that up until 1967 it was still illegal in sixteen states for people from different racial backgrounds to marry.

We make these arguments about class so that we won't have to face up to two of the most painful—yet obvious—truths about the society we live in: (1) Our dominant culture is built upon a racist ideology that sustains and promotes a race-based power hierarchy, and (2) by not acknowledging the hierarchy that we all participate in, we help reinforce that racist hegemony every day. What a tangled web of lies we weave.

Yet just acknowledging and wanting to change a culture of racism is only half the battle. Taking responsibility for how it plays out in our private lives is somewhat more challenging. This entails taking an honest look at our friendships and romantic relationships and examining how larger forces shape our desires and social interactions. Because even though most of us refuse to admit it, attraction isn't colorblind.

I agree with critics who say that just having "friends" of a different color doesn't necessarily make you a more open-minded person. I know plenty of people who pull the "I have a black/Chinese/Cherokee friend" card when the cocktail party discussion turns to race, yet their circle of close friends and their history of dating reveals they've never ventured outside of their own kind in their most intimate relationships (see blackpeopleloveus.com for more on this topic). Tokenism is never a pretty sight, particularly when you're the token. On the other hand, you have to start somewhere, and taking the risk of getting to know someone of a different race or ethnicity is at least a step in the right direction.

What I bump up against time and time again is this sort of white liberal hypocrisy, where people stick to their own in their private lives, yet claim they feel solidarity with groups of indigenous people halfway across the globe with whom they will never have a meaningful conversation. This was an ongoing theme at my predominantly white and very liberal university, where everyone was in solidarity with the Zapatistas in Chiapas and the factory workers in China and the starving children in Africa. But when discussions about the sorry state of diversity on our own campus or the racist undercurrents (including an active KKK that regularly distributed leaflets) of the town itself came up, people could only shift uncomfortably in their seats. It's too easy to claim solidarity with people of different backgrounds from afar—you don't have to take chances and endure the discomfort of having your own perspective and unconscious assumptions about race challenged. Examining and breaking down the racial boundaries in our personal lives is just as important as addressing injustices on a global scale.

Now that I've graduated and moved to San Francisco, I've found the same willful blindness in the workplace—particularly within the news media. We pay a lot of lip-service to fighting racial discrimination and the need for diversity, yet there are few to no people of color in high-level positions on the masthead.

We want so badly to believe that institutional racism is something that is going on "out there" in the world, when in fact it has tangled roots in our private lives. Whether we want to acknowledge it or not we all have a choice to be either accomplices or everyday revolutionaries. It's time to face the fact that the small, unconscious choices we make in our private lives—like who we feel safe sitting next to on the bus, who we choose to be our colleagues at work, and yes, even who we choose as our intimate friends and lovers—become the blueprints for the shape and color of our society as a whole.

Suggestions for Further Reading

Foner, Nancy. *New Immigrants in New York.* New York: Columbia University Press, 2001.

Fox, Geoffrey F. *Hispanic Nation: Culture, Politics and the Constructing of Identity.* University of Arizona Press, 1997.

Lee, Stacy J. *Unraveling the "Model Minority" Stereotype: Listening to Asian American Youth.* New York: Teachers College Press, 1996.

Morales, Ed. *Living in Spanglish: The Search for Latino Identity in America.* New York: St. Martin's Press, 2003.

Pedraza, Siliva, and Ruben Rumbaut. *Origins and Destinies: Immigration, Race, and Ethnicity in America.* Florence, KY: Wadsworth, 1995.

Portes, Alejandro. *Legacies: The Immigrant Second Generation.* Berkeley: University of California Press, 2001.

Roediger, David R. *Working Towards Whiteness: How America's Immigrants Become White. The Strange Journey from Ellis Island to the Suburbs.* New York: Basic Books, 2005.

Schmid, Carol L. *The Politics of Language: Conflict, Identity and Cultural Pluralism in Comparative Perspective.* New York: Oxford University Press, 2001.

Schmidt, Ronald, Sr. *Language Policy and Identity Politics in the United States.* Philadelphia: Temple University Press, 2000.

Sniderman, Paul M., and Thomas Piazza. *Black Pride, Black Prejudice.* Princeton University Press, 2002.

Suarez-Orozco, Marcele M., and Mariela M. Paez, eds. *Latinos: Remaking America.* University of California Press and Harvard University, David Rockefeller Center of Latin American Studies, 2002.

Tuan, Mia. *Forever Foreigners or Honorary Whites? The Asian American Experience Today.* New Brunswick, NJ: Rutgers University Press, 1999.

Waldinger, Roger. *Strangers at the Gates.* Berkeley: University of California Press, 2001.

PART IV

Discrimination in Everyday Life

The systems of oppression we have been studying, racism, sexism, heterosexism, and class privilege, express themselves in everyday life in a variety of ways. Sometimes they are reflected in the prejudiced attitudes that people carry with them into the workplace or the community, sometimes they erupt in racist, sexist, or homophobic utterances that reach us across the playground or through our car radio. Sometimes they are in evidence in the discriminatory policies and practices of government and business as they carry out their routine operations. In Part IV of the text we will have an opportunity to read newspaper stories and other materials that describe discrimination against individuals or groups because of their race/ethnicity, gender, sexual orientation, class position, or some combination of these.

Refusing to hire a qualified person because of his or her race/ethnicity, gender, or sexual orientation, or refusing to rent that person an apartment or sell them a home, are fairly straightforward examples of discrimination. Most people would agree that such behavior is unfair or unjust. But once we move beyond these clear-cut cases, it becomes difficult to reach agreement. Is the joke told by a popular radio personality that portrays women or gays in a derogatory way sexist, racist, and homophobic, or is it merely a joke? Does the fact that most major U.S. corporations have few if any women in senior management positions in itself indicate discriminatory hiring policies? Is the underrepresentation of women of all colors and men of color in the United States

Congress de facto evidence of racism and sexism in society, or does it merely reflect a shortage of qualified individuals? Who determines what it means to be qualified? How do we arrive at the criteria according to which students are admitted to colleges and professional schools, or by which senior management is hired? Is it possible that the very criteria employed already reflect a subtle but pervasive race, class, and gender bias? Can individuals and institutions be racist, sexist, and homophobic in the course of their normal, everyday operation quite apart from—even without—their conscious or explicit intent? These are just some of the questions that are raised by the newspaper articles that appear in Part IV.

Selection 1 is an excerpt from a 1981 report issued by the United States Commission on Civil Rights. It provides a historical overview of the kinds of discrimination against women and "minorities" that is part of our shared history. In addition, it offers some categories and distinctions that will prove useful as we read about the cases in the news articles that follow. According to this report, discrimination can take many forms. It can exist at the level of individual attitudes and behavior, as when a doctor refuses to treat patients because of their sexual orientation. It can be carried out through the routine application of the rules, policies, and practices of organizations when they unfairly prevent members of certain groups from, for example, receiving a promotion or being given highly valued work assignments. And it can be carried out by the day-to-day, unexamined practices of schools, government agencies, and other institutions so that it is so pervasive within the social structure as to constitute structural discrimination. Structural discrimination refers to an interlocking cycle of discrimination where discrimination in one area, for example, education, leads to discrimination in other areas, such as employment and housing, creating a cycle of discrimination and disadvantage from which it is difficult to emerge.

As the articles in this part make clear, discrimination of every type is a fact of life in every area of contemporary society. Why then do so many people, in particular, so many young people, seem to believe that racism and sexism are largely things of the past? Perhaps because so many people mistakenly believe that whether an act is discriminatory or racist can be determined by examining the motives of the person involved rather than by looking at the consequences of the act itself. (If you haven't already looked at the Tatum and Bonilla-Silva articles in Part II, you might want to do so now.) In fact, racism and sexism can be unintentional as well as intentional and good people who mean well can inadvertently do and say things that are racist and sexist or homophobic. For example, the recruiter who fails to hire a woman because they believe that women will be uncomfortable functioning within the prevailing company culture, may indeed have meant well, but intentions aside, this is a clear example of discrimination because it effectively denies women access to certain jobs. If the company culture is not welcoming to women, the right thing to do is to change that culture, not to deny women employment.

As the members of the U.S. Commission on Civil Rights point out, even superficially "color-blind" or "gender-neutral," organizational practices can result in placing women and men of color or white women at a disadvantage. Seemingly innocuous height requirements for a particular job may discriminate disproportionately against members of certain ethnic groups or women; "standard" ways of posting job openings may exclude those who are not part of the "old boys' network," and even those of us who mean no harm can reinforce heterosexism, racism, sexism, or class privilege by our unexamined and seemingly innocent choices. As the news clippings and other articles in this part make clear, racism, sexism, heterosexism, and class privilege are part of both our past and our present, part of our history and part of everyday life. Learning to recognize discrimination is an essential prerequisite for acting to end it.

THE PROBLEM
Discrimination

U.S. Commission on Civil Rights

Making choices is an essential part of everyday life for individuals and organizations. These choices are shaped in part by social structures that set standards and influence conduct in such areas as education, employment, housing, and government. When these choices limit the opportunities available to people because of their race, sex, or national origin, the problem of discrimination arises.

Historically, discrimination against minorities and women was not only accepted but it was also governmentally required. The doctrine of white supremacy used to support the institution of slavery was so much a part of American custom and policy that the Supreme Court in 1857 approvingly concluded that both the North and the South regarded slaves "as beings of an inferior order, and altogether unfit to associate with the white race, either in social or political relations; and so far inferior, that they had no rights which the white man was bound to respect."[1] White supremacy survived the passage of the Civil War amendments to the Constitution and continued to dominate legal and social institutions in the North as well as the South to disadvantage not only blacks,[2] but other racial and ethnic groups as well—American Indians, Alaskan Natives, Asian and Pacific Islanders and Hispanics.[3]

While minorities were suffering from white supremacy, women were suffering from male supremacy. Mr. Justice Brennan has summed up the legal disabilities imposed on women this way:

> [T]hroughout much of the 19th century the position of women in our society was, in many respects, comparable to that of blacks under the pre–Civil War slave codes. Neither slaves nor women could hold office, serve on juries, or bring suit in their own names, and married women traditionally were denied the legal capacity to hold or convey property or to serve as legal guardians of their own children.[4]

In 1873 a member of the Supreme Court proclaimed, "Man is, or should be, woman's protector and defender. The natural and proper timidity and delicacy which belongs to the female sex evidently unfits it for many of the occupations of civil life."[5] Such romantic paternalism has alternated with fixed notions of male

From *Affirmative Action in the 1980s*. U.S. Commission on Civil Rights 65 (January 1981): 9–15.

superiority to deny women in law and in practice the most fundamental of rights, including the right to vote, which was not granted until 1920;[6] the Equal Rights Amendment has yet to be ratified.[7]

White and male supremacy are no longer popularly accepted American values. The blatant racial and sexual discrimination that originated in our conveniently forgotten past, however, continues to manifest itself today in a complex interaction of attitudes and actions of individuals, organizations, and the network of social structures that make up our society.

Individual Discrimination

The most common understanding of discrimination rests at the level of prejudiced individual attitudes and behavior. Although open and intentional prejudice persists, individual discriminatory conduct is often hidden and sometimes unintentional.[8] Some of the following are examples of deliberately discriminatory actions by consciously prejudiced individuals. Some are examples of unintentionally discriminatory actions taken by persons who may not believe themselves to be prejudiced but whose decisions continue to be guided by deeply ingrained discriminatory customs.

- Personnel officers whose stereotyped beliefs about women and minorities justify hiring them for low level and low paying jobs exclusively, regardless of their potential experience or qualifications for higher level jobs.[9]
- Administrators, historically white males, who rely on "word-of-mouth" recruiting among their friends and colleagues, so that only their friends and protégés of the same race and sex learn of potential job openings.[10]
- Employers who hire women for their sexual attractiveness or potential sexual availability rather than their competence, and employers who engage in sexual harassment of their female employees.[11]
- Teachers who interpret linguistic and cultural differences as indications of low potential or lack of academic interest on the part of minority students.[12]
- Guidance counselors and teachers whose low expectations lead them to steer female and minority students away from "hard" subjects, such as mathematics and science, toward subjects that do not prepare them for higher paying jobs.[13]
- Real estate agents who show fewer homes to minority buyers and steer them to minority or mixed neighborhoods because they believe white residents would oppose the presence of black neighbors.[14]
- Families who assume that property values inevitably decrease when minorities move in and therefore move out of their neighborhoods if minorities do move in.[15]
- Parole boards that assume minority offenders to be more dangerous or more unreliable than white offenders and consequently more frequently deny parole to minorities than to whites convicted of equally serious crimes.[16]

These contemporary examples of discrimination may not be motivated by conscious prejudice. The personnel manager is likely to deny believing that minorities and women can only perform satisfactorily in low level jobs and at the same time allege that other executives and decision makers would not consider them for higher level positions. In some cases, the minority or female applicants may not be aware that they have been discriminated against—the personnel manager may inform them that they are deficient in experience while rejecting their applications because of prejudice; the white male administrator who recruits by word-of-mouth from his friends or white male work force excludes minorities and women who never learn of the available positions. The discriminatory results these activities cause may not even be desired. The guidance counselor may honestly believe there are no other realistic alternatives for minority and female students.

Whether conscious or not, open or hidden, desired or undesired, these acts build on and support prejudicial stereotypes, deny their victims opportunities provided to others, and perpetuate discrimination, regardless of intent.

Organizational Discrimination

Discrimination, though practiced by individuals, is often reinforced by the well-established rules, policies, and practices of organizations. These actions are often regarded simply as part of the organization's way of doing business and are carried out by individuals as just part of their day's work.

Discrimination at the organizational level takes forms that are similar to those on the individual level. For example:

- Height and weight requirements that are unnecessarily geared to the physical proportions of white males and, therefore, exclude females and some minorities from certain jobs.[17]
- Seniority rules, when applied to jobs historically held only by white males, make more recently hired minorities and females more subject to layoff—the "last hired, first fired" employee—and less eligible for advancement.[18]
- Nepotistic membership policies of some referral unions that exclude those who are not relatives of members who, because of past employment practices, are usually white.[19]
- Restrictive employment leave policies, coupled with prohibitions on part-time work or denials of fringe benefits to part-time workers, that make it difficult for the heads of single parent families, most of whom are women, to get and keep jobs and meet the needs of their families.[20]
- The use of standardized academic tests or criteria, geared to the cultural and educational norms of the middle-class or white males, that are not relevant indicators of successful job performance.[21]
- Preferences shown by many law and medical schools in the admission of children of wealthy and influential alumni, nearly all of whom are white.[22]

- Credit policies of banks and lending institutions that prevent the granting of mortgage monies and loans in minority neighborhoods, or prevent the granting of credit to married women and others who have previously been denied the opportunity to build good credit histories in their own names.[23]

Superficially "color-blind" or "gender-neutral," these organizational practices have an adverse effect on minorities and women. As with individual actions, these organizational actions favor white males, even when taken with no conscious intent to affect minorities and women adversely, by protecting and promoting the status quo arising from the racism and sexism of the past. If, for example, the jobs now protected by "last hired, first fired" provisions had always been integrated, seniority would not operate to disadvantage minorities and women. If educational systems from kindergarten through college had not historically favored white males, many more minorities and women would hold advanced degrees and thereby be included among those involved in deciding what academic tests should test for. If minorities had lived in the same neighborhoods as whites, there would be no minority neighborhoods to which mortgage money could be denied on the basis of their being minority neighborhoods.

In addition, these barriers to minorities and women too often do not fulfill legitimate needs of the organization, or these needs can be met through other means that adequately maintain the organization without discriminating. Instead of excluding all women on the assumption that they are too weak or should be protected from strenuous work, the organization can implement a reasonable test that measures the strength actually needed to perform the job or, where possible, develop ways of doing the work that require less physical effort. Admissions to academic and professional schools can be decided not only on the basis of grades, standardized test scores, and the prestige of the high school or college from which the applicant graduated, but also on the basis of community service, work experience, and letters of recommendation. Lending institutions can look at the individual and his or her financial ability rather than the neighborhood or marital status of the prospective borrower.

Some practices that disadvantage minorities and women are readily accepted aspects of everyday behavior. Consider the "old boy" network in business and education built on years of friendship and social contact among white males, or the exchanges of information and corporate strategies by business acquaintances in racially or sexually exclusive country clubs and locker rooms paid for by the employer.[24] These actions, all of which have a discriminatory impact on minorities and women, are not necessarily acts of conscious prejudice. Because such actions are so often considered part of the "normal" way of doing things, people have difficulty recognizing that they are discriminating and therefore resist abandoning these practices despite the clearly discriminatory results. Consequently, many decision makers have difficulty considering, much less accepting, nondiscriminatory alternatives that may work just as well or better to advance legitimate organizational interests but without systematically disadvantaging minorities and women.

This is not to suggest that all such discriminatory organizational actions are spurious or arbitrary. Many may serve the actual needs of the organization. Physical size or strength at times may be a legitimate job requirement; sick leave and insurance policies must be reasonably restricted; educational qualifications are needed for many jobs; lending institutions cannot lend to people who cannot reasonably demonstrate an ability to repay loans. Unless carefully examined and then modified or eliminated, however, these apparently neutral rules, policies, and practices will continue to perpetuate age-old discriminatory patterns into the structure of today's society.

Whatever the motivation behind such organizational acts, a process is occurring, the common denominator of which is unequal results on a very large scale. When unequal outcomes are repeated over time and in numerous societal and geographical areas, it is a clear signal that a discriminatory process is at work.

Such discrimination is not a static, one-time phenomenon that has a clearly limited effect. Discrimination can feed on discrimination in self-perpetuating cycles.[25]

- The employer who recruits job applicants by word-of-mouth within a predominantly white male work force reduces the chances of receiving applications from minorities and females for open positions. Since they do not apply, they are not hired. Since they are not hired, they are not present when new jobs become available. Since they are not aware of new jobs, they cannot recruit other minority or female applicants. Because there are no minority or female employees to recruit others, the employer is left to recruit on his own from among his predominantly white and male work force.[26]

- The teacher who expects poor academic performance from minority and female students may not become greatly concerned when their grades are low. The acceptance of their low grades removes incentives to improve. Without incentives to improve, their grades remain low. Their low grades reduce their expectations, and the teacher has no basis for expecting more of them.[27]

- The realtor who assumes that white home owners do not want minority neighbors "steers" minorities to minority neighborhoods. Those steered to minority neighborhoods tend to live in minority neighborhoods. White neighborhoods then remain white, and realtors tend to assume that whites do not want minority neighbors.[28]

- Elected officials appoint voting registrars who impose linguistic, geographic, and other barriers to minority voter registration. Lack of minority registration leads to low voting rates. Lower minority voting rates lead to the election of fewer minorities. Fewer elected minorities leads to the appointment of voting registrars who maintain the same barriers.[29]

Structural Discrimination

Such self-sustaining discriminatory processes occur not only within the fields of employment, education, housing, and government but also between these structural areas. There is a classic cycle of structural discrimination that reproduces itself.

Discrimination in education denies the credentials to get good jobs. Discrimination in employment denies the economic resources to buy good housing. Discrimination in housing confines minorities to school districts providing inferior education, closing the cycle in a classic form.[30]

With regard to white women, the cycle is not as tightly closed. To the extent they are raised in families headed by white males, and are married to or live with white males, white women will enjoy the advantages in housing and other areas that such relationships to white men can confer. White women lacking the sponsorship of white men, however, will be unable to avoid gender-based discrimination in housing, education, and employment. White women can thus be the victims of discrimination produced by social structures that is comparable in form to that experienced by minorities.

This perspective is not intended to imply that either the dynamics of discrimination or its nature and degree are identical for women and minorities. But when a woman of any background seeks to compete with men of any group, she finds herself the victim of a discriminatory process. Regarding the similarities and differences between the discrimination experienced by women and minorities, one author has aptly stated:

> [W]hen two groups exist in a situation of inequality, it may be self-defeating to become embroiled in a quarrel over which is more unequal or the victim of greater oppression. The more salient question is how a condition of inequality for both is maintained and perpetuated—through what means is it reinforced?[31]

The following are additional examples of the interaction between social structures that affect minorities and women:

- The absence of minorities and women from executive, writing, directing, news reporting, and acting positions in television contributes to unfavorable stereotyping on the screen, which in turn reinforces existing stereotypes among the public and creates psychological roadblocks to progress in employment, education, and housing.[32]

- Living in inner-city high crime areas in disproportionate numbers, minorities, particularly minority youth, are more likely to be arrested and are more likely to go to jail than whites accused of similar offenses, and their arrest and conviction records are then often used as bars to employment.[33]

- Because of past discrimination against minorities and women, female and minority-headed businesses are often small and relatively new. Further disadvantaged by contemporary credit and lending practices, they are more likely than white male–owned businesses to remain small and be less able to employ full-time specialists in applying for government contracts. Because they cannot monitor the availability of government contracts, they do not receive such contracts. Because they cannot demonstrate success with government contracts, contracting officers tend to favor other firms that have more experience with government contracts.[34]

Discriminatory actions by individuals and organizations are not only pervasive, occurring in every sector of society, but also cumulative with effects limited neither to the time nor the particular structural area in which they occur. This process of discrimination, therefore, extends across generations, across organizations, and across social structures in self-reinforcing cycles, passing the disadvantages incurred by one generation in one area to future generations in many related areas.[35]

These interrelated components of the discriminatory process share one basic result: the persistent gaps seen in the status of women and minorities relative to that of white males. These unequal results themselves have real consequences. The employer who wishes to hire more minorities and women may be bewildered by charges of racism and sexism when confronted by what appears to be a genuine shortage of qualified minority and female applicants. The guidance counselor who sees one promising minority student after another drop out of school or give up in despair may be resentful of allegations of racism when there is little he or she alone can do for the student. The banker who denies a loan to a female single parent may wish to do differently, but believes that prudent fiscal judgment requires taking into account her lack of financial history and inability to prove that she is a good credit risk. These and other decision makers see the results of a discriminatory process repeated over and over again, and those results provide a basis for rationalizing their own actions, which then feed into that same process.

When seen outside the context of the interlocking and intertwined effects of discrimination, complaints that many women and minorities are absent from the ranks of qualified job applicants, academically inferior and unmotivated, poor credit risks, and so forth, may appear to be justified. Decision makers like those described above are reacting to real social problems stemming from the process of discrimination. But many too easily fall prey to stereotyping and consequently disregard those minorities and women who have the necessary skills or qualifications. And they erroneously "blame the victims" of discrimination,[36] instead of examining the past and present context in which their own actions are taken and the multiple consequences of these actions on the lives of minorities and women.

The Process of Discrimination

Although discrimination is maintained through individual actions, neither individual prejudices nor random chance can fully explain the persistent national patterns of inequality and underrepresentation. Nor can these patterns be blamed on the persons who are at the bottom of our economic, political, and social order. Overt racism and sexism as embodied in popular notions of white and male supremacy have been widely repudiated, but our history of discrimination based on race, sex, and national origin has not been readily put aside. Past discrimination continues to have present effects. The task today is to identify those effects and the forms and dynamics of the discrimination that produced them.

Discrimination against minorities and women must now be viewed as an interlocking process involving the attitudes and actions of individuals and the organizations and social structures that guide individual behavior. That process, started by past events, now routinely bestows privileges, favors, and advantages on white males and imposes disadvantages and penalties on minorities and women. This process is also self-perpetuating. Many normal, seemingly neutral, operations of our society create stereotyped expectations that justify unequal results; unequal results in one area foster inequalities in opportunity and accomplishment in others; the lack of opportunity and accomplishment confirms the original prejudices or engenders new ones that fuel the normal operations generating unequal results.

As we have shown, the process of discrimination involves many aspects of our society. No single factor sufficiently explains it, and no single means will suffice to eliminate it. Such elements of our society as our history of *de jure* discrimination, deeply ingrained prejudices,[37] inequities based on economic and social class,[38] and the structure and function of all our economic, social, and political institutions[39] must be continually examined in order to understand their part in shaping today's decisions that will either maintain or counter the current process of discrimination.

It may be difficult to identify precisely all aspects of the discriminatory process and assign those parts their appropriate importance. But understanding discrimination starts with an awareness that such a process exists and that to avoid perpetuating it, we must carefully assess the context and consequences of our everyday actions. . . .

NOTES

1. Dred Scott v. Sandford, 60 U.S. (19 How.) 393, 408 (1857).
2. For a concise summary of this history, see U.S. Commission on Civil Rights, *Twenty Years After Brown*, pp. 4–29 (1975); *Freedom to the Free: 1863, Century of Emancipation* (1963).
3. The discriminatory conditions experienced by these minority groups have been documented in the following publications by the U.S. Commission on Civil Rights: *The Navajo Nation: An American Colony* (1975); *The Southwest Indian Report* (1973); *The Forgotten Minority: Asian Americans in New York City* (State Advisory Committee Report 1977); *Success of Asian Americans: Fact or Fiction?* (1980); *Stranger in One's Land* (1970); *Toward Quality Education for Mexican Americans* (1974); *Puerto Ricans in the Continental United States: An Uncertain Future* (1976).
4. Frontiero v. Richardson, 411 U.S. 677, 684–86 (1973), citing L. Kanowitz, *Women and the Law: The Unfinished Revolution*, pp. 5–6 (1970), and G. Myrdal, *An American Dilemma* 1073 (20th Anniversary Ed., 1962). Justice Brennan wrote the opinion of the Court, joined by Justices Douglas, White, and Marshall. Justice Stewart concurred in the judgment. Justice Powell, joined by Chief Justice Burger and Justice Blackmun, wrote a separate concurring opinion. Justice Rehnquist dissented. See also H. M. Hacker, "Women as a Minority Group," *Social Forces*, vol. 30 (1951), pp. 60–69; W. Chafe, *Women and Equality: Changing Patterns in American Culture* (New York: Oxford University Press, 1977).
5. Bradwell v. State, 83 U.S. (16 Wall) 130, 141 (1873) (Bradley, J., concurring), quoted in *Frontiero, supra* note 4.
6. U.S. Const. amend. XIX.
7. See U.S. Commission on Civil Rights, *Statement on the Equal Rights Amendment* (December 1978).

8. See, e.g., R. K. Merton, "Discrimination and the American Creed," in R. K. Merton, *Sociological Ambivalence and Other Essays* (New York: The Free Press, 1976), pp. 189–216. In this essay on racism, published for the first time more than 30 years ago, Merton presented a typology which introduced the notion that discriminatory actions are not always directly related to individual attitudes of prejudice. Merton's typology consisted of the following: Type I—the unprejudiced nondiscriminator; Type II—the unprejudiced discriminator; Type III—the prejudiced nondiscriminator; Type IV—the prejudiced discriminator. In the present context, Type II is crucial in its observation that discrimination is often practiced by persons who are not themselves prejudiced, but who respond to, or do not oppose, the actions of those who discriminate because of prejudiced attitudes (Type IV). See also D. C. Reitzes, "Prejudice and Discrimination: A Study in Contradictions," in *Racial and Ethnic Relations*, ed. H. M. Hughes (Boston: Allyn and Bacon, 1970), pp. 56–65.

9. See R. M. Kanter and B. A. Stein, "Making a Life at the Bottom," in *Life in Organizations, Workplaces as People Experience Them*, ed. Kanter and Stein (New York: Basic Books, 1976), pp. 176–90; also L. K. Howe, "Retail Sales Worker," ibid., pp. 248–51; also R. M. Kanter, *Men and Women of the Corporation* (New York: Basic Books, 1977).

10. See M. S. Granovetter, *Getting a Job: A Study of Contract and Careers* (Cambridge: Harvard University Press, 1974), pp. 6–11; also A. W. Blumrosen, *Black Employment and the Law* (New Brunswick, N.J.: Rutgers University Press, 1971), p. 232.

11. See U.S. Equal Employment Opportunity Commission, "Guidelines on Discrimination Because of Sex," 29 C.F.R. §1604.4 (1979); L. Farley, *Sexual Shakedown: The Sexual Harassment of Women on the Job* (New York: McGraw-Hill, 1978), pp. 92–96, 176–79; C. A. Mackinnon, *Sexual Harassment of Working Women* (New Haven: Yale University Press, 1979), pp. 25–55.

12. See R. Rosenthal and L. F. Jacobson, "Teacher Expectations for the Disadvantaged," *Scientific American*, 1968 (b) 218, 219–23; also D. Bar Tal, "Interactions of Teachers and Pupils," in *New Approaches to Social Problems*, ed. I. H. Frieze, D. Bar Tal, and J. S. Carrol (San Francisco: Jossey Bass, 1979), pp. 337–58; also U.S. Commission on Civil Rights, *Teachers and Students, Report V: Mexican American Education Study. Differences in Teacher Interaction with Mexican American and Anglo Students* (1973), pp. 22–23.

13. Ibid.

14. U.S. Department of Housing and Urban Development, "Measuring Racial Discrimination in American Housing Markets: The Housing Market Practices Survey" (1979); D. M. Pearce, "Gatekeepers and Home Seekers: Institutional Patterns in Racial Steering," *Social Problems*, vol. 26 (1979), pp. 325–42; "Benign Steering and Benign Quotas: The Validity of Race Conscious Government Policies to Promote Residential Integration," 93 *Harv. L. Rev.* 938, 944 (1980).

15. See M. N. Danielson, *The Politics of Exclusion* (New York: Columbia University Press, 1976), pp. 11–12; U.S. Commission on Civil Rights, *Equal Opportunity in Suburbia* (1974).

16. See L. L. Knowles and K. Prewitt, eds., *Institutional Racism in America* (Englewood Cliffs, N.J.: Prentice Hall, 1969), pp. 58–77, and E. D. Wright, *The Politics of Punishment* (New York: Harper and Row, 1973). Also, S. V. Brown, "Race and Parole Hearing Outcomes," in *Discrimination in Organizations*, ed. R. Alvarez and K. G. Lutterman (San Francisco: Jossey Bass, 1979), pp. 355–74.

17. Height and weight minimums that disproportionately exclude women without a showing of legitimate job requirement constitute unlawful sex discrimination. See Dothard v. Rawlinson, 433 U.S. 321 (1977); Bowe v. Colgate Palmolive Co., 416 F.2d 711 (7th Cir.

1969). Minimum height requirements used in screening applicants for employment have also been held to be unlawful where such a requirement excludes a significantly higher percentage of Hispanics than other national origin groups in the labor market and no job relatedness is shown. See Smith v. City of East Cleveland, 520 F.2d 492 (6th Cir. 1975).

18. U.S. Commission on Civil Rights, *Last Hired, First Fired* (1976); Tangren v. Wackenhut Servs., Inc., 480 F. Supp. 539 (D. Nev. 1979).

19. U.S. Commission on Civil Rights, *The Challenge Ahead, Equal Opportunity in Referral Unions* (1977), pp. 84–89.

20. A. Pifer, "Women Working: Toward a New Society," pp. 13–34, and D. Pearce, "Women, Work and Welfare: The Feminization of Poverty," pp. 103–24, both in K. A. Fernstein, ed., *Working Women and Families* (Beverly Hills: Sage Publications, 1979). Disproportionate numbers of single-parent families are minorities.

21. See Griggs v. Duke Power Company, 401 U.S. 424 (1971); U.S. Commission on Civil Rights, *Toward Equal Educational Opportunity: Affirmative Admissions Programs at Law and Medical Schools* (1978), pp. 10–12; I. Berg, *Education and Jobs: The Great Training Robbery* (Boston: Beacon Press, 1971), pp. 58–60.

22. See U.S. Commission on Civil Rights, *Toward Equal Educational Opportunity: Affirmative Admissions Programs at Law and Medical Schools* (1978), pp. 14–15.

23. See U.S. Commission on Civil Rights, *Mortgage Money: Who Gets It? A Case Study in Mortgage Lending Discrimination in Hartford, Conn.* (1974); J. Feagin and C. B. Feagin, *Discrimination American Style, Institutional Racism and Sexism* (Englewood Cliffs, N.J.: Prentice Hall, 1976), pp. 78–79.

24. See *Club Membership Practices by Financial Institutions: Hearing before the Comm. on Banking, Housing and Urban Affairs, United States Senate,* 96th Cong., 1st Sess. (1979). The Office of Federal Contract Compliance Programs of the Department of Labor has proposed a rule that would make the payment or reimbursement of membership fees in a private club that accepts or rejects persons on the basis of race, color, sex, religion, or national origin a prohibited discriminatory practice. 45 Fed. Reg. 4954 (1980) (to be codified in 41 C.F.R. §60–1.11).

25. See U.S. Commission on Civil Rights, *For All the People . . . By All the People* (1969), pp. 122–23.

26. See note 10.

27. See note 12.

28. See notes 14 and 15.

29. See Statement of Arthur S. Flemming, Chairman, U.S. Commission on Civil Rights, before the Subcommittee on Constitutional Rights of the Committee on the Judiciary of the U.S. Senate on S.407, S.903, and S.1279, Apr. 9, 1975, pp. 15–18, based on U.S. Commission on Civil Rights, *The Voting Rights Act: Ten Years After* (January 1975).

30. See, e.g., U.S. Commission on Civil Rights, *Equal Opportunity in Suburbia* (1974).

31. Chafe, *Women and Equality,* p. 78.

32. U.S. Commission on Civil Rights, *Window Dressing on the Set* (1977).

33. See note 16; Gregory v. Litton Systems, Inc., 472 F.2d 631 (9th Cir. 1972); Green v. Mo.-Pac. R.R., 523 F.2d 1290 (8th Cir. 1975).

34. See U.S. Commission on Civil Rights, *Minorities and Women as Government Contractors,* pp. 20, 27, 125 (1975).

35. See, e.g., A. Downs, *Racism in America and How to Combat It* (U.S. Commission on Civil Rights, 1970); "The Web of Urban Racism," in *Institutional Racism in America,* ed. Knowles and Prewitt (Englewood Cliffs, N.J.: Prentice Hall, 1969), pp. 134–76. Other

factors in addition to race, sex, and national origin may contribute to these interlocking institutional patterns. In *Equal Opportunity in Suburbia* (1974), this Commission documented what it termed "the cycle of urban poverty" that confines minorities in central cities with declining tax bases, soaring educational and other public needs, and dwindling employment opportunities, surrounded by largely white, affluent suburbs. This cycle of poverty, however, started with and is fueled by discrimination against minorities. See also W. Taylor, *Hanging Together, Equality in an Urban Nation* (New York: Simon & Schuster, 1971).

36. The "self-fulfilling prophecy" is a well-known phenomenon. "Blaming the victim" occurs when responses to discrimination are treated as though they were the causes rather than the results of discrimination. See Chafe, *Women and Equality*, pp. 76–78; W. Ryan, *Blaming the Victim* (New York: Pantheon Books, 1971).

37. See, e.g., J. E. Simpson and J. M. Yinger, *Racial and Cultural Minorities* (New York: Harper and Row, 1965), pp. 49–79; J. M. Jones, *Prejudice and Racism* (Reading, Mass.: Addison Wesley, 1972), pp. 60–111; M. M. Tumin, "Who Is Against Desegregation?" in *Racial and Ethnic Relations*, ed. H. Hughes (Boston: Allyn and Bacon, 1970), pp. 76–85; D. M. Wellman, *Portraits of White Racism* (Cambridge: Cambridge University Press, 1977).

38. See, e.g., D. C. Cox, *Caste, Class and Race: A Study in Social Dynamics* (Garden City, N.Y.: Doubleday, 1948); W. J. Wilson, *Power, Racism and Privilege* (New York: Macmillan, 1973).

39. H. Hacker, "Women as a Minority Group," *Social Forces*, vol. 30 (1951), pp. 60–69; J. Feagin and C. B. Feagin, *Discrimination American Style*; Chafe, *Women and Equality*; J. Feagin, "Indirect Institutionalized Discrimination," *American Politics Quarterly*, vol. 5 (1977), pp. 177–200; M. A. Chesler, "Contemporary Sociological Theories of Racism," in *Towards the Elimination of Racism*, ed. P. Katz (New York: Pergamon Press, 1976); P. Van den Berghe, *Race and Racism: A Comparative Perspective* (New York: Wiley, 1967); S. Carmichael and C. Hamilton, *Black Power* (New York: Random House, 1967); Knowles and Prewitt, *Institutional Racism in America*; Downs, *Racism in America and How to Combat It.*

2

ABERCROMBIE SETTLES CLASS-ACTION SUIT

Abercrombie & Fitch has agreed to a multimillion-dollar deal to settle accusations that the retail clothing giant promoted whites at the expense of minorities.

The settlement of this class-action lawsuit requires the company pay $40 million to Latino, African American, Asian American and women applicants and employees who charged the company with discrimination. It also requires Abercrombie

Reprinted by permission of Carol N. Vu and *Northwest Asian Weekly*.

& Fitch to institute policies and programs to promote diversity in its workforce and to prevent discrimination based on race or gender.

Plaintiff Anthony Ocampo, a recent Stanford University graduate, said he was pleased with the settlement. He had been told by an Abercrombie & Fitch employee that he couldn't be hired because "there's already too many Filipinos."

Ocampo said, "It is important that Abercrombie seek out employees of color and provide them with training and opportunities for promotion."

Fellow plaintiff Jennifer Lu agrees. She claims she and five other Asian American employee were terminated following a visit by senior management to their Costa Mesa, Calif., store. They were replaced by white sales staff. "I am looking forward to seeing a more diverse Abercrombie—one that actually reflects the look of America," Lu said.

The U.S. Equal Employment Opportunity Commission estimates that the suit would affect more than 10,000 Hispanic, Asian or black men and women who have worked for, or applied for a position, at the retailer. The EEOC was among the plaintiffs in the lawsuit.

"This agreement promises to transform this company, whose distinctiveness will no longer stem from an all-white image and workforce," said Thomas A. Saenz, vice president of litigation at the Mexican American Legal Defense and Educational Fund.

The first lawsuit was filed last June in San Francisco by Hispanic and Asian groups charging that Abercrombie & Fitch hires a disproportionately white sales force, puts minorities in less-visible jobs and cultivates a virtually all-white image in its catalogues and elsewhere. It was on behalf of nine young adults of color, including students and graduates of Stanford University and the University of California.

A second, similar lawsuit was filed against the company last November in New Jersey.

The settlement also requires the store pursue "benchmarks" for the hiring and promotion of Latino, African Americans, Asian Americans and women. The company must hire 25 recruiters who will seek out minority employees. It is barred from targeting specific fraternities and sororities for recruitment purposes, a practice that allegedly ensured a predominantly white sales staff.

A vice president for diversity will also be named, and marketing materials will begin to include more people of color.

The Ohio-based retailer has a workforce of 22,000 and more than 700 stores, including many in the Greater Seattle area.

The monetary awards to the class members will be based on the number of claimants who come forward and the kind of discrimination they faced. But, said defense attorney Martin J. D'Urso, "the true value of this settlement goes far beyond the money being paid to class members. The changes that are being made . . . will help transform Abercrombie into the type of company that, I believe, its customers want and the law demands."

Notices will be placed on the Internet and in major magazines to alert class members around the country. Individuals who feel they are part of the class should call 866-854-4175 or visit www.abercrombieclaims.com.

Abercrombie & Fitch has been blamed for racial prejudice before. In the spring of 2002, it removed T-shirts from its store shelves after Asian Americans deemed them racist. One of the shirts showed two slant-eyed men wearing conical hats, underneath the slogan "Wong Brothers Laundry Service: Two Wongs Can Make It White." The shirts pushed Asian Americans, especially college students, to protest in front of Abercrombie & Fitch stores across the country.

3

APPAREL FACTORY WORKERS WERE CHEATED, STATE SAYS

Steven Greenhouse

It was one of the worst sweatshops that state inspectors have visited in years, they said, sometimes requiring its 100 employees to work seven days a week, sometimes for months in a row.

The factory, in Queens — which made women's apparel for Banana Republic, the Gap, Macy's, Urban Apparel and Victoria's Secret — handed out instructions to its workers telling them to give false answers about working conditions when government inspectors visited.

Wage violations were so widespread, state labor officials said at a news conference on Wednesday, that the factory, Jin Shun, cheated its workers of $5.3 million. The case made by the State Labor Department against Jin Shun is one of the biggest involving back pay that it has ever brought.

According to state officials, most employees, virtually all of them Chinese immigrants, were paid just $250 when they worked their typical 66-hour, six-day weeks, amounting to $3.79 an hour, far below the state's $7.15-an-hour minimum wage. They received more when they were required to work seven-day weeks.

No one answered the phone at the factory on Wednesday afternoon.

In addition to claiming minimum wage and overtime violations, the Labor Department accused the factory of falsifying time records and coaching employees to lie to investigators, and of not paying a mandatory extra amount when employees worked more than 10 hours in a day.

Two Chinese immigrants who worked at the factory said that during one busy stretch they worked 120 days straight.

State officials said that the instructions given to employees, written in English and Mandarin, told them that if government inspectors ever asked them how many hours they worked each week, they were to respond, "Not sure, depends on the workload."

The instructions told the workers that if inspectors asked how much they earned, they should respond, "I don't remember, because sometimes I work more hours and sometimes less."

The instruction sheet told the workers that if they were asked, "What is your hourly wage?" they were to answer, "Not sure, but always over $7.75 depending on the job complexity." Even though the workers were paid at a fixed rate per piece of work performed and partly in cash, they were told to answer that they were always paid by the hour and through direct deposit.

The state labor commissioner, M. Patricia Smith, said that the factory, at 47–51 33rd Street, in Long Island City, also used other strategies to deceive investigators.

She said that Jin Shun falsified time records by making employees punch one timecard on Monday through Wednesday and a second one for the rest of the week, so that neither timecard showed the total number of hours worked each week. The employer provided just one set of cards to investigators.

"This factory paid sweatshop wages, kept fake records and coached employees to lie, even though it had signed retailer codes of conduct to comply with the law," Ms. Smith said. "Although there appear to be great advances in the industry with retailers' having codes of conduct, that's just a first step. There really has to be aggressive enforcement and monitoring" by government officials and the factory's customers.

Macy's said it was investigating the matter and was "very concerned about allegations" being raised by the Labor Department.

Robin Olshavsky, a spokeswoman for Limited Brands, which owns Victoria's Secret, said, "Our primary concern in a situation like this is the well-being of the workers involved." She said that the company had a zero-tolerance policy for "vendors and factories that are unwilling or unable to work with us to achieve such compliance."

Dan Henkle, senior vice president of social responsibility at the Gap, which also owns Banana Republic, said, "We plan to fully cooperate with authorities to ensure the workers are treated fairly." He said the company had no current production at the factory and was suspending future production there "until this investigation is satisfactorily resolved."

The Labor Department announced that on Wednesday morning it placed special tags on more than 10,000 items of Jin Shun's apparel, stating that the garments were produced under unlawful conditions.

Within hours of that tagging, the clothing company Urban Apparel paid state officials $60,000 to have the tags removed. The money covered the amount of wage violations that the department found had occurred when employees were making the tagged garments.

One former worker, who spoke on the condition of anonymity because she feared retribution by management, said that after working several seven-day weeks, she took off one Sunday to see a doctor. "When I showed up at work the next day, the boss asked me, 'How come you didn't show up yesterday?' " she said. "I tell him, 'I was sick. I needed to see a doctor,' and the boss said, 'If you don't follow my orders, if you don't come to work, then we don't need you to come back any more," and fired her.

Another worker said, "The employer instructed us when the Labor Department visited the factory: 'Don't tell them the truth. Don't tell them you receive cash payments from the employer.' When the boss told me these things, I figured something was not right."

Several workers said that their bosses allowed them only 30 minutes for lunch but subtracted an hour from their time cards. When the managers knew that monitors from private companies that bought Jin Shun's apparel were to visit, they told the employees to take an hour, not 30 minutes, for lunch.

State officials said that about $2.4 million of the $5.3 million in wage violations occurred while the factory was operating under a previous name, Venture 47. They said the factory's owners recently changed its name to Garlee NY.

Ms. Smith said that her department began investigating Jin Shun last November and that investigators obtained the factory's production records and compared them with employee time records.

"We could then see that the timecards we were getting had to be false," Ms. Smith said. "If they weren't false, it meant those workers were making a garment a minute."

4

Refusal to Fire Unattractive Saleswoman Led to Dismissal, Suit Contends

Steven Greenhouse

It was not the kind of order that Elysa Yanowitz, a regional sales manager for a giant cosmetics company, was used to hearing.

After a top executive of her company, L'Oréal, visited the perfume department of a Macy's store in San Jose, she said, he ordered her to fire a saleswoman for not being sexy enough. In court papers, Ms. Yanowitz said his words were, "Get me somebody hot."

A few weeks later when the executive, John Wiswall, general manager of L'Oréal's designer fragrance division, again visited the store, he discovered that she had not dismissed the saleswoman, and, Ms. Yanowitz said, he told her, "Didn't I tell you to get rid of her?"

Later, Ms. Yanowitz said in a sworn statement, as the two passed an attractive blond woman, Mr. Wiswall said, "Get me one that looks like that."

"It was disturbing to me as a professional woman that he would make such a demand," Ms. Yanowitz said. "It was bad enough that he gave me no legitimate reason to fire a capable, perfectly presentable employee. But to refer in an offensive manner to a saleswoman who was almost young enough to be his granddaughter was disgusting."

Ms. Yanowitz continued to refuse to dismiss the saleswoman, who was one of the region's highest-selling sales associates, and soon after, her bosses soured on her. They told Ms. Yanowitz that she had become a liability and was making mistake after mistake, though the year before she had been L'Oréal's regional sales manager of the year.

Ms. Yanowitz, 56, began suffering from high blood pressure. She took a long medical leave, and after three months L'Oreal replaced her.

Throughout a four-year court battle, Ms. Yanowitz has insisted that L'Oréal improperly retaliated against her and was preparing the groundwork to fire her because she refused to dismiss the saleswoman.

L'Oréal's lawyers argue that Mr. Wiswall and other company officials did nothing illegal or wrong. In their court papers, they argued that L'Oréal did not retaliate against Ms. Yanowitz, but merely reprimanded her for errors and oversights.

In her lawsuit, Ms. Yanowitz argued that Mr. Wiswall had violated California's fair employment law, which bars sexual discrimination, when he sought to fire the saleswoman. She further contended that it was illegal for L'Oréal to retaliate against her for not carrying out an order she believed violated the law.

In a far-reaching decision that could make it harder for employers to fire workers because of how they look, a California appeals court accepted Ms. Yanowitz's argument. The ruling last month by a three-judge panel of the Court of Appeals for the First Appellate District in San Francisco reinstated her claim of retaliation, which had been dismissed by the trial court.

As part of its ruling, the panel wrote, "An explicit order to fire a female employee for failing to meet a male executive's personal standards for sexual desirability is sex discrimination."

The court added, "A lower-level manager's refusal to carry out that order is protected activity, and an employer may not retaliate against her for that refusal."

L'Oréal's lawyers said they would ask the state Supreme Court to review the ruling. But they praised the appellate court for affirming the dismissal of some of Ms. Yanowitz's claims, among them that L'Oréal had negligently inflicted emotional distress on her.

"Most of plaintiff's claims were dismissed without a trial," said William J. Carroll, a lawyer for L'Oréal. "We are seeking appellate review of the one remaining claim. We believe the court will rule in our favor."

He did not confirm or deny that Mr. Wiswall made the statements he is accused of making.

If the Supreme Court decides not to hear the appeal, the case may go to trial to determine whether L'Oréal retaliated against Ms. Yanowitz.

Jennifer Brown, legal director of the NOW Legal Defense and Education Fund, said the case, although decided under California law, could have implications nationwide. Ms. Brown said similar rulings could be made under federal sex discrimination laws, noting that federal courts have ruled that it is illegal for an airline to impose far more stringent weight limits on female flight attendants than on male ones.

"This case is a very clear statement that directing that a woman be fired based on sexual attractiveness is sexual discrimination when those same standards are not being applied to men," Ms. Brown said. "This is a stark reminder to employers that attractiveness cannot be used as a criterion for employment unless the same standards are applied for both sexes."

Experts on sexual discrimination law note that employers are allowed to take attractiveness into account for female employees when it is a bona fide qualification, as with fashion models or movie stars.

To buttress the case that there was improper retaliation, Ms. Yanowitz's lawyer, her husband, Herbert W. Yanowitz, uncovered evidence that soon after she refused to fire the saleswoman, L'Oréal officials began asking her subordinates to provide negative information about her.

"After Elysa refused to fire the salesperson, they became very vindictive," Mr. Yanowitz said. "For Elysa, it was a matter of principle. She thought it would be illegal, immoral, and counterproductive to discharge a highly productive salesperson simply because of physical characteristics."

L'Oréal argued in court papers that Ms. Yanowitz's performance grew steadily worse after she received the sales manager award.

5

WHERE "ENGLISH ONLY" FALLS SHORT

Stacy A. Teicher

Companies Scramble to Cope with Multiple Languages in the Workplace

They were the go-to people when customers needed advice in Spanish about eyeshadow or perfume. But when Hispanic employees wanted to speak Spanish to one another, they say it was forbidden—even on lunch breaks.

Five women who worked for the cosmetics store Sephora in New York filed complaints, and the Equal Employment Opportunity Commission (EEOC) sued last fall on their behalf. They argue the policy is too restrictive and amounts to national-origin discrimination, which is illegal under the Civil Rights Act of 1964.

"All of the [women say] how hurtful it is to be told that you can't speak your own language," says EEOC attorney Raechel Adams. "Language is so closely tied to their culture and their ethnicity. [Ironically,] they were expected to assist Spanish-speaking customers."

As companies hire from an ever more diverse labor pool, they reap the benefits of bilingualism, but they're also running into a Babel of problems. Already, a fifth of the nation's population speaks something other than English as their primary language (in some areas, it's two-fifths). Many of them have limited English proficiency that can lead to costly mistakes or low productivity. Managers worry about compromised safety or the quality of customer service. And if some workers use a foreign language to mock others, morale can break down.

There's no quick fix. Some employers go to the expense of offering classes to improve workers' English. Others turn the tables and train supervisors in languages most often spoken by workers in their industry. What seems the simplest answer to some—an English-only policy—is tricky because conflicts between court rulings and EEOC guidelines leave a lot of gray areas.

In the case of the five New York Hispanics, Sephora denied that it had an English-only rule or discriminated in any way. The court is awaiting the store's answer to the complaint.

English-only policies generate few official grievances. In 2002, the EEOC received 228 such complaints out of about 9,000 claims of national-origin discrimination. But observers say that many more workers who feel silenced don't take action for fear of losing their jobs.

Often what determines fairness is how a policy is implemented and whether there's an atmosphere of ethnic tension. In a case settled recently for $1.5 million, Hispanic housekeepers at a casino were not allowed to speak Spanish. A janitor reported that he had to hide in closets to train new employees who understood only Spanish. Others told of harassment by supervisors who called them "wetbacks," accused them of stealing, and fired them for objecting to the English policy. The Colorado Central Station Casino in Black Hawk did not return calls seeking comment. In the settlement, it denied wrongdoing but agreed to remedies such as posting notices declaring there is no English-only rule.

For bilingual people, suppressing the tendency to talk in both languages can be difficult. They may know enough English to get by in their jobs, but to talk about family or other topics with friends, their primary language offers them a much richer vocabulary.

"It's called code-switching," says Nina Perales, regional counsel of the Mexican-American Legal Defense Fund (MALDEF), which joined the EEOC in the suit against the casino. "You might switch languages for reason of emphasis or because you're more comfortable explaining certain things in one language versus the other." And sometimes it's even done unconsciously, linguists say.

But when conversations are restricted, "there's almost an issue of dehumanization," says Karl Krahnke, a linguistics professor at Colorado State University. "They are not being viewed as humans with the same social needs as anybody else."

Some insist those complexities shouldn't keep employers from creating a language policy if they think it's good for business. "I speak four languages . . . but a business has the right to establish rules for whatever reason—it could be safety, it could be social . . . so other [workers] won't feel insulted," says Mauro E. Mujica, chairman of U.S. English in Washington, D.C. His organization promotes official-English policies, which exist in 27 states and apply only to government, not the private sector. But workplace policies, he says, should not extend to people's personal time.

No Navajo

Another case takes the debate out of the immigration context. At R.D.'s Drive-In in Page, Ariz., it wasn't a "foreign" language that the boss restricted, but a native one: Navajo.

The town borders the Navajo Nation reservation, and nearly 90 percent of the restaurant's employees are Navajo, though the owners, the Kidman family, are not.

Speaking on the Kidman's behalf, Joe Becker of the Mountain States Legal Foundation in Denver says the family asked employees to sign a language policy in the summer of 2000. Their reason: There were complaints from customers and staff about rude comments being made in Navajo.

The agreement read: "The owner of this business can speak and understand only English. While the owner is paying you as an employee, you are required to use English at all times . . . [except] when the customer cannot understand English. If you feel unable to comply with this requirement, you may find another job."

Elva Josley and three others took exception to the rule. Ms. Josley had worked for the Kidmans for nearly three years and their families were close friends. But this, she says, was hurtful. She says the Kidmans never told her there had been complaints about things being said in Navajo.

Legacy of Suppression

"A lot of Native American people were sent to boarding schools and told not to speak their own language . . . and they were trying to make Christians out of these 'savages,'" she says. "I [said to the Kidmans]: 'It's not fair, because you people are the ones who came to our land and you can't tell us not to be who we are.'" Without native languages, she says, the US wouldn't have had the help of the code talkers during World War II.

The EEOC sued the diner, and Josley hopes the case will be settled soon and will send a message to employers: "Everyone's human and deserves to be respected . . . and next time people will think twice before doing something like this."

6

WOMEN IN THE STATE POLICE: TROUBLE IN THE RANKS

Jonathan Schuppe

For Victoria Grant, it was the deer testicles in her locker.

For Kimberly Zollitsch, it was the nails in her tires.

For Amy Johnson, it was the name-calling and obscene Valentine signed by a commanding officer.

At a time when the New Jersey State Police is trying to eliminate racial profiling, the agency finds itself grappling with another issue of discrimination. Female troopers say they are harassed by fellow troopers, and the State Police record for hiring women is one of the worst in the nation.

Grant, Zollitsch and Johnson are veteran state troopers who left the force in the last four years and sued, citing years of relentless harassment by male troopers.

Yet other female troopers, such as Capt. Gayle Cameron and Lt. Col. Lori Hennon-Bell, who have been on patrol now for 23 years, say they have had rewarding careers, and that the agency is a better place for women than when they signed on.

But there is general agreement that there are troubling trends.

Today the agency includes 100 women, or 3.7 percent of its 2,708-member force. The female/male ratio ranks 11th from the bottom among state law enforcement agencies, according to 2001 FBI figures. A recent survey of 247 large police forces placed the New Jersey State Police at 235.

There are other numbers that raise concern.

In 2001, a report commissioned by the State Police but never made public found that 80 percent of women troopers—as well as a majority of men—had experienced "sexually harassing behavior" ranging from dirty jokes to unwanted sexual advances.

Attorney General Peter Harvey says the solution lies in recruiting.

"We know discrimination is an aspect of American life that permeates many institutions," said Harvey. "I submit that the real problem is we have to be more consistent in our recruitment efforts, and then promoting consistently talented women up the line."

The troopers union has a harsher view.

"It is shameful and embarrassing that we're not doing a better job in our recruiting of women," said Kenneth McClelland, president of the State Troopers Fraternal Association.

Stress Leave

Kimberly Zollitsch is one of nine female troopers who have sued the State Police in the last five years.

After 15 years on the force, she ended an extended stress leave this summer by retiring with a psychological disability. She says her troubles were prompted by nearly nonstop sexual harassment. As a rookie, she attributed the behavior to hazing. She figured she could roll with it.

"The State Police was known as the best of the best, and to be one of the few females, to add to the number, was inspiring," she said.

But the harassment didn't stop, she said.

In a lawsuit filed in December 2001, Zollitsch recounted how women in the academy were brutalized in boxing matches by bigger men, and forced to go on training runs in white shorts while menstruating. Instructors jogging behind jeered at their female colleagues. While on road patrol, Zollitsch said in her lawsuit, she regularly saw male troopers watching pornographic movies in the barracks.

One colleague took a picture of her buttocks, copied it and posted it around her station in Bridgeton. At Port Norris, her locker and gear were vandalized the night before an inspection. Nails were driven through the tires of her personal car.

One night in December 1999, Zollitsch finished her shift and never returned. Neither the attorney general nor the State Police would comment on the specifics of her case.

But, in a February 2000 letter to her, the Attorney General's Office told Zollitsch that it had substantiated several of her allegations, including her contention she was called derogatory names, that her equipment was smashed and her tires flattened. The letter, reviewed by *The Star-Ledger*, also says two commanders failed to stop troopers from harassing her. But by that time, some of those responsible had retired and were beyond discipline. She doesn't know whether anyone was punished.

"For a long time I guess I just told myself they'll get tired of this and I'll get seniority and it will stop," Zollitsch recalled. "I tried to get through it with the attitude that they're not going to win and I liked doing my job. But a lot of little things built upon themselves to the point where I couldn't take it anymore."

A Success

Gayle Cameron is one of the success stories. She joined the State Police in 1980 when there were only two female troopers.

That year, the State Police announced with great fanfare the nation's first all-female trooper class, a one-shot attempt to boost the number of women. Cameron and 103 other women signed up for five months of intense training at the State Police training academy in Sea Girt. Only 30 made it to graduation day.

Eighteen members of that class, the 96th in State Police history, remain on the force. They include 10 sergeants, four lieutenants, two captains and a lieutenant colonel.

"We were groundbreakers," said Cameron, now a captain in the State Police's Records and Identification Section. "People thought women wouldn't be able to do the job."

Cameron remembers the 96th class graduating to a triumphant sendoff—national media attention and a crowd of supporters that included the state's top law enforcement officials. Attorney General John Degnan told the graduates they would "serve as shining examples for coming generations of women who blaze similar paths and continue to break down the barriers of sexism."

The women soon discovered that the male troopers saw them as second-class troopers or "trooperettes." There were no women's bathrooms or locker rooms. They had to wear uniforms tailored for men.

To the male troopers, the modified push-ups and chin-ups, female-only self-defense drills and other changes in the academy meant the women hadn't earned their dues.

In the stations, some male troopers refused to speak to the women, or called them vulgar nicknames. Others refused to join them on patrols.

Cameron, who was a 23-year-old former teacher from Massachusetts when she enlisted, said discrimination didn't overshadow what she called "a rewarding, worthwhile experience" in the State Police.

Cameron excelled. She became a detective, investigating casinos and organized crime, before winning a coveted assignment on Gov. Christie Whitman's security detail. She investigated discrimination complaints in the Equal Employment Opportunity/Affirmative Action Office and helped the force develop recruiting strategies.

Cameron said today's State Police is a much better place to work than when she joined.

"I think for a number of years we did not do what we could have done to make this a welcoming environment for men, women and minorities who wouldn't have been the typical trooper," Cameron said. "We could have done things better. But I think we are doing it better now and taking the issue seriously."

No Choice

Amy Johnson, also of the 1980 class, says the workplace was so hard on women, many faced this choice: Take a stand or quit. Eventually, she says, she had to do both.

Johnson says she made the mistake of complaining about what she saw as unfair criticism of her patrol reports. Her locker was trashed and lingerie catalogues were left in her mailbox. Supervisors belittled her in front of subordinates and locked her out of a station exercise room.

One commander sent her a Valentine's Day card. "Ah, Valentine's Day! Seems like a good time to use a man, then toss him aside like an old candy wrapper," the card read. The commander wrote, "This card fits you," adding a four-letter slur.

"I was a physical and mental wreck," she recalled.

Johnson says she created some of her own problems, namely by shooting her gun into the air one night while off duty. She was fired, but says her male colleagues who pulled similar stunts didn't lose their jobs. She appealed her dismissal and was reinstated.

Johnson eventually made sergeant, but she says the promotion came with a cost: several stress leaves and three sexual harassment complaints. She retired in 1999 and sued for discrimination a year later.

"I think we've helped the women of the future by saying, 'Enough is enough.'"

In an April 2000 letter to Johnson, a copy of which was reviewed by *The Star-Ledger*, Attorney General John Farmer said an investigation had substantiated several of her complaints, including the vulgar Valentine.

For Victoria Grant, who also joined in 1980, "enough" came four years ago. In 1999, she filed a lawsuit in which she alleged that troopers put dead birds and deer testicles in her locker and mailbox, and dressed a mannequin in her uniform along with pages from pornographic magazines. Grant, who retired this year, declined to be interviewed for this story.

7

BLACKS VS. LATINOS AT WORK

Miriam Jordan

Donnie Gaut, an African-American with 12 years of warehouse experience, applied for a job in 2002 at Farmer John Meats, a large Los Angeles pork processor. When he was turned down for the position, a job stocking goods that paid $7 an hour, Mr. Gaut decided the problem wasn't his résumé—it was his race. He filed a complaint with the U.S. Equal Employment Opportunity Commission, the federal agency that enforces antidiscrimination laws in the workplace.

Last October, the EEOC secured a $110,000 settlement from the company to be shared by Mr. Gaut and six other black applicants who were rejected for production jobs at Farmer John based on their race, according to the agency.

The EEOC says it found that the pork packer, owned by Clougherty Packing Co., had been almost exclusively hiring Hispanics for warehouse, packing and production jobs. Clougherty was acquired by Hormel Foods Corp. in 2004.

In response to questions, Clougherty Packing said in a statement that settlement of the case "in no way suggests the company did anything wrong." It said the packer wanted to avoid "what would have been costly and protracted litigation."

A new wave of race-discrimination cases is appearing in the workplace: African-Americans who feel that they are being passed over for Hispanics.

This kind of case marks a shift from years past, when blacks were likely to seek legal action against employers who showed preferential treatment toward whites. The cases highlight mounting tension between Hispanics and blacks as they compete for resources and job opportunities.

Recently, the federal agency announced it also secured a $180,000 settlement from Zenith National Insurance Corp., a national workers-compensation specialist, to be divided among 10 blacks who applied for a mailroom job at its headquarters in Woodland Hills, Calif. The job was offered to a Latino man with no mailroom experience, according to the EEOC.

Henry Shields, an attorney for Zenith, said the insurance company had adopted EEOC recommendations for improving its hiring practices "as a means of furthering its goals of equal opportunity." Mr. Shields declined to comment on the specifics of the case.

"There used to be a reluctance to bring cases against other minorities," says Anna Park, the EEOC regional attorney who oversaw both the Zenith and the Farmer John cases. "It's no longer a white-black paradigm. This is a new trend."

The situation is exacerbated by strong stereotypes that have set in among some employers about the pluses and minuses of hiring from each pool of minority workers. "There is a perception that Latinos closer to the immigrant experience might work harder than black persons," says Joe Hicks, who is African-American and vice president of Community Advocates, a nonpartisan group that aims to advance interracial dialogue.

John Trasvina, vice president for law and policy at the Mexican-American Defense League, an advocacy group that works on civil rights issues, says that some Latinos may be viewed as "preferred applicants." He believes there is a feeling among some employers that Latinos can be exploited because, in their view, they tend to be immigrants who are more likely to accept low wages and be less aware of their rights than blacks. Says Mr. Trasvina: "Employers sometimes pit one group of employees against the other."

California—where Hispanic immigrants have been moving into black working-class pockets of the state's cities for decades—is at the leading edge of this growing trend. As Latinos migrate eastward, to such states as Louisiana, Georgia and North Carolina, the competition with blacks for blue-collar jobs is likely to grow.

Hispanics have become the second-largest population group in the U.S.— ahead of African-Americans but behind Caucasians—thanks to the influx of immigrants from Latin America. In some cities, like Los Angeles, collaboration between African-American and Latino leaders is on the rise when it is mutually beneficial.

But as Latinos grab the attention of marketers and gain political clout, many African-Americans feel that their influence is waning, and that the decline is disproportionate and unfair.

Tension has spilled into the workplace. In New Orleans, city officials have raised concerns that employers are hiring Latino immigrants for low wages to do the hurricane cleanup instead of tapping the native-born, mainly black, workforce. Last October, New Orleans Mayor Ray Nagin asked local business leaders: "How do I ensure that New Orleans is not overrun by Mexican workers?"

Workers from all backgrounds—whites, blacks, Asians and others—use networks within their ethnic groups to find employment. Hispanic workers often bring in other family members or people from their neighborhoods or home regions to join them on a job. In sectors like construction, this can be an aid to employers who can tap their workers to help them find a fresh supply of laborers.

The flip side is that employers can become vulnerable to lawsuits if it's determined that they have been shutting out qualified applicants based on their race.

In the Zenith National Insurance case, Charles Dennis, who applied for a mailroom job he spotted in a newspaper's classified section in 2001, says his interview with a Hispanic manager "went great." He first became suspicious that something wasn't right when, in a follow-up call, the company told him the $10-an-hour position was put on hold.

Then, a few weeks later, Mr. Dennis—who had worked in another large insurer's mailroom—got a call from an employment agency telling him they had "the perfect job" for him, he recalls. It turned out to be the same position. He says the agency then called back and told him that Zenith "just didn't want to go with me."

Mr. Dennis took his case to the EEOC, which began to investigate. It found that Mr. Dennis and several other black applicants with relevant experience were passed over in favor of a Latino candidate, whose previous work amounted to mainly "swabbing decks on aircraft carriers" in the Navy, according to Ms. Park, the EEOC attorney.

In the case of Farmer John Meats, the EEOC said that it found that the employer had an all-Hispanic hiring staff and recruited new hires by word of mouth.

One of the Latinos hired to work in Farmer John Meats instead of the black candidates had been a gardener, according to Ms. Park. Both discrimination lawsuits were brought against the employers under Title VII of the Civil Rights Act of 1964. The message for employers is that "all individuals deserve to compete for jobs on a level playing field," she says.

8

Manhattan Store Owner Accused of Underpaying and Sexually Harassing Workers

Steven Greenhouse

Three immigrant women yesterday filed a federal lawsuit that accused a Manhattan store owner of paying them far less than the $5.15-an-hour minimum wage and telling them he would not grant them raises unless they had sex with him.

The lawsuit asserts that the women, who worked as cashiers and stocked merchandise, were paid as little as $30 for a 10-hour day, or $3 an hour, and were told they were to blame for their low pay because they refused to have sex with the boss.

The lawsuit, brought against three jointly owned stores in Upper Manhattan, describes a pervasive atmosphere of sexual harassment, with the owner telling the women that he kept a bed in the basement of one store for sex.

Deyanira Espinal, 38, a Dominican immigrant, said in court papers that when she asked for a raise last October, the stores' owner "told me he would give me a raise only if I had sex with him."

She added, "I did not have sex with him, and therefore I did not receive a raise."

Ms. Espinal said in an interview: "I felt bad, bad, bad. I have two daughters, and here he was making this proposition, and I needed the job."

Ms. Espinal said the owner once grabbed her in the store basement in an attempt to assault her sexually.

Later, he reduced her schedule to three days a week from six days to punish her for spurning his advances, she said.

The lawsuit, filed in Federal District Court in Manhattan, was brought against the three stores—two Ramco stores and a National Discount store—and against their owner, Albert Palacci.

Mr. Palacci denied the accusations. "That's not true," he said. "We don't have those things here."

He insisted that the harassment charges were baseless. "This is the worst thing you can hear," he said. "It's a lie 100 percent."

He said that some people have worked at his stores for more than two decades. "We pay top money," he said. "Some people will say things because they want to get money from you."

The Women's Rights Project of the American Civil Liberties Union filed the lawsuit after the women approached the group to complain that they were being underpaid, harassed and not receiving overtime.

"We were abused very unjustly on the job," said Maria Araceli Flores, 22, a Mexican immigrant who worked at the stores. "I had to put up with it out of necessity. I have a 5-year-old daughter to support."

The lawsuit accuses Mr. Palacci of false imprisonment, alleging that he once took two of the women to a house, locked the door and ordered them to undress. The suit further alleges that when the women refused, he took off his clothes, told the women to look at him and do whatever he told them. When they refused, the lawsuit asserts, he grabbed the women and threw them on the bed, but they again refused to submit.

Jennifer Arnett, a staff lawyer with the Women's Rights Project, said these abuses were far too common in New York City.

"This is not an isolated instance, especially in this area, where there are a lot of immigrant workers," she said. "This sort of abuse is running rampant, with workers being paid $30, $40 for 10-, 12-hour days and a lot of sexual harassment."

In the court papers, Angela Berise Peralta, a Dominican immigrant, said that once when she went into a store basement to seek some merchandise, she saw a bed there and Mr. Palacci asked her to have sex with him, but she refused.

On another occasion, she alleged, she accompanied him to a trade show in Manhattan, and he asked her to go to a hotel, adding, "I can give you what the young guys cannot."

Patricia Smith, director of the Attorney General's Labor Bureau, said, "Sexual harassment happens in a lot of small retailers because there aren't a lot of people around to witness it."

Ms. Peralta, 22, said she was paid $30 for working 10-hour days, while the other two women said they were paid $40 for 10-hour days.

"It was too much work and very little money," Ms. Peralta said.

Ms. Espinal said she was fired in March for refusing the owner's advances. "Mr. Palacci threatened me by telling me that I should do what he wanted me to do because I had children to support," Ms. Espinal said in the lawsuit.

She now works for another retailer in Upper Manhattan, she said, that pays her $40 for 11-hour days.

9

MUSLIM-AMERICAN RUNNING BACK OFF THE TEAM AT NEW MEXICO STATE

Matthew Rothschild

This was supposed to be Muammar Ali's year at New Mexico State. "Muammar Ali, who led the team with 561 yards rushing, will get even more opportunities," predicted SI.com in its NCAA football preview.

But he has no opportunities now. He's off the team.

On October 9, he "received a message on his phone answering machine at his home that his jersey was being pulled and that he was released," says a letter from his attorney, George Bach, of the ACLU of New Mexico, to the university.

That letter, dated October 25, alleges that Head Coach Hal Mumme engaged in religious discrimination.

"Coach Mumme questioned Mr. Ali repeatedly about Islam and specifically its ties to Al-Qaeda," the letter states. This made Mr. Ali uncomfortable, it says.

And then, after the team's first game, "despite being the star tailback for several years, Mr. Ali was relegated to fifth string and not even permitted to travel with the team," the letter says.

There were only two other Muslim players on the team, and they were also released, it says. The letter adds that the coach "regularly has players recite the Lord's Prayer after each practice and before each game."

Ali's father, Mustafa Ali, says the trouble started at a practice over the summer when the coach told the players to pray.

"My son and two other players who were Muslim, they were praying in a different manner, and the coach asked them, 'What are you doing?' They said, 'We're Muslims. This is how we pray.' That had a lot to do with how things went south."

Mustafa Ali says things escalated after his son had a personal meeting with Coach Mumme where the coach "questioned him about Al-Islam and Al-Qaeda." His son talked to him about the conversation.

"He told me it was very weird," Mustafa Ali recalls. "It disturbed him quite a bit. He didn't understand why it had anything to do with football."

After that meeting, the coach "never spoke to my son again," Mustafa Ali says.

Reprinted by permission from The Progressive Media Project, 409 E. Main Street, Madison, WI 53703. www.Progressive.org

"And as they moved into summer camp football, my son noticed that he wasn't getting the ball as much and wasn't playing as big a role," he says.

This surprised Mustafa Ali.

"In 2004, he was honorable mention All American in his sophomore year," he says. "He was the fastest, strongest, quickest person on the team."

His son "just knew there was something wrong," Mustafa Ali says.

When his son got cut, "he was upset, he was upset. The coach never gave a reason. None."

I asked to speak to his son, but Mustafa Ali said that would not be possible. "He's not talking to the media at this time," he said. "He's a very shy person."

New Mexico State isn't talking, either.

"The university has received the grievance," says Jerry Nevarez, specialist at the Office of Institutional Equity at New Mexico State.

"It is investigating the grievance, and it will have no further comment until the investigation is done."

Bruce Kite, the school's general counsel, did not return a phone call for comment.

Tyler Dunkel, director of athletic media relations for New Mexico State, said: "We're not commenting on that because there's an investigation going on and to ensure the integrity of the investigation we're not commenting on it until the investigation is finished."

Dunkel expects that to be "in the next couple of weeks."

I asked whether I could talk to Coach Mumme.

Said Dunkel: "No way."

10

TENNESSEE JUDGE TELLS IMMIGRANT MOTHERS: LEARN ENGLISH OR ELSE

Ellen Barry

A judge hearing child-abuse and neglect cases in Tennessee has given an unusual instruction to some immigrant mothers who have come before him: Learn English or else.

Most recently, it was an 18-year-old woman from Oaxaca, Mexico, who had been reported to the Department of Children's Services for failing to immunize her toddler and show up for appointments. At a hearing last month to monitor the mother's custody of the child, Wilson County Judge Barry Tatum instructed the woman to learn English and to use birth control, the *Lebanon Democrat* newspaper reported.

Last October, Tatum gave a similar order to a Mexican woman who had been cited for neglect of her 11-year-old daughter, said a lawyer who is representing the woman in her appeal. Setting a court date six months away, the judge told the woman she should be able to speak English at a fourth-grade level by that meeting. If she failed, he warned, he would begin the process of termination of parental rights.

"The court specially informs the mother that if she does not make the effort to learn English, she is running the risk of losing any connection—legally, morally and physically—with her daughter forever," reads a court order from the hearing, according to Jerry Gonzalez, the Nashville attorney who represents the woman.

Tatum's orders have become the subject of debate in this Tennessee community, which has seen an influx of non-English speakers over the past decade. Civil-rights advocates, including the American Civil Liberties Union, have called his orders discriminatory and unconstitutional. But many of Tatum's neighbors cheered the principle behind his act, saying new immigrants should be encouraged to assimilate more fully into American life.

Juvenile court proceedings are often more informal than adult cases, and it's not unusual for judges to give lifestyle advice to parents who come before them in neglect or abuse cases. And, when written down and signed by the judge, those instructions take on the force of a court order.

Such orders should pertain to behavior that contributes to abuse and neglect, said Susan Brooks, an expert on family law at Vanderbilt University Law School. Brooks said she was not familiar with Tatum's orders, but typically the inability to speak English would not fall into that category. The state Supreme Court regards the right to raise one's own children as fundamental, she added.

"That's treading on sacred ground," she said.

Tatum did not respond to interview requests from the *Los Angeles Times*, but he has explained that he gave the orders in hopes that the parents would make a greater effort to assimilate into American society, opening more opportunities to their children. He has given similar orders to non-English-speaking parents in as many as five cases.

He said he has never removed a child from a parent because the parent did not speak English.

Because records from juvenile court are sealed, further details of the cases were not available.

In Lebanon, a city 20 miles east of Nashville with a population of just more than 20,000, it was once rare to hear a foreign accent, much less a foreign language. Now Lebanon has become home to more than 1,200 foreign-born agricultural and manufacturing workers, including about 400 whose primary language is Mixteco, a language indigenous to Mexico.

Though the judge's order may have been a mistake, "the general sentiment is if people are going to be in this country, we all have a moral obligation to learn to speak the language," said Bob Bright, 61, who runs an insurance agency in Lebanon.

"I know if I was in Mexico I would make an effort to learn Hispanic."

In the October case, Tatum made a clear link between the mother's English abilities and her parental rights, said Gonzalez, the mother's attorney.

In the case, an 11-year-old girl had been placed with a foster family after allegations of neglect, Gonzalez said. The mother, who spoke only Mixteco, asked the court to arrange counseling, and the judge denied that request, instead giving the women a deadline for basic mastery of English.

11

Goodbye to Pat Morita, Best Supporting Asian

Lawrence Downes

Pat Morita, the Japanese-American actor, died on Thanksgiving Day [2005] in Las Vegas. He was 73. News reports over the weekend were not specific about the cause of death or funeral details. Also not clear was what Hollywood would do now that Mr. Morita is gone.

The movie and TV industry has never had many roles for Asian-American men, and it seemed for a while that they all went to Mr. Morita. He made his debut as "Oriental No. 2" in "Thoroughly Modern Millie" in 1967 and never stopped working. He hit two peaks—as Arnold the diner owner on TV's "Happy Days" and the wise old Mr. Miyagi in the "Karate Kid" movies—and spent the rest of nearly 40 years roaming an endless forest of bit parts.

He was Mahi Mahi, the pidgin-talking cabby in "Honeymoon in Vegas," Lamont Sanford's friend Ah Chew in "Sanford and Son," Brian the waiter in "Spy Hard," Chin Li the Chinese herbalist in "The Karate Dog."

Whenever a script called for a little Asian guy to drive a taxi, serve drinks or utter wise aphorisms in amusingly broken English, you could count on Mr. Morita to be there.

Those who knew Mr. Morita say he was a man of uncommon decency and good humor. He fulfilled the actor's prime directive, to keep busy.

But it's distressing to think that the life's work of one of the best-known, hardest-working Asian-American actors is mostly a loose collection of servile supporting roles.

I know nothing about Mr. Morita's ambitions; if he had a longing to interpret Eugene O'Neill on Broadway, I have not heard of it. But actors generally have to work within the range of what's available. And with Asian-Americans, particularly men, what's available generally stinks.

Mr. Morita was one of the last survivors of a generation of Asian-American actors who toiled within a system that was interested only in the stock Asian. Harold Sakata played Oddjob in "Goldfinger" and was typecast as a mute brute forever after. Philip Ahn played houseboys and villains for decade upon decade.

Some actors—well, a couple—broke out, like George Takei, Mr. Sulu in "Star Trek," and Jack Soo on "Barney Miller." B. D. Wong's role on "Law & Order: Special Victims Unit" is a major improvement, but it will be a long, long time before we erase the memory of the bucktoothed, jabbering Mickey Rooney in "Breakfast at Tiffany's," or Sidney Toler as Charlie Chan.

Watch Rob Schneider play Ula, a leering Hawaiian in the Adam Sandler movie "50 First Dates," with a pidgin accent by way of Cheech and Chong, and you get the sense that Hollywood still believes that there is no ethnic caricature a white actor can't improve upon.

Mr. Morita, who was born Noriyuki Morita to migrant farmworkers in California and was sent to an internment camp in Arizona during World War II, never gave the sense of bearing a racial burden.

He had a comic's perspective and sense of humor, and would play his parts—Chinese, Japanese, Korean, whatever—with relaxed professionalism. As a standup comedian in the 1960s, he called himself "the Hip Nip," and he once told a group of Pearl Harbor survivors in a Waikiki nightclub that he was sorry about messing up their harbor.

Mr. Miyagi remains everybody's idea of a positive character. Who can forget "wax on, wax off," his wise counsel linking car care to karate? But still, it bother me Miyagi-san so wise, but find so hard use articles, pronouns when talk.

Mr. Morita's legacy may soon take a posthumous turn for the better. He has a role in an unreleased movie, "Only the Brave," about Japanese-American soldiers of the famed 442nd Regimental Combat Team, one of the most decorated units in World War II. He plays a Buddhist priest who is imprisoned in Hawaii after Pearl Harbor.

Lane Nishikawa, who wrote, directed, produced and acted in the film, which is now making the rounds of festivals in search of a distributor, said it told its story from the Asian-American point of view—an unusual perspective, by past or current standards.

With its wide pool of Asian-American talent, including Mr. Morita, Tamlyn Tomita and Jason Scott Lee, the film promises to be at least different from the other movie about the 442nd.

That one—"Go for Broke!"—was made in 1951 and starred Van Johnson, with a large, and utterly forgotten, supporting cast.

ARSONIST SENTENCED FOR HATE CRIMES

Tom Kertscher

In a case that invoked the Vietnam War, America's promise of freedom and the tragedy of Sept. 11, a 23-year-old Manitowoc man who helped burn a house down was sentenced Tuesday to nearly 19 years in prison.

The Hmong victims and the judge spoke eloquently about what the crimes, and the punishment, said about this country.

Andrew Franz, the first of the seven white perpetrators to be sentenced in the hate crimes case, stayed silent.

Franz, a two-time burglar who has served prison time, had pleaded guilty in October to two hate crimes and a gun charge in the Hmong case. He said at the time that the 1998 arson, as well as an unfulfilled murder plot, were meant to "send a message" that Asians in the Manitowoc area should leave him and his friends alone.

On Tuesday in Milwaukee, U.S. District Judge Charles Clevert also spoke of sending a message, but first he listened to three of the victims.

Chao Lee, 43, began to cry before finishing her first thought. On July 28, 1998, she recalled, she, her husband and their six children ran into the night as their home went up in flames. Franz had ignited gasoline that he and one of his friends had poured on the porch.

"All that came out was our bodies," Lee said.

All of the family's possessions, including the sacred Hmong clothing she was saving for her burial, were lost.

Like other victims in the case, Lee and her family had resettled in the Manitowoc area from their native Laos after the war in Vietnam. Many Hmong fought with Americans and faced almost certain death had they remained in their homeland after the Communists took over.

"We came here seeking peace, but this is not peace," Lee said.

After the fire, the family had to live for a time with Lee's parents, a total of 12 in a tiny home.

"Every night one of the kids asked us, 'When can we go home?' But there is no home . . . nothing but ashes," said Lee, whose family moved into a new home.

Lee's testimony was translated by her oldest child, 20-year-old Xiong Lee. The last to escape the home, he said he would have perished had his mother not gone back inside to find him.

One who saw combat with the CIA in Vietnam was Humphrey Chang, 57, who was wounded twice during the war. Three days before the Lee fire, Franz and two of his co-defendants, armed with shotguns, had gone to Two Rivers intending to shoot Asians. They ignited an explosive outside Chang's home, hoping it would flush people out, but no one fled and no shots were fired.

"America is a country where freedom began," Chang said. Americans cannot allow such racial terrorism, "the act of killing innocent life for the only reason of hate," he said.

Franz and his friends said they had planned the arson and the shooting as revenge for an earlier fight between Asians and whites at a Manitowoc park. His father, Michael Franz, said that he and his son were sorry "for what happened" and that since the crimes his son had "really turned his life around."

Bobbi Bernstein, a civil rights prosecutor from Washington, D.C., and local Assistant U.S. Attorney Brian Pawlak said Franz's assistance to the FBI was pivotal in bringing charges against the six co-defendants. They recommended a roughly 17-year sentence.

Franz, who remained composed as he watched the victims speak, shed tears as he spoke with family and friends during a break in the hearing. But after Franz refused a second offer to speak, the judge told him he had seen no sign of remorse and spoke of the need to deter "this despicable" type of crime.

"Last Friday night in Salt Lake, a tattered American flag was paraded into the Olympic stadium as a reminder that this country had been attacked and that hate, unrelenting hate and total disregard for life, can have very tragic and lasting consequences," Clevert said.

"Given those considerations, it is important that this court impose a sentence as a reminder, a lifetime reminder for you and anyone who learns of your crime, that this court and our courts will deal with this type of crime very strongly and with the firm belief that we have to stamp out the kind of hate displayed in your case."

Franz will serve at least 85% of his 19-year term before being eligible for probation.

Later in the day, Judge J.P. Stadtmueller sentenced 21-year-old Augustine LaBarge of Manitowoc to 10 years in prison, one month less than the maximum for his lesser role in both crimes.

Four more adults will be sentenced. The record of the seventh defendant, a juvenile, is sealed.

13

My Black Skin Makes My White Coat Vanish

Mana Lumumba-Kasongo

The first time it happened I was a brand-spanking-new M.D., filled with an intern's enthusiasm. Proudly wearing my pristine white coat and feeling sure that I was going to save the world, I walked into my patient's room.

"Hello, I'm Dr. Kasongo. How can I help you?" I asked cheerfully. The patient was a pleasant African-American woman whose chief complaint was abdominal pain. I spent the next 10 minutes taking her history, examining her thoroughly and doing a rectal exam to spot signs of internal bleeding. I explained that I'd treat her pain, check her blood work and urine samples, and go from there. "That's great," she said with a smile. "When is the doctor going to see me?"

I frowned. Hadn't she heard me? Hadn't I just administered an invasive exam on her posterior? "I *am* the doctor," I told her, making myself smile again. Did she sense my newness? Was it my lack of confidence that made it hard for her to believe I had a medical degree? I decided that even though I was a 30-year-old intern, it must be the youthful appearance I inherited from my ageless mother that was confusing her.

That was four years ago. There have been many such incidents since then, ranging from the irritating to the comical, and I no longer have much doubt that what baffled my patient was the color of my skin. Several months later, I was having dinner at an upscale hotel in Las Vegas with a friend, when she started choking on a piece of food. As she flailed her arms in obvious distress, frantic cries of "Is there a doctor in the room?" rang out from nearby tables. I assured everyone that I was a doctor and administered the Heimlich maneuver successfully. Even as my friend regained her bearings, people at the surrounding tables kept screaming for a physician. Once the "real doctors"—two white males—came to the table and saw that her airway was clear, they told the staff that it appeared that I was in fact a doctor and that my friend was going to be fine. Yet, far from comforting them, this information produced only quizzical looks.

Over the years, the inability of patients and others to believe that I am a doctor has left me utterly demoralized. Their incredulity persists even now that I am a senior resident, working in one of the world's busiest hospital emergency rooms. How can it be that with all the years of experience I have, all the procedures I've performed and all the people I've interacted with in emergency situations, I still get what I call "the look"? It's too predictable. I walk in the room and introduce myself, then wait for the patient—whether he or she is black, white or Asian—to steal glances at the ID card that is attached to my scrubs or white coat. (I've thought of having it changed to read something like: *It's true. I'm a real doctor. Perhaps you've seen a black one on TV?*)

I remember talking to one of the white, male attending physicians in my training program after he witnessed one such encounter. "Listen," he said, trying to comfort me, "I can walk in wearing a T shirt and jeans and I'll always be seen as the doctor, even without an introduction. You will not." My heart sank as I thought of Malcolm X's words, "Do you know what white racists call black Ph.D.'s? N- - - -r!"

Only a small portion of the growing number of female doctors—not quite 4 percent—look like me. Perhaps that's why, for most people, "doctor" still doesn't fit the stereotypical image of a black woman in this country. Unfortunately, black children may be even more adversely affected by this than white ones. That point was driven home to me months ago, when a 6-year-old black girl refused to let me treat her when her mother brought her to the emergency room and left us alone. She insisted on being seen by a white doctor, leaving me feeling both embarrassed and humiliated.

Throughout the years, I've spoken to other female doctors about their experiences. While my white, female colleagues sometimes get "the look," it doesn't happen nearly as often as it does for black, female doctors. My African-American peers have their own ways of dealing with it; some even preempt suspicious patients by saying, "Yes, I am a doctor, and you can check online when you get home."

I've decided to try not to be bothered by my patients' attitudes. Like all doctors, I've worked hard to get to where I am. And occasionally I see that there is hope for humanity. A few months ago I treated a white, eighty-something man who had pneumonia. As I set up his IV line, I noticed that he was staring at me. Finally he said, "It must have been very hard for you to make it." After a pause, he added, "A woman—and black." We both laughed. Someone understood.

14

CLOSING DOORS ON AMERICANS' HOUSING CHOICES

Margery Austin Turner and Carla Herbig

Newspapers and TV commentaries around the country have been buzzing with alarm about skyrocketing housing prices. But for many Americans, spiraling home prices and rents aren't the only barriers to housing opportunity and choice. Discrimination—by landlords, real estate agents and mortgage lenders—stands in the way of too many families searching for a place to live.

Discrimination isn't as overt as it once was; often it is so subtle that victims don't even recognize it. Real estate agents no longer tell African Americans that they are unwelcome in a white subdivision. But an African-American couple visiting a real estate agent is shown fewer homes and less affluent neighborhoods than a comparable white couple. And landlords don't tell disabled applicants not to apply. But a deaf woman, using a TTY system to gather information about advertised rentals, can't get anybody to accept her calls or answer her questions.

Compelling evidence that discrimination persists comes from a recent series of "paired-testing" studies by the Urban Institute. In a paired test, two people (one minority and one white, or one disabled and one non-disabled) pose as equally qualified homeseekers. Both call or visit a real estate agent or landlord to ask about a house or apartment advertised as available. Both make exactly the same request and record all the information and service they receive.

Because the only difference between these two customers is their race or disability status, they should receive the same information and assistance. Systematic differences in treatment—telling the minority customer that an apartment is no longer available when the white customer is told he could move in next month, for example—provide direct evidence of discrimination. Paired testing catches housing providers in the act of discriminating.

More than 20 percent of the times that African-American and Hispanic renters ask about advertised apartments, they receive less information and assistance than comparable whites. Landlords only tell them about some of the apartments on the market and don't let them inspect everything that's available.

From Urban.org, September 18, 2005. Reprinted by permission.

African-American and Hispanic homebuyers face the same sort of discriminatory treatment from real estate agents. In addition, they are sometimes steered away from the most affluent and predominantly white neighborhoods, where comparable whites are shown homes. They are also less likely to get help—from either their real estate agent or their mortgage lender—with the complexities of mortgage financing.

Asian-American homeseekers also receive inferior treatment, especially in the homeownership market. And Native Americans who try to rent housing outside tribal lands face discrimination in almost one of every three inquiries.

Racial and ethnic minorities aren't the only Americans whose housing choices are blocked by discrimination in the marketplace. Paired testing reveals even higher levels of discrimination against deaf people when they try to inquire about advertised apartments, using TTY technology, and against wheelchair users when they visit apartment buildings in search of rental housing.

While many forms of discrimination occur less frequently today than they did a decade ago, the discrimination that persists is serious, making it much harder for minority and disabled homeseekers to find the homes and apartments they want in neighborhoods of their choice.

Public education provides one essential step toward a solution. A recent Urban Institute survey found that almost 50 percent of American adults don't know that steering homebuyers to neighborhoods on the basis of race is illegal, and more than 4 out of 10 are unaware of key protections for the disabled. People who may be victims of discrimination need to know their rights; landlords and real estate agents need to understand what actions are prohibited; and all of us need to speak out against practices that limit freedom of choice.

But education alone isn't enough. Even if people know their rights, they can't exercise them if they aren't aware they have been discriminated against. Federal and state governments should provide more support for local fair housing groups that use paired testing to regularly monitor landlords and real estate agencies and bring lawsuits against those who violate the law. Housing discrimination won't end until violators know they are likely to be caught and penalized.

15

THE SEGREGATED CLASSROOMS OF A PROUDLY DIVERSE SCHOOL

Jeffrey Gettleman

Columbia High School seems to have it all—great sports teams, great academics, famous alumni and an impressive campus with Gothic buildings. But no one boasts about one aspect of this blue-ribbon school, that its classrooms are largely segregated.

Though the school is majority black, white students make up the bulk of the advanced classes, while black students far outnumber whites in lower-level classes, statistics show.

"It's kind of sad," said Ugochi Opara, a senior who is president of the student council. "You can tell right away, just by looking into a classroom, what level it is."

This is a reality at many high schools coast to coast and one of the side effects of aggressive leveling, the increasingly popular practice of dividing students into ability groups.

But at Columbia High, the students nearly revolted. Two weeks ago, a black organization on campus planned a walkout to protest the leveling system. Word soon spread to the principal, who pleaded with the students not to go. The student leaders decided to hold an assembly instead, in which they lashed out at the racial gap.

The student uproar is now forcing district officials to take a hard look at the leveling system and decide how to strike a balance between their two main goals—celebrating diversity and pushing academic achievement.

Educators say that leveling allows smarter students to be challenged while giving struggling ones the special instruction they need. But many students, especially those in the lower levels, which often carry a stigma, say such stratification makes the rocky adolescent years only harder. And at Columbia High, there is no dispute that it is precisely the leveling system that has led to racial segregation.

Anthony Paolini, a senior at Columbia, is one of the few white students in a lower-level math class. The fact that most of his classmates are black does not bother him, he said. But the low expectations do.

"It makes you feel like you're in a hole," he said.

The school, about 15 minutes from downtown Newark, draws from the cosmopolitan towns of Maplewood and South Orange. Some students live in million-dollar homes. Others rely on government lunches. Of 2,024 students, 58 percent are black, 35 percent white, 4 percent Hispanic and 3 percent Asian. The public school sends more than 90 percent of graduates to college, has a dropout rate of less than half a percent and won a national Blue Ribbon award from the federal government for its academic excellence during the 1992–93 school year. Notable alumni include the actor Zach Braff and the singer Lauryn Hill, and the fact that the two stars, one white, one black, graduated in the same class is seen as a symbol of the diversity Columbia strives to project.

But racial tension is becoming more of an issue. In recent years, the number of black students in the school district has eclipsed the number of white students even though Maplewood and South Orange still are majority white. In the past year, the district has been sued twice for discrimination: once by two former black students who said they were mistreated by teachers after a food-fight in the cafeteria, and also by a group of teachers, mostly black, who accused the principal, who is white, of racial bias.

The superintendent of the district, Peter P. Horoschak, acknowledged that there were, in a sense, two Columbias. The de facto segregation is most visible at the extremes. Statistics for this year show that while a Level 5 math class, the highest, had 79 percent white students, a Level 2 math class, the lowest, had 88 percent black students. Levels 3 and 4 tend to be more mixed, though a school board member, Mila M. Jasey, said, "Some white parents tell me that they know their kid belongs in a Level 3 class but they don't want them to be the only white kid in the class."

Though parents and students are granted some input, students are supposed to be placed in levels primarily based on grades and test scores. Many black students complain that they are unfairly relegated to the lower levels and unable to move up.

Quentin Williams, the 17-year-old leader of the Martin Luther King Association at the school, calls it "contemporary segregation." He said that his organization, one of the largest on campus, had tried to meet with the administration over the issue several times but "got the runaround."

So in mid-March his group planned to walk out of school. They even had the backing of several parents, who volunteered to help. As the date approached, Quentin, a senior, said he felt "a lot of pressure coming in from a lot of different angles."

Student leaders eventually decided that holding an assembly would give them a better opportunity to publicly confront administrators, especially the principal, Renee Pollack. At the assembly, which was mandatory for all students, she stood in front of the student body and apologized for saying anything that might have been construed as insensitive.

Ms. Pollack said later that complaints about her were being spread by teachers on her own staff.

"They were trying to manipulate the kids in order to get at me," said Ms. Pollack, who has been the principal for three years and is up for tenure this month.

The flashpoint of the assembly came when Nathan Winkler, a skinny, intense senior who says he wants to be governor some day, grabbed the microphone and announced that he had no sympathy for people in lower levels because all it took was hard work to move up.

His short outburst was like a cleaver, splitting the student body in two. Many blacks booed him. Many whites cheered. He was then accused of using the term "you people" in his speech—though he did not, according to a videotape of the assembly. After the assembly, he said, he was stalked in the hallways.

He now admits that he spoke out of fear.

"I felt extremely isolated during that assembly," he said. "For the first time I was aware of being part of the minority. White kids are outnumbered at Columbia. I knew that, but I hadn't really felt it before."

Student leaders and administrators are now discussing ways to narrow the so-called achievement gap, like granting students more say in which level they are in; better identifying which level students belong in; expanding a summer school program for students who want to take upper-level classes. Administrators say they had been working on all this before the walkout threat.

"But the students forced the issue," Ms. Pollack acknowledged.

Ms. Pollack also pointed out that this year, more students of color from Columbia have been accepted into Ivy League universities than white students, with two Hispanic, three black and two white students gaining early admission.

The debate over leveling here boils down to fairness. Is it fair just to ensure equal access to upper-level classes? Or does fairness go farther than that and require administrators to truly level the playing field so that the racial makeup of upper classes better resembles the racial makeup of the school?

Stewart Hendricks, a senior whose father is from Guyana and whose mother is Swiss, said that some teachers do seem to have lower expectations for black students but that he did not let them get him down.

"The purpose of high school is to prepare you for the real world," he said. "And in the real world, you can't listen to other peoples' expectations, because in the real world, people are just waiting for you to fail."

Because of his mixed racial heritage, he said, "I guess you can say I'm in the middle of all this."

And in a way, that is why he sympathizes with the principal.

"She's got an entire black population that wants to get rid of the leveling system and an entire white population who would leave this town if they did that," he said. "What's she supposed to do?"

16

RACE AND FAMILY INCOME OF STUDENTS INFLUENCE GUIDANCE COUNSELORS' ADVICE, STUDY FINDS

Eric Hoover

The race and famly income of prospective college applicants influence the advice that high-school guidance counselors give them, according to a study released on Monday.

Counselors were more likely to recommend community colleges to middle-class black students with sub-par academic records than to middle-class white students with similar records, the study found. Among wealthier students with poor academic records, however, counselors were more likely to urge white students than black students to attend community colleges.

The study also found that counselors were more likely to recommend community colleges to middle-class students than to wealthier ones, and they recommended four-year colleges more strongly to upper-class students than to middle-class students.

The findings are based on the results of a three-year study sponsored by the National Commission for Cooperative Education, which sent surveys to 20,000 high-school counselors throughout the nation. Respondents received one of 16 profiles of fictional students specifying race, gender, family income, and academic performance. The counselors were asked to indicate how strongly they would recommend that the student seek more information about, visit, and apply to a four-year college and a community college. The results were based on a sample of approximately 1,700 responses.

The study, "High School Guidance Counselors: Facilitators or Pre-Emptors of Social Stratification in Education," was conducted by Frank Linnehan, an associate professor of management at Drexel University; Christy Weer, a Ph.D. candidate at Drexel; and Paul J. Stonely, the commission's president. The researchers plan to present their findings at a meeting of the Academy of Management in August.

17

College Choices Are Limited for Students from Needy Families, Report Says

Stephen Burd

Most students from low-income families never consider going to college, and those who do tend to go to community and for-profit colleges, according to a report released on Tuesday by the Pell Institute for the Study of Opportunity in Higher Education.

Officials at the Pell Institute say that the report, "Indicators of Opportunity in Higher Education," is the first of what will be an annual look at the ability of needy students to go to college and graduate. The institute is part of the Council for Opportunity in Education, which lobbies on behalf of the federal TRIO programs for disadvantaged students.

"This is the first national report of its kind that measures available opportunities for low-income students to access and succeed in higher education," said Arnold L. Mitchem, the council's president. "It clearly illustrates that our nation must take steps right now to seriously expand programs that improve access to higher education so that we can open the doors of postsecondary education for all students."

Using data collected by the Higher Education Research Institute at the University of California at Los Angeles in its annual survey of college freshmen, the report examines where students at different economic levels are going to college. It found that, in recent academic years:

- At community colleges, 20 percent of all students were from families with annual incomes under $25,000, 59 percent were from families earning $25,000 to $74,999, and 21 percent were from those making $75,000 and above.

- At private two-year institutions, 22 percent of all students were from the lowest-income group, 50 percent were from the middle-income group, and 28 percent were from the highest-income group.

- At public four-year colleges, 11 percent were from the lowest-income group, 48 percent were from the middle-income group, and 41 percent were from the highest-income group.
- At private four-year colleges, 8 percent were from the lowest-income group, 35 percent were from the middle-income group, and 57 percent were from the highest-income group.

The report also cites data from the U.S. Education Department's National Postsecondary Student Aid Study that show that 6 percent of all low-income students attend private for-profit institutions, compared with 2 percent of middle-income students and 1 percent of high-income students.

The report says that there appears to be an "increased stratification by students' income, meaning that low-income students are increasingly attending two-year and non-degree-granting institutions." If low-income students are unable to go to four-year colleges and obtain a bachelor's degree, the report says, "their aspirations and achievements will be limited."

18

WEALTHY OFTEN WIN THE RACE FOR MERIT-BASED COLLEGE AID

Jay Mathews

A father recently wrote to Dickinson College complaining that although the school admitted his daughter, it did not offer her any scholarship money, which two of its competitors had. The family's income was $250,000 a year, but the father figured that the Carlisle, Pa., college would kick in some financial aid rather than risk losing a student with excellent grades and test scores.

Robert J. Massa, Dickinson's vice president for enrollment and college relations, said the father's request did not surprise him. It was typical of the rising tide of "merit" or "non-need-based" scholarships—a zero-sum game, Massa said, that is hurting the quality of undergraduate education.

"Family expectations of price incentives are rampant, and my colleagues and I take the bait," he said.

A 2003 study by the Indianapolis-based Lumina Foundation for Education reported that from 1995 to 2000, scholarship aid to students from families making $40,000 or less increased 22 percent in 1999 dollars. At the same time, scholarship aid for students in families making $100,000 or more a year increased 145 percent.

Experts have said the growth in merit scholarships—grants for students with good grades or test scores—stems from two factors: the escalating competition between private colleges for accomplished students and state efforts to encourage enrollment in public universities by giving scholarships to all residents with decent grade-point averages.

Sandy Baum, professor of economics at Skidmore College in Saratoga Springs, N.Y., and senior policy analyst for the New York-based nonprofit College Board, said the private colleges' use of non-need-based aid encourages wealthy applicants and discourages those with little money. "If the private colleges don't refocus more dollars on students with high-level needs," she said, "they are going to become places that are totally closed to low-income students."

A few educators, such as Massa, are trying to turn the tide by reducing the number of merit scholarships they give to students, even if that handicaps them in the battle for prime undergraduates. "The bottom line is that society is no better off if a kid goes to Dickinson or goes to the University of Richmond," Massa said.

That quote is not to be found anywhere on Dickinson's Web site, with its pictures of eager high school students touring the campus. But the 2,200-undergraduate institution has a fine reputation and a surplus of good applicants—it accepts only half of those who apply—so Massa has been able to cut back on merit scholarships without reducing the quality of his freshman classes.

Merit aid recipients in Dickinson's freshman class of 600 decreased from 104 in 1999 to 64 last year. At the same time, the average SAT scores of those freshmen increased from 1189 to 1274, and minority enrollment increased from 4 percent to 15 percent.

Supporters of merit scholarships say students' high school academic accomplishments deserve the same kind of financial recognition that heavily recruited athletes get. They also note that state-sponsored merit programs appear to be persuading more students than ever, including low-income students, to give college a try.

In a chapter of a new book, *College Choices: The Economics of Where to Go, When to Go and How to Pay for It,* Susan Dynarski, assistant professor of public policy at Harvard University's John F. Kennedy School of Government, said that "since the early 1990s, more than a dozen states have established broad-based merit aid programs." The typical program gives tuition and fee money to residents who have at least a "B," or 3.0, grade-point average.

One of the most successful programs, the HOPE Scholarships in Georgia, paid $277 million in state lottery proceeds to 75,000 students from 2000 to 2001, Dynarski said.

Baum said, "The merit programs appear to be more effective than need-based aid at achieving this goal" of low-income enrollment in part because need-based scholarships, unlike merit aid, require families to fill out complicated forms.

Those results have convinced many governors and state legislatures that merit aid is a good idea. Many private college educators agree, even if it seems that they are sometimes subsidizing the wealthy. Much private-college merit aid goes to families that are making financial sacrifices, even if they don't qualify for need-based aid, college administrators have said.

19

A DEATH IN PATCHOGUE

New York Times Editorial

Marcelo Lucero was killed late Saturday night near the commuter railroad station in Patchogue, N.Y., a middle-class village in central Long Island. He was beaten and stabbed. The friend who crouched beside him in a parking lot as he lay dying, soaked in blood, said Mr. Lucero, who was 37, had come to the United States 16 years ago from Ecuador.

The police arrested seven teenage boys, who they said had driven into the village from out of town looking for Latinos to beat up. The police said the mob cornered Mr. Lucero and another man, who escaped and later identified the suspects to the police. A prosecutor at the arraignment on Monday quoted the young men as having said: "Let's go find some Mexicans." They have pleaded not guilty.

The county executive, Steve Levy, quickly issued a news release denouncing this latest apparent hate crime in Suffolk County. That should be the first and least of the actions he and other leaders take.

A possible lynching in a New York suburb should be more than enough to force this country to acknowledge the bitter chill that has overcome Latinos in these days of rage against illegal immigration.

The atmosphere began to darken when Republican politicians decided a few years ago to exploit immigration as a wedge issue. They drafted harsh legislation to criminalize the undocumented. They cheered as vigilantes streamed to the border to confront the concocted crisis of Spanish-speaking workers sneaking in to steal jobs and spread diseases. Cable personalities and radio talk-show hosts latched on to the issue. Years of effort in Congress to assemble a responsible overhaul of the immigration system failed repeatedly. Its opponents wanted only to demonize and punish the Latino workers on which the country had come to depend.

A campaign of raids and deportations, led by federal agents with help from state and local posses, has become so pervasive that nearly 1 in 10 Latinos, including citizens and legal immigrants, have told of being stopped and asked about their immigration status, according to the Pew Hispanic Center. Now that the economy is in free fall, the possibility of scapegoating is deepening Hispanic anxiety.

It is not yet clear how closely connected Mr. Lucero's murder is to this broad wave of xenophobia. But there is both a message and opportunity here for officials like Mr. Levy, an immigration hard-liner whose relations with his rapidly growing Latino immigrant constituency have been strained by past crises and confrontations.

Deadly violence represents the worst fear that immigrants deal with every day, but it is not the only one. It must be every leader's task to move beyond easy outrage and take on the difficult job of understanding and defending a community so vulnerable to sudden outbreaks of hostility and terror.

20

ON L.I., RAID STIRS DISPUTE OVER INFLUX OF IMMIGRANTS

Bruce Lambert

Among the many tenants crammed into the basement, one slept on a mattress atop a heating oil tank. The front door was blocked by furniture. Garbage piled up outside. Extension cords snaked and dangled everywhere, one draped across a propane tank with a religious candle burning nearby. None of the smoke detectors worked.

Those were just a few of the conditions that investigators say that they found at 33 Woodmont Place, where, Brookhaven town officials said, up to 64 people were living in a 900-square-foot rooming house zoned for one family. There were 44 beds in the home.

But Brookhaven and Suffolk County authorities were not greeted with unanimous praise after arresting the owner and shuttering the squalid house last week.

Instead, the crackdown reopened Farmingville's civic wounds over the influx of thousands of Mexican laborers, many of them illegal immigrants, into this blue-collar Long Island suburb. Often they live in overcrowded houses, and the town said it was investigating 123 other suspected cases.

"This has reignited the whole issue of hatred for immigrants in that community," said the Rev. Allan B. Ramirez, an advocate for illegal immigrants.

On the other side, some longtime homeowners cheered the enforcement as sorely overdue protection of their way of life.

Steve Levy, executive of Suffolk County, said, "We're going to stand up for the people of this county who have been exploited in their neighborhoods." The raid also rescued the immigrants from inhumane and potentially disastrous conditions, he said.

But the Mexicans, who are now homeless, accused Mr. Levy of racism, complaining that he left them with no place to live. "If he shut down a home with 30 or 40 dogs, would he have put them out on the street," asked Mr. Ramirez, "or would he have found a home for them?"

To protest the raid, the Mexicans planned to march on Sunday afternoon to call for an end to such evictions and to demand a meeting with Mr. Levy.

But Mr. Levy has refused to budge. "I will not meet with them on this matter," he said. "It's absurd to even discuss the notion we would keep such a facility open. I'm not one who's going to be intimidated by their antics or marches. Bring it on."

On Thursday night, Farmingville's renewed polarization played out on opposite ends of Waverly Avenue.

At the Sequoya Middle School, color photographs of the rooming house violations were displayed on a stage as about 60 residents and a score of town officials and political candidates gathered for a meeting of the Greater Farmingville Community Association, a homeowner group. Critical of past government inaction, the crowd repeatedly applauded the crackdown.

"We're mad as hell, and we're not going to take it anymore," said Ray Wysolmierski, the group's president. Referring to the Mexicans, he said, "This is an invasion and occupation." In the past he has called them "terrorists."

That same night, in an unmarked building a few miles north on Waverly, dozens of Mexicans met under the auspices of the United Day Laborers of Long Island and the Workplace Project, nonprofit groups that aid immigrants.

Their session was private, but about 11 p.m. someone emerged with a flier announcing the march and headlined, "Say NO to forced homelessness."

Some tenants say they were locked out and unable to retrieve their belongings. "I came home from work and couldn't get into my house," said a man who gave only a first name, Emiliano. Town officials say that arrangements have been made for the former residents to obtain their possessions.

The relocation issue is the source of another dispute. County officials indicated that Brookhaven was responsible, but the town denies having social service jurisdiction. Town officials said that they had contacted various charities, but that there was not enough time for them to help.

Tensions peaked in Farmingville in 2000 after two out-of-towners pretended to hire two Mexican workers in a group house on Granny Road, next to Woodmont, then nearly beat them to death. In 2003 teenagers set fire to the house next door, and a Mexican family sleeping inside barely escaped.

Politicians have grappled with the volatile issue. Mr. Levy, a Democrat, rejected a proposed hiring hall for day laborers, earning praise from some homeowners but criticism from liberals and minority groups.

Brookhaven has long been a Republican powerhouse, but after corruption scandals, the party faces a tough election this fall. Accused of lax code enforcement in the past, the town is taking an aggressive stance.

Homeowners have staged their own protests, picketing Mexican laborers who congregate on street corners seeking work from landscaping and construction contractors. Neighbors complain of excess traffic, and say the men are sometimes rude.

At night some Mexicans play loud music, drink and get rowdy, some neighbors say. At 33 Woodmont Place, with dozens of tenants but only two bathrooms, men often went outside to urinate, town investigators reported. Some neighbors said that men sometimes defecated in cans and buried the waste in the backyard.

But advocates for the Mexican workers say that most of them avoid trouble and simply want to earn money for their families back home. The 28 men found at 33 Woodmont Place last Sunday had no arrest warrants pending the police said.

Neighbors began complaining about 33 Woodmont a year ago, prompting investigations, tickets for fire and building code violations, and court orders for compliance.

The owner, Rosalina Dias, 31, refused to obey, officials say, so they arrested her on contempt of court charges. She is being defended by Bertil Peterson, a lawyer for the Coalition of Landlords, Homeowners and Merchants, a Long Island property rights group that fights government controls. Its president, Paul Palmieri, said that Ms. Dias's only comment was to deny the charges.

Property records show that Ms. Dias paid $86,000 for the house in 1999. The authorities say she charged up to $250 month to each tenant, for a total monthly income exceeding $9,000. At that rate, she would recover the costs about every ten months.

Ms. Dias's own home, at 6 Marlo Road in Selden, is a large two-story structure with a basement and a stone and stucco facade. The front entrance has 11 wide granite steps lined by a balustrade. A one-and-a-half story two-car garage, about the size of the rooming house on Woodmont, is set off by an artificial stone waterfall.

21

MORE BLACKS LIVE WITH POLLUTION

The Associated Press

An Associated Press analysis of a little-known government research project shows that black Americans are 79 percent more likely than whites to live in neighborhoods where industrial pollution is suspected of posing the greatest health danger.

Residents in neighborhoods with the highest pollution scores also tend to be poorer, less educated and more often unemployed than those elsewhere in the country, AP found.

"Poor communities, frequently communities of color but not exclusively, suffer disproportionately," said Carol Browner, who headed the Environmental Protection Agency during the Clinton administration when the scoring system was developed. "If you look at where our industrialized facilities tend to be located, they're not in the upper middle class neighborhoods."

With help from government scientists, AP mapped the risk scores for every neighborhood counted by the Census Bureau in 2000. The scores were then used to compare risks between neighborhoods and to study the racial and economic status of those who breathe America's most unhealthy air.

President Clinton ordered the government in 1993 to ensure equality in protecting Americans from pollution, but more than a decade later, factory emissions still disproportionately place minorities and the poor at risk, AP found.

In 19 states, blacks were more than twice as likely as whites to live in neighborhoods where air pollution seems to pose the greatest health danger, the analysis showed.

More than half the blacks in Kansas and nearly half of Missouri's black population, for example, live in the 10 percent of their states' neighborhoods with the highest risk scores. Similarly, more than four out of every 10 blacks in Kentucky, Minnesota, Oregon and Wisconsin live in high-risk neighborhoods.

And while Hispanics and Asians aren't overrepresented in high-risk neighborhoods nationally, in certain states they are. In Michigan, for example, 8.3 percent of the people living in high-risk areas are Hispanic, though Hispanics make up 3.3 percent of the statewide population.

All told, there are 12 states where Hispanics are more than twice as likely as non-Hispanics to live in neighborhoods with the highest risk scores. There are seven states where Asians are more than twice as likely as whites to live in the most polluted areas.

The average income in the highest risk neighborhoods was $18,806 when the Census last measured it, more than $3,000 less than the nationwide average.

One of every six people in the high-risk areas lived in poverty, compared with one of eight elsewhere, AP found.

Unemployment was nearly 20 percent higher than the national average in the neighborhoods with the highest risk scores, and residents there were far less likely to have college degrees.

Research over the past two decades has shown that short-term exposure to common air pollution worsens existing lung and heart disease and is linked to diseases like asthma, bronchitis and cancer. Long-term exposure increases the risks.

* * *

The Associated Press analyzed the health risk posed by industrial air pollution using data from the U.S. Environmental Protection Agency and the Census Bureau.

EPA uses toxic chemical air releases reported by factories to calculate a health risk score for each square kilometer of the United States. The scores can be used to compare risks from long-term exposure to factory pollution from one area to another.

The scores are based on:

- The amount of toxic pollution released by each factory.
- The path the pollution takes as it spreads through the air.
- The level of danger to humans posed by each different chemical released.
- The number of males and females of different ages who live in the exposure paths.

The scores aren't meant to measure the actual risks of getting sick or the actual exposure to toxic chemicals. Instead, they are designed to help screen for polluted areas that may need additional study of potential health problems, EPA said.

The AP mapped the health risk scores to the census blocks used during the 2000 population count, using a method developed in consultation with EPA. The news service then compared racial and socioeconomic makeup with risk scores in the top 5 percent to the population elsewhere.

Similar analyses were done in each state, comparing the 10 percent of neighborhoods with the highest risk scores to the rest in the state.

To match the 2000 Census data, the AP used health risk scores calculated from industrial pollution reports that companies filed for EPA's 2000 Toxic Release Inventory. It often takes several years for EPA to learn of and correct inaccurate reports from factories, and the 2000 data were more complete than data from more recent reports that were still being corrected.

The AP adjusted the 2000 health risk scores in Census blocks around some plants that filed incorrect air release reports in 2000, after plant officials provided corrected data.

Counties that had the highest potential health risk from industrial air pollution in 2000, according to an AP analysis of government records.   The health risk varies from year to year based on the level of factory emissions, the opening of new plants and the closing of older plants.

1. Washington County, Ohio
2. Wood County, W.Va.
3. Muscatine County, Iowa
4. Leflore County, Miss.
5. Cowlitz County, Wash.
6. Henry County, Ind.
7. Tooele County, Utah
8. Scott County, Iowa
9. Gila County, Ariz.
10. Whiteside County, Ill.

Factories whose emissions created the most potential health risk for residents in surrounding communities in 2000, according to an AP analysis of government records.

1. Eramet Marietta Inc., Marietta, Ohio
2. Titan Wheel Corp., Walcott, Iowa (closed in 2003)
3. Eastman Kodak Co., Rochester, N.Y.
4. American Minerals Inc., El Paso, Texas
5. F.W. Winter Inc., Camden, N.J.
6. Meridian Rail Corp., Cicero, Ill.
7. Carpenter Tech. Corp., Reading, Pa.
8. Longview Aluminum LLC, Longview, Wash. (closed in 2001)
9. DDE Louisville, Louisville, Ky.
10. Lincoln Electric Co., Cleveland

On the Net:

The Environmental Protection Agency: http://www.epa.gov
Details of the EPA's Risk Screening Environmental Indicators Project at: http://www.epa.gov/opptintr/rsei/views.html

22

LESBIAN SUES SCHOOL DISTRICT OVER HARASSMENT

Judy Peet

All she ever wanted, Nancy Wadington said, was an education.

Instead, the Holmdel teenager said she got a daily lesson in humiliation from classmates who called her names, threw bottles at her, urinated in her backpack and pushed her down a flight of stairs.

Wadington, 18, is a lesbian. She was when she started Holmdel High School in 2001 and when she left after nearly three years of what her mother called "a living nightmare."

Yesterday, Lambda Legal, a national gay rights organization, filed suit on behalf of Wadington, charging that Holmdel school officials knew about the abuse and ignored it.

The lawsuit is the first in New Jersey asking for a jury to determine monetary damages for anti-gay harassment in the schools, which is illegal under the state's civil rights laws.

"It is an atrocity that school officials would ignore laws in New Jersey, which are touted as being the most comprehensive nondiscrimination laws on the books," Alphonso David, a Lambda staff attorney, said at a news conference announcing the suit.

Holmdel officials said they were unaware of Wadington's allegations and first learned of them from court papers yesterday.

"If it's true, of course it's distressing," said school board attorney Martin Barger, who has represented the Monmouth County district since 1978. "But it wasn't ignored at the highest level because we never heard of it."

Superintendent Maureen Flaherty said the school code of conduct explicitly bans harassment based on various factors, including sexual orientation, and requires principals to report all harassment.

She said she never heard of Wadington. The principal during the time Wadington was a student has since left the district.

Though the lawsuit may be the first seeking a jury trial in a case involving alleged gay-bashing in New Jersey schools, there is precedent.

In 1998, a Wisconsin school district paid $1 million to a student who suffered similarly after a federal appeals court ruled that schools are liable for ignoring anti-gay harassment.

Last year, the New Jersey Division on Civil Rights ordered the Toms River Regional School District to pay $50,000 to a boy who was slapped, punched and taunted by classmates who thought he was gay. The district was also fined $10,000 and ordered to upgrade its policies.

Wadington's suit said the abuse began in 2001 when she was in ninth grade. Wadington was not the only gay or lesbian student at Holmdel High, but was the only one "outed" by one of her classmates, said David, who did not allow his client to answer questions.

David said the classmates—whom he identified as a small cluster of males and females—called Wadington names and threw food and bottles at her in the cafeteria. She and her mother complained several times, but "school officials took no effective measures in response."

In the spring of ninth grade, Wadington's backpack was stolen. It was found in one of the boys' bathrooms, covered with urine. Soon after that, her locker was broken into and her books and belongings scattered around the school hallway, spat on and damaged, according to the lawsuit.

Wadington complained and was again told nothing could be done. "Instead school administrators charged Nancy for the books that had been destroyed," the complaint stated.

When she was in 10th grade, the abuse became physical, culminating when students, who were not identified, pushed her down a flight of stairs, according to the lawsuit.

Her mother, Barbara, continued to beg for help from school authorities, but without success, David said. He did not comment on whether the family attempted to contact the school board or superintendent.

By her junior year, Wadington was so upset that a counselor at the local YMCA intervened with school administrators, according to court papers. The school placed Wadington on home instruction for the rest of the year.

The school also classified her as "emotionally disturbed" and transferred her for her senior year to Collier High School, a private school for special education students.

The suit seeks compensatory damages for physical and emotional pain and suffering. It also seeks an order forcing Holmdel to implement better anti-discrimination policies.

23

Director Accuses Police Complaint Board of Bias

Christine Hauser

The executive director of the Civilian Complaint Review Board, the independent city agency that investigates allegations of police misconduct, is accusing other board officials of discriminating against her because she is black.

The director, Joan M. Thompson, said, according to documents her lawyer sent to the board, that she was "subjected to discriminatory remarks"; that she was referred to as a "black bitch"; and that two deputy directors said she was hired because of her race and would "turn the agency black."

Ms. Thompson, 62, who started working for the board about a year ago, said that when she told the head of the agency's board, Franklin Stone, on Dec. 12, 2007, about the disparaging remarks, Ms. Stone replied "in a screaming manner that she didn't believe me," the documents said.

Ms. Stone formed a committee in June to review Ms. Thompson's job performance, Ms. Thompson wrote, adding, "Not only has there never been a black executive director in the history of the C.C.R.B., but no prior executive director had ever been evaluated."

Ms. Thompson's lawyer, Alan Serrins, sent the board a letter on Friday outlining the charge of discrimination, along with a form that is used to file complaints with the federal Equal Employment Opportunity Commission. The form was filled out; the lawyer wrote that he and Ms. Thompson would file the complaint with the federal commission unless the board moved quickly to "resolve this situation in an amicable fashion."

A spokesman for the board, Phil Weitzman, said, "We do not comment on personnel matters or actual or threatened lawsuits." He referred inquiries to the city's Law Department, which represents the board in such matters.

Georgia Pestana, the chief of labor and employment law in the Law Department, said, "It is unfortunate that this complaint has been made, and if Ms. Thompson pursues the litigation we will address it at that point."

In completing the form, Ms. Thompson did not say whether she had heard the comments directly or secondhand, or whether she had seen them in writing. Mr. Serrins declined to comment.

Ms. Thompson wrote that the problems started in November 2007 and continued through June. She said she was yelled at in front of the staff, prevented from opening mail and told she was incompetent. She has continued to report for work.

The allegations might seem incongruous for an agency that investigates misconduct like abuse of force and discourtesy by officers.

The board can recommend action by the Police Department, but has no power to carry it out. It has about 180 employees, most of whom are in investigations, and 13 board members named by the mayor, the City Council and the police commissioner. The board interviewed finalists for the executive director's job before hiring Ms. Thompson last year.

Ms. Thompson is responsible for daily operations, like reviewing cases and transcripts of board meetings. When the board hired her, it said in a statement that she had "worked for years fighting discrimination" in equal-opportunity compliance jobs at the Department of Education and the New York City Police Department.

Suggestions for Further Reading

See daily papers as well as weekly and monthly national magazines for continuing accounts of discrimination and harassment, as well as signs of change.

The Economics of Race, Class, and Gender

Although it is fashionable to deny the existence of rich and poor and to proclaim us all "middle class," class divisions are real and the gap between rich and poor in the United States is growing at an alarming rate. In, fact it's wider now than at any time since World War II. How does this impact on the lives of people living in the United States today? What kind of economic realities do we face as we seek to feed, clothe, house, and educate ourselves and our families? As we have already seen, being born into a particular class, racial/ethnic group, and sex has repercussions that affect every aspect of a person's life. In Part V we attempt to understand something of their impact by turning our attention from lottery winners' windfalls and sports stars' salaries often spotlighted in the media to statistics that reveal the economic realities faced by most ordinary people in their daily lives. Selection 1 by Holly Sklar, "Imagine a Country," provides a dramatic and thought-provoking introduction to this part.

The 1990s was an incredible decade for economic growth, but the start of the new century saw workers' pensions, 401K plans, and dot.com millionaires vanish overnight while the proportion of Americans living in poverty rose significantly. The story of the new century continues to be a persistent increase in the gap between rich and poor, a gap that has been increasing slowly but steadily since 1973. Selections 2, 3, 8, and 12 report on the most recent rises in this gap and paint a bleak picture of how ordinary families are faring in this economy. Among the most disturbing figures presented: The United States is now the third most unequal industrialized society after Russia and Mexico; for the first time on record, household incomes failed to increase for five

303

straight years; the poverty rate rose in 2004 for working-age people 18 to 64; the wealth gap between white families and Blacks and Hispanics has increased; and fewer people are getting health insurance from their employers. Commenting on current economic trends, a resident scholar at a conservative Washington, DC, research group observed that "gains have gone to capital and not to workers." And according to Chuck Collins and Felice Yeskel, this is no accident. They attribute the widening economic disparities in the United States to three decades of public policies designed to benefit major corporations at the expense of the rest of us.

In Selection 5, *New York Times* Op Ed columnist Bob Herbert takes a look at the growing problem of hunger in the United States. According to a report by the Department of Agriculture, more than 12 million families or approximately 11.2 percent of all U.S. households have a hard time feeding themselves. Herbert finds this particularly egregious in a country as wealthy as ours and asks why the fact that so many low-income working families cannot meet their basic needs isn't framed as a problem of major proportions worthy of national attention.

The next three articles all focus on poverty and race. The first turns our attention to race and extreme inequality and the next makes clear that any attempts to claim that we are now in a post-racial period are not credible. In the third article, Henry Louis Gates Jr. suggests that there is a significant correlation between property ownership and achievement. He argues that people who own property feel a sense of ownership in the future and that people without property often live in a culture without hope. Gates, like many others, points to differences in accumulated wealth to explain differences in standards of living and quality of life enjoyed by different racial/ethnic groups.

Current data on home ownership, poverty rates, and family income broken down according to ethnicity is provided in Selections 9 and 10, which paint a detailed picture of the economic realities faced by Latinos and Asian Americans in the United States. Taking us behind the broad generalizations frequently offered by the media, these two articles examine the unique situations of various Latino and Asian American ethnic groups and explore the specific history of discrimination and the social, cultural, and economic factors that lie behind the racial wealth gap in this country.

Selections 11 and 12 examine the wage gap first through the lens of gender and then through lenses of race/ethnicity and other variables. Ruth Conniff's article, "Women Losing Ground," explores the many factors that impact on women's economic situations. A series of charts and graphs presents an overview of the way differences in race/ethnicity and sex affect occupation and earnings in the United States today. These materials graphically illustrate the persistence of a wage gap between women and men over many years. If you have already read some of the newspaper accounts of cases of discrimination included in Part IV, this data may not come as such a surprise. But other data provided by The Wage Project will surprise you. Current statistics that highlight differences in earnings correlated with sex tell us that female college graduates in general earn $24,963 a year *less* than male graduates and over a lifetime this amounts to a $1.2 million gap in earnings between women and men who hold a college degree. Taken together, the material in this selection documents a persistent wage gap based on race and sex over many years and suggests that racism and sexism, not ability or qualifications, have determined which jobs women and men do and how much worth is attached to their work.

In sharp contrast to the reality that the articles and statistics in this section describe, the mythology of the American Dream continues to assure us that hard work and ability, not family background or connections, is the key to success. In Selection 14, "The Sons Also Rise," Princeton professor Paul Krugman reports on a recent study that once again contradicts this myth. Krugman tells us that "the children of today's wealthy" have "a huge advantage over those who chose the wrong parents." And he repeats the sobering news we have already seen, that "the spectacular increase in American inequality has made the gap between the rich and the middle class wider, and hence more difficult to cross, than it was in the past."

Selection 15, "The Education of Jessica Rivera," tells the story of a 20-year-old college student who, during an earlier time period, might well have provided us with an inspiring example of upward mobility through hard work and determination. Rivera's story is heartbreaking in many respects and suggests the pointless and punitive nature of many recent changes in welfare policy. As conservative politicians carry out a war against the poor that denies those on welfare or in prison the opportunity to acquire a college education and a better life, it is no wonder that the gap between rich and poor is growing ever wider and ever harder to cross.

And this unequal treatment starts well before a student ever thinks of seeking to enroll in higher education. Selection 16 reports on the "Savage Inequalities" of school funding across the county, which continues to see wealthy, white school districts receiving significantly more funding than poor districts and districts with large numbers of students of color. You may find it interesting to jump ahead to Part VIII and read the article entitled "Still Separate, Still Unequal: American Apartheid Education" by Jonathan Kozol.

The relationship between poverty or income inequality and poor health is explored in a sobering article by Alejandro Reuss entitled "Cause of Death: Inequality." According to the findings he presents, there is a high correlation between life expectancy, chronic disease, death by injury, and generally poor health and low income or low status. Perhaps most surprising for many of us will be Reuss's assertion that those of us who are worse off in the United States are not well off by comparison with people in other countries. While that may be true with respect to consumer goods he reports, it is decidedly not true with respect to health and heath care. His conclusion: inequality can kill.

Part V concludes with an essay by Alejandro Portes that looks at the plight of immigrant children in the United States today. Despite the recent and on-going debate about our immigration policy, U.S. business is dependent upon immigrant workers to fill a host of menial jobs in agribusiness, hotels, landscaping, and other low-paying work. While paying such wages may be in the short-term interests of corporations and businesses seeking high profits, the economic benefits these corporations and businesses derive is creating a "rainbow underclass." As Portes observes, the very "low wages that make foreign workers so attractive to employers translate into poverty and inferior schooling for their children." The cumulative effects of growing up in poverty, along with the effects of race discrimination experienced by so many immigrant children, suggest a dire future both for these children and for society at large.

Imagine a Country — 2009

Holly Sklar

Imagine a country where one out of four children is born into poverty, and wealth is being redistributed upward. Since the 1970s, the richest 1 percent of households has nearly doubled its share of the nation's wealth. The top 1 percent has more wealth than the bottom 90 percent of households combined.

It's not Jamaica.

Imagine a country whose national intelligence agency says, "Since 1975, practically all the gains in household income have gone to the top 20% of households." Especially the very top.

Imagine a country where economic inequality has gone back to the future circa the 1920s. By 2006, the richest 1 percent had increased their share of the nation's income to the second-highest level on record. The only year higher was 1928—on the eve of a great depression.

Imagine a country where more and more jobs are keeping people in poverty instead of out of poverty.

Imagine a country where healthcare aides can't afford to take sick days. Where farm workers and security guards turn to overwhelmed food banks to help feed their families, and homelessness is rising among working families.

Imagine a country where some are paid so little their children go without necessities—while others are paid so much their grandchildren could live in luxury without having to work at all.

Imagine a country where the 400 richest taxpayers quadrupled their incomes between 1992 and 2006, adjusted for inflation. The richest 400 taxpayers had an average 2006 adjusted gross income of $263 million each—more than $5 million a week—on their federal income tax returns (excluding tax-exempt interest income from state and local government bonds).

Imagine a country where taxes were cut so much that the nation's richest bosses pay lower effective rates than workers. The 400 richest taxpayers paid an average federal tax rate of 17 percent in 2006—down from 26 percent in 1992.

Imagine a country that gave tax breaks to millionaires while millions of people went without health insurance and the infrastructure built by earlier generations of taxpayers fell apart. Tax cuts saved the top 1 percent nearly half a trillion dollars between 2001 and 2008. The $79.5 billion in tax cuts for the top 1 percent in

2008 was more than the budgets of the nation's department of education and environmental protection agency combined.

Imagine a country giving tax breaks to billionaires and millionaires while going into massive debt with other countries.

It's not Egypt.

Imagine a country where worker productivity went up, but workers' wages went down.

In the words of the national labor department, "As the productivity of workers increases, one would expect worker compensation [wages and benefits] to experience similar gains." Between 1947 and 1973, worker productivity rose 104 percent and the minimum wage rose 101 percent, adjusted for inflation. But between 1973 and 2008, as worker productivity rose 87 percent, the average hourly wage fell 10 percent and the minimum wage fell 16 percent.

Imagine a country where minimum wage increases have been so little, so late that minimum wage workers earn less today, adjusting for inflation, than they did in 1956.

Imagine a country where the minimum wage has become a poverty wage instead of an anti-poverty wage. The minimum wage has lagged so far behind necessities that keeping a roof overhead is a constant struggle and family health coverage would cost nearly all the annual income of a full-time worker at minimum wage.

Imagine a country with poverty rates higher than they were in the 1970s. Imagine a country that sets the official poverty line well below the actual cost of minimally adequate housing, healthcare, food, and other necessities. On average, households need more than double the official poverty threshold to meet basic needs.

It's not Mexico.

Imagine a country where some of the worst CEOs make millions more in a year than the best CEOs of earlier generations made in their lifetimes.

In 1980, CEOs of major corporations made an average 45 times the pay of average full-time workers. In 1991, when CEOs made 140 times as much as workers, a prominent pay expert said the CEO "is paid so much more than ordinary workers that he hasn't got the slightest clue as to how the rest of the country lives." In 2003, a leading business magazine put a pig in a pinstriped suit on the cover and headlined its CEO pay roundup, "Have they no shame? Their performance stank last year, yet most CEOs got paid more than ever." In 2007, CEOs made 353 times the pay of average workers.

It's not England.

Imagine a country where wages have fallen despite greatly increased education. Since 1973, the share of workers without a high school degree has plummeted and the percentage with at least four years of college has more than doubled. But the 2008 average hourly wage was 10 percent below 1973, adjusted for inflation.

Imagine a country where college tuition and fees increased three times more than median family income from 1982 to 2007. Student borrowing has more than doubled in just the last decade. Students from lower-income families receive smaller grants from colleges and universities than students from upper-income families.

Imagine a country where households headed by persons under age 44 had lower median net worth (assets minus debt) in 2007 than in 1989, adjusted for inflation.

Imagine a country where more and more two-paycheck households are struggling to afford a home, college, healthcare, and retirement, once normal for middle-class households with one paycheck. Middle-class households are a medical crisis, outsourced job, or busted pension away from bankruptcy.

Households tried to prop themselves up in the face of falling real wages by maxing out work hours, credit cards, and home equity loans. Consumer spending makes up about 70 percent of the economy. An economy fueled by rising debt rather than rising wages is a house of cards.

Imagine a country where underpaid workers are bailing out banks and corporations run by overpaid, undertaxed bosses who milked their companies and country like cash cows and crashed the world economy.

While workers across the nation were losing jobs, homes, and health insurance, a big investment firm paid nearly 700 employees more than $1 million each in bonuses, amounting to a $3.6 billion bonus bonanza in 2008 while the firm lost $27 billion.

It's not Germany.

Imagine a country where more workers are going back to the future of sweatshops and day labor. Corporations are replacing full-time jobs with disposable "contingent workers." They include temporary employees, on-call workers, contract workers, "leased" employees—some of them fired and then "rented" back at a large discount by the same company—and involuntary part-time workers who want permanent, full-time work.

How do workers, increasingly forced to migrate from job to job at low- and variable-wage rates, without health insurance or paid vacation, much less a pension, care for themselves and their families, pay for college, save for retirement, plan a future, build strong communities?

Imagine a country that negotiated "free trade" agreements helping corporations trade freely on cheap labor at home and abroad.

Imagine a country becoming a nation of Scrooge-Marts and outsourcers—with an increasingly low-wage, underemployed workforce instead of a growing middle class.

It's not Canada.

Imagine a country where polls show most workers would join a union if they could, but for decades employers routinely violated workers' rights to organize.

A leading business magazine observed in 2004, "While labor unions were largely responsible for creating the broad middle class after World War II . . . that's not the case today. Most . . . employers fiercely resist unionization, which, along with other factors, has helped slash union membership to just 13% of the workforce, vs. a midcentury peak of more than 35%." Full-time workers who were union members had median 2008 weekly earnings of $886 compared with just $691 for workers not represented by unions.

It's not South Korea.

Imagine a country where nearly two-thirds of women with children under age 6 and more than three-fourths of women with children ages 6–17 are in the labor force, but affordable childcare and after-school programs are scarce. Apparently, kids are expected to have three parents: Two parents with jobs to pay the bills, and another parent to be home in mid-afternoon when school lets out, as well as all summer.

Imagine a country where women working full time earn 78 cents for every dollar men earn. Women don't pay 78 cents on a man's dollar for their education, rent, food, or healthcare. The gender wage gap has closed just 14 cents since 1955, when women earned 64 cents for every dollar earned by men. There's still another 22 cents to go.

The average female high school graduate who works full time from ages 25 to 65 will earn about $450,000 less than the average male high school graduate. The gap widens to $900,000 for full-time workers with bachelor's degrees. In the words of a 2002 government report, "Men with professional degrees may expect to earn almost $2 million more than their female counterparts over their work-life."

Imagine a country where childcare workers, mostly women, typically make less than baggage porters and bellhops and much less than animal trainers. Out of 801 occupations surveyed by the labor department, only 20 have lower median wages than childcare workers.

Imagine a country where 97 percent of the CEOs and 84 percent of the corporate officers at the largest 500 companies are men. Never mind that companies with a higher share of women in their senior management teams financially outperform companies with lower representation.

Imagine a country where discrimination against women is pervasive from the bottom to the top of the pay scale, and it's not because women are on the "mommy track." In the words of a leading business magazine, "At the same level of management, the typical woman's pay is lower than her male colleague's—even when she has the exact same qualifications, works just as many years, relocates just as often, provides the main financial support for her family, takes no time off for personal reasons, and wins the same number of promotions to comparable jobs."

Imagine a country where instead of rooting out discrimination, many policy makers blame women for their disproportionate poverty. If women earned as much as similarly qualified men, poverty in single-mother households would be cut in half.

It's not Japan.

Imagine a country where violence against women is so epidemic it is their leading cause of injury. Nearly a third of all murdered women are killed by husbands, boyfriends, and ex-partners. Researchers say, "Men commonly kill their female partners in response to the woman's attempt to leave an abusive relationship."

The country has no equal rights amendment.

It's not Pakistan.

Imagine a country whose school system is rigged in favor of the already privileged, with lower caste children tracked by race and income into the most deficient and demoralizing schools and classrooms. Public school budgets are heavily determined by private property taxes, allowing higher income districts to spend more than poorer ones. In the state with the largest gap, state and local spending per pupil in districts with the lowest child poverty rates was $2,792 greater in 2006 than districts with the highest child poverty rates. The difference amounts to more than $1 million for a typical elementary school of 400 students—money that could be used for needed teachers, books, computers, and other resources.

In rich districts, kids take modern libraries, laboratories, and computers for granted. In poor districts, they are rationing out-of-date textbooks and toilet paper. Rich schools often look like country clubs—with manicured sports fields and swimming pools. In poor districts, schools often look more like jails—with concrete grounds and grated windows. College prep courses, art, music, physical education, field trips, and foreign languages are often considered necessities for the affluent, luxuries for the poor.

It's not India.

Imagine a country where the infant death rate for children in the nation's capital is higher than for children in Kerala, India.

Imagine a country whose constitution once counted black slaves as worth three-fifths of whites. Today, black per capita income is about three-fifths of whites.

Imagine a country where racial disparities take their toll from birth to death. The black infant mortality rate is more than double that of whites. Black life expectancy is five years less. The official black unemployment rate is about twice that of whites and the black poverty rate is triple that of whites.

Imagine a country where the government subsidized decades of segregated suburbanization for whites while the inner cities, left to people of color, were treated as outsider cities—separate, unequal, and disposable. Recent studies have documented continuing discrimination in housing, education, employment, banking, insurance, healthcare, and criminal justice.

Imagine a country where the typical white household has about six times the net worth of the typical household of color. In 2007, median household net worth—*including home equity*—was $170,400 for white households and just $27,800 for households of color. Black households had a median net worth of just $17,000. That was before the housing bubble burst.

It's not South Africa.

Imagine a country that doesn't count you as unemployed just because you're unemployed. To be counted in the official unemployment rate you must be actively searching for work. The government doesn't count people as "unemployed" if they are so discouraged from long and fruitless job searches that they have given up looking. It doesn't count as "unemployed" those who couldn't look for work in the past month because they had no childcare, for example. If you need a full-time job but are working part-time—whether 1 hour or 34 hours weekly—because that's all you can find, you're counted as employed.

A leading business magazine observed, "Increasingly the labor market is filled with surplus workers who are not being counted as unemployed."

Imagine a country where there is a shortage of jobs, not a shortage of work. Millions of people need work and urgent work needs people—from staffing after-school programs and community centers, to creating affordable housing, to strengthening levees, repairing bridges, and building mass transit, to cleaning up pollution and converting to renewable energy.

It's not France.

Imagine a country with full prisons instead of full employment. The jail and prison population has more than quadrupled since 1980, when one in every 453 residents was incarcerated. By 2007, the figure had jumped to one in every 131. The figures are even grimmer when it comes to adults in prison or jail or on probation or parole: one in every 31 adults is under some form of correctional control.

Imagine a country that is number one in the world when it comes to locking up its own people. It has less than 5 percent of the world's population, but 23 percent of the world's incarcerated population.

Imagine a country where prison is a growth industry. State governments spend an average $29,000 a year to keep someone in prison, while cutting cost-effective programs of education, job training, employment, community development, and mental illness and addiction treatment to keep them out. In the words of a national center on institutions and alternatives, this nation has "replaced the social safety net with a dragnet."

It's not China.

Imagine a country that imprisons black people at a rate much higher than South Africa did under apartheid. One out of nine black men ages 25–29 are locked up in prisons or jails compared to one out of 59 white men in the same age group. Across age groups, black men were six to eight times more likely than white men to be incarcerated, the nation's bureau of justice statistics reports. The overall incarceration rate for black women is four times higher than for white women.

Meanwhile, one out of ten black men and women were unemployed according to the official count in 2008. This includes nearly one out of three black people ages 16-19, and one out of six ages 20-24. Remember, to be counted in the official unemployment rate you must be actively looking for a job and not finding one. "Surplus" workers are increasingly being criminalized.

Imagine a country whose justice department observed, "The fact that the legal order not only countenanced but sustained slavery, segregation, and discrimination for most of our Nation's history—and the fact that the police were bound to uphold that order—set a pattern for police behavior and attitudes toward minority communities that has persisted until the present day." Racial profiling and "driving while black" are well-known terms.

Imagine a country where from first arrests to third strikes resulting in lifetime sentences—often for nonviolent petty crimes—blacks and Latinos are arrested and imprisoned in massively disproportionate numbers.

Imagine a country waging a racially biased "War on Drugs." Although blacks and whites engage in drug offenses at comparable rates, a human rights group reports, blacks are ten times more likely than whites to enter prison for drug offenses. Two out of three people in the country are white but two out of three state prisoners convicted of drug offenses are black or Latino, according to government data. Between 1999 and 2007, 80 percent or more of all drug arrests were for possession, not sales.

A study in a prominent medical journal found that drug and alcohol rates were slightly higher for pregnant white women than pregnant black women, but black women were about ten times more likely to be reported to authorities by private doctors and public health clinics—under a mandatory reporting law. Poor women were also more likely to be reported.

It is said that truth is the first casualty in war, and the "War on Drugs" is no exception. Contrary to stereotype, "The typical cocaine user is white, male, a high school graduate employed full time and living in a small metropolitan area or suburb," says the nation's former drug czar. A leading newspaper reported that law officers and judges say, "Although it is clear that whites sell most of the nation's cocaine and account for 80% of its consumers, it is blacks and other minorities who continue to fill up [the] courtrooms and jails, largely because, in a political climate that demands that something be done, they are the easiest people to arrest." They are the easiest to scapegoat.

It's not Australia.

Imagine a country that ranks first in the world in wealth and military power, and just 40th in child mortality (under age five), tied with United Arab Emirates, Slovakia, Serbia, and Lithuania, and behind countries such as Cuba, Thailand, Portugal, and Singapore. If the government were a parent, it would be guilty of child abuse. Thousands of children die preventable deaths.

Imagine a country where healthcare is managed for healthy profit. Between 1999 and 2008, the average cost of insurance premiums more than doubled. Other industrialized countries have universal health coverage. But in this nation, one out of five people under age 65 had no health insurance, public or private, at any time in 2007. One out of three people under age 65 were uninsured for some or all of 2007–2008.

"The absence of health insurance is hazardous to your health," says the Institute of Medicine. "Uninsured people, children as well as adults, suffer worse health and die sooner than those with insurance."

Lack of health insurance typically means lack of preventive healthcare and delayed or second-rate treatment. The uninsured are at much higher risk for chronic disease and disability, and uninsured adults have a 25 percent greater chance of dying (adjusting for demographic, socioeconomic, and health characteristics). Uninsured women with breast cancer have a 30 percent to 50 percent higher risk of dying than insured women, for example. Severely injured car crash victims who are uninsured receive less care in the hospital and have a 39 percent higher mortality rate than privately insured patients.

Imagine a country where healthcare is literally a matter of life and death, but every day more than 2,000 babies are born without health insurance. The country's northern neighbor, which has universal healthcare, has a life expectancy that is three years longer.

Imagine a country where many descendants of its first inhabitants live on reservations strip-mined of natural resources and have a higher proportion of people in poverty than any other ethnic group.

Imagine a country where centuries of plunder and lies are masked in expressions like "Indian giver." Where the military still dubs enemy territory "Indian country."

Imagine a country that has less than 5 percent of the world's population and less than 3 percent of world's oil reserves, but consumes 24 percent of the world's oil. While automakers from other countries raced to make more fuel-efficient vehicles, this nation churned out bigger gas-guzzlers and drove its auto industry off a cliff.

Imagine a country with a carbon footprint that is two times that of the UK, five times that of China, and over 15 times that of India. It long obstructed international action against catastrophic climate change and continues to subsidize fossil fuels such as the oxymoronic "clean coal."

It's not Brazil.

Imagine a country whose senate and house of representatives are not representative of the nation. They are overwhelmingly white and male, and increasingly wealthy. More than one out of three house members are millionaires, according to financial disclosure records that don't even include the value of their primary residences. More than 60 percent of the senators are millionaires, but no senators are women of color. If the senate reflected the population, only one would be a millionaire.

Imagine a country that's ranked just 69th — right behind Uzbekistan — when it comes to the percentage of women in national legislative bodies. Just 17 percent of its senate and house of representatives were women in 2009.

If the 100-member senate reflected the population it would have 51 women and 49 men, including 66 whites, 15 Latinos, 13 blacks, 5 Asian and Pacific Islanders, and 1 Native American. Instead, it has 17 women and 83 men, including 95 whites, 2 Latinos, 1 black, 2 Asian and Pacific Islanders, and no Native Americans.

Imagine a country whose leaders misused a fight against terrorism as camouflage for trampling its bill of rights and undermining democracy. The most fundamental civil liberties, including the right not to be thrown into prison indefinitely on the secret word of government officials, were tossed aside.

Imagine a country that spends nearly as much on the military as the rest of the world combined. It also leads the world in arms exports.

In this same country, a five-star general who became president had warned in 1961, "In the councils of government, we must guard against the acquisition of unwarranted influence, whether sought or unsought, by the military-industrial complex . . . We must never let the weight of this combination endanger our liberties or democratic processes. We should take nothing for granted. Only an alert and knowledgeable citizenry can compel the proper meshing of the huge industrial and military machinery of defense with our peaceful methods and goals, so that security and liberty may prosper together."

It's not Russia.

It's the United States.

The words of Dr. Martin Luther King, Jr., call down to us today.

A true revolution of values will soon cause us to question the fairness and justice of many of our past and present policies. We are called to play the Good Samaritan on life's roadside; but . . . one day the whole Jericho road must be transformed so that men and women will not be beaten and robbed as they make their journey through life. . . .

A true revolution of values will soon look uneasily on the glaring contrast of poverty and wealth. . . . There is nothing but a lack of social vision to prevent us from paying an adequate wage to every American citizen whether he be a hospital worker, laundry worker, maid or day laborer.

SELECTED SOURCES

BP Statistical Review of World Energy, 2008.

Business Week, annual reports on executive pay.

Catalyst, New York, reports on women in business.

Center for American Women and Politics, Rutgers University, New Jersey.

Center for Arms Control and Non-Proliferation, Washington, DC.

Center for Defense Information, Washington, DC.

Center on Budget and Policy Priorities, Washington, DC.

Ira J. Chasnoff, et al., "The Prevalence of Illicit-Drug or Alcohol Use During Pregnancy and Discrepancies in Mandatory Reporting," *New England Journal of Medicine*, April 26, 1990.

Children's Defense Fund, Washington, DC.

CIA World Factbook, United States profile.

Citizens for Tax Justice, Washington, DC.

Congressional Budget Office.

Michelle Conlin and Aaron Bernstein, "Working . . . and Poor," *Business Week*, May 31, 2004.

Graef S. Crystal, *In Search of Excess: The Overcompensation of American Executives* (New York: Norton, 1992/1991).

Economic Policy Institute, Washington, DC.

Education Trust, *The Funding Gap*, 2008 edition.

President Dwight D. Eisenhower, Farewell Radio and Television Address to the American People, January 17, 1961.

Families USA, *Americans at Risk: One in Three Uninsured*, March 2009.

Anne B. Fisher, "When Will Women Get To The Top?" *Fortune*, September 21, 1992.

Forbes, annual reports on executive pay.

Human Rights Watch, *Decades of Disparity: Drug Arrests and Race in the United States* (March 2009) and *Targeting Blacks* (May 2008).

Institute of Medicine, National Academy of Sciences, *America's Uninsured Crisis* (2009) and earlier reports on the consequences of lack of health insurance.

International Centre for Prison Studies, King's College, London, UK.

Henry J. Kaiser Family Foundation reports on health insurance coverage and costs.

Martin Luther King, Jr., *Where Do We Go From Here: Chaos or Community?* (Harper & Row, 1967).

Jonathan Kozol, *The Shame of the Nation: The Restoration of Apartheid Schooling in America* (New York: Crown, 2005) and *Savage Inequalities: Children in America's Schools* (New York: Crown, 1991).

Leadership Conference on Civil Rights, Washington, DC.

Peter Medoff and Holly Sklar, *Streets of Hope: The Fall and Rise of an Urban Neighborhood* (Boston: South End Press, 1994).

National Center for Public Policy and Higher Education, *Measuring Up 2008: The National Report Card on Higher Education*.

National Center on Institutions and Alternatives, Baltimore, MD.

Pew Center on the States, *One in 31: The Long Reach of American Corrections*, 2009, and *One in 100: Behind Bars in America 2008*.

Emmanuel Saez, "Striking it Richer: The Evolution of Top Incomes in the United States," March 15, 2008, and updated data tables for 1913-2006.

Sentencing Project, Washington, DC, reports on racial disparity in criminal justice.

Holly Sklar and Paul Sherry, *A Just Minimum Wage: Good for Workers, Business and Our Future* (American Friends Service Committee/National Council of Churches, 2005).

Holly Sklar, Laryssa Mykyta and Susan Wefald, *Raise the Floor: Wages and Policies That Work For All of Us* (Boston: South End Press, 2002).

United Nations Children's Fund, *The State of the World's Children* 2009.

United Nations Development Program, *Human Development Report 2007/2008: Fighting Climate Change*.

Jerry Useem, "Have They No Shame?" *Fortune*, April 28, 2003.

U.S. Census Bureau.

U.S. Centers for Disease Control and Prevention, National Center for Health Statistics.

U.S. Department of Health and Human Services, Substance Abuse and Mental Health Services Administration, *National Survey on Drug Use and Health*.

U.S. Department of Justice, Bureau of Justice Statistics.

U.S. Department of Labor, Bureau of Labor Statistics.

U.S. Federal Reserve Board, Survey of Consumer Finances.

U.S. Internal Revenue Service, "The 400 Individual Income Tax Returns Reporting the Highest Adjusted Gross Incomes Each Year, 1992-2006," January 2009.

Hubert Williams and Patrick V. Murphy, "The Evolving Strategy of Police: A Minority View," *Perspectives on Policing*, U.S. Department of Justice (January 1990).

2

INCOME GAP IS WIDENING, DATA SHOWS

David Cay Johnson

Income inequality grew significantly in 2005, with the top 1 percent of Americans—those with incomes that year of more than $348,000—receiving their largest share of national income since 1928, analysis of newly released tax data shows.

The top 10 percent, roughly those earning more than $100,000, also reached a level of income share not seen since before the Depression.

While total reported income in the United States increased almost 9 percent in 2005, the most recent year for which such data is available, average incomes for those in the bottom 90 percent dipped slightly compared with the year before, dropping $172, or 0.6 percent.

The gains went largely to the top 1 percent, whose incomes rose to an average of more than $1.1 million each, an increase of more than $139,000, or about 14 percent.

The new data also shows that the top 300,000 Americans collectively enjoyed almost as much income as the bottom 150 million Americans. Per person, the top group received 440 times as much as the average person in the bottom half earned, nearly doubling the gap from 1980.

Prof. Emmanuel Saez, the University of California, Berkeley, economist who analyzed the Internal Revenue Service data with Prof. Thomas Piketty of the Paris School of Economics, said such growing disparities were significant in terms of social and political stability.

"If the economy is growing but only a few are enjoying the benefits, it goes to our sense of fairness," Professor Saez said. "It can have important political consequences."

Last year, according to data from other sources, incomes for average Americans increased for the first time in several years. But because those at the top rely heavily on the stock market and business profits for their income, both of which were strong last year, it is likely that the disparities in 2005 are the same or larger now, Professor Saez said.

He noted that the analysis was based on preliminary data and that the highest-income Americans were more likely than others to file their returns late, so his data might understate the growth in inequality.

The disparities may be even greater for another reason. The Internal Revenue Service estimates that it is able to accurately tax 99 percent of wage income but that it captures only about 70 percent of business and investment income, most of which flows to upper-income individuals, because not everybody accurately reports such figures.

The Bush administration argued that its tax policies, despite cuts that benefited those at the top more than others, had not added to the widening gap but "made the tax code more progressive, not less." Brookly McLaughlin, the chief Treasury Department spokeswoman, said that this year "the share of income taxes paid by lower-income taxpayers will be lower than it would have been without the tax relief, while the share of income taxes for higher-income taxpayers will be higher."

Treasury Secretary Henry M. Paulson Jr., she noted, has acknowledged that income disparities have increased, but, along with a "solid consensus" of experts, attributed that shift largely to "the rapid pace of technological change [that] has been a major driver in the decades-long widening of the income gap in the United States."

Others argued that public policies had played a role in the shift. Robert Greenstein, executive director of the Center on Budget and Policy Priorities, an advocacy group for the poor, said that the data understates the widening disparity between the top 1 percent and the rest of the country.

He said that in addition to rising incomes and reduced taxes, the equation should take into account cuts in fringe benefits to workers and in government services that middle-class and poor Americans rely on more than the affluent. These include health care, child care and education spending.

"The nation faces some very tough choices in coming years," he said. "That such a large share of the income gains are going to the very top, at a minimum, raises serious questions about continuing to provide tax cuts averaging over $150,000 a year to people making more than a million dollars a year, while saying we do not have enough money" to provide health insurance to 47 million Americans and cutting education benefits.

A major issue likely to be debated in Congress in the year ahead is whether reversing the Bush tax cuts would slow investment and, if so, how much that would cost the economy.

Mr. Greenstein's organization will release a report today showing that for Americans in the middle, the share of income taken by federal taxes has been essentially unchanged across four decades. By comparison, it has fallen by half for those at the very top of the income ladder.

Because the incomes of those at the top have grown so much more than those below them, their share of total income tax revenue has risen despite the reduced rates.

The analysis by the two professors showed that the top 10 percent of Americans collected 48.5 percent of all reported income in 2005.

That is an increase of more than 2 percentage points over the previous year and up from roughly 33 percent in the late 1970s. The peak for this group was 49.3 percent in 1928.

The top 1 percent received 21.8 percent of all reported income in 2005, up significantly from 19.8 percent the year before and more than double their share of income in 1980. The peak was in 1928, when the top 1 percent reported 23.9 percent of all income.

The top tenth of a percent and top one-hundredth of a percent recorded even bigger gains in 2005 over the previous year. Their incomes soared by about a fifth in one year, largely because of the rising stock market and increased business profits.

The top tenth of a percent reported an average income of $5.6 million, up $908,000, while the top one-hundredth of a percent had an average income of $25.7 million, up nearly $4.4 million in one year.

3

MEET THE WEALTH GAP

Gabriel Thompson

For a delivery worker, perched on a bicycle with plastic bags of food dangling from each handlebar, Manhattan's East Side offers many opportunities for a trip to the emergency room. I learn this one May afternoon as I trail 26-year-old Apolinar Perez, a chubby-faced Mexican immigrant who skillfully steers his black mountain bike through the chaos. A taxi switches lanes without warning, nearly clipping my front wheel. Suit-clad men and women stride purposefully into the street, too wrapped up in their phone conversations to notice they're crossing against the light. A black Suburban with tinted windows screeches to a halt in front of us, directly in the path of the bike lane.

Perez arrived in New York City five years ago, after crossing the Texas border in the back of a truck while hidden beneath a pile of children's toys. Since then, he's delivered food for the same Italian restaurant, working eleven hours a day, six days a week. Pay couldn't be simpler: before heading home each night, one of the managers hands him a $20 bill. That's an hourly wage of $1.82—well below the

Reprinted with permission from the June 30, 2008, issue of *The Nation*. Research support for this article was provided by the Investigative Fund of The Nation Institute.

state's $4.85 minimum wage for delivery workers. The rest of his earnings come through tips, which average $60 a shift. There's no overtime or healthcare, no sick days or workers' comp. I inquire about any benefits I might be forgetting. "For Christmas they give me $50," he says. "Sometimes."

I first encounter Perez as he is locking up his bike in front of 500 Park Avenue, a large, glassy building that serves as the headquarters for the hedge fund Caxton Associates, which manages more than $11 billion. Caxton was founded in 1983 by Bruce Kovner, a broad-shouldered 63-year-old with bushy eyebrows and a ruddy face who was among the top-ten highest-paid hedge-fund managers in 2006, with an income of $715 million. Though he has never shied away from public involvement—Kovner is chair of the American Enterprise Institute (AEI)—he does shy away from the press (an assistant told me he never speaks to the media). Perez wraps a chain around his bike's frame and attaches it to a post, then grabs two orders of pasta and heads through the revolving doors. Every lunch hour in Manhattan, the very poor meet the very rich. Today, wealth will be distributed downward, slightly: Perez emerges with a $2 tip. "I usually don't get very good tips from the fancy buildings," he will later tell me.

Four blocks away from the offices of Caxton Associates is 590 Madison Avenue, a forty-three-story building made of steel and granite, boasting a backup generator that can service its corporate tenants for four days without refueling. Behind a desk on the first floor stands security guard Timothy Williams. Williams, who has been an employee of TNM Protection for a year, is a 24-year-old African-American who, like Perez, lives in the Bronx, the borough with the lowest rents in New York City. After graduating from high school in 2002 he joined the Army, partly in the hope that it would help pay for college. He served in Iraq from August 2004 to July 2005, fighting the war that Kovner's AEI so aggressively pushed. AEI "Freedom Scholar" Michael Ledeen hoped the United States would turn the Middle East "into a caldron," and AEI fellow Richard Perle promised that Iraq's oil would pay for the reconstruction. "Maybe it won't work perfectly," admitted AEI vice president Danielle Pletka on the eve of the invasion, "but does that mean we shouldn't try?"

Williams, though, is disillusioned. "I was for going into Afghanistan, but I'm against Iraq," he tells me at the beginning of a noon-to-midnight shift. Wearing a dark suit with an American flag pin affixed to his lapel, he says that his time in Iraq convinced him that the mission wasn't working, which is one of the reasons he cast his primary vote for Obama.

Now back home, he's earning $12.50 an hour, with no union and no healthcare. "This is just a job I'll have for a little bit," he explains. He's able to get by with the help of the $1,300 monthly checks he receives from the GI Bill, which also covers his tuition at Monroe College, a private school in the Bronx geared toward working students, where he's pursuing an associate's degree. He plans to join the NYPD and hopes one day to become a lawyer. In the meantime, he has joined the National Guard—"I see the military as a place where I can actually have a career"—and recently learned he'll be sent back to Iraq next year.

Journey twenty-nine floors up from where Williams stands guard and the growing disparities of wealth again come into stark contrast. Here you will find the headquarters of Paulson & Company, a $32 billion hedge fund, this one run by

John Paulson, the highest-paid individual in 2007. By short-selling the subprime market, he earned $3.7 billion last year. (In January, after a year in which 2.2 million households filed for foreclosure, Paulson told the *Wall Street Journal,* "I've never been involved in a trade with such unlimited upside.")

For Williams, who would likely shepherd Paulson to safety in the event of a building emergency, that upside is hard to discern: he would have to work more than twenty years as a security guard to earn what Paulson made last year in one hour.

On the East Side of Manhattan two very distinct classes of New Yorkers cross paths every day: the working poor (undocumented immigrants and citizens alike), who cook, deliver, secure and protect—for little money and no benefits—and the titans of finance, hedge-fund executives and heads of private-equity firms, who stare at numbers on screens while moving other people's money in and out of stocks and commodities or buying and selling companies, and whose wealth is expanding so quickly they have difficulty figuring out what to do with it.

While workers in the first group struggle to survive on wages that don't get much higher than $10 an hour, the financial elite continue to break income records. The just-released 2007 earnings figures find the top five hedge-fund managers all clearing $1.5 billion. As *Alpha* magazine notes, "The top 25 on the list earned an average $892 million, up from $532 million in 2006"—in a year when the economy began to stall, the group needing no help ended up nearly doubling its income. The top ten earners alone made a combined $16.1 billion, more than the GDP of Nicaragua.

4

BILLIONAIRES R US

Chuck Collins and Felice Yeskel

Fall is inequality season. Every autumn, as the leaves change color, we get a vivid new picture of the trends that pull us apart as a country.

This year is no different. But after almost three decades of incrementally widening disparities of wealth and income, it's worth noting that we've entered a new version of economic apartheid, American-style. Let's call it Inequality 2.0.

The United States is now the third most unequal industrialized society after Russia and Mexico. This is not a club we want to be part of. Russia is a recovering kleptocracy, with a post-Soviet oligarchy enriched by looting. And Mexico, despite joining the rich-nations club of the Organization for Economic and Community Development, has some of the most glaring poverty in the hemisphere.

In 2004, after three years of economic recovery, the U.S. Census reports that poverty continues to grow, while the real median income for full-time workers has declined. Since 2001, when the economy hit bottom, the ranks of our nation's poor have grown by 4 million, and the number of people without health insurance has swelled by 4.6 million to over 45 million.

Income inequality is now near all-time highs, with over 50 percent of 2004 income going to the top fifth of households, and the biggest gains going to the top 5 percent and 1 percent of households. The average CEO now takes home a paycheck 431 times that of their average worker.

At the pinnacle of U.S. wealth, 2004 saw a dramatic increase in the number of billionaires. According to *Forbes Magazine*, there are now 374 U.S. billionaires. The growth in billionaires took a dramatic leap since the early 1980s, when the average net worth of the individuals on the Forbes 400 list was $400 million. Today, the average net worth is $2.8 billion. Wal-Mart's Walton family now has 771,287 times more than the median U.S. household.

Does inequality matter? One problem is that concentrations of wealth and power pose a danger to our democratic system. The corruption of politics by big money might explain why for the last five years the president and Congress have been more interested in repealing the federal estate tax, paid only by multi-millionaires, than on reinforcing levees along the Gulf Coast.

Now, to pay for hurricane reconstruction and the war in Iraq, Congress is considering cuts in programs that help poor people, such as Medicaid and Food Stamps. They have not yet considered fairer ways of reducing the deficit by reversing special tax breaks for the rich, such as the recent cuts in capital gains and dividend taxes.

Inequality is non-partisan. The pace of inequality has grown steadily over three decades, under both Republican and Democratic administrations and Congresses. The Gini index, the global measure of inequality, grew as quickly under President Clinton as it has under President George W. Bush. Widening disparities in the U.S. are the result of three decades of bi-partisan public policies that have tilted the rules of the economy to the benefit of major corporations and large asset owners at the expense of people whose security comes from a paycheck.

Public policies in trade, taxes, wages and social spending can make a difference in mitigating national and global trends toward prolonged inequality. But our priorities are moving in the wrong direction.

For example, the failure to raise the minimum wage from its 1997 level of $5.15 an hour guarantees continued income stagnation for the working poor for years to come. The president and Congress's focus on tax cuts for the wealthy and their disinterest in government spending to expand equal opportunity sets the stage for Inequality Version 3.0.

We shouldn't tolerate this drift toward an economic apartheid society.

5

Shhh, Don't Say "Poverty"

Bob Herbert

Former Senator Phil Gramm, a Republican from Texas who was known for his orneriness, once said, "We're the only nation in the world where all our poor people are fat."

That particular example of compassionate conservatism came to mind as I looked over a report from the Department of Agriculture showing that more than 12 million American families continue to struggle, and not always successfully, to feed themselves.

The 12 million families represent 11.2 percent of all U.S. households. "At some time during the year," the report said, "these households were uncertain of having, or unable to acquire, enough food for all their members because they had insufficient money or other resources."

Of the 12 million families that worried about putting food on the table, 3.9 million had members who actually went hungry at some point last year. "The other two-thirds . . . obtained enough food to avoid hunger using a variety of coping strategies," the report said, "such as eating less varied diets, participating in federal food assistance programs, or getting emergency food from community food pantries or emergency kitchens."

These are dismal statistics for a country as well-to-do as the United States. But we don't hear much about them because hunger is associated with poverty, and poverty is not even close to becoming part of our national conversation. Swift boats, yes. Sex scenes on "Monday Night Football," most definitely. The struggle of millions of Americans to feed themselves? Oh no. Let's not go there.

What does that tell you about American values?

We are surrounded by poor and low-income people. (The definitions can be elastic and easily blurred, but essentially we're talking about individuals and families that don't have enough money to cover the essentials—food, shelter, clothing, transportation and so forth.) Many of them are full-time workers, and some have more than one job.

A new study by the Center for an Urban Future, a nonprofit research group, found that more than 550,000 families in New York—a quarter of all working families in the state—had incomes that were too low to cover their basic needs.

We just had a bitterly contested presidential election, but this very serious problem (it's hardly confined to New York) was not a major part of the debate.

According to the study: "Most low-income working families do not conform to the popular stereotype of the working poor as young, single, fast-food workers: 88 percent of low-income working families include a parent between 25 and 54 years old. Married couples head 53 percent of these families nationwide. Important jobs such as health aide, janitor and child care worker pay a poverty wage."

In its introduction, the study says, "The implied bargain America offers its citizens is supposed to be that anyone who works hard and plays by the rules can support his or her family and move onward and upward."

If that was the bargain, we've broken it again and again. Low-income workers have always been targets for exploitation, and that hasn't changed. The *Times's* Steven Greenhouse had a troubling front-page article in last Friday's paper about workers at restaurants, supermarkets, call centers and other low-paying establishments who are forced to go off the clock and continue working for periods of time without pay.

The federal government has not raised the minimum wage since 1997, and has made it easier for some employers to deny time-and-a-half pay to employees who work overtime.

Franklin Roosevelt, in his second Inaugural Address, told a rain-soaked crowd, "The test of our progress is not whether we add more to the abundance of those who have much; it is whether we provide enough for those who have too little."

I can hear the politicians in today's Washington having a hearty laugh at that sentiment.

There are advocates and even some politicians hard at work addressing the myriad problems faced by beleaguered workers and their families. But they get very little in the way of attention or resources from the most powerful sectors of society. So the health care workers who can't afford health insurance will continue emptying bedpans for a pittance. And the janitors will clean up faithfully after the big shots who ignore them.

These are rough times for the American dream. But times change, and the people who have broken faith with the dream won't be in power forever.

6

RACE AND EXTREME INEQUALITY

Dedrick Muhammad

The current presidential campaign has sparked a lot of conversation about race, but it has primarily been at the symbolic and interpersonal level. It has failed to probe the underlying substance of racial economic disparities and the slow rate of progress toward equity in wealth and wages. Too many Americans naïvely see the strong presidential candidacy of Illinois Senator Barack Obama as evidence of the resolution of the racial divide.

Since 1968, the year Martin Luther King Jr. was assassinated, the income gap between blacks and whites has narrowed by just three cents on the dollar. In 2005 the median per capita income in the United States stood at $16,629 for blacks and $28,946 for whites. At this slow rate of progress, we will not achieve income equality for 537 years. And if politicians continue to dismantle government checks on income and wealth concentration, even these modest gains may be reversed.

Extreme inequality in the overall economy exacerbates income and wealth disparities between whites and people of color. These disparities remain shockingly wide and especially evident when we examine the polarization of assets and wealth in the United States. The black homeownership rate, for instance, sits at 47 percent and the Latino rate at 49.7 percent, compared with 75 percent for whites.

African-American families in the United States have a median net worth of $20,600, only 14.6 percent of the $140,700 median white net worth. The median net worth for Latino families is $18,600, only 13.2 percent of median white net worth. Between 1983 and 2004, the most recent year for which official federal data are available, median black and Latino wealth inched up from 7 percent to 10 percent of median white wealth. At this rate, we will not achieve wealth equality for 634 years.

Even more disturbing, the tiny wealth gains of recent decades are evaporating as the subprime mortgage meltdown continues to spread. According to Home Mortgage Disclosure Act data, blacks are three times as likely as whites to have received a subprime loan and four times as likely to have refinanced from a subprime lender. Figures for Latinos are just as depressing. According to the Center for Responsible Lending, Latinos will lose between $75 billion and $98 billion in home-value wealth from subprime loans. Blacks will lose between $71 billion and $92

Reprinted with permission from the July 11, 2008, issue of *The Nation*.

billion. United for a Fair Economy has called this family net-worth catastrophe the "greatest loss of wealth for people of color in modern U.S. history."

The subprime fiasco is rippling through communities of color like miniature Hurricane Katrinas. And we are witnessing only the beginning of the impact: foreclosure, displacement, family upheaval, the devaluation of entire neighborhoods, eroding local tax bases, the decline of local services.

Our nation needs to make a dramatic reinvestment in broadening wealth and opportunity—for all Americans. In the decades after FDR's New Deal, such investments—including low-interest home-buyer loans, grants for college education and small-business subsidies—helped tens of millions of families enter the middle class. But these wealth-building programs directly or indirectly excluded people of color. They thus bolstered the economic supremacy of whites, continuing the American legacy of racist inequality.

Since the end of legal segregation and discrimination, we have not seen comparable government investment programs that could benefit people of color. We urgently need such programs, including matching savings plans to build assets and purchase homes. We can afford them—but only if we stop investing America's resources in the wealthiest people, leaving the rest of Americans to survive on a trickle.

7

POST-RACIAL? NOT YET

Fred McKissak Jr.

Moments after CNN declared Barack Obama the next President of the United States, I called my parents. I could tell my father was beaming. Through Obama he could see the future for his grandsons and their peers—a collective sense of inclusion that has eluded the race for so long.

My mother cried when she recited the litany of things they'd lived through: Emmett Till, four little girls in Birmingham, Schwerner, Goodman, and Chaney, Bloody Sunday, JFK, MLK, RFK, Chicago in '68, Detroit, Watts, Newark, and Katrina. Then, as folks would say, the spirit hit her.

"Yes, we can," she yelled. "Yes, we can. Yes, we can. Yes-we-can."

It was an unforgettable moment.

Reprinted by permission of *The Progressive*, 409 E. Main Street, Madison, WI 53703.

But after a night's sleep, I couldn't help but think that now we're going to hear, as we did after Obama's triumph in the Iowa caucuses, the absurd talk about post-racial America.

Exactly how can we be in post-racial America when nearly 40 percent of black children under the age of five live at or below the poverty line?

How are we in post-racial America when the level of school seregation for Hispanics is the highest in forty years and segregation of African Americans is back to levels not seen since the late 1960s?

How are we in post-racial America when the gaps in wealth, income, education, and health care have widened over the last eight years?

In 2006, 20.3 percent of African Americans were not covered by health insurance, compared with only 10.8 percent of whites. For Hispanics, a whopping 34.1 percent were not covered.

In 2007, the unemployment rate for blacks was twice as high as that for whites.

We are all Americans, but the pain of poverty is disproportionately cracking the backs of minorities.

There are those who insist that the gap in wealth, income, health care, and education is due to an inherent culture of victimization. If people of color only worked harder, they'd be fine, we are told.

But it's a flawed premise. This economy has never provided enough jobs for everyone. The funding of education gives a leg up to those who grow up in wealthy districts. Having health insurance isn't practical for those without the means. And institutional racism persists.

Now is not the time to avert our eyes from the prize. Indeed, the nation needs to refocus its attention on tearing down the walls that keep us from truly living in post-racial America.

"Our union can be perfected," Obama told the multitude gathered in Grant Park and the legions watching from New Orleans to Nairobi. "What we've already achieved gives us hope for what we can and must achieve tomorrow."

His election and his words redeem the sacrifices of my parents' generation and bear the fruit of the protests at lunch counters and on Southern roads.

The prize is not won, but we are on a path to get there.

8

Forty Acres and a Gap in Wealth

Henry Louis Gates Jr.

Last week, the Pew Research Center published the astonishing finding that 37 percent of African-Americans polled felt that "blacks today can no longer be thought of as a single race" because of a widening class divide. From Frederick Douglass to the Rev. Dr. Martin Luther King Jr., perhaps the most fundamental assumption in the history of the black community has been that Americans of African descent, the descendants of the slaves, either because of shared culture or shared oppression, constitute "a mighty race," as Marcus Garvey often put it.

"By a ratio of 2 to 1," the report says, "blacks say that the values of poor and middle-class blacks have grown more dissimilar over the past decade. In contrast, most blacks say that the values of blacks and whites have grown more alike."

The message here is that it is time to examine the differences between black families on either side of the divide for clues about how to address an increasingly entrenched inequality. We can't afford to wait any longer to address the causes of persistent poverty among most black families.

This class divide was predicted long ago, and nobody wanted to listen. At a conference marking the 40th anniversary of Daniel Patrick Moynihan's infamous report on the problems of the black family, I asked the conservative scholar James Q. Wilson and the liberal scholar William Julius Wilson if ours was the generation presiding over an irreversible, self-perpetuating class divide within the African-American community.

"I have to believe that this is not the case," the liberal Wilson responded with willed optimism. "Why go on with this work otherwise?" The conservative Wilson nodded. Yet, no one could imagine how to close the gap.

In 1965, when Moynihan published his report, suggesting that the out-of-wedlock birthrate and the number of families headed by single mothers, both about 24 percent, pointed to dissolution of the social fabric of the black community, black scholars and liberals dismissed it. They attacked its author as a right-wing bigot. Now we'd give just about anything to have those statistics back. Today, 69 percent of black babies are born out of wedlock, while 45 percent of black households with children are headed by women.

How did this happen? As many theories flourish as pundits—from slavery and segregation to the decline of factory jobs, crack cocaine, draconian drug laws and outsourcing. But nobody knows for sure.

I have been studying the family trees of 20 successful African-Americans, people in fields ranging from entertainment and sports (Oprah Winfrey, the track star Jackie Joyner-Kersee) to space travel and medicine (the astronaut Mae Jemison and Ben Carson, a pediatric neurosurgeon). And I've seen an astonishing pattern: 15 of the 20 descend from at least one line of former slaves who managed to obtain property by 1920—a time when only 25 percent of all African-American families owned property.

Ten years after slavery ended, Constantine Winfrey, Oprah's great-grandfather, bartered eight bales of cleaned cotton (4,000 pounds) that he picked on his own time for 80 acres of prime bottomland in Mississippi. (He also learned to read and write while picking all that cotton.)

Sometimes the government helped: Whoopi Goldberg's great-great-grandparents received their land through the Southern Homestead Act. "So my family got its 40 acres and a mule," she exclaimed when I showed her the deed, referring to the rumor that freed slaves would receive land that had been owned by their masters.

Well, perhaps not the mule, but 104 acres in Florida. If there is a meaningful correlation between the success of accomplished African-Americans today and their ancestors' property ownership, we can only imagine how different black-white relations would be had "40 acres and a mule" really been official government policy in the Reconstruction South.

The historical basis for the gap between the black middle class and underclass shows that ending discrimination, by itself, would not eradicate black poverty and dysfunction. We also need intervention to promulgate a middle-class ethic of success among the poor, while expanding opportunities for economic betterment.

Perhaps Margaret Thatcher, of all people, suggested a program that might help. In the 1980s, she turned 1.5 million residents of public housing projects in Britain into homeowners. It was certainly the most liberal thing Mrs. Thatcher did, and perhaps progressives should borrow a leaf from her playbook.

The telltale fact is that the biggest gap in black prosperity isn't in income, but in wealth. According to a study by the economist Edward N. Wolff, the median net worth of non-Hispanic black households in 2004 was only $11,800—less than 10 percent that of non-Hispanic white households, $118,300. Perhaps a bold and innovative approach to the problem of black poverty—one floated during the Civil War but never fully put into practice—would be to look at ways to turn tenants into homeowners. Sadly, in the wake of the subprime mortgage debacle, an enormous number of houses are being repossessed. But for the black poor, real progress may come only once they have an ownership stake in American society.

People who own property feel a sense of ownership in their future and their society. They study, save, work, strive and vote. And people trapped in a culture of tenancy do not.

The sad truth is that the civil rights movement cannot be reborn until we identify the causes of black suffering, some of them self-inflicted. Why can't black leaders organize rallies around responsible sexuality, birth within marriage, parents reading to their children and students staying in school and doing homework? Imagine Al Sharpton and Jesse Jackson distributing free copies of Virginia Hamilton's collection of folktales "The People Could Fly" or Dr. Seuss, and demanding that black parents sign pledges to read to their children. What would it take to make inner-city schools havens of learning?

John Kenneth Galbraith once told me that the first step in reversing the economic inequalities that blacks face is greater voter participation, and I think he was right. Politicians will not put forth programs aimed at the problems of poor blacks while their turnout remains so low.

If the correlation between land ownership and success of African-Americans argues that the chasm between classes in the black community is partly the result of social forces set in motion by the dismal failure of 40 acres and a mule, then we must act decisively. If we do not, ours will be remembered as the generation that presided over a permanent class divide, a slow but inevitable process that began with the failure to give property to the people who had once been defined as property.

9

THE ECONOMIC REALITY OF BEING LATINO/A IN THE UNITED STATES

Meizhu Lui and others

Latinos in the United States tend to be described as one large, predominantly immigrant community that displays lagging socioeconomic status compared to the white population. This media-driven perception of the Hispanic population in the United States is misleading. Latinos are diverse in a variety of ways: country of origin; generational status (many were here prior to the establishment of the first thirteen colonies); and class mobility. . . .

Taken as a whole, without regard for length of time in the United States (first generation versus fifth generation), 57.35 percent of all Latino families fall into the zero to $40,000 income bracket.[1] Approximately 40 percent of the Latino population in the United States is foreign born. And contrary to popular belief,[2] . . . native-born Latinos have a 73.5 percent high school completion rate. . . .

Wealth building behaviors among Latinos in the United States rest squarely on a strong work ethic, on collective family and extended kin efforts, and a strong entrepreneurial spirit. These are exactly the behaviors demanded in an ownership society. Yet, the gap between Latino families (13.6 percent) and white families (34 percent) earning $80,000 or more is substantial, as is the home ownership rate, which for whites is 74 percent and for Latinos is only 44 percent. . . .

Income and Latino Families

Between 2000 and 2003, Latino median household income declined 4.8 percent, from $36,032 to $34,272.[2] Of the 11.8 million Latino households in 2003, 9.4 million are families, and the income distribution for families indicates that 57 percent of these families annually earn $40,000 or less. Thirty percent of Latino families have five or more members. Moreover, 35 percent of the Latino population is eighteen years of age or younger—fourteen million. Of the almost forty million Latinos, over half—21.5 million—reside in states along the U.S.-Mexico border in Texas, New Mexico, Arizona, and California.

FIGURE 1
Family Median, Mean, and Per Capita Income (in 2001 dollars)

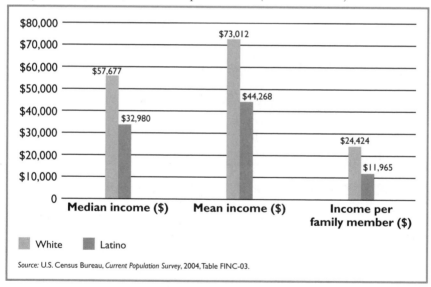

Source: U.S. Census Bureau, *Current Population Survey*, 2004, Table FINC-03.

Family formation among Latinos continues to display non-nuclear and extended-kin or pseudo-kin arrangements. Family formation among Latinos has implications for income parity, budgeting for necessary family expenditures, and wealth-building opportunities. In 2003, Latino families without children had an average of three people in the household; for those with children, the average number of people in the family unit totaled five compared to non-Hispanic white families, which had an average of three people in families with children. Family status plays a significant role in normalizing immigration status, in sponsoring family members, and in reunifying families. Moreover, living arrangements in large families contribute to economies of scale, lowering the costs of housing and transportation. Larger families generally have more earners in the household, which contributes to income flow and wealth accumulation. The downside of extended and pseudo-kin family arrangements is the communal nature of pooling resources to acquire assets. In the United States, most laws, financial products and services, housing and housing services, insurance and binding contracts are between individuals. The emphasis on individual property rights, and correspondingly individual liability, devalues communal property and communal asset-building activities. The communal pooling of resources is not recognized by financial data collection agencies and government social services. The collective manner in which family economic survival strategies have evolved in the working-poor Latino community are not within the scope of what the U.S. government defines as a nuclear family, which poses a significant problem for Latinos transitioning from poverty status into financially stable circumstances.

FIGURE 2

Latino Groups Annual Income, 2000–2001 (consumer expenditure survey in 2001 dollars)

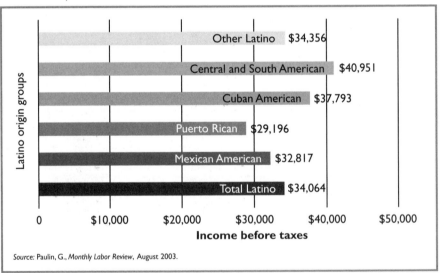

Source: Paulin, G., *Monthly Labor Review*, August 2003.

Latino income stability, as for other communities, continues to depend heavily upon access to educational opportunities. The income earned based on educational attainment—the financial return on education—still reflects a disparity across different racial and ethnic groups. These lingering inequalities remind us that education is one route out of poverty, while not a guarantee of equal pay.

Legislation, policies, and judicial rulings at the federal, state, and local levels have adversely affected the income and economic stability of Latino families. These include rules barring Latino workers from speaking Spanish on the job; laws preventing undocumented immigrant Latino workers from being treated as native-born workers (in the U.S. Supreme Court decision of March 2002, *Hoffman Plastic Compounds, Inc. v. National Labor Relations Board*); laws setting state minimum wage laws at the federal minimum wage level or below; policies creating regressive sales and payroll taxes for those earning minimum wage and setting asset eligibility requirements for the Earned Income Tax Credit and other social service programs that do not take into account Latino families' communal asset building.

Migrant workers, day laborers, seasonal workers, and recently arrived Latino immigrant families pool their resources in order to purchase assets as a group, while listing the asset under an individual name to meet financial requirements such as getting auto loans. For example, three brothers pool their funds together for the purchase of a van that can transport their families to their place of employment during the harvest cycle. The oldest brother purchases the vehicle, which can cost from $28,000 to $32,000. This asset makes the oldest brother ineligible for subsidized low-income housing and possibly for the Earned Income Tax Credit. Federal and state asset eligibility rules do not take into account the communal pooling of resources that occur among many Latino working families and extended kin.

FIGURE 3
Median Income in 2002, Population 25 Years and Over

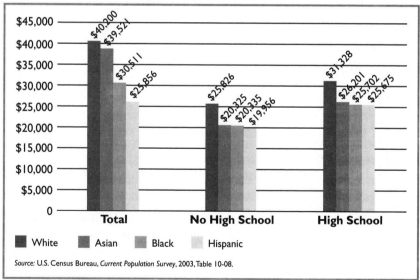

Source: U.S. Census Bureau, *Current Population Survey*, 2003, Table 10-08.

NOTES

1. *U.S. Census Bureau Current Population Survey*, 2003.
2. *U.S. Census Bureau Current Population Survey*, 2003.

10

THE ECONOMIC REALITY OF BEING ASIAN AMERICAN

Meizhu Lui and others

If we were to imagine the racial economic structure as a solar system with whites in the center like the sun around which all other races revolve like planets, Asian Americans for the first one hundred years would have been in the outermost orbit; they were Pluto. All people of color were closer to each other in terms of economic status than any of them were to whites. But since 1965, Asians have moved closer to whites economically—they are now Mars—while other people of color are still far away in the outer orbits. But despite their proximate success, the social, political, and economic profile of Asians is quite different from that of whites. For example, even though the median incomes for whites and Asians are similar, Asians do not occupy the same range of professions as whites and are less likely to own homes. They are missing from the higher ranks of business and politics. Policies and practices from years past still affect their status, as does the turmoil of current world events and the shifting alliances in U.S. foreign policy.

Asians Need Not Apply

The most important exclusionary policy was already in place when the first Asians arrived in the 1840's. Only white people could become citizens. One of the first pieces of legislation passed by the newly founded United States of America, the 1790 Naturalization Law, stated that only "a free white person" could begin the naturalization process that would lead to citizenship. Over time, the 1790 law would be used to designate immigrants from one Asian country after another as nonwhite, which kept them from wealth-building opportunities offered to white immigrants only, the chosen future citizens of the United States.

Other policies specifically targeting Asians prevented them from sustained asset building in their new country. From the mid-1800s to the mid-1900s, many discriminatory state and local laws were passed; federal court decisions upheld those anti-Asian practices, such as Asian-only taxes, or laws restricting Asians from owning land.[1]

Finally, the classification of Asians as ineligible for citizenship played a part in the formulation of immigration laws that restricted the entry of Asians into the United States.[2] This stymied Asian population growth, as well as their political power and collective wealth-building potential. Asian men with families were prohibited from sending for their wives and children; other Asian men who were single were reluctant to go back to their homeland to find and return with a wife, because the law often did not allow re-entry. When families can't come in, then money flows out, sent home to support those left behind. . . .

Asian Wealth: Bipolar Disorder

While the mean and median assets of blacks, whites, and Latinos are available, there are no comparable figures for Asians. Even in the new data source book, *The New Face of Asian Pacific America: Numbers, Diversity and Change in the 21st Century,* wealth and asset data are missing.[3] However, we can draw some limited conclusions from the available information.

FIGURE 1
Poverty Rate of Asian Nationalities in the United States

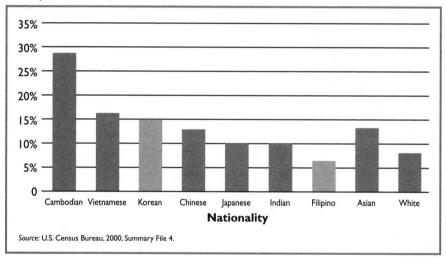

Source: U.S. Census Bureau, 2000, Summary File 4.

The Asian population has a unique economic profile. It is "bipolar" with people concentrated at both ends of the economic strata—like an hourglass. There is a greater percentage of people in the higher quintiles (fifths) and in the lower quintiles than other racial groups, and a smaller percentage in the middle income and wealth brackets. If we were to look at just income figures, it would seem that Asians are doing even better than whites. But if we were to look at just poverty rates, it would seem that Asians are doing *worse* than whites.

For Asians, statistical averages obscure the fact that the Asian demographic is top- and bottom-heavy. From looking at the aggregated numbers, some conclude that Asian Americans are "outwhiting whites." This is misleading, because it masks the differences in economic status among Asians—wealth gaps exists within the Asian category itself—and because it causes Asians who live in extreme poverty to be overlooked by the general public and by policy makers. Nearly 30 percent of Cambodians live in poverty, one of the highest poverty rates of all nationalities in the United States. However, it is still true that overall Asians have leapfrogged over other groups of color in economic status.

Asian Americans in the Economy: A Different Reality

How Data Obscures Asian Realities

From the numbers, it looks like Asian Americans are number one. In 1990, it was reported that Asians had a median income of $36,000, while whites had only $31,100. Why is that?

First, Asians do not live everywhere whites live. Over half of the Asian population lives in just three states: California (4.2 million), New York (1.2 million), and Hawaii (0.7 million). In those states, Asians are mostly concentrated in urban and suburban areas. If Asian income is higher than average, it's partly because very few Asians are working in states with low wages and low costs of living. If you compare whites and Asians in those cities with the highest Asian density, then the median income for Asians becomes $37,200, and for whites it is $40,000. Although lagging whites, Asians are indeed economically better off than African Americans or Latinos; in those same cities, the median income for blacks is $24,100, and for Latinos, $25,600.[4]

A second factor is the difference in family size between Asians and whites. Asian households are larger, so if you looked at income per person (per capita), Asian income would be less than that of whites. (See Figures 2 and 3.) For example, in Hawaii, the average white family size was 2.46 people, while that of Asians was 2.97, and that of Native Hawaiians was 3.75.

A third factor is that a few Asians have achieved enormous wealth. Charles Wang, the CEO of Computer Associates, took home $655 million in 1999. He was the only nonwhite among the 150 highest paid CEOs in 2005. Average that into all Asian salaries, and he pulls the average up.[5]

Finally, the distribution of income and wealth differs widely by nationality. Asian Indians are largely clustered at the higher end of the economic spectrum; Cambodians are at the bottom. (Sometimes the bipolarity exists *within* a population, such as the Chinese. There are many new arrivals living in extreme poverty, while many established Chinese professionals enjoy high standards of living.)

FIGURE 2
Median Household Income of Various Asian Nationalities in the United States

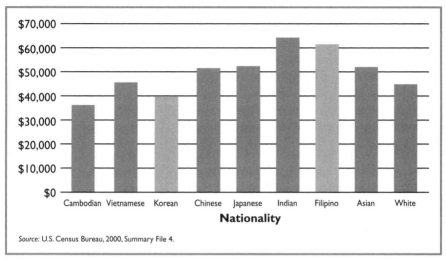

Source: U.S. Census Bureau, 2000, Summary File 4.

FIGURE 3
Per Capita Income, 1999

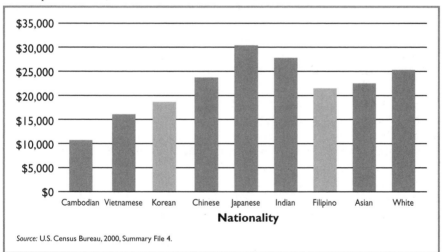

Source: U.S. Census Bureau, 2000, Summary File 4.

New Arrivals Skew the Picture

Since most wealth comes from inheritance, it is harder to talk about wealth accumulation in the United States when there are such a large number of immigrants in the Asian demographic. Some come with no money at all, others may bring wealth with them from home, so their wealth status cannot be credited or blamed

on U.S. policies. The 2000 census recorded 11.9 million U.S. residents who identified themselves as Asian alone or in combination with one or more other races,
making up just over 4 percent of the total population. In 1990, the population was
7.3 million. With such a rate of growth, obviously many are relatively recent arrivals. Two out of three Asians, or eight million, in the United States have parents
who were born abroad and were not U.S. citizens. Of those, only half are naturalized citizens. Since this article is concerned with the intergenerational accumulation and transfer of wealth that took place within the United States, the large
numbers of immigrants make the current Asian economic data comparable only
to Latinos.

For example, recent Chinese immigrants represent the third largest group of
immigrants to the United States, after Mexicans and Filipinos. Between 1965 and
1984, a total of 419,373 Chinese immigrants arrived, almost as many as the 426,000
Chinese who came between 1849 and 1930. The Chinese community went from
being 61 percent American-born in 1965 to 63 percent foreign-born in 1984, from
citizen to immigrant once again.[6] Between 1984 and 1990, the Chinese population in the United States doubled again, to 1,645,000.[7] In 2000, the Chinese numbered 2,314,537; add in those who identified as a mixture of Chinese and another
race, and the total was 2,734,841. When we look at the data for the Chinese, both
recent immigrants and older residents are combined.

The only Asian group that is not a population of immigrants is Japanese Americans. Because of the Marshall Plan after World War II, in which the United States
invested in rebuilding the Japanese economy, there has been no economic or political reason for the Japanese to leave their home country.

Income

If you took every Asian household in the United States and lined them up from
the lowest to the highest income, the family in the middle has the median income.
If you took all incomes, added them together, and then divided by the number of
households, you would have the mean, or average, income. The "Asian" bar in the
graph is the average of all Asian nationalities.

As mentioned, an Asian household is usually larger than a white household,
since Asians bring their extended family structure with them when they arrive, and
live in larger groups by choice. Because families often arrive with few resources,
sometimes they do not have the choice of having adequate living space. When a
landlord is busted for violating housing codes, sometimes there are three families
living in a one-family apartment. The median household income chart (Figure 2)
shows that only two Asian nationalities earn *less* than whites.

Per capita income data tell a more realistic story. Looking at the incomes of
each working person, only two Asian nationalities earn *more* than whites.

At the top end of the Asian economic hourglass, second- and third-generation
Asian Americans have unquestionably made economic leaps far beyond their immigrant parents' economic status.

Some immigrants who have come to work as professionals have arrived close to the top. South Asians (people from Bangladesh, Bhutan, India, the Maldives, Nepal, Pakistan, and Sri Lanka) are the best example of immigrants who have high incomes and wealth. Most have immigrated since the 1965 Immigration Act took effect. According to the 2000 Census, there are over two million South Asians in the United States today.

All subgroups of South Asians have very high levels of education compared to the general U.S. population. Many Indian physicians, pharmacists, nurses, and other medical professionals were allowed to immigrate during the 1970s. Also, many Indians came as foreign students, completed their master's or Ph.D. programs, and changed their status to permanent residents.[8] In 1990, 30 percent of Asian Indian workers were in professional occupations, compared to 14 percent of white workers. They are more highly represented in the professional category than any other immigrant/minority group, and medical professionals make up a large proportion of that category. Two factors other than education have been important to Asian Indians' high-income occupational level. First, they are fluent in English (as a result of British colonization), and second is many of them have completed graduate programs in the United States.[9] Their skills are highly sought after. In 2001, Microsoft and other high-tech companies lobbied hard to get federal officials to double the number of foreign high-tech specialists allowed to come to the United States to work. Forty-four percent of those were from India.[10]

But once again, international factors have affected the South Asian community. Racist attacks against Asian Americans spiked significantly across the country after the World Trade Center was attacked on September 11; singled out as targets were Indian and Pakistani Americans, especially Sikh Americans, a religious group often mistakenly perceived to be Arab because many Sikh men wear turbans and have long beards. In some places, South Asian businesses have been burned to the ground.[11] As with the Chinese during the McCarthy era, they have been investigated, harassed, arrested, and deported. It is the latest example of how being perceived as foreign can threaten the economic security of Asian groups.

While some Asian subgroups are in well-paid professional jobs, as a group they do not attain the income levels of whites. At both the top and the bottom of the employment ladder, it is still commonly assumed that Asians will work harder for less pay than whites, so they are still considered a good deal for white employers. Professionals bump up against a racial glass ceiling, so that they cannot reach the top of the management ladder—still a white male preserve. In 1991, Congress created a Federal Glass Ceiling Commission, and its 1995 study found, for example, that "Asian/Pacific Islanders held less than one one-hundredth of one percent of all corporate directorships."[12] Asians are also limited to fewer occupations and industries. They are three times more likely to be scientists and engineers than their numbers would predict; in those fields, they also hit a glass ceiling.[13]

Success as professionals has not come to all Asians. Compared to the Chinese, the recent Filipino immigration has been largely invisible, and yet it has been much larger. Over the last three decades, the Philippines sent more immigrants to the United States than any other Asian country and, until recently, was the second largest source of U.S. immigrants after Mexico. In 1990, Filipino Americans numbered over 1.4 million, up 90 percent from 770,000 in 1980.[14] In 2000, it was the second largest subgroup of Asians, with 2,364,815 people (including Filipinos of mixed race).[15] The recent wave is due to the economic crisis in the Philippines.

Many Filipino immigrants are well-educated professionals such as engineers, scientists, accountants, teachers, lawyers, nurses, and doctors.[16] But for those not recruited for a job, coming to America can result in downward mobility. According to Stephanie Yan, the daughter of Filipino immigrants, before emigrating many doctors in the Philippines study to be nurses, jobs they are more likely to find in the United States.

Filipinos from professional backgrounds are findings jobs in the lowest-paid sectors of the workforce—nannies, maids, home care workers, and food service workers. When looking at Filipinos as a whole, they remain in subordinate positions in relation to some other Asian groups and whites, whether educated or less educated, skilled or unskilled.[17]

Asians are the least likely to be unemployed. In 1990, 67 percent of all Asian Americans compared with 65 percent of all Americans were working. Again, these numbers mask differences in ethnicity; for example, the Hmong people from Laos had only a 29.3 percent labor participation rate, while Asian Indian men had an 84 percent rate.

At the bottom end of the scale, Asians also experience greater poverty rates than the general population. About 14 percent of all Asians lived in poverty in 1989; the rate for the nation was 10 percent. Again, there are enormous ethnic differences. The 1990 Census data revealed that 47 percent of Cambodians, 66 percent of Hmong, 67 percent of Laotians, and 3 percent of Vietnamese were impoverished. While at one end of the scale Asians do better than other minorities, at the low end, poverty rates among Southeast Asians are much higher than those of other minority groups such as African Americans (21 percent) and Latinos (23 percent).[18]

Education

Education continues to be an important part of the Asian strategy for social and economic advancement. Even low-wage parents doing manual labor place all their eggs in their children's educational baskets. Forty-four percent of Asians and Pacific Islanders (API) age twenty-five and over had a bachelor's degree or higher in 2000. The rate for all adults twenty-five and over was 26 percent. Eighty-six percent were high school graduates; the rate for all U.S. residents was 84 percent for all adults age twenty-five or higher. One in seven APIs over the age of twenty-five, or one million people, has an advanced degree.

However, the returns on their educational investments are not equal to whites. In 1988, the U.S. Commission on Civil Rights reported, according to Deborah Woo, that "after controlling for education, work experience, English ability, urban residence, and industry of employment . . . 'Asian descent' continued to have a negative effect on one's chances of moving into management."[19] Moreover, in a National Science Foundation survey of eighty-eight thousand scientists and engineers, they found that even when Asians did become managers, whites in similar positions earned *twice* as much.[20]

Looking at income data from California, where most Asians reside and work, one can see that if Asians are a model minority, as claimed by many, they are not getting the benefits that would be expected. Whites with no high school diploma, can expect to earn $26,115 a year; Asians, $18,517. Whites with a bachelor's degree can expect $44,426; Asians, $33,758. With a doctorate, whites earn $77,877; Asians, $59,603.[21] While this earnings gap is smaller than it is for black and Latino graduates, there's still a significant penalty for being Asian American.

NOTES

1. Gotanda, Neil. "Exclusion and Inclusion: Immigration and American Orientalism." In *Across the Pacific: Asian Americans and Globalization*, edited by Evelyn Hu-DeHart. Philadelphia: Temple University Press, 1999, p. 138.

2. Hutchinson, Edward Prince. *Legislative History of American Immigration Policy: 1798–1965*. Philadelphia: University of Pennsylvania Press, 1981, p. 66.

3. Lai, Eric, and Dennis Arguelles. *The New Face of Asian Pacific America: Numbers, Diversity and Change in the 21st Century*. San Francisco: Asian Week, 2003.

4. Woo, Deborah. *Glass Ceilings and Asian Americans: The New Face of Workplace Barriers*, Walnut Creek, CA: AltaMira Press, 2000, p. 34.

5. United for a Fair Economy, "Estate Tax Action Center," http://www.faireconomy.org/estatetax/ (accessed December 19, 2004).

6. Takaki, R. *Strangers from a Different Shore*. Boston: Little, Brown, and Co., 1998, p. 421.

7. Wong, Morrison G. "Chinese Americans." In *Asian Americans: Contemporary Trends and Issues*, edited by P.G. Min. Thousand Oaks, CA: Sage Publications, 1995.

8. Sheth, Manju. "Asian Indian Americans." In *Asian Americans: Contemporary Trends and Issues*, edited by P.G. Min. Thousand Oaks, CA: Sage Publications, 1995, p. 177.

9. Ibid., p. 178.

10. Zia, Helen. *Asian American Dreams: The Emergence of an American People*. New York: Farrar, Straus, and Giroux, 2000, p. 210.

11. Marosi, Richard. "Study Finds Deadly Spike in Racial Violence Against Asian Americans," *Los Angeles Times*, March 11, 2002, p. A18.

12. Glass Ceiling Commission. *Good for Business: Making Full Use of the Nation's Human Capital*. A Fact-Finding Report of the Federal Glass Ceiling Commission, Washington, D.C., March 1995, p. 143. http://www.ilr.cornell.edu/library/downloads/keyWorkplace Documents/GlassCeilingFactFindingEnvironmentalScan.pdf (accessed December 10, 2004).

13. Woo, 2000, p. 58.

14. Agbayani-Siewert, P., and Revilla, L. "Filipino Americans." In *Asian Americans: Contemporary Trends and Issues*, edited by P.G. Min. Thousand Oaks, CA: Sage Publications, 1995, pp. 134, 142.

15. U.S. Census Bureau. 2000 Decennial Census, Summary File 1. Accessed through American Factfinder utility: http://factfinder.census.gov/servlet/BasicFactsServlet.

16. Takaki, 1998, pp. 431–433.

17. Kitano, Harry H.L., and Roger Daniels. *Asian Americans: Emerging Minorities.* Englewood Cliffs, NJ: Prentice-Hall, 1988, p. 86.

18. O'Reily, Richard, and Maureen Lyons. *Analysis of U.S. Census Data, 1993.* Cited on http://www.bol/ucla.edu/~tiffloui/glassceil.htm (accessed December 21, 2004).

19. Woo, 2000, pp. 54–55.

20. Ibid., p. 63.

21. O'Reily and Lyons, 1993.

11

WOMEN LOSING GROUND

Ruth Conniff

Forget about Michelle Obama, Cindy McCain, and the culture war over what a First Lady should look like: fist-bumping teammate or decorative sidekick. The biggest women's issue of the election season is not even reproductive rights. It's the economy.

For the first time since the 1970s, women's work force participation has been heading steadily downward.

Under the headline "U.S. Employers Pushing Women Out of Work Force," Sharon Johnson of *Women's e-news* reports that women are losing ground. "From the 1950s through the 1990s, the percentage of U.S. women in the paid work force steadily increased. But that trend has begun to reverse, and today 3.3 million fewer women are working than would be if the trend had continued," she writes.

Contrary to conventional analysis, women are not opting out" because they want to stay at home, Johnson reports. Instead, women's policy groups say the problem is a workplace that is hostile to women, especially mothers. "The real explanation, they contend, is a workplace that fails women on some basic interlocking fronts: inflexible scheduling requirements, job discrimination, lack of child care, lack of parental leave, lack of sick leave," Johnson says.

The Center for WorkLife Law in San Francisco found that in 13,000 cases, "mothers were 79 percent less likely to be hired and 100 percent less likely to be promoted because they are held to a higher standard than non-mothers in their companies," according to Johnson's summary.

Reprinted by permission of *The Progressive*, 409 E. Main Street, Madison, WI 53703.

Women now grow up expecting to be full participants in society, with the same career expectations as men. But sexism persists, and society has not adjusted to the reality of two-career families. Women still take the brunt of domestic and childrearing duties, madly scrambling to balance their competing responsibilities. Our country still treats raising a family as a private matter, even if June Cleaver and the family wage are history. At best, flex time, on-site child care, and family leave are seen as expensive perks, and employees who take advantage of them are often the first to be downsized—with repercussions across society.

A front-page story in *The New York Times*, "Women Are Now Equal as Victims of Poor Economy," adds more to the story. Median income for women has fallen over a period of several years—from $15.04 an hour in 2004 to $14.84 in 2007. After decades of steady progress, the *Times* reports, women across all economic and social strata are working less and earning less, and their families are making do with lower incomes as a result. While women's work force participation kept growing even through previous recessions, the *Times* headline refers to the fact that today women, like men, are seeing their overall numbers at work decline as a result of low wages and the perception that staying on the job under current economic conditions is not worth it. In particular, women, like men, are losing manufacturing jobs. Nor are they making an easy transition to other sectors.

As mothers lose ground at work, families are suffering.

The New York Times took a lot of flak a few years ago for a 2003 story in the Sunday magazine on the "opt-out revolution," by Lisa Belkin. Belkin portrayed latte-sipping, high-income suburban moms as choosing family over work. It turned out that the numbers did not support the "trend" asserted by that story.

In its July 21 news piece on women's economic slide, the *Times* notes that a lot of the variation in women's work force participation in recent years has been pushed by women at the other end of the economic spectrum from Belkin's subjects—welfare recipients who were pushed into jobs by welfare reform legislation. "Now, as the economy weakens and employers shrink their payrolls, many of these women struggle to find work," reports the *Times*.

Advocates for the poor warned back in the early 1990s that there could be dire consequences from welfare reform legislation, which operated on the assumption that everyone would be better off if poor, single mothers were pushed into the first available full-time job. With no child care system in place—let alone high-quality, universally available care—and no provisions that allowed former welfare mothers to get the kind of education and training that could lead to high-paying, benefits-providing jobs, the idea that workfare alone would "end the cycle of poverty" always seemed illusory. But the economic boom, and the failure of states to keep statistics on what happened to the people they pushed off the welfare rolls, obscured the consequences of welfare reform.

The feminization of poverty is leaping out at economists and reporters now, with the economy turning sour.

According to the *Times*, it is often unclear why middle-income women drop out of work, since "men are rarely thought of as dropping out to run the household, [but] that is often the assumption when women pull out."

More than cultural assumptions, mothers face some very concrete problems as they struggle to raise children and support their families. For example, child care for infants and toddlers can easily cost as much as $15,000 a year. Add to that the extreme difficulty of finding the kind of environment where you can actually feel good about leaving your baby all day, and mix in shrinking wages and benefits, long commutes, inflexible employers, and a workpalce that is not set up to deal with the inevitable crises of sick children and other family hassles.

The problem with the "opt-out" story line, as E. J. Graff pointed out in an excellent critique of Belkin's piece for the *Columbia Journalism Review*, is that women's response to all this pressure is presented as a rather pleasant, personal choice to kick back and let dad bring home the paycheck while spending more time at the gym.

The reality is that most families badly need women's earnings to stay afloat. The answer is not to muse about how a few affluent women manage their careers and cultural expectations, but how we, as a society, make life workable for families under extreme economic, social, and emotional stress. Men, women, and children alike badly need a more modern approach to these problems. As the current recession hits home, it's high time we did something about it.

12

LILLY'S BIG DAY

Gail Collins

President Obama is scheduled to sign the Lilly Ledbetter Fair Pay Act into law today.

"I'm so excited I can hardly stand it," Ledbetter said recently after the bill passed the Senate.

Obama told her story over and over when he campaigned for president: How Ledbetter, now 70, spent years working as a plant supervisor at a tire factory in Alabama. How, when she neared retirement, someone slipped her a pay schedule that showed her male colleagues were making much more money than she was. A jury found her employer, the Goodyear Tire and Rubber Company, to be really,

really guilty of pay discrimination. But the Supreme Court, in a 5-to-4 decision led by the Bush appointees, threw out Ledbetter's case, ruling that she should have filed her suit within 180 days of the first time Goodyear paid her less than her peers.

(Let us pause briefly to contemplate the chances of figuring out your co-workers' salaries within the first six months on the job.)

Until the Supreme Court stepped in, courts generally presumed that the 180-day time limit began the last time an employee got a discriminatory paycheck, not the first. In an attempt at bipartisan comity, the Senate decided to simply restore the status quo, rejecting House efforts to make the law tougher. Even then, only five Republican senators voted for it—four women and Arlen Specter of Pennsylvania, who is currently the most threatened of the deeply endangered species known as moderate Republicans.

Ledbetter, who was widowed in December, won't get any restitution of her lost wages; her case can't be retried. She's now part of a long line of working women who went to court and changed a little bit of the world in fights that often brought them minimal personal benefit.

Another was Eulalie Cooper, a flight attendant who sued Delta Air Lines in the mid-'60s when she was fired for being married. Not only did a Louisiana judge uphold the airline industry's bizarre rules requiring stewardesses to be young and single, Cooper was denied unemployment benefits on the grounds that by getting married she left her job "voluntarily."

But she began a pattern of litigation that eventually ended the industry's insistence that women needed to look like sex objects in order to properly care for passengers on airplanes. Next time you talk about US Airways Flight 1549's spectacular landing on the Hudson River, remember that the three flight attendants who kept calm in the ditched plane were all women in their 50s and give a nod to people like Eulalie Cooper.

Patricia Lorance, an Illinois factory worker, went to court after her union and employer secretly agreed to new seniority rules that discriminated against the women who had been promoted in the post-Civil Rights Act era of the 1970s. Like Ledbetter, she lost her court fight because of a ridiculous ruling about timing, which had to be fixed by Congress.

Working at a series of lower-paying jobs after the factory closed, and then disabled by physical ailments, Lorance lost track of her case long before it finally wound its way through the Supreme Court. "But to this day, I am rather proud of myself because I was not a dumb person. I believe in just standing up and fighting for your own rights," she said in a phone interview.

Ledbetter's real soul sister is Lorena Weeks of Wadley, Ga. Weeks, now 80, had worked two jobs to support her orphaned siblings, then struggled with her husband to set enough money aside to assure their children would be able to go to college. A longtime telephone employee, she applied for a higher-paying job overseeing equipment at the central office. Both her union and the management said the job was unsuitable for a woman because it involved pushing 30-pound equipment on a dolly, even though Weeks regularly toted around a 34-pound typewriter at her clerical job.

Weeks v. Southern Bell helped smash employers' old dodge of keeping women out of higher-paying positions by claiming that they required qualifications only men could fulfill. But it was a long, painful fight during which Weeks was terrified that she might lose her job entirely. "I felt like I was so alone, and yet I knew I was doing what God wanted me to do. Going back to the fact my momma had died working so hard. And I knew women worked and needed a place in the world," she said.

It's a good day for the feisty working women who went to court to demand their rights and the frequently underpaid lawyers who championed them. They're strangers to one another; most of them made their stands and then returned to their ordinary lives. But they're a special sorority all the same. And Lilly Ledbetter got to go to the inauguration and dance with the new president.

"Tell her congratulations," said Lorena Weeks.

13

THE WAGE GAP AND ITS COSTS

What Is the Wage Gap?

The wage gap is the difference between the wages of women and men. Full-time working women still get paid—on average—only 77 cents for each dollar full-time working men get paid.

And this is a conservative estimate. The Institute for Women's Policy Research found that women workers in their primary earning ages between 26 and 59 years old make only 38% of what men earn if part-time work and years out of the work force due to family care are taken into account.

Two decades ago, full-time women workers earned 59 cents for every dollar earned by men. The common explanation was that the gender wage gap existed because of a "merit gap." Women, this theory went, were not as educated as men,

Differences in Earnings Between Women and Men, 1960–2002

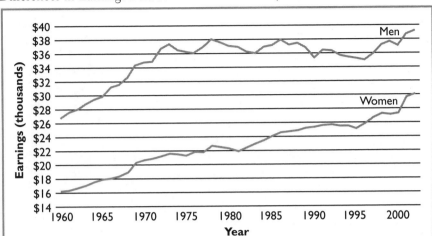

hadn't worked as long, or were working in stopgap jobs until they got married, while men were family breadwinners. With increases in women's education and employment, the wage gap did begin to narrow, although part of the narrowing was accounted for by declines in male wages.

But, in 1994, despite a booming economy, the wage gap widened. Worse, over the next several years women continued to lose ground. This flew in the face of the merit gap theory. More than forty million American working women were educated, experienced, and holding full-time jobs comparable to men's. Like men, these women had families dependent on their earnings.

Why, instead of catching up, were hard-working women suddenly falling further behind? Over the course of the decade, many women's earnings rose. Yet, on average, women's earnings did not go up as much as men's did. Women's real wages grew 94 percent—while men's real wages had grown 160 percent.

If women's earnings could not catch up to men's in a time of nearly unreal prosperity, at a time when women's qualifications had caught up, what was holding them back? The answer is simple: discrimination.

Who Is Affected by the Wage Gap?

While most women suffer from the wage gap, it does not affect all women equally. According to 2004 Median Annual Earning U.S. Census data, African American women earn only 68 cents for every dollar a man earns, while Hispanic women earn only 57 cents to the male dollar.

But young women do not escape the wage gap either. If you graduated from college in 2000, your pay started much farther behind men's than the pay of

Wage Gap by Race

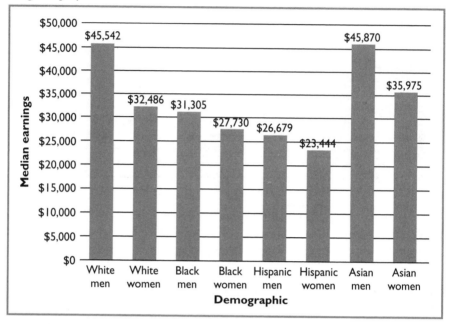

women who graduated a decade earlier. In 1991, the wage gap between young women and men with college degrees was only 9 percent, or a few thousand dollars difference. But in 2000, the wage gap for young women and men with these same credentials was 31 percent.

Wage Gap by Age

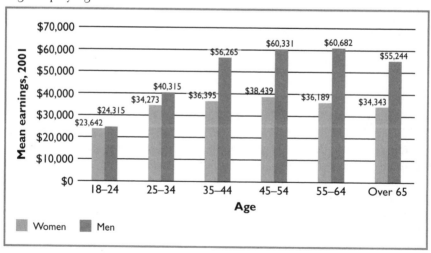

Wage Gap by Education

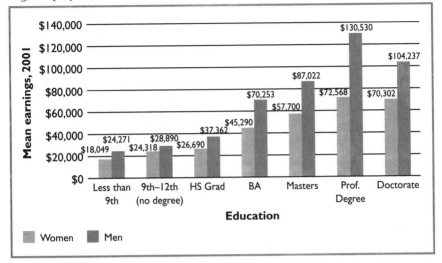

What Are the Costs of the Wage Gap?

Because of the wage gap, more women than men fear—and experience—poverty, or teeter right on the edge. They are missing almost a quarter of their rightful earnings—money that few women can afford to miss.

Eleven million older American women (and only four million older men) make do with less than $8,300 a year, the federal definition of poverty. Nearly three times as many women as men live at subsistence level in their old age.

The wage gap isn't some meaningless abstraction. It adds up. It takes a personal toll. Discrimination is costing women (and their loved ones) the paychecks, pensions, and security that they need and deserve.

- A high school graduate loses $700,000. A young woman graduates from high school this year and goes straight to work at $20,000 a year. Over her lifetime, she will make $700,000 less than the young man graduating with her.
- A college graduate loses $1.2 million. A young woman graduates from college into a $30,000 starting salary. Over her lifetime, she will make $1.2 million less than the young man getting his diploma in line right behind her.
- A professional school graduate loses $2 million. A young woman gets a degree in business, medicine, or law and graduates into a $70,000 starting salary (along with staggering student loan debts). Over her lifetime, she will make $2 million less than the young man at her side.

What would you, your daughter, your mother, your niece, your grandmother, or your sister do with another $700,000, or $1,200,000, or $2,000,000 over your lifetime?

High School Graduate Woman

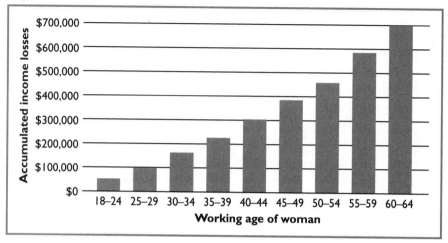

College Graduate Woman

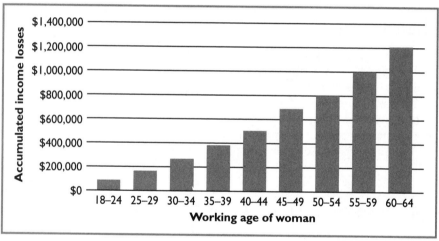

Why Is There a Wage Gap?

The wage gap is the result of a variety of forms of sex discrimination in the workplace, including discrimination in hiring, promotion and pay, sexual harassment, occupational segregation, bias against mothers, and other ways in which women workers and women's work are undervalued.

Hiring, Promotion, Pay

First comes what most people think of as sex discrimination: the simple and straightforward refusal to hire, promote, or fairly pay women who are just as qualified as men.

Sexual Harassment

Few people realize that sexual harassment also constitutes wage discrimination. After long and repeated sexual harassment, women leave or lose their jobs, potential raises, promotions, opportunities, emotional stability, ability to work, and sometimes their lives.

Occupational Segregation

In 2000, two-thirds of all U.S. working women were still crowded into twenty-one of the 500 occupational categories. And, then women's work is consistently paid less than men's work. Are janitors really worth more than nurses' aides, parking lot attendants more than child care workers, construction laborers more than bookkeepers and cashiers? According to American payrolls, they are.

Taxing Motherhood

Many people believe that the wage gap exists because women choose to care for children. But do they really choose to be paid less for doing the same work they did before giving birth? Forget the mommy track: too many women find themselves shunted unwillingly onto the mommy sidetrack. Frustrated women talk about how, once they came back from maternity leave, colleagues began to treat them as unreliable and unpromotable—almost willfully overlooking any evidence of productivity.

Undervaluing Women Workers

Everyday, women workers' suggestions are dismissed—only to be discussed seriously when made by a man. Or when employers turn to old boy networks rather than public postings to recruit new talent. Or when interviews or screening tests prize male strengths or deeper voices, even though women's strengths and communication styles could accomplish the job just as well.

14

THE SONS ALSO RISE

Paul Krugman

America, we all know, is the land of opportunity. Your success in life depends on your ability and drive, not on who your father was.

Just ask the Bush brothers. Talk to Elizabeth Cheney, who holds a specially created State Department job, or her husband, chief counsel of the Office of Management and Budget. Interview Eugene Scalia, the top lawyer at the Labor Department, and Janet Rehnquist, inspector general at the Department of Health and Human Services. And don't forget to check in with William Kristol, editor of *The Weekly Standard,* and the conservative commentator John Podhoretz.

What's interesting is how little comment, let alone criticism, this roll call has occasioned. It might be just another case of kid-gloves treatment by the media, but I think it's a symptom of a broader phenomenon: inherited status is making a comeback.

It has always been good to have a rich or powerful father. Last week my Princeton colleague Alan Krueger wrote a column for *The Times* surveying statistical studies that debunk the mythology of American social mobility. "If the United States stands out in comparison with other countries," he wrote, "it is in having a more static distribution of income across generations with fewer opportunities for advancement." And Kevin Phillips, in his book "Wealth and Democracy," shows that robber-baron fortunes have been far more persistent than legend would have it.

But the past is only prologue. According to one study cited by Mr. Krueger, the heritability of status has been increasing in recent decades. And that's just the beginning. Underlying economic, social and political trends will give the children of today's wealthy a huge advantage over those who chose the wrong parents.

For one thing, there's more privilege to pass on. Thirty years ago the C.E.O. of a major company was a bureaucrat—well paid, but not truly wealthy. He couldn't give either his position or a large fortune to his heirs. Today's imperial C.E.O.'s, by contrast, will leave vast estates behind—and they are often able to give their children lucrative jobs, too. More broadly, the spectacular increase in American inequality has made the gap between the rich and the middle class wider, and hence more difficult to cross, than it was in the past.

Meanwhile, one key doorway to upward mobility—a good education system, available to all—has been closing. More and more, ambitious parents feel that a public school education is a dead end. It's telling that Jack Grubman, the former Salomon Smith Barney analyst, apparently sold his soul not for personal wealth but for two places in the right nursery school. Alas, most American souls aren't worth enough to get the kids into the 92nd Street Y.

Also, the heritability of status will be mightily reinforced by the repeal of the estate tax—a prime example of the odd way in which public policy and public opinion have shifted in favor of measures that benefit the wealthy, even as our society becomes increasingly class-ridden.

It wasn't always thus. The influential dynasties of the 20th century, like the Kennedys, the Rockefellers and, yes, the Sulzbergers, faced a public suspicious of inherited position; they overcame that suspicion by demonstrating a strong sense of noblesse oblige, justifying their existence by standing for high principles. Indeed, the Kennedy legend has a whiff of Bonnie Prince Charlie about it; the rightful heirs were also perceived as defenders of the downtrodden against the powerful.

But today's heirs feel no need to demonstrate concern for those less fortunate. On the contrary, they are often avid defenders of the powerful against the downtrodden. Mr. Scalia's principal personal claim to fame is his crusade against regulations that protect workers from ergonomic hazards, while Ms. Rehnquist has attracted controversy because of her efforts to weaken the punishment of healthcare companies found to have committed fraud.

The official ideology of America's elite remains one of meritocracy, just as our political leadership pretends to be populist. But that won't last. Soon enough, our society will rediscover the importance of good breeding, and the vulgarity of talented upstarts.

For years, opinion leaders have told us that it's all about family values. And it is—but it will take a while before most people realize that they meant the value of coming from the right family.

15

THE EDUCATION OF JESSICA RIVERA

Kim Phillips-Fein

Jessica Rivera (not her real name) is a slight, composed 20-year-old Hunter College student. She grew up in the Bronx, raised by her mother and extended family. No one in her family has completed college, so Rivera was thrilled to get accepted to Hunter College, one of the best schools in the City University of New York. "It was my top choice," she says.

In the legendary heyday of City College in the 1930s and '40s, Rivera's could have been a classic story of upward mobility. Had she enjoyed similar opportunities, she might even have wound up with Irving Howe and Daniel Bell, "arguing the world" in the cafeteria alcoves. But Rivera's mother—who was injured at the Bronx factory that she worked at many years ago—is on public assistance. When Rivera turned 18, welfare caseworkers told her she would have to report for twenty to thirty hours a week to the city's Work Experience Program (WEP) if she wanted to keep collecting the benefits she and her mother depend on. "They offered me jobs working in the park, cleaning toilets, cleaning transportation." The long hours would have made it nearly impossible to continue at Hunter as a full-time student. At 18, Rivera was faced with a choice between quitting school for a dead-end job and losing her family's income.

For middle-class Americans, society offers myriad incentives for higher education: scholarships, interest-free loans and the "Hope" tax credits. But for women on welfare, it's a different story. In September the 1996 welfare reform law was up for Congressional reauthorization. The vote did not happen then, because of divergences between a bill in the Senate, written by moderate Republicans and Democrats, and the Bush Administration's vision of welfare reform, reflected in a House bill. The welfare law expired September 30, and no compromise bill or temporary legislation is yet ready to take its place.

One of the sticking points was that the Senate legislation would have made it easier for welfare recipients to go to college. Bush, however, told the *New York Times* in July that he does not think a college education teaches "the importance of work," nor does he think it can "[help] people achieve the dignity necessary so that they can live a free life, free from government control." Now that all three branches of government are controlled by Republicans, it seems likely that the Bush Administration's vision will soon be reflected in law.

The Personal Responsibility and Work Opportunity Reconciliation Act of 1996 mandates that recipients of public assistance work in return for their checks. They must either find jobs or, failing this, participate in state-run work programs for a minimum of thirty hours a week (split between twenty hours of paid or unpaid work, and ten hours of participation in other programs like job-search services). Should states fail to meet this work requirement, they face the loss of federal grants. (Many cities, like New York, have raised the number of required work hours above the federal minimum—in the case of New York, to thirty-five per week. It's called a "simulated work week.")

Under the 1996 law, college education cannot be substituted for any part of the primary work requirement. In New York City the result is clear: Before welfare reform, 28,000 CUNY students were on welfare. By spring 2002, 5,000 were—a decline even steeper than the celebrated 60 percent drop in New York City's welfare rolls. Today, although nearly 60 percent of welfare recipients in the city lack a high school diploma or a GED, only 2 percent are enrolled in ESL or GED programs, and fewer than 4 percent are engaged in full-time education or training. "New York City has one of the most sophisticated systems of higher education in the country, but welfare recipients are essentially shut out of it," says Wendy Bach, an attorney at the Urban Justice Center who works with welfare recipients.

The basic presumption behind welfare reform is the harsh moral logic of the workhouse. Welfare recipients, so the theory goes, are poor because they lack the discipline to hold down a job. But women who are struggling to seize hold of a little bit of upward mobility have a different experience: They feel like they work all the time.

Patricia Williams, a 32-year-old Brooklyn native and mother of a gorgeous, energetic 18-month-old girl, graduated from Hunter last year. She plans to go back to school someday for a master's. "I want to run a high-quality daycare center," says Williams, who was orphaned at an early age. When she started working, she did temp jobs—"everything from assembling the folders for the new Macy's event to setting up perfume samples to shelling nuts." After a while she decided to get an associate's degree in computer services. Lacking parents who could help her out, she applied for welfare as a kind of financial aid. "I went on public assistance to get ahead." After completing her degree, she enrolled at Hunter. But then came welfare reform, and she had to enter WEP.

William's first assignment under WEP was housekeeping at a community senior-citizen center in downtown Manhattan. It wasn't a job she would have chosen—she lives in Brooklyn and commutes to Hunter, on the Upper East Side, for school. But she got up at 5:30 every morning to be at work at 7:30, "cleaning bathrooms and gathering garbage." At noon, she went uptown for class, then back downtown in the late afternoon for another stint of maid work. At the community center, "they knew me as Pat the WEP worker," she said. "They didn't know that I had my associate's, or that I was working toward my bachelor's."

The final straw came in her last semester at Hunter. She asked her supervisor for a change in her schedule, so that she could fulfill a student teaching requirement she needed in order to graduate. "I said I would work late, on weekends." When WEP refused, she quit. Immediately, she lost her food stamps and Medicaid. At a hearing downtown, she says, she asked a city representative, "Is it fair that I am being pulled out of school to do a dead-end WEP job?" The city worker replied, "You need to know what commitment is and what it takes to report to work. . . .

Even as New York moves to the center of the national debate over welfare policy, local politicians are starting to respond to pressure to change the law—much of which is coming from welfare recipients themselves. In 2000 the Welfare Rights Initiative (WRI), a Hunter-based organization of current and former welfare recipients, successfully lobbied the state legislature to enact a bill permitting work-study and internships to substitute for work requirements. In spring 2002 Gifford Miller, the Speaker of the City Council, proposed a bill allowing welfare recipients to substitute college course work for WEP. Meanwhile, in Maine, legislators have used state-level funds to support college students on welfare. The program (called Parents as Scholars) has been very successful. The women it serves earn a median wage of $11.71 upon graduation—compared with $8 for women before entering college; they are also more likely to work in jobs that offer health benefits. Ninety percent of Maine women who earned a degree while on welfare have left the rolls, with every indication that they will stay off.

But while innovative local programs are all to the good, the restrictive federal policies with regard to college for welfare recipients are part of a larger social shift toward a constriction of access to higher education for poor and working-class Americans. . . .

When Bush ran for president in 2000, he described himself as the "education President," because ever since Horatio Alger, education has been touted as the key to upward mobility. But in truth, the question of who has access to college has always been deeply social and political. College enrollments exploded during the great postwar boom, in the heyday of high union density and the welfare state, and today's college gap simultaneously reflects and perpetuates the haughty isolation of the rich.

Young women like Jessica Rivera, though, clearly benefit from whatever changes local organizations can make. Just when she was about to give up on school, Rivera learned about WRI. With legal help provided by the advocacy group, she successfully pleaded her case before a hearing officer to substitute work-study hours for WEP under the state law. The rising junior says she isn't yet sure what she wants to major in, but she knows she wants to get a master's degree—even, someday, a PhD. "Who wants to be on welfare? I'm going to have my own job and be independent—I don't need to depend on anybody," she says cheerfully. But, at the same time, when she thinks about her mother, Rivera's face grows sad and reflective. With a gentleness that seems to contradict her spunk, she softly says, "Some people just have to be on welfare." It is anybody's guess what our President—whose Poppy surely paid for Yale—thinks young women like Rivera will learn about responsibility or commitment picking up trash in Central Park.

16

"SAVAGE INEQUALITIES" REVISITED

Bob Feldman

Richer, Whiter School Districts Are Still Getting More Public Funds, While the Federal Government Looks the Other Way

In the late 1980s, I taught health and social studies in a New York City public school. My students came largely from African-American and Caribbean families, and the school was located in a high-poverty district. Because funding was so tight, we had no textbooks for a required eighth-grade health class, no classroom maps for seventh- and eighth-grade history classes, and no photocopying machines that teachers or students could use for free. There was also no school newspaper or yearbook, and the school band had fewer than twenty instruments.

The conditions in this school illustrated a crisis of funding inequality in the U.S. public school system. In his 1991 book *Savage Inequalities*, Jonathan Kozol, a longtime critic of unequal education, famously exposed this crisis. He noted, for instance, that schools in the rich suburbs of New York City spent more than $11,000 per pupil in 1987, while those in the city itself spent only $5,500. The story was the same throughout the country: per-capita spending for poor students and students of color in urban areas was a fraction of that in richer, whiter suburbs just miles away.

Over ten years after *Savage Inequalities* was first published, how close has the U.S. public school system come to providing equitable funding for all students — funding that is at least equal between districts, or better yet, higher in poorer areas that have greater needs?

Not very far, according to a new report by the Washington, D.C.-based Education Trust. Entitled "The Funding Gap: Low-Income and Minority Students Receive Fewer Dollars," the report examines state and local expenditures in 15,000 school districts during 1999–2000. Since federal funds account for only 7% of public school resources, this study of state and local spending zeroes in on the source of funding inequality.

According to the Education Trust study, the poorest 25% of school districts in each state receive an average of $966 less in state and local funds per pupil than

Reprinted by permission of *Dollars & Sense*, a progressive economics magazine, available at www.dollarsandsense.org. Bob Feldman is a *Dollars & Sense* intern.

the richest 25%. This gap has narrowed by $173 since 1997, but it does not reflect uniform progress: in nine of 47 states examined, the gap widened by at least $100. In states like New York and Illinois, spending differences remain staggering, totaling $2,152 and $2,060 per student, respectively. These figures, like all those in the study, are adjusted to account for the greater expense of educating students in poor districts and areas with a high cost of living. (See Chart 1.)

Funding inequality puts students of color at a special disadvantage. In two-thirds of states in the Education Trust study, the quarter of school districts with the highest percentage of students of color received at least $100 less in state and local funding than the quarter of districts with the lowest percentage of students of color. New York topped the charts for racial inequality: the quarter of districts with the highest percentage of students of color received $2,034 less in state and local funds per student than the quarter of districts enrolling the smallest percentage. (See Chart 2.)

Between 1997 and 2000, 30 of the 47 states studied did move toward providing equal or greater funding for students in poorer districts—and some states made significant progress. Why did this happen? According to Michael Rebell, executive director of the Campaign for Fiscal Equity, lawsuits have produced some changes. New Jersey, for instance, began channeling funds to its poorest districts after a court challenge; as of 2000, the state government provided roughly three times as

CHART 1
Poor Students Get Less: States with Largest Per-Student Funding Gaps, and U.S. Average

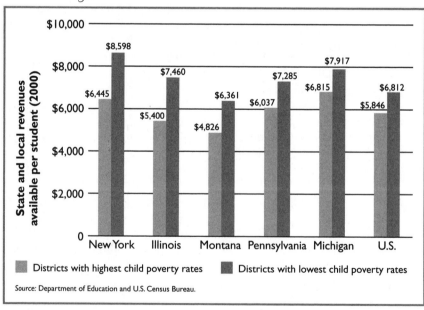

Source: Department of Education and U.S. Census Bureau.

CHART 2
Students of Color Get Less: States with Largest Per-Student Funding Gaps, and U.S. Average

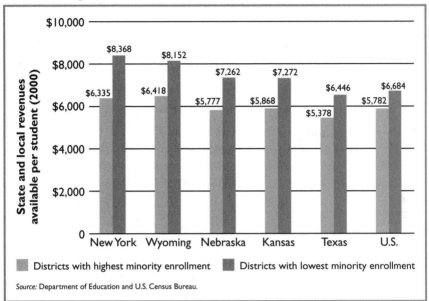

Source: Department of Education and U.S. Census Bureau.

much per-capita funding to the poorest quarter of districts as it did to the richest quarter. While the state government's targeted funds are counterbalanced by wildly unequal local resources, students in the poorest quarter of districts now receive a net of $324 more per capita than those in the richest quarter. States like Oregon have achieved similar results not by targeting poorer districts, but by assuming a greater share of responsibility for school funding state-wide. Strategies like New Jersey's and Oregon's help explain the narrowing funding gap, and could be models for other states.

Rebell notes, however, that state-level remedies are fundamentally limited: among states, they are "complex and uneven," and nationally, they leave millions of students unaffected. A more powerful solution might be for the federal government to fund the public school system directly, as governments do in Canada, Japan, and most social democratic countries of Western Europe. Today, the U.S. government does channel money to poor districts through Title I, the largest single federal investment in education. But Title I funds are not intended to equalize funding within states: the federal government leaves that responsibility to state and local authorities, who plainly do not comply.

The needs of students would be justly served by federally guaranteed funding, but current state and federal policies guarantee something very different. As Jonathan Kozol explained a decade ago, "The present system guarantees that those who can buy a $1 million home in an affluent suburb will also be able to provide their children with superior schools." The U.S. public school system is still rigged in favor of students from richer, whiter districts; and as Rebell remarks, the United States remains "the only major developed country in the world that exhibits this shameful pattern of educational inequity."

RESOURCES

Jonathan Kozol, *Savage Inequalities: Children in America's Schools* (Crown Publishers, 1991).

Educational Leadership, December 1, 1993 interview with Jonathan Kozol. ⟨www.ACCESSednetwork.org⟩.

"The Funding Gap: Low-Income and Minority Students Receive Fewer Dollars," The Education Trust, Inc., ⟨www.edtrust.org⟩.

17

CAUSE OF DEATH: INEQUALITY

Alejandro Reuss

Inequality Kills

You won't see inequality on a medical chart or a coroner's report under "cause of death." You won't see it listed among the top killers in the United States each year. All too often, however, it is social inequality that lurks behind a more immediate cause of death, be it heart disease or diabetes, accidental injury or homicide. Few of the top causes of death are "equal opportunity killers." Instead, they tend to strike poor people more than rich people, the less educated more than the highly educated, people lower on the occupational ladder more than those higher up, or people of color more than white people.

Statistics on mortality and life expectancy do not provide a perfect map of social inequality. For example, in 2002, the life expectancy for women in the United States was about five years longer than the life expectancy for men, despite the

Reprinted by permission of *Dollars & Sense*, a progressive economics magazine, available at www.dollarsandsense.org.

many ways in which women are subordinated to men. Take most indicators of so-cioeconomic status, however, and most causes of death, and it's a strong bet that you'll find illness and injury (or "morbidity") and mortality increasing as status decreases.

Among people between the ages of 25 and 64, those with less than a high school diploma (or equivalent) had an age-adjusted mortality rate more than three times that of people with at least some college, as of 2003. Those without a high school diploma had more than triple the death rate from chronic noncommunicable diseases (e.g., heart disease), more than $3\frac{1}{2}$ times the death rate from injury, and nearly six times the death rate from HIV/AIDS, compared to those with at least some college. People with incomes below the poverty line were nearly twice as likely to have had an asthma attack in the previous year (among those previously diagnosed with asthma) as people with incomes at least twice the poverty line. Poor people were over $2\frac{1}{2}$ times as likely to suffer from a chronic condition that limited their activity and over three times as likely to characterize their own health as "fair" or "poor" (rather than "good" or "very good"), compared to those with incomes over double the poverty line. African Americans have higher death rates than whites from cancer ($\frac{1}{4}$ higher), heart disease ($\frac{1}{3}$ higher), stroke ($\frac{1}{2}$ higher), diabetes (twice as high), homicide (more than 5 times as high), and AIDS (more than 8 times as high). The infant mortality rate for African Americans was, in 2002–2003, over twice as high as for whites. In all, the lower you are in a social hierarchy, the worse your health and the shorter your life are likely to be.

The Worse off in the United States Are Not Well off by World Standards

You often hear it said that even poor people in rich countries like the United States are rich compared to ordinary people in poor countries. While that may be true when it comes to consumer goods like televisions or telephones, which are widely available even to poor people in the United States, it's completely wrong when it comes to health.

In a 1996 study published in the *New England Journal of Medicine*, University of Michigan researchers found that African-American females living to age 15 in Harlem had a 65% chance of surviving to age 65. That is less than the probability at birth of surviving to age 65 for women in India, according to 2000–2005 data. Meanwhile, Harlem's African-American males reaching age 15 had only a 37% chance of surviving to age 65. That is less than the probability at birth of surviving to age 65 for men in Haiti. Among both African-American men and women, diseases of the circulatory system and cancers were the leading causes of death.

It takes more income to achieve a given life expectancy in a rich country like the United States than it does to achieve the same life expectancy in a less afflu-ent country. So the higher money income of a low-income person in the United States, compared to a middle-income person in a poor country, does not necessarily translate into a longer life span. The average income per person in African-American households ($15,200), for example, is about three times the per capita income of Peru. As of 2002, however, the life expectancy for African-American men in the United States was about 69 years, less than the average life expectancy in Peru. The infant mortality rate for African Americans, 13.5 per 1000 live births, is between that of Uruguay and Bulgaria, both of which have per capita incomes around $8,000.

Health Inequalities in the United States Are Not Just About Access to Health Care

Nearly one sixth of the U.S. population below age 65 lacks health insurance of any kind, private or Medicaid. Among those with incomes below 1½ times the poverty line, over 30% lack health coverage of any kind, compared to 10% for those with incomes more than twice the poverty line. African Americans under age 65 were about 1½ times as likely as whites to lack health insurance; Latinos, nearly three times as likely. Among those aged 55 to 64, uninsured people were about ⅔ as likely as insured people to have seen a primary-care doctor in the last year, and less than half as likely to have seen a specialist, as of 2002–2003. Among women over 40, about 55% of those with incomes below the poverty line had gotten a mammogram in the last two years, compared to 75% of those with incomes over twice the poverty line, as of 2003. Obviously, disparities in access to health care are a major health problem.

But so are environmental hazards; communicable diseases; homicide and accidental death; and smoking, lack of exercise, and other risk factors. These dangers all tend to affect lower-income people more than higher-income, less-educated people more than more-educated, and people of color more than whites. African-American children between the ages of 3 and 10 were nearly twice as likely to have had an asthma attack in the last year as white children, among those previously diagnosed with asthma. The frequency of attacks is linked to air pollution. Among people between ages 25 and 64, those without a high school diploma had over five times the death rate from communicable diseases, compared to those with at least some college. African-American men were, as of 2003, more than seven times as likely to fall victim to homicide as white men; African-American women, more than four times as likely as white women. People without a high school diploma (or equivalent) were nearly three times as likely to smoke as those with at least a bachelor's degree, as of 2003. People with incomes below the poverty line were nearly twice as likely to get no exercise as people with incomes over double the poverty line.

Michael Marmot, a pioneer in the study of social inequality and health, notes that so-called diseases of affluence—disorders, like heart disease or diabetes, associated with high-calorie and high-fat diets, lack of physical activity, etc. increasingly typical in rich societies—are most prevalent among the *least* affluent people in these societies. While recognizing the role of such "behavioral" risk factors as smoking in produceing poor health, he argues, "It is not sufficient . . . to ask what contribution smoking makes to generating the social gradient in ill health, but we must ask, why is there a social gradient in smoking?" What appear to be individual "lifestyle" decisions often reflect a broader social epidemiology.

Greater Income Inequality Goes Hand in Hand with Poorer Health

Numerous studies suggest that the more unequal the income distribution in a country, state, or city, the lower the life expectancies for people at all income levels. A 1996 study published in the *American Journal of Public Health*, for example, shows that U.S. metropolitan areas with low per capita incomes and low levels of income inequality have lower mortality rates than areas with high median incomes and high levels of income inequality. Meanwhile, for a given per capita income range, mortality rates always decline as inequality declines.

R.G. Wilkinson, perhaps the researcher most responsible for relating health outcomes to overall levels of inequality (rather than individual income levels), argues that greater income inequality causes worse health outcomes independent of its effects on poverty. Wilkinson and his associates suggest several explanations for this relationship. First, the bigger the income gap between rich and poor, the less inclined the well-off are to pay taxes for public services they either do not use or use in low proportion to the taxes they pay. Lower spending on public hospitals, schools, and other basic services does not affect wealthy people's life expectancies very much, but it affects poor people's life expectancies a great deal. Second, the bigger the income gap between rich and poor, the lower the overall level of social cohesion. High levels of social cohesion are associated with good health outcomes for several reasons. For example, people in highly cohesive societies are more likely to be active in their communities, reducing social isolation, a known health risk factor.

Numerous researchers have criticized Wilkinson's conclusions, arguing that the real reason income inequality tends to be associated with worse health outcomes is that it is associated with higher rates of poverty. But even if they are right and income inequality causes worse health simply by bringing about greater poverty, that hardly makes for a defense of inequality. Poverty and inequality are like partners in crime. "Whether public policy focuses primarily on the elimination of poverty or on reduction in income disparity," argue Wilkinson critics Kevin Fiscella and Peter Franks, "neither goal is likely to be achieved in the absence of the other."

Differences in Status May Be Just as Important as Income Levels

Even after accounting for differences in income, education, and other factors, the life expectancy for African Americans is less than that for whites, U.S. researchers are beginning to explore the relationship between high blood pressure among

African Americans and the racism of the surrounding society. African Americans tend to suffer from high blood pressure, a risk factor for circulatory disease, more often than whites. Moreover, studies have found that, when confronted with racism, African Americans suffer larger and longer-lasting increases in blood pressure than when faced with other stressful situations. Broader surveys relating blood pressure in African Americans to perceived instances of racial discrimination have yielded complex results, depending on social class, gender, and other factors.

Stresses cascade down social hierarchies and accumulate among the least empowered. Even researchers focusing on social inequality and health, however, have been surprised by the large effects on mortality. Over 30 years ago, Michael Marmot and his associates undertook a landmark study, known as Whitehall I, of health among British civil servants. Since the civil servants shared many characteristics regardless of job classification—an office work environment, a high degree of job security, etc.—the researchers expected to find only modest health differences among them. To their surprise, the study revealed a sharp increase in mortality with each step down the job hierarchy—even from the highest grade to the second highest. Over ten years, employees in the lowest grade were three times as likely to die as those in the highest grade. One factor was that people in lower grades showed a higher incidence of many "lifestyle" risk factors, like smoking, poor diet, and lack of exercise. Even when the researchers controlled for such factors, however, more than half the mortality gap remained.

Marmot noted that people in the lower job grades were less likely to describe themselves as having "control over their working lives" or being "satisfied with their work situation," compared to those higher up. While people in higher job grades were more likely to report "having to work at a fast pace," lower-level civil servants were more likely to report feelings of hostility, the main stress-related risk factor for heart disease. Marmot concluded that "psycho-social" factors—the psychological costs of being lower in the hierarchy—played an important role in the unexplained mortality gap. Many of us have probably said to ourselves, after a trying day on the job, "They're killing me." Turns out it's not just a figure of speech. Inequality kills—and it starts at the bottom.

RESOURCES

Health, United States, 2005, with Chartbook on Trends in the Health of Americans, National Center for Health Statistics, www.cdc.gov/nchs.

Health, United States, 1998, with Socioeconomic Status and Health Chartbook, National Center for Health Statistics, www.cdc.gov/nchs.

Human Development Report 2005, UN Development Programme, hdr.undp.org.

Human Development Report 2000, UN Development Programme, hdr.undp.org.

World Development Indicators 2000, World Bank.

Lisa Berkman, "Social Inequalities and Health: Five Key Points for Policy-Makers to Know," February 5, 2001, Kennedy School of Government, Harvard University.

Ichiro Kawachi, Bruce P. Kennedy, and Richard G. Wilkinson, eds., *The Society and*

Population Health Reader, Volume I: Income Inequality and Health. New York: The New Press, 1999.

Michael Marmot, "Social Differences in Mortality: The Whitehall Studies," in Alan D. Lopez, Graziella Caselli, and Tapani Valkonen, eds., *Adult Mortality in Developed Countries: From Description to Explanation.* New York: Oxford University Press, 1995.

Michael Marmot, "The Social Pattern of Health and Disease," in David Blane, Eric Brunner, and Richard Wilkinson, eds., *Health and Social Organization: Towards a Health Policy for the Twenty-First Century.* New York: Routledge, 1996.

Arline T. Gronimus et al., "Excess Mortality Among Blacks and Whites in the United States, *The New England Journal of Medicine,* 335(21), November 21, 1996.

Nancy Krieger, Ph.D., and Stephen Sidney, M.D., "Racial Discrimination and Blood Pressure: The CARDIA Study of Young Black and White Adults," *American Journal of Public Health,* 86(10), October 1996.

18

IMMIGRATION'S AFTERMATH

Alejandro Portes

It is well known by now that immigration is changing the face of America. The U.S. Census Bureau reports that the number of foreign-born persons in the United States surged to 28 million in 2000 and now represents 12 percent of the total population, the highest figures in a century. In New York City, 54 percent of the population is of foreign stock—that is, immigrants and children of immigrants. The figure increases to 62 percent in the Los Angeles metropolitan area and to an amazing 72 percent in Miami. All around us, in these cities and elsewhere, the sounds of foreign languages and the sights of a kaleidoscope of cultures are readily apparent. But the long-term consequences are much less well known.

A driving force behind today's immigrant wave is the labor needs of the American economy. While those needs encompass a substantial demand for immigrant engineers and computer programmers in high-tech industries, the vast majority of today's immigrants are employed in menial, low-paying jobs. The reasons why employers in agribusiness, construction, landscaping, restaurants, hotels, and many other sectors want this foreign labor are quite understandable. Immigrants provide an abundant, diligent, docile, vulnerable, and low-cost labor pool where native workers willing to toil at the same harsh jobs for minimum pay have all but disappeared.

The same agribusiness, industrial, and service firms that profit from this labor have extracted from Congress ingenious loopholes to ensure the continued immigrant flow, both legal and undocumented. Most notable is the requirement, created by the Immigration Reform and Control Act of 1986, that employers must certify that their employees have proper documents without having to establish their validity. Predictably, an entire industry of fraudulent papers has emerged. Would-be workers at construction sites and similar places often are told to go get "their papers" and return the following day. Through such subterfuges, firms demanding low-wage labor have continued to receive a steady supply, thus guaranteeing their profitability.

Defenders of this free flow portray it as a win-win process: Immigrants seeking a better life and the businesses that need their labor both gain. Opponents denounce it as a kind of invasion, as if employees did not welcome these workers. But this debate sidesteps a more consequential one: What becomes of the children of these immigrants? Business may think of them as nothing but cheap labor—indeed, that's why many business groups support pure bracero programs of temporary "guestworkers." But the vast majority of these immigrants want what everyone else wants: families.

So the short-term benefits of migration must be balanced against what happens next. The human consequences of immigration come in the form of children born to today's immigrants. Immigrant children and children of immigrants already number 14.1 million—one in five of all Americans aged 18 and under—and that figure is growing fast. A large proportion of this new second generation is growing up under conditions of severe disadvantage. The low wages that make foreign workers so attractive to employers translate into poverty and inferior schooling for their children. If these youngsters were growing up just to replace their parents as the next generation of low-paid manual workers, the present situation could go on forever. But this is not how things happen.

Children of immigrants do not grow up to be low-paid foreign workers but U.S. citizens, with English as their primary language and American-style aspirations. In my study with Rubén G. Rumbaut of more than 5,200 second-generation children in the Miami and San Diego school systems, we found that 99 percent spoke fluent English and that by age 17 less than a third maintained any fluency in their parents' tongues. Two-thirds of these youths had aspirations for a college degree and a professional-level occupation. The proportion aspiring to a postgraduate education varied significantly by nationality, but even among the most impoverished groups the figures were high.

The trouble is that poor schools, tough neighborhoods, and the lack of role models to which their parents' poverty condemns them make these lofty aspirations an unreachable dream for many. Among Mexican parents, the largest group in our survey as well as in the total immigrant population, just 2.6 percent had a college education. Even after controlling for their paltry human capital, Mexican immigrants' incomes are significantly lower than those of workers with comparable education and work experience. Similar conditions were found among other sizable immigrant groups such as Haitians, Laotians, Nicaraguans, and Cambodians. Children born to these immigrants are caught between the pitiful jobs held by their parents and an American future blocked by a lack of resources and suitable training. Add to this the effects of race discrimination—because the majority of today's second generation is nonwhite by present U.S. standards—and the stage is set for serious trouble.

The future of children growing up under these conditions is not entirely unknown, for there are several telling precedents. Journalistic and scholarly writings concerning the nearly five million young inner-city Americans who are not only unemployed but unemployable—and the more than 300,000 young men of color who crowd the American prison system—commonly neglect to mention that this underclass population did not materialize out of thin air but is the human aftermath of earlier waves of labor migration. The forebears of today's urban underclass were the southern-black and Puerto Rican migrants who moved to the industrializing cities of the Northeast and Midwest in the mid-twentieth century in search of unskilled factory employment. They too willingly performed the poorly paid menial jobs of the time and were, for that reason, preferred by industrial employers. Yet when their children and grandchildren grew up, they found the road into the American middle class blocked by poverty, lack of training, and discrimination. The entrapment of this redundant population in American inner cities is the direct source of the urban underclass and the nightmarish world of drugs, gangs, and violence that these cities battle every day.

Children of poor immigrants are encountering similar and even more difficult conditions of blocked opportunity and external discrimination. In the postindustrial era, the American labor market has come to resemble a metaphoric hourglass, with job opportunities concentrated at the top (in professional and technical fields requiring an advanced education) and at the bottom (in low-paid menial services and agriculture). New migrants respond by crowding into the bottom of the hourglass, but their children, imbued with American-style aspirations, resist accepting the same jobs. This means that they must bridge in the course of a single generation the gap between their parents' low education and the college-level training required to access well-paid nonmenial jobs. Those who fail, and there are likely to be many, are just a step short of the same labor market redundancy that has trapped descendants of earlier black and Puerto Rican migrants.

Assimilation under these conditions does not lead upward into the U.S. middle class but downward into poverty and permanent disadvantage. This outcome is not the fault of immigrant parents or their children but of the objective conditions with which they must cope. All immigrants are imbued with a strong success drive—otherwise they wouldn't have made the uncertain journey to a new land—and all have high ambitions for their children. But family values and a strong work ethic do not compensate for the social conditions that these children face.

Parents' educational expectations are quite high, even higher than their children's. Expectations vary significantly by nationality, but among all groups, 50 percent or more of parents believe that their offspring will attain a college degree. Yet the resources required to achieve this lofty goal—parental education, family income, quality of schools attended—often are not there. The differences found among immigrant nationalities . . . show the wide disparities in parents' income and education and in their children's attendance at poor inner-city schools. Groups that comprise the largest and fastest-growing components of contemporary immigration, primarily Mexicans, have the lowest human-capital endowments and incomes, and their children end up attending mostly inner-city schools.

Effects of these disparities do not take long to manifest themselves in the form of school achievement and the probability of dropping out of school. Parental education and occupation are consistently strong predictors of children's school achievement. Each additional point in parental socioeconomic status (a composite of parents' education, occupation, and home ownership) increases math-test scores by 8 percentile points and reading by 9 points in early adolescence (after controlling for other variables). Living in a family with both parents present also increases performance significantly and reduces the chances of leaving school. Growing up in an intact family and attending a suburban school in early adolescence cuts down the probability of dropping out of high school by a net 11 percent, or approximately half the average dropout rate (again controlling for other variables).

Differences in academic outcomes illustrate . . . math-test scores and school-inactivity rates of immigrants' children, again broken down by nationality. While the correlation is not perfect, the groups with the lowest family incomes and educational endowments—and highest probability of attending inner-city schools—also tend to produce the most disadvantaged children, both in terms of test scores and the probability of achieving a high-school diploma.

At San Diego's Hoover High, there's a group that calls itself the Crazy Brown Ladies. They wear heavy makeup, or "ghetto paint," and reserve derision for classmates striving for grades ("schoolgirls" is the Ladies' label for these lesser beings). Petite Guatemalan-born Iris de la Puente never joined the Ladies, but neither did she make it through high school. The daughter of a gardener and a seamstress, she has lived alone with her mother for several years, since her father was deported and did not return. Mrs. de la Puente repeatedly exhorted Iris to stay in school, but her message was empty. The pressure of work kept the mother away from home for many hours, and her own modest education and lack of English fluency did not give her a clue how to help Iris. By ninth grade, the girl's grade-point average had fallen to a C and she was just hanging in there, hoping for a high-school diploma. When junior year rolled around, it was all over. "Going to college would be nice, but it was clear that it was not for me," Iris said. Getting a job, no matter how poorly paid, became the only option. As far as the immigrant second generation is concerned, it simply is not true that "where there's a will, there's a way." No matter how ambitious parents and children are, no matter how strong their family values and dreams of making it in America, the realities of poverty, discrimination, and poor schools become impassable barriers for many. Like Iris de la Puente, these youths find that the dream of a college education is just that. The same children growing up in inner cities encounter a ready alternative to education in the drug gangs and street culture that already saturate their environment. The emergence of a "rainbow underclass" that includes the offspring of many of today's immigrants is an ominous but distinct possibility.

The short-term economic benefits of immigration are easy to understand and equally easy to appropriate by the urban firms, ranches, and farms that employ this labor, ensuring their profitability. Absent heroic social supports, the long-term consequences are borne by children growing up under conditions of severe disadvantage and by society at large. If the United States wants to keep indulging its addiction to cheap foreign workers, it had better do so with full awareness of what comes next. For immigrants and their children are people, not just labor, and they cannot be dismissed so easily when their work is done. The aftermath of immigration depends on what happens to these children. The prospect for many, given the obstacles at hand, appear dim.

Suggestions for Further Reading

Albelda, Randy, et al. *Unlevel Playing Fields: Understanding Wage Inequality and Discrimination* (2nd Ed.). Boston: Economic Affairs Bureau, 2004.

Amott, Theresa L., and Julie Atthaei. *Race, Gender, and Work: A Multicultural History of Women in the U.S.* (Revised Ed.). Boston: South End Press, 1999.

Anderson, Sarah, et al. *A Decade of Executive Excess: The 1990s.* Boston: United for a Fair Economy, 1999.

Aronowitz, Stanley. *How Class Works.* New Haven, CT: Yale University Press, 2004.

Bergmann, Barbara R. *The Economic Emergence of Women,* 2nd Ed. New York: Palgrave Macmillan, 2005.

Cashin, Sheryll. *The Failures of Integration: How Race and Class Are Undermining the American Dream.* Public Affairs, 2005.

Children's Defense Fund. *The State of America's Children.* Children's Defense Fund, 25 E Street NW, Washington, DC, 20001. Published annually.

Dantzinger, Sheldon H., and Robert H. Haveman. *Understanding Poverty.* Boston: Harvard University Press, 2002.

DeMott, Benjamin. *The Imperial Middle.* New York: William Morrow, 1990.

Domhoff, G. William. *Who Rules America: Power, Politics and Social Change.* New York: McGraw-Hill, 2006.

Ehrenreich, Barbara. *Bait and Switch: The (Futile) Pursuit of the American Dream.* New York: Metropolitan Books, 2005.

Ehrenreich, Barbara. *Nickel and Dimed.* New York: Owl Books, 2002.

Gans, Herbert J. *The War Against the Poor.* New York: Basic Books, 1995.

Goldin, Claudia, and Leonard Katz. *The Race Between Education and Technology.* Cambridge, MA: Belknap Press, 2008.

Hacker, Andrew. *Two Nations: Black and White, Separate, Hostile, Unequal.* New York: Scribner, 2003.

Hays, Sharon. *Flat Broke with Children: Women in the Age of Welfare Reform.* New York: Oxford University Press, 2004.

Keister, Lisa A. *Wealth in America: Trends in Wealth Inequality.* Cambridge: Cambridge University Press, 2000.

Kessler Harris, Alice. *In Pursuit of Equity: Women, Men, and the Quest for Economic Citizenship in Twentieth-Century America.* New York: Oxford University Press, 2001.

Kozol, Jonathan. *Savage Inequalities: Children in America's Schools.* New York: Crown Publishers, 1991.

MacLean, Nancy. *Freedom Is Not Enough.* Cambridge, MA: Harvard University Press, 2008.

Mishel, Lawrence, et al. *The State of Working America 2000–2001.* Ithaca, NY: Cornell University Press, 2001.

Newman, Katherine S. *No Shame in My Game: The Working Poor in the Inner City.* New York: Vintage Books, 2000.

New York Times and Bill Keller. *Class Matters.* New York: Times Books, 2005.

Phillips, Kevin. *Wealth in America: A Political History of the American Rich.* New York: Broadway Books, 2002.

Polakrow, Valerie. *Lives on the Edge: Single Women and Their Children in the Other America.* Chicago: University of Chicago Press, 1993.

Rank, Mark Robert. *One Nation Underprivileged: Why American Poverty Affects Us All*. New York: Oxford University Press, 2005.

Sernau, Scott. *Worlds Apart: Social Inequalities in a New Century*. California: Pine Forge Press, 2001.

Shapiro, Thomas M. *The Hidden Costs of Being African American: How Wealth Perpetuates Inequality*. London: Oxford University Press, 2003.

Sidel, Ruth. *Unsung Heroines: Single Mothers and the American Dream*. Berkeley: University of California Press, 2006.

Shipler, David K. *The Working Poor: Invisible in America* (Reprint Ed.). New York: Vintage Books, 2005.

Wolff, Edward N. *Top Heavy: The Increasing Inequality of Wealth in America and What Can Be Done About It* (2nd Ed.). New York: New Press, 2002.

In addition to these books, the following organizations are good sources for obtaining current statistics analyzed in terms of race, class, and gender:

Asian Nation   asian-nation.org
The Association for American Indian Affairs
Children's Defense Fund   www.childrensdefense.org
United for a Fair Economy   www.faireconomy.org
Institute for Women's Policy Research   www.iwpr.org
Institute for Gay and Lesbian Strategic Studies   iglss.org
The National Urban League   www.nul.org
The National Committee on Pay Equity   www.pay-equity.org
U.S. Bureau of Labor Statistics   www.bls.gov

Many Voices, Many Lives: Some Consequences of Race, Class, and Gender Inequality

S tatistics can tell us a lot about life in any given society, yet they paint only part of the picture. They can tell us that more than 110,000 Japanese Americans were herded into relocation camps during World War II, but they can tell us little of the lives lived in those camps or of the repercussions years later from those lives. They can tell us that every day four women die in this country as a result of domestic violence, but they cannot convey what it means to live in an abusive relationship. Statistics can tell us a story with numbers, but they cannot translate those numbers into lived experience. For that, we must turn to stories about people's lives.

Who will tell these stories? For many years, and not so long ago, the voices of the majority of people in our society were missing from the books in libraries and on our course reading lists. The experiences of women from all racial and ethnic groups regardless of their class position were missing, as were the history, culture, and experience of many men. In their place were the writings and teachings of a relatively small group—predominantly privileged, white, and male—who offered their experience and their perspective as if it were universal. Ironically, even books about breast-feeding and childbirth were written exclusively by male "experts" who defined and described a reality they had never known. White sociologists, psychologists, and anthropologists set themselves up as experts on Native American, Latina, Hispanic, Black, and Asian American experience and culture, offering elaborate, critical accounts of the family structure and lifestyle of each group. Novels chronicling the growth to manhood of young white males from the upper or middle class were routinely assigned in high school and college English courses and examined for "universal themes," while novels about the experiences of men of color, working people, lesbian, gay, bisexual, and transgendered people and women of all groups were relegated to "special interest" courses and treated as marginal. In short, by definition, serious scholarship, "real" science, and "great" literature were what had been produced by well-to-do white males and often focused exclusively on their experiences—accounts of the lives of other groups, if available at all, were rarely written by members of those groups.

We are fortunate that more accounts of the lives of ordinary people have become available over the past 20 or 30 years, largely as a result of the creation of Women's Studies, Ethnic Studies, and LGBT Studies as academic disciplines. These accounts fill in some of the gaps in the limited experience each of us brings to our study of race, class, gender, and sexuality. The selections in Part VI are offered as a way of putting flesh and blood around the often bare-bones statistics provided in Part V. They provide us with an opportunity to move outside the limits of our particular identity, at least for a few minutes, and find out what the world looks like from someone else's perspective. In Part VI we get a glimpse of what it was like to be a young Native American girl torn from her family and community and sent to live at a typical Indian boarding school many years ago. We hear about life as a young Japanese American growing up on the West Coast during World War II when Yuri Kochiyama shares her experiences, first in California and then in a relocation camp in Jerome, Arkansas. We listen in as Mona Fayad talks about what it means to be an Arab American woman in the United States today and see how the socially constructed stereotypes associated with such women impact on her sense of herself. We stand on a cardboard box with Dave Grossman down the street from his junior high school as the seventh-grader proudly announces that he is gay. And we walk the streets of Brooklyn, New York, with June Jordan as she reflects upon her own childhood and the childhood boxer Mike Tyson knew a 25-minute bus ride from her house. We explore the current debate about the implications and consequences of Proposition 8 banning gay marriage, become aware of the fact that her college experience is not always his, and read a painful, multi-layered account of what Helena María Viramontes titles "Beach Blanket Baja," a story it is impossible to summarize adequately.

Each of these essays, and the others in Part VI as well, provide us with unique opportunities to look at everyday life in the United States using the lenses of race, gender, class, and sexuality to call our attention to things we may not have noticed before. In addition, they broaden our range of vision to include some of the other factors that can have significant impact on life choices: among them are religion, age, physical condition, and geographical location. Some of these factors are touched upon or highlighted as well in these readings. Sometimes these factors play a major role in shaping the way others treat us, in determining how much we are paid, what kinds of educational opportunities are available to us, and where and how we live. In other contexts, these variables will be less significant, perhaps even irrelevant. Reading about them adds another dimension to our understanding of the complex set of additional factors that interact with issues of race, class, gender, and sexuality.

But even as we acknowledge how much there is to learn from looking at the lives and experiences of many different people, there is also a danger in this project—the danger of overgeneralizing. It is easy to take the particular experience or the particular beliefs of one member of a group and attribute them to all members of that group. Many students who are members of a religious, racial, or ethnic minority have had the uncomfortable experience of being asked to speak for all members of that minority group at some point in their college experience. Failing to see members of minority groups as individuals is typical of a society in which stereotyping flourishes. On the other hand, for the purposes of studying issues of race, class, gender, and sexuality, it is often necessary to look beyond individual differences and generalize about "Native Americans" or "Chicanas" or "men" in order to highlight aspects of their experience that are more typical of that group's experience than of others. As we have already seen, it would be naive to think that the individual exists in a vacuum, untouched by the racism, sexism, heterosexism, and class bias in society. Unless we understand something about the ways different *groups* experience life in the United States, we will never adequately understand the particular experiences of individual people.

The essays in this part have been selected because they give us a sense of the diversity of life experience in the United States at the same time that they reflect some of the consequences of the inequalities documented in Part V. For the most part, these articles, poems, and essays need no introduction. They speak for themselves.

Civilize Them with a Stick

Mary Brave Bird (Crow Dog) with Richard Erdoes

Gathered from the cabin, the wickiup, and the tepee,
partly by cajolery and partly by threats,
partly by bribery and partly by force,
they are induced to leave their kindred
to enter these schools and take upon themselves
the outward appearance of civilized life.
—Annual report of the Department of Interior, 1901

It is almost impossible to explain to a sympathetic white person what a typical old Indian boarding school was like; how it affected the Indian child suddenly dumped into it like a small creature from another world, helpless, defenseless, bewildered, trying desperately and instinctively to survive and sometimes not surviving at all. I think such children were like the victims of Nazi concentration camps trying to tell average, middle-class Americans what their experience had been like. Even now, when these schools are much improved, when the buildings are new, all gleaming steel and glass, the food tolerable, the teachers well trained and well-intentioned, even trained in child psychology—unfortunately the psychology of white children, which is different from ours—the shock to the child upon arrival is still tremendous. Some just seem to shrivel up, don't speak for days on end, and have an empty look in their eyes. I know of an eleven-year-old on another reservation who hanged herself, and in our school, while I was there, a girl jumped out of the window, trying to kill herself to escape an unbearable situation. That first shock is always there.

Although the old tiyospaye has been destroyed, in the traditional Sioux families, especially in those where there is no drinking, the child is never left alone. It is always surrounded by relatives, carried around, enveloped in warmth. It is treated with the respect due to any human being, even a small one. It is seldom forced to do anything against its will, seldom screamed at, and never beaten. That much, at least, is left of the old family group among full-bloods. And then suddenly a bus or car arrives, full of strangers, usually white strangers, who yank the child out of the arms of those who love it, taking it screaming to the boarding school. The only word I can think of for what is done to these children is kidnapping.

Even now, in a good school, there is impersonality instead of close human contact; a sterile, cold atmosphere, an unfamiliar routine, language problems, and above all the mazaskan-skin, that damn clock—white man's time as opposed to Indian time, which is natural time. Like eating when you are hungry and sleeping when you are tired, not when that damn clock says you must. But I was not taken to one of the better, modern schools. I was taken to the old-fashioned mission school at St. Francis, run by the nuns and Catholic fathers, built sometime around the turn of the century and not improved a bit when I arrived, not improved as far as the buildings, the food, the teachers, or their methods were concerned.

In the old days, nature was our people's only school and they needed no other. Girls had their toy tipis and dolls, boys their toy bows and arrows. Both rode and swam and played the rough Indian games together. Kids watched their peers and elders and naturally grew from children into adults. Life in the tipi circle was harmonious—until the whiskey peddlers arrived with their wagons and barrels of "Injun whiskey." I often wished I could have grown up in the old, before-whiskey days.

Oddly enough, we owed our unspeakable boarding schools to the do-gooders, the white Indian-lovers. The schools were intended as an alternative to the outright extermination seriously advocated by Generals Sherman and Sheridan, as well as by most settlers and prospectors overrunning our land. "You don't have to kill those poor benighted heathen," the do-gooders said, "in order to solve the Indian Problem. Just give us a chance to turn them into useful farmhands, laborers, and chambermaids who will break their backs for you at low wages." In that way the boarding schools were born. The kids were taken away from their villages and pueblos, in their blankets and moccasins, kept completely isolated from their families—sometimes for as long as ten years—suddenly coming back, their short hair slick with pomade, their necks raw from stiff, high collars, their thick jackets always short in the sleeves and pinching under the arms, their tight patent leather shoes giving them corns, the girls in starched white blouses and clumsy, high-buttoned boots—caricatures of white people. When they found out—and they found out quickly—that they were neither wanted by whites nor by Indians, they got good and drunk, many of them staying drunk for the rest of their lives. I still have a poster I found among my grandfather's stuff, given to him by the missionaries to tack up on his wall. It reads:

1. Let Jesus save you.
2. Come out of your blanket, cut your hair, and dress like a white man.
3. Have a Christian family with one wife for life only.
4. Live in a house like your white brother. Work hard and wash often.
5. Learn the value of a hard-earned dollar. Do not waste your money on giveaways. Be punctual.
6. Believe that property and wealth are signs of divine approval.

7. Keep away from salons and strong spirits.
8. Speak the language of your white brother. Send your children to school to do likewise.
9. Go to church often and regularly.
10. Do not go to Indian dances or to the medicine man.

The people who were stuck upon "solving the Indian Problem" by making us into whites retreated from this position only step by step in the wake of Indian protests.

The mission school at St. Francis was a curse for our family for generations. My grandmother went there, then my mother, then my sisters and I. At one time or other every one of us tried to run away. Grandma told me once about the bad times she had experienced at St. Francis. In those days they let students go home only for one week every year. Two days were used up for transportation, which meant spending just five days out of three hundred and sixty-five with her family. And that was an improvement. Before grandma's time, on many reservations they did not let the students go home at all until they had finished school. Anybody who disobeyed the nuns was severely punished. The building in which my grandmother stayed had three floors, for girls only. Way up in the attic were little cells, about five by five by ten feet. One time she was in church and instead of praying she was playing jacks. As punishment they took her to one of those little cubicles where she stayed in darkness because the windows had been boarded up. They left her there for a whole week with only bread and water for nourishment. After she came out she promptly ran away, together with three other girls. They were found and brought back. The nuns stripped them naked and whipped them. They used a horse buggy whip on my grandmother. Then she was put back into the attic—for two weeks.

My mother had much the same experiences but never wanted to talk about them, and then there I was, in the same place. The school is now run by the BIA—the Bureau of Indian Affairs—but only since about fifteen years ago. When I was there, during the 1960s, it was still run by the Church. The Jesuit fathers ran the boys' wing and the Sisters of the Sacred Heart ran us—with the help of the strap. Nothing had changed since my grandmother's days. I have been told recently that even in the '70s they were still beating children at that school. All I got out of school was being taught how to pray. I learned quickly that I would be beaten if I failed in my devotions or, God forbid, prayed the wrong way, especially prayed in Indian to Wakan Tanka, the Indian Creator.

The girls' wing was built like an F and was run like a penal institution. Every morning at five o'clock the sisters would come into our large dormitory to wake us up, and immediately we had to kneel down at the sides of our beds and recite the prayers. At six o'clock we were herded into the church for more of the same. I did not take kindly to the discipline and to marching by the clock, left-right, left-right. I was never one to like being forced to do something. I do something because I feel like doing it. I felt this way always, as far as I can remember, and my sister Barbara felt the same way. An old medicine man once told me: "Us Lakotas are not like dogs who can be trained, who can be beaten and keep on wagging their tails, licking the hand that whipped them. We are like cats, little cats, big cats, wildcats, bobcats, mountain lions. It doesn't matter what kind, but cats who can't be tamed, who scratch if you step on their tails." But I was only a kitten and my claws were still small.

Barbara was still in the school when I arrived and during my first year or two she could still protect me a little bit. When Barb was a seventh-grader she ran away together with five other girls, early in the morning before sunrise. They brought them back in the evening. The girls had to wait for two hours in front of the mother superior's office. They were hungry and cold, frozen through. It was wintertime and they had been running the whole day without food, trying to make good their escape. The mother superior asked each girl, "Would you do this again?" She told them that as punishment they would not be allowed to visit home for a month and that she'd keep them busy on work details until the skin on their knees and elbows had worn off. At the end of her speech she told each girl, "Get up from this chair and lean over it." She then lifted the girls' skirts and pulled down their underpants. Not little girls either, but teenagers. She had a leather strap about a foot long and four inches wide fastened to a stick, and beat the girls, one after another, until they cried. Barb did not give her that satisfaction but just clenched her teeth. There was one girl, Barb told me, the nun kept on beating and beating until her arm got tired.

I did not escape my share of the strap. Once, when I was thirteen years old, I refused to go to Mass. I did not want to go to church because I did not feel well. A nun grabbed me by the hair, dragged me upstairs, made me stoop over, pulled my dress up (we were not allowed at the time to wear jeans), pulled my panties down, and gave me what they called "swats"—twenty-five swats with a board around which Scotch tape had been wound. She hurt me badly.

My classroom was right next to the principal's office and almost every day I could hear him swatting the boys. Beating was the common punishment for not doing one's homework, or for being late to school. It had such a bad effect upon me that I hated and mistrusted every white person on sight, because I met only one kind. It was not until much later that I met sincere white people I could relate to and be friends with. Racism breeds racism in reverse.

2

THEN CAME THE WAR

Yuri Kochiyama

I was red, white, and blue when I was growing up. I taught Sunday school, and was very, very American. But I was also very provincial. We were just kids rooting for our high school.

My father owned a fish market. Terminal Island was nearby, and that was where many Japanese families lived. It was a fishing town. My family lived in the city proper. San Pedro was very mixed, predominantly white, but there were blacks also.

I was nineteen at the time of the evacuation. I had just finished junior college. I was looking for a job, and didn't realize how different the school world was from the work world. In the school world, I never felt racism. But when you got into the work world, it was very difficult. This was 1941, just before the war. I finally did get a job at a department store. But for us back then, it was a big thing, because I don't think they had ever hired an Asian in a department store before. I tried, because I saw a Mexican friend who got a job there. Even then they didn't hire me on a regular basis, just on Saturdays, summer vacation, Easter vacation, and Christmas vacation. Other than that, I was working like the others—at a vegetable stand, or doing part-time domestic work. Back then, I only knew of two Japanese American girl friends who got jobs as secretaries—but these were in Japanese companies. But generally you almost never saw a Japanese American working in a white place. It was hard for Asians. Even for Japanese, the best jobs they felt they could get were in Chinatowns, such as in Los Angeles. Most Japanese were either in some aspect of fishing, such as in the canneries, or went right from school to work on the farms. That was what it was like in the town of San Pedro. I loved working in the department store, because it was a small town, and you got to know and see everyone. The town itself was wonderful. People were very friendly. I didn't see my job as work—it was like a community job.

Everything changed for me on the day Pearl Harbor was bombed. On that very day—December 7—the FBI came and they took my father. He had just come home from the hospital the day before. For several days we didn't know where they

From Joann Faung Jean Lee, *Asian American Experiences in the United States: Oral Histories of First to Fourth Generation Americans from China, the Philippines, Japan, India, the Pacific Islands, Vietnam and Cambodia.* © 1991 Joann Faung Jean Lee. Reprinted by permission of McFarland & Company, Inc., Publishers, Jefferson, NC 28640. www.mcfarlandpub.com

had taken him. Then we found out that he was taken to the federal prison at Terminal Island. Overnight, things changed for us. They took all men who lived near the Pacific waters, and had nothing to do with fishing. A month later, they took every fisherman from Terminal Island, sixteen and over, to places—not the regular concentration camps—but to detention centers in places like South Dakota, Montana, and New Mexico. They said that all Japanese who had given money to any kind of Japanese organization would have to be taken away. At that time, many people were giving to the Japanese Red Cross. The first group was thirteen hundred Isseis—my parents' generation. They took those who were leaders of the community, or Japanese school teachers, or were teaching martial arts, or who were Buddhist priests. Those categories which would make them very "Japanesey," were picked up. This really made a tremendous impact on our lives. My twin brother was going to the University at Berkeley. He came rushing back. All of our classmates were joining up, so he volunteered to go into the service. And it seemed strange that here they had my father in prison, and there the draft board okayed my brother. He went right into the army. My other brother, who was two years older, was trying to run my father's fish market. But business was already going down, so he had to close it. He had finished college at the University of California a couple of years before.

They took my father on December 7th. The day before, he had just come home from the hospital. He had surgery for an ulcer. We only saw him once, on December 13. On December 20th they said he could come home. By the time they brought him back, he couldn't talk. He made guttural sounds and we didn't know if he could hear. He was home for twelve hours. He was dying. The next morning, when we got up, they told us that he was gone. He was very sick. And I think the interrogation was very rough. My mother kept begging the authorities to let him go to the hospital until he was well, then put him back in the prison. They did finally put him there, a week or so later. But they put him in a hospital where they were bringing back all these American Merchant Marines who were hit on Wake Island. So he was the only Japanese in that hospital, so they hung a sheet around him that said, Prisoner of War. The feeling where he was was very bad.

You could see the hysteria of war. There was a sense that war could actually come to American shores. Everybody was yelling to get the "Japs" out of California. In Congress, people were speaking out. Organizations such as the Sons and Daughters of the Golden West were screaming "Get the 'Japs' out." So were the real estate people, who wanted to get the land from the Japanese farmers. The war had whipped up such a hysteria that if there was anyone for the Japanese, you didn't hear about it. I'm sure they were afraid to speak out, because they would be considered not only just "Jap" lovers, but unpatriotic.

Just the fact that my father was taken made us suspect to people. But on the whole, the neighbors were quite nice, especially the ones adjacent to us. There was already a six AM to six PM curfew and a five mile limit on where we could go from our homes. So they offered to do our shopping for us, if we needed.

Most Japanese Americans had to give up their jobs, whatever they did, and were told they had to leave. The edict for 9066—President Roosevelt's edict* for evacuation—was in February 1942. We were moved to a detention center that April. By then the Japanese on Terminal Island were just helter skelter, looking for anywhere they could go. They opened up the Japanese school and Buddhist churches, and families just crowded in. Even farmers brought along their chickens and chicken coops. They just opened up the places for people to stay until they could figure out what to do. Some people left for Colorado and Utah. Those who had relatives could do so. The idea was to evacuate all the Japanese from the coast. But all the money was frozen, so even if you knew where you wanted to go, it wasn't that simple. By then, people knew they would be going into camps, so they were selling what they could, even though they got next to nothing for it.

We were fortunate, in that our neighbors, who were white, were kind enough to look after our house, and they said they would find people to rent it, and look after it till we got back. But these neighbors were very, very unusual.

We were sent to an assembly center in Arcadia, California, in April. It was the largest assembly center on the West Coast, having nearly twenty thousand people. There were some smaller centers with about six hundred people. All along the West Coast—Washington, Oregon, California—there were many, many assembly centers, but ours was the largest. Most of the assembly centers were either fairgrounds, or race tracks. So many of us lived in stables, and they said you could take what you could carry. We were there until October.

Even though we stayed in a horse stable, everything was well organized. Every unit would hold four to six people. So in some cases, families had to split up, or join others. We slept on army cots, and for mattresses they gave us muslin bags, and told us to fill them with straw. And for chairs, everybody scrounged around for carton boxes, because they could serve as chairs. You could put two together and it could be a little table. So it was just makeshift. But I was amazed how, in a few months, some of those units really looked nice. Japanese women fixed them up. Some people had the foresight to bring material and needles and thread. But they didn't let us bring anything that could be used as weapons. They let us have spoons, but no knives. For those who had small children or babies, it was rough. They said you could take what you could carry. Well, they could only take their babies in their arms, and maybe the little children could carry something, but it was pretty limited.

I was so red, white, and blue, I couldn't believe this was happening to us. America would never do a thing like this to us. This is the greatest country in the world. So I thought this is only going to be for a short while, maybe a few weeks or something, and they will let us go back. At the beginning no one realized how long this would go on. I didn't feel the anger that much because I thought maybe this was the way we could show our love for our country, and we should not make too

*Executive Order No. 9066 does not mention detention of Japanese specifically, but was used exclusively against the Japanese. Over 120,000 Japanese were evacuated from the West Coast.

much fuss or noise, we should abide by what they asked of us. I'm a totally different person now than I was back then. I was naïve about so many things. The more I think about it, the more I realize how little you learn about American history. It's just what they want you to know.

At the beginning, we didn't have any idea how temporary or permanent the situation was. We thought we would be able to leave shortly. But after several months they told us this was just temporary quarters, and they were building more permanent quarters elsewhere in the United States. All this was so unbelievable. A year before we would never have thought anything like this could have happened to us—not in this country. As time went by, the sense of frustration grew. Many families were already divided. The fathers, the heads of the households, were taken to other camps. In the beginning, there was no way for the sons to get in touch with their families. Before our group left for the detention camp, we were saying goodbye almost every day to other groups who were going to places like Arizona and Utah. Here we finally had made so many new friends—people who we met, lived with, shared the time, and got to know. So it was even sad on that note and the goodbyes were difficult. Here we had gotten close to these people, and now we had to separate again. I don't think we even thought about where they were going to take us, or how long we would have to stay there. When we got on the trains to leave for the camps, we didn't know where we were going. None of the groups knew. It was later on that we learned so and so ended up in Arizona, or Colorado, or some other place. We were all at these assembly centers for about seven months. Once they started pushing people out, it was done very quickly. By October, our group headed out for Jerome, Arkansas, which is on the Texarkana corner.

We were on the train for five days. The blinds were down, so we couldn't look out, and other people couldn't look in to see who was in the train. We stopped in Nebraska, and everybody pulled the blinds to see what Nebraska looked like. The interesting thing was, there was a troop train stopped at the station too. These American soldiers looked out, and saw all these Asians, and they wondered what we were doing on the train. So the Japanese raised the windows, and so did the soldiers. It wasn't a bad feeling at all. There was none of that "you Japs" kind of thing. The women were about the same age as the soldiers—eighteen to twenty-five, and we had the same thing on our minds. In camps, there wasn't much to do, so the fun thing was to receive letters, so on our train, all the girls who were my age, were yelling to the guys, "Hey, give us your address where you're going, we'll write you." And they said, "Are you sure you're going to write?" We exchanged addresses and for a long time I wrote to some of those soldiers. On the other side of the train, I'll never forget there was this old guy, about sixty, who came to our window and said, "We have some Japanese living here. This is Omaha, Nebraska." This guy was very nice, and didn't seem to have any ill feelings for Japanese. He had calling cards, and he said "Will any of you people write to me?" We said, "Sure," so he threw in a bunch of calling cards, and I got one, and I wrote to him for years. I wrote to him about what camp was like, because he said, "Let me know what it's like wherever you end up." And he wrote back, and told me what was happening in Omaha, Nebraska. There were many, many interesting experiences too. Our mail was generally not censored, but all the mail from the soldiers was. Letters meant everything.

When we got to Jerome, Arkansas, we were shocked because we had never seen an area like it. There was forest all around us. And they told us to wait till the rains hit. This would not only turn into mud, but Arkansas swamp lands. That's where they put us—in swamp lands, surrounded by forests. It was nothing like California.

I'm speaking as a person of twenty who had good health. Up until then, I had lived a fairly comfortable life. But there were many others who didn't see the whole experience the same way. Especially those who were older and in poor health and had experienced racism. One more thing like this could break them. I was at an age where transitions were not hard—the point where anything new could even be considered exciting. But for people in poor health, it was hell.

There were army-type barracks, with two hundred to two hundred and five people to each block and every block had its own mess hall, facility for washing clothes, showering. It was all surrounded by barbed wire, and armed soldiers. I think they said only seven people were killed in total, though thirty were shot, because they went too close to the fence. Where we were, nobody thought of escaping because you'd be more scared of the swamps—the poisonous snakes, the bayous. Climatic conditions were very harsh. Although Arkansas is in the South, the winters were very, very cold. We had a pot bellied stove in every room and we burned wood. Everything was very organized. We got there in October, and were warned to prepare ourselves. So on our block, for instance, males eighteen and over could go out in the forest to chop down trees for wood for the winter. The men would bring back the trees, and the women sawed the trees. Everybody worked. The children would pile up the wood for each unit.

They told us when it rained, it would be very wet, so we would have to build our own drainage system. One of the barracks was to hold meetings, so block heads would call meetings. There was a block council to represent the people from different areas.

When we first arrived, there were some things that weren't completely fixed. For instance, the roofers would come by, and everyone would hunger for information from the outside world. We wanted to know what was happening with the war. We weren't allowed to bring radios; that was contraband. And there were no televisions then. So we would ask the workers to bring us back some papers, and they would give us papers from Texas or Arkansas, so for the first time we would find out about news from the outside.

Just before we went in to the camps, we saw that being a Japanese wasn't such a good thing, because everybody was turning against the Japanese, thinking we were saboteurs, or linking us with Pearl Harbor. But when I saw the kind of work they did at camp, I felt so proud of the Japanese, and proud to be Japanese, and wondered why I was so white, white when I was outside, because I was always with white folks. Many people had brothers or sons who were in the military and Japanese American servicemen would come into the camp to visit the families, and we felt so proud of them when they came in their uniforms. We knew that it would only be a matter of time before they would be shipped overseas. Also what made us feel proud was the forming of the 442 unit.*

I was one of these real American patriots then. I've changed now. But back then, I was all American. Growing up, my mother would say we're Japanese. But I'd say, "No, I'm American." I think a lot of Japanese grew up that way. People would say to them, "You're Japanese," and they would say, "No, we're Americans." I don't even think they used the hyphenated term "Japanese-American" back then. At the time, I was ashamed of being Japanese. I think many Japanese Americans felt the same way. Pearl Harbor was a shameful act, and being Japanese Americans, even though we had nothing to do with it, we still somehow felt we were blamed for it. I hated Japan at that point. So I saw myself at that part of my history as an American, and not as a Japanese or Japanese American. That sort of changed while I was in the camp.

I hated the war, because it wasn't just between the governments. It went down to the people, and it nurtured hate. What was happening during the war were many things I didn't like. I hoped that one day when the war was over there could be a way that people could come together in their relationships.

Now I can relate to Japan in a more mature way, where I see its faults and its very, very negative history. But I also see its potential. Scientifically and technologically it has really gone far. But I'm disappointed that when it comes to human rights she hasn't grown. The Japan of today—I feel there are still things lacking. For instance, I don't think the students have the opportunity to have more leeway in developing their lives.

We always called the camps "relocation centers" while we were there. Now we feel it is apropos to call them concentration camps. It is not the same as the concentration camps of Europe; those we feel were death camps. Concentration camps were a concentration of people placed in an area, and disempowered and disenfranchised. So it is apropos to call what I was in a concentration camp. After two years in the camp, I was released.

Going home wasn't much of a problem for us because our neighbors had looked after our place. But for most of our Japanese friends, starting over again was very difficult after the war.

I returned in October of 1945. It was very hard to find work, at least for me. I wasn't expecting to find anything good, just something to tide me over until my boyfriend came back from New York. The only thing I was looking for was to work in a restaurant as a waitress. But I couldn't find anything. I would walk from one end of the town to the other, and down every main avenue. But as soon as they found out I was Japanese, they would say no. Or they would ask me if I was in the union, and of course I couldn't be in the union because I had just gotten there.

---

*American soldiers of Japanese ancestry were assembled in two units: the 442 Regimental Combat Team and the 100th Infantry Battalion. The two groups were sent to battle in Europe. The 100th Battalion had over 900 casualties and was known as the Purple Heart Battalion. Combined, the units received 9,486 purple hearts and 18,143 individual decorations.

Anyway, no Japanese could be in the union, so if the answer was no I'm not in the union, they would say no. So finally what I did was go into the rough area of San Pedro—there's a strip near the wharf—and I went down there. I was determined to keep the jobs as long as I could. But for a while, I could last maybe two hours, and somebody would say "Is that a 'Jap'?" And as soon as someone would ask that, the boss would say, "Sorry, you gotta go. We don't want trouble here." The strip wasn't that big, so after I'd go the whole length of it, I'd have to keep coming back to the same restaurants, and say, "Gee, will you give me another chance." I figure, all these servicemen were coming back and the restaurants didn't have enough waitresses to come in and take these jobs. And so, they'd say "Okay. But soon as somebody asks who you are, or if you're a 'Jap,' or any problem about being a 'Jap,' you go." So I said, "Okay, sure. How about keeping me until that happens?" So sometimes I'd last a night, sometimes a couple of nights that no one would say anything. Sometimes people threw cups at me or hot coffee. At first they didn't know what I was. They thought I was Chinese. Then someone would say, "I bet she's a 'Jap'." And I wasn't going to say I wasn't. So as soon as I said "Yeah," then it was like an uproar. Rather than have them say, "Get out," I just walked out. I mean, there was no point in fighting it. If you just walked out, there was less chance of getting hurt. But one place I lasted two weeks. These owners didn't want to have to let me go. But they didn't want to have problems with the people.

And so I did this until I left for New York, which was about three months later. I would work the dinner shift, from six at night to three in the morning. When you are young you tend not to take things as strongly. Everything is like an adventure. Looking back, I felt the people who were the kindest to me were those who went out and fought, those who just got back from Japan or the Far East. I think the worst ones were the ones who stayed here and worked in defense plants, who felt they had to be so patriotic. On the West Coast, there wasn't hysteria anymore, but there were hostile feelings towards the Japanese, because they were coming back. It took a while, but my mother said that things were getting back to normal, and that the Japanese were slowly being accepted again. At the time, I didn't go through the bitterness that many others went through, because it's not just what they went through, but it is also what they experienced before that. I mean, I happened to have a much more comfortable life before, so you sort of see things in a different light. You see that there are all kinds of Americans, and that they're not all people who hate Japs. You know too that it was hysteria that had a lot to do with it.

All Japanese, before they left camp, were told not to congregate among Japanese, and not to speak Japanese. They were told by the authorities. There was even a piece of paper that gave you instructions. But then people went on to places like Chicago where there were churches, so they did congregate in churches. But they did ask people not to. I think psychologically the Japanese, having gone through a period where they were so hated by everyone, didn't even want to admit they were Japanese, or accept the fact that they were Japanese. Of course, they would say they were Japanese Americans. But I think the psychological damage of the wartime period, and of racism itself, has left its mark. There is a stigma to being Japanese. I think that is why such a large number of Japanese, in particular Japanese American women, have married out of the race. On the West Coast I've heard people say that sixty to seventy percent of the Japanese women have married, I guess, mostly whites. Japanese men are doing it too, but not to that degree. I guess Japanese Americans just didn't want to have that Japanese identity, or that Japanese part. There is definitely some self-hate, and part of that has to do with the racism that's so deeply a part of this society.

Historically, Americans have always been putting people behind walls. First there were the American Indians who were put on reservations, Africans in slavery, their lives on the plantations, Chicanos doing migratory work, and the kinds of camps they lived in, and even, too, the Chinese when they worked on the railroad camps where they were almost isolated, dispossessed people—disempowered. And I feel those are the things we should fight against so they won't happen again. It wasn't so long ago—in 1979—that the feeling against the Iranians was so strong because of the takeover of the U.S. embassy in Iran, where they wanted to deport Iranian students. And that is when a group called Concerned Japanese Americans organized, and that was the first issue we took up, and then we connected it with what the Japanese had gone through. This whole period of what the Japanese went through is important. If we can see the connections of how often this happens in history, we can stem the tide of these things happening again by speaking out against them.

Most Japanese Americans who worked years and years for redress never thought it would happen the way it did. The papers have been signed, we will be given reparation, and there was an apology from the government. I think the redress movement itself was very good because it was a learning experience for the Japanese people; we could get out into our communities and speak about what happened to us and link it with experiences of other people. In that sense, though, it wasn't done as much as it should have been. Some Japanese Americans didn't even learn that part. They just started the movement as a reaction to the bad experience they had. They don't even see other ethnic groups who have gone through it. It showed us, too, how vulnerable everybody is. It showed us that even though there is a Constitution, that constitutional rights could be taken away very easily.

3

YELLOW

Frank Wu

Writing Race

I'd like to be as honest as possible in explaining why and how race matters, because it shapes every aspect of my life—and everyone else's. I'd like to do so in a manner that allows my white relatives and my white friends to understand and empathize.

I have learned how naïve I was to have supposed that children grew out of their race and to have expected that adults could not possibly be racist. The lives of people of color are materially different than the lives of whites, but in the abiding American spirit we all prefer to believe that our individualism is most important.

As a member of a minority group everywhere in my country except among family or through the self-conscious effort to find other Asian Americans, I alternate between being conspicuous and vanishing, being stared at or looked through. Although the conditions may seem contradictory, they have in common the loss of control. In most instances, I am who others perceive me to be rather than how I perceive myself to be. Considered by the strong sense of individualism inherent to American society, the inability to define one's self is the greatest loss of liberty possible. We Americans believe in an heroic myth from the nineteenth century, whereby moving to the frontier gives a person a new identity. Even if they do not find gold, silver, or oil, men who migrate to the West can remake their reputations. But moving to California works only for white men. Others cannot invent themselves by sheer will, because no matter how idiosyncratic one's individual identity, one cannot overcome the stereotype of group identity.

Sometimes I have an encounter that demonstrates how easily people can be transfixed by a racial stereotype. In a casual aside, a business colleague, who I thought knew me well enough to know better, may make an earnest remark revealing that his attempt to connect with me can come only through race. Although they rarely mention their personal lives, people always will make it a point to tell me about the hit movie they saw last night or the museum exhibit they toured over the weekend if it had a vaguely Asian theme, whether Chinese, Japanese, Korean, Vietnamese, or whatever, because, "It reminded me of you." They tell me I resemble the cellist Yo-Yo Ma or their five-year-old son's friend in school. Or in a passing instant, a white boy or a black boy, whom I would credit with childhood innocence, can rekindle my memory of the ordinary intolerance of days past. At an airport or riding on a subway, boys will see me and suddenly strike a karate pose, chop at the air, throw a kick, and utter some sing-song gibberish, before turning around and running away. Martin Luther King Jr. asked to be judged by the content of his character rather than the color of his skin, but in these surreal episodes I am not judged by the content of my character because the dealings have no content except for the racial image. Worse, it is as trivial for others as it is traumatic to me. I may as well be a stage prop. University of California at Berkeley literature professor Elaine Kim has recounted being told by a white friend who'd read Maxine Hong Kingston's *The Woman Warrior*, one of the earliest works of Asian American novels to become a staple of literature courses, that only through the book did she come to understand Kim.[1] The fictional character becomes more believable than a real person, as though it is easier to know Asian Americans through the representation than through the reality.

At other times, I will have another type of encounter in the anonymous rush of contemporary life, one that confirms that people can be oblivious to folks who don't resemble them.[2] To present an analogy, most motorcyclists and bicyclists who ride regularly on city streets are accustomed to the situation in which they will make prolonged eye contact with a driver, who then blithely proceeds to cut off the bike or turn directly in front of it. The person behind the wheel may have seen the rider but responds only to vehicles like her own; anything else doesn't register. Likewise, waiting in line, I am amazed when a white person, sometimes well-dressed and distinguished looking and sometimes not, cuts in front of me or expects to be given VIP treatment. I am galled by not only the action but also the sense of entitlement that this person radiates. I want to say, "Hello? Did you not see the rest of us back here, or did you take it for granted that you were more important?" Of course, sometimes people are momentarily distracted or generally impolite. It happens often enough, however, in cases where it is fair to surmise that race and gender are involved. When whites are disrespected by other whites—for example, when they are ushered to a deserted area of the restaurant near the kitchen—they generally are not plagued by the suspicion that it is for racial reasons. It is easier for them to write off an incident as the consequence of incivility rather than another indication of something worse. Even if people of color are spurned for reasons other than race, the maltreatment harkens back to race because of the uncertainty of the matter. People of color are held to a double standard. Asian Americans are impudent if we presume to behave as others have done without doubting their right; what is assertive and commanding when it comes from a white male is bossy and presumptuous from an Asian American female. . . .

My premise is straightforward. Race is more than black and white, literally and figuratively. Yellow belongs. Gray predominates. I advance these arguments together, and they are mutually reinforcing. Being neither black nor white, Asian Americans do not automatically side with either blacks or whites. Columbia University professor Gary Okihiro once asked, "is yellow black or white?"[3] Chang-Lin

Tien, who was the first Asian American to head a major research university, recalled arriving in the United States in 1956. He says that when he was a graduate student, "I never rode the city buses" in Louisville, Kentucky. He was humiliated when he boarded one and saw that "whites rode in the front and 'coloreds' rode in the rear." He asked, "Just where exactly did an Asian fit in?" He did not wish to be consigned to the back of the bus, but neither did he believe that even if he dared to sit down in the front of the bus, he could stay there in good conscience.[4] Theirs are the best type of question, because they have no answers. . . .

In race matters, words matter, too. Asian Americans have been excluded by the very terms used to conceptualize race. People speak of "American" as if it means "white" and "minority" as if it means "black." In that semantic formula, Asian Americans, neither black nor white, consequently are neither American nor minority. I am offended, both as an academic and as an Asian American. Asian Americans should be included for the sake of truthfulness, not merely to gratify our ego. Without us—and needless to say, without many others—everything about race is incomplete.

It isn't easy to call people on their unconscious errors. If I point out that they said "American" when they meant "white," they will brush it off with, "Well, you know what I mean," or "Why are you bringing up race?" Yet it is worth pondering exactly what they do mean. What they have done through negligence, with barely any awareness, is equate race and citizenship. They may even become embarrassed once the effect is noticed. Asian Americans were upset when the MSNBC website printed a headline announcing that "American beats out Kwan" after Tara Lipinsky defeated Michelle Kwan in figure skating at the 1998 Winter Olympics.[5] Like gold medalist Lipinsky, Kwan is an American. By implying that Kwan was a foreigner who had been defeated by an "American," the headline in effect announced that an Asian American had been defeated by a white American in a racialized contest. If two white Americans compete against each other in a sporting event—say, rivals Nancy Kerrigan and Tonya Harding—it would be preposterous for the result to be described as one of them defeated by an "American." If Kwan had won, it also would be unlikely for the victory to be described as "American beats out Lipinsky" or "Asian beats out white." Movie producer Christopher Lee recalls that when studio executives were considering making a film version of *Joy Luck Club*, they shied away from it because "there are no Americans in it." He told his colleagues, "There are Americans in it. They just don't look like you."[6]

NOTES

1. Elaine H. Kim, *Asian American Literature: An Introduction to the Writings and Their Social Context* (Philadelphia: Temple University Press, 1982), xix.

2. "Miss Manners," the advice columnist, has addressed this issue, but she prefers to assume that these incidents are not racial. See Judith Martin, "Anger, Fear and Loathing at Airport and at Dinner," *Washington Post*, July 22, 1998, D16.

3. Gary Y. Okihiro, *Margins and Mainstreams: Asians in American History and Culture* (Seattle: University of Washington Press, 1994), 31–63.

4. Chang-Lin Tien, "Affirming Affirmative Action," Perspectives on Affirmative Action . . . and Its Impact on Asian-Pacific Americans (Los Angeles: Leadership Education for Asian Pacifics, 1996), 19.

5. Joann Lee, "Mistaken Headline Underscores Racial Presumptions," *Editor & Publisher*, April 25, 1998, 64.

6. Howard Chua-Eoan, "Profiles in Outrage: America Is Home, But Asian Americans Feel Treated as Outlanders with Unproven Loyalties," *Time*, September 25, 2000, 40.

4

THE MYTH OF THE LATIN WOMAN
I Just Met a Girl Named María

Judith Ortiz Cofer

On a bus trip to London from Oxford University where I was earning some graduate credits one summer, a young man, obviously fresh from a pub, spotted me and as if struck by inspiration went down on his knees in the aisle. With both hands over his heart he broke into an Irish tenor's rendition of "María" from *West Side Story*. My politely amused fellow passengers gave his lovely voice the round of gentle applause it deserved. Though I was not quite as amused, I managed my version of an English smile: no show of teeth, no extreme contortions of the facial muscles—I was at this time of my life practicing reserve and cool. Oh, that British control, how I coveted it. But María had followed me to London, reminding me of a prime fact of my life: you can leave the Island, master the English language, and travel as far as you can, but if you are a Latina, especially one like me who so obviously belongs to Rita Moreno's gene pool, the Island travels with you.

This is sometimes a very good thing—it may win you that extra minute of someone's attention. But with some people, the same things can make *you* an island—not so much a tropical paradise as an Alcatraz, a place nobody wants to visit. As a Puerto Rican girl growing up in the United States and wanting like most children to "belong," I resented the stereotype that my Hispanic appearance called forth from many people I met.

Our family lived in a large urban center in New Jersey during the sixties, where life was designed as a microcosm of my parents' casas on the island. We spoke in Spanish, we ate Puerto Rican food bought at the bodega, and we practiced strict Catholicism complete with Saturday confession and Sunday mass at a church where our parents were accommodated into a one-hour Spanish mass slot, performed by a Chinese priest trained as a missionary for Latin America.

As a girl I was kept under strict surveillance, since virtue and modesty were, by cultural equation, the same as family honor. As a teenager I was instructed on how to behave as a proper señorita. But it was a conflicting message girls got, since the Puerto Rican mothers also encouraged their daughters to look and act like women and to dress in clothes our Anglo friends and their mothers found too "mature" for our age. It was, and is, cultural, yet I often felt humiliated when I appeared at an American friend's party wearing a dress more suitable to a semiformal than to a playroom birthday celebration. At Puerto Rican festivities, neither the music nor the colors we wore could be too loud. I still experience a vague sense of letdown when I'm invited to a "party" and it turns out to be a marathon conversation in hushed tones rather than a fiesta with salsa, laughter, and dancing—the kind of celebration I remember from my childhood.

I remember Career Day in our high school, when teachers told us to come dressed as if for a job interview. It quickly became obvious that to the barrio girls, "dressing up" sometimes meant wearing ornate jewelry and clothing that would be more appropriate (by mainstream standards) for the company Christmas party than as daily office attire. That morning I had agonized in front of my closet, trying to figure out what a "career girl" would wear because, essentially, except for Marlo Thomas on TV, I had no models on which to base my decision. I knew how to dress for school: at the Catholic school I attended we all wore uniforms; I knew how to dress for Sunday mass, and I knew what dresses to wear for parties at my relatives' homes. Though I do not recall the precise details of my Career Day outfit, it must have been a composite of the above choices. But I remember a comment my friend (an Italian-American) made in later years that coalesced my impressions of that day. She said that at the business school she was attending the Puerto Rican girls always stood out for wearing "everything at once." She meant, of course, too much jewelry, too many accessories. On that day at school, we were simply made the negative models by the nuns who were themselves not credible fashion experts to any of us. But it was painfully obvious to me that to the others, in their tailored skirts and silk blouses, we must have seemed "hopeless" and "vulgar." Though I now know that most adolescents feel out of step much of the time, I also know that for the Puerto Rican girls of my generation that sense was intensified. The way our teachers and classmates looked at us that day in school was just a taste of the culture clash that awaited us in the real world, where prospective employers and men on the street would often misinterpret our tight skirts and jingling bracelets as a come-on.

Mixed cultural signals have perpetuated certain stereotypes—for example, that of the Hispanic woman as the "Hot Tamale" or sexual firebrand. It is a one-dimensional view that the media have found easy to promote. In their special vocabulary, advertisers have designated "sizzling" and "smoldering" as the adjectives of choice for describing not only the foods but also the women of Latin America. From conversations in my house I recall hearing about the harassment that Puerto Rican women endured in factories where the "boss men" talked to them as if sexual innuendo was all they understood and, worse, often gave them the choice of submitting to advances or being fired.

It is custom, however, not chromosomes, that leads us to choose scarlet over pale pink. As young girls, we were influenced in our decisions about clothes and colors by the women—older sisters and mothers who had grown up on a tropical island where the natural environment was a riot of primary colors, where showing your skin was one way to keep cool as well as to look sexy. Most important of all, on the island, women perhaps felt freer to dress and move more provocatively, since, in most cases, they were protected by the traditions, mores, and laws of a Spanish/Catholic system of morality and machismo whose main rule was: *You may look at my sister, but if you touch her I will kill you.* The extended family and church structure could provide a young woman with a circle of safety in her small pueblo on the island; if a man "wronged" a girl, everyone would close in to save her family honor.

This is what I have gleaned from my discussions as an adult with older Puerto Rican women. They have told me about dressing in their best party clothes on Saturday nights and going to the town's plaza to promenade with their girlfriends in front of the boys they liked. The males were thus given an opportunity to admire the women and to express their admiration in the form of *piropos*: erotically charged street poems they composed on the spot. I have been subjected to a few piropos while visiting the Island, and they can be outrageous, although custom dictates that they must never cross into obscenity. This ritual, as I understand it, also entails a show of studied indifference on the woman's part; if she is "decent," she must not acknowledge the man's impassioned words. So I do understand how things can be lost in translation. When a Puerto Rican girl dressed in her idea of what is attractive meets a man from the mainstream culture who has been trained to react to certain types of clothing as a sexual signal, a clash is likely to take place. The line I first heard based on this aspect of the myth happened when the boy who took me to my first formal dance leaned over to plant a sloppy overeager kiss painfully on my mouth, and when I didn't respond with sufficient passion said in a resentful tone: "I thought you Latin girls were supposed to mature early"—my first instance of being thought of as a fruit or vegetable—I was supposed to *ripen*, not just grow into womanhood like other girls.

It is surprising to some of my professional friends that some people, including those who should know better, still put others "in their place." Though rarer, these incidents are still commonplace in my life. It happened to me most recently during a stay at a very classy metropolitan hotel favored by young professional couples for their weddings. Late one evening after the theater, as I walked toward my room with my new colleague (a woman with whom I was coordinating an arts program), a middle-aged man in a tuxedo, a young girl in satin and lace on his arm, stepped directly into our path. With his champagne glass extended toward me, he exclaimed, "Evita!"

Our way blocked, my companion and I listened as the man half-recited, half-bellowed "Don't Cry for Me, Argentina." When he finished, the young girl said: "How about a round of applause for my daddy?" We complied, hoping this would bring the silly spectacle to a close. I was becoming aware that our little group was attracting the attention of the other guests. "Daddy" must have perceived this too, and he once more barred the way as we tried to walk past him. He began to shout-sing a ditty to the tune of "La Bamba"—except the lyrics were about a girl named María whose exploits all rhymed with her name and gonorrhea. The girl kept saying "Oh, Daddy" and looking at me with pleading eyes. She wanted me to laugh along with the others. My companion and I stood silently waiting for the man to end his offensive song. When he finished, I looked not at him but at his daughter. I advised her calmly never to ask her father what he had done in the army. Then I walked between them and to my room. My friend complimented me on my cool handling of the situation. I confessed to her that I really had wanted to push the jerk into the swimming pool. I knew that this same man—probably a corporate executive, well educated, even worldly by most standards—would not have been likely to regale a white woman with a dirty song in public. He would perhaps have checked his impulse by assuming that she could be somebody's wife or mother, or at least *somebody* who might take offense. But to him, I was just an Evita or a María: merely a character in his cartoon-populated universe.

Because of my education and my proficiency with the English language, I have acquired many mechanisms for dealing with the anger I experience. This was not true for my parents, nor is it true for the many Latin women working at menial jobs who must put up with stereotypes about our ethnic group such as: "They make good domestics." This is another facet of the myth of the Latin woman in the United States. Its origin is simple to deduce. Work as domestics, waitressing, and factory jobs are all that's available to women with little English and few skills. The myth of the Hispanic menial has been sustained by the same media phenomenon that made "Mammy" from *Gone with the Wind* America's idea of the black woman for generations; María, the housemaid or counter girl, is now indelibly etched into the national psyche. The big and the little screens have presented us with the picture of the funny Hispanic maid, mispronouncing words and cooking up a spicy storm in a shiny California kitchen.

This media-engendered image of the Latina in the United States has been documented by feminist Hispanic scholars, who claim that such portrayals are partially responsible for the denial of opportunities for upward mobility among Latinas in the professions. I have a Chicana friend working on a Ph.D. in philosophy at a major university. She says her doctor still shakes his head in puzzled amazement at all the "big words" she uses. Since I do not wear my diplomas around my neck for all to see, I too have on occasion been sent to that "kitchen," where some think I obviously belong.

One such incident that has stayed with me, though I recognize it as a minor offense, happened on the day of my first public poetry reading. It took place in Miami in a boat-restaurant where we were having lunch before the event. I was nervous and excited as I walked in with my notebook in my hand. An older woman motioned me to her table. Thinking (foolish me) that she wanted me to autograph a copy of my brand new slender volume of verse, I went over. She ordered a cup of coffee from me, assuming that I was the waitress. Easy enough to mistake my poems for menus, I suppose. I know that it wasn't an intentional act of cruelty, yet of all the good things that happened that day, I remember that scene most clearly, because it reminded me of what I had to overcome before anyone would take me seriously. In retrospect I understand that my anger gave my reading fire, that I have almost always taken doubts in my abilities as a challenge—and that the result is, most times, a feeling of satisfaction at having won a convert when I see the cold, appraising eyes warm to my words, the body language change, the smile that indicates that I have opened some avenue for communication. That day I read to that woman and her lowered eyes told me that she was embarrassed at her little faux pas, and when I willed her to look up at me, it was my victory, and she graciously allowed me to punish her with my full attention. We shook hands at the end of the reading, and I never saw her again. She has probably forgotten the whole thing but maybe not.

Yet I am one of the lucky ones. My parents made it possible for me to acquire a stronger footing in the mainstream culture by giving me the chance at an education. And books and art have saved me from the harsher forms of ethnic and racial prejudice that many of my Hispanic *compañeras* have had to endure. I travel a lot around the United States, reading from my books of poetry and my novel, and the reception I most often receive is one of positive interest by people who want to know more about my culture. There are, however, thousands of Latinas without the privilege of an education or the entrée into society that I have. For them life is a struggle against the misconceptions perpetuated by the myth of the Latina as whore, domestic, or criminal. We cannot change this by legislating the way people look at us. The transformation, as I see it, has to occur at a much more individual level. My personal goal in my public life is to try to replace the old pervasive stereotypes and myths about Latinas with a much more interesting set of realities. Every time I give a reading, I hope the stories I tell, the dreams and fears I examine in my work, can achieve some universal truth which will get my audience past the particulars of my skin color, my accent, or my clothes.

I once wrote a poem in which I called us Latinas "God's brown daughters." This poem is really a prayer of sorts, offered upward, but also, through the human-to-human channel of art, outward. It is a prayer for communication, and for respect. In it, Latin women pray "in Spanish to an Anglo God/with a Jewish heritage," and they are "fervently hoping/that if not omnipotent,/at least He be bilingual."

5

THE ARAB WOMAN AND I

Mona Fayad

I am haunted by a constant companion called The Arab Woman. When I shut myself alone in my home, she steps out of the television screen to haunt me. In the movies, she stares down at me just as I am starting to relax. As I settle in a coffee shop to read the newspaper, she springs out at me and tries to choke me. In the classroom, when I tell my students that I grew up in Syria, she materializes suddenly as the inevitable question comes up: "Did you wear a veil?" That is when she appears in all her glory: the Faceless Veiled Woman, silent, passive, helpless, in need of rescue by the west. But there's also that other version of her, exotic and seductive, that follows me in the form of the Belly Dancer.

As a construct invented by the west, this two-in-one Arab Woman is completely intractable. Her voice drowns mine. It is no use pointing out that in Syria, Arab school girls wear khaki uniforms and are required for school credit to work on urban improvement projects, planting trees and painting walls. Or that Syrian television is constantly running ads for women to join the army. As I try to assert my experience of being an Arab woman, the Arab Woman tries to make me write about *her*. For a brief moment, I give in.

My one personal encounter in Syria with a fully veiled woman happens during my third year at the University of Damascus. I take a bus home. (Yes, we do have buses in the Middle East. We did away with camels as a means of transportation five years ago.) A veiled woman climbs aboard, the only one on the bus. I pay her no attention until she rushes up and embraces me enthusiastically. "Mona, how wonderful to see you!"

I know the voice, but somehow I can't place it. Realizing my predicament, she raises the veil for a minute. It's Mona, a friend of mine from university that I haven't seen recently. A bouncing, energetic person, she is very active socially. I have never seen her veiled. I ask if it's a recent decision.

"Not really. I come from a conservative neighborhood, so I prefer to wear the veil when I arrive there." She shrugs. "My family isn't very concerned, but I prefer to do it this way."

Reprinted by permission of South End Press.

The old souk (market) in downtown Kuwait is one of my favorite places to go. The tradition of bargaining is still in practice. It's a sharp contrast to the cold, impersonal supermarkets that have now almost completely eradicated the social exchanges that have been a part of buying and selling in the Middle East for centuries. In this section of town, many women wear burqas or are completely veiled since they belong to an older generation. Here the real haggling happens, and the high-pitched shouting of women dins the lower and more cracked voices of the men. "What a cheat," the woman announces to whoever is willing to listen. "Can you believe how much he's asking for this worthless piece of cloth?"

In another corner, two women selling men's underwear laugh good-naturedly as they target a young man whose embarrassment is apparent. "How *big* did you say you were?"

These are some veiled Arab women. Neither silent nor passive, they have a place within their culture, like women all across the world. But once again, The Arab Woman has intruded, preventing me from talking about myself, pushing me to feed you what you want to hear.

Part of the reason I obey her is that it's easier to be exotic. To talk about an ordinary Arab woman, one who wears pants or a plain dress or a suit and walks around looking like everyone else is uninteresting, to say the least. I feel pressured to produce something *special*, something different. I try to shut out The Arab Woman who is controlling my thoughts. She is asking me for facts, figures, ways of classifying women so they can be clearly placed in boxes and the doors can be shut on them once and for all. She wants order, a rational explanation, something easy to understand.

After much thinking, it occurs to me that it is you who veil the Arab woman, it is you who make her into a passive victim, it is you who silence her. Arab women get on with our lives. I try to get on with my life, but it is difficult to constantly confront what I am not.

I am not The Arab Woman. And, further, I cannot represent Arab women. Each Arab woman must represent herself, with the range of identities that include Syrian or Saudi Arabian, Berber or Copt, bedouin or society woman from Beirut, Druze or Alawite, villager in the Upper Nile or Minister of Culture from Damascus. We're not an object that can be crushed together and concentrated for Western consumption in a box labelled: Organic Arab Woman.

There's no doubt within *me* that I'm an Arab woman. The problem is whether you will believe me.

6

BEACH BLANKET BAJA

Helena María Viramontes

In our East Los Angeles working-class neighborhoods of the '50s and '60s, no one thought of summer vacations or sleep-away camps as a possibility.

Right after the school year was over and before we were driven to the Central Valley to pick raisin grapes for the summer, we'd hunt down discarded bottles to redeem for the deposits, roll up our swimsuits in a towel taquito, locate our one Esther Williams bathing cap (mandatory in the public pool, and which we had to take turns wearing) for our sojourn to the Belvedere Park plunge located a quarter-mile from our home. One dime paid for our admittance, while a precious nickel bought a Big Hunk candy bar, which, later on when we were sun-toasted, sugar-starved and spent by hours of water play, delivered the energy for us to walk back home.

My parents grew up in one of the largest and oldest Mexican-American communities in the nation. Immigrant belief prevailed, despite the fact that both Mom and Dad were born in the United States. We were poor, but it was a poverty that we were unaware of since everyone around us was the same. The fact that our family was Catholic and large once made the headlines of *The East Los Angeles Tribune*, where a photo of my smiling mother announced the birth of her 11th child at Beverly Hospital.

Work was a given, and labor of any kind was highly valued. My father was a hod carrier who bore the weight of 60 pounds of wet cement on his back while expertly climbing scaffolds braced against buildings under construction.

My mother was our cook, consoler, healer, launderer and caregiver. I became a dutiful daughter, like most of my sisters. We all felt strong empathy for her. We howled whenever we'd watch Donna Reed on television vacuuming in stilettos and full petticoat dresses. If we were lucky enough to catch an Annette Funicello and Frankie Avalon "Beach Party" movie, my older sisters would remark to one another in frustration and with a hint of jealousy: "Where do they get all that free time?"

Our Tío José was a great drinking friend of my father's. He was a stout man who had a fondness for whiskey, a frequent visitor who arrived with pocketfuls of lollipops that he distributed to the younger ones. Sometimes he brought along his two handsome teenage sons as an added bonus. My older sisters were prohibited from dating, so they entertained mutual crushes on Larry and Joe Junior while playing their 45s on the turntable and munching potato chips. On one such visit in 1964, when I was 10, my father announced that we were all to spend a weekend in Ensenada, Mexico, with José and his family.

My mother was, at first, skeptical: It would be no easy feat to transport a total of 16 people, the majority of them children, but Tío José had worked out a plan. He would drive his Pontiac, accompanied by his wife, Tía Lola, and his children. My father would drive Joe Junior's clunky Chevy, and my oldest brother, Gil, would be in charge of driving our father's white Ford pickup.

Gas and food? Everything was much cheaper across the border. Lodging? Camping under the stars!

Grumbling ceaselessly, my mother packed her good menudo knife, along with her tamale pot for the slow-cooking tripe, and most of her kitchen setup. She had grown up in the fields, traveling with our grandparents who were following the California crops. And although she still used her own mother's cast-iron stove, the one with removable legs for easier transport to migrant labor camps—it still amazed us all that Grandma made both tortillas and bread in this odd-looking apparatus—the stove was kept home.

We children quickly became stupid with vacation delirium. At dawn on the day of departure, we scuttled to pile the truck with our clothes-filled paper bags (we did not own luggage), cardboard boxes containing bread and peanut butter, coffee, chips, snacks and other nonperishables, including a set of dishes and a metal bucket to wash them in. Like Steinbeck's Joads heading out for something better, we joined the caravan for the two-hour drive to cross the border to Tijuana, then another two-hour drive along the bumpy, winding and ill-repaired Carretera 1 to Ensenada.

I was the fifth to the youngest, the invisible child, and for a reason I cannot recall, my mother allowed me to ride with her inside the truck. This is what I remember: the alacrity with which we were waved across the border by a Mexican immigration officer, the muddle of the Tijuana streets and the astounding poverty of the Mexican children as we stopped to buy more groceries, then the unknotting of the streets into the main highway where we passed the shantytowns, or *las colonias*, on the outskirts of the city. Seeing houses molded from cardboard and garbage, tins and bushes, children whose filthy faces were snot-smeared, men without legs scooting themselves around, brought on a terror larger than my empathy. And although I could not turn away, I sat closer to the warm folds of my mother.

Once we entered the winding carretera, my mother's nerves shot up. "Slow down!" she demanded of my brother. "Watch out!" But I caught my mother's proud smile; her first-born son, as thin as wire, sitting upright and rigid, eternally focused on the road, light sprigs of a mustache, a young man now.

Finally, the caravan of vehicles drove into an empty stretch of beach, parked side by side with trunks facing the surf, and the tedious work of unloading began. Our father prepared the campsite while my older sisters paired off with Larry and

Joe Junior to find firewood. My father and Tío José opened a bottle of tequila and took swigs back and forth while working.

We younger ones ran over a series of dunes and into the surf with absolutely no regard for time. We body surfed, built sand castles, chased the waves as if they were monsters and we were their intended victims, body slammed our nakedness against the froth, buried one another—on and on our illustrious and profound play went.

By late afternoon, caped in our towels, we returned to the campsite, trembling and hungry. Apparently, my mother had sent my father to find firewood since my sisters had not returned, and by then annoyance had replaced her worry. In the meantime, we ate cold bologna sandwiches and Ho-Hos and drank Kool-Aid, but we remained hungry until my father returned with planks of wood so uniformly cut that they could have easily been a section of a picket fence. (They were.)

Already boozy, Tío José started the pit fire, and we roasted marshmallows or hot dogs. In between the licks of flame, my lost sisters and the brothers returned, and I saw patches of sand on MaryAnn's hair. Words were exchanged. Later, as MaryAnn sat beside me, her face held such beguile against the crackling of the fire, I thought her more beautiful than Annette Funicello.

Our collective trance broke when Tío José, in a fit of alcoholic anger, got a hold of my mother's menudo knife and threatened to kill my aunt. His wobbling roars and verbal assaults were almost hilarious (he could barely stand up straight) had he not been wielding the huge machete.

His swings to and fro forced all of us, including Tía Lola, to dodge behind the dunes while my mother and father tried to settle Tío down. These were things that adults did all the time. The affliction of split personalities, the mysterious explosions of emotions, nuclear rages that we were often exposed to—confusing and terrifying—made us into children who wavered in their faith in God because He, too, was an adult and prone to similar fits. Crouched behind a sand dune, Larry told us quite calmly: "My dad does this every Saturday."

Perhaps it was the pot of strong coffee and Kahlúa or simple exhaustion that lowered my Tío into a deaf-defying snore. Then we all readied for bed as if nothing out of the ordinary had happened.

In the truck bed, seven of us lay atop thick Mexican blankets. Even at such a tender age, my younger brother Frank's sinuses rattled like marbles in a jar, hence the nightly bickering as to who would sleep next to him. This night it was to be me, and I considered myself lucky since he kept me awake to witness the stars, inhale the scent of the sea and listen to the smoothing mellow waves broaching the shore. From the truck, I admired the shattered bits of moon on the skin of the water.

While others slept soundly, I could hear Tío's snores in the distance and my sweet brother's gurgling, and I felt as if I was the only person in the world who was awake. I thought about the stars and the beyondness of them, and the darkness, which made up the unknown.

We have no photos of this one family vacation, but the images of Gil behind the steering wheel of the truck, the sand on MaryAnn's hair and Tío's machete threats are easily summoned and deliver a sense of gratitude. Unfortunately, upon our return to the United States, the long lines at the border crossing allowed anxieties to grow to monstrous proportions.

At the gateway, a United States immigration officer studied us. He remained silent even as he reached over and grabbed away a piece of sugar cane I had been sucking on. I began to cry. My mother said nothing to him about his rudeness, and I could see by her trembling as she handed over the documents that she was afraid of something.

"Are you an American citizen?" he demanded. Gil knew to stare straight ahead as the officer deliberated whether to search us or allow us to cross into our own country while I complained and whined. All my mother could muster during the two-hour drive home was: "Behave next time." Since that day, I never have.

7

CROSSING THE BORDER WITHOUT LOSING YOUR PAST

Oscar Casares

SAN MIGUEL DE ALLENDE, Mexico   Along with it being diez y seis de septiembre, Mexican Independence Day, today is my father's 89th birthday. Everardo Issasi Casares was born in 1914, a little more than a hundred years after Miguel Hidalgo y Costilla rang the church bells of Dolores, summoning his parishioners to rise up against the Spaniards.

This connection has always been important in my family. Though my father was born in the United States, he considers himself a Mexicano. To him, ancestry is what determines your identity. If you have Mexican blood, you are Mexican, whether you were born in Mexico City or New York City. This is not to say he denies his American citizenship—he votes, pays taxes and served in the Army. But his identity is tied to the past. His family came from Mexico, so like them he is Mexicano, punto, end of discussion.

In my hometown, Brownsville, Tex., almost everyone I know is Mexicano: neighbors, teachers, principals, dropouts, doctors, lawyers, drug dealers, priests. Rich and poor, short and tall, fat and skinny, dark- and light-skinned. Every year our Mexican heritage is celebrated in a four-day festival called Charro Days. Men grow beards; mothers draw moustaches on their little boys and dress their little girls like Mexican peasants; the brave compete in a jalapeño-eating contest. But the celebration also commemorates the connection between two neighboring countries, opening with an exchange of gritos (traditional cowboy calls you might hear in a Mexican movie) between a representative from Matamoros, Mexico, standing on one side of the International Bridge and a Brownsville representative standing on the other.

Like many Americans whose families came to this country from somewhere else, many children of Mexican immigrants struggle with their identity, as our push to fully assimilate is met with an even greater pull to remain anchored to our family's country of origin. This is especially true when that country is less than a quarter of a mile away—the width of the Rio Grande—from the new one. We learn both cultures as effortlessly as we do two languages. We learn quickly that we can exist simultaneously in both worlds, and that our home exists neither here nor there but in the migration between these two forces.

But for Mexican-Americans and other immigrants from Spanish-speaking countries who have been lumped into categories like Latino or Hispanic, this struggle has become even more pronounced over the last few years as we have grown into the largest minority group in the United States. Our culture has been both embraced and exploited by advertisers, politicians and the media. And as we move, individually, from our small communities, where our identity is clear, we enter a world that wants to assign us a label of its choosing.

When I left Brownsville in 1985 to start at the University of Texas at Austin one of the first things I was asked was, "What are you?" "I'm Mexican," I told the guy, who was thrown off by my height and light skin. "Really, what part of Mexico are you from?" he asked, which led me to explain I was really from Brownsville, but my parents were Mexican. "Really, what part of Mexico?" Here again I had to admit they weren't really born in Mexico and neither were my grandparents or great-grandparents. "Oh," he said, "you're Mexican-American, is what you are."

Mexican-American. I imagined a 300-mile-long hyphen that connected Brownsville to Austin, a bridge between my old and new world. Not that I hadn't seen this word combination, Mexican-American, on school applications, but I couldn't remember the words being spoken to me directly. In Brownsville, I always thought of myself as being equally Mexican and American.

When I graduated that label was again redefined. One of my first job interviews was at an advertising agency, where I was taken on a tour: the media department, the creative department, the account-service department, the Hispanic department. This last department specialized in marketing products to Spanish-speaking consumers. In the group were men and women from Mexico, Puerto Rico and California, but together they were Hispanic. I was hired to work in another department, but suddenly, everyone was referring to me as Hispanic.

Hispanic? Where was the Mexican in me? Where was the hyphen? I didn't want to be Hispanic. The word reminded me of those Mexican-Americans who preferred to say their families came from Spain, which they felt somehow increased their social status. Just hearing the word Hispanic reminded me, too, of people who used the word Spanish to refer to Mexicans. "The Spanish like to get wild at their fiestas," they would say, or "You Spanish people sure do have a lot of babies."

In this same way, the word Hispanic seemed to want to be more user friendly, especially when someone didn't want to say the M word: Mexican. Except it did slip out occasionally. I remember standing in my supervisor's office as he described calling the police after he saw a car full of "Mexicans" drive through his suburban neighborhood.

Away from the border, the word Mexican had come to mean dirty, shiftless, drunken, lustful, criminal. I still cringe whenever I think someone might say the word. But usually it happens unexpectedly, as though the person has pulled a knife on me. I feel the sharp words up against my gut. Because of my appearance, people often say things in front of me they wouldn't say if they knew my real ethnicity—not Hispanic, Latino or even Mexican-American. I am, like my father, Mexican, and on this day of independence, I say this with particular pride.

8

THE EVENT OF BECOMING

Jewelle L. Gomez

When I was about eleven years old I was visiting the small city in Rhode Island where my mother lived with my stepfather. Pawtucket was a failing mill town, predominantly white, of various ethnicities. Its working-class homes were spiraling downward in the late 1950s, before the phenomenon of gentrification. It was a cheap and manageable town for my fair-skinned, straight-haired mother, who resembles the Wampanoag side of the family more than I do. It had seemed like a comfortable place for her and her white husband.

One day, while sitting on the steps outside my mother's home I was approached by a boy a bit younger than I. He eyed me warily and asked what nationality I was. I replied that I was an American. He looked puzzled, then said, "No, I mean what nationality are you?"

Reprinted by permission of the author.

I was adamant. "American."

"No," he said, "you know what I mean."

The beginning of anger stretched my words tightly in the air.

"You said what nationality, that means nation. I'm from America, so I'm American. What are you?"

He looked at me in fear and then disgust and said, "You don't know what you're talking about," then ran down the street to his own stoop.

He went back, I'm sure, to his white parents who'd sent him. He had the air of a child on a mission he did not quite understand, but he knew I had not responded satisfactorily. I was sure that he'd expected me to say I was a "nigger," just as his father and mother had probably identified me. The look of expectation in his eyes was a betrayal. In siding with his parents' ignorance he betrayed our natural alliance as children. I felt crushed.

But I had a major advantage over that child. I knew what he was doing and he did not. As a black person in the United States—even as a child—I recognized a trap being set by a white person. I saw, at eleven years old, what black meant to white America, and I knew that by stating my blackness I might set in motion a series of events that had historically never meant anything good for me. So, precocious little wench that I was even then, I whipped out another identity I knew would stump him and his parents, whose devious hand I sensed guided his bumbling inquiries.

And lest my behavior be dismissed today as fanciful paranoia, the fact is that within months of that encounter my mother and her family were besieged with hate phone calls; garbage was dumped and burned on her tiny lawn. Her neighbors threatened her home and her life when they realized that by American I also meant black.

So the question of identity and its complexities is not just an academic one for me. I never had the privilege of relaxedly theorizing who I was in this world, even as a child. Each hypothesis I might create was met with a specifically defined reality and the question of survival. Interestingly enough, this reality and the experiences it offered me did not seduce me into an insistence on a rigidly guarded identity. I recognized the wondrous spectrum of elements that begin the construction of my identity—lesbian, African American, Wampanoag, Ioway, Bostonian—to just begin. Coming of age during the political movement of the 1960s helped me learn an early appreciation of the power and the value of identification. But the complexity of identity didn't escape me. After all, my mother was an acceptable neighbor on one day and a target of violence the next, simply because of others' interpretation of her identity. This life lesson also helped me develop a critical stance toward any element that was viewed as fixed, unmitigated, or eternal.

Now that I've been given the opportunity to do some theorizing, I'd like to share some linked but not necessarily linearly related thoughts and feelings on my two responses to the question of identity—appreciation and caution.

First, I suggest that the question of identity as posed in this country is one that would be almost unrecognizable in other countries. Most nations begin from a more articulate definition of who its citizens are, rightly or wrongly, and then develop attitudes and institutions which allow for assorted variations, as well as for colonialism. In the eighteenth and nineteenth centuries the concept of a "British subject" became so expansive that it could, at one time, have taken in just about every existing ethnic group. I'm not suggesting that the British have been especially liberal in their acceptance of immigrant African or Caribbean "subjects" any more than the citizens of Germany today absorb Asian and African immigrant workers. But those nations start from a unified whole—whether real or imagined—and the United States does not.

The idea of "American" (and I, of course, use that word imprecisely when I use it to speak only of U.S. citizens) embodies resilient refugees from many other shores. Consequently the struggle for identity is more focused, more strident for citizens of the United States. We are continually, as a nation, seeking a way to pull together the unifying threads that make us a nation. And when we speak of Americans we think of an amazing array of mostly European immigrants who escaped their countries, explicitly choosing the United States because of its mythology. Most often the United States has been extolled as a place where one could escape the oppressions of the past (religious, economic, social, judicial) and create a new life, that is, a new identity.

It is this tabula rasa ideal that sets much of the tone for the development of the American national persona. After being bathed in the fire and water of a transatlantic journey and surviving to step on to the frightening and alien shores of America, the new arrivals must surely have deemed it only fair that life be allowed to begin anew. And that idea of newness, that disconnection from all that went before, alongside the sense of a vast expanse of wilderness (supposedly unclaimed) shaped the embryonic American identity.

That American identity most often comes into greatest relief when we speak of the deeds of explorers/exploiters such as the Pilgrims, cowboys, and settlers of the western migration or those who survive victimization—European immigrants who endured antagonism to become successful. Both mythologies were shaped to emphasize a simplistic heroism—good against bad. Personal fortitude and ingenuity winning out over mindless evil or ignorance. John Wayne versus the wild Indians; Horatio Alger versus poverty. In this country politicians play most successfully to people's belief in this mythology. The good citizens are asked to defeat the forces of evil: antifamily homosexuals, pornographers, the lazy poor, the violent people of color, all those too "weak" to overcome their circumstance. The polyethnic nature of our beginnings makes such fractionalizations an easy strategy.

There has been much discussion in literary circles in the past few years of the deconstruction of words and ideas, stripping them down to allow them to stand independent of meaning, stark against a page; that old tabula rasa, if you will. We learn much when we are able to look at roots and at the flotsam and jetsam that have little meaning in and of themselves, but that linger in the wake of words and ideas. We strip away the attendant realities until we look at the empty space that lies there, waiting to form itself into motion, object, concept.

But people are not artichokes. It is very helpful in a therapeutic situation to peel each leaf and get to the heart of what has formed a personality. But in human social interaction it is by exploring the full construction and interaction of the layers of character that we find the heart. To twist an old geometry principle—the whole equals more than the sum of its parts.

Any writer or literary critic would acknowledge that it is those layers both personal and social that make our fictional characters memorable. When most effective our stories reflect the plurality of who we are both individually and as a nation. Because of who I am when I wrote my novel *The Gilda Stories*, the questions of real (fictional) life and those of national identity had to be considered. I made the choice not to discard but to utilize those questions in developing the plot, themes, and characters. If a youthful-looking, dark-skinned woman is walking down a lonely country road at night and encounters two men dressed like beds, that is, wearing sheets and hoods, with what dilemma are they presented? Well, two conflicting desires begin: both are rooted in fear and need for a sense of power. So there is murder and there is rape. The conflict: whether to rape her or kill her. Of course the resolution is that they can do both, first rape, then lynch. They assume that they can accomplish both deeds successfully, anonymously, because history has shown them it's possible.

But shortly into the encounter they realize they have misidentified their prey. Like the little boy on my mother's stoop, they see only what they've been told to see. On that road she is not simply a lone dark woman; she is that and more. She is someone with powers—physical or mystical, or maybe just a gun. She is a lone dark woman who is also more than simply that description, and the inability of those men to absorb a constructive concept of who she is will cost them their lives. For them identity is reached through a reductionist theory. It says that black women are one particular set of things: powerless, sexual prey, not intelligent. These men are unable to see her identity in a constructive way, that is, a circle of elements forming a whole. But whether this encounter takes place in the eighteenth century or the twentieth century, whether it is on a dark country road or in a U.S. Senate judiciary hearing room, the definition of the identity of that lone dark woman will not (for the white males who've intercepted her) be broad enough to include other things she might be—a crack shot, a black belt in karate, a reputable lawyer who'll no longer be silent about harassment, a vampire.

Many of us who've been categorized and oppressed fear that to identify oneself as a specific thing—black, lesbian, Jewish, Italian, American—is to reduce yourself to a single element that excludes all other possible elements. The concept of identity as a reductionist rather than constructive expression is continually reinforced in this culture, where ethnic or social identity is rarely used as part of a normative stance. Sociological surveys pinpoint specific identities in order to categorize and assess and market information. The Kinseys, the Nielsens, the Bureau of the Census introduce the slots into which we must all fit. And once we are slotted, wheels will turn and things will happen. Homosexuals will be known as lonely white men, television shows with all-black casts and no laugh track will not be produced, and candidates for office will decide on which neighborhood to focus their campaign. We have come to accept negative social consequences from such identification.

Why is that, when evidence also shows that creating specifics doesn't have to be limiting or exclusionary? The success of the film and television business depends on precisely that principle—anyone in the world should be able to identify with Shirley Temple, Sylvester Stallone, or a purple dinosaur. The concept of "world literature" also presumes such identification. People rarely think, What an ethnic oddity Leopold Bloom is, let's drop Joyce from the canon; or, the working poor of Victorian England are irrelevant so don't bother reading Dickens. We can accept the perspectives of Joyce or Dickens as extremely specific and at the same time broad and relevant. We now must insist on giving the same credence and value to other perspectives, including our own.

Marilyn Frye speaks of "the event of becoming a lesbian (as) a reorientation of attention in a kind of ontological conversion." When we use this constructive approach, identification becomes a shift in perspective rather than a closing of one's eyes. To identify ourselves can open a way into discussion. Rather than reducing us to familiar elements, it can offer an introduction into the many layers that construct who we are. To say that I am a lesbian is not the same as saying that I am *only* a lesbian. Identifying myself as a lesbian shifts the emphasis, suggesting a place to begin, not a place to end.

I first read James Baldwin's *Giovanni's Room* around 1961 and was not surprised to find that it was about gay men. In one section one of the characters, seated in a bar, coyly observes the patrons and says, "All these men, all these men and so few women. Doesn't that seem strange to you?" "Ah," said Giovanni, "no doubt the women are waiting at home."

Because I knew myself to be a lesbian I identified with the men in that bar, eyeing each other in a way that was forbidden. I experienced the thrill of recognition of my place with these people. I saw the hot mix of limbs and sweat that was the reason for being there and found joy in it. At the same time I transmuted the experience and was able to understand that I was also at home with the women—the women who I knew were not merely waiting. Our imagination allows each of us this possibility of being party to both experiences.

Perhaps it would be easier for us to acknowledge the many places where we reside if we could learn to accept the basic, natural permutation that is our lives. We are perpetually defining and redefining ourselves. The baby, the youth, the teenager. I am now learning my identity as middle-aged in preparation for my identity as an elder. These are precise identities that we take on, reshape, fill up as we need to over the course of our alloted time on this planet. As we move into the next definition, what we have been does not evaporate to make way for the next phase. It is embedded in who we are. That infamous inner child! We can hold on to all those other things we've been and make what we are more whole. My identity as a lesbian is tied up with James Baldwin's literary representation of gay men; with Mercedes McCambridge, a particularly dykey actress of the 1940s; with Gwen, my high femme best friend from high school; as well as with Stephen, the heroine of *The Well of Loneliness*. My early experience of lesbians as women in flannel shirts and Frye boots gives more resonance to my experience today of lesbians in three-piece suits or in transparent body stockings. When I can reconcile those experiences, those identifications, I have created a larger whole, not a smaller self.

I enjoy being called a lesbian, a writer, a Virgo, a Bostonian, a woman, an African American, or any of the other identities for which I qualify. And I will gleefully correct you if you seem to indicate that one of those must preclude the others. The little boy questioning me in Pawtucket didn't understand what he saw or heard when I called myself an American, which is sort of the equivalent of saying "all of the above."

9

THIS PERSON DOESN'T SOUND WHITE

Ziba Kashef

Kofi? Mani? Sule? Bijan?

Choosing a name for my future son has turned out to be much more complicated than I thought when I started searching online for possibilities.

Reza? Omar? Darius? Malcolm?

While I entertained the sound and significance of each potential moniker (Kofi is Twi for "born on Friday"—what if he's born on Tuesday?), I started to wonder about the consequences of giving him an obviously "ethnic" name. It would reflect his multiracial heritage (black, Iranian, Irish, Hungarian) and hopefully contribute to his sense of cultural pride. But the name would also likely be misspelled, mispronounced, and misunderstood in a country that is largely still ignorant and suspicious of otherness.

My own name, Ziba (zee-bah), has mainly evoked expressions of admiration (How unusual!) and curiosity (How do you spell that?). But on occasion, the rev-

ColorLines Magazine, Culture Section, vol. 6, no. 3, Fall 2003.

elation that it is Persian, as is my father, has been met with awkward silence or stares. A Middle Eastern name is not particularly welcome in the U.S., especially in the current anti-Muslim/Arab/Middle East political environment.

So as I contemplate my son's name, I'm torn between the desire to emphasize his ethnicity and the desire to minimize the potential for profiling and discrimination against him. While racial discrimination has been understood historically as a practice based on an individual's skin color, recent research is showing that it is also often based on a person's name or speech, with the same destructive effects.

What's in a Name?

A name—and the racial group associated with it—can make the difference between getting a job interview and remaining unemployed, according to one recent study. Researchers at the University of Chicago Graduate School of Business and the Massachusetts Institute of Technology sent 5,000 fake resumes in response to a variety of ads in two major newspapers—the *Boston Globe* and the *Chicago Tribune*. Names on the resumes were selected to sound either distinctively Anglo (e.g., Brendan Baker) or African American (e.g., Jamal Jones). The study revealed that the fictitious job seekers with white names were 50 percent more likely to get calls for interviews. Those stats translate into the need for blacks to mail 15 resumes for every 10 resumes sent by whites in order to land one interview. Sadly, this pattern of affirmative action for white job hunters emerged even among federal contractors and firms that advertised themselves as "equal opportunity" employers.

Besides changing their names, there appears to be little black applicants can do to level the playing field. As part of the study, researchers created two sets of resumes—high quality and low quality—to reflect the actual pool of job seekers looking for work in fields ranging from sales, administrative support, clerical services, and customer services. But even having a higher quality resume with such credentials as volunteer experience, computer skills, and special honors failed to improve the black applicants' chances of getting their foot in the door. "The payback that an African American applicant gets from building these skills is much lower than the payback a white applicant would get," the University of Chicago's associate professor Marianne Bertrand noted in a summary of the study.

African and African American names aren't the only ones singled out for prejudice, of course, and the job sphere isn't the only realm in which such discrimination gets played out. In the American-Arab Anti-Discrimination Committee's (ADC) "Report on Hate Crimes and Discrimination Against Arab Americans: The Post-September 11 Backlash," the authors noted that among the dozens of instances of discrimination by airlines that occurred between September 2001 and October 2002, "the passenger's name or perceived ethnicity" alone was often sufficient cause for unprovoked removal from a flight. Discrimination often took place whether or not the passenger was actually Arab or Muslim, resulting in many South Asians and others falling victim to the ignorance of the pilot or another passenger. According to the ADC, one Indian Canadian woman was removed from a plane because her last name was mispronounced as "Attah" and therefore perceived as Middle Eastern. Other passengers were prevented from traveling because their names were similar to those on the FBI watch list.

This type of profiling quickly spread with Jim-Crow-like effects. "We've found that persons named Osama are being regularly denied services, whether in restaurants, stores, or other areas," says the ADC's media director Laila Al-Qatami. Another example recorded by the ADC describes how an Indian American couple were handcuffed and interrogated after purchasing Broadway tickets and specifying that their seats be located in the middle of the theater. Their crime? The "foreign name and accent" of the ticket buyer had made the ticket agent suspicious enough to call the police.

While the ADC has documented more than 700 violent incidents and 800 cases of employment discrimination against Arab Americans since 9/11, many more go unreported and unchallenged. "It is hard to easily label what happens as discrimination. For example, if a person is denied housing or not offered a position with a company," notes Al-Qatami, "can this be linked to discrimination or is the candidate not truly qualified? It is a fine line."

Linguistic Profiling

Names aren't the only potential cues to a person's racial identity: speech may also reveal—or conceal—ethnicity. While searching for housing in the predominantly white neighborhood of Palo Alto, California, in the mid-1990s, John Baugh made appointment after appointment over the phone only to be turned away at the landlord's door. "I was told that there was nothing available," says the Stanford University professor of education and linguistics, who happens to be African American. It didn't take long for him to realize that prospective owners were mistaking his phone voice for that of a white person and inviting him to view apartments. When he showed up for the appointments, he was repeatedly told that there had been some misunderstanding.

This personal affront piqued Baugh's professional curiosity. While it's established that landlords have long discriminated against prospective tenants on the basis of skin color, Baugh decided to test whether they did so on the basis of brief telephone conversations. Using three distinct dialects he learned while growing up in Los Angeles—African American Vernacular English, Chicano English and Standard American English—he placed calls in response to ads for apartments in five Northern California neighborhoods. During those calls, he used various pseudonyms, such as Juan Ramirez for the Chicano English dialect. What emerged was clearer proof of bias against the black and Chicano dialects in predominantly white locales. "[The] research demonstrates that voice is a surrogate for race in many instances when people choose to discriminate over the telephone or use the telephone as the means of discrimination," he explains. Two University of Pennsylvania sociologists uncovered similar results in a separate study of rental housing discrimination.

With his evidence, Baugh, who wrote the book *Beyond Ebonics: Linguistic Pride and Racial Prejudice* (Oxford University Press), has been able to help bolster the claims of a dozen housing discrimination victims in court. Baugh and his colleagues at Stanford are also currently investigating linguistic profiling in education and employment. He cites examples of elementary and secondary school students being placed on non-academic reading tracks based on their accents. "The linguistic profiling that is taking place does have direct educational consequences for the child," he adds—consequences that can affect their ability to later compete in the job market.

Double-Edged Discrimination Data

Research that verifies the persistence of prejudice against people of color because of names and speech can have both positive and negative consequences. On the one hand, employers and landlords can be challenged in court, and in the best-case scenarios, they can also become more aware of subconscious discriminatory practices in order to change them. Shanna L. Smith of the National Fair Housing Alliance, which documents reports of housing discrimination nationwide, has gone so far as to encourage companies to offer employees sensitivity training so they can avoid discriminating and resulting lawsuits, according to an article in *Legal Affairs*.

But Baugh acknowledges that the validation of racial identification by voice can also have negative effects. Prejudiced property owners who have gotten wind of his research can simply discriminate more carefully by either making some appointments with people of color when they have no intention of renting to them, or claiming that despite the evidence, they personally can't identify a person's race by the sound of his or her voice. "I had hoped that this research would expose and eliminate the discrimination but it's far more complicated than that," he says. "If the result . . . is that landlords grant appointments and then deny someone housing face to face, that, to me, is not a real improvement." On the other hand, he points to instances in which criminal courts have allowed police officers and witnesses to identify a suspect solely by the sound of his voice—i.e., I heard the voice of a black/Latino man. This has happened in rape cases when the victim could not see her attacker and other cases in which police used wiretaps but did not actually see a suspect. Such testimony has succeeded and rarely been challenged in criminal cases. "This issue of voice identification has cut both ways against minority speakers," he explains. "It cuts against them as defendants and it cuts against them as plaintiffs."

While blacks have long been the victims of such bias, Latinos, Asians, and Arab Americans—not to mention other vulnerable groups such as the elderly and disabled—are similarly profiled, experts note. Evidence of discrimination and laws to prevent it (such as the Fair Housing Act and Civil Rights Act) have failed to eradicate "talking while black" and other examples of linguistic racism. They remain largely invisible acts of bigotry—bloodless crimes that injure people of color while quietly reinforcing and perpetuating segregation and white supremacy. Perhaps by the time my future son is an adult, some 50 years after legal discrimination officially ended, he will grow up in a society where his ethnic name and heritage is truly accepted and not punished.

10

FAMILY TIES AND THE ENTANGLEMENTS OF CASTE

Joseph Berger

As an Indian immigrant, Dr. Bodh Das faced an excruciating challenge. His three daughters had been exposed to America's freewheeling mating rituals, but he wanted to find them husbands the old-fashioned way—within the Hindu caste into which he was born.

With his eldest daughter, Abha—the one who had spent the least time growing up in America—he hit the jackpot, getting her to return to India in 1975 to wed a man she had never met but who hailed not only from the same Kayashta subcaste but also from the same obscure offshoot. With his second daughter, Bibha, he was less successful. She married a Kayashta, but from a different branch.

"So there was some transgression in this marriage," Dr. Das, a silver-haired cardiologist in the Bronx, said with a wry stoicism worthy of another father who struggled with three modern-minded marriageable daughters, Tevye of "Fiddler on the Roof."

Dr. Das's third daughter, Rekha, the most Americanized, strayed even further. She refused to return to India to find her mate and married a man outside her father's caste whom she met in school. It was what Indians call "a love marriage." And Dr. Das's losing battle to uphold tradition is about to suffer yet another setback: a grandson plans to marry a non-Indian Christian from Chicago whom he met at Harvard.

As Dr. Das's experience shows, the peculiarly Indian system of stratifying its people into hierarchical castes—with Brahmins at the top and untouchables at the bottom—has managed to stow away on the journey to the United States, a country that prides itself on its standard of egalitarianism, however flawed the execution. But the caste system, weakening for a half-century in India, is withering here under the relentless forces of assimilation and modernity. While it persists, its vestiges today often seem more a matter of sentiment than cultural imperative.

To be sure, not just marital arrangements but business relations are sometimes colored by caste. Arun K. Sinha, a member of the Kurmi caste, is owner of the Foods of India store, a shop on Curry Hill at Lexington Avenue and 28th Street in Manhattan. He complains that wholesalers from a Gujarati caste insist that he pay cash rather than extend the credit they give to merchants from their own clan.

E. Valentine Daniel, a professor of anthropology at Columbia University, says some Indian executives will not hire untouchables, now usually called Dalits, or downtrodden, no matter their qualifications. "It's even more than a glass ceiling, it's a tin roof," he said.

Mr. Daniel, former director of Columbia's South Asian Institute, told of the resistance he faced among upper-caste Indians on an academic committee when he wanted to name an endowed chair in Indian political economics after a noted untouchable, Dr. B. R. Ambedkar, a Columbia graduate who helped draft the Indian Constitution, which decades ago abolished the caste system.

Sometimes, the caste distinctions, recognizable by family names and places of origin, linger as a form of social snobbery. Keerthi Vadlamani, a 23-year-old chemical engineer from an affluent Brahmin family in the south-central Indian city of Hyderabad, said, "Some people are stupid enough not to mingle with a Dalit, to cold-shoulder them."

"You won't invite them home, you won't go over to their home," he said.

Other upper-caste Indians here say that they do not bother to probe someone's caste and that most compatriots will do business with anyone. Few Indians would admit to such behavior as refusing to eat in a restaurant because its food was cooked by an untouchable, something many upper-caste Indians might have done 50 years ago.

Mostly caste survives here as a kind of tribal bonding, with Indians finding kindred spirits among people who grew up with the same foods and cultural signals. Just as descendants of the Pilgrims use the Mayflower Society as a social outlet to mingle with people of congenial backgrounds, a few castes have formed societies like the Brahmin Samaj of North America, where meditation and yoga are practiced and caste traditions like vegetarianism and periodic fasting are explained to the young.

"Right now my children are living in a mixed-up society," said Pratima Sharma, president of the New Jersey chapter of Brahmin Samaj and a 39-year-old software trainer with two daughters, 9 and 3. "That's why I went into the Brahmin group, because I wanted to give my children the same values."

The exquisitely complex Indian caste system dates back thousands of years to the origins of Hinduism. Hindus tell of a deity who transformed himself into a human society arranged according to a cooperative division of labor. The deity's head turned into the Brahmin caste of priests and scholars, his hands into the Kshatriya caste of warriors and administrators, his thighs into the merchant and landholding Vaishyas, and his feet into Shudras, the skilled workers and peasants. Hindu notions of ritual purity and pollution defined how these four broad castes could interact and reserved an underclass rung for the untouchables, who worked in the most "polluting" jobs like cleaning streets or toilets.

Whatever its economic and religious foundations, the caste system—which in time sprouted more than 3,000 jati, or subcastes, tinged by geography, language and employment—became ironbound. Until recent decades, village untouchables would step out of view whenever a Brahmin walked by, and tea stalls would reserve separate dishware for Dalit. The rigid system confined people in lower castes to poverty, said Dr. Parmatma Saran, a professor of sociology at Baruch College, so that economic class often paralleled caste.

After India gained independence from Britain in 1947, the legal forms of caste were abolished, and lower castes began benefiting from favorable quotas for government jobs and college entry. By the mid-1960's, the social aspects of the system were also slackening among urban and educated sectors of Indian society, precisely the groups that furnished most of the doctors, engineers and other professionals who began coming to the United States under preferences in immigration law.

Then something surprising happened here. Madhulika S. Khandelwal, director of the Asian American Center at Queens College, said that the continuing influx of immigrants brought in less-educated relatives who tended to sustain caste distinctions, and created masses of caste members who could associate conveniently with one another. In the 2000 census, there were 454,686 Indians in the New York–New Jersey–Connecticut metropolitan area.

Ads in New York City's Indian newspapers testify to the persistence of caste, with one family advertising for a "Brahmin bride" and another seeking an "alliance for U.S.-educated, professionally accomplished" Bengali Kayashta daughter.

"The underlying hope is that you have a woman or man from the same caste," Dr. Khandelwal said of such matchmaking ads. "That way the marriage supports the family tradition. You are assuring, to the best of your ability, to live through those traditions expressed in food, dress, vocabulary and other things."

Still, the exposure of younger Indians to American ways continues to chip away at even these caste traditions. Mr. Vadlamani, the chemical engineer, said members of his Brahmin family "find it hard to digest that I eat meat, that I date girls not in the same caste." His parents, significantly, do not object.

Ranjana Pathak, a quality-control chemist on Long Island, maintains many Brahmin traditions. Last week, she was eating only fruit to mark an Indian festival. But she has found other traditions hurtful. Though she agreed to an arranged marriage, her in-laws disapproved her coming from a lower subcaste of Brahmins.

"Until today it has left a bitter taste in my mouth, and those are things you never forget," she said. "That's why I won't do it to my children."

There are, of course, young people attached to the old ways. Hariharan Janakiraman, a 31-year-old software engineer who lives in Queens, is a Brahmin from the

Vadama branch, which emphasizes teaching. Choosing engineering was his one rebellion. But he intends to let his parents select his wife from his caste.

His parents, he said, will consult his horoscope and that of the bride and make sure their planets and attendant moons are aligned. They will, he said, ask the prospective bride to prepare some food and sing and dance, the latter to make sure all her limbs work.

"If I marry people from other castes, my uncle and aunt won't have a good impression of my parents, so I won't do that," he said. "If I get married to a Dalit girl, the way she was brought up is different from the way I was brought up, so some incompatibility will result."

Dalits say they still on occasion sense upper-caste scorn. Pinder Paul is a spirited 50-year-old Punjabi Sikh (the Sikh faith absorbed some caste distinctions) who came to New York City in 1985 and worked as a dishwasher at Tad's Steaks. Now he and his wife spend seven days a week running the Chirping Chicken outlet he owns in Astoria. He could cite no instance of outright discrimination, but said looks and gestures sometimes betray upper-caste condescension.

"Our friends who came here from India from the upper classes, they're supposed to leave this kind of thing behind, but unfortunately they brought it with them," he said.

Yet in a paradoxical demonstration of the stubborn resilience of caste, Mr. Paul is active with a local Dalit group and said he would prefer that his son marry a Dalit.

"We want to stay in our community," he said.

11

WHAT I LEARNED ABOUT JEWS

Joe Wood

The preacher begins his tale, then reads some history: You are black and proud and you will remember that somewhere along the way some of the people in our line were made very low and not tough at all. I recall: We laughed at the whites when their backs were turned, and our mother spit out the lemon seeds under the porch because she said someday a tree with its natty leaves would lick light there long after we

Reprinted with the permission of the Estate of Joe Wood, Jr.

moved to the city. We were slaves then and maybe we are still today, slaves, our black-
ness a badge of terrifying knowledge, a certificate of human accomplishment, its pos-
sibility and strength, like a god or a flame inside cupped hands, not something to
flee from like a dead body or a bad smell.

While Jews, along with Italians and the Irish, have in most of the century's ren-
derings of American history been assigned the role of "immigrant," and as such are
permitted a history before America, Negroes were made in America. That left us with
a blank place where a history should be: no place to put our peoplehood and few
ways to understand the situation. So we patched our wounds with the pages of the
Bible. So in church, our hospital, we tell the tale over and over again; how much we
resemble the ancient Jews, how we too are slaves awaiting deliverance. We hold this
tale more dear than did the pilgrims who made us slaves—but what of the Jews, who
would certainly want their story back?

It was simple and plain. You'd heard that the Jews controlled jazz, the media, the Democratic Party, the civil rights movement and Harlem real estate, and you wondered. You knew this didn't explain why the police beat you up or why the public education system was a mess or why your neighborhood was without cable and regular garbage pickup, but still you wondered.

"Don't let them call you an anti-Semite, sista," he said. "You'll never work again."

"Jewish people run Hollywood, just like they do *The New York Times*," you said.

"Definitely," he said.

"If that's the way it works, why can't I say it?"

"You know why," he said. "The Jews got it sewed up, and refuse to admit it. I'm tired of reading about Israel and the Holocaust. And about how they worked in the civil rights movement. My theory is they produced the civil rights movement and they pumped up King and all them preachers as a public relations diversion so no one would notice them buying mortgages."

"Well . . . ," you said, scratching your nose. You felt guilty whenever someone talked about "the Jews."

He picked up the slack. "I read where the Anti-Defamation League said the whiteboys are the ones writing 'Heil Hitler' and 'Jewboy' and stuff like that on the synagogues. Niggas got better sense than that."

"True," you said.

There was a silence.

"The Jews," he said, pausing. "My theory is the Holocaust messed them up. No matter how comfortable life starts to feel, they always bring back the Nazis. Or use them as an excuse to beat down niggas."

"Six million is a lot of million," you said, in a light voice.

"I'm telling you, Holocaust got them psychotic. But I want to hear them talk about how many million of us died getting here. Six million's only a drop in the ocean compared to what we went through. I want to know how many of us died on their slave ships. They never teach about that Holocaust."

Then he continued. "You don't hate them sometimes?"

Very quickly you said, "No."

"Good. Well I do. I'll be honest. I hate them sometimes. Because they were the minstrels. Al Jolson was a Jew and the Beastie Boys are Jews. Somebody even told me Elvis was a Jew. They bought our stuff for a dime and made a mint off it. Fats Waller to Chuck Berry to all them rappers—it's the Jews making the money. They act like your friend, but they're the No. 1 pimps of niggas. You got to admit that."

"Jewish people definitely don't have a monopoly on that."

"But the Jews were the ones who made Hollywood: Selznick and Goldwyn and Mayer—Jews. It's a fact. Undeniable. Now it's to the point where they don't even have to slander us anymore. They got their Negro minstrels to say what they want in their papers and magazines and they give 'em a dollar and a prize and it's nothing but Negro smiles. You know what I'm saying—they hate niggas because they know we got their number."

You felt the pull of the words. Down. And then you felt guilty inside, because you wanted to say something more, to separate yourself, and you couldn't, so you smiled—even though you knew there was a limit to your solidarity with the brotha. James Baldwin got it right when he wrote about the special disappointment you've reserved for the Jews—also ex-slaves, but that's where your complicity ended. You knew Jewish people didn't cause more black problems than other whites did. You remembered the preacher's story of the mother and her lemon tree, our collective selfhood. This was the real story, and it actually had very little to do with Jews. You remembered, and you comforted yourself by saying your blackness and his blackness was why you smiled, but suddenly you felt the urge to spit something out.

I read a lot as a kid. I was a curious and obedient boy who paid close attention to his parents' exhortations about the improvement of the race. I had a role to play. My parents were determined to see their children become doctors or lawyers or captains of industry or something to help black people to be proud, so I tried hard, very hard—I brought all my books to bed. My mother drove my sister and me to the library, and my father drove us to private school, and when I lay down I would open the books: the Bible, Edith Wharton, Malcolm X, *The New Republic*, James Joyce, Yukio Mishima, Gerard Manley Hopkins, James Baldwin, Spiderman, Tom Wolfe, *Playboy*, Maya Angelou, John le Carré, Kurt Vonnegut.

I also read Norman Mailer's tales and Saul Bellow's stories and Norman Podhoretz's "My Negro Problem—and Ours." Podhoretz's essay described and tried to defend a racist Jew's racism. I still think of that piece whenever I hear talk of black anti-Semitism. But as I bring my own Jewish story to light now, I will refrain from harping on any "Jewish problem"; I will instead try to tell the truth, which is more complicated than words like "problem" allow.

For I grew up feeling a little like a Jew. Most of the children at Riverdale School in the Bronx were Jewish, and I went there for 10 years. I tried to fit in and did. I listened to the same music and wore the same clothes and laughed at Woody Allen movies for the same reasons as my peers. I lived on the other side of town, but I knew the difference between the words "meshugga" and "zaftig"—I spoke the language of my environment. I even adopted my classmates' views of the world.

I shared, for instance, my Jewish schoolmates' dislike of WASPs even though I hadn't met many. The WASPs mainly went to Collegiate and places outside the city like Hotchkiss or Andover, and only the dumbest of their children came to Riverdale. Most of the school's administrators were of Anglo heritage, and this was a problem for many of the Jewish parents. My peers followed their parents' lead. I remember them saying the goyim "ruled the country," then saying "You're a Jew" during a dispute about money; or fawning over Nordic facial features, making fun of the WASPs with Jewish noses. This perspective resembled the distaste for whites expressed around my neighborhood, a blend of vocal contempt and private admiration.

Our parents didn't particularly care for whites, but they weren't hostile in an active way. No one would have acted funny or said anything to any of the block's remaining few, the ones who hadn't moved to Jersey or Westchester. Mostly, you heard talk about Jamaicans or the islanders we derisively called 'Ricans. The whites usually discussed were the Italians, who still had some shops in the area. They were reputedly mafia and were to be avoided if possible, though they were admired for their sense of family and their piety.

But there wasn't much talk of Jews, even in church. I remember a Catholic friend saying they were the ones who betrayed Christ, and it made sense. We had all learned that Jews were the ones who had inhabited the long dark before the coming of the Lord. But no preacher or Sunday school teacher ever said anything directly against Jewish people when I was around, except that we were oppressed, like the blood of Abraham.

When our parents talked about Jews, the topic was usually commerce. You might be able to go to Delancey Street and "Jew down" a shopkeeper, it was said, but you'd probably fail, because they're too smart with money. The Jew doesn't care about anybody but himself. The Jew keeps money and power inside the Jewish community. If you hire a Jewish accountant, he's going to recommend a Jewish lawyer. *Believe me.* Black people, our parents emphasized, need to learn how to stick together the way the Jews do.

This casual collection of attitudes hardened over time at school, where I encountered Jews every day. No matter how Jewish I felt, I could not completely ignore my difference. Lines between black people and Jews were partly hidden, but they were always there. I remember an outraged conversation about the Holocaust among some of the older children on the bus ride back to our side of town. One of the Jewish students had the nerve to argue that the Holocaust was far worse than slavery, and everyone agreed the kid was *arrogant.* From then on I used this word often—I began to record all events that proved it. There was the pity in the voices of otherwise lovely people when the subject of black America came up. There were the patronizing parents who wanted their daughter to date me because, "Why should it matter?" There was the outright racism of certain vicious classmates. In ninth grade, Scott W. told me in the library that I should be glad I'm not still in

Africa—if it weren't for Europe I would still be chucking spears. Another classmate said that while black people were gifted at sports and music, Jews had provided the world with intellectual genius. As proof, he ticked off three names: Freud, Einstein, Marx. I got very angry.

For a long time I wondered whether the Jews were really chosen by God, as one of my Jewish classmates suggested. The argument seemed watertight. Wherever Jews were given the chance they have shown themselves to be smarter than anyone else. *Look at how well we've done in America and everywhere else we've gone. Look at the Jews. Look.*

This was reinforced by Riverdale's unofficial story: There exists a WASP-Jewish-black hierarchy, and it is the real ordering structure of the world. It explained our school, the paltry numbers of blacks, the predominance of Jewish students, the continuing dominance of WASP administrators. Everything we saw seemed natural. The blacks were an undiscussed underclass, the Jews were the electorate, the WASPs democracy's vanishing counsel. Each group seemed chosen for its role by nature and God.

But things shifted drastically when I went to college. On entering Yale I studied my Jewish peers, and kept a firm eye on the school's pretensions to Oxford and Cambridge, the way students were asked to call some administrators "Master," as if slavery never happened. Yale was, to say the least, a problematic institution for black students, a cold place that required all sorts of submission, but it was also difficult for Jewish students, and to a degree I hadn't expected.

What I saw challenged any belief I had in Jewish chosenness. For the first time in my life I found myself in a school where Jews were simply one smart group of many. There were also smart people who were blacks and had grown up like me in the rarefied precincts of middle-class whiteness. Black students from cities with high concentrations of Jewish people were familiar with Jewish anxieties about "old" wealth and other WASP virtues, and we also considered anti-Semitism to be a very bad thing. It is fair, however, to say that most of us felt a decidedly grudging admiration for Jewish people. My ideas about Jewish supremacy remained a mix of anger and belief until I witnessed so many of my Jewish classmates folding in the face of Yale's anti-Semitism. I guess I had never had the secret stake my Jewish high-school classmates had in admiring WASPs; seeing Jewish peers genuflect removed any illusions of Jewish chosenness.

Dan and I roomed together during our junior and senior years at Yale. We became close friends even though we competed a lot over grades and once over a woman's affections. We love each other like brothers. Our kinship is not simple. There is the difference in class: Dan is from Wisconsin and his mother is a judge, his father a geneticist; I am from the Bronx and my parents are social workers. While Dan is a serious cyclist and hiker, I am the sort who watches movies and reads. Also, differences lurk within our similarities. In high school, I was one of a very small number of black people at a school of Jews; Dan was a Jew among many Christians. I'm not a nationalist, cultural or otherwise, and Dan is not religious.

But alienation has had radically different effects on our lives. While I find more to despise about America each day, Dan's outsider status hasn't affected his love of the country; he believes in this place. There are many divisions between us, and they are real. But so is our bond.

The summer after junior year Dan went to South Africa to monitor what the Government called trials. I remember him working on the application at my desk; I still have a print he gave me of black and white figures tearing down a great house of cards, "Rise and Destruction of Power." Dan took humanism to South Africa and brought me back a distant blackness, as he did when he gave me Miles Davis or Billie Holiday records to check out. There is a passage in John Edgar Wideman's *Brothers and Keepers* in which the author describes wanting to beat down a whiteboy for knowing more about the blues than he did. I understand his rage, but I hardly felt it. Mostly I loved learning about what I didn't know, sometimes covering up how much I was learning, sometimes questioning my friend's authority or authenticity, but always in the main feeling thankful. I believe it is the same mix of sensations Dan felt for me when I talked. I had, after all, grown up among a lot of Jewish people, and he hadn't; his parents had moved from New York to the Midwest. The references I brought from the city contained a curious and appealing atavism: I was a strange native informant reporting on his ancestral home, and he was a native alien of mine.

If Dan was "black" in any way, it was in precisely the same way that I was a "Jew." Our lives were shaped by cross-cultural consumption and the force of political sympathies, neither of which, in the end, necessarily makes you a real group member. Suburban Jewish guys who like black culture—it's a common enough phenomenon, I suppose, as were black kids in the old ghettos who grew up knowing a little Yiddish. Still, our ethnic "guest appearances" counted for something, since they did help make us who we were. Dan and I had chosen each other, after all, because we understood.

Last spring I went to visit Dan in Seattle, where he was clerking for a Federal judge. There was almost no news in that green and fragrant city about blacks and Jews and how we like to fight. It was only Dan and me and my thoughts and the smell of fruit blossoms wafting in through the open window.

I wondered how Dan came to be my brother. Brother. It means something else now. As with the word "immigrant," which in New York no longer means Jews or Italians so much as Dominicans and Haitians and Mexicans and Southeast Asians. Who is a "real" immigrant today, and who is an alien? Who deserves to become a member of the American tribe?

There is a line, a neoconservative "political correctness," on this question. Richard Cohen of *The Washington Post*, for example, had this to say about the boycotts of Asian grocers by blacks: "What a diversion all this picketing and boycotting is. And what a tragedy to boot. In New York, Washington and other cities, certain blacks talk about Asians as if they were involved in a conspiracy against them: Where do they get the money to buy these stores? Certain black leaders curse Asians or, just for good measure, Jews. They are constantly on the lookout for scapegoats. They have so thoroughly accepted the ethic of victimization that they blame others for a situation that they themselves can rectify: open some stores." I think the president of a Korean grocers' group was more to the point when he told a reporter, "We are no different than the Jews, Italians and other Europeans."

Family is made of the people family says are family. Folks like Cohen and the store owner are clearly trying to embrace each other, and leave Negroes outside. They say, *Look at those hard-working Jewish immigrants and sullen, menacing Negroes and remember: the story hasn't changed. Put Dominicans and Haitians and Mexicans here on the problem side, away, and let in the huddled Koreans and Eastern Europeans and (white) Cubans—the good ones. They are most like the "model" immigrants who came here early in the century. They deserve to be American. They should be family.*

It is as stupid a story as the Rev. Louis Farrakhan's foolishness about Jews, and certainly more dangerous. If family is made of the people family says are family, and if "family" and "immigrant" do not include people who are deemed problematic, collective responsibility for crime, segregated housing, the failure of public education—for all of which blacks are routinely blamed—just disappears. The paradigm is old and familiar.

Dan and I come from better traditions. Today, he is a death penalty defense lawyer. Once in a while, he and I get to talking about pooling our talents to elect him senator from Wisconsin or something. It would make sense: we want more people to get a better deal, especially the most despised, who are so often black. Somehow along the way, Dan and I grew up and examined the stories we'd been told. Thus far, our research has helped usher Dan, the progressive Jew, and me, the progressive black, into the same camp.

But I don't mean to mislead you about my thinking. Politics and the other crossings of our heritages are only part of what Dan and I share. Our brotherhood is made of ethnic sympathies, but it also has nothing to do with our being black or Jewish or any of that, and I love Dan not because he's Jewish or, in some sense, black, and not because I am black or, in some sense, Jewish. While our tribes, and their memories, and their stories, did make us, they also have nothing to do with it. The heart, after all, is raised on a mess of stories, and then it writes its own.

12

PIGSKIN, PATRIARCHY, AND PAIN

Don Sabo

I am sitting down to write as I've done thousands of times over the last decade. But today there's something very different. I'm not in pain.

A half-year ago I underwent back surgery. My physician removed two disks from the lumbar region of my spine and fused three vertebrae using bone scrapings from my right hip. The surgery is called a "spinal fusion." For seventy-two hours I was completely immobilized. On the fifth day, I took a few faltering first steps with one of those aluminum walkers that are usually associated with the elderly in nursing homes. I progressed rapidly and left the hospital after nine days completely free of pain for the first time in years.

How did I, a well-intending and reasonably gentle boy from western Pennsylvania, ever get into so much pain? At a simple level, I ended up in pain because I played a sport that brutalizes men's (and now sometimes women's) bodies. *Why* I played football and bit the bullet of pain, however, is more complicated. Like a young child who learns to dance or sing for a piece of candy, I played for rewards and payoffs. Winning at sport meant winning friends and carving a place for myself within the male pecking order. Success at the "game" would make me less like myself and more like the older boys and my hero, Dick Butkus. Pictures of his hulking and snarling form filled my head and hung over my bed, beckoning me forward like a mythic Siren. If I could be like Butkus, I told myself, people would adore me as much as I adored him. I might even adore myself. As an adolescent I hoped sport would get me attention from the girls. Later, I became more practical-minded and I worried more about my future. What kind of work would I do for a living? Football became my ticket to a college scholarship which, in western Pennsylvania during the early 'sixties, meant a career instead of getting stuck in the steelmills.

From *Sex, Violence and Power in Sports: Rethinking Masculinity*, Michael A. Messner and Donald F. Sabo, eds. (Freedom, CA: The Crossing Press). © 1994. Reprinted by permission of Don Sabo. Don Sabo, Ph.D., is professor of sociology at D'Youville College where he also directs the Center for Research on Physical Acitivity, Sport & Health.

The Road to Surgery

My bout with pain and spinal "pathology" began with a decision I made in 1955 when I was 8 years old. I "went out" for football. At the time, I felt uncomfortable inside my body—too fat, too short, too weak. Freckles and glasses, too! I wanted to change my image, and I felt that changing my body was one place to begin. My parents bought me a set of weights, and one of the older boys in the neighborhood was solicited to demonstrate their use. I can still remember the ease with which he lifted the barbell, the veins popping through his bulging biceps in the summer sun, and the sated look of strength and accomplishment on his face. This was to be the image of my future.

That Fall I made a dinner-table announcement that I was going out for football. What followed was a rather inauspicious beginning. First, the initiation rites. Pricking the flesh with thorns until blood was drawn and having hot peppers rubbed in my eyes. Getting punched in the gut again and again. Being forced to wear a jockstrap around my nose and not knowing what was funny. Then came what was to be an endless series of proving myself: calisthenics until my arms ached; hitting hard and fast and knocking the other guy down; getting hit in the groin and not crying. I learned that pain and injury are "part of the game."

I "played" through grade school, co-captained my high school team, and went on to become an inside linebacker and defensive captain at the NCAA Division I level. I learned to be an animal. Coaches took notice of animals. Animals made first team. Being an animal meant being fanatically aggressive and ruthlessly competitive. If I saw an arm in front of me, I trampled it. Whenever blood was spilled, I nodded approval. Broken bones (not mine of course) were secretly seen as little victories within the bigger struggle. The coaches taught me to "punish the other man," but little did I suspect that I was devastating my own body at the same time. There were broken noses, ribs, fingers, toes and teeth, torn muscles and ligaments, bruises, bad knees, and busted lips, and the gradual pulverizing of my spinal column that, by the time my jock career was long over at age 30, had resulted in seven years of near-constant pain. It was a long road to the surgeon's office.

Now surgically freed from its grip, my understanding of pain has changed. Pain had gnawed away at my insides. Pain turned my awareness inward. I blamed myself for my predicament; I thought that I was solely responsible for every twinge and sleepless night. But this view was an illusion. My pain, each individual's pain, is really an expression of a linkage to an outer world of people, events, and forces. The origins of our pain are rooted *outside*, not inside, our skins.

The Pain Principle

Sport is just one of the many areas in our culture where pain is more important than pleasure. Boys are taught that to endure pain is courageous, to survive pain is manly. The principle that pain is "good" and pleasure is "bad" is crudely evident in the "no pain, no gain" philosophy of so many coaches and athletes. The "pain principle" weaves its way into the lives and psyches of male athletes in two fundamental ways. It stifles men's awareness of their bodies and limits our emotional expression. We learn to ignore personal hurts and injuries because they interfere with the "efficiency" and "goals" of the "team." We become adept at taking the feelings that boil up inside us—feelings of insecurity and stress from striving so hard for success—and channeling them in a bundle of rage which is directed at opponents and enemies. This posture toward oneself and the world is not limited to "jocks." It is evident in the lives of many nonathletic men who, as tough guys, deny their authentic physical or emotional needs and develop health problems as a result.

Today, I no longer perceive myself as an *individual* ripped off by athletic injury. Rather, I see myself as just *one more man among many men* who got swallowed up by a social system predicated on male domination. Patriarchy has two structural aspects. First, it is an hierarchical system in which men dominate women in crude and debased, slick and subtle ways. Feminists have made great progress exposing and analyzing this dimension of the edifice of sexism. But it is also a system of *intermale dominance*, in which a minority of men dominates the masses of men. This intermale dominance hierarchy exploits the majority of those it beckons to climb its heights. Patriarchy's mythos of heroism and its morality of power-worship implant visions of ecstasy and masculine excellence in the minds of the boys who ultimately will defend its inequities and ridicule its victims. It is inside this institutional framework that I have begun to explore the essence and scope of "the pain principle."

Taking It

Patriarchy is a form of social hierarchy. Hierarchy breeds inequity and inequity breeds pain. To remain stable, the hierarchy must either justify the pain or explain it away. In a patriarchy, women and the masses of men are fed the cultural message that pain is inevitable and that pain enhances one's character and moral worth. This principle is expressed in Judeo-Christian beliefs. The Judeo-Christian god inflicts or permits pain, yet "the Father" is still revered and loved. Likewise, a chief disciplinarian in the patriarchal family, the father has the right to inflict pain. The "pain principle" also echoes throughout traditional western sexual morality; it is better to experience the pain of *not* having sexual pleasure than it is to have sexual pleasure.

Most men learn to heed these cultural messages and take their "cues for survival" from the patriarchy. The Willie Lomans of the economy pander to the prophets of profit and the American Dream. Soldiers, young and old, salute their neo-Hun generals. Right-wing Christians genuflect before the idols of righteousness, affluence, and conformity. And male athletes adopt the visions and values that coaches are offering: to take orders, to take pain, to "take out" opponents, to take the game seriously, to take women, and to take their place on the team. And if they can't "take it," then the rewards of athletic camaraderie, prestige, scholarship, pro contracts, and community recognition are not forthcoming.

Becoming a football player fosters conformity to male-chauvinistic values and self-abusing lifestyles. It contributes to the legitimacy of a social structure based on patriarchal power. Male competition for prestige and status in sport and elsewhere leads to identification with the relatively few males who control resources and are able to bestow rewards and inflict punishment. Male supremacists are not born, they are made, and traditional athletic socialization is a fundamental contribution to this complex social-psychological and political process. Through sport, many males, indeed, learn to "take it"—that is, to internalize patriarchal values which, in turn, become part of their gender identity and conception of women and society.

My high school coach once evoked the pain principle during a pregame pep talk. For what seemed an eternity, he paced frenetically and silently before us with fists clenched and head bowed. He suddenly stopped and faced us with a smile. It was as though he had approached a podium to begin a long-awaited lecture. "Boys," he began, "people who say that football is a 'contact sport' are dead wrong. Dancing is a contact sport. Football is a game of pain and violence! Now get the hell out of here and kick some ass." We practically ran through the wall of the locker room, surging in unison to fight the coach's war. I see now that the coach was right but for all the wrong reasons. I should have taken him at his word and never played the game!

13

THE SLAVE SIDE OF SUNDAY

Dave Zirin

For most sports fans, heaven would be to play in the National Football League. We see money, fame and no expectations of social responsibility beyond showing up on Sunday ready to play. In the mind of the fantasy sports fan, it means a big house, a garage full of cars and the promise of sexual gratification. The last thing any fan would believe—or want to believe—is that racism is endemic to the culture of the NFL.

Reprinted with permission from the January 20, 2006, issue of *The Nation*. For subscription information, call 1-800-333-8536. Portions of each week's *Nation* magazine can be accessed at http://www.thenation.com.

That's the contention of NFL veteran Anthony Prior, whose new book, *The Slave Side of Sunday*, invokes an explosive metaphor to describe life in the NFL. Prior played six NFL seasons with the New York Jets, the Oakland Raiders and the Minnesota Vikings, and developed a reputation as a cornerback with blinding speed, if not blinding stats.

Prior contends that the NFL is rife with a racism that is both deeply institutionalized and largely unchallenged. "I was frustrated by not seeing the truth in print," Prior told me in a recent interview. "And I believe that if you want to see it, you should write it."

Prior is a self-published author. In addition to *The Slave Side of Sunday*, his publishing house, Stone Hold Books, produced *Faith on 40 Yards: Behind the Silver & Gold of the NFL* in 2003. The starting point for his new book is the much-derided 2003 statement by Tampa Bay all-pro defensive tackle Warren Sapp that the NFL acts as a "slavemaster" to its players. Sapp was pilloried for his comments, but Prior argues that there is a lot more truth to Sapp's statement than meets the eye.

Prior knows that, like Sapp, he will receive criticism for his statements. And on the face of it, his argument does seem ridiculous, if not offensive: How can people who make mega-salaries and play before adoring crowds be likened to slaves? Prior's response is that the answer lies in the lack of control NFL players are allowed to have in their daily lives and in the mega-industry they have helped create. He sees this lack of control being intimately tied with a dynamic where 65 percent of the players are African-American, yet only 18 percent of coaches, 6 percent of general managers and no owners are anything other than white.

"Black players have created a billion-dollar market but have no voice in the industry, no power. That sounds an awful lot like slavery to me," he says. "On plantations slaves were respected for their physical skills but were given no respect as thinking beings. On the football field, we are treated as what appears like gods, but in fact this is just the 'show and tell' of the management for their spectators. In reality, what is transpiring is that black athletes are being treated with disrespect and degradation. As soon we take off that uniform, behind the dressing room doors, we are less than human. We are bought and sold. Traded and drafted, like our ancestors, and the public views this as a sport, ironically the same attitude as people had in the slavery era."

Prior names no names, but he contends that coaches and other authority figures in the game use racism to bully African-American players in an effort to instill obedience. "I've heard coaches call players 'boy,' 'porch monkeys,' 'sambos,'" he says. "Players don't get tested on their athleticism as much as they get tested on their manhood. Many players rail against this. They say, 'I'm being treated like a goddamn slave.' However, as soon as the coach is present, their life becomes doing whatever possible to please this man.

"The intimidation is immense. . . . I've seen players benched because a coach saw them with a white woman, or overheard a criticism of his incompetence, or because a player didn't go to Bible study. I've been in film sessions where coaches would try to get a rise out of players by calling them 'boy' or 'Jemima,' and players are so conditioned to not jeopardize their place, they just take it. It's my under-standing that management by intimidation is illegal, so why do we allow this to occur? I believe that due to the nature of the race of players who are being intim-idated, people tend to overlook this. That is why I wrote this book. People must understand that this is not just intimidation, this is pure racism."

Prior says Southern-born athletes are particularly vulnerable. "Southern Black players call the coach 'boss' or even 'master.' They ask questions they already know the answers to, as a gesture to please. They let themselves be abused in all man-ner to keep their jobs. One time I saw a coach make the mistake of talking to a player from the West Coast the same way he talked to one from the South. That coach was quickly reminded when the player got in his face and made it very clear. 'I am a man and you will respect me as a man.' Words to live by."

Another institution that raises Prior's ire is Athletes in Action, an evangelical Christian group that is a presence in high school, college athletics and even the professional sports. Before the big game on Super Bowl Sunday, Athletes in Action is sponsoring an NFL-sanctioned prayer breakfast in Detroit.

I call [them] Hypocrites in Action. Almost every time, the minister is white, and the subject matter is right off the plantation," Prior says. "One time I went over to the Bible study and asked, 'What's the subject matter?' I was told, 'Living in Obedience.' I just said, 'No thank you, I don't want to be brainwashed today.' On some teams, prayer becomes obligation, and God and Jesus become little more than a lucky rabbit's foot. Unfortunately, religion is used as a crutch to prey upon players who intend to be true to their faith but end up being slaves to it. This is a wrongfully instilled practice. I wouldn't have issue with this if the tools given were truly in good nature for the progression of mankind, not the regression of players."

Neither the NFL nor Athletes in Action returned calls for comment on Prior's allegations.

Prior says he has written the book as a way to advance the idea that African-American players can organize themselves to fight racism beyond the playing field. "As individuals we must create a collective. NFL's black players have a tremendous strength. This is a power we are scared to exercise yet dream to live." He believes that a workplace action on the eve of the Super Bowl could bring real change. Cer-tainly, the thought of football players holding the multibillion-dollar spectacle hostage and making demands on the NFL ownership to give more back to the im-poverished communities that produce their all-pros is a daring notion. The ques-tion is whether Prior and those who agree with him would risk the fruits of Super Bowl glory for the greater good of those who will never see an NFL contract.

14

HOW TO SELL HUMVEES TO MEN

Mary Beckman

Women have used the tactic for years: Call a guy a sissy, and he'll try and fix the sputtering carburetor. Now, a new study demonstrates just how sensitive men can be to attacks on their manhood. The result might shed light on how males are adjusting to changing roles in society.

Freud argued that people respond to attacks on their identity by exaggerating the threatened trait. Scientists have noted since the 1950s that men who were insecure about their masculinity were more likely to be racist and authoritarian, though few sociologists have tested this by manipulating men's insecurities experimentally.

To investigate the effects of psychological emasculation, sociologist Robb Willer at Cornell University in Ithaca, New York, and colleagues gave 111 Cornell undergraduates a gender identity survey, and regardless of the answers, told half that they appeared extremely feminine and half that they seemed terribly masculine. The researchers then surveyed students' attitudes towards politics, homosexuality, and car purchasers. Males who were told they were effeminate were more likely to support the Iraq war, Bush's handling of the war, and a ban on gay marriage. Threatened men also expressed greater interest in buying an SUV, and they were willing to pay up to $7,000 more for the vehicle than their nonthreatened peers. Female students, on the other hand, had similar responses regardless of where they were told they fell on the gender continuum, Willer will report at the American Sociological Association's annual meeting in Philadelphia on 15 August.

Sociologist Michael Kimmel of Stony Brook University in New York advises against generalizing the results of the study to all American males. "There's no way that 20-year-old college guys are secure in their masculinity," he says. Older men wouldn't show the same effect, he predicts. But social historian Rocco Capraro of Hobart and William Smith Colleges, Geneva, New York, says that if the work holds up in additional studies, the results suggest men aren't gracefully accepting their changing role in society. As women move into traditionally male domains, men are taking up more female roles and are being put on the defensive. But instead of fighting back with hypermasculinity, men should accept the changing times, Capraro says. And leave the engine to their female mechanic.

Reprinted with permission from *Science* 8/4/05. Copyright 2005 AAAS.

15

HE DEFIES YOU STILL
The Memoirs of a Sissy

Tommi Avicolli

You're just a faggot
No history faces you this morning
A faggot's dreams are scarlet
Bad blood bled from words that scarred[1]

Scene One

A homeroom in a Catholic high school in South Philadelphia. The boy sits quietly in the first aisle, third desk, reading a book. He does not look up, not even for a moment. He is hoping no one will remember he is sitting there. He wishes he were invisible. The teacher is not yet in the classroom so the other boys are talking and laughing loudly.

Suddenly, a voice from beside him:

"Hey, you're a faggot, ain't you?"

The boy does not answer. He goes on reading his book, or rather pretending he is reading his book. It is impossible to actually read the book now.

"Hey, I'm talking to you!"

The boy still does not look up. He is so scared his heart is thumping madly; it feels like it is leaping out of his chest and into his throat. But he can't look up.

"Faggot, I'm talking to you!"

To look up is to meet the eyes of the tormentor.

Suddenly, a sharpened pencil point is thrust into the boy's arm. He jolts, shaking off the pencil, aware that there is blood seeping from the wound.

"What did you do that for?" he asks timidly.

"Cause I hate faggots," the other boy says, laughing. Some other boys begin to laugh, too. A symphony of laughter. The boy feels as if he's going to cry. But he must not cry. Must not cry. So he holds back the tears and tries to read the book again. He must read the book. Read the book.

When the teacher arrives a few minutes later, the class quiets down. The boy does not tell the teacher what has happened. He spits on the wound to clean it, dabbing it with a tissue until the bleeding stops. For weeks he fears some dreadful infection from the lead in the pencil point.

Scene Two

The boy is walking home from school. A group of boys (two, maybe three, he is not certain) grab him from behind, drag him into an alley and beat him up. When he gets home, he races up to his room, refusing dinner ("I don't feel well," he tells his mother through the locked door) and spends the night alone in the dark wishing he would die. . . .

These are not fictitious accounts—I *was* that boy. Having been branded a sissy by neighborhood children because I preferred jump rope to baseball and dolls to playing soldiers, I was often taunted with "hey sissy" or "hey faggot" or "yoo hoo honey" (in a mocking voice) when I left the house.

To avoid harassment, I spent many summers alone in my room. I went out on rainy days when the street was empty.

I came to like being alone. I didn't need anyone, I told myself over and over again. I was an island. Contact with others meant pain. Alone, I was protected. I began writing poems, then short stories. There was no reason to go outside anymore. I had a world of my own.

In the schoolyard today
they'll single you out
Their laughter will leave your ears ringing
like the church bells
which once awed you.[2] . . .

School was one of the more painful experiences of my youth. The neighborhood bullies could be avoided. The taunts of the children living in those endless repetitive row houses could be evaded by staying in my room. But school was something I had to face day after day for some two hundred mornings a year.

I had few friends in school. I was a pariah. Some kids would talk to me, but few wanted to be known as my close friend. Afraid of labels. If I was a sissy, then he had to be a sissy, too. I was condemned to loneliness.

Fortunately, a new boy moved into our neighborhood and befriended me; he wasn't afraid of the labels. He protected me when the other guys threatened to beat me up. He walked me home from school; he broke through the terrible loneliness. We were in third or fourth grade at the time.

We spent a summer or two together. Then his parents sent him to camp and I was once again confined to my room.

Scene Three

High school lunchroom. The boy sits at a table near the back of the room. Without warning, his lunch bag is grabbed and tossed to another table. Someone opens it and confiscates a package of Tastykakes; another boy takes the sandwich. The empty bag is tossed back to the boy who stares at it, dumbfounded. He should be used to this; it has happened before.

Someone screams, "faggot," laughing. There is always laughter. It does not annoy him anymore.

There is no teacher nearby. There is never a teacher around. And what would he say if there were? Could he report the crime? He would be jumped after school if he did. Besides, it would be his word against theirs. Teachers never noticed anything. They never heard the taunts. Never heard the word, "faggot." They were the great deaf mutes, pillars of indifference; a sissy's pain was not relevant to history and geography and god made me to love honor and obey him, amen.

Scene Four

High school Religion class. Someone has a copy of *Playboy*. Father N. is not in the room yet; he's late, as usual. Someone taps the boy roughly on the shoulder. He turns. A finger points to the centerfold model, pink fleshy body, thin and sleek. Almost painted. Not real. The other asks, mocking voice, "Hey, does she turn you on? Look at those tits!"

The boy smiles, nodding meekly; turns away.

The other jabs him harder on the shoulder, "Hey, whatsamatter, don't you like girls?"

Laughter. Thousands of mouths; unbearable din of laughter. In the Arena: thumbs down. Don't spare the queer.

"Wanna suck my dick? Huh? That turn you on, faggot!"

The laughter seems to go on forever. . . .

Behind you, the sound of their laughter
echoes a million times
in a soundless place
They watch how you walk/sit/stand/breathe.[3] . . .

What did being a sissy really mean? It was a way of walking (from the hips rather than the shoulders); it was a way of talking (often with a lisp or in a high-pitched voice); it was a way of relating to others (gently, not wanting to fight, or hurt anyone's feelings). It was being intelligent ("an egghead" they called it sometimes); getting good grades. It meant not being interested in sports, not playing football in the street after school; not discussing teams and scores and playoffs. And it involved not showing fervent interest in girls, not talking about scoring with tits or *Playboy* centerfolds. Not concealing naked women in your history book; or porno books in your locker.

On the other hand, anyone could be a "faggot." It was a catch-all. If you did something that didn't conform to what was the acceptable behavior of the group, then you risked being called a faggot. If you didn't get along with the "in" crowd, you were a faggot. It was the most commonly used put-down. It kept guys in line. They became angry when somebody called them a faggot. More fights started over someone calling someone else a faggot than anything else. The word had power. It toppled the male ego, shattered his delicate facade, violated the image he projected. He was tough. Without feeling. Faggot cut through all this. It made him vulnerable. Feminine. And feminine was the worst thing he could possibly be. Girls were fine for fucking, but no boy in his right mind wanted to be like them. A boy was the opposite of girl. He was not feminine. He was not feeling. He was not weak.

Just look at the gym teacher who growled like a dog; or the priest with the black belt who threw kids against the wall in rage when they didn't know their Latin. They were men, they got respect.

But not the physics teacher who preached pacifism during lectures on the nature of atoms. Everybody knew what he was—and why he believed in the anti-war movement.

My parents only knew that the neighborhood kids called me names. They begged me to act more like the other boys. My brothers were ashamed of me. They never said it, but I knew. Just as I knew that my parents were embarrassed by my behavior.

At times, they tried to get me to act differently. Once my father lectured me on how to walk right. I'm still not clear on what that means. Not from the hips, I guess, don't "swish" like faggots do.

A nun in elementary school told my mother at Open House that there was "something wrong with me." I had draped my sweater over my shoulders like a girl, she said. I was a smart kid, but I should know better than to wear my sweater like a girl!

My mother stood there, mute. I wanted her to say something, to chastise the nun; to defend me. But how could she? This was a nun talking—representative of Jesus, protector of all that was good and decent.

An uncle once told me I should start "acting like a boy" instead of like a girl. Everybody seemed ashamed of me. And I guess I was ashamed of myself, too. It was hard not to be.

Scene Five

Priest: Do you like girls, Mark?
Mark: Uh-huh.

Priest: I mean *really* like them?
Mark: Yeah—they're okay.
Priest: There's a role they play in your salvation. Do you understand it, Mark?
Mark: Yeah.
Priest: You've got to like girls. Even if you should decide to enter the seminary, it's important to keep in mind God's plan for a man and a woman.[4] . . .

Catholicism of course condemned homosexuality. Effeminacy was tolerated as long as the effeminate person did not admit to being gay. Thus, priests could be effeminate because they weren't gay.

As a sissy, I could count on no support from the church. A male's sole purpose in life was to father children—souls for the church to save. The only hope a homosexual had of attaining salvation was by remaining totally celibate. Don't even think of touching another boy. To think of a sin was a sin. And to sin was to put a mark upon the soul. Sin—if it was a serious offense against god—led to hell. There was no way around it. If you sinned, you were doomed.

Realizing I was gay was not an easy task. Although I knew I was attracted to boys by the time I was about eleven, I didn't connect this attraction to homosexuality. I was not queer. Not I. I was merely appreciating a boy's good looks, his fine features, his proportions. It didn't seem to matter that I didn't appreciate a girl's looks in the same way. There was no twitching in my thighs when I gazed upon a beautiful girl. But I wasn't queer.

I resisted that label—queer—for the longest time. Even when everything pointed to it, I refused to see it. I was certainly not queer. Not I.

We sat through endless English classes, and History courses about the wars between men who were not allowed to love each other. No gay history was ever taught. No history faces you this morning. You're just a faggot. Homosexuals had never contributed to the human race. God destroyed the queers in Sodom and Gomorrah.

We learned about Michelangelo, Oscar Wilde, Gertrude Stein—but never that they were queer. They were not queer. Walt Whitman, the "father of American poetry," was not queer. No one was queer. I was alone, totally unique. One of a kind. Were there others like me somewhere? Another planet, perhaps?

In school, they never talked of the queers. They did not exist. The only hint we got of this other species was in religion class. And even then it was clouded in mystery—never spelled out. It was sin. Like masturbation. Like looking at *Playboy* and getting a hard-on. A sin.

Once a progressive priest in senior year religion class actually mentioned homosexuals—he said the word—but was into Erich Fromm, into homosexuals as pathetic and sick. Fixated at some early stage; penis, anal, whatever. Only heterosexuals passed on to the nirvana of sexual development.

No other images from the halls of the Catholic high school except those the other boys knew: swishy faggot sucking cock in an alley somewhere, grabbing asses in the bathroom. Never mentioning how much straight boys craved blowjobs, it was part of the secret.

It was all a secret. You were not supposed to talk about the queers. Whisper maybe. Laugh about them, yes. But don't be open, honest; don't try to understand. Don't cite their accomplishments. No history faces you this morning. You're just a faggot   faggot   no history   just a faggot

Epilogue

The boy marching down the Parkway. Hundreds of queers. Signs proclaiming gay pride. Speakers. Tables with literature from gay groups. A miracle, he is thinking. Tears are coming loose now. Someone hugs him.

> *You could not control*
> *the sissy in me*
> *nor could you exorcise him*
> *nor electrocute him*
> *You declared him illegal illegitimate*
> *insane and immature*
> *But he defies you still.*[5]

NOTES

1. From the poem "Faggot" by Tommi Avicolli, published in *GPU News*, September 1979.

2. *Ibid.*

3. *Ibid.*

4. From the play *Judgment of the Roaches* by Tommi Avicolli, produced in Philadelphia at the Gay Community Center, the Painted Bride Arts Center and the University of Pennsylvania; aired over WXPN-FM, in four parts; and presented at the Lesbian/Gay Conference in Norfolk, VA, July 1980.

5. From the poem "Sissy Poem," published in *Magic Doesn't Live Here Anymore* (Philadelphia: Spruce Street Press, 1976).

16

WITH NO IMMEDIATE CAUSE

Ntozake Shange

every 3 minutes a woman is beaten
every five minutes a
woman is raped/every ten minutes
a lil girl is molested
yet i rode the subway today
i sat next to an old man who
may have beaten his old wife
3 minutes ago or 3 days/30 years ago
he might have sodomized his
daughter but i sat there
cuz the young men on the train
might beat some young women
later in the day or tomorrow
i might not shut my door fast
enuf/push hard enuf
every 3 minutes it happens
some woman's innocence
rushes to her cheeks/pours from her mouth
like the betsy wetsy dolls have been torn
apart/their mouths
menses red & split/every
three minutes a shoulder
is jammed through plaster and the oven door/
chairs push thru the rib cage/hot water or
boiling sperm decorate her body
i rode the subway today
& bought a paper from a
man who might
have held his old lady onto
a hot pressing iron/i dont know
maybe he catches lil girls in the
park & rips open their behinds

with steel rods/i can't decide
what he might have done i only
know every 3 minutes
every 5 minutes every 10 minutes/so
i bought the paper
looking for the announcement
the discovery/of the dismembered
woman's body/the
victims have not all been
identified/today they are
naked and dead/refuse to
testify/one girl out of 10's not
coherent/i took the coffee
& spit it up/i found an
announcement/not the woman's
bloated body in the river/floating
not the child bleeding in the
59th street corridor/not the baby
broken on the floor/

>   *"there is some concern*
>   *that alleged battered women*
>   *might start to murder their*
>   *husbands & lovers with no*
>   *immediate cause"*

i spit up i vomit i am screaming
we all have immediate cause
every 3 minutes
every 5 minutes
every 10 minutes
every day
women's bodies are found
in alleys & bedrooms/at the top of the stairs
before i ride the subway/buy a paper/drink
coffee/i must know/
have you hurt a woman today
did you beat a woman today
throw a child across a room
>   *are the lil girl's panties*
>   *in yr pocket*
did you hurt a woman today

i have to ask these obscene questions
the authorities require me to
establish
immediate cause

17

REQUIEM FOR THE CHAMP

June Jordan

Mike Tyson comes from Brooklyn. And so do I. Where he grew up was about a twenty-minute bus ride from my house. I always thought his neighborhood looked like a war zone. It reminded me of Berlin—immediately after World War II. I had never seen Berlin except for black-and-white photos in *Life* magazine, but that was bad enough: Rubble. Barren. Blasted. Everywhere you turned your eyes recoiled from the jagged edges of an office building or a cathedral, shattered, or the tops of apartment houses torn off, and nothing alive even intimated, anywhere. I used to think, "This is what it means to fight and really win or really lose. War means you hurt somebody, or something, until there's nothing soft or sensible left."

For sure I never had a boyfriend who came out of Mike Tyson's territory. Yes, I enjoyed my share of tough guys and/or gang members who walked and talked and fought and loved in quintessential Brooklyn ways: cool, tough, and deadly serious. But there was a code as rigid and as romantic as anything that ever made the pages of traditional English literature. A guy would beat up another guy or, if appropriate, he'd kill him. But a guy talked different to a girl. A guy made other guys clean up their language around "his girl." A guy brought ribbons and candies and earrings and tulips to a girl. He took care of her. He walked her home. And if he got serious about that girl, and even if she was only twelve years old, then she became his "lady." And woe betide any other guy stupid enough to disrespect that particular young Black female.

But none of the boys—none of the young men—none of the young Black male inhabitants of my universe and my heart ever came from Mike Tyson's streets or avenues. We didn't live someplace fancy or middle-class, but at least there were ten-cent gardens, front and back, and coin Laundromats, and grocery stores, and soda parlors, and barber shops, and Holy Roller churchfronts, and chicken shacks, and dry cleaners, and bars-and-grills, and a takeout Chinese restaurant, and all of that usable detail that does not survive a war. That kind of seasonal green turf and daily-life supporting pattern of establishments to meet your needs did not exist inside the gelid urban cemetery where Mike Tyson learned what he thought he needed to know.

I remember when the City of New York decided to construct a senior housing project there, in the childhood world of former heavyweight boxing champion Mike Tyson. I remember wondering, "Where in the hell will those old people have to go in order to find food? And how will they get there?"

I'm talking godforsaken. And much of living in Brooklyn was like that. But then it might rain or it might snow and, for example, I could look at the rain forcing forsythia into bloom or watch how snowflakes can tease bare tree limbs into temporary blossoms of snow dissolving into diadems of sunlight. And what did Mike Tyson ever see besides brick walls and garbage in the gutter and disintegrating concrete steps and boarded-up windows and broken car parts blocking the sidewalk and men, bitter, with their hands in their pockets, and women, bitter, with their heads down and their eyes almost closed?

In his neighborhood, where could you buy ribbons for a girl, or tulips?

Mike Tyson comes from Brooklyn. And so do I. In the big picture of America, I never had much going for me. And he had less. I only learned, last year, that I can stop whatever violence starts with me. I only learned, last year, that love is infinitely more interesting, and more exciting, and more powerful, than really winning or really losing a fight. I only learned, last year, that all war leads to death and that all love leads you away from death. I am more than twice Mike Tyson's age. And I'm not stupid. Or slow. But I'm Black. And I come from Brooklyn. And I grew up fighting. And I grew up and I got out of Brooklyn because I got pretty good at fighting. And winning. Or else, intimidating my would-be adversaries with my fists, my feet, and my mouth. And I never wanted to fight. I never wanted anybody to hit me. And I never wanted to hit anybody. But the bell would ring at the end of another dumb day in school and I'd head out with dread and a nervous sweat because I knew some jackass more or less my age and more or less my height would be waiting for me because she or he had nothing better to do than to wait for me and hope to kick my butt or tear up my books or break my pencils or pull hair out of my head.

This is the meaning of poverty: when you have nothing better to do than to hate somebody who, just exactly like yourself, has nothing better to do than to pick on you instead of trying to figure out how come there's nothing better to do. How come there's no gym/no swimming pool/no dirt track/no soccer field/no ice-skating rink/ no bike/no bike path/no tennis courts/no language arts workshop/no computer science center/no band practice/no choir rehearsal/no music lessons/no basketball or baseball team? How come neither one of you has his or her own room in a house where you can hang out and dance and make out or get on the telephone or eat and drink up everything in the kitchen that can move? How come nobody on your block and nobody in your class has any of these things?

I'm Black. Mike Tyson is Black. And neither one of us was ever supposed to win anything more than a fight between the two of us. And if you check out the mass-media material on "us," and if you check out the emergency-room reports on "us," you might well believe we're losing the fight to be more than our enemies have decreed. Our enemies would deprive us of everything except each other:

hungry and furious and drug-addicted and rejected and ever convinced we can never be beautiful or right or true or different from the beggarly monsters our enemies envision and insist upon, and how should we then stand, Black man and Black woman, face to face?

Way back when I was born, Richard Wright had just published *Native Son* and, thereby, introduced white America to the monstrous produce of its racist hatred.

Poverty does not beautify. Poverty does not teach generosity or allow for sucker attributes of tenderness and restraint. In white America, hatred of Blackfolks has imposed horrible poverty upon us.

And so, back in the thirties, Richard Wright's Native Son, Bigger Thomas, did what he thought he had to do: he hideously murdered a white woman and he viciously murdered his Black girlfriend in what he conceived as self-defense. He did not perceive any options to these psychopathic, horrifying deeds. I do not believe he, Bigger Thomas, had any other choices open to him. Not to him, he who was meant to die like the rat he, Bigger Thomas, cornered and smashed to death in his mother's beggarly clean space.

I never thought Bigger Thomas was okay. I never thought he should skate back into my, or anyone's, community. But I did and I do think he is my brother. The choices available to us dehumanize. And any single one of us, Black in this white country, we may be defeated, we may become dehumanized, by the monstrous hatred arrayed against us and our needy dreams.

And so I write this requiem for Mike Tyson: international celebrity, millionaire, former heavyweight boxing champion of the world, a big-time winner, a big-time loser, an African-American male in his twenties, and, now, a convicted rapist.

Do I believe he is guilty of rape?

Yes I do.

And what would I propose as appropriate punishment?

Whatever will force him to fear the justice of exact retribution, and whatever will force him, for the rest of his damned life, to regret and to detest the fact that he defiled, he subjugated, and he wounded somebody helpless to his power.

And do I therefore rejoice in the jury's finding?

I do not.

Well, would I like to see Mike Tyson a free man again?

He was never free!

And I do not excuse or condone or forget or minimize or forgive the crime of his violation of the young Black woman he raped!

But did anybody ever tell Mike Tyson that you talk different to a girl? Where would he learn that? Would he learn that from U.S. Senator Ted Kennedy? Or from hotshot/scot-free movie director Roman Polanski? Or from rap recording star Ice Cube? Or from Ronald Reagan and the Grenada escapade? Or from George Bush in Panama? Or from George Bush and Colin Powell in the Persian Gulf? Or from the military hero flyboys who returned from bombing the shit out of civilian cities in Iraq and then said, laughing and proud, on international TV: "All I need, now, is a woman"? Or from the hundreds of thousands of American football fans? Or from the millions of Americans who would, if they could, pay surrealistic amounts of money just to witness, up close, somebody like Mike Tyson beat the brains out of somebody?

And what could which university teach Mike Tyson about the difference between violence and love? Is there any citadel of higher education in the country that does not pay its football coach at least three times as much as the chancellor and six times as much as its professors and ten times as much as its social and psychological counselors?

In this America where Mike Tyson and I live together and bitterly, bitterly, apart, I say he became what he felt. He felt the stigma of a priori hatred and intentional poverty. He was given the choice of violence or violence: the violence of defeat or the violence of victory. Who would pay him to rehabilitate innercity housing or to refurbish a bridge? Who would pay him what to study the facts of our collective history? Who would pay him what to plant and nurture the trees of a forest? And who will write and who will play the songs that tell a guy like Mike Tyson how to talk to a girl?

What was America willing to love about Mike Tyson? Or any Black man? Or any man's man?

Tyson's neighborhood and my own have become the same no-win battleground. And he has fallen there. And I do not rejoice. I do not.

18

HER COLLEGE EXPERIENCE IS NOT HIS

Linda Sax

At a time when national attention is focused on the relative numbers of women and men on college campuses, little is known about the characteristics of the two genders and how aspects of college further shape those characteristics. The popular messages are oversimplified: Gender equity has been achieved, women are an academic success story, and men are experiencing an educational crisis.

Each of those messages has some truth, but they tend to convey the status of women and men as a zero-sum game: If one gender is succeeding, the other must

Reprinted by permission of the author, Linda J. Sax, Associate Professor, UCLA.

be failing. The reality is that both genders face obstacles and challenges in their pursuit of higher education, and we need a deeper understanding of the nuances and implications of the gender gap in college.

As a scholar in gender issues, I have studied survey responses of more than eight million students who participated over the past four decades in the freshman survey of the Cooperative Institutional Research Program at the University of California at Los Angeles. I have also examined longitudinal information obtained by the College Student Survey of students who entered college in 1994 and were followed up in 1998. Such data have enabled me to assess how gender shapes the characteristics of women and men entering college, how both genders experience college, and how college influences them. And I have found that women and men differ significantly from each other—and in ways that raise many questions for further research:

Connection to family. It has largely been assumed that leaving home is equally important for both genders, but we have found that it may be especially beneficial for female students, who develop greater scholarly confidence, stronger leadership skills, and a healthy sense of emotional well-being. For men, whether they live close to home or thousands of miles away is less relevant.

Today, however, students and parents stay in frequent contact with each other. The challenge facing colleges is how to encourage women to develop a healthy sense of independence at the same time that they stay connected to their parents.

Questions for future research: Do women turn to their families because of academic or social difficulties? Does their dependence on their families inhibit their personal and academic development? How do the type and frequency of student–parent communications relate to students' personal, academic, and social development?

Student–faculty interactions. Gender differences fall into three main categories. First, while interactions with faculty members encourage liberalism, political engagement, and a commitment to social activism among all students, we generally find that the more time men spend engaged in one-on-one interactions with faculty members, the more liberal they become in their political views and the greater concern they develop about race relations and the welfare of the larger society.

Second, men who work with faculty members on research or receive advice, encouragement, and support from them hold more egalitarian views on gender roles. They become less supportive of the notion that "the activities of married women are best confined to the home and family." For women, the opposite is true: Those who spend more time with faculty members, especially in the context of research, become *more* committed to traditional gender roles.

A third theme relates to professors' influence on women's sense of confidence and well-being. Feeling dismissed by faculty members in the classroom has negative consequences for women's long-term academic aspirations, confidence in math, and even physical health.

Faculty members would benefit from a better understanding of the implications of their actions for students. They need to recognize that even when they believe they are treating male and female students the same way, the two genders may internalize those interactions differently.

Questions for future research: Does the nature of student–faculty interactions depend on where those interactions take place—in the classroom, a faculty office, a research lab, or elsewhere? Why and how do research experiences influence students' gender-role attitudes? What sorts of messages do professors send—intentionally or not—regarding women's social roles? What specific faculty actions lead women to feel they are not being taken seriously? What are effective strategies for promoting healthier student–faculty relations and for promoting safe spaces in the classroom? How does all this depend on the faculty member's gender?

Presence of female faculty members. It is often stated that female students benefit from greater numbers of women on college faculties—and, in fact, attending institutions with more female professors strengthens female students' scholarly confidence, motivation to achieve, and grade-point average. Yet the presence of female professors appears to bring a broader range of benefits to male students, including gains in mathematical confidence, scientific orientation, leadership ability, and emotional well-being. An obvious implication of those findings would be for colleges to hire more female faculty members. That could be an opportunity to shape the academic climate, as female faculty members have been shown to be generally more concerned than male faculty members with students' emotional development, character development, and self-understanding.

Questions for future research: Could the trend of males' benefiting more from the presence of female faculty members result from such professors treating their male students more favorably than their female students? Or, taking another perspective, might the developmental benefits accrued to men result from having less exposure to male faculty members? Are these findings due to a larger climate shift that occurs when an institution employs more female faculty members? In other words, how does the representation of female faculty members shape the culture of departments and institutions, and what impact does that have on male and female students?

Academic engagement. In high school, women devote more time than men do to studying, homework, and a range of academic and extracurricular activities. Women also place greater value than men do on the intellectual benefits of going to college, such as the opportunity to learn more about what interests them and to prepare themselves for graduate school. Women's superior record of academic achievement and intellectual engagement creates a gender gap that holds steady over the course of college.

But although men are less academically engaged than women, the influence of academic engagement is stronger for them. The time that men spend preparing for class has a greater impact on their grades, academic confidence, critical thinking skills, and motivation to achieve. And the more time that men devote to their studies, the more interested they become in the larger political and cultural contexts that surround them, while the same is not true for women. Certainly, studying matters for women as well, but it seems to make more of a difference for men.

Clearly, colleges need to consider strategies for encouraging greater academic engagement among male students. As Jillian Kinzie, the associate director of the Center for Postsecondary Research and National Survey of Student Engagement Institute, and her colleagues suggested in a 2007 research paper on gender and student engagement, colleges should involve men more in "learning communities, first-year seminars, writing-intensive courses, student–faculty research, study abroad, internships, and capstone seminars."

Questions for future research: How much do colleges consider the different academic needs of male and female learners? Should strategies for promoting student engagement be the same for both?

The impact of diversity programs. My research found that experiences with diversity both inside and outside the classroom are more liberalizing, motivating, and eye-opening for men than women. For example, attending racial or cultural awareness workshops or engaging in social diversity—dating, dining, studying, or living with someone of a different race or ethnicity—contributes more strongly to men's desire to improve race relations. In addition, taking ethnic studies courses and participating in racial awareness and cultural awareness workshops give rise to more-progressive gender-role attitudes among male students.

Yet, at the same time, such activities are also often accompanied by heightened feelings of discomfort in male students. Campuses should provide appropriate resources for such students—following up with them in the weeks or even months after their participation in diversity programming to gauge whether they may need counseling or other support.

Questions for future research: Why are men more challenged and conflicted by diversity experiences than women? What specific aspects of diversity programming lead to such outcomes?

Careers and majors. Colleges often find it difficult to attract more women to pursue the traditionally male fields of engineering and computer science. Large numbers of women opt out of the science and engineering pipeline before they attend college, often because of factors beyond colleges' control, such as family influences and early educational experiences.

But colleges are in a position to recruit and retain women who have the ability and preparation for science and engineering careers yet who may nevertheless select other career paths. They have an opportunity to educate students about the ways in which math and science can help improve society and the human condition, particularly at a time of tremendous progress in computer and biological technologies. The more that higher-education institutions can connect scientific concepts to issues that women tend to care about—education, the environment, human rights—the more likely women will become scientists and create change in those areas.

Strategies to increase the number of women in science include summer internships, mentorships, professional development workshops, and online networks of women in science. They are usually viewed, however, as programmatic supplements rather than integrated into the mainstream curriculum. In fact, we know far less about how to transform the broader culture of academic science.

Questions for future research: How can we make science more appealing to women? What are the characteristics of programs that successfully educate students about the connection between scientific concepts and larger societal concerns?

Besides those aspects of college life, female and male college students' experiences in higher education differ in several other key ways. For example, female students' average income has fallen further behind men's, so they are substantially more concerned than their male counterparts about whether they will have enough money to complete college. Thus, colleges should evaluate whether they allocate student aid and work-study opportunities fairly to women and men, which types of work experiences are most beneficial, and the extent to which women and men have equal access to the most desirable positions. We should study, for example, whether having a job in the campus bookstore relates to a different set of outcomes than working in the admissions office, in the recreation center, or at the local coffeehouse or a retail store.

Also, despite the fact that college women earn better grades and exhibit a stronger academic orientation than their male counterparts, they tend to suffer from comparatively low academic confidence. In fact, women rate themselves lower than men on nearly every assessment of their academic abilities. Further, these gender differences grow during college. We should learn more about why women rate themselves lower—because they believe they are less capable, or are they simply reluctant to describe themselves as having high ability—and what conditions account for the widening gender gap in academic self-confidence.

Finally, compared with men, women enter college with higher levels of self-reported stress and lower ratings of their physical and emotional health. Such gender gaps remain significant over four years of college and reflect the fact that men spend more time on activities that can be considered ways to relieve stress (playing sports and video games, partying, and watching television) while women often devote themselves to a range of responsibilities that tend to induce stress (studying, homework, community service, and family responsibilities). Colleges should encourage all students to strike a healthier balance between academics, extracurricular activities, and leisure. We also need to develop a better understanding of what it means for a student to maintain balance.

Although women have a numerical advantage in college, both genders face challenges to their adjustment and development. Just as we need to be concerned about high stress and low self-esteem among women, we must be concerned about growing academic disengagement among men.

And while we aim to encourage all students to become engaged and involved, we must be mindful that the dynamics of those experiences can be quite different for the two genders, especially when it comes to students' interactions with their professors. Thus, institutional efforts aimed at improving the college experience for both genders must consider the distinct needs of each.

19

GAY MARRIAGE IS A QUESTION OF LOVE

Keith Olbermann

Finally tonight as promised, a Special Comment on the passage, last week, of Proposition Eight in California, which rescinded the right of same-sex couples to marry, and tilted the balance on this issue, from coast to coast.

Some parameters, as preface. This isn't about yelling, and this isn't about politics, and this isn't really just about Prop. 8. And I don't have a personal investment in this: I'm not gay, I had to strain to think of one member of even my very extended family who is, I have no personal stories of close friends or colleagues fighting the prejudice that still pervades their lives.

And yet to me this vote is horrible. Horrible. Because this isn't about yelling, and this isn't about politics. This is about the human heart, and if that sounds corny, so be it.

If you voted for this proposition or support those who did or the sentiment they expressed, I have some questions, because, truly, I do not understand. Why does this matter to you? What is it to you? In a time of impermanence and fly-by-night relationships, these people over here want the same chance at permanence and happiness that is your option. They don't want to deny you yours. They don't want to take anything away from you. They want what you want—a chance to be a little less alone in the world.

Only now you are saying to them—no. You can't have it on these terms. Maybe something similar. If they behave. If they don't cause too much trouble. You'll even give them all the same legal rights—even as you're taking away the legal right, which they already had. A world around them, still anchored in love and marriage, and you are saying, no, you can't marry. What if somebody passed a law that said you couldn't marry?

I keep hearing this term "re-defining" marriage. If this country hadn't re-defined marriage, black people still couldn't marry white people. Sixteen states had laws on the books which made that illegal in 1967. 1967.

The parents of the President-Elect of the United States couldn't have married in nearly one third of the states of the country their son grew up to lead. But it's worse than that. If this country had not "re-defined" marriage, some black people still couldn't marry black people. It is one of the most overlooked and cruelest parts of our sad story of slavery. Marriages were not legally recognized, if the people were slaves. Since slaves were property, they could not legally be husband and wife, or mother and child. Their marriage vows were different: not "Until Death, Do You Part," but "Until Death or Distance, Do You Part." Marriages among slaves were not legally recognized.

You know, just like marriages today in California are not legally recognized, if the people are gay.

And uncountable in our history are the number of men and women, forced by society into marrying the opposite sex, in sham marriages, or marriages of convenience, or just marriages of not knowing, centuries of men and women who have lived their lives in shame and unhappiness, and who have, through a lie to themselves or others, broken countless other lives, of spouses and children, all because we said a man couldn't marry another man, or a woman couldn't marry another woman. The sanctity of marriage.

How many marriages like that have there been and how on earth do they increase the "sanctity" of marriage, rather than render the term meaningless?

What is this, to you? Nobody is asking you to embrace their expression of love. But don't you, as human beings, have to embrace . . . that love? The world is barren enough.

It is stacked against love, and against hope, and against those very few and precious emotions that enable us to go forward. Your marriage only stands a 50-50 chance of lasting, no matter how much you feel and how hard you work.

And here are people overjoyed at the prospect of just that chance, and that work, just for the hope of having that feeling. With so much hate in the world, with so much meaningless division, and people pitted against people for no good reason, this is what your religion tells you to do? With your experience of life and this world and all its sadnesses, this is what your conscience tells you to do?

With your knowledge that life, with endless vigor, seems to tilt the playing field on which we all live, in favor of unhappiness and hate . . . this is what your heart tells you to do? You want to sanctify marriage? You want to honor your God and the universal love you believe he represents? Then spread happiness—this tiny, symbolic, semantical grain of happiness—share it with all those who seek it. Quote me anything from your religious leader or book of choice telling you to stand against this. And then tell me how you can believe both that statement and another statement, another one which reads only "do unto others as you would have them do unto you."

You are asked now, by your country, and perhaps by your creator, to stand on one side or another. You are asked now to stand, not on a question of politics, not on a question of religion, not on a question of gay or straight. You are asked now to stand, on a question of love. All you need do is stand, and let the tiny ember of love meet its own fate.

You don't have to help it, you don't have it applaud it, you don't have to fight for it. Just don't put it out. Just don't extinguish it. Because while it may at first look like that love is between two people you don't know and you don't understand and maybe you don't even want to know. It is, in fact, the ember of your love, for your fellow person just because this is the only world we have. And the other guy counts, too.

This is the second time in ten days I find myself concluding by turning to, of all things, the closing plea for mercy by Clarence Darrow in a murder trial. But what he said, fits what is really at the heart of this:

> "I was reading last night of the aspiration of the old Persian poet, Omar Khayyám," he told the judge. "It appealed to me as the highest that I can vision. I wish it was in my heart, and I wish it was in the hearts of all: So I be written in the Book of Love; I do not care about that Book above. Erase my name, or write it as you will, So I be written in the Book of Love."

20

EIGHT IS ENOUGH

Patricia J. Williams

For some years now, the biotechnology of fertility enhancement has been exalted as God's gift to the biblically barren. A relentless narrative of entitlement intertwined with prayerfulness has framed infertility as a tragedy, an oppression, an agony, a disease. Some have proclaimed a "right" to a "natural," biologically related child, a child "like me." Unusually large Middle American families—some with up to eighteen children—are offered movie deals and television programs.

Reprinted with permission from the March 2, 2009, issue of *The Nation*.

Against the backdrop of a cold, impersonal and lonely world, these well-feathered and overly populated nests look villagey and warm. It's an undeniably seductive vision, even if other options like adoption and fostering are almost never mentioned. Also less discussed are the side effects of this mad race for biological generation at all costs: the likelihood of multiple births, low birth weight and birth defects; the ethics of using poorer women as fetal hatcheries; the health risks to young women who have their "Ivy League" eggs extracted for handsome sums of cash.

There are loads of good reasons to think about regulating these medical procedures; we should have come up with something other than a "free market" for them years ago. But now, with the birth of Nadya Suleman's octuplets in Bellflower, California, we are confronting a perfect storm of eugenic outcry. With a plunging economy, all the well-rehearsed elements of the "undeserving" welfare queen are lined up: Suleman is single, disabled, unemployed, on food stamps and has six other children under the age of 8, one of whom is reportedly autistic. She lives in a matchbox-size house with her resentful parents, who think she's insane. Toss in that funny, foreign-sounding name—which turns out to be, gasp, Iraqi!—and the backlash is in full swing.

No doubt Suleman has emotional problems. But rather than caring about her mental health, much of the media are content to pillory her as a drain on the public dole—selfish, frivolous, calculating and cruel. No Brangelina-style accolades of "God Bless 'Em" in *People* magazine. Just impassioned calls to cut off her remaining sources of income and to criminally prosecute the doctor who fertilized her. *The Atlanta Journal-Constitution* even ran an op-ed calling for the government to appoint a legal advocate for every child born to an unmarried woman, since the "lack of a father's guidance" must be "a major cause of [children's] suffering." Furthermore, in the case of Suleman's children, "the legal advocate would file suit against the fertility clinic or a physician who knowingly contributed to their abuse—life in a multiple-child household headed by a single woman."

Nadya Suleman's saga, in other words, has highlighted a deep cognitive dissonance about whether children are "assets" or eternal expenditure, divine joy or devilish curse in a time of dwindling planetary resources. When I first heard of Suleman, my immediate thought was of Andrea and Rusty Yates—married, fundamentalist Christian believers in that ubiquitous story line about going forth and multiplying no matter what. After caring for and home-schooling five very young children with no assistance but prayer, and with accumulating signs of postpartum psychosis, Andrea Yates woke up one morning and drowned all her children with quiet efficiency.

And so the specter of psychotic breakdown haunts me when I think of the Suleman abode: one autistic child, plus 2-year-old twins, plus four other kids ages 3 to 7, plus eight newborns ranging from one to three pounds, plus a grandfather who has gone back to Iraq to earn more money for the family, plus a grandmother furious at the medical professionals who "assisted" her daughter, plus a surreally chipper Nadya, who despite the miserable odds remains enrolled as a graduate student in, of all things, pediatric counseling. This situation is undeniably sheer madness, but the public discussion seems fixated on the question of whether she can "afford" so many kids, as though if she was rich, this would be sane.

This past fall *The New York Times Magazine* ran a cover story by Alex Kuczynski, fashion writer and self-confessed "cosmetic surgery addict." Her wish to have a child was framed by fierce determinism, the "natural outgrowth" of marriage to her husband—without whom she "would skip the child." Kuczynski is married to a man whose "sperm had a track record"—six other children by two prior wives. She, the third bride and twenty years her husband's junior, described herself as engaged in nothing less than a "battle for my fertility"; having a biological child was "necessary," a "mad desire," a "compulsion" and "proof" of the marital bond, without which she faced "wrecked hopes" and an "abyss of grief." Indeed, to die "without having created a life is to die two deaths: the death of yourself and the death of the immense opportunity that is a child." When she thinks she's pregnant, she feels a "shiver of victorious accomplishment. . . . my own fecundity triumphant." When she tells people she's not, she feels "barren, decrepit, desexualized," "branded with a scarlet 'I' for 'Infertile,'" "the dried-up crone with a uterus full of twigs."

Just because Kuczynski is married and wealthy does not make her less obsessive or more profound than Suleman. Kuczynski sounds like a sad, silly child mooning over "fertile but fit" stars like Halle Berry, Nicole Kidman, Salma Hayek and "John Edwards's sometime mistress," who all had babies in their 40s. Likewise, Suleman takes heart looking at Angelina Jolie. Suleman and Kuczynski represent disturbing emotional extremes. But that should not excuse the rest of us from examining the oppressive competitive natality that seems to have gripped us—the fantasies of "baby bumps" and breeding, always breeding, yet more of "our kind." Our culture's antifeminist backlash and its unrealistic aspirations have bewitched Kuczynski and Suleman, these two young women who are so addled and so suggestible, so endowed and yet so impoverished. All these years after the age of "liberation," perhaps it is time to revisit the myths we still concoct about childless women's worth.

21

OUT OF THE CLOSET, BUT NOT OUT OF MIDDLE SCHOOL

Libby Copeland

On the last day of seventh grade, Dave Grossman mounted some cardboard boxes down the street from his junior high school and held a one-boy rally.

I'm sick of pretending, he announced into a cheap loudspeaker.

I'm gay.

The affair was a bit botched. Dave's principal, fearing a "disruption," asked him to move his makeshift stage and rainbow flags away from school grounds. The event caused barely an eye-roll from his peers, who scattered from school eager to inaugurate summer.

Still, there was Dave with his loudspeaker and his conviction. Like a soap opera character haunted by a secret past, he had been living two lives. In school, he was a straight kid with straight A's. After classes, he rode the Metro downtown and hung with gay friends past dinner time. He says few people could believe that at 13, he was so certain he was gay.

Two years later, Dave puts it like this: "It was a lot of built-up frustration over everyone saying, 'You're too young, you're too young, you're too young.'"

In the national debate about gay and bisexual identity, age is a volatile fault line along which schools are being forced to pick sides. Gay-youth advocacy groups say the average age of kids who "come out" has decreased substantially in recent years. Whereas once a teenager might have come out in senior year with a burn-your-bridges disinhibition, now that same teenager is making his homosexuality public in middle school or ninth grade.

Puberty is a roulette wheel of biding time and spurting growth. One preteen is sexually active while her classmate is still collecting stickers. American girls are hitting puberty far earlier than they were a century ago, and there's growing awareness of a disconnection between physical and mental maturity. Add the perennial dilemmas of sex education—how much kids should learn, how soon, from whom—and you have a recipe for controversy.

What happens when a middle school student—in braces, in a training bra, inexperienced—announces that she's gay?

It's happening. Ritch Savin-Williams, a developmental psychologist at Cornell University, used data from nine independent studies conducted over the last 20 years to conclude that the average age at which young men label their same-sex attractions as gay dropped from almost 20 in 1979 to just 13 in 1998. They may not, however, definitively call themselves gay until a few years later.

"Every time we sample these kids, the average age is getting younger," says Savin-Williams. "What's different is that now gay kids are becoming like straight kids—they know that they're gay before they have sex."

At Longfellow Middle School in Falls Church, Dave Grossman forced the issue that advocacy groups, educators and mental health providers have been debating for several years: Should the nation's struggle over sex and morality play out inside schools, involving kids in a debate that can be loudspeaker loud? Or should such issues be fought at the ballot box, from church pulpits and at home?

Longfellow's principal, Gail Womble, respected Dave's desire to come out, if not his venue. In the end, she was relieved that Dave said his piece without causing an uproar.

"I did have concerns about how middle school students would meet that kind of disclosure," says Womble, who has since moved to Rachel Carson Middle School in Fairfax. "At this age, we have kids who are old enough to be exploring those feelings and other kids who are still playing with Barbie dolls."

Dave's mother was disgusted by what she felt were "outrageous" banishing dictums imposed on her son, like making Dave move his stage across the street. Donna Brown Grossman says Womble also asked Dave to cover a T-shirt reading "Nobody Knows I'm Gay," and would not let him pass out homemade pamphlets promoting his rally.

"Her reaction was one thing that made me feel that I had to take my child out of the public school system," says Grossman, 48, who subsequently transferred her son to Thornton Friends, a private Quaker school. As school systems debate whether to allow gay support groups, or pass anti-harassment policies on behalf of gays, or show their faculty the controversial documentary "It's Elementary: Talking About Gay Issues in School," proponents on both sides point to the tender age of the youngsters as evidence of the rectitude of their positions.

Gay-rights advocacy groups and much of the mental health community cite 12-year-old gay youngsters as proof that being homosexual is "natural." Christian conservative groups argue that young adolescents bombarded by hormones and pop images of sexuality are especially susceptible to gay "recruiting."

"Those kids are incredibly impressionable, and I think certainly the younger the age, the more they can be swayed," says Peter LaBarbera, editor of the Lambda Report on Homosexuality, which argues that the declining age at which youngsters are coming out is largely the product of gay propaganda inside schools.

"There's different gradations. Love, sexuality: It's a very tangled web."

This is Ellen Sweeney, 18, an assured young woman who was co-leader of the gay discussion group at Sidwell Friends, a private school in Northwest Washington, during this, her senior year. She began to question her own sexuality in seventh grade, joined the discussion group in high school, and recently, has taught workshops to middle school students on gay issues. Incidentally, Sweeney is straight. But, she says, "I question myself up until this day."

This open attitude toward sexuality is a splinter in the skin of many who oppose gay discussion groups. They ask, what if youngsters who would otherwise be straight are encouraged to question, and ultimately, to declare themselves gay?

In the last few years in the Washington area, at least 15 gay discussion groups have cropped up in high schools and one middle school. The majority of the groups are in Montgomery County, where, amid a storm of controversy three years ago, the school board added gay students and teachers to the list of people protected from discrimination. The groups, which range from sanctioned clubs to informal lunch gatherings, serve as sounding boards—to examine homophobia, for example, or the feelings of a member who says she has been "questioning."

The problem with such discussions, opponents say, is that they don't offer an alternative to open-armed acceptance of homosexuality. Janet Folger, national director of the Center for Reclaiming America, an arm of Coral Ridge Ministries, says if gay issues must be part of the school climate, youngsters should at least be exposed to "ex-gays" and told of the health risks of homosexuality.

As things stand, "there is no balance," Folger says. "There is no message of hope . . . that you can walk away from it."

Like many area private schools, Edmund Burke School in the District doesn't see it that way. When a gay-issues discussion group was created there this year, middle school students were included in the weekly lunch meetings. Hugh Taft-Morales, the group's faculty adviser, said the group has "no agenda."

"They are already talking about this," he says. "What we're doing is taking responsibility as adults to raise the level of the discussion."

Although no exhaustive data can be found on discussion groups in schools, the New York-based Gay, Lesbian and Straight Educational Network keeps tabs on clubs that register with it. Its national list has blossomed from roughly 150 high school "Gay/Straight Alliances" last year to about 400 this year, concentrated mainly in Massachusetts, California and the New York City area. In Maryland and Virginia, there are seven registered high school alliances.

"Some people feel it's not our job," says Pamela Latt, principal of Centreville High School, which is on track to become the third high school in Virginia with a registered gay/straight alliance. Centreville has had a gay counseling group for two years, but a few students have been pushing for more.

"Having a counseling group sort of sends the wrong message," says Caroline Zuscheck, 17, a straight student involved in the effort. "It's like if you have an eating disorder or a problem with depression."

But although the principal supports starting an alliance next year, she also has reservations. On one hand, she says, it will contribute to a healthier environment for gay teenagers, a high-risk group. But Latt knows she is treading on important toes in conservative Centreville, where some School Board and community members have already voiced discomfort with a school-sanctioned club. "I don't blame people for being very cautious and careful," she says.

Latt is conflicted for other reasons. She is Catholic and has puzzled over whether homosexuality is wrong (she doesn't think so) and what causes it (she doesn't know). At any rate, she says, the alliance is about "saving lives," not promoting homosexuality. But perhaps in an ideal world, this messy moral stew wouldn't fall into the principal's lap.

"This really shouldn't be a part of my job," Latt says finally. "But I don't think I have a choice."

Amy Levy and her son remember the moment differently. The way Will tells it, his mom was nagging him, Why don't you have a girlfriend? The way Levy tells it, Will's confession came straight out of the clear blue sky.

Never mind why. That moment changed everything. One minute, the mother is dropping her son off in the car. The next, he tells her, "I'm gay," and hops out.

He is 14.

For Levy, 50, that belly-flop into reality challenged a lot of rules. Will was the first openly gay student at his tiny Bethesda private school, which has no specific policies on the issue. In an attempt to carve a comfortable space for himself, Will, now 16, met with teachers. Levy met with teachers. Teachers met with other teachers.

Levy says Will's coming out made them all dissect their feelings about homosexuality. "Do you really believe in what you thought you believed in when it becomes part of your life?" she wonders. (To protect her son, Levy asked that Will's last name, which is different from hers, not be published.)

Gay-rights advocates say this type of discussion is a door slowly creaking open, a departure from past decades when an unofficial "don't ask, don't tell" policy reigned in high schools and middle schools.

At a recent meeting for gay Montgomery County youths, two adults leading the session reminisced about how different it once was: one man, one woman, both in their forties or fifties, both of whom married at 23, both of whom divorced, both of whom realized only in adulthood that they were, in fact, gay.

They listened to the teenagers and then ticked off each belated milestone in their own closeted lives, as if to say, All those years lost.

Dave Grossman is a slight, blue-eyed youth with an energy and intelligence that sometimes gets the better of him. He skipped eighth grade, and, after ninth, went to Simon's Rock, a college in Great Barrington, Mass., designed for kids of high school age. Now he's transferring to American University, entering his second year of college at 15.

While he was growing up, Dave says, instinct told him he liked other boys. He just knew, natural as corn. In fourth grade, he says, "I came to my senses. I was just staring benignly at the boy across from me."

At 11, Dave found online chat rooms and located the gay bulletin board in short order.

At 12, he told his parents, because there was no reason not to, because now he knew for sure, and the knowledge pressed in on him. It was after synagogue on a late summer night. The date sticks in his mind—August 30, 1996. He recalls his mother crying with the shock and the strangeness. "She was like, 'Wow, I didn't even know you had a sexuality.'"

And Dave started his journey, because he saw himself as a young man with a sexuality and an image to build, and he shed his baby fat, his glasses and his gawky hair and hatched a plan to let people know that he had found himself. A stage, a loudspeaker, a grand announcement.

"I was going to do something," he says. "Something that was extravagant."

A showdown of sorts—even if there were few people around to watch. A showdown, at the very least, with the person who mattered.

22

FOR YOU, MY LOVELY, A FACE-LIFT

Natasha Singer

Last year Helena Rasin's grandmother gave her $200 for Christmas. This year her grandmother gave her a new nose.

"A nose job is the best Christmas present ever because you'll have it forever," Ms. Rasin, 25, a drug company representative in Los Angeles, said two weeks ago while at home recuperating from her rhinoplasty. "It's not like some sweater you don't like and have to take back to the store. Even with the bandages still on, I can already tell I look cuter."

For a denizen of a looks-centric milieu like Los Angeles, Ms. Rasin, who emigrated from Ukraine in 1992, may seem like a plastic surgery late bloomer. Many of her peers had their noses bobbed back in high school and did not get cosmetic procedures this year, Ms. Rasin said. Instead they gave them to family members.

"It's kind of in now, it's kind of hip this year to give surgery," Ms. Rasin said.

December has always been a busy month for plastic surgeons, whose schedules fill with patients seeking a little streamlining before the holiday party season or in advance of body-baring beach vacations. But this year, rather than going under the knife themselves, an increasing number of people conferred nips and tucks upon their loved ones, doctors say. Children financed $15,000 face-lifts for their parents. Sisters shelled out $500 for each other's Botox treatments. And wives sent husbands to cosmetic dentists for $40,000 sets of porcelain tooth veneers.

But among some doctors and social critics the idea of buying loved ones new and improved body parts raises moral and psychological questions about the consequences of amending someone else's appearance, especially if the gift was not requested. Critics worry that giving friends or relatives permanent body alterations could negatively affect romantic relationships or family dynamics, and some doctors turn away as many as one in three patients out of concern they are being pressured to undergo the procedures.

Gift giving may also cause patients to overlook the medical risks involved in cosmetic procedures.

"It is an unlikely possibility, but these are presents you could die from," said Virginia L. Blum, the author of *Flesh Wounds: the Culture of Cosmetic Surgery.*

Since the 1970's affluent parents have quietly arranged for their teenage daughters to have nose jobs during the holiday vacation. But overt gifts of plastic surgery between adults were almost unheard of before the advent of television shows like "Extreme Makeover" four years ago. The exact number of people buying cosmetic procedures for others is unknown. But in a survey of about 100 facial surgeons conducted by the American Academy of Facial Plastic and Reconstructive Surgery, 49 percent said they had seen patients in 2004 who received cosmetic surgery as a gift, up from 31 percent in 2001. The practice goes on year-round, thanks to birthdays and anniversaries, but seems to peak during the Christmas and Hanukkah season.

"We're seeing more and more women in their 20's and 30's who have loose tummies and hollow breasts as a result of having babies," said Dr. Linda Li, a plastic surgeon in Beverly Hills, Calif. "The women want to restore themselves by having surgery, and their husbands are giving it to them."

Dr. Li, a regular on the makeover show "Dr. 90210," said she has about 30 new patients this month who are receiving surgery as a gift. Some have appointments for $7,000 breast augmentations. Others, she said, will have multiple surgeries in a single session: a $23,000 combination of a tummy tuck, liposuction, breast implants and eye lifts, for instance.

"The way we view cosmetic surgery has really changed," Dr. Li said. "If you can shop for your own new tummy, new chest and new teeth, you can buy them for someone else too."

But some people wince at the idea that cosmetic treatments might become gifts as sought after as Xbox video game consoles or iPod nanos. As cosmetic enhancement enters the realm of consumer goods, critics say, it becomes part of the competitive sport that is shopping. Keeping up with the Joneses becomes keeping up with their noses.

"We have a desperate need to get our flat screen TV's, our updated electronics, our liposuction and our breast implants to keep up with the lives of the rich and famous," said Sean Jablonski, a supervising writer for "Nip/Tuck," the fictional plastic surgery show that dissects the underbelly of cosmetic culture. A recent episode featured Santa Claus wanting to endow a comely elf named Circe with double-D breast implants. "Plastic surgery is now so accepted and infused in our social landscape that we can broach improving someone else as long as it's wrapped as a gift," Mr. Jablonski said.

Many doctors say surgical gift giving reduces medicine to a service industry as accessible as fast food. And that may cause patients to overlook the fact that any invasive operation can have complications, including infection, scarring, brain damage (from anesthesia) and death.

"Cosmetic surgery has slipped so far away from the realm of serious medicine that buying it seems as trivial as purchasing a garment or a hairdo," said Dr. Adam Searle, the president of the British Association of Aesthetic Plastic Surgeons.

This month he and his colleagues sent out a press release excoriating a British plastic surgery chain called Transform Medical Group for offering gift certificates for everything from lip augmentation to liposuction. Dr. Searle said buying gift certificates for any medical procedure, be it plastic surgery or a hernia operation, is inappropriate. American plastic surgery societies condemn selling gift certificates for procedures, although they condone them for skin care products or doctors' consultations.

"A decision to have plastic surgery should be between a patient and a doctor," and not commercialized with gift certificates, said Dr. Mark L. Jewell, a plastic surgeon in Oregon who is the president of the American Society for Aesthetic Plastic Surgery.

Television shows like "Extreme Makeover" and "The Swan" may inspire viewers to bestow enhanced body parts upon one another, said Dr. Richard Ellenbogen, a plastic surgeon in Beverly Hills. "The wish-fulfillment format of these television shows has made it comfortable for people to give surgery to each other," he said. "You give the gift to your wife or your girlfriend and she becomes the swan."

But just as makeover shows enumerate a person's purported faults before correcting them, a person who offers a cosmetic procedure to a loved one may implicitly criticize the recipient's looks.

"All along you've been thinking that your own perky and not so smallish breasts are fine," said Daphne Merkin, an author in New York City whose book *Dreaming of Hitler* contains essays on beauty and identity. "Then someone says, 'Honey, I'm going to improve you by giving you new breasts.' I presume this could lead to a divorce. No one is going to be flattered by such a gift because a judgment is being made about you."

Ms. Blum, an associate professor of English at the University of Kentucky in Louisville, said makeover shows have turned Americans into would-be surgeons who constantly examine one another for signs of aging. "The makeover shows have made us feel safer about insulting each other's body parts because correction seems just around the corner," she said.

Some recipients are unenthusiastic about the gift of surgery. Last month a man who wanted to give his girlfriend breast implants took her for a consultation with Dr. Peter B. Fodor, a plastic surgeon in Los Angeles who is the immediate past president of the American Society for Aesthetic Plastic Surgery. Dr. Fodor said he turned the couple away because he could tell by the woman's body language, and by her concern that big implants might cause her breasts to sag, that her boyfriend was trying to coerce her into the procedure by paying for it.

"If she gets new breasts she doesn't want just for the boyfriend's sake and then the relationship ends, it will be hell for her in every way," Dr. Fodor said. "If she keeps the implants, they will remind her of him. If she has the implants removed, she will have big scars." He said he turns down about 30 percent of gift surgery patients. "Gifts only work if the patient would have wanted the surgery anyway."

Often it is the patient who seeks the gift of a lift. Take Grace Gao Macnow, the 54-year-old owner of Graceful Services Spa in Midtown Manhattan. For several years she had been telling her daughter, Li Huang, that she wanted cosmetic surgery to reduce the wrinkles around her eyes and mouth. This month Ms. Huang spent about $15,000 on a mini face-lift and eyelid lifts for her mother, she said.

"If I can make her happy, money is not an issue," said Ms. Huang, who just opened her own spa downtown. "Now my mother is showing off, telling our relatives that her daughter really cares about her because I bought her a face-lift."

Dr. Robert C. Silich, the plastic surgeon who performed Ms. Macnow's face-lift this month, said he found it "sweet that the daughter is giving this as a gift."

But Ms. Blum said the idea of gift surgeries reminded her of old diamond advertisements that had slogans like "Show her how much you love her."

"The idea was the bigger the diamond, the bigger your love," Ms. Blum said. "It was brilliant marketing. Are gift procedures the surgical equivalent?"

23

Before Spring Break,
The Anorexic Challenge

Alex Williams

"I really gotta start losing weight before spring break," a 15-year-old from Long Island wrote in her blog on Xanga.com, a social networking site. "Basically today I went 24 hours without food and then I ate green beans and a little baked ziti. Frankly I'm proud of myself, not to mention the 100 situps on the yoga ball and the 100 I'll do before sleep. . . . Yey for me."

A Californian, 18, wrote: "I'm at 108 right now. Spring break is in about 3 weeks and I want to be down to at least 99–100. That can easily be done."

From a writer identifying herself as Workhardgetskinny: "I only did 100 crunches but I'm trying to do 200 more before bed. . . . 2 full days till spring break!"

The discussion took place in one of Xanga's blog rings, a string of Web logs connected by a common theme, in this case a spring break challenge, in which young women pledged to shed a lot of weight before their trips to the beaches of Florida and Mexico.

Their home pages were decorated with images of gaunt supermodels and pipe-cleaner-thin celebrities like Nicole Richie. Declarations like "Food Is Poison" and "Diet Coke Is Love" blared like banner advertisements across screens. Participants also shared their daily indulgences. One writer confessed to eating "one cracker, one strawberry and a little bit of soup" in a 24-hour period. Another recounted a lunch that consisted of a slice of mango and a stick of gum.

For most students spring break represents the promise of a beer-soaked respite from Northern cold and midterm stress, a time to let go and revive. But for a subculture of students with eating disorders, this annual weeklong bacchanalia, unfolding across Florida, Mexico and the Caribbean during March and April, represents the summit of deprivation and self-denial.

Though not widely discussed—sufferers of eating disorders often spend years in denial about their condition, and therapists treating them can rarely isolate any single reason for these complex psychological syndromes—those who treat eating disorders say spring break is one of the most dangerous times of the year for young women struggling with their weight and eating.

"This is a trigger time for youth to start to obsess about weight and body image," said Margo Maine, a clinical psychologist in West Hartford, Conn., who specializes in eating disorders. She said she observes a spike in weight anxiety every year among her younger patients before spring break. "By the beginning of February people are starting to talk about their bodies and getting ready for spring break. Even girls who are simply around that talk can't get away from it."

The fantasy of achieving a "bikini-ready" body on a deadline is an intoxicating incentive, according to those who have experienced and observed the behavior. And in a school setting, in which tightly knit groups of young women are all vacationing together, diets easily become competitive or, as Dr. Maine put it, contagious.

For Ashley Filipp, a recent college graduate and recovering anorexic and bulimic, the warmup to spring break when she was a student in Colorado represented, she said, "the big time of the year." She added, "You start realizing that you have been packing on the winter pounds, the insulation, and now it's time to lose them."

Starting in her senior year of high school, Ms. Filipp, 24, recalled preparing for her annual spring break trip to Mexico at least 100 days beforehand. "As soon as we would make our plans, my best friend and I would start counting 'How many days to Cancun?'" recalled Ms. Filipp, who now works as a crisis helpline counselor for the National Association of Anorexia Nervosa and Associated Disorders in Highland Park, Ill.

By the time Ms. Filipp entered college, she said, there was no shortage of students eager to join her in what became a pre-spring-break ritual. In January and February, she said, the scene inside her sorority house at times resembled an Olympics of extreme weight loss. Some students would subsist on little more than lettuce flavored with calorie-free spray butter flavoring. Others would purge by vomiting or swallowing laxatives. Obsessive exercise was common.

The group dieting that is relatively ad hoc among friends and sorority sisters takes a more organized form on the Internet, where spring break has become a popular topic on Web sites and message boards maintained by devotees of a controversial underground movement known as "pro-ana," or pro-anorexia, who sometimes identify themselves in public by wearing red bracelets. There are hundreds of pro-ana Web sites promoting and supporting the "anorexic lifestyle," despite aggressive efforts to shut them down by eating-disorder activists. In addition the pro-anas are also present on social network sites like MySpace.com, Xanga and Livejournal.com, where blog rings topics range as widely as emo music and parasailing.

On Xanga groups of pro-ana members who link their blogs by a common interest in extreme weight loss sometimes participate in a perverse distortion of Weight Watchers. Instead of accumulating points for food eaten, points are granted for restraint: a point for every day survived under 500 calories; 6 points for every day under 100 calories; 2 points for each diet pill taken; a point for every photo of a skinny celebrity on a home page, known as "thinspiration" or "thinspo." The points are gained during group challenges aimed at losing weight before spring break. Other challenges have focused on prom season, the holidays and summer.

Not all those discussing weight loss on the site fit the criteria of anorexics or identify themselves with the pro-ana underground. Xanga is one of many meeting places on the Web for weight-related discussion rings. John Hiler, its chief executive, said in an e-mail message: "We have zero desire to host any 'pro-ana' groups. If users report them to us, we delete them from our system."

Still, some therapists suggest that pro-ana Web pages can have some value, serving as support groups for young anorexics, who feel they have no place else to turn. Experts who treat eating disorders worry that healthy girls and young women who use spring break as an excuse to dabble in dangerous dieting techniques can tip over into self-destructive behavior. "You take that typical 15-year-old, who is taking her anxiety into spring break, if there are other issues in her life or her family, she's a prime candidate for anorexia or bulimia," said Doug Bunnell, the director of treatment for the Renfrew Center eating disorders program in Wilton, Conn. "Their first diet can blossom into a real nightmare."

The online pro-ana networks can be especially dangerous, experts say, because participants can offer irresponsible advice behind a mask of anonymity. Several eating-disorder therapists interviewed said they considered all the pro-ana material on the Web highly dangerous, particularly when spiced with the spirit of a contest.

"There's been no good research to date on how these sites actually impact teenagers," said Dr. Rebecka Peebles, a pediatrician who specializes in the treatment of adolescent eating disorders at Lucile Packard Children's Hospital in Palo Alto, Calif., and who is conducting a study of pro-ana and "pro-mia" (bulimia) Web sites. "But I can tell you anecdotally that some of my patients felt very triggered by these point challenges. That level of competition is just very hard to resist."

On Xanga, a 20-year-old sophomore at an undisclosed college who included photographs of herself looking attractive, shapely and healthy, wrote, "Spring break is comin' up mid march and I wanna look super hot." She explained that she wanted to plummet from 133 pounds to 110 by the time she and her friends took off for Mexico, in part by reducing her daily food intake to 500 calories, about a third of what is recommended for a young woman, as well as exercising. But, she added, "I always get sick when I run and don't eat enough. Does that happen to you guys?"

"Yes," one respondent wrote, "if I eat under 300 calories and work out for several days, I start to feel sick. I hate that, but I end up eating a little bit because I don't want to faint. Luv & support."

Though it is not possible to estimate the number of young women participating in extreme spring break weight-loss contests, or to assess how the popularity of such contests has grown, eating disorder experts say that the rise of spring break as a cultural phenomenon might play a role.

"Every year spring break seems to get bigger and bigger," Dr. Maine said, adding that body-image pressure also rises. She said the expectation that you have to "party like a rock star and be over the top" also "includes looking like a rock star," that is, fashionably, even dangerously, skinny.

It's also an opportunity to show a little skin, and parade in front of the opposite sex.

"It's showoff time," said Eileen Adams, a psychologist and treatment specialist at Remuda Ranch, a Bible-based eating disorder center in Wickenburg, Ariz. "That puts a lot of pressure on young people."

And most young women are already feeling pressure, at least when it comes to body-image anxieties. Eating disorder associations say that about 86 percent of the approximately 10 million American girls and women—and one million boys and men—who suffer from an eating disorder reported the onset of their condition by 20.

The pressure has only become worse over the years, therapists said, as spring break has become more sexualized at beaches like South Padre Island, Tex., or Cancun or on MTV. String bikini and wet T-shirt contests make a simple weeklong break from teachers and exams look more like a Mardi Gras for the 18-to-21 set.

Some therapists said the letting-go ethic of spring break in general can also serve as a dangerous excuse for students to push the frontiers of good sense and self-preservation. Bulimics in particular are at risk, Dr. Bunnell of the Renfrew Center said, since they tend to be drawn to extremes, as exemplified by their binge and purge cycles. Anorexics, by contrast, are generally motivated by issues of control; they are often reserved, socially anxious perfectionists, who attempt to master their food intake because they feel they cannot control other aspects of their lives. For them, he said, "anything that intensifies body image anxiety will encourage them to be symptomatic."

The difficulty for parents and educators is to distinguish between routine pre-spring break dieting and something worse. "If a child is just going on a spring diet to lose a few pounds, she'll be in a fine mood," said Maria Rago, a clinical psychologist and the director of the eating disorders program at Linden Oaks Hospital at Edward Hospital, a mental health center in Naperville, Ill. By contrast dieters slipping into dangerous territory "will become irritable, preoccupied," she said. "They'll skip meals, and stop eating with the family. It's an entire change of mood and mind-set."

Sometimes that change of mood can happen right after spring break, as opposed to before.

On a Xanga blog ring called the Bikini Coming Soon Challenge, one 19-year-old related the anxieties she was experiencing only days after returning from a week on the beach with friends: "Tonight I was looking on Facebook at people's albums from spring break. I saw the guy's album that I kind of was starting to like before spring break. In his album were pictures of all these pretty girls—tan, skinny, looked perfect in their bikinis—and all these guys were commenting on the pics: 'She is so hot!' or 'wooowww!!' Stuff like that. Seriously, that's what I want.

"This just makes me want to lose so much weight and then have those guys see me."

She concluded: "I hate boys, I hate my body. Goodnight."

24

MY FIRST TIME

Allana Allen

I arrived in Provincetown on Sunday, the first day of Fantasia Fair, and couldn't even bring myself to walk into the inn where I had reserved my room, even though I was in boy clothes. I was so scared I drove past the inn twice and eventually parked in a public lot so I could walk around the town to go CD spotting before I could decide whether I had the nerve to try it myself. Either there were no other crossdressers in Provincetown that day, or they were so passable I certainly wouldn't fit in.

Disheartened, with tears welling in my eyes, I walked back to the car, where I sat for a very long time, trying to decide what to do. I had all but decided to forget this silly fantasy and make the three-hour drive back home when it came to me that the worst-case scenario was that I could simply check into my room and spend a pleasant week in this lovely little tourist town on Cape Cod—as a man. It took me more than two hours before I had enough nerve just to check in.

Locked safely inside my room, I somehow found the courage to unpack the four suitcases of women's clothing and lingerie I had brought with me. As I unpacked, hanging each item in the tiny closet or folding it neatly into the two drawers of the small dresser, Allana fought her way to the surface. What would it hurt if I dressed here in my room? The transformation was somehow different this time than it had ever been before. For more than forty years I had slapped myself together haphazardly, and it had always been good enough. Something deep inside me, something I couldn't reach or even understand, was telling me that this time good enough wasn't good enough. This time I wasn't dressing to look like a woman. This time, I was a woman getting dressed. I tried to let go and let Allana come to the surface as she had never been allowed to before. The inner struggle was one of the hardest things I had ever done, but slowly she fought her way out. In time, I stood before the dresser mirror looking and feeling more like a woman than I ever had before. It took me another hour and a large pair of woman's sunglasses to hide behind before I found the courage to actually open the door and walk out of my room.

Literally trembling in my panties, I fretfully walked the length of the hallway in my high heels, praying no one would open a door, step into the hall, and see

Reprinted by permission of the International Foundation for Gender Education.

me. My legs trembled as I descended the staircase to the lobby, and my eyes looked neither left nor right as I took the four or five steps from the stairs to the front door. Riddled with apprehension and nervousness, and overwhelmed with absolute fear, Allana pushed us out the door and I stepped into the real world, dressed as a woman, for the very first time in my life.

I headed for Fantasia Fair headquarters at the Crown & Anchor Inn, just a couple of blocks away. It was the longest walk of my life. My heart was pounding so hard I truly thought it would leap right out of my chest. Commercial Street, the main drag (no pun intended) in Provincetown, was filled with people. I just knew they could tell I wasn't a real woman. My stomach was one gigantic knot and my legs tumbled with every step as I walked, but I marched on, keeping my eyes on the ground and looking up only to make sure I didn't stumble in my high heels. After what seemed an eternity, I finally reached the C&A and quickly headed for the side door. The apprehension of what lay behind that door was nothing compared to the complete and overwhelming fear I was feeling out in the open.

Inside, I found a large meeting room similar to a small theater. A long table had been set along one wall, and three women sat behind it, papers covering every inch of the tabletop. Around the room were men and women (?) filling out forms.

When you spend your entire life inside a box, and the only time you ever express your inner self is when you are alone, the opportunity for conversation simply doesn't happen. As a result, you never really know what the woman within sounds like. I approached the table, never even considering to try to disguise my voice, and actually spoke for the first time ever in my life while dressed as a woman. In my own husky male voice I quavered out a nervous, "Hi, I'm here for Fantasia Fair."

I was greeted without so much as a strange glance, and as naturally as if they were talking to a real woman.

"Have you been to FanFair before?" I was asked.

"No" I replied, my masculine voice still quaking. I was handed a packet of papers and asked to fill them out at one of the smaller tables and bring them back.

If it wasn't for the fact that I was so nervous, this could just as easily have been an everyday transaction at my local bank. There was such a calming sense of normalcy in the air that I could hardly believe what was happening. I filled out the papers and returned them to the same woman. Another woman started handing me more papers and began to explain that this one was a guide to the Fair and included a map of all the places in Provincetown where I would be going—these were lunch tickets for the different restaurants around town where the women would be eating. On and on she went, with me hearing less than ten percent of what she was saying because I was still so nervous.

The last thing she told me was that there would be a welcoming cocktail party at Crowne Pointe Inn at 5:30 and that she expected to see me there. It was now approximately 3:00. Somehow, I had managed to make it this far without so much as causing a raised eyebrow. I was still nervous and still scared to death, because now I had to walk Commercial Street again to get back to my inn! I donned my sunglasses once more to hide my true identity, and ventured out into the open for the second time in my life!

The trip back to the inn was no easier than the trip down, and I was wet with perspiration, despite the cold ocean breeze, by the time I reached my inn. I quickly ascended the staircase to my room without looking left or right. To this day, I couldn't tell you if anyone was in the lobby or even standing behind the desk.

I reached my room, slammed the door, and realized I had not breathed since I had left the C&A. BUT I HAD DONE IT! And I was so proud of myself! I selected a black skirt suit with white stripes and a zippered jacket top to wear to the cocktail party, then spent the next two hours getting ready. When I was done, I checked myself out in the mirror—and went out anyway!

The one-block walk to Crowne Pointe was so short that I didn't have time to get scared. Besides, I was starting (mind you, only STARTING) to feel a little better. After all, I had managed to stroll outdoors twice already and no one had laughed at me, pointed fingers, or even snickered. I was amazed! The cocktail party was absolutely fabulous! I had never been to one before, not even as a man. I was greeted at the door by the owners of Crowne Point, who very graciously welcomed me and THANKED me for coming. Nothing in my entire life had ever made me feel so much like a lady. I was directed to a bar where I was handed a cosmopolitan (a delicious pink mixed drink that looked very feminine and was served in a fluted glass). I began to mingle.

Some of the other Fair attendees were already there. Most seemed comfortable in this surrounding. People chatted over here and laughed and joked over there. I quickly noticed to my surprise that most didn't even try to disguise their voices. Some of the women were very beautiful and some were simply passable, but the vast majority were girls like me who would have a hard time sneaking past a blind man without being discovered.

As I walked toward the rear of the house to what appeared to be the sitting area, I passed through a huge, beautiful, formal dining room with a banquet-sized table at one end and a baby grand piano at the other. The sitting room itself was lavishly appointed with beautiful furniture. I felt like a debutante. I meekly squeaked out a few polite hellos as I walked past people and found a place to sit. Another woman struck up a conversation with me as if I were her long lost sister, and I soon started to become comfortable in this surrounding. It felt as if we were just a bunch a women out for an elegant evening. Across the room, two beautiful genetic women were chatting away and laughing with two of our girls. When one of them walked past me, she paused to tell me my suit was gorgeous, and introduced herself. I nervously thanked her, but when she looked deeply into my eyes, I nearly died. She called her friend over, introduced her as her lesbian partner, then said, "Doesn't she have the most beautiful eyes you ever saw?" I could hardly believe my ears. I was being complimented by a real woman!

They began giving me pointers on eye makeup to enhance my eyes and beauty tips on eye shadow and face makeup. One of them took the zipper of my jacket and slid it down a bit to expose my (lack of) cleavage, explaining that if I took some makeup and put a little here and there it would give the illusion of cleavage. Then she pointed out that next time I should wear a black bra under the outfit. Perhaps I should have been embarrassed by that, but I wasn't. It was my first GIRL TALK, and I loved it. They made me feel so comfortable, like one of the gals, and we chatted like this was the way it was supposed to be! Little by little, the rooms filled, until you could barely move, and little by little, more and more of Allana came to the surface. My knees went together automatically as my ankles crossed and slipped under my chair. My hands found themselves folded femininely in my lap, and I began to feel more comfortable in my female persona than I ever had in my life. This was Allana, and she was finally home!

When you've hidden inside the box for more than forty years, as I have, and it has become your entire, comfortable little crossdressing world, it's hard to even imagine that anything else exists. When your secret life has become so routine that your second self, screaming to come out, amounts to nothing more than another trip to the back of the closet to drag out those dusty suitcases where you keep your life hidden from view like one of Aunt Sophie's reindeer sweaters, and you double- and triple-check to make sure you've put it all away again so nothing is missed that might out you to your family and friends, even the mere idea of a life outside the box seems like a cruel joke.

To allow yourself to think, for even a second, that there might be a place outside that box, outside your secret little world, where you could go and be who you want to be in a real-world setting, surrounded by people who are literally aching to give you all the support, encouragement, and love you could ever dream of, would surely be nothing more than fantasy.

But to suddenly find that it's not just some joke, it's not just a fantasy, that it's real, and does exist, to finally not just peek over the top edge of the box, but come out of the box completely and, for one preciously fleeting week of your life, experience the pure magical wonder of it, to be literally reborn and be able to hold in your hands everything you ever dreamed of and be allowed for the very first time to be a whole person, is such a wonderfully life-altering experience that it's well worth the personal hell it costs to then have to give it all up and go back into the box! It took me three years to build up the courage to attend the Fair because I had never, that's right, NEVER set foot out of the house dressed as a woman before. You want to talk scared? I was petrified! That first day, Sunday, was the turning point for me. Monday served to further build my confidence. By Tuesday, I was waltzing down Commercial Street and all over Provincetown with my "head up and tits out," walking my best female walk and looking people in the eye as I greeted them with a smile and a pleasant hello in a softer version of my own voice. In fact, I was so comfortable by Wednesday that I stopped a local woman on the street to ask directions.

"Excuse me," I asked, "but have I passed Napi's Restaurant?"

"No sir, er, ma'am," she blushingly replied.

I laughed, patted her femininely on the arm, and said "that's okay . . . I'm not sure yet, either."

We both laughed, and she said, "In that case, good morning. It's right down at the next corner." I thanked her, and as I began to walk away she said, "I hope you enjoy the week." I almost cried.

On Saturday night, the last night of the Fair, there was a very elegant final banquet and awards ceremony. One award, Miss Cinderella, is voted on by everyone who attends the Fair. This award goes to the first-timer who best overcame her fears and went on to enjoy her female identity throughout the Fair. By the night of the banquet I was so comfortable in my female identity that I was feeling as if this was the way life was supposed to be for crossdressers. Everything was just so natural that I felt like a princess in a fairy tale. I was stunned when I heard I was a runner-up for Miss Cinderella!

No, I didn't win it, and I didn't expect to, either. So many other wonderful sisters who were also there for their first Fair had overcome much more difficult obstacles than I. Besides, I wasn't trying to win an award, I was just enjoying, for the first time in my life, the freedom of being me. Still, I couldn't believe so many had actually voted for me. I cried like a lady!

EVERYONE in Provincetown was so nice to us and so accepting that it would be almost impossible to be uncomfortable there. I'm convinced that there is nowhere else in the world where I could have come so far in such a short period of time. During the week, I made many new friends and bonded with so many sisters. It was absolutely amazing! Everyone had the same story. Everyone knew where you were coming from. Everyone could identify with you. I met transgendered folks from all over the United States, from Mexico, Colombia, Canada, England, and even from as far away as Scandinavia, and every one of them was my girlfriend instantly! It's like a wonderful, worldwide, secret sorority, but instead of a secret handshake, we use skirts to identify each other.

Some were passable, others (like me) weren't. Some were tall, some short, some fat, some thin. Some had wonderful female voices and others sounded like truck drivers. One even had a full male beard! And every single one of them, EVERY ONE! was open, warm, friendly, unassuming, non-judgmental, completely accepting, and ready to offer a huge warm, heart-felt hug at the drop of a hat! Throughout my lifetime, I have truly felt that I have been in the right place at exactly the right time only three times. The first two times were at the hospitals when my sons were born. The last was my first Fantasia Fair!

It's hard to describe what it's like to come out of the box for the very first time in your life, or to explain the overwhelming depth of suppressed emotions that come flooding to the surface in torrential waves when it finally happens. Unless you have experienced it yourself, it's impossible to convey in written words the wonderful feeling of absolute freedom to actually be the woman who has hidden deep inside the darkest recesses of your being for your entire life. It is an unequalled opportunity to explore your inner self, to evaluate your life, to learn who you truly are, and to laugh and to cry.

The hardest part of Fantasia Fair for all first-timers isn't taking that first step outdoors—it's leaving the Fair! They call it the pink fog—that extraordinary sense of self you acquire during the Fair—the feeling of normalcy, wholeness, and oneness, a feeling that everything is now right in the world. It fills us with hopes and dreams and, sadly, the fantasy that we don't ever have to go back into the box. For some that is true; Fantasia Fair is a turning point in their lives from which they never return. They go on to live their lives outside the box, being who they want to be. For others like me, sadly, it is not. Social pressures, work demands, and family relationships are too great to overcome and make it impossible for us to remain outside. The pink fog has special meaning to those of us who must pack our lives, our selves, back into those dusty suitcases and bury them deep into the back of the closet, back into the box once more. We must go on with only the memory of who we really are. We struggle each day to hold on to the identity and the love we found that week in Provincetown, as, day by day, it slips further and further from our grasp.

We try to return to who we were before the Fair, but that's impossible. To paraphrase a few lines from *The Velveteen Rabbit*: "Real isn't how you are made, real is what you become, and once you become real, you can never be unreal again." So a song on the radio, the faint scent of a certain perfume, the sound of high heels clicking across a room, or the fleeting memory of a special moment at the Fair wells up inside you until you find yourself driving down the road with tears streaming down your face.

25

THE CASE OF SHARON KOWALSKI AND KAREN THOMPSON
Ableism, Heterosexism, and Sexism

Joan L. Griscom

In November, 1983, Sharon Kowalski was in a head-on collision with a drunk driver, suffered a severe brain-stem injury, became paralyzed, and lost the ability to speak. Sharon was in a committed partnership with Karen Thompson. Serious conflict soon developed between Karen and Kowalski's parents, erupting in a series of lawsuits that lasted eight years. Karen fought to secure adequate rehabilitation for

Reprinted with the permission of the author.

Sharon as well as access to friends and family of her choice. In 1985, acting under Minnesota guardianship laws, Sharon's father placed her in a nursing home without adequate rehabilitation services and prohibited Karen and others from visiting her. Karen continued to fight through the courts and the media. In 1989, Sharon was finally transferred to an appropriate rehabilitation facility, reunited with lover and friends, and, in 1991, finally allowed her choice to live with Karen.

In this article I tell the story of Sharon Kowalski and Karen Thompson. While the story shows violations of their human rights, it is more than a story of two individuals. The injustices they encountered were modes of oppression that operate at a social-structural level and affect many other people. These oppressions include ableism, discrimination against disabled persons; heterosexism, the structuring of our institutions to legitimate only heterosexual relationships; and sexism, discrimination against women. Their story shows the power of structural discrimination, the intertwining of both our medical and legal systems in ways that denied both of them the fullest quality of life.

A History of the Events

By November 1983, Sharon and Karen had lived in partnership for almost four years. Karen was thirty-six, teaching physical education at St. Cloud State University, devoutly religious, conservative. Sharon was twenty-seven, a fine athlete who had graduated from St. Cloud in physical education and just accepted a staff coaching position. She had grown up in the Iron Mine area of Minnesota, a conservative world where women are expected to marry young. Defying such expectations, she became first in her family to attend college, earning tuition working part-time in the mines. After she and Karen fell in love, they exchanged rings, bought a house together, and vowed lifetime commitment.

After the accident Sharon lay in a coma for weeks, and doctors were pessimistic about her recovery. Karen spent hours, daily, talking to her, reading the Bible, massaging and stretching her neck, shoulders, and hands. It is essential to massage and stretch brain-injured persons in comas, for their muscles tend to curl up tightly and incur permanent damage. Early in 1984, Karen saw Sharon moving her right index finger, and found that she could indicate answers to questions by moving it. Later she began to tap her fingers, then slowly learned to write letters and words.

The Kowalski parents became suspicious of the long hours Karen was spending with her, and increasingly Karen feared they would try to exclude her from Sharon's life. After consulting a psychologist, she wrote them a letter explaining their love, in hopes they would understand her importance to Sharon. They reacted with shock, denial, and rage. As the nightmare deepened, Karen consulted a lawyer and learned she had no legal rights, unless she won guardianship. In March, 1984, she therefore filed for guardianship, and Donald Kowalski counterfiled.

Guardianship was awarded to Kowalski, but Karen was granted equal access to medical and financial information and full visitation rights. She continued to participate in both physical and occupational therapy. Sharon improved slowly; Karen made her an alphabet board, and she began to spell out answers to questions. Later she began to communicate by typewriter, and in August spoke a few words. But conflicts continued. The day after the court decision Kowalski incorrectly told Karen she did not have visitation rights, and later tried to cancel her work with Sharon's therapists. When Karen and others took Sharon out on day passes, he objected, subsequently testifying in court that he did not want her out in public. In October, Sharon was moved further away, and Kowalski filed to gain full power as guardian. Karen counterfiled to remove him as guardian.

Months elapsed while the legal battles were fought. Sharon was moved several times, regressed in her skills, and became clinically depressed. The Minnesota Civil Liberties Union (MCLU) entered the case, arguing that under the First Amendment Sharon's rights of free speech and free association were being violated. A tri-county Handicap Services Program submitted testimony of Sharon's capacity to communicate, including a long conversation in which she stated she was gay and Karen was her lover. At Sharon's request, the MCLU asked to represent her and suggested she might testify for herself. The court refused both requests, finding that Sharon lacked understanding to make decisions for herself. In July, 1985, Kowalski was awarded full guardianship. Within a day, he denied visitation to Karen, other friends, the MCLU, and disability rights groups; in two days he transferred her to a nursing home near his home with only minimal rehabilitation facilities. In August, 1985, Karen saw Sharon for what would be the last time for over three years.

As this summary indicates, the medical system failed Sharon in at least three respects. First, it failed to supply rehabilitation in the years when it was vital to her recovery. Stark in the medical record is the fact that this woman who was starting to stand and to feed herself was locked away for over three years with an implanted feeding tube, left insufficiently stretched so that muscles that had been starting to work curled back on themselves again. Second, she was deprived of the bombardment of emotional and physical stimulation needed to regenerate her cognitive faculties. Once in the nursing home, for example, she was forbidden regenerative outside excursions. Third, although medical staff often recognized Sharon's unusual response to Karen, they failed to explain to her parents its importance. Despite an urgent need for counseling to assist the parents, none, except for one court-mandated session, took place.

The failure of the medical system was consistently supported by the legal system. Initially the court ruled that Sharon must have access to a young-adult rehabilitation ward. But once Kowalski won full guardianship, he was able to move her to a nursing home without such a ward. In 1985 the Office of Health Facility Complaints investigated Sharon's right to choose visitors, a right guaranteed by the Minnesota Patient Bill of Rights, and found that indeed her right was being violated. However, the appeals court held that the Patient Bill of Rights was inapplicable, since the healthcare facility was not restricting the right of visitation, the guardian was.

The deficiencies of guardianship law are a central problem in this case. First, a guardian can restrict a person's rights, without legal recourse. As is often said, under present laws a guardian can lock up a person and throw away the key. This is a national problem, affecting the disabled, the elderly, anyone presumed incompetent. Second, guardians are inadequately supervised. Under Minnesota law, a guardian is required to have the ward tested annually for competence. Kowalski never did, and for over three years the courts did not require him to. In 1985, Karen first filed a motion to hold him in contempt for failure to arrange testing and for failure to heed Sharon's wishes for visitation. The courts routinely rejected such motions.

Between 1985 and 1988, Karen and the MCLU pursued repeated appeals to various Minnesota courts, all denied. Karen began to seek help from the media, also disability, gay/lesbian, women's, and church groups. She recognized that the legal precedents could be devastating for others, e.g., gay/lesbian couples or unmarried heterosexual couples. The reserved, closeted, conservative professor was slowly transformed into a passionate public speaker in her quest to secure freedom and rehabilitation for Sharon; and slowly she gained national attention. The alternative press responded; national groups such as the National Organization for Women were supportive; the National Committee to Free Sharon Kowalski formed, with regional chapters. Finally the mainstream media began publishing concerned articles; Karen appeared on national TV programs; state and national politicians, including Jesse Jackson, spoke out. Meanwhile Sharon remained in the nursing home, cut off from friends, physically regressed, psychologically depressed.

The first break in the case came in February, 1988. In response to a new motion from Karen, requesting that Sharon be tested for competence, testing was ordered. In January, 1989, she was moved to the Miller-Dwan Medical Center for a 60-day evaluation. Kowalski unsuccessfully argued in court against both the move and the testing. Sharon immediately expressed her wish to see Karen. On February 2, 1989, Karen visited her for the first time in three and a half years, an event which made banner headlines in the alternative press across the nation. She was, however, highly depressed, with numerous physical problems: for example, her feet had curled up so tightly that she was no longer able to stand. More significant was her cognitive ability; to this day, her short-term memory loss remains considerable.

The competency evaluation nevertheless demonstrated that she could communicate on an adult level and had significant potential for rehabilitation. The report recommended "her return to pre-morbid home environment," and added:

> We believe Sharon has shown areas of potential and ability to make rational choices in many areas of her life. She has consistently indicated a desire to return home . . . to live with Karen Thompson again.

Donald Kowalski subsequently resigned as guardian, for both financial and health reasons, and the parents stopped attending medical conferences. In June, 1989, Sharon was transferred to a long-term rehabilitation center for brain-injured young adults. Here she had extensive occupational, physical, and speech therapy. Again Karen spent hours with her and took her out on trips. She had surgery on her legs, feet, toes, left shoulder and arm to reverse the results of three years of inadequate care. She began to use a speech synthesizer and a motorized wheelchair.

Karen subsequently filed for guardianship. Medical staff testified unanimously that Sharon was capable of deciding for herself what relationships she wanted and where she wished to live. They testified that she was capable of living outside an institution and Karen was best qualified to care for her in a home environment. Witnesses for the Kowalskis opposed the petition. The judge appeared increasingly uncomfortable with the national publicity. While in 1990 he allowed Sharon and Karen to fly out to San Francisco where each received a Woman of Courage Award from the National Organization for Women, he refused Sharon permission to attend the first Disability Pride Day in Boston. He issued a gag order against Karen, which was overturned on appeal. Finally, in April, 1991, he denied Karen guardianship and awarded it to a supposedly "neutral third party," a former classmate of Sharon who lived near the Kowalski parents and had testified against Karen in a 1984 hearing. This decision raised the alarming possibility that Sharon might be returned to the inadequate facility. Karen appealed it.

In December, 1991, the appeals court reversed the judge's ruling and granted guardianship to Karen, on two bases: first, the medical testimony that Sharon was able to make her own choices; and second, the fact that the two women are "a family of affinity" that deserves respect. This is a major decision in U.S. legal history, setting important legal precedents both for disabled people and gay/lesbian families. Sharon and Karen now live together.

The Three Modes of Oppression

Sharon and Karen were denied their rights by three interacting systems of oppression: ableism, heterosexism, and sexism. Originally Karen believed that their difficulties were merely personal problems. All her life she had believed that our social institutions are basically fair, designed to support individual rights. In the book she co-authored with Julie Andrzejewski[1], she documented her growing awareness that widespread social/political forces were involved in their supposedly personal problems and that the oppression they experienced was systemic.

Ableism was rampant throughout. Sharon's inability to speak was often construed as incompetence, and her particular kinds of communication were not recognized. Quite early Karen noticed some did not speak to Sharon, some talked loudly as if she was deaf, others spoke to her as if she were a child. One doctor discussed her in her presence as if she was not there. When Karen later asked how she felt about this, she typed out "Shitty." Probably one reason she responded to Karen more than anyone was that Karen talked extensively and read to her, played music, asked questions, and constantly consulted her wishes. Although the MCLU and the Handicap Services Program submitted transcripts of long conversations with her, the courts did not accept these as evidence of competence, relying instead on testimony from people who had much less interaction with her. A major article in the St. Paul *Pioneer Press* (1987) described the Kowalskis visiting the room "where their eerily silent daughter lies trapped in her twisted body." Eerily silent? This is the person who typed out "columbine" when asked her favorite flower, answered arithmetical questions correctly, and responded to numerous questions about her life, feelings, and wishes. She also communicates nonverbally in many ways: gestures, smiles, tears, and laughter.

Thanks to ableism, Sharon was often stereotyped as helpless. The presumption of helplessness "traps" her far more severely than her "twisted body." Once a person is labeled helpless, there is no need to consult her wishes, consider her written communications, hear her testimony. When Sharon arrived at Miller-Dwan for competency testing, Karen reported with joy that staff was giving her information and allowing her choices, even if her choice was to do nothing. Most seriously, if a person is seen as helpless, then there is no potential for rehabilitation. As Ellen Bilofsky[2] has written, Sharon was presumed "incompetent until proven competent." If Karen's legal motion for competency testing had not been accepted, Sharon might have remained in the nursing home indefinitely, presumed incompetent.

Finally, ableism can lead to keeping disabled persons hidden, literally out of sight. Kowalski argued against day passes, resisted Karen's efforts to take Sharon out, and testified he would not take her to a church or shopping center because he did not wish to put her "on display . . . in her condition." Although medical staff could see that outside trips provided Sharon with pleasure and stimulation, both important for cognitive rehabilitation, they cooperated with the father in denying them. According to an article in the *Washington Post*, he once said, "What the hell difference does it make if she's gay or lesbian or straight or anything because she's laying there in diapers? . . . let the poor kid rest in peace."

Invisible in the nursing home, cut off from lover and friends, Sharon had little chance to demonstrate competence. The wonder is that after three and a half years of loss, loneliness, and lack of care, she was able to emerge from her depression and respond to her competency examiners. To retain her capacity for response, through such an experience, suggests a strong spirit.

The second mode of oppression infusing this case is heterosexism, the structuring of our institutions so as to legitimate heterosexuality only. Glaringly apparent is the failure to recognize gay/lesbian partnerships. When Karen was first to arrive at the hospital after the accident, she was not allowed access to Sharon or even any information, because she was not "family." Seeing her anguish, a Roman Catholic priest interceded, brought information, and arranged for a doctor to speak with her. Although the two women considered themselves married, in law they were not, and therefore lacked any legal rights as a couple. If heterosexual, there would have been no denial of visitation, no long nightmare of the three-and-a-half year separation. While unmarried heterosexual partners might have trouble securing guardianship, married partners would not.

Because of heterosexism, Sharon's emotional need for her partner and Karen's rehabilitative effect on her were not honored. Because of Sharon's response, Karen was often included in the therapeutic work. Yet, prior to 1989, medical staff often refused to testify to this positive effect. Perhaps they feared condoning the same-sex relationship, perhaps they wished to stay out of the conflict. One neurologist, Dr. Keith Larson, did testify, although stipulating that he spoke as friend of the court, not as witness for Karen.

> The reason I'm here today is . . . to deliver an observation that I have agonized over and thought a great deal about, and prayed a little bit. . . . I cannot help but say that Sharon's friend, Karen, can get out of Sharon physical actions, attempts at vocalization, and longer periods of alertness and attention than can really any of our professional therapists.

Why was it necessary to "agonize" over this testimony? Pray about it? Make such a tremendous effort? Clearly, were one of the partners male, Larson would have had no difficulty. He simply would have reported that the patient responded to her partner. Some medical staff did testify positively, without effort; and after 1989, testimony from medical personnel was strong and unanimous. However, repeatedly, the courts ignored it.

Finally, heterosexism is evident in a consistent tendency to exaggerate the role of sex in same-sex relationships. Many believe that the lives of gay/lesbian people revolve around sex, though evidence from all social-psychological research is that homosexual people are no more sexually active than heterosexual people. Further, gay/lesbian sex is often perceived as sexual exploitation rather than an expression of mutual caring. The final denial of Karen's visitation rights was based on the charge that she might sexually abuse Sharon. A physician hired by the Kowalskis, Dr. William L. Wilson, leveled this charge:

> Karen Thompson has been involved in bathing Sharon Kowalski behind a closed door for a prolonged period of time. . . . Ms. Thompson has [also] alleged a sexual relationship with Sharon Kowalski that existed prior to the accident. Based on this knowledge and my best medical judgment . . . I feel that visits by Karen Thompson at this time would expose Sharon Kowalski to a high risk of sexual abuse.

Accordingly, Wilson directed the nursing home staff not to let Karen visit. Even though under statutes, Karen could have continued to visit while the court decisions were under appeal, the nursing home was obliged to obey the doctor's order.

In this instance, ableism and heterosexism merge. If they were unmarried heterosexual partners, sexual abuse probably would not have been an issue. If married, the issue would not exist. Ableism often denies disabled persons their sexuality, though a person does not lose her sexuality simply because she becomes disabled. Also, a person who loses the capacity to speak has a special need for touching. What were Sharon's sexual rights? When she was starting to emerge from the coma, she once reached out and touched Karen's breast, and later placed Karen's hand on her breast. At the time Karen did not dare ask medical advice for fear of revealing their relationship. Even to raise such questions might have exposed her to more charges of sexual abuse.

While same-sex relationships are often called "anti-family" in our heterosexist society, actually such relationships create family, in that they create stable emotional and economic units. Family, in this sense, may be defined as a kin-like unit of two or more persons related by blood, marriage, adoption, or primary commitment, who usually share the same household. Sharon and Karen considered themselves married. Karen's long pilgrimage over almost nine years testifies to an extraordinary depth of commitment. Sharon consistently said she was gay, Karen was her lover, she wanted to live with her. While marriage has historically occurred between two sexes, history cannot determine its definition. In U.S. history, marriage between black and white persons was forbidden for centuries. In 1967, when the Supreme Court finally declared miscegenation laws unconstitutional, there were still such laws in sixteen states.

Sexism is sufficiently interfused with heterosexism that they are hard to separate. Often sexism enforces a social role on women in which they are subordinated to men. Women in the Minnesota world where Sharon grew up were expected to marry young and submit to their husbands' authority, an intrinsically sexist model. According to this model, her partnership with Karen was illegitimate. Sexism also is apparent in awarding guardianship to the father. Had Sharon been a man rather than a twenty-eight-year-old "girl," such a decision might be less possible; but in a sexist society, it is appropriate to assign an adult woman to her male parent. Finally, our society devalues friendship, especially between women. Once, very early, a doctor advised Karen to forget Sharon. The gist of his remarks was that "Sharon's parents will always be her parents. They have to deal with this, but you don't. Maybe you should go back to leading your own life." Friendship between the two women was unimportant. Ableism as well as sexism is apparent in these remarks.

This case makes clear that the modes of oppression work simultaneously. Like Audre Lorde[3], I argue that "there is no hierarchy of oppression." Disability was not more important than sexuality in curtailing Sharon's freedoms; they worked together seamlessly, in her life as in the legal and medical systems. Admittedly, any individual's perspective on the case may reflect the issue most central to her or his life: e.g., the gay press, reporting the case, emphasized heterosexism, and the disability rights press emphasized ableism. Working in coalition on this case, some women were ill at ease with disability rights activists; and some disability rights groups were anxious about associating with gay/lesbian issues. But there are lesbians and gays in the disabled community, and disabled folks in women's groups. Karen experienced the inseparability of the issues once when invited to speak to a Presbyterian group. They asked her to speak only about ableism since they had already "done" gay/lesbian concerns. She tried, but found it nearly impossible; she had to censor her material, ignore basic facts, leave out crucial connections.

In each mode of oppression, one group of persons takes power over another, and this power is institutionalized. Disabled people, women, gay men and lesbians, and others are all to some degree denied their full personhood by the structures of our society. Their choices can be denied, their sexuality is controlled. On the basis of ableism, heterosexism, and sexism, both Karen Thompson's and Sharon Kowalski's opportunities for the fullest quality of life were taken from them. Sharon lost cognitive ability that might have been saved. As the Minnesota Civil Liberties Union put it, "The convicted criminal loses only his or her liberty; Sharon Kowalski has lost the right to choose whom she may see, who she may like, and who she may love." To change this picture took nearly nine years of struggle by a partner who lived out her vow of lifetime commitment and the work of many committed persons and groups.

Conclusion

Many national groups joined the struggle to provide rehabilitation for Sharon and bring her home, including disability rights activists, gays and lesbians, feminists and male supporters, and civil rights groups. In addition there were thousands of people drawn to this case by simple human rights. After all, any of us could be hit by a drunk driver, become disabled, and in the process lose our legal and medical rights. The Kowalski/Thompson case stands as a warning that in our deeply divided society, freedom is still a privilege and rights are fragile.

People living in nontraditional families need legal protection to secure legal and medical rights. Karen Thompson stresses the importance of making your relationships known to your family of birth, if possible, and informing them of your wishes in case of disability or death. Also, it is essential to execute a durable power of attorney, a document that stipulates a person to make medical and financial decisions for you, in case of need. Copies should be given to your physician. While requirements vary between states and powers of attorney are not always enforceable, they may protect your rights. Information about how to execute them may be found in your public library, in consultation with a competent lawyer, or in Appendix B of the book *Why Can't Sharon Kowalski Come Home?*

NOTES

1. Karen Thompson and Julie Andrzejewski. *Why Can't Sharon Kowalski Come Home?* San Francisco: Spinster/Aunt Lute, 1988. All quotations in text are from this book.

2. Ellen Bilofsky. "The Fragile Rights of Sharon Kowalski." *Health/PAC Bulletin*, 1989, 19, 4–16.

3. Audre Lorde. "There Is No Hierarchy of Oppressions." *Interracial Books for Children Bulletin*, 1983, 14, 9.

26

LAME

Joyce Davies

Several words describe the person who cannot walk in an ordinary fashion. My own personal preference is "physically limited" for a rather formal description and plain, old-fashioned "lame" as a short (and somehow *loving*) adjective. "Orthopedically handicapped" is fair enough. But here I conjure up visions of huge rehabilitation clinics or state senators reading amendments in proper medical and legal terms. The two words together are exact but cold. "Handicapped" alone is far too inclusive to apply with much realism to those who cannot walk well, for it has become a grab-bag word that embraces an enormous population of deaf, blind, speech-impaired, and mentally impaired individuals.

"Disabled" goes "handicapped" one better. Here there are legal overtones. To be classified as "disabled" one usually needs a medical stamp to prove inability to earn a living, and this can apply to anyone who is out of commission from a physical or mental illness. Yet both "handicapped" and "disabled" are handy tags to hang on those who get around with crutches or a walker or a wheelchair. They slip out in ordinary conversation and who am I to mind? I use the words myself.

But "crippled" is an ugly and stumbling word. There is no dignity there at all—only a picture of someone twisted, pitiful, poor, and not very bright. This is a personal prejudice that took hold long ago for reasons sunk deep in the subconscious. But I find when I use "crippled," I am stressing the harshness and purely *physical* fact of paralysis. The word, in its dark intensity, blots out the power and the hope of the spirit.

Of course, "lame" is not an accurate description for a person who cannot walk at all; only paralyzed applies here. But, oh, the hope for improvement embodied in the word "lame"! Perhaps that is one of its appealing connotations, suggesting a mild affliction, though sometimes a stretching of the truth. Once I received a letter from a friend who had a slow recovery from a fall, and she mentioned with beautiful carelessness that we had so much in common with our children and "our lameness." I treasure her conception of me not as disabled or crippled or even handicapped, but simply lame. She is right. To be able to walk with crutches, even though one must resort to a wheelchair in some situations, should classify a person as "lame" if she wishes.

I should like to resurrect the word "lame" because it is gentle and informal. Though there is often more to it than that, we who walk with difficulty are primarily lame and far more fortunate than those thousands of men, women, and children who cannot leave their wheelchairs at all. If "lame" should seem a vague term like "thin" or "fat" or "pretty," so much the better. Most of us would like nothing more than to melt in with the crowd—unlabeled, almost unnoticed.

We had a cat once who appeared, half-starved, at the door to request family membership along with three other cats. One of her paws took a very long time to reach the ground, so she devised an alternate way to walk, scorning the slow limp, and she simply hopped like a rabbit with her three strong legs. Still she had to rest a lot. Fortunately for her, cats have few responsibilities beyond self-preservation and cleanliness and she could accomplish those near the house. The other cats were quite gentle with her, as if they sensed she couldn't handle a hard fight. Yet she was expected to make her own way. No one put a supper dish under her nose or pushed her onto safe high ground in the midst of a dog attack.

And so it was for many of us who went home from a long hospitalization [for polio] thirty years ago. There was no real follow-up care as there is now. We were on our own, especially if we lived far from therapists and the orthopedic specialists who were working full time on new polio cases anyway.

It became a very personal matter between you and your stubborn body. Certain maneuvers failed, and so you tried others. There was a bit of black magic to these first attempts because you didn't plan consciously to get up from a chair in a specific way that came as an inspiration in the middle of the night. Rather you were propelled by a mysterious force—the driving power of muscles unknown to you—to move your body this way or that until something worked. Babies know this. Their first tentative steps are individual tries at speeding life up a bit. They see people *walking*—a truly fascinating activity. No one lectures them with the scientific approach of a quadracep muscle straining to pull in a forward motion. First one little leg, then another; try and fail; try and fail. If babies stopped to analyze or criticize each attempt, the discouragement level would be too much. Instead their innocent minds shed worry and gather faith that nature has a formula for walking—never mind what it might be.

During my first few weeks at home I discovered from nowhere that I could lock my leg braces, turn around in a chair, stiffen my arms, push with the strong left bicep muscle, and back off to a standing position. This opened up a whole new world. I could grab my crutches and practice walking any old time. Alone. Nature (that old black magic) was on my side. Together we backed into a way of life with the premise that any attempt at motion was better than none at all. Even with an incorrect gait, frightening falls, and the speed of a tortoise, the upright approach beat years in a wheelchair.

My ingenious husband designed stools, ramps, arm slings, and kitchen equipment so that we could remain an independent family. Having been separated too long by war and a wayward virus, we wanted to take care of each other again. There was a strong natural incentive to adjust. But, for my part, I did a most imperfect job. I was asked many times during the first year at home, and am still asked, "How in the world do you manage?" The answer remains, "Not very well. Just average." Sometimes an abundance of love rather than determination makes things possible, if not smooth-running.

27

C. P. ELLIS

Studs Terkel

We're in his office in Durham, North Carolina. He is the business manager of the International Union of Operating Engineers. On the wall is a plaque: "Certificate of Service, in recognition to C. P. Ellis, for your faithful service to the city in having served as a member of the Durham Human Relations Council. February 1977."

At one time, he had been president (exalted cyclops) of the Durham chapter of the Ku Klux Klan . . .

He is fifty-three years old.

My father worked in a textile mill in Durham. He died at forty-eight years old. It was probably from cotton dust. Back then, we never heard of brown lung. I was about seventeen years old and had a mother and sister depending on somebody to make a livin'. It was just barely enough insurance to cover his burial. I had to quit school and go to work. I was about eighth grade when I quit.

My father worked hard but never had enough money to buy decent clothes. When I went to school, I never seemed to have adequate clothes to wear. I always left school late afternoon with a sense of inferiority. The other kids had nice

From *American Dreams* by Studs Terkel. Reprinted by permission of Donaldio & Olson, Inc. Copyright © 1980 by Studs Terkel.

clothes, and I just had what Daddy could buy. I still got some of those inferiority feelin's now that I have to overcome once in a while.

I loved my father. He would go with me to ball games. We'd go fishin' together. I was really ashamed of the way he'd dress. He would take this money and give it to me instead of putting it on himself. I always had the feeling about somebody looking at him and makin' fun of him and makin' fun of me. I think it had to do somethin' with my life.

My father and I were very close, but we didn't talk about too many intimate things. He did have a drinking problem. During the week, he would work every day, but weekend he was ready to get plastered. I can understand when a guy looks at his paycheck and looks at his bills, and he's worried hard all the week, and his bills are larger than his paycheck. He'd done the best he could the entire week, and there seemed to be no hope. It's an illness thing. Finally you just say: "The heck with it. I'll just get drunk and forget it."

My father was out of work during the depression, and I remember going with him to the finance company uptown, and he was turned down. That's something that's always stuck.

My father never seemed to be happy. It was a constant struggle with him just like it was for me. It's very seldom I'd see him laugh. He was just tryin' to figure out what he could do from one day to the next.

After several years pumping gas at a service station, I got married. We had to have children. Four. One child was born blind and retarded, which was a real additional expense to us. He's never spoken a word. He doesn't know me when I go to see him. But I see him, I hug his neck. I talk to him, tell him I love him. I don't know whether he knows me or not, but I know he's well taken care of. All my life, I had work, never a day without work, worked all the overtime I could get and still could not survive financially. I began to say there's somethin' wrong with this country. I worked my butt off and just never seemed to break even.

I had some real great ideas about this great nation. (Laughs.) They say to abide by the law, go to church, do right and live for the Lord, and everything'll work out. But it didn't work out. It just kept gettin' worse and worse.

I was workin' a bread route. The highest I made one week was seventy-five dollars. The rent on our house was about twelve dollars a week. I will never forget: outside of this house was a 265-gallon oil drum, and I never did get enough money to fill up that oil drum. What I would do every night, I would run up to the store and buy five gallons of oil and climb up the ladder and pour it in that 265-gallon drum. I could hear that five gallons when it hits the bottom of that oil drum, splatters, and it sounds like it's nothin' in there. But it would keep the house warm for the night. Next day you'd have to do the same thing.

I left the bread route with fifty dollars in my pocket. I went to the bank and I borrowed four thousand dollars to buy the service station. I worked seven days a week, open and close, and finally had a heart attack. Just about two months before the last payments of that loan. My wife had done the best she could to keep it runnin'. Tryin' to come out of that hole, I just couldn't do it.

I really began to get bitter. I didn't know who to blame. I tried to find somebody. I began to blame it on black people. I had to hate somebody. Hatin' America is hard to do because you can't see it to hate it. You gotta have somethin' to look at to hate. (Laughs.) The natural person for me to hate would be black people, because my father before me was a member of the Klan. As far as he was concerned, it was the savior of the white people. It was the only organization in the world that would take care of the white people. So I began to admire the Klan.

I got active in the Klan while I was at the service station. Every Monday night, a group of men would come by and buy a Coca-Cola, go back to the car, take a few drinks, and come back and stand around talkin'. I couldn't help but wonder: Why are these dudes comin' out every Monday? They said they were with the Klan and have meetings close-by. Would I be interested? Boy, that was an opportunity I really looked forward to! To be part of somethin'. I joined the Klan, went from member to chaplain, from chaplain to vice-president, from vice-president to president. The title is exalted cyclops.

The first night I went with the fellas, they knocked on the door and gave the signal. They sent some robed Klansmen to talk to me and give me some instructions. I was led into a large meeting room, and this was the time of my life! It was thrilling. Here's a guy who's worked all his life and struggled all his life to be something, and here's the moment to be something. I will never forget it. Four robed Klansmen led me into the hall. The lights were dim, and the only thing you could see was an illuminated cross. I knelt before the cross. I had to make certain vows and promises. We promised to uphold the purity of the white race, fight communism, and protect white womanhood.

After I had taken my oath, there was loud applause goin' throughout the buildin', musta been at least four hundred people. For this one little ol' person. It was a thrilling moment for C. P. Ellis.

It disturbs me when people who do not really know what it's all about are so very critical of individual Klansmen. The majority of 'em are low-income whites, people who really don't have a part in something. They have been shut out as well as the blacks. Some are not very well educated either. Just like myself. We had a lot of support from doctors and lawyers and police officers.

Maybe they've had bitter experiences in this life and they had to hate somebody. So the natural person to hate would be the black person. He's beginnin' to come up, he's beginnin' to learn to read and start votin' and run for political office. Here are white people who are supposed to be superior to them, and we're shut out.

I can understand why people join extreme right-wing or left-wing groups. They're in the same boat I was. Shut out. Deep down inside, we want to be part of this great society. Nobody listens, so we join these groups.

At one time, I was state organizer of the National Rights party. I organized a youth group for the Klan. I felt we were getting old and our generation's gonna die. So I contacted certain kids in schools. They were havin' racial problems. On the first night, we had a hundred high school students. When they came in the door, we had "Dixie" playin'. These kids were just thrilled to death. I begin to hold weekly meetin's with 'em, teachin' the principles of the Klan. At that time, I believed Martin Luther King had Communist connections. I began to teach that Andy Young was affiliated with the Communist party.

I had a call one night from one of our kids. He was about twelve. He said: "I just been robbed downtown by two niggers." I'd had a couple of drinks and that really teed me off. I go downtown and couldn't find the kid. I got worried. I saw two young black people. I had the .32 revolver with me. I said: "Nigger, you seen a little young white boy up here? I just got a call from him and was told that some niggers robbed him of fifteen cents." I pulled my pistol out and put it right at his head. I said: "I've always wanted to kill a nigger and I think I'll make you the first one." I nearly scared the kid to death, and he struck off.

This was the time when the civil rights movement was really beginnin' to peak. The blacks were beginnin' to demonstrate and picket downtown stores. I never will forget some black lady I hated with a purple passion. Ann Atwater. Every time I'd go downtown, she'd be leadin' a boycott. How I hated—pardon the expression, I don't use it much now—how I just hated that black nigger. (Laughs.) Big, fat, heavy woman. She'd pull about eight demonstrations, and first thing you know they had two, three blacks at the checkout counter. Her and I have had some pretty close confrontations.

I felt very big, yeah. (Laughs.) We're more or less a secret organization. We didn't want anybody to know who we were, and I began to do some thinkin'. What am I hidin' for? I've never been convicted of anything in my life. I don't have any court record. What am I, C. P. Ellis, as a citizen and a member of the United Klansmen of America? Why can't I go the city council meeting and say: "This is the way we feel about the matter? We don't want you to purchase mobile units to set in our schoolyards. We don't want niggers in our schools."

We began to come out in the open. We would go to the meetings, and the blacks would be there and we'd be there. It was a confrontation every time. I didn't hold back anything. We began to make some inroads with the city council-men and county commissioners. They began to call us friend. Call us at night on the telephone: "C. P., glad you came to that meeting last night." They didn't want integration either, but they did it secretively, in order to get elected. They couldn't stand up openly and say it, but they were glad somebody was sayin' it. We visited some of the city leaders in their home and talk to 'em privately. It wasn't long before councilmen would call me up: "The blacks are comin' up tonight and makin' outrageous demands. How about some of you people showin' up and have a little balance?" I'd get on the telephone: "The niggers is comin' to the council meeting tonight. Persons in the city's called me and asked us to be there."

We'd load up our cars and we'd fill up half the council chambers, and the blacks the other half. During these times, I carried weapons to the meetings, out-side my belt. We'd go there armed. We would wind up just hollerin' and fussin' at each other. What happened? As a result of our fightin' one another, the city council still had their way. They didn't want to give up control to the blacks nor the Klan. They were usin' us.

I began to realize this later down the road. One day I was walkin' downtown and a certain city council member saw me comin'. I expected him to shake my hand because he was talkin' to me at night on the telephone. I had been in his home and visited with him. He crossed the street. Oh shit, I began to think, somethin's wrong here. Most of 'em are merchants or maybe an attorney, an insurance agent, people like that. As long as they kept low-income whites and low-income blacks fightin', they're gonna maintain control.

I began to get that feeling after I was ignored in public. I thought: Bullshit, you're not gonna use me anymore. That's when I began to do some real serious thinkin'.

The same thing is happening in this country today. People are being used by those in control, those who have all the wealth. I'm not espousing communism. We got the greatest system of government in the world. But those who have it simply don't want those who don't have it to have any part of it. Black and white. When it comes to money, the green, the other colors make no difference. (Laughs.)

I spent a lot of sleepless nights. I still didn't like blacks. I didn't want to associate with 'em. Blacks, Jews, or Catholics. My father said: "Don't have anything to do with 'em." I didn't until I met a black person and talked with him, eyeball to eyeball, and met a Jewish person and talked to him, eyeball to eyeball. I found out they're people just like me. They cried, they cussed, they prayed, they had desires. Just like myself. Thank God, I got to the point where I can look past labels. But at that time, my mind was closed.

I remember one Monday night Klan meeting. I said something was wrong. Our city fathers were using us. And I didn't like to be used. The reactions of the others was not too pleasant: "Let's just keep fightin' them niggers."

I'd go home at night and I'd have to wrestle with myself. I'd look at a black person walkin' down the street, and the guy'd have ragged shoes or his clothes would be worn. That began to do somethin' to me inside. I went through this for about six months. I felt I just had to get out of the Klan. But I wouldn't get out.

Then something happened. The state AFL-CIO received a grant from the Department of HEW, a $78,000 grant: how to solve racial problems in the school system. I got a telephone call from the president of the state AFL-CIO. "We'd like to get some people together from all walks of life." I said: "All walks of life? Who you talkin' about?" He said: "Blacks, whites, liberals, conservatives, Klansmen, NAACP people."

I said: "No way am I comin' with all those niggers. I'm not gonna be associated with those type of people." A White Citizens Council guy said: "Let's go up there and see what's goin' on. It's tax money bein' spent." I walk in the door, and there was a large number of blacks and white liberals. I knew most of 'em by face 'cause I seen 'em demonstratin' around town. Ann Atwater was there. (Laughs.) I just forced myself to go in and sit down.

The meeting was moderated by a great big black guy who was bushy-headed. (Laughs.) That turned me off. He acted very nice. He said: "I want you all to feel free to say anything you want to say." Some of the blacks stand up and say it's white racism. I took all I could take. I asked for the floor and I cut loose. I said: "No, sir, it's black racism. If we didn't have niggers in the schools, we wouldn't have the problems we got today."

I will never forget. Howard Clements, a black guy, stood up. He said: "I'm certainly glad C. P. Ellis come because he's the most honest man here tonight." I said: "What's that nigger tryin' to do?" (Laughs.) At the end of that meeting, some blacks tried to come up shake my hand, but I wouldn't do it. I walked off.

Second night, same group was there. I felt a little more easy because I got some things off my chest. The third night, after they elected all the committees, they want to elect a chairman. Howard Clements stood up and said: "I suggest we elect two co-chairpersons." Joe Beckton, executive director of the Human Relations Commission, just as black as he can be, he nominated me. There was a reaction from some blacks. Nooo. And, of all things, they nominated Ann Atwater, that big old fat black gal that I had just hated with a purple passion, as co-chairman. I thought to myself: Hey, ain't no way I can work with that gal. Finally, I agreed to accept it, 'cause at this point, I was tired of fightin', either for survival or against black people or against Jews or against Catholics.

A Klansman and a militant black woman, co-chairmen of the school committee. It was impossible. How could I work with her? But after about two or three days, it was in our hands. We had to make it a success. This gave me another sense of belongin', a sense of pride. This helped this inferiority feelin' I had. A man who has stood up publicly and said he despised black people, all of a sudden he was willin' to work with 'em. Here's a chance for a low-income white man to be somethin'. In spite of all my hatred for blacks and Jews and liberals, I accepted the job. Her and I began to reluctantly work together. (Laughs.) She had as many problems workin' with me as I had workin' with her.

One night, I called her: "Ann, you and I should have a lot of differences and we got 'em now. But there's somethin' laid out here before us, and if it's gonna be a success, you and I are gonna have to make it one. Can we lay aside some of these feelin's?" She said: "I'm willing if you are." I said: "Let's do it."

My old friends would call me at night: "C. P., what the hell is wrong with you? You're sellin' out the white race." This begin to make me have guilt feelin's. Am I doin' right? Am I doin' wrong? Here I am all of a sudden makin' an about-face and tryin' to deal with my feelin's, my heart. My mind was beginnin' to open up. I was beginnin' to see what was right and what was wrong. I don't want the kids to fight forever.

We were gonna go ten nights. By this time, I had went to work at Duke University, in maintenance. Makin' very little money. Terry Sanford give me this ten days off with pay. He was president of Duke at the time. He knew I was a Klansman and realized the importance of blacks and whites getting along.

I said: "If we're gonna make this thing a success, I've got to get to my kind of people." The low-income whites. We walked the streets of Durham, and we knocked on doors and invited people. Ann was goin' into the black community. They just wasn't respondin' to us when we made these house calls. Some of 'em were cussin' us out. "You're sellin' us out, Ellis, get out of my door. I don't want to talk to you." Ann was gettin' the same response from blacks: "What are you doin' messin' with that Klansman?"

One day, Ann and I went back to the school and we sat down. We began to talk and just reflect. Ann said: "My daughter came home cryin' every day. She said her teacher was makin' fun of me in front of the other kids." I said: "Boy, the same thing happened to my kid. White liberal teacher was makin' fun of Tim Ellis's father, the Klansman. In front of other peoples. He came home cryin'." At this point—(he pauses, swallows hard, stifles a sob)—I begin to see, here we are, two people from the far ends of the fence, havin' identical problems, except hers bein' black and me bein' white. From that moment on, I tell ya, that gal and I worked together good. I begin to love the girl, really. (He weeps.)

The amazing thing about it, her and I, up to that point, had cussed each other, bawled each other, we hated each other. Up to that point, we didn't know each other. We didn't know we had things in common.

We worked at it, with the people who came to these meetings. They talked about racism, sex education, about teachers not bein' qualified. After seven, eight nights of real intense discussion, these people, who'd never talked to each other before, all of a sudden came up with resolutions. It was really somethin', you had to be there to get the tone and feelin' of it.

At that point, I didn't like integration, but the law says you do this and I've got to do what the law says, okay? We said: "Let's take these resolutions to the school board." The most disheartening thing I've ever faced was the school system refused to implement any one of these resolutions. These were recommendations from the people who pay taxes and pay their salaries. (Laughs.)

I thought they were good answers. Some of 'em I didn't agree with, but I been in this thing from the beginning, and whatever comes of it, I'm gonna support it. Okay, since the school board refused, I decided I'd just run for the school board.

I spent eighty-five dollars on the campaign. The guy runnin' against me spent several thousand. I really had nobody on my side. The Klan turned against me. The low-income whites turned against me. The liberals didn't particularly like me. The blacks were suspicious of me. The blacks wanted to support me, but they couldn't muster up enough to support a Klansman on the school board. (Laughs.) But I made up my mind that what I was doin' was right, and I was gonna do it regardless what anybody said.

It bothered me when people would call and worry my wife. She's always supported me in anything I wanted to do. She was changing, and my boys were too. I got some of my youth corps kids involved. They still followed me.

I was invited to the Democratic women's social hour as a candidate. Didn't have but one suit to my name. Had it six, seven, eight years. I had it cleaned, put on the best shirt I had and a tie. Here were all this high-class wealthy candidates shakin' hands. I walked up to the mayor and stuck out my hand. He give me that handshake with that rag type of hand. He said: "C. P., I'm glad to see you." But I could tell by his handshake he was lyin' to me. This was botherin' me. I know I'm a low-income person. I know I'm not wealthy. I know they were sayin': "What's this little ol' dude runnin' for school board?" Yet they had to smile and make like they're glad to see me. I begin to spot some black people in that room. I automatically went to 'em and that was a firm handshake. They said: "I'm glad to see you, C. P." I knew they meant it—you can tell about a handshake.

Every place I appeared, I said I will listen to the voice of the people. I will not make a major decision until I first contacted all the organizations in the city. I got 4,640 votes. The guy beat me by two thousand. Not bad for eighty-five bucks and no constituency.

The whole world was openin' up, and I was learnin' new truths that I had never learned before. I was beginnin' to look at a black person, shake hands with him, and see him as a human bein'. I hadn't got rid of all this stuff. I've still got a little bit of it. But somethin' was happenin' to me.

It was almost like bein' born again. It was a new life. I didn't have these sleepless nights I used to have when I was active in the Klan and slippin' around at night. I could sleep at night and feel good about it. I'd rather live now than at any other time in history. It's a challenge.

Back at Duke, doin' maintenance, I'd pick up my tools, fix the commode, unstop the drains. But this got in my blood. Things weren't right in this country, and what we done in Durham needs to be told. I was so miserable at Duke, I could hardly stand it. I'd go to work every mornin' just hatin' to go.

My whole life had changed. I got an eighth-grade education, and I wanted to complete high school. Went to high school in the afternoons on a program called PEP—Past Employment Progress. I was about the only white in class, and the oldest. I begin to read about biology. I'd take my books home at night, 'cause I was determined to get through. Sure enough, I graduated. I got the diploma at home.

I come to work one mornin' and some guy says: "We need a union." At this time I wasn't pro-union. My daddy was anti-labor, too. We're not gettin' paid much, we're havin' to work seven days in a row. We're all starvin' to death. The next day, I meet the international representative of the Operating Engineers. He give me authorization cards. "Get these cards out and we'll have an election." There was eighty-eight for the union and seventeen no's. I was elected chief steward for the union.

Shortly after, a union man come down from Charlotte and says we need a full-time rep. We've got only two hundred people at the two plants here. It's just barely enough money comin' in to pay your salary. You'll have to get out and organize more people. I didn't know nothin' about organizin' unions, but I knew how to organize people, stir people up. (Laughs.) That's how I got to be business agent for the union.

When I began to organize, I began to see far deeper. I began to see people again bein' used. Blacks against whites. I say this without any hesitancy: management is vicious. There's two things they want to keep: all the money and all the say-so. They don't want these poor workin' folks to have none of that. I begin to see management fightin' me with everything they had. Hire anti-union law firms, badmouth unions. The people were makin' a dollar ninety-five an hour, barely able to get through weekends. I worked as a business rep for five years and was seein' all this.

Last year, I ran for business manager of the union. He's elected by the workers. The guy that ran against me was black, and our membership is seventy-five percent black. I thought: Claiborne, there's no way you can beat that black guy. People know your background. Even though you've made tremendous strides, those black people are not gonna vote for you. You know how much I beat him? Four to one. (Laughs.)

The company used my past against me. They put out letters with a picture of a robe and a cap: Would you vote for a Klansman? They wouldn't deal with the issues. I immediately called for a mass meeting. I met with the ladies at an electric component plant. I said: "Okay, this is Claiborne Ellis. This is where I come from. I want you to know right now, you black ladies here, I was at one time a member of the Klan. I want you to know, because they'll tell you about it."

I invited some of my old black friends. I said: "Brother Joe, Brother Howard, be honest now and tell these people how you feel about me." They done it. (Laughs.) Howard Clements kidded me a little bit. He said: "I don't know what I'm doin' here, supportin' an ex-Klansman." (Laughs.) He said: "I know what C. P. Ellis come from. I knew him when he was. I knew him as he grew, and growed with him. I'm tellin' you now: follow, follow this Klansman." (He pauses, swallows hard.) "Any questions?" "No," the black ladies said. "Let's get on with the meeting, we need Ellis." (He laughs and weeps.) Boy, black people sayin' that about me. I won one thirty-four to forty-one. Four to one.

It makes you feel good to go into a plant and butt heads with professional union busters. You see black people and white people join hands to defeat the racist issues they use against people. They're tryin' the same things with the Klan. It's still happenin' today. Can you imagine a guy who's got an adult high school diploma runnin' into professional college graduates who are union busters? I gotta compete with 'em. I work seven days a week, nights, and on Saturday and Sunday. The salary's not that great, and if I didn't care, I'd quit. But I care and I can't quit. I got a taste of it. (Laughs.)

I tell people there's a tremendous possibility in this country to stop wars, the battles, the struggles, the fights between people. People say: "That's an impossible dream. You sound like Martin Luther King." An ex-Klansman who sounds like Martin Luther King. (Laughs.) I don't think it's an impossible dream. It's happened in my life. It's happened in other people's lives in America.

I don't know what's ahead of me. I have no desire to be a big union official. I want to be right out here in the field with the workers. I want to walk through their factory and shake hands with that man whose hands are dirty. I'm gonna do all that one little ol' man can do. I'm fifty-two years old, and I ain't got many years left, but I want to make the best of 'em.

When the news came over the radio that Martin Luther King was assassinated, I got on the telephone and begin to call other Klansmen. We just had a real party at the service station. Really rejoicin' 'cause that son of a bitch was dead. Our troubles are over with. They say the older you get, the harder it is for you to change. That's not necessarily true. Since I changed, I've set down and listened to tapes of Martin Luther King. I listen to it and tears come to my eyes 'cause I know what he's sayin' now. I know what's happenin'.

POSTSCRIPT: The phone rings. A conversation. . . .

"This was a black guy who's director of Operation Breakthrough in Durham. I had called his office. I'm interested in employin' some young black person who's interested in learnin' the labor movement. I want somebody who's never had an opportunity, just like myself. Just so he can read and write, that's all."

Suggestions for Further Reading

Anzaldua, Gloria, ed. *Making Faces, Making Soul: Creative and Critical Perspectives by Women of Color.* San Francisco: Aunt Lute Books, 1990.

Azoulay, Katya Gibel. *Black, Jewish, and Interracial.* Durham: Duke University Press, 1997.

Baumgarder, Jennifer. *Look Both Ways.* New York: Farrar, Straus and Giroux, 2008.

Bean, Joseph. *In the Life: A Black Gay Anthology.* Boston: Alyson Publications, 1986.

Brown, R. M. *RubyFruit Jungle.* New York: Bantam, 1977.

Clausen, Jan. *Apples and Oranges: My Journey to Sexual Identity.* Boston: Houghton Mifflin, 1999.

Cofer, Judith Ortiz. *The Latin Deli.* Athens: University of Georgia Press, 1993.

Crozier-Hogle, Lois, et al. *Surviving in Two Worlds: Contemporary Native American Voices.* Austin: University of Texas Press, 1997.

Davis, Lennard. *The Disability Reader.* New York: Routledge, 1997.

Delgado, Richard, and Jean Stefancic. *The Latino/a Condition: A Critical Reader.* New York: New York University Press, 1998.

Danticat, Edwidge. *Breath, Eyes, Memory.* New York: Vintage Books, 1994.

Eugenidies, Jeffrey. *Middlesex: A Novel.* New York: Picador, 2003.

Findlen, Barbara. *Listen Up: Voices from the Next Feminist Generation* (2nd ed.). Berkeley, CA: Seal Press, 2001.

Fong, Timothy, and Larry Shingawa. *Asian American Experiences and Perspectives.* Englewood Cliffs, NJ: Prentice Hall, 2000.

Gwaltney, J. Drylongso. *A Self-Portrait of Black America.* New York: Vintage Books, 1981.

Haley, Alex. *The Autobiography of Malcolm X.* New York: Grove Press, 1964.

Jen, Gish. *Typical American.* New York: Penguin, 1992.

Kim, Elaine H., and Lilia V. Villanueva. *Making More Waves: New Writings by Asian American Women.* Boston: Beacon Press, 1997.

Kimmel, Michael S., and Michael A. Messner, eds. *Men's Lives.* New York: Macmillan, 1997.

Kingston, Maxine Hong. *The Woman Warrior.* New York: Vintage Books, 1981.

Lahiri, Jhumpa. *The Namesake.* New York: Mariner Books, 2003.

Linton, Simi. *My Body Politic.* Ann Arbor: University of Michigan Press, 2005.

Moody, A. *Coming of Age in Mississippi.* New York: Dell, 1968.

Nam, Vickie. *Yell-Oh Girls!* New York: HarperCollins, 2001.

Native Americans 500 Years After. Photographs by Joseph C. Farner, text by Michael Dorris. New York: Thomas Crowell, 1975.

Obama, Barack. *Dreams of My Father.* New York: Three Rivers Press, 2004.

Portas, Alejandros. *Legacies: The Story of the Immigrant Second Generation.* Berkeley: University of California Press, 2001.

Rebollendo, Tey Diana, and Eliana S. Rivero, eds. *Infinite Divisions: An Anthology of Chicana Literature.* Tucson: University of Arizona Press, 1993.

Reid, John. *The Best Little Boy in the World.* New York: G.P. Putnam's Sons, 1973.

Rivera, E. *Family Installments: Memories of Growing Up Hispanic.* New York: Penguin, 1983.

Rubin, L. B. *Worlds of Pain: Life in the Working Class Family.* New York: Basic Books, 1976.

Santiago, Esmeralda. *When I Was Puerto Rican.* New York: Vintage Books, 1993.

Shulman, A. K. *Memoirs of an Ex-Prom Queen.* New York: Knopf, 1972.

Silko, L. M. *Ceremony.* New York: New American Library, 1972.

Smith, B., ed. *Home Girls: A Black Feminist Anthology.* New York: Kitchen Table/Women of Color Press, 1983.

Turkel, Studs. *Working.* New York: Avon Books, 1972.

Warshaw, Robin. *I Never Called It Rape.* New York: Harper & Row, 1988.

Winged Words: American Indian Writers Speak. Lincoln: University of Nebraska Press, 1990.

Wu, Frank. *Yellow: Race in America Beyond Black and White.* New York: Basic Books, 2003.

Zahava, Irene, ed. *Speaking for Ourselves: Short Stories by Jewish Lesbians.* Freedom, CA: Crossing Press, 1990.

Zhou, Min, and James V. Gatewood, eds. *Contemporary Asian Americans: A Multidisciplinary Reader.* New York: New York University Press, 2000.

Zia, Helen. *Asian American Dreams: The Emergence of an American People.* New York: Farrar, Straus and Giroux, 2000.

PART VII

How It Happened: Race and Gender Issues in U.S. Law

History holds the key to both the past and the present. By studying history we can understand how what happened in the past is reflected in the present, and we can distinguish between discriminatory or unjust contemporary policies and practices that represent accidental or aberrant abridgement of rights and those that are part of a pattern of racism and sexism. But whose history shall we study?

History can be written from many different perspectives. The life stories of so-called great men will vary greatly, depending on whether the biographers are their mothers, their wives, their lovers, their peers, their children, or their servants. Each perspective contributes something unique and essential to the portrait. Furthermore, historians now ask why history should be the study of "great men" exclusively, as they increasingly turn their attention to the lives of ordinary people in order to produce a more inclusive and hence more accurate account of the past.

We can even question who decides what counts as history. It was once the case that the war diaries of generals were regarded as important historical documents, whereas the diaries written by women giving an account of their daily lives were ignored or discarded. What made one document invaluable and the other irrelevant? Traditional historians adopted a fairly narrow, Eurocentric perspective on the past and used it as the basis for writing what was then alleged to provide an "objective" and "universal" picture of the past. These texts left out important information and consigned the majority of people in U.S. society to the margins of history. This approach failed to reflect the ways in which women, people of all colors, and working people created the wealth and culture of this country.

It is commonly believed that history involves collecting and studying facts. But what counts as a "fact," and who decides which facts are important? Whose interests are served or furthered by these decisions? For many years, one of the first "facts" that grade-school children learned was that Christopher Columbus discovered America. Yet this "history" is neither clear nor incontrovertible. It is a piece of the past examined from the point of view of white Europeans; it is in their interest to persuade others to believe it, since this "fact" undermines the claims of others. Native Americans might well ask how Columbus could have discovered America in 1492 if they had already been living here for thousands of years. Teaching children that bit of fiction about Columbus served to render Native Americans invisible and thus tacitly excused or denied the genocide carried out by European settlers.

During the contemporary period, many new approaches to history have arisen to remedy the omissions and distortions of the past. Women's history, black history, lesbian and gay history, ethnic history, labor history, and others all propose to transform traditional history so that it more accurately reflects the reality of people's lives, both past and present.

Part VII does not attempt to provide a comprehensive history of the American Republic since its beginning. Rather, it traces the legal status of people of color and women since the first Europeans came to this land. After a preliminary reading (Selection 1) that represents an overview of legal issues as they apply to Native Americans in particular, this Part proceeds by presenting legal documents that highlight developments in legal status. In a few cases, these documents are supplemented with materials that help paint a clearer picture of the issues involved or their implications.

Much is left out by adopting this framework for our study. Most significantly, discussions of the actual political and social movements that brought about the changes in the legal realm are omitted. For this reason, students are urged to supplement their study of the legal documents with the rich accounts of social history from the *Suggestions for Further Reading* at the end of Part VII.

However, the legal documents themselves are fascinating. They make it possible to reduce the record of hundreds of years of history to a manageable size. We can thus form a picture of the rights and status of many so-called minority groups in this country, a picture that contrasts sharply with the one usually offered in high school social studies classes. Most importantly, the documents can help us answer the question raised by material in the first six parts of this text: How did it happen that all women and all people of color came to have such limited access to power and opportunity?

The readings here show that, from the country's inception, the laws and institutions of the United States were designed to create and maintain the privileges of wealthy white males. The discrimination documented in the early parts of this book is no accident. It has a long and deliberate history. Understanding this history is essential if we are to create a more just and democratic society.

On July 4, 1776, the thirteen colonies set forth a declaration of independence from Great Britain. In that famous document, the founders of the Republic explained their reasons for separating from the homeland and expressed their hopes for the new Republic. In lines that are rightly famous and often quoted, the signatories proclaimed that "all Men are created equal, that they are endowed by their Creator with certain unalienable Rights, that among these are Life, Liberty and the Pursuit of Happiness." They went on to assert that "to secure these Rights, Governments are instituted among Men, deriving their just Powers from the Consent of the Governed." When these words were written, however, a large portion of the population of the United States had no legal rights whatsoever. Native Americans, women, indentured servants, poor white men who did not own property, and, of course, Negroes held as slaves could not vote, nor were they free to exercise their liberty or pursue their happiness in the same way that white men with property could. When the authors of the Declaration of Independence proclaimed that all men were created equal and endowed with unalienable rights, they meant "men" quite literally and white men specifically. Negroes held in slavery, as it turned out, were worth "three fifths of all other Persons," a figure stipulated in Article 1, Section 2, of the United States Constitution (see Selection 3). This section of the Constitution, which is often referred to as the "three-fifths compromise," undertook to establish how slaves would be counted for the purposes of determining taxes as well as for calculating representation of the states in Congress.

Faced with the need for an enormous work force to cultivate the land, the European settlers first tried to enslave the American Indian population. Later, the settlers brought over large numbers of "indentured workers" from Europe. These workers were poor white men, women, and children, some serving prison sentences at home, who were expected to work in the colonies for a certain period of time and then receive their freedom. When neither of these populations proved suitable, the settlers began importing African Negroes to serve their purposes.

Records show that the first African Negroes were brought to this country as early as 1526. Initially, the Negroes appear to have had the same status as indentured servants, but the laws reflect a fairly rapid distinction between the two groups. Maryland law made this distinction as early as 1640; Massachusetts legally recognized slavery in 1641; Virginia passed a law making Negroes slaves for life in 1661; and so it went until the number of slaves grew to roughly 600,000 at the time of the signing of the Declaration of Independence.[1] Numerous legal documents, such as An Act for the Better Ordering and Governing of Negroes and Slaves, passed in South Carolina in 1712 and excerpted in Selection 2, prescribed the existence of the slaves, as did the acts modeled on An Act Prohibiting the Teaching of Slaves to Read, a North Carolina statute reprinted here in Selection 4.

When the early European settlers came to this country, there were approximately 2.5 million Native Americans living on the land that was to become the United States. These peoples were divided among numerous separate and autonomous tribes, each with its own highly developed culture and history. The white settlers quickly lumped these diverse peoples into a single and inferior category, "Indians," and set about destroying their culture and seizing their lands. The Indian Removal Act of 1830 was fairly typical of the kinds of laws that were passed to carry out the appropriation of Indian lands. Believing the Indians to be inherently inferior to whites, the U.S. government had no hesitation about legislating the removal of the Indians from valuable ancestral lands to ever more remote and barren reservations. The dissolution of the Indian tribal system was further advanced by the General Allotment Act (Dawes Act) of 1887, which divided tribal landholdings among individual Indians and thereby successfully undermined the tribal system and the culture of which it was a part. In addition, this act opened up lands within the reservation area for purchase by the U.S. government, which then made those lands available to white settlers for homesteading. Many supporters of the allotment policy, who were considered "friends" of the Indians, argued that the benefits of individual ownership would have a "civilizing effect" on them.[2] Instead, it ensured a life of unrelenting poverty for most because it was usually impossible for a family to derive subsistence from the use of a single plot of land, without the support of the tribal community.

While John Adams was involved in writing the Declaration of Independence, his wife, Abigail Adams, took him to task for failing to accord women the same rights and privileges as men: "I cannot say that you are very generous to the ladies; for whilst you are proclaiming peace and good will to men, emancipating all nations, you insist upon retaining an absolute power over wives."[3] Although law and custom consistently treated women as if they were physically and mentally inferior to men, the reality of women's lives was very different. Black female slaves were forced to perform the same inhuman fieldwork as black male slaves and were expected to do so even in the final weeks of pregnancy. They were routinely beaten and abused without regard for the supposed biological fragility of the female sex. White women settlers gave birth to large numbers of children, ten and twelve being quite common and as many as twenty births not being unusual. And they did so in addition to working side by side with men to perform all those duties necessary to ensure survival in a new and unfamiliar environment. When her husband died, a woman often assumed his responsibilities as well. It was not until well into the 1800s, primarily as a result of changes brought about by the Industrial Revolution, that significant class differences began to affect the lives and work of white women.

As women, both black and white, became increasingly active in the antislavery movement during the 1800s, many noticed certain similarities between the legal status of women and the legal status of people held as slaves. Participants at the first women's rights convention, held in Seneca Falls, New York, in 1848, listed women's grievances and specified their demands. At this time, married women were regarded as property of their husbands and had no direct legal control over their own wages, their property, or even their children. The Declaration of Sentiments issued in Seneca Falls was modeled on the Declaration of Independence in the hope that men would extend the declaration's rights to women. It is reprinted in this Part (as Selection 5) along with readings from a variety of sources from the period that reflect the most typical male responses to women's demand for the vote and other rights (see Selection 6). Similar emotional attacks are still used today to ridicule and then dismiss contemporary feminist demands.

The abysmal legal status of women and people of color in the United States during the nineteenth century is graphically documented in a series of court decisions reproduced in this Part. In *People* v. *Hall,* 1854 (excerpted in Selection 7), the California Supreme Court decided that a California statute barring Indians and Negroes from testifying in court cases involving whites also applied to Chinese Americans. The judges asserted that the Chinese are "a race of people whom nature has marked as inferior, and who are incapable of progress or intellectual development beyond a certain point." The extent of anti-Chinese feeling in parts of the United States can be further inferred from portions of the California Constitution adopted in 1876 (see Selection 14).

In a more famous case, *Dred Scott* v. *Sandford,* 1857 (Selection 8), the United States Supreme Court was asked to decide whether Dred Scott, a Negro, was a citizen of the United States with the rights that that implied. Scott, a slave who had been taken from Missouri, a slave state, into the free state of Illinois for a period of time, argued that because he was free and had been born in the United States, he was therefore a citizen. The Court ruled that this was not the case and, using reasoning that strongly parallels *People* v. *Hall,* offered a survey of U.S. law and custom to show that Negroes were never considered a part of the people of the United States. In *Bradwell* v. *Illinois,* 1873 (summarized in Selection 12), the Supreme Court ruled that women could not practice law and used the opportunity to carefully distinguish the rights and prerogatives of women from those of men. The Court maintained that "civil law, as well as nature herself, has always recognized a wide difference in the respective spheres and destinies of man and woman" and went on to argue that women belong in the "domestic sphere."

During the period in which these and other court cases were brought, the United States moved toward and ultimately fought a bloody civil war. It was allegedly fought "to free the slaves," but much more was at stake. The Civil War reflected a struggle to the death between the Southern aristocracy, whose wealth was based on land and whose power rested on a kind of feudal economic-political order, and the Northern capitalists, who came into being by virtue of the Industrial Revolution and who wished to restructure the nation's economic-political institutions to better serve the needs of the new industrial order. Chief among these needs was a large and mobile work force for the factories in the North. Hundreds of thousands of soldiers died in the bloody conflict, while other men purchased army deferments and used the war years to amass tremendous personal wealth. On the Confederate side, men who owned fifty or more slaves were exempted from serving in the army, whereas wealthy Northern men were able to purchase deferments from the Union for the sum of $300. Among those who purchased deferments and went on to become millionaires as a result of war profiteering were John D. Rockefeller, Andrew Carnegie, J. Pierpont Morgan, Philip Armour, James Mellon, and Jay Gould.[4]

In September 1862, President Abraham Lincoln signed the Emancipation Proclamation (Selection 9) as part of his efforts to bring the Civil War to an end by forcing the Southern states to concede. It did not free all slaves; it freed only those in states or parts of states in rebellion against the federal government. Only in September 1865, after the conclusion of the war, were all people held as slaves freed by the Thirteenth Amendment (Selection 10). However, Southern whites did not yield their privileges easily. Immediately after the war, the Southern states began to pass laws known as "The

Black Codes," which attempted to reestablish the relations of slavery. Some of these codes are described in this Part in Selection 11, written by the distinguished historian W. E. B. Du Bois.

In the face of such efforts to deny the rights of citizenship to black men, Congress passed the Fourteenth Amendment (Selection 10) in July 1868. This amendment, which continues to play a major role in contemporary legal battles over discrimination, includes a number of important provisions. It explicitly extended citizenship to all those born or naturalized in the United States and guaranteed all citizens "due process" and "equal protection" of the law. In addition, it canceled all debts incurred by the Confederacy in its unsuccessful rebellion while recognizing the validity of the debts incurred by the federal government. This meant that wealthy Southerners who had extended large sums of money or credit to the Confederacy would lose it, whereas wealthy Northern industrialists would be repaid.

Southern resistance to extending the rights and privileges of citizenship to black men persisted, and the Southern states used all their powers, including unbridled terror and violence, to subvert the intent of the Thirteenth and Fourteenth Amendments. The Fifteenth Amendment (Selection 10), which explicitly granted the vote to black men, was passed in 1870 but was received by the Southern states with as little enthusiasm as had greeted the Thirteenth and Fourteenth Amendments.

As the abolitionist movement grew and the Civil War became inevitable, many women's rights activists, also active in the struggle to end slavery, argued that the push for women's rights should temporarily defer to the issue of slavery. In fact, after February 1861, no women's rights conventions were held until the end of the war. Although black and white women had long worked together in both movements, the question of which struggle took precedence created serious splits among women's rights activists, including such strong black allies as Frederick Douglass and Sojourner Truth. Some argued that the evils of slavery were so great that they took precedence over the legal discrimination experienced by middle-class white women. They resented attempts by Elizabeth Cady Stanton and others to equate the condition of white women with that of Negroes held in slavery and argued, moreover, that the women's rights movement had never been concerned with the extraordinary suffering of black women or the special needs of working women. The explicitly racist appeals made by some white women activists as they sought white men's support for women's suffrage did nothing to bridge this schism. While black men received the vote in 1868, at least on paper, women would have to continue their fight until the passage of the Nineteenth Amendment (Selection 17) in 1920. As a result, many women and blacks saw each other as adversaries or obstacles in their struggle for legal equality, deflecting their attention from the privileged white men who provoked the conflict and whose power was reinforced by it.

One special cause for bitterness was the Fourteenth Amendment's reference to "male inhabitants" and the right to vote. This was the first time that voting rights had explicitly been rendered gender-specific. The Fourteenth Amendment was tested in 1875 by *Minor* v. *Happersett* (Selection 13), in which the Court was asked to rule directly on the question of whether women had the vote by virtue of their being citizens of the United States. The Court ruled unanimously that women did not have the vote, arguing that women, like criminals and mental defectives, could legitimately be denied the vote by the states.[5] In a somewhat similar case, *Elk* v. *Wilkins,* 1884 (Selection 15), John Elk, an American Indian who had left his tribe and lived among whites, argued that he was a citizen by virtue of the Fourteenth Amendment and should not be denied the right to vote by the state of Nebraska. The Supreme Court ruled that neither the Fourteenth nor the Fifteenth Amendment applied to Elk. Native Americans became citizens of the United States three years later, under one of the provisions of the Dawes Act of 1887.

Unsuccessful in their attempts to reinstate some form of forced servitude by passage of "The Black Codes," Southern states began to legalize the separation of the races in all aspects of public and private life. In *Plessy* v. *Ferguson,* 1896 (Selection 16), the Supreme Court was asked to rule on whether segregation by race in public facilities violated the Thirteenth and Fourteenth Amendments. In a ruling that was to cruelly affect several generations of black Americans, the Supreme Court decided that restricting Negroes to the use of "separate but equal" public accommodations did not deny them equal protection of the law. This decision remained in effect for almost sixty years until *Brown* v. *Board of Education of Topeka,* 1954 (Selection 19). In the historic *Brown* decision, the Court ruled, in effect, that "separate" could not possibly be "equal." Nonetheless, abolishing segregation on paper was one thing; actually bringing about the integration of public facilities was another. The integration of public schools, housing, and employment in both the North and the South has been a long and often bloody struggle that continues to this day.

The racist attitudes toward Chinese Americans, reflected in the nineteenth-century California statutes and constitution, as we have already seen, extended toward Japanese Americans as well. This racism erupted during the twentieth century after the bombing of Pearl Harbor by Japan on December 7, 1941. Anti-Japanese feelings ran so high that President Franklin Roosevelt issued an executive order allowing the military to designate "military areas" from which it could then exclude any persons it chose. On March 2, 1942, the entire West Coast was designated as such an area, and within a few months everyone of Japanese ancestry (defined as those having as little as one-eighth Japanese blood) was evacuated. More than 110,000 people of Japanese descent, most of them American citizens, were forced to leave their homes and jobs and to spend the war years in so-called relocation camps behind barbed wire.[6] Although the United States was also at war with Germany, no such barbaric treatment was afforded German Americans. The military evacuation of Japanese Americans was challenged in *Korematsu* v. *United States,* 1944. In its decision, excerpted in Selection 18, the Supreme Court upheld the forced evacuation.

The twentieth century has seen the growth of large and diverse movements for race and gender justice. These movements precipitated the creation of a number of commissions and government agencies that were to research and enforce equal treatment for people of color and women, the passage of a number of statutes to this end, and a series of Supreme Court decisions. For women, one of the most significant Court decisions of the recent past was *Roe* v. *Wade,* 1973 (Selection 20), which, for the first time, gave women the right to terminate pregnancy by abortion. Rather than affirming a woman's right to control her body, however, the *Roe* decision is based on the right to privacy. The impact of *Roe* was significantly blunted by *Harris* v. *McRae,* 1980, in which the Court ruled that the right to privacy did not require public funding of medically necessary abortions for women who could not afford them. In practice, this meant that middle-class women who chose abortion could exercise their right but that many poor white women and women of color could not. The single biggest defeat for the women's movement of this period was the failure to pass the much misunderstood Equal Rights Amendment, which is reprinted in Selection 21.

More recently, the Supreme Court was asked to reconsider *Bowers* v. *Hardwick,* which had upheld the Texas statute making it a crime for two persons of the same sex to engage in certain intimate sexual contact. In 2003, *Lawrence* v. *Texas* reversed the Bowers decision ruling it legal for homosexuals to choose to enter upon relationships in the confines of their homes and their private lives and still retain dignity as free persons.

NOTES

1. W. Z. Foster, *The Negro People in American History* (New York: International Publishers, 1954), p. 37.

2. U.S. Commission on Civil Rights, *Indian Tribes: A Continuing Quest for Survival,* a report of the United States Commission on Civil Rights, June 1981, p. 34.

3. Letter to John Adams, May 7, 1776.

4. H. Wasserman, *Harvey Wasserman's History of the United States* (New York: Harper & Row, 1975), p. 3.

5. E. Flexner, *Century of Struggle* (Cambridge, MA: Harvard University Press, 1976), p. 172.

6. R. E. Cushman and R. F. Cushman, *Cases in Constitutional Law* (New York: Appleton-Century-Crofts, 1958), p. 127.

1

INDIAN TRIBES
A Continuing Quest for Survival

U.S. Commission on Human Rights

Traditional civil rights, as the phrase is used here, include those rights that are secured to individuals and are basic to the United States system of government. They include the right to vote and the right to equal treatment without discrimination on the basis of race, religion, or national origin, among others, in such areas as education, housing, employment, public accommodations, and the administration of justice.

In order to understand where American Indians stand today with respect to these rights, it is important to look at historical developments of the concept of Indian rights along with the civil rights movement in this country. The consideration given to these factors here will not be exhaustive, but rather a brief look at some of the events that are most necessary to a background understanding of this area.

A basic and essential factor concerning American Indians is that the development of civil rights issues for them is in reverse order from other minorities in this country. Politically, other minorities started with nothing and attempted to obtain a voice in the existing economic and political structure. Indians started with everything and have gradually lost much of what they had to an advancing alien civilization. Other minorities have had no separate governmental institutions. Their goal primarily has been and continues to be to make the existing system involve them and work for them. Indian tribes have always been separate political entities interested in maintaining their own institutions and beliefs. Their goal has been to prevent the dismantling of their own systems. So while other minorities have sought integration into the larger society, much of Indian society is motivated to retain its political and cultural separateness.

Although at the beginning of the colonization process Indian nations were more numerous and better adapted to survival on this continent than the European settlers, these advantages were quickly lost. The colonization period saw the rapid expansion of non-Indian communities in numbers and territory covered and a shift in the balance of strength from Indian to non-Indian communities and governments. The extent to which Indians intermingled with non-Indian society varied by time period, geographical location, and the ability of natives and newcomers

Indian Tribes: A Continuing Quest for Survival, a report of the United States Commission on Civil Rights, June 1981, p. 34. Reprinted by permission.

to get along with one another. As a general matter, however, Indians were viewed and treated as members of political entities that were not part of the United States. The Constitution acknowledges this by its separate provision regarding trade with the Indian tribes.[1] Indian tribes today that have not been forcibly assimilated, extinguished, or legally terminated still consider themselves to be, and are viewed in American law, as separate political units.

The Racial Factor

An important element in the development of civil rights for American Indians today goes beyond their legal and political status to include the way they have been viewed racially. Since colonial times Indians have been viewed as an "inferior race"; sometimes this view is condescendingly positive—the romanticized noble savage—at other times this view is hostile—the vicious savage—at all times the view is racist. All things Indian are viewed as inherently inferior to their counterparts in the white European tradition. Strong racist statements have appeared in congressional debates, Presidential policy announcements, court decisions, and other authoritative public utterances. This racism has served to justify a view now repudiated, but which still lingers in the public mind, that Indians are not entitled to the same legal rights as others in this country. In some cases, racism has been coupled with apparently benevolent motives, to "civilize" the "savages," to teach them Christian principles. In other cases, the racism has been coupled with greed; Indians were "removed" to distant locations to prevent them from standing in the way of the development of the new Western civilization. At one extreme the concept of inferior status of Indians was used to justify genocide; at the other, apparently benevolent side, the attempt was to assimilate them into the dominant society. Whatever the rationale or motive, whether rooted in voluntary efforts or coercion, the common denominator has been the belief that Indian society is an inferior lifestyle.

> It sprang from a conviction that native people were a lower grade of humanity for whom the accepted cannons [*sic*] of respect need not apply; one did not debase oneself by ruining a native person. At times, this conviction was stated explicitly by men in public office, but whether expressed or not, it generated decision and action.[2]

Early assimilationists like Thomas Jefferson proceeded from this assumption with benevolent designs.

> Thus, even as they acknowledged a degree of political autonomy in the tribes, their conviction of the natives' cultural inferiority led them to interfere in their social, religious, and economic practices. Federal agents to the tribes not only negotiated treaties and tendered payments; they pressured husbands to take up the plow and wives to learn to spin. The more conscientious agents offered gratuitous lectures on the virtues of monogamy, industry, and temperance.

The same underlying assumption provided the basis for Andrew Jackson's attitude. "I have long viewed treaties with the Indians an absurdity not to be reconciled to the principles of our government," he said. As President he refused to enforce the decisions of the U.S. Supreme Court upholding Cherokee tribal autonomy, and he had a prominent role in the forced removal of the Cherokees from Georgia and the appropriation of their land by white settlers. Other eastern tribes met a similar fate under the Indian Removal Act of 1830.[3]

Another Federal Indian land policy, enacted at the end of the 19th century and followed until 1934, that shows the virulent effect of racist assumptions was the allotment of land parcels to individual Indians as a replacement for tribal ownership. Many proponents of the policy were considered "friends of the Indians," and they argued that the attributes of individual land ownership would have a great civilizing and assimilating effect on American Indians. This action, undertaken for the benefit of the Indians, was accomplished without consulting them. Had Congress heeded the views of the purported beneficiaries of this policy, allotment might not have been adopted. Representatives of 19 tribes met in Oklahoma and unanimously opposed the legislation, recognizing the destructive effect it would have upon Indian culture and the land base itself, which was reduced by 90 million acres in 45 years.

An important principle established by the allotment policy was that the Indian form of land ownership was not "civilized," and so it was the right of the Government to invalidate that form. It is curious that the principle of the right to own property in conglomerate form for the benefit of those with a shareholder's undivided interest in the whole was a basis of the American corporate system, then developing in strength. Yet a similar form of ownership when practiced by Indians was viewed as a hallmark of savagery. Whatever the explanation for this double standard, the allotment policy reinforced the notion that Indians were somehow inferior, that non-Indians in power knew what was best for them, and that these suppositions justified the assertion that non-Indians had the power and authority to interfere with the basic right to own property.

Religion is another area in which non-Indians have felt justified in interfering with Indian beliefs. The intent to civilize the natives of this continent included a determined effort to Christianize them. Despite the constitutional prohibition, Congress, beginning in 1819, regularly appropriated funds for Christian missionary efforts. Christian goals were visibly aligned with Federal Indian policy in 1869 when a Board of Indian Commissioners was established by Congress under President Grant's administration. Representative of the spectrum of Christian denominations, the independently wealthy members of the Board were charged by the Commissioner of Indian Affairs to work for the "humanization, civilization and Christianization of the Indians." Officials of the Federal Indian Service were supposed to cooperate with this Board.

The benevolent support of Christian missionary efforts stood in stark contrast to the Federal policy of suppressing tribal religions. Indian ceremonial behavior was misunderstood and suppressed by Indian agents. In 1892 the Commissioner of Indian Affairs established a regulation making it a criminal offense to engage in such ceremonies as the sun dance. The spread of the Ghost Dance religion, which promised salvation from the white man, was so frightening to the Federal Government that troops were called in to prevent it, even though the practice posed no threat to white settlers.

The judiciary of the United States, though it has in many instances forthrightly interpreted the law to support Indian legal claims in the face of strong, sometimes violent opposition, has also lent support to the myth of Indian inferiority. For example, the United States Supreme Court in 1883, in recognizing the right of tribes to govern themselves, held that they had the exclusive authority to try Indians for criminal offenses committed against Indians. In describing its reasons for refusing to find jurisdiction in a non-Indian court in such cases, the Supreme Court said:

> It [the non-Indian court] tries them, not by their peers, nor by the customs of their people, nor the law of their land, but by *superiors* of a different race, according to the law of a social state of which they have an imperfect conception, and which is opposed to the traditions of their history, to the habits of their lives, to the strongest prejudices of their *savage nature*; one which measures the red man's revenge by the maxims of the white man's morality.[4] (emphasis added)

In recognizing the power of the United States Government to determine the right of Indians to occupy their lands, the Supreme Court expressed the good faith of the country in such matters with these words: "the United States will be governed by such considerations of justice as will control a Christian people in their treatment of an ignorant and dependent race."[5]

Another example of racist stereotyping to be found in the courts is this example from the Supreme Court of Washington State:

> The Indian was a child, and a dangerous child, of nature, to be both protected and restrained. . . . True, arrangements took the form of treaty and of terms like "cede," "relinquish," "reserve." But never were these agreements between equals . . . [but rather] that "between a superior and an inferior."[6]

This reasoning, based on racism, has supported the view that Indians are wards of the Government who need the protection and assistance of Federal agencies and it is the Government's obligation to recreate their governments, conforming them to a non-Indian model, to establish their priorities, and to make or approve their decisions for them.

Indian education policies have often been examples of the Federal Government having determined what is "best" for Indians. Having judged that assimilation could be promoted through the indoctrination process of white schools, the Federal Government began investing in Indian education. Following the model established by army officer Richard Pratt in 1879, boarding schools were established where Indian children were separated from the influences of tribal and home life. The boarding schools tried to teach Indians skills and trades that would be useful in white society, utilizing stern disciplinary measures to force assimilation. The tactics used are within memory of today's generation of tribal leaders who recall the policy of deterring communication in native languages. "I remember being punished many times for . . . singing one Navajo song, or a Navajo word slipping out of my tongue just in an unplanned way, but I was punished for it."

Federal education was made compulsory, and the policy was applied to tribes that had sophisticated school systems of their own as well as to tribes that really needed assistance to establish educational systems. The ability of the tribal school to educate was not relevant, given that the overriding goal was assimilation rather than education.

Racism in Indian affairs has not been sanctioned recently by political or religious leaders or other leaders in American society. In fact, public pronouncements over the last several decades have lamented past evils and poor treatment of Indians.[7] The virulent public expressions of other eras characterizing Indians as "children" or "savages" are not now acceptable modes of public expression. Public policy today is a commitment to Indian self-determination. Numerous actions of Congress and the executive branch give evidence of a more positive era for Indian policy.[8] Beneath the surface, however, the effects of centuries of racism still persist. The attitudes of the public, of State and local officials, and of Federal policymakers do not always live up to the positive pronouncements of official policy. Some decisions today are perceived as being made on the basis of precedents mired in the racism and greed of another era. Perhaps more important, the legacy of racism permeates behavior and that behavior creates classic civil rights violations. . . .

NOTES

1. U.S. Const. Art. 1, §8.
2. D'Arcy McNickel, *Native American Tribalism* (New York: Oxford University Press, 1973), p. 56.
3. Act of May 28, 1830, ch. 148, 4 Stat. 411.
4. *Ex Parte Crow Dog*, 109 U.S. 556, 571 (1883).
5. *Missouri, Kansas, and Texas Railway Co. v. Roberts*, 152 U.S. 114, 117 (1894).
6. *State v. Towessnute*, 154 P. 805, 807 (Wash. Sup. Ct. 1916), quoting *Choctaw Nation v. United States*, 119 U.S. 1, 27 (1886).
7. See, e.g., President Nixon's July 8, 1970, Message to the Congress, Recommendations for Indian Policy, H. Doc. No. 91–363, 91st Cong., 2d sess.
8. Ibid; Indian Self-Determination and Education Assistance Act, Pub. L. No. 93–638, 88 Stat. 2203 (1975); Indian Child Welfare Act of 1978, Pub. L. No. 95–608, 92 Stat. 3096; U.S. Department of the Interior, *Report on the Implementation of the Helsinki Final Act* (1979).

AN ACT FOR THE BETTER ORDERING AND GOVERNING OF NEGROES AND SLAVES, SOUTH CAROLINA, 1712

Colonial America had a role for the Negro. But the presence of a servile population, presumably of inferior stock, made it necessary to adopt measures of control. As might be expected, the southern colonies had the most highly developed codes governing Negroes. In 1712 South Carolina passed "An Act for the better ordering and governing of Negroes and Slaves." This comprehensive measure served as a model for slave codes in the South during the colonial and national periods. Eight of its thirty-five sections are reproduced below.

Whereas, the plantations and estates of this province cannot be well and sufficiently managed and brought into use, without the labor and service of negroes and other slaves; and forasmuch as the said negroes and other slaves brought unto the people of this Province for that purpose, are of barbarous, wild, savage natures, and such as renders them wholly unqualified to be governed by the laws, customs, and practices of this Province; but that it is absolutely necessary, that such other constitutions, laws and orders, should in this Province be made and enacted, for the good regulating and ordering of them, as may restrain the disorders, rapines and inhumanity, to which they are naturally prone and inclined, and may also tend to the safety and security of the people of this Province and their estates; to which purpose,

I. *Be it therefore enacted,* by his Excellency William, Lord Craven, Palatine, and the rest of the true and absolute Lords and Proprietors of this Province, by and with the advice and consent of the rest of the members of the General Assembly, now met at Charlestown, for the South-west part of this Province, and by the authority of the same, That all negroes, mulatoes, mustizoes or Indians, which at any time heretofore have been sold, or now are held or taken to be, or hereafter shall be bought and sold for slaves, are hereby declared slaves; and they, and their children, are hereby made and declared slaves, to all intents and purposes; excepting all such negroes, mulatoes, mustizoes or Indians, which heretofore have been, or hereafter shall be, for some particular merit, made and declared free, either by the

From Thomas Cooper and David J. McCord, eds., *Statutes at Large of South Carolina* (10 vols., Columbia, 1836–1841), VII, 352–357.

Governor and council of this Province, pursuant to any Act or law of this Province, or by their respective owners or masters; and also, excepting all such negroes, mulatoes, mustizoes or Indians, as can prove they ought not to be sold for slaves. And in case any negro, mulatoe, mustizoe or Indian, doth lay claim to his or her freedom, upon all or any of the said accounts, the same shall be finally heard and determined by the Governor and council of this Province.

II. And for the better ordering and governing of negroes and all other slaves in this Province, *Be it enacted* by the authority aforesaid, That no master, mistress, overseer, or other person whatsoever, that hath the care and charge of any negro or slave, shall give their negroes and other slaves leave, on Sundays, hollidays, or any other time, to go out of their plantations, except such negro or other slave as usually wait upon them at home or abroad, or wearing a livery; and every other negro or slave that shall be taken hereafter out of his master's plantation, without a ticket, or leave in writing, from his master or mistress, or some other person by his or her appointment, or some white person in the company of such slave, to give an account of his business, shall be whipped; and every person who shall not (when in his power) apprehend every negro or other slave which he shall see out of his master's plantation, without leave as aforesaid, and after apprehended, shall neglect to punish him by moderate whipping, shall forfeit twenty shillings, the one half to the poor, to be paid to the church wardens of the Parish where such forfeiture shall become due, and the other half to him that will inform for the same, within one week after such neglect; and that no slave may make further or other use of any one ticket than was intended by him that granted the same, every ticket shall particularly mention the name of every slave employed in the particular business, and to what place they are sent, and what time they return; and if any person shall presume to give any negro or slave a ticket in the name of his master or mistress, without his or her consent, such person so doing shall forfeit the sum of twenty shillings; one half to the poor, to be disposed of as aforesaid, the other half to the person injured, that will complain against the person offending, within one week after the offence committed. And for the better security of all such persons that shall endeavor to take any runaway, or shall examine any slave for his ticket, passing to and from his master's plantation, it is hereby declared lawful for any white person to beat, maim or assult, and if such negro or slave cannot otherwise be taken, to kill him, who shall refuse to shew his ticket, or, by running away or resistance, shall endeavor to avoid being apprehended or taken.

III. *And be it further enacted* by the authority aforesaid, That every master, mistress or overseer of a family in this Province, shall cause all his negro houses to be searched diligently and effectually, once every fourteen days, for fugitive and runaway slaves, guns, swords, clubs, and any other mischievous weapons, and finding any, to take them away, and cause them to be secured; as also, for clothes, goods, and any other things and commodities that are not given them by their master, mistress, commander or overseer, and honestly come by; and in whose custody they find any thing of that kind, and suspect or know to be stolen goods, the same they shall seize and take into their custody, and a full and ample description of the particulars thereof, in writing, within ten days after the discovery thereof, either to the provost marshall, or to the clerk of the parish for the time being, who is hereby required to receive the same, and to enter upon it the day of its receipt, and the particulars to file and keep to himself; and the clerk shall set upon the posts of the church door, and the provost marshall upon the usual public places, or places of notice, a short brief, that such lost goods are found; whereby, any person that hath lost his goods may the better come to the knowledge where they are; and the owner going to the marshall or clerk, and proving, by marks or otherwise, that the goods lost belong to him, and paying twelve pence for the entry and declaration of the same, if the marshall or clerk be convinced that any part of the goods certified by him to be found, appertains to the party inquiring, he is to direct the said party inquiring to the place and party where the goods be, who is hereby required to make restitution of what is in being to the true owner; and every master, mistress or overseer, as also the provost marshall or clerk, neglecting his duty in any the particulars aforesaid, for every neglect shall forfeit twenty shillings.

IV. And for the more effectual detecting and punishing such persons that trade with any slave for stolen goods, *Be it further enacted* by the authority aforesaid, That where any person shall be suspected to trade as aforesaid, any justice of the peace shall have power to take from him suspected, sufficient recognizance, not to trade with any slave contrary to the laws of this Province; and if it shall afterwards appear to any of the justices of the peace, that such person hath, or hath had, or shipped off, any goods, suspected to be unlawfully come by, it shall be lawful for such justice of the peace to oblige the person to appear at the next general sessions, who shall there be obliged to make reasonable proof, of whom he brought, or how he came by, the said goods, and unless he do it, his recognizance shall be forfeited. . . .

VII. And *whereas*, great numbers of slaves which do not dwell in Charlestown, on Sundays and holidays resort thither, to drink, quarrel, fight, curse and swear, and profane the Sabbath, and using and carrying of clubs and other mischievous weapons, resorting in great companies together, which may give them an opportunity of executing any wicked designs and purposes, to the damage and prejudice of the inhabitants of this Province; for the prevention whereof, *Be it enacted* by the authority aforesaid, That all and every the constables of Charlestown, separately on every Sunday, and the holidays at Christmas, Easter and Whitsonside, together with so many men as each constable shall think necessary to accompany him, which he is hereby empowered for that end to press, under the penalty of twenty shillings to the person that shall disobey him, shall, together with such persons, go through all or any the streets, and also, round about Charlestown, and as much further on the neck as they shall be informed or have reason to suspect any meeting or concourse of any such negroes or slaves to be at that time, and to enter into any house, at Charlestown, or elsewhere, to search for such slaves, and as many of them as they can apprehend, shall cause to be publicly whipped in Charlestown, and then to be delivered to the marshall, who for every slave so whipped and delivered to him by the constable, shall pay the constable five shillings, which five shillings shall be repaid the said marshall by the owner or head of that family to which the said negro or slave, doth belong, together with such other charges as shall become due to him for keeping runaway slaves; and the marshall shall in all respects keep and dispose of such slave as if the same was delivered to him as a runaway, under the same penalties and forfeiture as hereafter in that case is provided; and every constable of Charlestown which shall neglect or refuse to make search as aforesaid, for every such neglect shall forfeit the sum of twenty shillings. . . .

IX. *And be it further enacted* by the authority aforesaid, That upon complaint made to any justice of the peace, of any heinous or grievous crime, committed by any slave or slaves, as murder, burglary, robbery, burning of houses, or any lesser crimes, as killing or stealing any meat or other cattle, maiming one the other, stealing of fowls, provisions, or such like trespasses or injuries, the said justice shall issue out his warrant for apprehending the offender or offenders, and for all persons to come before him that can give evidence; and if upon examination, it probably appeareth, that the apprehended person is guilty, he shall commit him or them to prison, or immediately proceed to tryal of the said slave or slaves, according to the form hereafter specified, or take security for his or their forthcoming, as the case shall require, and also to certify to the justice next to him, the said cause, and to require him, by virtue of this Act, to associate himself to him, which said justice is hereby required to do, and they so associated, are to issue their summons to three sufficient freeholders, acquainting them with the matter, and appointing them a day, hour and place, when and where the same shall be heard and determined, at which day, hour and place, the said justices and freeholders shall cause the offenders and evidences to come before them, and if they, on hearing the matter, the said freeholders being by the said justices first sworn to judge uprightly and according to evidence, and diligently weighing and examining all evidences, proofs and testimonies (and in case of murder only, if on violent presumption and circumstances), they shall find such negro or other slave or slaves guilty thereof, they shall give sentence of death, if the crime by law deserve the same, and forthwith by their warrant cause immediate execution to be done, by the common or any other executioner, in such manner as they shall think fit, the kind of death to be inflicted to be left to their judgment and discretion; and if the crime committed shall not deserve death, they shall then condemn and adjudge the criminal or criminals to any other punishment, but not extending to limb or disabling him, without a particular law directing such punishment, and shall forthwith order execution to be done accordingly.

X. And in regard great mischiefs daily happen by petty larcenies committed by negroes and slaves of this Province, *Be it further enacted* by the authority aforesaid, That if any negro or other slave shall hereafter steal or destroy any goods, chattels, or provisions whatsoever, of any other person than his master or mistress, being under the value of twelve pence, every negro or other slave so offending, and being brought before some justice of the peace of this Province, upon complaint of the party injured, and shall be adjudged guilty by confession, proof, or probable circumstances, such negro or slave so offending, excepting children, whose punishment is left wholly to the discretion of the said justice, shall be adjudged by such justice to be publicly and severely whipped, not exceeding forty lashes; and if such negro or other slave punished as aforesaid, be afterwards, by two justices of the peace, found guilty of the like crimes, he or they, for such his or their second offence, shall either have one of his ears cut off, or be branded in the forehead with a hot iron, that the mark thereof may remain; and if after such punishment, such negro or slave for his third offence, shall have his nose slit; and if such negro or other slave, after the third time as aforesaid, be accused of petty larceny, or of any of the offences before mentioned, such negro or other slave shall be tried in such manner as those accused of murder, burglary, *etc.* are before by this Act provided for to be tried, and in case they shall be found guilty a fourth time, of any of the offences before mentioned, then such negro or other slave shall be adjudged to suffer death, or other punishment, as the said justices shall think fitting; and any judgment given for the first offence, shall be a sufficient conviction for the first offence; and any after judgment after the first judgment, shall be a sufficient conviction to bring the offender within the penalty of the second offence, and so for inflicting the rest of the punishments; and in case the said justices and freeholders, and any or either of them, shall neglect or refuse to perform the duties by this Act required of them, they shall severally, for such their defaults, forfeit the sum of twenty-five pounds. . . .

XII. *And it is further enacted* by the authority aforesaid, That if any negroes or other slaves shall make mutiny or insurrection, or rise in rebellion against the authority and government of this Province, or shall make preparation of arms, powder, bullets or offensive weapons, in order to carry on such mutiny or insurrection, or shall hold any counsel or conspiracy for raising such mutiny, insurrection or rebellion, the offenders shall be tried by two justices of the peace and three freeholders, associated together as before expressed in case of murder, burglary, *etc.*, who are hereby empowered and required to try the said slaves so offending, and inflict death, or any other punishment, upon the offenders, and forthwith by their warrant cause execution to be done, by the common or any other executioner, in such manner as they shall think fitting; and if any person shall make away or conceal any negro or negroes, or other slave or slaves, suspected to be guilty of the beforementioned crimes, and not upon demand bring forth the suspected offender or offenders, such person shall forfeit for every negro or slave so concealed or made away, the sum of fifty pounds; *Provided, nevertheless,* that when and as often as any of the beforementioned crimes shall be committed by more than one negro, that shall deserve death, that then and in all such cases, if the Governor and council of this Province shall think fitting, and accordingly shall order, that only one or more of the said criminals should suffer death as exemplary, and the rest to be returned to the owners, that then, the owners of the negroes so offending, shall bear proportionably the loss of the said negro or negroes so put to death, as shall be allotted them by the said justices and freeholders; and if any person shall refuse his part so allotted him, that then, and in all such cases, the said justices and freeholders are hereby required to issue out their warrant of distress upon the goods and chattels of the person so refusing, and shall cause the same to be sold by public outcry, to satisfy the said money so allotted him to pay, and to return the overplus, if any be, to the owner; *Provided, nevertheless,* that the part allotted for any person to pay for his part or proportion of the negro or negroes so put to death, shall not exceed one sixth part of his negro or negroes so excused and pardoned; and in case that shall not be sufficient to satisfy for the negro or negroes that shall be put to death, that the remaining sum shall be paid out of the public treasury of this Province.

3

THE "THREE-FIFTHS COMPROMISE"
The U.S. Constitution, Article I, Section 2

One of the major debates in the Constitutional Convention hinged on the use of slaves in computing taxes and fixing representation. Southern delegates held that slaves should be computed in determining representation in the House, but that they should not be counted in determining a state's share of the direct tax burden. The northern delegates' point of view was exactly the opposite. A compromise was reached whereby three-fifths of the slaves were to be counted in apportionment of representation and in direct taxes among the states. Thus the South was victorious in obtaining representation for its slaves, even though delegate Luther Martin might rail that the Constitution was an insult to the Deity "who views with equal eye the poor African slave and his American master." The "three-fifths compromise" appears in Article I, Section 2.

Representatives and direct Taxes shall be apportioned among the several States which may be included within this Union, according to their respective Numbers, which shall be determined by adding to the whole Number of free Persons, including those bound to Service for a Term of Years, and excluding Indians not taxed, three fifths of all other Persons.

4

AN ACT PROHIBITING THE TEACHING OF SLAVES TO READ

To keep the slaves in hand, it was deemed necessary to keep them innocent of the printed page. Otherwise, they might read abolitionist newspapers that were smuggled in, become dissatisfied, forge passes, or simply know too much. Hence most states passed laws prohibiting anyone from teaching slaves to read or write. The North Carolina statute was typical.

An Act to Prevent All Persons from Teaching Slaves to Read or Write, the Use of Figures Excepted

Whereas the teaching of slaves to read and write, has a tendency to excite dissatisfaction in their minds, and to produce insurrection and rebellion, to the manifest injury of the citizens of this State:

Therefore,

Be it enacted by the General Assembly of the State of North Carolina, and it is hereby enacted by the authority of the same, That any free person, who shall hereafter teach, or attempt to teach, any slave within the State to read or write, the use of figures excepted, or shall give or sell to such slave or slaves any books or pamphlets, shall be liable to indictment in any court of record in this State having jurisdiction thereof, and upon conviction, shall, at the discretion of the court, if a white man or woman, be fined not less than one hundred dollars, nor more than two hundred dollars, or imprisoned; and if a free person of color, shall be fined, imprisoned, or whipped, at the discretion of the court, not exceeding thirty-nine lashes, nor less than twenty lashes.

II. *Be it further enacted,* That if any slave shall hereafter teach, or attempt to teach, any other slave to read or write, the use of figures excepted, he or she may be carried before any justice of the peace, and on conviction thereof, shall be sentenced to receive thirty-nine lashes on his or her bare back.

III. *Be it further enacted,* That the judges of the Superior Courts and the justices of the County Courts shall give this act in charge to the grand juries of their respective counties.

From *Acts Passed by the General Assembly of the State of North Carolina at the Session of 1830–1831* (Raleigh, 1831), 11.

Declaration of Sentiments and Resolutions, Seneca Falls Convention, 1848

The Declaration of Sentiments, adopted in July 1848 at Seneca Falls, New York, at the first woman's rights convention, is the most famous document in the history of feminism. Like its model, the Declaration of Independence, it contains a bill of particulars. Some people at the meeting thought the inclusion of disfranchisement in the list of grievances would discredit the entire movement, and when the resolutions accompanying the Declaration were put to a vote, the one calling for the suffrage was the only one that did not pass unanimously. But it did pass and thus inaugurated the woman's suffrage movement in the United States.

Declaration of Sentiments

When, in the course of human events, it becomes necessary for one portion of the family of man to assume among the people of the earth a position different from that which they have hitherto occupied, but one to which the laws of nature and of nature's God entitle them, a decent respect to the opinions of mankind requires that they should declare the causes that impel them to such a course.

We hold these truths to be self-evident: that all men and women are created equal; that they are endowed by their Creator with certain inalienable rights; that among these are life, liberty, and the pursuit of happiness; that to secure these rights governments are instituted, deriving their just powers from the consent of the governed. Whenever any form of government becomes destructive of these ends, it is the right of those who suffer from it to refuse allegiance to it, and to insist upon the institution of a new government, laying its foundation on such principles, and organizing its powers in such form, as to them shall seem most likely to effect their safety and happiness. Prudence, indeed, will dictate that governments long established should not be changed for light and transient causes; and accordingly all experience hath shown that mankind are more disposed to suffer, while evils are sufferable, than to right themselves by abolishing the forms to which they were accustomed. But when a long train of abuses and usurpations, pursuing invariably the same object, evinces a design to reduce them under absolute despotism, it is their duty to throw off such government, and to provide new guards for their future security. Such has been the patient sufferance of the women under this government, and such is now the necessity which constrains them to demand the equal station to which they are entitled.

The history of mankind is a history of repeated injuries and usurpations on the part of man toward woman, having in direct object the establishment of an absolute tyranny over her. To prove this, let facts be submitted to a candid world.

He has never permitted her to exercise her inalienable right to the elective franchise.

He has compelled her to submit to laws, in the formation of which she had no voice.

He has withheld from her rights which are given to the most ignorant and degraded men—both natives and foreigners.

Having deprived her of this first right of a citizen, the elective franchise, thereby leaving her without representation in the halls of legislation, he has oppressed her on all sides.

He has made her, if married, in the eye of the law, civilly dead.

He has taken from her all right in property, even to the wages she earns.

He has made her, morally, an irresponsible being, as she can commit many crimes with impunity, provided they be done in the presence of her husband. In the covenant of marriage, she is compelled to promise obedience to her husband, he becoming, to all intents and purposes, her master—the law giving him power to deprive her of her liberty, and to administer chastisement.

He has so framed the laws of divorce, as to what shall be the proper causes, and in case of separation, to whom the guardianship of the children shall be given, as to be wholly regardless of the happiness of women—the law, in all cases, going upon the false supposition of the supremacy of man, and giving all power into his hands.

After depriving her of all rights as a married woman, if single, and the owner of property, he has taxed her to support a government which recognizes her only when her property can be made profitable to it.

He has monopolized nearly all the profitable employments, and from those she is permitted to follow, she receives but a scanty remuneration. He closes against her all the avenues to wealth and distinction which he considers most honorable to himself. As a teacher of theology, medicine, or law, she is not known.

He has denied her the facilities for obtaining a thorough education, all colleges being closed against her.

He allows her in Church, as well as State, but a subordinate position, claiming Apostolic authority for her exclusion from the ministry, and, with some exceptions, from any public participation in the affairs of the Church.

He has created a false public sentiment by giving to the world a different code of morals for men and women, by which moral delinquencies which exclude women from society, are not only tolerated, but deemed of little account in man.

He has usurped the prerogative of Jehovah himself, claiming it as his right to assign for her a sphere of action, when that belongs to her conscience and to her God.

He has endeavored, in every way that he could, to destroy her confidence in her own powers, to lessen her self-respect, and to make her willing to lead a dependent and abject life.

Now, in view of this entire disfranchisement of one-half the people of this country, their social and religious degradation—in view of the unjust laws above mentioned, and because women do feel themselves aggrieved, oppressed, and fraudulently deprived of their most sacred rights, we insist that they have immediate admission to all the rights and privileges which belong to them as citizens of the United States.

In entering upon the great work before us, we anticipate no small amount of misconception, misrepresentation, and ridicule; but we shall use every instrumentality within our power to effect our object. We shall employ agents, circulate tracts, petition the State and National legislatures, and endeavor to enlist the pulpit and the press in our behalf. We hope this Convention will be followed by a series of Conventions embracing every part of the country.

Resolutions

WHEREAS, The great precept of nature is conceded to be, that "man shall pursue his own true and substantial happiness." Blackstone in his Commentaries remarks, that this law of Nature being coeval with mankind, and dictated by God himself, is of course superior in obligation to any other. It is binding over all the globe, in all countries and at all times; no human laws are of any validity if contrary to this, and such of them as are valid, derive all their force, and all their validity, and all their authority, mediately and immediately, from this original; therefore,

Resolved, That such laws as conflict, in any way, with the true and substantial happiness of woman, are contrary to the great precept of nature and of no validity, for this is "superior in obligation to any other."

Resolved, That all laws which prevent woman from occupying such a station in society as her conscience shall dictate, or which place her in a position inferior to that of man, are contrary to the great precept of nature, and therefore of no force or authority.

Resolved, That woman is man's equal—was intended to be so by the Creator, and the highest good of the race demands that she should be recognized as such.

Resolved, That the women of this country ought to be enlightened in regard to the laws under which they live, that they may no longer publish their degradation by declaring themselves satisfied with their present position, nor their ignorance, by asserting that they have all the rights they want.

Resolved, That inasmuch as man, while claiming for himself intellectual superiority, does accord to woman moral superiority, it is pre-eminently his duty to encourage her to speak and teach, as she has an opportunity, in all religious assemblies.

Resolved, That the same amount of virtue, delicacy, and refinement of behavior that is required of woman in the social state, should also be required of man, and the same transgressions should be visited with equal severity on both man and woman.

Resolved, That the objection of indelicacy and impropriety, which is so often brought against woman when she addresses a public audience, comes with a very ill-grace from those who encourage, by their attendance, her appearance on the stage, in the concert, or in feats of the circus.

Resolved, That woman has too long rested satisfied in the circumscribed limits which corrupt customs and a perverted application of the Scriptures have marked out for her, and that it is time she should move in the enlarged sphere which her great Creator has assigned her.

Resolved, That it is the duty of the women of this country to secure to themselves their sacred right to the elective franchise.

Resolved, That the equality of human rights results necessarily from the fact of the identity of the race in capabilities and responsibilities.

Resolved, therefore, That, being invested by the Creator with the same capabilities, and the same consciousness of responsibility for their exercise, it is demonstrably the right and duty of woman, equally with man, to promote every righteous cause by every righteous means; and especially in regard to the great subjects of morals and religion, it is self-evidently her right to participate with her brother in teaching them, both in private and in public, by writing and by speaking, by any instrumentalities proper to be used, and in any assemblies proper to be held; and this being a self-evident truth growing out of the divinely implanted principles of human nature, any custom or authority adverse to it, whether modern or wearing the hoary sanction of antiquity, is to be regarded as a self-evident falsehood, and at war with mankind.

[All the preceding resolutions had been drafted by Elizabeth Cady Stanton. At the last session of the convention Lucretia Mott offered the following, which, along with all the other resolutions except the ninth, was adopted unanimously.—*Ed.*]

Resolved, That the speedy success of our cause depends upon the zealous and untiring efforts of both men and women, for the overthrow of the monopoly of the pulpit, and for the securing to woman an equal participation with men in the various trades, professions, and commerce.

6

THE ANTISUFFRAGISTS
Selected Papers, 1852–1887

Editorial, New York *Herald* (1852)

The farce at Syracuse has been played out. . . .

Who are these women? What do they want? What are the motives that impel them to this course of action? The *dramatis personae* of the farce enacted at Syracuse present a curious conglomeration of both sexes. Some of them are old maids, whose personal charms were never very attractive, and who have been sadly slighted by the masculine gender in general; some of them women who have been badly mated, whose own temper, or their husbands', has made life anything but agreeable to them, and they are therefore down upon the whole of the opposite sex; some, having so much of the virago in their disposition, that nature appears to have made a mistake in their gender—mannish women, like hens that crow; some of boundless vanity and egotism, who believe that they are superior in intellectual ability to "all the world and the rest of mankind," and delight to see their speeches and addresses in print; and man shall be consigned to his proper sphere—nursing the babies, washing the dishes, mending stockings, and sweeping the house. This is "the good time coming." Besides the classes we have enumerated, there is a class of wild enthusiasts and visionaries—very sincere, but very mad—having the same vein as the fanatical Abolitionists, and the majority, if not all of them, being, in point of fact, deeply imbued with the anti-slavery sentiment. Of the male sex who attend these Conventions for the purpose of taking part in them, the majority are henpecked husbands, and all of them ought to wear petticoats. . . .

How did woman first become subject to man as she now is all over the world? By her nature, her sex, just as the negro is and always will be, to the end of time, inferior to the white race, and, therefore, doomed to subjection; but happier than she would be in any other condition, just because it is the law of her nature. The women themselves would not have this law reversed. . . .

What do the leaders of the Woman's Rights Convention want? They want to vote, and to hustle with the rowdies at the polls. They want to be members of Congress, and in the heat of debate to subject themselves to coarse jests and indecent language. . . . They want to fill all other posts which men are ambitious to occupy—

From "The Woman's Rights Convention—The Last Act of the Drama," editorial, New York *Herald*, September 12, 1852.

to be lawyers, doctors, captains of vessels, and generals in the field. How funny it would sound in the newspapers, that Lucy Stone, pleading a cause, took suddenly ill in the pains of parturition, and perhaps gave birth to a fine bouncing boy in court! Or that Rev. Antoinette Brown was arrested in the middle of her sermon in the pulpit from the same cause, and presented a "pledge" to her husband and the congregation; or, that Dr. Harriot K. Hunt, while attending a gentleman patient for a fit of the gout or *fistula in ano,* found it necessary to send for a doctor, there and then, and to be delivered of a man or woman child—perhaps twins. A similar event might happen on the floor of Congress, in a storm at sea, or in the raging tempest of battle, and then what is to become of the woman legislator?

New York State Legislative Report (1856)*

Mr. Foote, from the Judiciary Committee, made a report on Women's rights that set the whole House in roars of laughter:

"The Committee is composed of married and single gentlemen. The bachelors on the Committee, with becoming diffidence, having left the subject pretty much to the married gentlemen, they have considered it with the aid of the light they have before them and the experience married life has given them. Thus aided, they are enabled to state that the ladies always have the best place and choicest titbit at the table. They have the best seat in the cars, carriages, and sleighs; the warmest place in the winter, and the coolest place in the summer. They have their choice on which side of the bed they will lie, front or back. A lady's dress costs three times as much as that of a gentleman; and, at the present time, with the prevailing fashion, one lady occupies three times as much space in the world as a gentleman.

"It has thus appeared to the married gentlemen of your Committee, being a majority (the bachelors being silent for the reason mentioned, and also probably for the further reason that they are still suitors for the favors of the gentler sex), that, if there is any inequality or oppression in the case, the gentlemen are the sufferers. They, however, have presented no petitions for redress; having, doubtless, made up their minds to yield to an inevitable destiny. . . ."

Orestes A. Brownson, The Woman Question (1869 and 1873)†

The conclusive objection to the political enfranchisement of women is, that it would weaken and finally break up and destroy the Christian family. The social

---

*This Report on Woman's Rights, made to the New York State Legislature and concerning a petition for political equality for women, was printed in an Albany paper in March 1856.

†This document consists of two articles by Orestes A. Brownson: "The Woman Question. Article I [from the *Catholic World,* May 1869]," in Henry F. Brownson, ed., *The Works of Orestes A. Brownson,* XVIII (Detroit, 1885), 388–89; and "The Woman Question. Article II [a review of Horace Bushnell, *Women's Suffrage: The Reform against Nature* (New York, 1869), from *Brownson's Quarterly Review* for October 1873]," in Henry F. Brownson, *op. cit.,* p. 403.

unit is the family, not the individual; and the greatest danger to American society is, that we are rapidly becoming a nation of isolated individuals, without family ties or affections. The family has already been much weakened, and is fast disappearing. We have broken away from the old homestead, have lost the restraining and purifying associations that gathered around it, and live away from home in hotels and boarding-houses. We are daily losing the faith, the virtues, the habits, and the manners without which the family cannot be sustained; and when the family goes, the nation goes too, or ceases to be worth preserving. . . .

Extend now to women suffrage and eligibility; give them the political right to vote and to be voted for; render it feasible for them to enter the arena of political strife, to become canvassers in elections and candidates for office, and what remains of family union will soon be dissolved. The wife may espouse one political party, and the husband another, and it may well happen that the husband and wife may be rival candidates for the same office, and one or the other doomed to the mortification of defeat. Will the husband like to see his wife enter the lists against him, and triumph over him? Will the wife, fired with political ambition for place or power, be pleased to see her own husband enter the lists against her, and succeed at her expense? Will political rivalry and the passions it never fails to engender increase the mutual affection of husband and wife for each other, and promote domestic union and peace, or will it not carry into the bosom of the family all the strife, discord, anger, and division of the political canvass? . . .

Woman was created to be a wife and a mother; that is her destiny. To that destiny all her instincts point, and for it nature has specially qualified her. Her proper sphere is home, and her proper function is the care of the household, to manage a family, to take care of children, and attend to their early training. For this she is endowed with patience, endurance, passive courage, quick sensibilities, a sympathetic nature, and great executive and administrative ability. She was born to be a queen in her own household, and to make home cheerful, bright, and happy.

We do not believe women, unless we acknowledge individual exceptions, are fit to have their own head. The most degraded of the savage tribes are those in which women rule, and descent is reckoned from the mother instead of the father. Revelation asserts, and universal experience proves that the man is the head of the woman, and that the woman is for the man, not the man for the woman; and his greatest error, as well as the primal curse of society is that he abdicates his headship, and allows himself to be governed, we might almost say, deprived of his reason, by woman. It was through the seductions of the woman, herself seduced by the serpent, that man fell, and brought sin and all our woe into the world. She has all the qualities that fit her to be a help-meet of man, to be the mother of his children, to be their nurse, their early instructress, their guardian, their life-long friend; to be his companion, his comforter, his consoler in sorrow, his friend in trouble, his ministering angel in sickness; but as an independent existence, free to follow her own fancies and vague longings, her own ambition and natural love of power, without masculine direction or control, she is out of her element, and a social anomaly, sometimes a hideous monster, which men seldom are, excepting through a woman's influence. This is no excuse for men, but it proves that women need a head, and the restraint of father, husband, or the priest of God.

Remarks of Senator George G. Vest in Congress (1887)*

MR. VEST. . . . If this Government, which is based on the intelligence of the people, shall ever be destroyed it will be by injudicious, immature, or corrupt suffrage. If the ship of state launched by our fathers shall ever be destroyed, it will be by striking the rock of universal, unprepared suffrage. . . .

The Senator who last spoke on this question refers to the successful experiment in regard to woman suffrage in the Territories of Wyoming and Washington. Mr. President, it is not upon the plains of the sparsely settled Territories of the West that woman suffrage can be tested. Suffrage in the rural districts and sparsely settled regions of this country must from the very nature of things remain pure when corrupt everywhere else. The danger of corrupt suffrage is in the cities, and those masses of population to which civilization tends everywhere in all history. Whilst the country has been pure and patriotic, cities have been the first cancers to appear upon the body-politic in all ages of the world.

Wyoming Territory! Washington Territory! Where are their large cities? Where are the localities in those Territories where the strain upon popular government must come? The Senator from New Hampshire [Henry W. Blair—*Ed.*], who is so conspicuous in this movement, appalled the country some months since by his ghastly array of illiteracy in the Southern States. . . . That Senator proposes now to double, and more than double, that illiteracy. He proposes now to give the negro women of the South this right of suffrage, utterly unprepared as they are for it.

In a convention some two years and a half ago in the city of Louisville an intelligent negro from the South said the negro men could not vote the Democratic ticket because the women would not live with them if they did. The negro men go out in the hotels and upon the railroad cars. They go to the cities and by attrition they wear away the prejudice of race; but the women remain at home, and their emotional natures aggregate and compound the race-prejudice, and when suffrage is given them what must be the result? . . .

I pity the man who can consider any question affecting the influence of woman with the cold, dry logic of business. What man can, without aversion, turn from the blessed memory of that dear old grandmother, or the gentle words and caressing hand of that dear blessed mother gone to the unknown world, to face in its stead the idea of a female justice of the peace or township constable? For my part I want when I go to my home—when I turn from the arena where man contends with man for what we call the prizes of this paltry world—I want to go back, not

---

*The remarks of Senator George G. Vest (Democrat, Missouri) may be found in the *Congressional Record*, 49th Cong., 2d sess., January 25, 1887, p. 986.

to be received in the masculine embrace of some female ward politician, but to the earnest, loving look and touch of a true woman. I want to go back to the jurisdiction of the wife, the mother; and instead of a lecture upon finance or the tariff, or upon the construction of the Constitution, I want those blessed, loving details of domestic life and domestic love.

. . . I speak now respecting women as a sex. I believe that they are better than men, but I do not believe they are adapted to the political work of this world. I do not believe that the Great Intelligence ever intended them to invade the sphere of work given to men, tearing down and destroying all the best influences for which God has intended them.

The great evil in this country to-day is in emotional suffrage. The great danger to-day is in excitable suffrage. If the voters of this country could think always coolly, and if they could deliberate, if they could go by judgment and not by passion, our institutions would survive forever, eternal as the foundations of the continent itself; but massed together, subject to the excitements of mobs and of these terrible political contests that come upon us from year to year under the autonomy of our Government, what would be the result if suffrage were given to the women of the United States?

Women are essentially emotional. It is no disparagement to them they are so. It is no more insulting to say that women are emotional than to say that they are delicately constructed physically and unfitted to become soldiers or workmen under the sterner, harder pursuits of life.

What we want in this country is to avoid emotional suffrage, and what we need is to put more logic into public affairs and less feeling. There are spheres in which feeling should be paramount. There are kingdoms in which the heart should reign supreme. That kingdom belongs to woman. The realm of sentiment, the realm of love, the realm of the gentler and the holier and kindlier attributes that make the name of wife, mother, and sister next to that of God himself.

I would not, and I say it deliberately, degrade woman by giving her the right of suffrage. I mean the word in its full signification, because I believe that woman as she is to-day, the queen of the home and of hearts, is above the political collisions of this world, and should always be kept above them. . . .

It is said that the suffrage is to be given to enlarge the sphere of woman's influence. Mr. President, it would destroy her influence. It would take her down from that pedestal where she is to-day, influencing as a mother the minds of her offspring, influencing by her gentle and kindly caress the action of her husband toward the good and pure.

7

PEOPLE V. HALL, 1854

Bias against Chinese and other colored "races" was endemic in nineteenth-century California, but perhaps no single document so well demonstrates that bias as this majority opinion handed down by the Chief Justice of the California Supreme Court. Since Chinese miners lived in small, segregated groups, the practical effect of this decision was to declare "open season" on Chinese, since crimes against them were likely to be witnessed only by other Chinese.

The People, Respondent, v.
George W. Hall, Appellant

The appellant, a free white citizen of this State, was convicted of murder upon the testimony of Chinese witnesses.

The point involved in this case, is the admissibility of such evidence.

The 394th section of the Act Concerning Civil Cases, provides that no Indian or Negro shall be allowed to testify as a witness in any action or proceeding in which a White person is a party.

The 14th section of the Act of April 16th, 1850, regulating Criminal Proceedings, provides that "No Black, or Mulatto person, or Indian, shall be allowed to give evidence in favor of, or against a white man."

The true point at which we are anxious to arrive, is the legal signification of the words, "Black, Mulatto, Indian and White person," and whether the Legislature adopted them as generic terms, or intended to limit their application to specific types of the human species.

Before considering this question, it is proper to remark the difference between the two sections of our Statute, already quoted, the latter being more broad and comprehensive in its exclusion, by use of the word "Black," instead of Negro.

Conceding, however, for the present, that the word "Black," as used in the 14th section, and "Negro," in 394th, are convertible terms, and that the former was intended to include the latter, let us proceed to inquire who are excluded from testifying as witnesses under the term "Indian."

When Columbus first landed upon the shores of this continent, in his attempt to discover a western passage to the Indies, he imagined that he had accomplished the object of his expedition, and that the Island of San Salvador was one of those

Islands of the Chinese sea, lying near the extremity of India, which had been described by navigators.

Acting upon this hypothesis, and also perhaps from the similarity of features and physical conformation, he gave to the Islanders the name of Indians, which appellation was universally adopted, and extended to the aboriginals of the New World, as well as of Asia.

From that time, down to a very recent period, the American Indians and the Mongolian, or Asiatic, were regarded as the same type of human species. . . .

. . . That this was the common opinion in the early history of American legislation, cannot be disputed, and, therefore, all legislation upon the subject must have borne relation to that opinion. . . .

. . . In using the words, "No Black, or Mulatto person, or Indian shall be allowed to give evidence for or against a White person," the Legislature, if any intention can be ascribed to it, adopted the most comprehensive terms to embrace every known class or shade of color, as the apparent design was to protect the White person from the influence of all testimony other than that of persons of the same caste. The use of these terms must, by every sound rule of construction, exclude every one who is not of white blood. . . .

. . . We have carefully considered all the consequences resulting from a different rule of construction, and are satisfied that even in a doubtful case we would be impelled to this decision on grounds of public policy.

The same rule which would admit them to testify, would admit them to all the equal rights of citizenship, and we might soon see them at the polls, in the jury box, upon the bench, and in our legislative halls.

This is not a speculation which exists in the excited and overheated imagination of the patriot and statesman, but it is an actual and present danger.

The anomalous spectacle of a distinct people, living in our community, recognizing no laws of this State except through necessity, bringing with them their prejudices and national feuds, in which they indulge in open violation of law; whose mendacity is proverbial; a race of people whom nature has marked as inferior, and who are incapable of progress or intellectual development beyond a certain point, as their history has shown; differing in language, opinions, color, and physical conformation; between whom and ourselves nature has placed an impassible difference, is now presented, and for them is claimed, not only the right to swear away the life of a citizen, but the further privilege of participating with us in administering the affairs of our Government. . . .

. . . For these reasons, we are of opinion that the testimony was inadmissible. . . .

8

DRED SCOTT V. SANDFORD, 1857

The question is simply this: Can a negro, whose ancestors were imported into this country, and sold as slaves, become a member of the political community formed and brought into existence by the Constitution of the United States, and as such become entitled to all the rights, and privileges, and immunities, guarantied by that instrument to the citizen? One of which rights is the privilege of suing in a court of the United States in the cases specified in the Constitution.

It will be observed, that the plea applies to that class of persons only whose ancestors were negroes of the African race, and imported into this country, and sold and held as slaves. The only matter in issue before this court, therefore, is whether the descendants of such slaves, when they shall be emancipated, or who are born of parents who had become free before their birth, are citizens of a State, in the sense in which the word citizen is used in the Constitution of the United States. And this being the only matter in dispute on the pleadings, the court must be understood as speaking in his opinion of that class only, that is, of those persons who are the descendants of Africans who were imported into this country, and sold as slaves.

It becomes necessary, therefore, to determine who were citizens of the several States when the Constitution was adopted. And in order to do this, we must recur to the Governments and institutions of the thirteen colonies, when they separated from Great Britain and formed new sovereignties, and took their places in the family of independent nations. We must inquire who, at that time, were recognised as the people or citizens of a State, whose rights and liberties had been outraged by the English Government; and who declared their independence, and assumed the powers of Government to defend their rights by force of arms.

In the opinion of the court, the legislation and histories of the times, and the language used in the Declaration of Independence, show, that neither the class of persons who had been imported as slaves, nor their descendants, whether they had become free or not, were then acknowledged as a part of the people, nor intended to be included in the general words used in that memorable instrument.

It is difficult at this day to realize the state of public opinion in relation to that unfortunate race, which prevailed in the civilized and enlightened portions of the world at the time of the Declaration of Independence, and when the Constitution

From Benjamin C. Howard, *Report of the Decision of the Supreme Court of the United States in the Case Dred Scott* . . . (Washington, 1857), 9, 13–14, 15–17, 60.

of the United States was formed and adopted. But the public history of every European nation displays it in a manner too plain to be mistaken.

They had for more than a century before been regarded as beings of an inferior order, and altogether unfit to associate with the white race, either in social or political relations; and so far inferior, that they had no rights which the white man was bound to respect; and that the negro might justly and lawfully be reduced to slavery for his benefit. He was bought and sold, and treated as an ordinary article of merchandise and traffic, whenever a profit could be made by it. This opinion was at that time fixed and universal in the civilized portion of the white race. It was regarded as an axiom in morals as well as in politics, which no one thought of disputing, or supposed to be open to dispute; and men in every grade and position in society daily and habitually acted upon it in their private pursuits, as well as in matters of public concern, without doubting for a moment the correctness of this opinion.

And in no nation was this opinion more firmly fixed or more uniformly acted upon than by the English Government and English people. They not only seized them on the coast of Africa, and sold them or held them in slavery for their own use, but they took them as ordinary articles of merchandise to every country where they could make a profit on them, and were far more extensively engaged in this commerce than any other nation in the world.

The opinion thus entertained and acted upon in England was naturally impressed upon the colonies they founded on this side of the Atlantic. And, accordingly, a negro of the African race was regarded by them as an article of property, and held, and bought and sold as such, in every one of the thirteen colonies which united in the Declaration of Independence, and afterwards formed the Constitution of the United States. The slaves were more or less numerous in the different colonies, as slave labor was found more or less profitable. But no one seems to have doubted the correctness of the prevailing opinion of the time.

The legislation of the different colonies furnishes positive and indisputable proof of this fact.

The language of the Declaration of Independence is equally conclusive:

It begins by declaring that, "when in the course of human events it becomes necessary for one people to dissolve the political bands which have connected them with another, and to assume among the powers of the earth the separate and equal station to which the laws of nature and nature's God entitle them, a decent respect for the opinions of mankind requires that they should declare the causes which impel them to the separation."

It then proceeds to say: "We hold these truths to be self-evident: that all men are created equal; that they are endowed by their Creator with certain unalienable rights; that among them is life, liberty, and the pursuit of happiness; that to secure these rights, Governments are instituted, deriving their just powers from the consent of the governed."

The general words above quoted would seem to embrace the whole human family, and if they were used in a similar instrument at this day would be so understood.

But it is too clear for dispute, that the enslaved African race were not intended to be included, and formed no part of the people who framed and adopted this declaration; for if the language, as understood in that day, would embrace them, the conduct of the distinguished men who framed the Declaration of Independence would have been utterly and flagrantly inconsistent with the principles they asserted; and instead of the sympathy of mankind, to which they so confidently appealed, they would have deserved and received universal rebuke and reprobation.

Yet the men who framed this declaration were great men—high in literary acquirements—high in their sense of honor, and incapable of asserting principles inconsistent with those on which they were acting. They perfectly understood the meaning of the language they used, and how it would be understood by others; and they knew that it would not in any part of the civilized world be supposed to embrace the negro race, which, by common consent, had been excluded from civilized Governments and the family of nations, and doomed to slavery. They spoke and acted according to the then established doctrines and principles, and in the ordinary language of the day, and no one misunderstood them. The unhappy black race were separated from the white by indelible marks, and laws long before established, and were never thought of or spoken of except as property, and when the claims of the owner or the profit of the trader were supposed to need protection.

The state of public opinion had undergone no change when the Constitution was adopted, as is equally evident from its provisions and language.

This brief preamble sets forth by whom it was formed, for what purposes, and for whose benefit and protection. It declares that it is formed by the *people* of the United States; that is to say, by those who were members of the different political communities in the several States; and its great object is declared to be to secure the blessings of liberty to themselves and their posterity. It speaks in general terms of the *people* of the United States, and of *citizens* of the several States, when it is providing for the exercise of the powers granted or the privileges secured to the citizen. It does not define what description of persons are intended to be included under these terms, or who shall be regarded as a citizen and one of the people. It uses them as terms so well understood, that no further description or definition was necessary.

But there are two clauses in the Constitution which point directly and specifically to the negro race as a separate class of persons, and show clearly that they were not regarded as a portion of the people or citizens of the Government then formed.

One of these clauses reserves to each of the thirteen States the right to import slaves until the year 1808, if it thinks proper. And the importation which it thus sanctions was unquestionably of persons of the race of which we are speaking, as the traffic in slaves in the United States had always been confined to them. And by the other provision the States pledge themselves to each other to maintain the right of property of the master, by delivering up to him any slave who may have escaped from his service, and be found within their respective territories. By the first above-mentioned clause, therefore, the right to purchase and hold this property is directly sanctioned and authorized for twenty years by the people who framed the Constitution. And by the second, they pledge themselves to maintain and uphold the right of the master in the manner specified, as long as the Government they then formed should endure. And these two provisions show, conclusively, that neither the description of persons therein referred to, nor their descendants, were embraced in any of the other provisions of the Constitution, for certainly these two clauses were not intended to confer on them or their posterity the blessings of liberty, or any of the personal rights so carefully provided for the citizen.

Upon the whole, therefore, it is the judgment of this court, that it appears by the record before us that the plaintiff in error is not a citizen of Missouri, in the sense in which that word is used in the Constitution; and that the Circuit Court of the United States, for that reason, had no jurisdiction in the case, and could give no judgment in it. Its judgment for the defendant must, consequently, be reversed, and a mandate issued, directing the suit to be dismissed for want of jurisdiction.

9

THE EMANCIPATION PROCLAMATION

Abraham Lincoln

Emancipation Proclamation by the President of the United States of America: A Proclamation

January 1, 1863

Whereas, on the twenty-second day of September, in the year of our Lord one thousand eight hundred and sixty two, a proclamation was issued by the President of the United States, containing, among other things, the following, to wit:

"That on the first day of January, in the year of our Lord one thousand eight hundred and sixty-three, all persons held as slaves within any State or designated part of a State, the people whereof shall then be in rebellion against the United States, shall be then, thenceforward, and forever free; and the Executive Government of the United States, including the military and naval authority thereof, will recognize and maintain the freedom of such persons, and will do no act or acts to repress such persons, or any of them, in any efforts they may make for their actual freedom.

"That the Executive will, on the first day of January aforesaid, by proclamation, designate the States and parts of States, if any, in which the people thereof, respectively, shall then be in rebellion against the United States; and the fact that any State, or the people thereof, shall on that day be, in good faith, represented in the Congress of the United States by members chosen thereto at elections wherein a majority of the qualified voters of such State shall have participated, shall, in the absence of strong countervailing testimony, be deemed conclusive evidence that such State, and the people thereof, are not then in rebellion against the United States."

Now, therefore I, Abraham Lincoln, President of the United States, by virtue of the power in me vested as Commander-in-Chief, of the Army and Navy of the United States in time of actual armed rebellion against authority and government of the United States, and as a fit and necessary war measure for suppressing said rebellion, do, on this first day of January, in the year of our Lord one thousand eight hundred and sixty-three, and in accordance with my purpose so to do publicly proclaimed for the full period of one hundred days, from the day first above mentioned, order and designate as the States and parts of States wherein the people thereof respectively, are this day in rebellion against the United States, the following, to wit:

Arkansas, Texas, Louisiana (except the Parishes of St. Bernard, Plaquemines, Jefferson, St. Johns, St. Charles, St. James[,] Ascension, Assumption, Terrebonne, Lafourche, St. Mary, St. Martin, and Orleans, including the City of New-Orleans), Mississippi, Alabama, Florida, Georgia, South-Carolina, North-Carolina, and Virginia (except the forty-eight counties designated as West Virginia, and also the counties of Berkley, Accomac, Northampton, Elizabeth-City, York, Princess Ann, and Norfolk, including the cities of Norfolk & Portsmouth [)]; and which excepted parts are, for the present, left precisely as if this proclamation were not issued.

And by virtue of the power, and for the purpose aforesaid, I do order and declare that all persons held as slaves within said designated States, and parts of States, are, and henceforward shall be free; and that the Executive Government of the United States, including the military and naval authorities thereof, will recognize and maintain the freedom of said persons.

And I hereby enjoin upon the people so declared to be free to abstain from all violence, unless in necessary self-defence; and I recommend to them that, in all cases when allowed, they labor faithfully for reasonable wages.

And I further declare and make known, that such persons of suitable condition, will be received into the armed service of the United States to garrison forts, positions, stations, and other places, and to man vessels of all sorts in said service.

And upon this act, sincerely believed to be an act of justice, warranted by the Constitution, upon military necessity, I invoke the considerate judgment of mankind, and the gracious favor of Almighty God.

In witness whereof, I have hereunto set my hand and caused the seal of the United States to be affixed.

Done at the City of Washington, this first day of January, in the year of our Lord one thousand eight hundred and sixty-three, and of the Independence of the United States of America the eighty-seventh.

By the President:
Abraham Lincoln

William H. Steward,
Secretary of State

10

UNITED STATES CONSTITUTION
Thirteenth (1865), Fourteenth (1868), and Fifteenth (1870) Amendments

Amendment XIII (Ratified December 6, 1865). *Section 1.* Neither slavery nor involuntary servitude, except as a punishment for crime whereof the party shall have been duly convicted, shall exist within the United States, or any place subject to their jurisdiction.

Section 2. Congress shall have power to enforce this article by appropriate legislation.

Amendment XIV (Ratified July 9, 1868). *Section 1.* All persons born or naturalized in the United States, and subject to the jurisdiction thereof, are citizens of the United States and of the state wherein they reside. No State shall make or enforce any law which shall abridge the privileges or immunities of citizens of the United States; nor shall any State deprive any person of life, liberty, or property, without due process of law; nor deny to any person within its jurisdiction the equal protection of the laws.

Section 2. Representatives shall be apportioned among the several states according to their respective numbers, counting the whole number of persons in each state, excluding Indians not taxed. But when the right to vote at any election for the choice of Electors for President and Vice-President of the United States, Representatives in Congress, the executive and judicial officers of a State, or the members of the Legislature thereof, is denied to any of the male inhabitants of such State, being twenty-one years of age, and, citizens of the United States, or in any way abridged, except for participation in rebellion, or other crime, the basis of representation therein shall be reduced in the proportion which the number of such male citizens shall bear to the whole number of male citizens twenty-one years of age in such State.

Section 3. No person shall be a Senator or Representative in Congress, or elector of President and Vice-President, or hold any office, civil or military, under the United States, or under any State, who, having previously taken an oath, as a member of Congress, or as an officer of the United States, or as an executive or judicial officer of any State, to support the Constitution of the United States, shall have engaged in insurrection or rebellion against the same, or given aid or comfort to the enemies thereof. But Congress may by a vote of two-thirds of each House, remove such disability.

Section 4. The validity of the public debt of the United States, authorized by law, including debts incurred for payment of pensions and bounties for services in suppressing insurrection or rebellion, shall not be questioned. But neither the United States nor any State shall assume or pay any debt or obligation incurred in aid of insurrection or rebellion against the United States, or any claim for the loss or emancipation of any slave; but all such debts, obligations, and claims, shall be held illegal and void.

Section 5. The Congress shall have power to enforce, by appropriate legislation, the provisions of this article.

Amendment XV (Ratified February 3, 1870). *Section 1.* The right of citizens of the United States to vote shall not be denied or abridged by the United States or by any State on account of race, color, or previous condition of servitude.

Section 2. The Congress shall have power to enforce this article by appropriate legislation.

11

THE BLACK CODES

W. E. B. Du Bois

The whole proof of what the South proposed to do to the emancipated Negro, unless restrained by the nation, was shown in the Black Codes passed after [President Andrew] Johnson's accession, but representing the logical result of attitudes of mind existing when Lincoln still lived. Some of these were passed and en-

From W.E.B. Du Bois, *Black Reconstruction* (New York: Harcourt Brace, 1935). Reprinted by permission of David G. Du Bois.

forced. Some were passed and afterward repealed or modified when the reaction of the North was realized. In other cases, as for instance, in Louisiana, it is not clear just which laws were retained and which were repealed. In Alabama, the Governor induced the legislature not to enact some parts of the proposed code which they overwhelmingly favored.

The original codes favored by the Southern legislatures were an astonishing affront to emancipation and dealt with vagrancy, apprenticeship, labor contracts, migration, civil and legal rights. In all cases, there was plain and indisputable attempt on the part of the Southern states to make Negroes slaves in everything but name. They were given certain civil rights: the right to hold property, to sue and be sued. The family relations for the first time were legally recognized. Negroes were no longer real estate.

Yet, in the face of this, the Black Codes were deliberately designed to take advantage of every misfortune of the Negro. Negroes were liable to a slave trade under the guise of vagrancy and apprenticeship laws; to make the best labor contracts, Negroes must leave the old plantations and seek better terms; but if caught wandering in search of work, and thus unemployed and without a home, this was vagrancy, and the victim could be whipped and sold into slavery. In the turmoil of war, children were separated from parents, or parents unable to support them properly. These children could be sold into slavery, and "the former owner of said minors shall have the preference." Negroes could come into court as witnesses only in cases in which Negroes were involved. And even then, they must make their appeal to a jury and judge who would believe the word of any white man in preference to that of any Negro on pain of losing office and caste.

The Negro's access to the land was hindered and limited; his right to work was curtailed; his right of self-defense was taken away, when his right to bear arms was stopped; and his employment was virtually reduced to contract labor with penal servitude as a punishment for leaving his job. And in all cases, the judges of the Negro's guilt or innocence, rights and obligations were men who believed firmly, for the most part, that he had "no rights which a white man was bound to respect."

Making every allowance for the excitement and turmoil of war, and the mentality of a defeated people, the Black Codes were infamous pieces of legislation.

Let us examine these codes in detail.[1] They covered, naturally, a wide range of subjects. First, there was the question of allowing Negroes to come into the state. In South Carolina the constitution of 1865 permitted the Legislature to regulate immigration, and the consequent law declared "that no person of color shall migrate into and reside in this State, unless, within twenty days after his arrival within the same, he shall enter into a bond, with two freeholders as sureties . . . in a penalty of one thousand dollars, conditioned for his good behavior, and for his support."

Especially in the matter of work was the Negro narrowly restricted. In South Carolina, he must be especially licensed if he was to follow on his own account any employment, except that of farmer or servant. Those licensed must not only prove their fitness, but pay an annual tax ranging from $10–$100. Under no circumstances could they manufacture or sell liquor. Licenses for work were to be granted by a judge and were revokable on complaint. The penalty was a fine double the amount of the license, one-half of which went to the informer.

Mississippi provided that "every freedman, free Negro, and mulatto shall on the second Monday of January, one thousand eight hundred and sixty-six, and annually thereafter, have a lawful home or employment, and shall have written evidence thereof . . . from the Mayor . . . or from a member of the board of police . . . which licenses may be revoked for cause at any time by the authority granting the same."

Detailed regulation of labor was provided for in nearly all these states.

Louisiana passed an elaborate law in 1865, to "regulate labor contracts for agricultural pursuits." Later, it was denied that this legislation was actually enacted but the law was published at the time and the constitutional convention of 1868 certainly regarded this statute as law, for they formally repealed it. The law required all agricultural laborers to make labor contracts for the next year within the first ten days of January, the contracts to be in writing, to be with heads of families, to embrace the labor of all the members, and to be "binding on all minors thereof." Each laborer, after choosing his employer, "shall not be allowed to leave his place of employment, until the fulfillment of his contract, unless by consent of his employer, or on account of harsh treatment, or breach of contract on the part of the employer; and if they do so leave, without cause or permission, they shall forfeit all wages earned to the time of abandonment. . . .

"In case of sickness of the laborer, wages for the time lost shall be deducted, and where the sickness is feigned for purposes of idleness, . . . and also should refusal to work be continued beyond three days, the offender shall be reported to a justice of the peace, and shall be forced to labor on roads, levees, and other public works, without pay, until the offender consents to return to his labor. . . .

"When in health, the laborer shall work ten hours during the day in summer, and nine hours during the day in winter, unless otherwise stipulated in the labor contract; he shall obey all proper orders of his employer or his agent; take proper care of his work mules, horses, oxen, stock; also of all agricultural implements; and employers shall have the right to make a reasonable deduction from the laborer's wages for injuries done to animals or agricultural implements committed to his care, or for bad or negligent work. Bad work shall not be allowed. Failing to obey reasonable orders, neglect of duty and leaving home without permission, will be deemed disobedience. . . . For any disobedience a fine of one dollar shall be imposed on the offender. For all lost time from work hours, unless in case of sickness, the laborer shall be fined twenty-five cents per hour. For all absence from home without leave, the laborer will be fined at the rate of two dollars per day. Laborers will not be required to labor on the Sabbath except to take the necessary care of stock and other property on plantations and do the necessary cooking and household duties, unless by special contract. For all thefts of the laborers from the employer of agricultural products, hogs, sheep, poultry or any other property of the employer, or willful destruction of property or injury, the laborer shall pay the employer double the amount of the value of the property stolen, destroyed or injured, one half to be paid to the employer, and the other half to be placed in the general fund provided for in this section. No live stock shall be allowed to laborers without the permission of the employer. Laborers shall not receive visitors during work hours. All difficulties arising between the employers and laborers, under this section, shall be settled, and all fines be imposed, by the former; if not satisfactory to the laborers, an appeal may be had to the nearest justice of the peace and two freeholders, citizens, one of said citizens to be selected by the employer and the other by the laborer; and all fines imposed and collected under this section shall be deducted from the wages due, and shall be placed in a common fund, to be divided among the other laborers employed on the plantation at the time when their full wages fall due, except as provided for above."

Similar detailed regulations of work were in the South Carolina law. Elaborate provision was made for contracting colored "servants" to white "masters." Their masters were given the right to whip "moderately" servants under eighteen. Others were to be whipped on authority of judicial officers. These officers were given authority to return runaway servants to their masters. The servants, on the other hand, were given certain rights. Their wages and period of service must be specified in writing, and they were protected against "unreasonable" tasks, Sunday and night work, unauthorized attacks on their persons, and inadequate food.

Contracting Negroes were to be known as "servants" and contractors as "masters." Wages were to be fixed by the judge, unless stipulated. Negroes of ten years of age or more without a parent living in the district might make a valid contract for a year or less. Failure to make written contracts was a misdemeanor, punishable by a fine of $5 to $50; farm labor to be from sunrise to sunset, with intervals for meals; servants to rise at dawn, to be careful of master's property and answerable for property lost or injured. Lost time was to be deducted from wages. Food and clothes might be deducted. Servants were to be quiet and orderly and to go to bed at reasonable hours. No night work or outdoor work in bad weather was to be asked, except in cases of necessity, visitors not allowed without the master's consent. Servants leaving employment without good reason must forfeit wages. Masters might discharge servants for disobedience, drunkenness, disease, absence, etc. Enticing away the services of a servant was punishable by a fine of $20 to $100. A master could command a servant to aid him in defense of his own person, family or property. House servants at all hours of the day and night, and at all days of the weeks, "must answer promptly all calls and execute all lawful orders. . . ."

Mississippi provided "that every civil officer shall, and every person may, arrest and carry back to his or her legal employer any freedman, free Negro, or mulatto who shall have quit the service of his or her employer before the expiration of his or her term of service without good cause; and said officer and person shall be entitled to receive for arresting and carrying back every deserting employee aforesaid the sum of five dollars, and ten cents per mile from the place of arrest to the place of delivery, and the same shall be paid by the employer and held as a set-off for so much against the wages of said deserting employee."

It was provided in some states, like South Carolina, that any white man, whether an officer or not, could arrest a Negro. "Upon view of a misdemeanor committed by a person of color, any person present may arrest the offender and take him before a magistrate, to be dealt with as the case may require. In case of a misdemeanor committed by a white person toward a person of color, any person may complain to a magistrate, who shall cause the offender to be arrested, and according to the nature of the case, to be brought before himself, or be taken for trial in the district court."

On the other hand, in Mississippi, it was dangerous for a Negro to try to bring a white person to court on any charge. "In every case where any white person has been arrested and brought to trial, by virtue of the provisions of the tenth section of the above recited act, in any court in this State, upon sufficient proof being made to the court or jury, upon the trial before said court, that any freedman, free Negro or mulatto has falsely and maliciously caused the arrest and trial of said white person or persons, the court shall render up a judgment against said freedman, free Negro or mulatto for all costs of the case, and impose a fine not to exceed fifty dollars, and imprisonment in the county jail not to exceed twenty days; and for a failure of said freedman, free Negro or mulatto to pay, or cause to be paid, all costs, fines and jail fees, the sheriff of the county is hereby authorized and required, after giving ten days' public notice, to proceed to hire out at public outcry, at the courthouse of the county, said freedman, free Negro or mulatto, for the shortest time to raise the amount necessary to discharge said freedman, free Negro or mulatto from all costs, fines, and jail fees aforesaid."

Mississippi declared that: "Any freedman, free Negro, or mulatto, committing riots, routs, affrays, trespasses, malicious mischief and cruel treatment to animals, seditious speeches, insulting gestures, language or acts, or assaults on any person, disturbance of the peace, exercising the functions of a minister of the gospel without a license from some regularly organized church, vending spirituous or intoxicating liquors, or committing any other misdemeanor, the punishment of which is not specifically provided for by law, shall, upon conviction thereof, in the county court, be fined not less than ten dollars, and not more than one hundred dollars, and may be imprisoned, at the discretion of the court, not exceeding thirty days. . . ."

The most important and oppressive laws were those with regard to vagrancy and apprenticeship. Sometimes they especially applied to Negroes; in other cases, they were drawn in general terms but evidently designed to fit the Negro's condition and to be enforced particularly with regard to Negroes.

The Virginia Vagrant Act enacted that "any justice of the peace, upon the complaint of any one of certain officers therein named, may issue his warrant for the apprehension of any person alleged to be a vagrant and cause such person to be apprehended and brought before him; and that if upon due examination said justice of the peace shall find that such person is a vagrant within the definition of vagrancy contained in said statute, he shall issue his warrant, directing such person to be employed for a term not exceeding three months, and by any constable of the county wherein the proceedings are had, be hired out for the best wages which can be procured, his wages to be applied to the support of himself and his family. The said statute further provides, that in case any vagrant so hired shall, during his term of service, run away from his employer without sufficient cause, he shall be apprehended on the warrant of a justice of the peace and returned to the custody of his employer, who shall then have, free from any other hire, the services of such vagrant for one month in addition to the original term of hiring, and that the employer shall then have power, if authorized by a justice of the peace, to work such vagrant with ball and chain. The said statute specified the persons who shall be considered vagrants and liable to the penalties imposed by it. Among those declared to be vagrants are all persons who, not having the wherewith to support their families, live idly and without employment, and refuse to work for the usual and common wages given to other laborers in the like work in the place where they are."

In Florida, January 12, 1866: "It is provided that when any person of color shall enter into a contract as aforesaid, to serve as a laborer for a year, or any other specified term, on any farm or plantation in this State, if he shall refuse or neglect to perform the stipulations of his contract by willful disobedience of orders, wanton impudence or disrespect to his employer, or his authorized agent, failure or refusal to perform the work assigned to him, idleness, or abandonment of the premises or the employment of the party with whom the contract was made, he or she shall be liable, upon the complaint of his employer or his agent, made under oath before any justice of the peace of the county, to be arrested and tried before the criminal court of the county, and upon conviction shall be subject to all the pains and penalties prescribed for the punishment of vagrancy."

In Georgia, it was ruled that "All persons wandering or strolling about in idleness, who are able to work, and who have no property to support them; all persons leading an idle, immoral, or profligate life, who have no property to support them and are able to work and do not work; all persons able to work having no visible and known means of a fair, honest, and respectable livelihood; all persons having a fixed abode, who have no visible property to support them, and who live by stealing or by trading in, bartering for, or buying stolen property; and all professional gamblers living in idleness, shall be deemed and considered vagrants, and shall be indicated as such, and it shall be lawful for any person to arrest said vagrants and have them bound over for trial to the next term of the county court, and upon conviction, they shall be fined and imprisoned or sentenced to work on the public works, for not longer than a year, or shall, in the discretion of the court, be bound out to some person for a time not longer than one year, upon such valuable consideration as the court may prescribe."

Mississippi provided "That all freedmen, free Negroes, and mulattoes in this state over the age of eighteen years, found on the second Monday in January, 1866, or thereafter, with no lawful employment or business, or found unlawfully assembling themselves together, either in the day or night time, and all white persons so assembling with freedmen, free Negroes or mulattoes, or usually associating with freedmen, free Negroes or mulattoes on terms of equality, or living in adultery or fornication with a freedwoman, free Negro or mulatto, shall be deemed vagrants, and on conviction thereof shall be fined in the sum of not exceeding, in the case of a freedman, free Negro or mulatto, fifty dollars, and a white man two hundred dollars and imprisoned, at the discretion of the court, the free Negro not exceeding ten days, and the white men not exceeding six months."

Sec. 5 provides that "all fines and forfeitures collected under the provisions of this act shall be paid into the county treasury for general county purposes, and in case any freedman, free Negro or mulatto, shall fail for five days after the imposition of any fine or forfeiture upon him or her, for violation of any of the provisions of this act to pay the same, that it shall be, and is hereby made, the duty of the Sheriff of the proper county to hire out said freedman, free Negro or mulatto, to any person who will, for the shortest period of service, pay said fine or forfeiture and all costs; *Provided,* a preference shall be given to the employer, if there be one, in which case the employer shall be entitled to deduct and retain the amount so paid from the wages of such freedman, free Negro or mulatto, then due or to become due; and in case such freedman, free Negro or mulatto cannot be hired out, he or she may be dealt with as a pauper. . . ."

In Alabama, the "former owner" was to have preference in the apprenticing of a child. This was true in Kentucky and Mississippi.

Mississippi "provides that it shall be the duty of all sheriffs, justices of the peace, and other civil officers of the several counties in this state to report to the probate courts of their respective counties semi-annually, at the January and July terms of said courts, all freedmen, free Negroes and mulattoes, under the age of eighteen, within their respective counties, beats, or districts, who are orphans, or whose parent or parents have not the means, or who refuse to provide for and support said minors, and thereupon it shall be the duty of said probate court to order the clerk of said court to apprentice said minors to some competent and suitable person, on such terms as the court may direct, having a particular care to the interest of said minors; *Provided,* that the former owner of said minors shall have the preference when, in the opinion of the court, he or she shall be a suitable person for that purpose. . . ."

"Capital punishment was provided for colored persons guilty of willful homicide, assault upon a white woman, impersonating her husband for carnal purposes, raising an insurrection, stealing a horse, a mule, or baled cotton, and housebreaking. For crimes not demanding death Negroes might be confined at hard labor, whipped, or transported; 'but punishments more degrading than imprisonment shall not be imposed upon a white person for a crime not infamous.'"[2]

In most states Negroes were allowed to testify in courts but the testimony was usually confined to cases where colored persons were involved, although in some states, by consent of the parties, they could testify in cases where only white people were involved. . . .

Mississippi simply reenacted her slave code and made it operative so far as punishments were concerned. "That all the penal and criminal laws now in force in this State, defining offenses, and prescribing the mode of punishment for crimes and misdemeanors committed by slaves, free Negroes or mulattoes, be and the same are hereby reenacted, and declared to be in full force and effect, against freedmen, free Negroes, and mulattoes, except so far as the mode and manner of trial and punishment have been changed or altered by law."

North Carolina, on the other hand, abolished her slave code, making difference of punishment only in the case of Negroes convicted of rape. Georgia placed the fines and costs of a servant upon the master. "Where such cases shall go against the servant, the judgment for costs upon written notice to the master shall operate as a garnishment against him, and he shall retain a sufficient amount for the payment thereof, out of any wages due to said servant, or to become due during the period of service, and may be cited at any time by the collecting officer to make answer thereto."

The celebrated ordinance of Opelousas, Louisiana, shows the local ordinances regulating Negroes. "No Negro or freedman shall be allowed to come within the limits of the town of Opelousas without special permission from his employer, specifying the object of his visit and the time necessary for the accomplishment of the same.

"Every Negro freedman who shall be found on the streets of Opelousas after ten o'clock at night without a written pass or permit from his employer, shall be imprisoned and compelled to work five days on the public streets, or pay a fine of five dollars.

"No Negro or freedman shall be permitted to rent or keep a house within the limits of the town under any circumstances, and anyone thus offending shall be ejected, and compelled to find an employer or leave the town within twenty-four hours.

"No Negro or freedman shall reside within the limits of the town of Opelousas who is not in the regular service of some white person or former owner, who shall be held responsible for the conduct of said freedman.

"No Negro or freedman shall be permitted to preach, exhort, or otherwise declaim to congregations of colored people without a special permission from the Mayor or President of the Board of Police, under the penalty of a fine of ten dollars or twenty days' work on the public streets.

"No freedman who is not in the military service shall be allowed to carry firearms, or any kind of weapons within the limits of the town of Opelousas without the special permission of his employer, in writing, and approved by the Mayor or President of the Board.

"Any freedman not residing in Opelousas, who shall be found within its corporate limits after the hour of 3 o'clock, on Sunday, without a special permission from his employer or the Mayor, shall be arrested and imprisoned and made to work two days on the public streets, or pay two dollars in lieu of said work."[3]

Of Louisiana, Thomas Conway testified February 22, 1866: "Some of the leading officers of the state down there—men who do much to form and control the opinions of the masses—instead of doing as they promised, and quietly submitting to the authority of the government, engaged in issuing slave codes and in promulgating them to their subordinates, ordering them to carry them into execution, and this to the knowledge of state officials of a higher character, the governor and others. And the men who issued them were not punished except as the military authorities punished them. The governor inflicted no punishment on them while I was there, and I don't know that, up to this day, he has ever punished one of them. These codes were simply the old black code of the state, with the word 'slave' expunged, and 'Negro' substituted. The most odious features of slavery were preserved in them. . . ."[4]

NOTES

1. Quotations from McPherson, *History of United States during Reconstruction*, pp. 29–44.
2. Simkins and Woody, *South Carolina during Reconstruction*, pp. 49, 50.
3. Warmoth, *War, Politics and Reconstruction*, p. 274.
4. *Report on the Joint Committee on Reconstruction*, 1866, Part IV, pp. 78–79.

12

BRADWELL V. ILLINOIS, 1873

Mid-nineteenth century feminists, many of them diligent workers in the cause of abolition, looked to Congress after the Civil War for an express guarantee of equal rights for men and women. Viewed in historical perspective, their expectations appear unrealistic. A problem of far greater immediacy faced the nation. Moreover, the common law heritage, ranking the married woman in relationship to her husband as "something better than his dog, a little dearer than his horse,"[1] was just beginning to erode. Nonetheless, the text of the fourteenth amendment appalled the proponents of a sex equality guarantee. Their concern centered on the abortive second section of the amendment, which placed in the Constitution for the first time the word "male." Threefold use of the word "male," always in conjunction with the term "citizens," caused concern that the grand phrases of the first section of the fourteenth amendment would have, at best, qualified application to women.[2]

For more than a century after the adoption of the fourteenth amendment, the judiciary, with rare exceptions, demonstrated utmost deference to sex lines drawn by the legislature. . . .

The Court's initial examination of a woman's claim to full participation in society through entry into a profession traditionally reserved to men came in 1873 in Bradwell v. Illinois.[3] Myra Bradwell's application for a license to practice law had been denied by the Illinois Supreme Court solely because she was a female. The Supreme Court affirmed this judgment with only one dissent, recorded but not explained, by Chief Justice Chase. Justice Miller's opinion for the majority was placed on two grounds: (1) since petitioner was a citizen of Illinois, the privileges and immunities clause of article IV, section 2 of the Federal Constitution[4] was inapplicable to her claim; and (2) since admission to the bar of a state is not one of the privileges and immunities of United States citizenship, the fourteenth amendment did not secure the asserted right. Justice Bradley, speaking for himself and Justices Swayne and Field, chose to place his concurrence in the judgment on broader grounds. He wrote[5]:

[T]he civil law, as well as nature herself, has always recognized a wide difference in the respective spheres and destinies of man and woman. Man is, or should be, woman's protector and defender. The natural and proper timidity and delicacy which belongs to the female sex evidently unfits it for many of the occupations of civil life. The constitution of the family organization, which is founded in the divine ordinance, as well as in the nature of things, indicates the domestic sphere as that which properly belongs to the domain and functions of womanhood. The harmony, not to say identity, of interests and views which belong, or should belong, to the family institution is repugnant to the idea of a woman adopting a distinct and independent career from that of her husband. So firmly fixed was this sentiment in the founders of the common law that it became a maxim of that system of jurisprudence that a woman had no legal existence separate from her husband, who was regarded as her head and representative in the social state and, notwithstanding some recent modifications of this civil status, many of the special rules of law flowing from and dependent upon this cardinal principle still exist in full force in most States. One of these is, that a married woman is incapable, without her husband's consent, of making contracts which shall be binding on her or him. This very incapacity was one circumstance which the Supreme Court of Illinois deemed important in rendering a married woman incompetent fully to perform the duties and trusts that belong to the office of an attorney and counsellor.

It is true that many women are unmarried and not affected by any of the duties, complications, and incapacities arising out of the married state, but these are exceptions to the general rule. The paramount destiny and mission of woman are to fulfil the noble and benign offices of wife and mother. This is the law of the Creator. And the rules of civil society must be adapted to the general constitution of things, and cannot be based upon exceptional cases.

The humane movements of modern society, which have for their object the multiplication of avenues for woman's advancement, and of occupations adapted to her condition and sex, have my heartiest concurrence. But I am not prepared to say that it is one of her fundamental rights and privileges to be admitted into every office and position, including those which require highly special qualifications and demanding special responsibilities. In the nature of things it is not every citizen of every age, sex, and condition that is qualified for every calling and position. It is the prerogative of the legislator to prescribe regulations founded on nature, reason, and experience for the due admission of qualified persons to professions and callings demanding special skill and confidence. This fairly belongs to the police power of the State; and, in my opinion, in view of the peculiar characteristics, destiny, and mission of woman, it is within the province of the legislature to ordain what offices, positions, and callings shall be filled and discharged by men, and shall receive the benefit of those energies and responsibilities, and that decision and firmness which are presumed to predominate in the sterner sex.

Although the method of communication between the Creator and the judge is never disclosed, "divine ordinance" has been a dominant theme in decisions justifying laws establishing sex-based classifications.[6] Well past the middle of the twentieth century laws delineating "a sharp line between the sexes"[7] were sanctioned by the judiciary on the basis of lofty inspiration as well as restrained constitutional interpretation. . . .

NOTES

1. Alfred, Lord Tennyson, *Locksley Hall* (1842); see Johnston, Sex and Property: The Common Law Tradition, The Law School Curriculum, and Developments Toward Equality, 47 N.Y.U.L. Rev. 1033, 1044–1070 (1972).
2. E. Flexner, *Century of Struggle* 142–55 (1959).
3. 83 U.S. (16 Wall.) 130, 21 L. Ed. 442 (1873).
4. Article IV, section 2 reads: "The Citizens of each State shall be entitled to all Privileges and Immunities of Citizens in the several States."
5. 83 U.S. (16 Wall.) at 141–42.
6. E.g., *State v. Heitman*, 105 Kan. 139, 146–47, 181 P. 630. 633–34 (1919); *State v. Bearcub*, 1 Or. App. 579, 580, 465 P. 2d 252, 253 (1970).
7. *Goesaert v. Cleary*, 335 U.S. 464, 466, 69 S. Ct. 198, 199, 93 L. Ed. 163, 165 (1948). *Goesaert* was disapproved in *Craig v. Boren*, 429 U.S. 190, 210 n. 23, 97 S. Ct. 451, 463, 50 L. Ed. 2d 397, 414 (1976).

13

MINOR V. HAPPERSETT, 1875

In this case the court held that although women were citizens, the right to vote was not a privilege or immunity of national citizenship before adoption of the 14th Amendment, nor did the amendment add suffrage to the privileges and immunities of national citizenship. Therefore, the national government could not require states to permit women to vote.

14

CALIFORNIA CONSTITUTION, 1876

In 1876, at the height of the anti-Chinese movement, California adopted a new constitution. Its anti-Chinese provisions, largely unenforceable, represent an accurate measure of public feeling.

Article XIX

Section 1. The Legislature shall prescribe all necessary regulations for the protection of the State, and the counties, cities, and towns thereof, from the burdens and evils arising from the presence of aliens, who are or may become vagrants, paupers, mendicants, criminals, or invalids afflicted with contagious or infectious diseases, and from aliens otherwise dangerous or detrimental to the well-being or peace of the State, and to impose conditions upon which such persons may reside in the State, and to provide means and mode of their removal from the State upon failure or refusal to comply with such conditions; provided, that nothing contained in this section shall be construed to impair or limit the power of the Legislature to pass such police laws or other regulations as it may deem necessary.

Selection 13 from *Congressional Quarterly's Guide to the U.S. Supreme Court,* 1979, p. 631.

Section 2. No corporation now existing or hereafter formed under the laws of this State, shall, after the adoption of this Constitution, employ, directly or indirectly, in any capacity, any Chinese or Mongolian. The Legislature shall pass such laws as may be necessary to enforce this provision.

Section 3. No Chinese shall be employed on any State, county, municipal, or other public work, except in punishment for crime.

Section 4. The presence of foreigners ineligible to become citizens of the United States is declared to be dangerous to the well-being of the State, and the Legislature shall discourage their immigration by all the means within its power. Asiatic coolieism is a form of human slavery, and is forever prohibited in this State; and all contracts for coolie labor shall be void. All companies or corporations, whether formed in this country or any foreign country, for the importation of such labor, shall be subject to such penalties as the Legislature may prescribe. The Legislature shall delegate all necessary power to the incorporated cities and towns of this State for the removal of Chinese without the limits of such cities and towns, or for their location within prescribed portions of those limits; and it shall also provide the necessary legislation to prohibit the introduction into this State of Chinese after the adoption of this Constitution. This section shall be enforced by appropriate legislation.

15

ELK V. WILKINS, NOVEMBER 3, 1884

John Elk, an Indian who had voluntarily separated himself from his tribe and taken up residence among the whites, was denied the right to vote in Omaha, Nebraska, on the grounds that he was not a citizen. The Supreme Court considered the question of whether Elk had been made a citizen by the Fourteenth Amendment and decided against him.

. . . The plaintiff, in support of his action, relies on the first clause of the first section of the Fourteenth Article of Amendment of the Constitution of the United States, by which "all persons born or naturalized in the United States, and subject to the jurisdiction thereof, are citizens of the United States and of the State wherein

From *Elk v. Wilkins*, 112 *United States Reports: Cases Adjudged in the Supreme Court* (New York: Banks & Brothers).

they reside"; and on the Fifteenth Article of Amendment, which provides that "the right of citizens of the United States to vote shall not be denied or abridged by the United States or by any State on account of race, color, or previous condition of servitude." . . .

The petition, while it does not show of what Indian tribe the plaintiff was a member, yet, by the allegations that he "is an Indian, and was born within the United States," and that "he had severed his tribal relation to the Indian tribes," clearly implies that he was born a member of one of the Indian tribes within the limits of the United States, which still exists and is recognized as a tribe by the government of the United States. Though the plaintiff alleges that he "had fully and completely surrendered himself to the jurisdiction of the United States," he does not allege that the United States accepted his surrender, or that he has ever been naturalized, or taxed, or in any way recognized or treated as a citizen, by the State or by the United States. Nor is it contended by his counsel that there is any statute or treaty that makes him a citizen.

The question then is, whether an Indian, born a member of one of the Indian tribes within the United States, is, merely by reason of his birth within the United States, and of his afterwards voluntarily separating himself from his tribe and taking up his residence among white citizens, a citizen of the United States, within the meaning of the first section of the Fourteenth Amendment of the Constitution. . . .

Indians born within the territorial limits of the United States, members of, and owing immediate allegiance to, one of the Indian tribes (an alien, though dependent, power), although in a geographical sense born in the United States, are no more "born in the United States and subject to the jurisdiction thereof," within the meaning of the first section of the Fourteenth Amendment, than the children of subjects of any foreign government born within the domain of that government, or the children born within the United States, of ambassadors or other public ministers of foreign nations.

This view is confirmed by the second section of the Fourteenth Amendment, which provides that "representatives shall be apportioned among the several States according to their respective numbers, counting the whole number of persons in each State, excluding Indians not taxed." Slavery having been abolished, and the persons formerly held as slaves made citizens, this clause fixing the apportionment of representatives has abrogated so much of the corresponding clause of the original Constitution as counted only three-fifths of such persons. But Indians not taxed are still excluded from the count, for the reason that they are not citizens. Their absolute exclusion from the basis of representation, in which all other persons are now included, is wholly inconsistent with their being considered citizens. . . .

The plaintiff, not being a citizen of the United States under the Fourteenth Amendment of the Constitution, has been deprived of no right secured by the Fifteenth Amendment, and cannot maintain this action.

16

PLESSY V. FERGUSON, 1896

After the collapse of Reconstruction governments, Southern whites began gradually to legalize the informal practices of segregation which obtained in the South. One such law was passed by the Louisiana legislature in 1890 and provided that "all railway companies carrying passengers . . . in this State shall provide separate but equal accommodations for the white and colored races."

Plessy v. Ferguson tested the constitutionality of this recent trend in Southern legislation. Plessy was a mulatto who, on June 7, 1892, bought a first-class ticket on the East Louisiana Railway for a trip from New Orleans to Covington, Louisiana, and sought to be seated in the "white" coach. Upon conviction of a violation of the 1890 statute, he appealed to the Supreme Court of Louisiana, which upheld his conviction, and finally to the U.S. Supreme Court, which pronounced the Louisiana law constitutional, on May 18, 1896. The defense of Plessy and attack on the Louisiana statute was in the hands of four men, the most famous of whom was Albion W. Tourgée. M. J. Cunningham, attorney general of Louisiana, was assisted by two other lawyers in defending the statute. The majority opinion of the Court was delivered by Justice Henry B. Brown. John Marshall Harlan dissented and Justice David J. Brewer did not participate, making it a 7–1 decision.

In his dissent to this decision Harlan asserted that "Our Constitution is colorblind, and neither knows nor tolerates classes among citizens. In respect of civil rights, all citizens are equal before the law." He offered the prophecy that "the judgment rendered this day will, in time, prove to be quite as pernicious as the decision made by this tribunal in the Dred Scott case."

The constitutionality of this act is attacked upon the ground that it conflicts both with the Thirteenth Amendment of the Constitution, abolishing slavery, and the Fourteenth Amendment, which prohibits certain restrictive legislation on the part of the States.

1. That it does not conflict with the Thirteenth Amendment, which abolished slavery and involuntary servitude, except as a punishment for crime, is too clear for argument. Slavery implies involuntary servitude—a state of bondage: the ownership of mankind as a chattel, or at least the control of the labor and services of one

From *Plessy v. Ferguson*, 163 U.S. 537 *United States Reports: Cases Adjudged in the Supreme Court* (New York, Banks & Brothers, 1896).

man for the benefit of another, and the absence of a legal right to the disposal of his own person, property and services. . . .

A statute which implies merely a legal distinction between the white and colored races—a distinction which is founded in the color of the two races, and which must always exist so long as white men are distinguished from the other race by color—has no tendency to destroy the legal equality of the two races, or reestablish a state of involuntary servitude. Indeed, we do not understand that the Thirteenth Amendment is strenuously relied upon by the plaintiff in error in this connection.

2. By the Fourteenth Amendment, all persons born or naturalized in the United States, and subject to the jurisdiction thereof, are made citizens of the United States and of the State wherein they reside; and the States are forbidden from making or enforcing any law which shall abridge the privileges or immunities of citizens of the United States, or shall deprive any person of life, liberty or property without due process of law, or deny to any person within their jurisdiction the equal protection of the laws. . . .

The object of the amendment was undoubtedly to enforce the absolute equality of the two races before the law, but in the nature of things it could not have been intended to abolish distinctions based upon color, or to enforce social, as distinguished from political equality, or a commingling of the two races upon terms unsatisfactory to either. Laws permitting, and even requiring, their separation in places where they are liable to be brought into contact do not necessarily imply the inferiority of either race to the other, and have been generally, if not universally, recognized as within the competency of the state legislatures in the exercise of their police power. The most common instance of this is connected with the establishment of separate schools for white and colored children, which has been held to be a valid exercise of the legislative power even by courts of States where the political rights of the colored race have been longest and most earnestly enforced. . . .

While we think the enforced separation of the races, as applied to the internal commerce of the State, neither abridges the privileges or immunities of the colored man, deprives him of his property without due process of law, nor denies him the equal protection of the laws, within the meaning of the Fourteenth Amendment, we are not prepared to say that the conductor, in assigning passengers to the coaches according to their race, does not act at his peril, or that the provision of the second section of the act, that denies to the passenger compensation in damages for a refusal to receive him into the coach in which he properly belongs, is a valid exercise of the legislative power. Indeed, we understand it to be conceded by the State's attorney, that such part of the act as exempts from liability the railway company and its officers is unconstitutional. The power to assign to a particular coach obviously implies the power to determine to which race the passenger belongs, as well as the power to determine who, under the laws of the particular State, is to be deemed a white, and who a colored person. . . .

It is claimed by the plaintiff in error that, in any mixed community, the reputation of belonging to the dominant race, in this instance the white race, is *property*, in the same sense that a right of action, or of inheritance, is property. Conceding this to be so, for the purposes of this case, we are unable to see how this statute deprives him of, or in any way affects his right to, such property. If he be a white man and assigned to a colored coach, he may have his action for damages against the company for being deprived of his so called property. Upon the other hand, if he be a colored man and be so assigned, he has been deprived of no property, since he is not lawfully entitled to the reputation of being a white man.

In this connection, it is also suggested by the learned counsel for the plaintiff in error that the same argument that will justify the state legislature in requiring railways to provide separate accommodations for the two races will also authorize them to require separate cars to be provided for the people whose hair is of a certain color, or who are aliens, or who belong to certain nationalities, or to enact laws requiring colored people to walk upon one side of the street, and white people upon the other, or requiring white men's houses to be painted white, and colored men's black, or their vehicles or business signs to be of different colors, upon the theory that one side of the street is as good as the other, or that a house or vehicle of one color is as good as one of another color. The reply to all this is that every exercise of the police power must be reasonable, and extend only to such laws as are enacted in good faith for the promotion for the public good, and not for the annoyance or oppression of a particular class. . . .

We consider the underlying fallacy of the plaintiff's argument to consist in the assumption that the enforced separation of the two races stamps the colored race with a badge of inferiority. If this be so, it is not by reason of anything found in the act, but solely because the colored race chooses to put that construction upon it. The argument necessarily assumes that if, as has been more than once the case, and is not unlikely to be so again, the colored race should become the dominant power in the state legislature, and should enact a law in precisely similar terms, it would thereby relegate the white race to an inferior position. We imagine that the white race, at least, would not acquiesce in this assumption. The argument also assumes that social prejudices may be overcome by legislation, and that equal rights cannot be secured to the negro except by an enforced commingling of the two races. We cannot accept this proposition. If the two races are to meet upon terms of social equality, it must be the result of natural affinities, a mutual appreciation of each other's merits and a voluntary consent of individuals.

17

UNITED STATES CONSTITUTION
Nineteenth Amendment (1920)

Amendment XIX (ratified August 18, 1920). *Section 1.* The right of citizens of the United States to vote shall not be denied or abridged by the United States or by any State on account of sex.

Section 2. Congress shall have power to enforce this Article by appropriate legislation.

18

KOREMATSU V. UNITED STATES, 1944

The present case involved perhaps the most alarming use of executive military authority in our nation's history. Following the bombing of Pearl Harbor in December 1941, the anti-Japanese sentiment on the West Coast brought the residents of the area to a state of near hysteria; and in February 1942, President Roosevelt issued an executive order authorizing the creation of military areas from which any or all persons might be excluded as the military authorities might decide. On March 2, the entire West Coast to a depth of about forty miles was designated by the commanding general as Military Area No. 1, and he thereupon proclaimed a curfew in that area for all persons of Japanese ancestry. Later he ordered the compulsory evacuation from the area of all persons of Japanese ancestry, and by the middle of the summer most of these people had been moved inland to "War Relocation Centers," the American equivalent of concentration camps. Congress subsequently made it a crime to violate these military orders. Of the 112,000 persons of Japanese ancestry involved, about 70,000 were native-born American citizens, none of whom had been specifically accused of disloyalty. Three cases were brought to the Supreme Court as challenging the right of the government to override in this manner the customary civil rights of these citizens. In Hirabayashi v. United States, 320 U.S. 81 (1943), *the*

Court upheld the curfew regulations as a valid military measure to prevent espionage and sabotage. "Whatever views we may entertain regarding the loyalty to this country of the citizens of Japanese ancestry, we cannot reject as unfounded the judgment of the military authorities and of Congress that there were disloyal members of that population, whose number and strength could not be precisely and quickly ascertained. We cannot say that the war-making branches of the Government did not have grounds for believing that in a critical hour such persons could not readily be isolated and separately dealt with, and constituted a menace to the national defense and safety. . . ." While emphasizing that distinctions based on ancestry were "by their very nature odious to a free people," the Court nonetheless felt "that in time of war residents having ethnic affiliations with an invading enemy may be a greater source of danger than those of a different ancestry."

While the Court, in the present case, held valid the discriminatory mass evacuation of all persons of Japanese descent, it also held in Ex parte Endo, 323 U.S. 283 (1944), *that an American citizen of Japanese ancestry whose loyalty to this country had been established could not constitutionally be held in a War Relocation Center but must be unconditionally released. The government had allowed persons to leave the Relocation Centers under conditions and restrictions that aimed to guarantee that there should not be "a dangerously disorderly migration of unwanted people to unprepared communities." Permission to leave was granted only if the applicant had the assurance of a job and a place to live, and wanted to go to a place "approved" by the War Relocation Authority. The Court held that the sole purpose of the evacuation and detention program was to protect the war effort against sabotage and espionage. "A person who is concededly loyal presents no problem of espionage or sabotage. . . . He who is loyal is by definition not a spy or a saboteur." It therefore follows that the authority to detain a citizen of Japanese ancestry ends when his loyalty is established. To hold otherwise would be to justify his detention not on grounds of military necessity but purely on grounds of race.*

Although no case reached the Court squarely challenging the right of the government to incarcerate citizens of Japanese ancestry pending a determination of their loyalty, the tenor of the opinions leaves little doubt that such action would have been sustained. The present case involved only the right of the military to evacuate such persons from the West Coast. Justice Murphy, one of the three dissenters, attacked the qualifications of the military to make sociological judgments about the effects of ancestry, and pointed out that the time consumed in evacuating these persons (eleven months) was ample for making an orderly inquiry into their individual loyalty.

Mr. Justice Black delivered the opinion of the Court, saying in part:

The petitioner, an American citizen of Japanese descent, was convicted in a federal district court for remaining in San Leandro, California, a "Military Area," contrary to Civilian Exclusion Order No. 34 of the Commanding General of the Western Command, U.S. Army, which directed that after May 9, 1942, all persons of Japanese ancestry should be excluded from that area. No question was raised as to petitioner's loyalty to the United States. The Circuit Court of Appeals affirmed, and the importance of the constitutional question involved caused us to grant certiorari.

It should be noted, to begin with, that all legal restrictions which curtail the civil rights of a single racial group are immediately suspect. That is not to say that all such restrictions are unconstitutional. It is to say that courts must subject them to the most rigid scrutiny. Pressing public necessity may sometimes justify the existence of such restrictions; racial antagonism never can.

In the instant case prosecution of the petitioner was begun by information charging violation of an Act of Congress, of March 21, 1942, 56 Stat. 173, which provides that ". . . whoever shall enter, remain in, leave, or commit any act in any military area or military zone prescribed, under the authority of an Executive order of the President, by the Secretary of War, or by any military commander designated by the Secretary of War, contrary to the restrictions applicable to any such area or zone or contrary to the order of the Secretary of War or any such military commander, shall, if it appears that he knew or should have known of the existence and extent of the restrictions or order and that his act was in violation thereof, be guilty of a misdemeanor and upon conviction shall be liable to a fine of not to exceed $5,000 or to imprisonment for not more than one year, or both, for each offense."

Exclusion Order No. 34, which the petitioner knowingly and admittedly violated, was one of a number of military orders and proclamations, all of which were substantially based upon Executive Order No. 9066, 7 Fed. Reg. 1407. That order, issued after we were at war with Japan, declared that "the successful prosecution of the war requires every possible protection against espionage and against sabotage to national-defense material, national-defense premises, and national-defense utilities. . . ."

One of the series of orders and proclamations, a curfew order, which like the exclusion order here was promulgated pursuant to Executive Order 9066, subjected all persons of Japanese ancestry in prescribed West Coast military areas to remain in their residences from 8 P.M. to 6 A.M. As is the case with the exclusion order here, that prior curfew order was designed as a "protection against espionage and against sabotage." In Kiyoshi Hirabayashi v. United States, 320 U.S. 81, we sustained a conviction obtained for violation of the curfew order. The Hirabayashi conviction and this one thus rest on the same 1942 Congressional Act and the same basic executive and military orders, all of which orders were aimed at the twin dangers of espionage and sabotage.

The 1942 Act was attacked in the Hirabayashi case as an unconstitutional delegation of power; it was contended that the curfew order and other orders on which it rested were beyond the war powers of the Congress, the military authorities and of the President, as Commander in Chief of the Army; and finally that to apply the curfew order against none but citizens of Japanese ancestry amounted to a constitutionally prohibited discrimination solely on account of race. To these questions, we gave the serious consideration which their importance justified. We upheld the curfew order as an exercise of the power of the government to take steps necessary to prevent espionage and sabotage in an area threatened by Japanese attack.

In the light of the principles we announced in the Hirabayashi case, we are unable to conclude that it was beyond the war power of Congress and the Executive to exclude those of Japanese ancestry from the West Coast war area at the time they did. True, exclusion from the area in which one's home is located is a far greater deprivation than constant confinement to the home from 8 P.M. to 6 A.M. Nothing short of apprehension by the proper military authorities of the gravest imminent danger to the public safety can constitutionally justify either. But exclusion from a threatened area, no less than curfew, has a definite and close relationship to the prevention of espionage and sabotage. The military authorities, charged with the primary responsibility of defending our shores, concluded that curfew provided inadequate protection and ordered exclusion. They did so, as pointed out in our Hirabayashi opinion, in accordance with Congressional authority to the military to say who should, and who should not, remain in the threatened areas.

In this case the petitioner challenges the assumptions upon which we rested our conclusions in the Hirabayashi case. He also urges that by May 1942, when Order No. 34 was promulgated, all danger of Japanese invasion of the West Coast had disappeared. After careful consideration of these contentions we are compelled to reject them.

Here, as in the Hirabayashi case, ". . . we cannot reject as unfounded the judgment of the military authorities and of Congress that there were disloyal members of that population, whose number and strength could not be precisely and quickly ascertained. We cannot say that the warmaking branches of the Government did not have ground for believing that in a critical hour such persons could not readily be isolated and separately dealt with, and constituted a menace to the national defense and safety, which demanded that prompt and adequate measures be taken to guard against it."

Like curfew, exclusion of those of Japanese origin was deemed necessary because of the presence of an unascertained number of disloyal members of the group, most of whom we have no doubt were loyal to this country. It was because we could not reject the finding of the military authorities that it was impossible to bring about an immediate segregation of the disloyal from the loyal that we sustained the validity of the curfew order as applying to the whole group. In the instant case, temporary exclusion of the entire group was rested by the military on the same ground. The judgment that exclusion of the whole group was for the same reason a military imperative answers the contention that the exclusion was in the nature of group punishment based on antagonism to those of Japanese origin. That there were members of the group who retained loyalties to Japan has been confirmed by investigations made subsequent to the exclusion. Approximately five thousand American citizens of Japanese ancestry refused to swear unqualified allegiance to the United States and to renounce allegiance to the Japanese Emperor, and several thousand evacuees requested repatriation to Japan.

We uphold the exclusion order as of the time it was made and when the petitioner violated it. . . . In doing so, we are not unmindful of the hardships imposed by it upon a large group of American citizens. . . . But hardships are part of war, and war is an aggregation of hardships. All citizens alike, both in and out of uniform, feel the impact of war in greater or lesser measure. Citizenship has its responsibilities as well as its privileges, and in time of war the burden is always heavier. Compulsory exclusion of large groups of citizens from their homes, except under circumstances of direst emergency and peril, is inconsistent with our basic governmental institution. But when under conditions of modern warfare our shores are threatened by hostile forces, the power to protect must be commensurate with the threatened danger. . . .

[The Court dealt at some length with a technical complication that arose in the case. On May 30, the date on which Korematsu was charged with remaining unlawfully in the prohibited area, there were two conflicting military orders outstanding, one forbidding him to remain in the area, the other forbidding him to leave but ordering him to report to an assembly center. Thus, he alleged, he was punished for doing what it was made a crime to fail to do. The Court held the orders not to be contradictory, since the requirement to report to the assembly center was merely a step in an orderly program of compulsory evacuation from the area.]

It is said that we are dealing here with the case of imprisonment of a citizen in a concentration camp solely because of his ancestry, without evidence or inquiry concerning his loyalty and good disposition towards the United States. Our task would be simple, our duty clear, were this a case involving the imprisonment of a loyal citizen in a concentration camp because of racial prejudice. Regardless of the true nature of the assembly and relocation centers—and we deem it unjustifiable to call them concentration camps with all the ugly connotations that term implies—we are dealing specifically with nothing but an exclusion order. To cast this case into outlines of racial prejudice, without reference to the real military dangers which were presented, merely confuses the issue. Korematsu was not excluded from the Military Area because of hostility to him or his race. He was excluded because we are at war with the Japanese Empire, because the properly constituted military authorities feared an invasion of our West Coast and felt constrained to take proper security measures, because they decided that the military urgency of the situation demanded that all citizens of Japanese ancestry be segregated from the West Coast temporarily, and finally, because Congress reposing its confidence in this time of war in our military leaders—as inevitably it must—determined that they should have the power to do just this. There was evidence of disloyalty on the part of some, the military authorities considered that the need for action was great, and time was short. We cannot—by availing ourselves of the calm perspective of hindsight—now say that at that time these actions were unjustified.

Affirmed.

Mr. Justice Frankfurter wrote a concurring opinion. Justices Roberts, Murphy, and Jackson each wrote a dissenting opinion.

Brown v. Board of Education of Topeka, 1954

Mr. Chief Justice Warren delivered the opinion of the Court.

These cases come to us from the States of Kansas, South Carolina, Virginia, and Delaware. They are premised on different facts and different local conditions, but a common legal question justifies their consideration together in this consolidated opinion.[1]

In each of the cases, minors of the Negro race, through their legal representatives, seek the aid of the courts in obtaining admission to the public schools of their community on a nonsegregated basis. In each instance, they had been denied admission to schools attended by white children under laws requiring or permitting segregation according to race. This segregation was alleged to deprive the plaintiffs of the equal protection of the laws under the Fourteenth Amendment. In each of the cases other than the Delaware case, a three-judge federal district court denied relief to the plaintiffs on the so-called "separate but equal" doctrine announced by this Court in *Plessy* v. *Ferguson*, 163 U.S. 537. Under that doctrine, equality of treatment is accorded when the races are provided substantially equal facilities, even though these facilities be separate. In the Delaware case, the Supreme Court of Delaware adhered to that doctrine, but ordered that the plaintiffs be admitted to the white schools because of their superiority to the Negro schools.

The plaintiffs contend that segregated public schools are not "equal" and cannot be made "equal," and that hence they are deprived of the equal protection of the laws. Because of the obvious importance of the question presented, the Court took jurisdiction.[2] Argument was heard in the 1952 Term, and reargument was heard this Term on certain questions propounded by the Court.[3] . . .

In approaching this problem, we cannot turn the clock back to 1868 when the Amendment was adopted, or even to 1896 when *Plessy* v. *Ferguson* was written. We must consider public education in the light of its full development and its present place in American life throughout the Nation. Only in this way can it be determined if segregation in public schools deprives these plaintiffs of the equal protection of the laws.

Today, education is perhaps the most important function of state and local governments. Compulsory school attendance laws and the great expenditures for education both demonstrate our recognition of the importance of education to our democratic society. It is required in the performance of our most basic public responsibilities, even service in the armed forces. It is the very foundation of good citizenship. Today it is a principal instrument in awakening the child to cultural values, in preparing him for later professional training, and in helping him to adjust normally to his environment. In these days, it is doubtful that any child may reasonably be expected to succeed in life if he is denied the opportunity of an education. Such an opportunity, where the state has undertaken to provide it, is a right which must be made available to all on equal terms.

We come then to the question presented: Does segregation of children in public schools solely on the basis of race, even though the physical facilities and other "tangible" factors may be equal, deprive the children of the minority group of equal educational opportunities? We believe that it does.

In *Sweatt* v. *Painter*, in finding that a segregated law school for Negroes could not provide them equal educational opportunities, this Court relied in large part on "those qualities which are incapable of objective measurement but which make for greatness in a law school." In *McLaurin* v. *Oklahoma State Regents*, the Court, in requiring that a Negro admitted to a white graduate school be treated like all other students, again resorted to intangible considerations: ". . . his ability to study, to engage in discussions and exchange views with other students, and in general, to learn his profession." Such considerations apply with added force to children in grade and high schools. To separate them from others of similar age and qualifications solely because of their race generates a feeling of inferiority as to their status in the community that may affect their hearts and minds in a way unlikely ever to be undone. The effect of this separation on their educational opportunities was well stated by a finding in the Kansas case by a court which nevertheless felt compelled to rule against the Negro plaintiffs:

> Segregation of white and colored children in public schools has a detrimental effect upon the colored children. The impact is greater when it has the sanction of the law; for the policy of separating the races is usually interpreted as denoting the inferiority of the negro group. A sense of inferiority affects the motivation of a child to learn. Segregation with the sanction of law, therefore, has a tendency to [retard] the educational and mental development of negro children and to deprive them of some of the benefits they receive in a racial[ly] integrated school system.[4]

Whatever may have been the extent of psychological knowledge at the time of *Plessy* v. *Ferguson*, this finding is amply supported by modern authority.[5] Any language in *Plessy* v. *Ferguson* contrary to this finding is rejected.

We conclude that in the field of public education the doctrine of "separate but equal" has no place. Separate educational facilities are inherently unequal. Therefore, we hold that the plaintiffs and others similarly situated for whom the actions have been brought are, by reason of the segregation complained of, deprived of the equal protection of the laws guaranteed by the Fourteenth Amendment. This disposition makes unnecessary any discussion whether such segregation also violates the Due Process Clause of the Fourteenth Amendment.

Because these are class actions, because of the wide applicability of this decision, and because of the great variety of local conditions, the formulation of decrees in these cases presents problems of considerable complexity. On reargument, the consideration of appropriate relief was necessarily subordinated to the primary question—the constitutionality of segregation in public education. We have now announced that such segregation is a denial of the equal protection of the laws. In order that we may have the full assistance of the parties in formulating decrees, the cases will be restored to the docket, and the parties are requested to present further argument on Questions 4 and 5 previously propounded by the Court for the reargument this Term.[6] The Attorney General of the United States is again invited to participate. The Attorneys General of the states requiring or permitting segregation in public education will also be permitted to appear as amici curiae upon request to do so by September 15, 1954, and submission of the briefs by October 1, 1954.

It is so ordered.

NOTES

1. In the Kansas case, *Brown v. Board of Education*, the plaintiffs are Negro children of elementary school age residing in Topeka. They brought this action in the United States District Court for the District of Kansas to enjoin enforcement of a Kansas statute which permits, but does not require, cities of more than 15,000 population to maintain separate school facilities for Negro and white students. Kan. Gen. Stat. §72-1724 (1949). Pursuant to that authority, the Topeka Board of Education elected to establish segregated elementary schools. Other public schools in the community, however, are operated on a nonsegregated basis. The three-judge District Court, convened under 28 U.S.C. §§2281 and 2284, found that segregation in public education has a detrimental effect upon Negro children, but denied relief on the ground that the Negro and white schools were substantially equal with respect to buildings, transportation, curricula, and educational qualifications of teachers. 98 F. Supp. 797. The case is here on direct appeal under 28 U.S.C. §1253. [The Topeka, Kansas, case would be analogous to a northern school case inasmuch as the school segregation that existed in Topeka was not mandated by state law, and some of the system was integrated. It would be eighteen years before the Court would accept another such case for review. *Keyes* v. *School District No. 1, Denver*, 445 F.2d 990 (10th Cir. 1971), *cert. granted*, 404 U.S. 1036 (1972)].

In the South Carolina case, *Briggs v. Elliot*, the plaintiffs are Negro children of both elementary and high school age residing in Clarendon County. They brought this action in the United States District Court for the Eastern District of South Carolina to enjoin enforcement of provisions in the state constitution and statutory code which require the segregation of Negroes and whites in public schools. S.C. Const., Art. XI, §7; S.C. Code §5377 (1942). The three-judge District Court, convened under 28 U.S.C. §§2281 and 2284, denied the requested relief. The court found that the Negro schools were inferior to the white schools and ordered the defendants to begin immediately to equalize the facilities. But the court sustained the validity of the contested provisions and denied the plaintiffs admission to the white schools during the equalization program. 98 F. Supp. 529. This Court vacated the District Court's judgment and remanded the case for the purpose of obtaining the court's views on a report filed by the defendants concerning the progress made in the equalization program. 342 U.S. 350. On remand, the District Court found that substantial equality had been achieved except for buildings and that the defendants were proceeding to rectify this inequality as well. 103 F. Supp. 920. The case is again here on direct appeal under 28 U.S.C. §1253.

In the Virginia case, *Davis* v. *County School Board*, the plaintiffs are Negro children of high school age residing in Prince Edward County. They brought this action in the United States District Court for the Eastern District of Virginia to enjoin enforcement of provisions in the state constitution and statutory code which require the segregation of Negroes and whites in public schools. Va. Const., §140; Va. Code §22-221 (1950). The three-judge District Court, convened under 28 U.S.C. §§2281 and 2284, denied the requested relief. The court found the Negro school inferior in physical plant, curricula, and transportation, and ordered the defendants forthwith to provide substantially equal curricula and transportation and to "proceed with all reasonable diligence and dispatch to remove" the inequality in physical plant. But, as in the South Carolina case, the court sustained the validity of the contested provisions and denied the plaintiffs admission to the white schools during the equalization program. 103 F. Supp. 337. The case is here on direct appeal under 28 U.S.C. §1253.

In the Delaware case, *Gebhart* v. *Belton*, the plaintiffs are Negro children of both elementary and high school age residing in New Castle County. They brought this action in the Delaware Court of Chancery to enjoin enforcement of provisions in the state constitution and statutory code which require the segregation of Negroes and whites in public schools. Del. Const., Art. X, §2; Del. Rev. Code §2631 (1935). The Chancellor gave judgment for the plaintiffs and ordered their immediate admission to schools previously attended only by white children, on the ground that the Negro schools were inferior with respect to teacher training, pupil-teacher ratio, extracurricular activities, physical plant, and time and distance involved in travel. 87 A.2d 862. The Chancellor also found that segregation itself results in an inferior education for Negro children (see note 4, infra), but did not rest his decision on that ground. Id., at 865. The Chancellor's decree was affirmed by the Supreme Court of Delaware, which intimated, however, that the defendants might be able to obtain a modification of the decree after equalization of the Negro and white schools had been accomplished. 91 A.2d 137, 152. The defendants, contending only that the Delaware courts had erred in ordering the immediate admission of the Negro plaintiffs to the white schools, applied to this Court for certiorari. The writ was granted, 344 U.S. 891. The plaintiffs, who were successful below, did not submit a cross-petition.

2. 344 U.S. 1, 141, 891.

3. 345 U.S. 972. The Attorney General of the United States participated both Terms as amicus curiae.

4. A similar finding was made in the Delaware case: "I conclude from the testimony that in our Delaware Society, State-imposed segregation in education itself results in the Negro children, as a class, receiving educational opportunities which are substantially inferior to those available to white children otherwise similarly situated." 87 A.2d 862, 865.

5. K. B. Clark, Effect of Prejudice and Discrimination on Personality Development (Midcentury White House Conference on Children and Youth, 1950); Witmer and Kotinsky, Personality in the Making (1952), c. VI; Deutscher and Chein, The Psychological Effects of Enforced Segregation: A Survey of Social Science Opinion, 26 J. Psychol. 259 (1948); Chein, What Are the Psychological Effects of Segregation Under Conditions of Equal Facilities?, 3 Int. J. Opinion and Attitude Res. 229 (1949); Brameld, Educational Costs, in Discrimination and National Welfare (MacIver, ed., 1949), 44–48; Frazier, The

Negro in the United States (1949), 674–681. And see generally Myrdal, An American Dilemma (1944).

6. "4. Assuming it is decided that segregation in public schools violates the Fourteenth Amendment

"(a) would a decree necessarily follow providing that, within the limits set by normal geographic school districting, Negro children should forthwith be admitted to schools of their choice, or

"(b) may this Court, in the exercise of its equity powers, permit an effective gradual adjustment to be brought about from existing segregated systems to a system not based on color distinctions?

"5. On the assumption on which questions 4(a) and (b) are based, and assuming further that this Court will exercise its equity powers to the end described in question 4(b),

"(a) should this Court formulate detailed decrees in these cases;

"(b) if so, what specific issues should the decrees reach;

"(c) should this Court appoint a special master to hear evidence with a view to recommending specific terms for such decrees;

"(d) should this Court remand to the courts of first instance with directions to frame decrees in these cases, and if so what general directions should the decrees of this Court include and what procedures should the courts of first instance follow in arriving at the specific terms of more detailed decrees?"

20

Roe v. Wade, 1973

This historic decision legalized a woman's right to terminate her pregnancy by abortion. The ruling was based upon the right of privacy founded on both the Fourteenth and Ninth Amendments to the Constitution. The Court ruled that this right of privacy protected the individual from interference by the state in the decision to terminate a pregnancy by abortion during the early portion of the pregnancy. At the same time, it recognized the interest of the state in regulating decisions concerning the pregnancy during the latter period as the fetus developed the capacity to survive outside the woman's body.

21

THE EQUAL RIGHTS AMENDMENT (DEFEATED)

Section 1. Equality of Rights under the law shall not be denied or abridged by the United States or any state on account of sex.

Section 2. The Congress shall have the power to enforce, by appropriate legislation, the provisions of this article.

Section 3. This amendment shall take effect two years after the date of ratification.

First introduced in Congress in 1923, the ERA was finally passed in 1972. However, because it failed to be ratified by the requisite number of states by its July 1982 deadline, the ERA never became part of the Constitution.

22

LAWRENCE ET AL. V. *TEXAS*, 2003

Responding to a reported weapons disturbance in a private residence, Houston police entered petitioner Lawrence's apartment and saw him and another adult man, petitioner Garner, engaging in a private, consensual sexual act. Petitioners were arrested and convicted of deviate sexual intercourse in violation of a Texas statute forbidding two persons of the same sex to engage in certain intimate sexual conduct. In affirming, the State Court of Appeals held, *inter alia*, that the statute was not unconstitutional under the Due Process Clause of the Fourteenth Amendment. The court considered *Bowers* v. *Hardwick*, 478 U.S. 186, controlling on that point.

Held: The Texas statute making it a crime for two persons of the same sex to engage in certain intimate sexual conduct violates the Due Process Clause. Pp. 3–18.

(a) Resolution of this case depends on whether petitioners were free as adults to engage in private conduct in the exercise of their liberty under the Due Process Clause. For this inquiry the Court deems it necessary to reconsider its *Bowers* holding. The *Bowers* Court's initial substantive statement—"The issue presented is whether the Federal Constitution confers a fundamental right upon homosexuals to engage in sodomy . . . ," 478 U.S., at 190—discloses the Court's failure to appreciate the extent of the liberty at stake. To say that the issue in *Bowers* was simply the right to engage in certain sexual conduct demeans the claim the individual put forward, just as it would demean a married couple were it said that marriage is just about the right to have sexual intercourse. Although the laws involved in *Bowers* and here purport to do not more than prohibit a particular sexual act, their penalties and purposes have more far-reaching consequences, touching upon the most private human conduct, sexual behavior, and in the most private of places, the home. They seek to control a personal relationship that, whether or not entitled to formal recognition in the law, is within the liberty of persons to choose without being punished as criminals. The liberty protected by the Constitution allows homosexual persons the right to choose to enter upon relationships in the confines of their homes and their own private lives and still retain their dignity as free persons. Pp. 3–6.

(b) Having misapprehended the liberty claim presented to it, the *Bowers* Court stated that proscriptions against sodomy have ancient roots. 478 U.S., at 192. It should be noted, however, that there is no longstanding history in this country of laws directed at homosexual conduct as a distinct matter. Early American sodomy laws were not directed at homosexuals as such but instead sought to prohibit nonprocreative sexual activity more generally, whether between men and women or men and men. Moreover, early sodomy laws seem not to have been enforced against consenting adults acting in private. Instead, sodomy prosecutions often involved predatory acts against those who could not or did not consent: relations between men and minor girls or boys, between adults involving force, between adults implicating disparity in status, or between men and animals. The longstanding criminal prohibition of homosexual sodomy upon which *Bowers* placed such reliance is as consistent with a general condemnation of nonprocreative sex as it is with an established tradition of prosecuting acts because of their homosexual character. Far from possessing "ancient roots," *ibid.*, American laws targeting same-sex couples did not develop until the last third of the 20th century. Even now, only nine States have singled out same-sex relations for criminal prosecution. Thus, the historical grounds relied upon in *Bowers* are more complex than the majority opinion and the concurring opinion by Chief Justice Burger there indicated. They are not without doubt and, at the very least, are overstated. The *Bowers* Court was, of course, making the broader point that for centuries there have been powerful voices to condemn homosexual conduct as immoral, but this Court's obligation is to define the liberty of all, not to mandate its own moral code, *Planned Parenthood of Southeastern Pa. v. Casey*, 505 U.S. 833, 850. The Nation's laws and traditions in the past half century are most relevant here. They show an emerging awareness that liberty gives substantial protection to adult persons in deciding how to conduct their private lives in matters pertaining to sex. See *County of Sacramento v. Lewis*, 523 U.S. 833, 857. Pp. 6–12.

(c) *Bowers'* deficiencies became even more apparent in the years following its announcement. The 25 States with laws prohibiting the conduct referenced in *Bowers* are reduced now to 13, of which 4 enforce their laws only against homosexual conduct. In those States, including Texas, that still proscribe sodomy (whether for same-sex or heterosexual conduct), there is a pattern of nonenforcement with respect to consenting adults acting in private. *Casey, supra*, at 851–which confirmed that the Due Process Clause protects personal decisions relating to marriage, procreation, contraception, family relationships, child rearing, and education–and *Romer v. Evans*, 517 U.S. 620, 624—which struck down class-based legislation directed at homosexuals—cast *Bowers'* holding into even more doubt. The stigma the Texas criminal statute imposes, moreover, is not trivial. Although the offense is but a minor misdemeanor, it remains a criminal offense with all that imports for the dignity of the persons charged, including notation of convictions on their records and on job application forms, and registration as sex offenders under state law. Where a case's foundations have sustained serious erosion, criticism from other sources is of greater significance. In the United States, criticism of *Bowers* has been substantial and continuing, disapproving of its reasoning in all respects, not just as to its historical assumptions. And, to the extent *Bowers* relied on values shared with a wider civilization, the case's reasoning and holding have been rejected by the European Court of Human Rights, and that other nations have taken action consistent with an affirmation of the protected right of homosexual adults to engage in intimate, consensual conduct. There has been no showing that in this country the governmental interest in circumscribing personal choice is somehow more legitimate or urgent. *Stare decisis* is not an inexorable command. *Payne v. Tennessee*, 501 U.S. 808, 828. *Bowers'* holding has not induced detrimental reliance of the sort that could counsel against overturning it once there are compelling reasons to do so. *Casey, supra*, at 855–856. *Bowers* causes uncertainty, for the precedents before and after it contradict its central holding. Pp. 12–17.

(d) *Bowers'* rationale does not withstand careful analysis. In his dissenting opinion in *Bowers* Justice Stevens concluded that (1) the fact a State's governing majority has traditionally viewed a particular practice as immoral is not a sufficient reason for upholding a law prohibiting the practice, and (2) individual decisions concerning the intimacies of physical relationships, even when not intended to produce offspring, are a form of "liberty" protected by due process. That analysis should have controlled *Bowers*, and it controls here. *Bowers* was not correct when it was decided, is not correct today, and is hereby overruled. This case does not involve minors, persons who might be injured or coerced, those who might not easily refuse consent, or public conduct or prostitution. It does involve two adults who, with full and mutual consent, engaged in sexual practices common to a homosexual lifestyle. Petitioners' right to liberty under the Due Process Clause gives them the full right to engage in private conduct without government intervention. *Casey, supra,* at 847. The Texas statute furthers no legitimate state interest which can justify its intrusion into the individual's personal and private life. Pp. 17–18.

41 S. W. 3d 349, reversed and remanded.

Kennedy, J., delivered the opinion of the Court, in which Stevens, Souter, Ginsburg, and Breyer, JJ., joined. O'Connor, J., filed an opinion concurring in the judgment. Scalia, J., filed a dissenting opinion, in which Rehnquist, C. J., and Thomas, J., joined. Thomas, J., filed a dissenting opinion.

23

FROM CRIMINALS AND PSYCHOPATHS TO THE FAMILY NEXT DOOR:
The Amazing Struggle for Lesbian and Gay Inclusion

Paula L. Ettelbrick

On November 4, 2008, while the majority of Americans were ecstatically celebrating the transcendent victory of Barack Obama as President of the United States, a sub-group of citizens—lesbians and gay men in California, predominantly—had their national fervor profoundly quelled by defeat. Californians, many of whom voted for Obama, voted 52–48% to overturn a groundbreaking California Supreme Court decision that put an end to the state's law barring same-sex couples from obtaining a civil marriage license. The Court's decision, only the second in the nation to proclaim that the state did not have the right to deny marriage to same-sex couples, opened the door to same-sex couples from around the world. Approximately 18,000 couples married in California. The voter initiative taking away that

Reprinted by permission of the author, Paula L. Ettelbrick, Executive Director, International Gay and Lesbian Human Rights Commission.

right, passed on November 4, put into question the status of those couples who married in the well-founded belief that it was legal.

How could this be? California is the "bluest" of states. It has the largest lesbian, gay, bisexual, and transgender (LGBT) community in the country, and it is larger than many countries in the world. Along with New Jersey, Vermont, Massachusetts, and Connecticut, it is considered the most supportive in protecting the legal rights of LGBT people. The California state legislature—twice—had democratically passed a marriage law that would include same-sex couples. Each time, the bill was vetoed by the Republican governor, Arnold Schwarzenegger. For a number of years, same-sex couples who registered as domestic partners in California had been provided with virtually all of the civil entitlements to marriage.

Yet, the ultimate social integration of gay and lesbian relationships, through marriage, remains elusive in California and vigorously opposed in most of the rest of the country. More than 40 states, such as Nebraska, Nevada, Kansas, Arizona, Florida, and Illinois, have passed laws or constitutional amendments to overtly ban same-sex marriage. Many have also banned any other recognition of lesbian and gay relationships, such as domestic partnerships (as exists in New Jersey) or civil unions (as exists in Vermont). Members of the United States Congress have proposed a federal constitutional amendment that would allow a national ban on same-sex marriage. In 1996, President Bill Clinton signed into law the Defense of Marriage Act (DOMA), which allows states to refuse to recognize same-sex marriages legally allowed in neighboring states, and bans any federal benefits generally given to married couples (tax breaks, social security) to be extended to legally married same-sex couples. The campaigns against civil marriage for same-sex couples have been fueled by vitriolic rhetoric about the devastating impact that lesbian and gay relationships would have on society, as well as delusional credit given to the much superior model of heterosexual marriage.

Within this national framework, even a majority of Californians simply were not ready to accept the overturning of the ultimate vestige of discrimination against LGBT people. While lesbian and gay *people* have gained greater acceptance in American society, their relationships have not. Ironically, interracial marriage between whites and people of color was also the last legal impediment to racial equality, ending only in 1967, 100 years after the end of slavery, when the United States Supreme Court declared an end to miscegenation laws.

At the same time, the fact that civil marriage for same-sex couples is even seriously considered and debated is, to many, an astounding achievement for a community of people that has been vilified as threats to the family and to society in general and stigmatized as psychopaths and deviants. The history of criminalizing and condemning sexual relationships between two men or two women and the development within medicine and psychology of treating lesbian and gay individuals as mentally ill colluded to completely ostracize any individual found or thought to be gay or lesbian.

The Criminals

It was not until 2003 that the United States Supreme Court put an end to the practice of criminalizing consensual, adult sexual relationships between two men or two women. In that case, the Court held Texas' sodomy law, which specifically outlawed so-called "homosexual sexual relationships," to be an unconstitutional invasion of personal privacy. As the supreme law of the land, the Court's ruling also struck down any remaining state laws in the United States that allowed for the arrest, conviction, and punishment of anyone who engaged in sexual activity with someone of the same sex. That ruling brought to an end a legal regime, inherited by the colonies from England, that at one time existed in every state in the union; and it was heralded as a major turnaround for the constitutional rights of lesbian, gay, bisexual, and transgender people in the country.

The case, *Lawrence v. Texas*, dealt with a law that was specifically targeted at "homosexual sex." But, its additional legal significance lies in the fact that the Supreme Court overturned its own previous decision from 1986 in the infamous *Bowers v. Hardwick* decision, where a slim majority of the Court had upheld the Georgia sodomy law as justified by the state's desire to promote morality. The Georgia law had outlawed oral and anal sex regardless of who the participants were, whether the couple was married or not, straight or gay. At the same time, the Court erroneously assumed that the crime of sodomy was a crime that only gay and lesbian people engage in, and ignored the explicit text of the law that infringes on the right of any citizen of Georgia to engage in nonprocreative sex. Every major newspaper in the country condemned the Court's decision in *Bowers* as an outrageous infringement on the right of citizens to sexual privacy.

Illinois became the first state, in 1961, to drop prohibitions on sodomy as part of a national effort to reform criminal laws in the United States. In 1986, when the Supreme Court ruled that the Georgia sodomy law was justified by the state's desire to promote morality, 25 states and the District of Columbia criminalized some form of sexual activity between two men or two women. In Michigan, for example, gay and lesbian couples could be sentenced to prison terms of up to 20 years. By the time the Supreme Court overturned itself in the Texas case, the number of states banning same-sex activity had dwindled to about a dozen, and were rarely if ever enforced directly. Nonetheless, the eradication of these laws handed the LGBT community a long sought victory and put an end to the arbitrary meddling of the state into the private sexual lives of consenting adults.

Sodomy laws, like fornication, cohabitation, and other laws banning any sexual activity other than marital intercourse, were part of a legal system that helped patrol the boundaries of acceptable sexuality and ensure that marital relationships remain dedicated to monogamy and procreation. Their impact does not lie only in the prospect of arrest and jail time. Courts have denied child custody to lesbians and gay men deemed criminals and, thus, unfit to be parents. People serving or seeking to serve their communities and country as firefighters, police officers, public service attorneys, teachers, child welfare officers, specialized national security agents, Arab-speaking translators, and military personnel have been barred because of the association between sexual orientation and criminality.

The Psychopaths

Laws criminalizing homosexuality were used to justify police harassment and violence against lesbians and gay men. But the medical and psychiatric profession's designation of homosexuality as a psychopathic personality trait justified a range of institutional abuses, stigma, and irrational fear of lesbians and gay men.

Police raids of gay and lesbian bars were common in the 1950s and 1960s in New York, San Francisco, and other cities where gay and lesbian communities were beginning to emerge publicly. While social and networking organizations had begun to emerge as early as 1924, when the Society for Human Rights was founded by Henry Gerber in Chicago, and in the late 1940s and the 1950s with the Mattachine Society for gay men and the Daughters of Bilitis for lesbians, they were largely private gatherings held in people's homes. Bars were among the only public venues available to men and women seeking relationships or simply finding and socializing with others like themselves. Regular raids of bars frequented by "known homosexuals" allowed the police and liquor authorities to control and intimidate the patrons, as well as the bar owners. In the extremely homophobic society of the time, the raids profoundly threatened the lives and well-being of lesbians and gay men. They were arrested, their names sometimes published in the local press, and their reputations often ruined in a time when being gay or lesbian was tantamount to being a criminal and social deviant. Jobs were lost, as well as families who did not understand.

It all started to turn around on the night of June 30, 1969, when New York City police raided a Greenwich Village bar, the Stonewall Inn. Instead of hiding their faces in shame, placidly accepting their fate, and hoping that the arrests would not result in convictions, the patrons—gay, lesbian, and transgender—fought back. The audacity of the resistance of those in the bar that night spread like wildfire throughout New York City, igniting a firestorm of long pent-up anger and outrage. Lesbian, gay, and transgender people from around the city descended on the bar in subsequent nights to fend off the police and establish a claim to dignified treatment that launched many of the gains made today. The so-called Stonewall Rebellion made news around the country, and the effects traveled across the Atlantic to emerging lesbian and gay organizations in Europe.

While a small and orderly group of lesbians and gay men had staged a picket outside the White House in 1965, Stonewall represented a more radical act: A true rebellion against the scorn and abuse that had become the norm. With this new level of political resistance, typical in that time of anti-war demonstrations, civil rights marches, women's rights organizing, and student rebellions, the lesbian and gay community faced numerous obstacles in its fight for social justice. Not the least of these was the official designation of homosexuality as a mental illness, as catalogued by the *Diagnostic and Statistical Manual* (DSM) and accepted throughout the medical and psychiatric professions.

While laws banning a range of nonprocreative, nonmarital sexual behaviors existed in every state, the emergence of a specific identity distinguishing between people whose primary sexual relationships were with people of the same sex and those attracted to members of the opposite sex did not develop until the mid-19th century. The terms "homosexual" and "heterosexual" were created by early social scientists and sexologists in Europe and the United States who were interested in studying human sexuality and observing the phenomenon of those whose sexual preferences deviated from what was considered the norm of male/female relationships. This relatively scientific study of sexual deviations, however, soon devolved into professional views that homosexuality represented not just a deviation from social standards, but a mental illness signified by antisocial behavior and the inability to develop "normal" relationships. Thus cast, inquiry turned to how to "correct" the behaviors.

The study of homosexuality turned into the promotion of homophobia. Institutionalization, electroshock, and corrective therapies were used to "treat" homosexuality and force behavior changes. Extreme social stigma kept all but the most recalcitrant (and financially independent) in the closet. Immigration laws, fueled by 1950s McCarthyism, banned homosexuals and others considered psychopathic personalities from entering the country. Lesbians and gay men were not considered outcasts merely because they were different, but rather they were deemed a danger to children, marriage, the family, and society in general. Homosexuality became associated with mental illness and antisocial behaviors. "Tests" to identify those with homosexual inclinations were conducted by city and government employers well into the 1970s to ferret out applicants for jobs in fire departments, police departments, and other civil service positions. Campaigns were waged to remove school teachers who were gay or were even simply supportive of gay rights from public schools for fear of their impact on children. Children were routinely removed from the custody of lesbian or gay parents who came out and divorced. In 1987, New Hampshire passed a law banning lesbians and gay men from being adoptive or foster parents. The law was upheld by the New Hampshire Supreme Court on the theory that lesbians and gay men were not appropriate role models for children.

The Stonewall generation of lesbian and gay activists knew that political and legal reforms to end discrimination and abuse of lesbians and gay men would be virtually impossible to attain without changing the designation of homosexuality as a mental disorder. Alfred Kinsey had caused a major stir by releasing his reports on human sexuality, which introduced his famous Kinsey Scale to gauge ranges of sexual behaviors and desires from "zero," which designated exclusive heterosexuality, to "six," which designated exclusive homosexuality. The Kinsey study showed a broad continuum of sexuality, with many "heterosexuals" revealing lesbian and homosexual behaviors and inclinations.

A small, but determined, number of researchers and mental health practitioners began chipping away at their colleagues' adoption of the illness framework for homosexuality. With their support, lesbian and gay activists approached the American Psychiatric Association (APA) to argue for a change to the *DSM*, used by mental health professionals as the guide to diagnosing mental illness. Changing the *DSM*'s designation of homosexuality as a mental disorder became an early strategic imperative, and in 1973, the APA modified its view of homosexuality enough to remove the professionally enforced stigma associated with same-sex attraction and relationships.

The Family Next Door

It would be a grand overstatement to say that the legal rights of lesbians and gay men have been vindicated. They have not. Nor have the rights of transgender people, those whose gender identity and expression do not conform to traditional views of male and female roles, been accepted in even the most minimal of ways in society. Despite the fact that the Supreme Court has overturned the criminal laws against homosexuality and has declared that deliberate and overtly hostile attempts to deny lesbian and gay citizens the right to advocate for non-discrimination laws are unconstitutional, American political culture is far from adding sexual orientation and gender identity to the list of personal characteristics that are unacceptable as a basis for bias, discrimination, and violence.

To date, there is no federal law banning discrimination on the basis of sexual orientation or gender identity. Only a dozen or so states prohibit discrimination based upon sexual orientation, though a growing number of cities ban both sexual orientation and gender identity discrimination. Although in 1990 the United States Congress repealed the ban on lesbians and gay men entering the country, the enactment in 1993 of the first federal law (as contrasted to the Department of Defense policy mandating discharge of gay and lesbian enlistees) barring lesbians and gay men from serving in the military and the 1996 enactment of the Defense of Marriage Act reinforced the continued legitimacy of targeting lesbian and gay people for overtly discriminatory treatment. Lesbians and gay men still encounter numerous obstacles to their rights to be parents or to maintain their parenting relationships. Lesbian, gay, bisexual, and transgender (LGBT) young people are primary targets for harassment and violence in schools, as are the children of LGBT parents. And the list goes on.

And yet, even without the range of civil rights laws that have helped reform society by banning discrimination and unequal treatment on the basis of race, national origin, and sex, many lesbians and gay men have succeeded in being viewed as simply the family next door. A far cry from the deviant, antisocial outcasts of a generation ago. While the public is still quite mixed with regard to extending marriage rights to same-sex couples, a vast majority believe that discrimination against LGBT people is unacceptable.

We are, after all, a "pull yourself up by your bootstraps" society. While this cultural value is too frequently used to unjustly chastise economically underprivileged members of society by ignoring the impact of stereotypes with regard to race, gender, and class on their struggle for a piece of the American pie, past civil rights battles have laid the groundwork for LGBT people to establish their own claim to equality. It has become axiomatic that employers should not discriminate on the basis of a personal characteristic that has no impact on one's ability to do the job, almost to the point that companies and employers have engaged in self-reform with regard to anti-LGBT discrimination regardless of the absence of legal imperative. Lesbian and gay families should have rights to health care, property rights, and other domestic partner benefits so readily afforded to married couples. Only one state, Florida, has steadfastly held to a policy of prohibiting lesbians and gay men from adopting children. In light of the sheer numbers of children in need of supportive homes, most states have tacitly welcomed any individual or couple willing and otherwise qualified to be an attentive parent. The majority of Fortune 500 corporations in the United States ban discrimination based on sexual orientation and extend a range of benefits to same-sex and opposite-sex domestic partners, as do a large number of major universities, non-profits, and city governments. In the last three presidential elections, the Democratic Party candidates have forthrightly promoted a full range of rights for LGBT people, including the right to be recognized as domestic partners.

The law is only one indicator of the acceptance of a community into the mainstream of society. Legal prohibitions against race or sex discrimination, for instance, have not completely resolved the tragic proportions of racism and sexism in social interactions or institutional practices. And while the obstacles facing LGBT people seeking full equality are still numerous, and the hostility to them in many parts of the country is still seething and palpable, the failure of the law to extend the full range of rights is not the only barometer of success or failure. The transformative impact of the Obama administration—the very first presidential administration not headed by a white male—has just begun to unfold in American society. And while it is never just one person who shifts social attitudes—even if he or she happens to be the President—the symbolic opportunity is there to separate from a past of discrimination and marginalization to a future of inclusion.

Suggestions for Further Reading

Acuna, Rudolpho. *Occupied America: A History of Chicanos,* 4th ed. Menlo Park, CA: Addison Wesley Longman, 2000.

Anderson, Karen. *Changing Women: A History of Racial Ethnic Women in Modern America.* New York: Oxford University Press, 1996.

Aptheker, Bettina. *Woman's Legacy: Essays on Race, Sex, and Class in American History.* Amherst: University of Massachusetts Press, 1982.

Baxendall, R., L. Gordon, and S. Reverby. *America's Working Women: A Documentary History—1600 to the Present.* New York: Random House, 1976.

Berry, Mary Frances. *Justice for All: The United States Commission on Civil Rights and the Continuing Struggle for Freedom in America.* New York: Knopf, 2009.

Boyer, R. O., and H. Morais. *Labor's Untold Story.* New York: United Electrical, Radio and Machine Workers of America, 1972.

Cluster, D., ed. *They Should Have Served that Cup of Coffee.* Boston: South End Press, 1979.

Cott, Nancy F. *Root of Bitterness: Documents of the Social History of American Women.* Boston: Northeastern Press, 1986.

Davis, Mike. *Prisoners of the American Dream: Politics and Economics in the History of the U.S. Working Class.* New York: Verso, 2000.

Deitz, James L. *Economic History of Puerto Rico: Institutional Change and Capitalist Development.* Princeton, NJ: Princeton University Press, 1986.

Duberman, Martin Baum, Martha Vicinus, and George Chauncey, Jr. *Hidden from History: Reclaiming the Gay and Lesbian Past.* New York: New American Library, 1989.

DuBois, Ellen, and Vicki Ruis. *Unequal Sisters,* 4th ed. New York: Routledge and Kegan Paul, 2007.

Fleischer, Doris Zames, and Frieda Zames. *The Disability Rights Movement from Charity to Confrontation.* Philadelphia: Temple University Press, 2001.

Flexner, Eleanor. *Century of Struggle.* Cambridge, MA: Harvard University Press, 1976.

Giddings, Paula. *When and Where I Enter: The Impact of Black Women on Race and Sex in America.* New York: Bantam Books, 1976.

Katz, Jonathan. *Gay American History: Lesbians and Gay Men in the U.S.: A Documentary History.* New York: Avon Books, 1984.

Kessler-Harris, Alice. *In Pursuit of Equity: Women, Men, and the Quest for Economic Citizenship in Twentieth-Century America.* New York: Oxford University Press, 2001.

Konig, Hans. *The Conquest of America: How the Indian Nations Lost Their Continent.* New York: Monthly Review Press, 1993.

Mintz, Sidney. *Caribbean Transformations.* Baltimore, MD: Johns Hopkins Press, 1974.

Perez, Emma. *The Decolonial Imaginary: Writing Chicanas into History.* Bloomington: Indiana University Press, 1999.

Robson, Ruthann. *Lesbian (Out)Law: Survival under the Rule of Law.* Ithaca, NY: Firebrand Books, 1992.

Takaki, Ronald. *A Different Mirror: Multicultural American History.* Boston: Little, Brown, 1993.

Takaki, Ronald. *From Different Shores: Perspectives on Race and Culture in America.* New York: Oxford University Press, 1987.

United States Commission on Human Rights. *Indian Tribes: A Continuing Quest for Survival.* Washington, DC: United States Commission on Human Rights, 1981.

Wagenheim, K., and O. J. Wagenheim, eds. *The Puerto Ricans: A Documentary History.* New York: Praeger, 1973.

PART VIII

Maintaining Race, Class, and Gender Hierarchies: Reproducing "Reality"

I n the end, the most effective forms of social control are always invisible. Tanks in the streets and armed militia serve as constant reminders that people are not free, and they provide a focus for anger and an impetus for rebellion. More effective by far are the beliefs and attitudes a society fosters to rationalize and reinforce prevailing distributions of power and opportunity. It is here that stereotypes and ideology have an important role to play. They shape how we see ourselves and others; they affect how we define social issues, and they determine who we hold responsible for society's ills. Each plays a part in persuading people that differences in wealth, power, and opportunity are reflections of natural differences among people, not the results of the economic and political organization of society. If stereotypes, ideology, and language are truly effective, they go beyond rationalizing inequality to rendering it invisible. Once again we find the social construction of gender, race, and class as hierarchy at the heart of a belief system that makes the prevailing distribution of wealth and opportunity appear natural and inevitable rather than arbitrary and alterable. In U.S. society the stereotypes and values transmitted through education and the media have played a critical role in perpetuating racism, sexism, heterosexism, and class privilege even at those times when the law has been used as a vehicle to fight discrimination rather than maintain it.

The selections in Part VIII examine some of the ways in which we are socialized to buy into belief systems that reinforce existing social roles and class positions and blunt social criticism. Stereotypes and beliefs or ideology are perpetuated by the institutions within which we live and grow. In addition to providing us with information and values, education, religion, and the family, along with the media, encourage us to adopt a particular picture of the world and our place in it. These institutions shape our perceptions of others and give us a sense of our own future. In effect, they construct what we take to be "reality."

The mass media selectively provides information, promotes certain values, and teaches us who and what we should regard as important. Along with other institutions, it shapes our definition of community, painting a picture of society divided between "us" and "them." By making inequities and suffering appear to be the result of personal or group deficiency rather than the consequences of injustice, stereotyping and ideology reconcile people to the status quo and prevent them from seeking change. Violence and the threat of violence reinforce ideology and threaten with pain or death those who challenge the prevailing system or its conventions and prescriptions.

In addition to creating and maintaining mistaken beliefs about the causes of unequal distribution of privilege, stereotypes can play an important role in reconciling individuals to discriminatory treatment. If stereotypes are truly effective, they can prevent the individual not only from recognizing discrimination but also even from encountering it by ensuring that he or she does not seek opportunities that are unavailable to members of his or her group.

In Selection 1 in Part VIII, "Self-Fulfilling Stereotypes," Mark Snyder uses examples from psychological research to show how important people's expectations are in shaping their perceptions of others and in determining how they behave. In particular, these studies raise serious questions about the "objectivity" of interviewers' evaluations of job candidates and applicants for admission to educational programs; the studies suggest that how we see others often says more about our own unconscious stereotyping and expectations than about the individuals being evaluated. As Snyder points out, some of the most interesting studies in the field of education show that teachers' expectations are at least as important as a child's innate ability in determining how well young children do in school. Taken together, Snyder's article and Richard D. Mohr's article, "Anti-Gay Stereotypes," that follows make it clear that the unconscious beliefs that people harbor can have powerful consequences for the life chances and well-being of others.

While some stereotyping is so crude that it can be easily dismissed, advertising has become extremely sophisticated in its ability to shape and manipulate unconscious attitudes and values. In "White Lies," Maurice Berger examines the portrayal of a "prototypical" black man in an ad campaign by one of America's more successful designers. After offering a subtle and thought-provoking analysis of the way in which black masculinity is constructed in the ad, Berger goes on to generalize about the relationship between such portrayals and the maintenance of prevailing relations of dominance and subordination in society. He argues that the cultural and social institutions that are controlled by white people continue to operate to protect white privilege.

While men in our society continue to be judged by the jobs they hold and their earning power, women continue to be judged according to a narrow and rigid standard of beauty. The messages that bombard young women from an early age continue to foster the belief that having a tiny waist is infinitely more important than earning an advanced degree or learning a technical skill. Although many women have made considerable strides in the world of work, the prevailing ideology continues to assert that being attractive (read "thin") enough to capture the right man is the real way to success. Aside from its heterosexist bias, this emphasis on physical appearance (and, consequently, on unhealthy standards for body weight) is simply one more way in which society keeps women in their place. In Selection 4, "Am I Thin Enough Yet?" Sharlene Hesse-Biber explores some of the consequences of the ways in which women have been encouraged to internalize an artificial and unattainable standard of beauty.

Sut Jhally takes the critique of advertising implicit throughout this part of the text to a whole new level in his essay, "Advertising at the Edge of the Apocalypse." In the course of his powerful and passionate indictment of our capitalist consumer culture, where production is organized around making the most profit possible rather than satisfying human needs, Sully paints a frightening picture of the cultural role of advertising in our society. He maintains that by teaching people that their happiness will be realized through buying more and more things, advertising serves the needs of the market and prevents us, both as individuals and as a society, from asking the hard questions we need to ask about the kind of world we really want to live in and what we really value. By denying collective values, emphasizing material life, and seeking short-term profits at the expense of long-term environmentally responsible planning, capitalism and advertising, he contends, are propelling us toward a catastrophic future.

It is helpful to read Jhally's critique of the culture of capitalism in conjunction with Michael Parenti's account of our society as a plutocracy, a system of rule by and for the rich, rather than a democracy, a system of rule by and for the people (Selection 6). In this book excerpt, Parenti offers us a detailed account of the ways in which our social institutions are organized to perpetuate rule by the rich and the ways in which we are socialized to embrace a system of beliefs that reinforces the existing social hierarchy. He suggests that all of us get a clear message that material success is the measure of person's worth and the related message that, by implication, the poor aren't worth very much and so we should not waste society's resources on them.

While Gregory Mantsios, the author of Selection 7, would undoubtedly agree with Parenti's conclusion, Mantsios argues that in addition to playing a major role in fostering racial, ethnic, gender, and class stereotypes, the media's programming and perspective impact on our ability to "see" class at all. "By ignoring the poor and blurring the lines between working people and the upper class," he writes "the news media creates a universal middle class." By adopting the perspective of those who are most privileged, it distorts the realities of daily life and encourages most of us to identify with the needs and interests of a privileged few.

It would be difficult if not impossible to underestimate the role that education plays in reproducing the social hierarchy. Jonathan Kozol, the author of Selection 8, has written numerous books about this role. His most recent book is appropriately titled *Shame of the Nation*. In the selection in this part he describes what he calls "the governmentally administered diminishment in the value of children of the poor." Kozol's thesis is that education in the United States continues to be separate and unequal to such an extent that it both constitutes and perpetuates a system of apartheid.

In Selection 9, William Chafe examines the impact of both race and gender stereotypes and ideology by drawing an analogy between sex and race. He argues persuasively that both racism and sexism function analogously as forms of social control. Although Chafe suggests he is comparing the experiences of white women with those of African Americans, a careful reading of his essay suggests that he is really comparing the experiences of white women with those of black men. The reader might be interested in exploring whether Chafe's claim about racism, sexism, and social control holds up equally well when we construct similar accounts of the experiences of African American women, as well as members of other racial/ethnic groups discussed in this book. Chafe begins by analyzing how stereotypes, ideology, and language can distort expectations, perceptions, and experience and then proceeds to ask whose interests are served by this distortion.

While Greg Mantsios talks about the media's ability to make class issues disappear, Angela Davis suggests that the criminal justice system in the United States performs a similarly magical feat by making social problems disappear. In her essay, "Masked Racism: Reflections on the Prison Industrial Complex," Davis examines the recent trend toward privatizing the nation's prison system and argues that imprisonment has become the government's response to social problems. She writes, "Homelessness, unemployment, drug addiction, mental illness, and illiteracy are only a few of the problems that disappear from public view when the human beings contending with them are relegated to cages."

In the final selection in Part VIII, William Ryan considers how stereotyping and ideology reinforce the status quo by directing people's attention away from the economic and social arrangements that perpetuate unequal treatment and by encouraging people to blame the victims of these institutions for their own misery. Ryan's essay examines a technique he calls "blaming the victim," which effectively allows people to recognize injustice without either assuming responsibility for it or acknowledging the need to make fundamental changes in social and economic institutions.

Often, people become overwhelmed and discouraged when they realize how much our unconscious images and beliefs affect the ways we see each other and the world; as a result, they fail to go on to analyze the consequences of ideology. Believing that people are naturally prejudiced and can't change is one more bit of ideology that prevents us from questioning prevailing social and economic arrangements and asking whether they serve the best interests of all. By dividing us from each other and misleading us about who profits from these arrangements, ideology and stereotypes imprison us in a false world. In Part IX of this book, a number of articles suggest ways we can move beyond race, class, and gender divisions to work together in order to bring about social change.

Self-Fulfilling Stereotypes

Mark Snyder

Gordon Allport, the Harvard psychologist who wrote a classic work on the nature of prejudice, told a story about a child who had come to believe that people who lived in Minneapolis were called monopolists. From his father, moreover, he had learned that monopolists were evil folk. It wasn't until many years later, when he discovered his confusion, that his dislike of residents of Minneapolis vanished.

Allport knew, of course, that it was not so easy to wipe out prejudice and erroneous stereotypes. Real prejudice, psychologists like Allport argued, was buried deep in human character, and only a restructuring of education could begin to root it out. Yet many people whom I meet while lecturing seem to believe that stereotypes are simply beliefs or attitudes that change easily with experience. Why do some people express the view that Italians are passionate, blacks are lazy, Jews materialistic, and lesbians mannish in their demeanor? In the popular view, it is because they have not learned enough about the diversity among these groups and have not had enough contact with members of the groups for their stereotypes to be challenged by reality. With more experience, it is presumed, most people of good will are likely to revise their stereotypes.

My research over the past decade convinces me that there is little justification for such optimism—and not only for the reasons given by Allport. While it is true that deep prejudice is often based on the needs of pathological character structure, stereotypes are obviously quite common even among fairly normal individuals. When people first meet others, they cannot help noticing certain highly visible and distinctive characteristics: sex, race, physical appearance, and the like. Despite people's best intentions, their initial impressions of others are shaped by their assumptions about such characteristics.

What is critical, however, is that these assumptions are not merely beliefs or attitudes that exist in a vacuum; they are reinforced by the behavior of both prejudiced people and the targets of their prejudice. In recent years, psychologists have collected considerable laboratory evidence about the processes that strengthen stereotypes and put them beyond the reach of reason and good will.

My own studies initially focused on first encounters between strangers. It did not take long to discover, for example, that people have very different ways of treating those whom they regard as physically attractive and those whom they consider physically unattractive, and that these differences tend to bring out precisely those kinds of behavior that fit with stereotypes about attractiveness.

In an experiment that I conducted with my colleagues Elizabeth Decker Tanke and Ellen Berscheid, pairs of college-age men and women met and became acquainted in telephone conversations. Before the conversations began, each man received a Polaroid snapshot, presumably taken just months before, of the woman he would soon meet. The photograph, which had actually been prepared before the experiment began, showed either a physically attractive woman or a physically unattractive one. By randomly choosing which picture to use for each conversation, we insured that there was no consistent relationship between the attractiveness of the woman in the picture and the attractiveness of the woman in the conversation.

By questioning the men, we learned that even before the conversations began, stereotypes about physical attractiveness came into play. Men who looked forward to talking with physically attractive women said that they expected to meet decidedly sociable, poised, humorous, and socially adept people, while men who thought that they were about to get acquainted with unattractive women fashioned images of rather unsociable, awkward, serious, and socially inept creatures. Moreover, the men proved to have very different styles of getting acquainted with women whom they thought to be attractive and those whom they believed to be unattractive. Shown a photograph of an attractive woman, they behaved with warmth, friendliness, humor, and animation. However, when the woman in the picture was unattractive, the men were cold, uninteresting, and reserved.

These differences in the men's behavior elicited behavior in the women that was consistent with the men's stereotyped assumptions. Women who were believed (unbeknown to them) to be physically attractive behaved in a friendly, likeable, and sociable manner. In sharp contrast, women who were perceived as physically unattractive adopted a cool, aloof, and distant manner. So striking were the differences in the women's behavior that they could be discerned simply by listening to tape recordings of the woman's side of the conversations. Clearly, by acting upon their stereotyped beliefs about the women whom they would be meeting, the men had initiated a chain of events that produced *behavioral confirmation* for their beliefs.

Similarly, Susan Anderson and Sandra Bem have shown in an experiment at Stanford University that when the tables are turned—when it is women who have pictures of men they are to meet on the telephone—many women treat the men according to their presumed physical attractiveness, and by so doing encourage the men to confirm their stereotypes. Little wonder, then, that so many people remain convinced that good looks and appealing personalities go hand in hand.

Sex and Race

It is experiments such as these that point to a frequently unnoticed power of stereotypes: the power to influence social relationships in ways that create the illusion of reality. In one study, Berna Skrypnek and I arranged for pairs of previously unacquainted students to interact in a situation that permitted us to control the information that each one received about the apparent sex of the other. The two people were seated in separate rooms so that they could neither see nor hear each other. Using a system of signal lights that they operated with switches, they negotiated a division of labor, deciding which member of the pair would perform each of several tasks that differed in sex-role connotations. The tasks varied along the dimensions of masculinity and femininity: sharpen a hunting knife (masculine), polish a pair of shoes (neutral), iron a shirt (feminine).

One member of the team was led to believe that the other was, in one condition of the experiment, male; in the other, female. As we had predicted, the first member's belief about the sex of the partner influenced the outcome of the pair's negotiations. Women whose partners believed them to be men generally chose stereotypically masculine tasks; in contrast, women whose partners believed that they were women usually chose stereotypically feminine tasks. The experiment thus suggests that much sex-role behavior may be the product of other people's stereotyped and often erroneous beliefs.

In a related study at the University of Waterloo, Carl von Baeyer, Debbie Sherk, and Mark Zanna have shown how stereotypes about sex roles operate in job interviews. The researchers arranged to have men conduct simulated job interviews with women supposedly seeking positions as research assistants. The investigators informed half of the women that the men who would interview them held traditional views about the ideal woman, believing her to be very emotional, deferential to her husband, home-oriented, and passive. The rest of the women were told that their interviewer saw the ideal woman as independent, competitive, ambitious, and dominant. When the women arrived for their interviews, the researchers noticed that most of them had dressed to meet the stereotyped expectations of their prospective interviewers. Women who expected to see a traditional interviewer had chosen very feminine-looking makeup, clothes, and accessories. During the interviews (videotaped through a one-way mirror) these women behaved in traditionally feminine ways and gave traditionally feminine answers to questions such as "Do you have plans to include children and marriage with your career plans?"

Once more, then, we see the self-fulfilling nature of stereotypes. Many sex differences, it appears, may result from the images that people create in their attempts to act out accepted sex roles. The implication is that if stereotyped expectations about sex roles shift, behavior may change, too. In fact, statements by people who have undergone sex-change operations have highlighted the power of such expectations in easing adjustment to a new life. As the writer Jan Morris said in recounting the story of her transition from James to Jan: "The more I was treated as a woman, the more woman I became."

The power of stereotypes to cause people to confirm stereotyped expectations can also be seen in interracial relationships. In the first of two investigations done at Princeton University by Carl Word, Mark Zanna, and Joel Cooper, white undergraduates interviewed both white and black job applicants. The applicants were actually confederates of the experimenters, trained to behave consistently from interview to interview, no matter how the interviewers acted toward them.

To find out whether or not the white interviewers would behave differently toward white and black job applicants, the researchers secretly videotaped each interview and then studied the tapes. From these, it was apparent that there were substantial differences in the treatment accorded blacks and whites. For one thing, the interviewers' speech deteriorated when they talked to blacks, displaying more errors in grammar and pronunciation. For another, the interviewers spent less time with blacks than with whites and showed less "immediacy," as the researchers called it, in their manner. That is, they were less friendly, less outgoing, and more reserved with blacks.

In the second investigation, white confederates were trained to approximate the immediate or the nonimmediate interview styles that had been observed in the first investigation as they interviewed white job applicants. A panel of judges who evaluated the tapes agreed that applicants subjected to the nonimmediate styles performed less adequately and were more nervous than job applicants treated in the immediate style. Apparently, then, the blacks in the first study did not have a chance to display their qualifications to the best advantage. Considered together, the two investigations suggest that in interracial encounters, racial stereotypes may constrain behavior in ways to cause both blacks and whites to behave in accordance with those stereotypes.

Rewriting Biography

Having adopted stereotyped ways of thinking about another person, people tend to notice and remember the ways in which that person seems to fit the stereotype, while resisting evidence that contradicts the stereotype. In one investigation that I conducted with Seymour Uranowitz, student subjects read a biography of a fictitious woman named Betty K. We constructed the story of her life so that it would fit the stereotyped images of both lesbians and heterosexuals. Betty, we wrote, never had a steady boyfriend in high school, but did go out on dates. And although we gave her a steady boyfriend in college, we specified that he was more of a close friend than anything else. A week after we had distributed this biography, we gave our subjects some new information about Betty. We told some students that she was now living with another woman in a lesbian relationship; we told others that she was living with her husband.

To see what impact stereotypes about sexuality would have on how people remembered the facts of Betty's life, we asked each student to answer a series of questions about her life history. When we examined their answers, we found that the students had reconstructed the events of Betty's past in ways that supported their own stereotyped beliefs about her sexual orientation. Those who believed that Betty was a lesbian remembered that Betty had never had a·steady boyfriend in high school, but tended to neglect the fact that she had gone out on many dates in college. Those who believed that Betty was now a heterosexual tended to remember that she had formed a steady relationship with a man in college, but tended to ignore the fact that this relationship was more of a friendship than a romance.

The students showed not only selective memories but also a striking facility for interpreting what they remembered in ways that added fresh support for their stereotypes. One student who accurately remembered that a supposedly lesbian Betty never had a steady boyfriend in high school confidently pointed to the fact as an early sign of her lack of romantic or sexual interest in men. A student who correctly remembered that a purportedly lesbian Betty often went out on dates in college was sure that these dates were signs of Betty's early attempts to mask her lesbian interests.

Clearly, the students had allowed their preconceptions about lesbians and heterosexuals to dictate the way in which they interpreted and reinterpreted the facts of Betty's life. As long as stereotypes make it easy to bring to mind evidence that supports them and difficult to bring to mind evidence that undermines them, people will cling to erroneous beliefs.

Stereotypes in the Classroom and Work Place

The power of one person's beliefs to make other people conform to them has been well demonstrated in real life. Back in the 1960s, as most people well remember, Harvard psychologist Robert Rosenthal and his colleague Lenore Jacobson entered elementary-school classrooms and identified one out of every five pupils in each room as a child who could be expected to show dramatic improvement in intellectual achievement during the school year. What the teachers did not know was that the children had been chosen on a random basis. Nevertheless, something happened in the relationships between teachers and their supposedly gifted pupils that led the children to make clear gains in test performance.

It can also do so on the job. Albert King, now a professor of management at Northern Illinois University, told a welding instructor in a vocational training center that five men in his training program had unusually high aptitude. Although these five had been chosen at random and knew nothing of their designation as high-aptitude workers, they showed substantial changes in performance. They were absent less often than were other workers, learned the basics of the welder's trade in about half the usual time, and scored a full 10 points higher than other trainees on a welding test. Their gains were noticed not only by the researcher and by the welding instructor, but also by other trainees, who singled out the five as their preferred coworkers.

Might not other expectations influence the relationships between supervisors and workers? For example, supervisors who believe that men are better suited to some jobs and women to others may treat their workers (wittingly or unwittingly) in ways that encourage them to perform their jobs in accordance with stereotypes about differences between men and women. These same stereotypes may determine who gets which job in the first place. Perhaps some personnel managers allow stereotypes to influence, subtly or not so subtly, the way in which they interview job candidates, making it likely that candidates who fit the stereotypes show up better than job seekers who do not fit them.

Unfortunately, problems of this kind are compounded by the fact that members of stigmatized groups often subscribe to stereotypes about themselves. That is what Amerigo Farina and his colleagues at the University of Connecticut found when they measured the impact upon mental patients of believing that others knew their psychiatric history. In Farina's study, each mental patient cooperated with another person in a game requiring teamwork. Half of the patients believed that their partners knew they were patients, the other half believed that their partners thought they were nonpatients. In reality, the nonpatients never knew a thing about anyone's psychiatric history. Nevertheless, simply believing that others were aware of their history led the patients to feel less appreciated, to find the task more difficult, and to perform poorly. In addition, objective observers saw them as more tense, more anxious, and more poorly adjusted than patients who believed that their status was not known. Seemingly, the belief that others perceived them as stigmatized caused them to play the role of stigmatized patients.

Consequences for Society

Apparently, good will and education are not sufficient to subvert the power of stereotypes. If people treat others in such a way as to bring out behavior that supports stereotypes, they may never have an opportunity to discover which of their stereotypes are wrong.

I suspect that even if people were to develop doubts about the accuracy of their stereotypes, chances are they would proceed to test them by gathering precisely the evidence that would appear to confirm them.

The experiments I have described help to explain the persistence of stereotypes. But, as is so often the case, solving one puzzle only creates another. If by acting as if false stereotypes were true, people lead others, too, to act as if they were true, why do the stereotypes not come to *be* true? Why, for example, have researchers found so little evidence that attractive people are generally friendly, sociable, and outgoing and that unattractive people are generally shy and aloof?

I think that the explanation goes something like this: Very few among us have the kind of looks that virtually everyone considers either very attractive or very unattractive. Our looks make us rather attractive to some people but somewhat less attractive to other people. When we spend time with those who find us attractive, they will tend to bring out our more sociable sides, but when we are with those who find us less attractive, they will bring out our less sociable sides. Although our actual physical appearance does not change, we present ourselves quite differently to our admirers and to our detractors. For our admirers we become attractive people, and for our detractors we become unattractive. This mixed pattern of behavior will prevent the development of any consistent relationship between physical attractiveness and personality.

Now that I understand some of the powerful forces that work to perpetuate social stereotypes, I can see a new mission for my research. I hope, on the one hand, to find out how to help people see the flaws in their stereotypes. On the other hand, I would like to help the victims of false stereotypes find ways of liberating themselves from the constraints imposed on them by other members of society.

2

ANTI-GAY STEREOTYPES

Richard D. Mohr

A . . . Gallup poll found that only one in five Americans reports having a gay acquaintance.[1] This finding is extraordinary given the number of practicing homosexuals in America. Alfred Kinsey's 1948 study of the sex lives of 5000 white males shocked the nation: 37 percent had at least one homosexual experience to orgasm in their adult lives; an additional 13 percent had homosexual fantasies to orgasm; 4 percent were exclusively homosexual in their practices; another 5 percent had virtually no heterosexual experience; and nearly 20 percent had at least as many homosexual as heterosexual experiences.[2] With only slight variations, these figures held across all social categories: region, religion, political belief, class, income, occupation, and education.

Two out of five men one passes on the street have had orgasmic sex with men. Every second family in the country has a member who is essentially homosexual, and many more people regularly have homosexual experiences. Who are homosexuals? They are your friends, your minister, your teacher, your bank teller, your doctor, your mail carrier, your secretary, your congressional representative, your sibling, parent, and spouse. They are everywhere, virtually all ordinary, virtually all unknown.

What follows? First, the country is profoundly ignorant of the actual experience of gay people. Second, social attitudes and practices that are harmful to gays have a much greater overall negative impact on society than is usually realized. Third, most gay people live in hiding—in the closet—making the "coming out" experience

the central fixture of gay consciousness and invisibility the chief social characteristic of gays.

Society's ignorance of gay people is, however, not limited to individuals' lack
of personal acquaintance with gays. Stigma against gay people is so strong that even
discussions of homosexuality are taboo. This taboo is particularly strong in aca-
deme, where it is reinforced by the added fear of the teacher as molester. So even
within the hearth of reason irrational forces have held virtually unchallenged and
largely unchallengeable sway. The usual sort of clarifying research that might be
done on a stigmatized minority has with gays only just begun—haltingly—in history, literature, sociology, and the sciences.

Yet ignorance about gays has not stopped people from having strong opinions
about them. The void which ignorance leaves has been filled with stereotypes. Society holds chiefly two groups of anti-gay stereotypes; the two are an oddly contradictory lot. One set of stereotypes revolves around alleged mistakes in an individual's
gender identity: lesbians are women that want to be, or at least look and act like,
men—bulldykes, diesel dykes; while gay men are those who want to be, or at least
look and act like, women—queens, fairies, limp-wrists, nellies. Gays are "queer,"
which, remember, means at root not merely weird but chiefly counterfeit—"he's
as queer as a three dollar bill." These stereotypes of mismatched or fraudulent genders provide the materials through which gays and lesbians become the butts of
ethnic-like jokes. These stereotypes and jokes, though derisive, basically view gays
and lesbians as ridiculous.

Another set of stereotypes revolves around gays as a pervasive, sinister, conspir-
atorial, and corruptive threat. The core stereotype here is the gay person as child
molester and, more generally, as sex-crazed maniac. These stereotypes carry with
them fears of the very destruction of family and civilization itself. Now, that which
is essentially ridiculous can hardly have such a staggering effect. Something must
be afoot in this incoherent amalgam.

Sense can be made of this incoherence if the nature of stereotypes is clarified.
Stereotypes are not *simply* false generalizations from a skewed sample of cases examined. Admittedly, false generalizing plays a part in most stereotypes a society holds.
If, for instance, one takes as one's sample homosexuals who are in psychiatric hospitals or prisons, as was done in nearly all early investigations, not surprisingly one will
probably find homosexuals to be of a crazed and criminal cast. Such false generalizations, though, simply confirm beliefs already held on independent grounds, ones
that likely led the investigator to the prison and psychiatric ward to begin with.
Evelyn Hooker, who in the mid-fifties carried out the first rigorous studies to use non-
clinical gays, found that psychiatrists, when presented with results of standard psychological diagnostic tests—but with indications of sexual orientation omitted—were
able to do no better than if they had guessed randomly in their attempts to distinguish gay files from nongay ones, even though the psychiatrists believed gays to be
crazy and supposed themselves to be experts in detecting craziness.[3] These studies
proved a profound embarrassment to the psychiatric establishment, the financial
well-being of which was substantially enhanced by "curing" allegedly insane gays.

Eventually the studies contributed to the American Psychiatric Association's dropping homosexuality from its registry of mental illnesses in 1973.[4] Nevertheless, the stereotype of gays as sick continues apace in the mind of America.

False generalizations *help maintain* stereotypes; they do not *form* them. As the history of Hooker's discoveries shows, stereotypes have a life beyond facts. Their origin lies in a culture's ideology—the general system of beliefs by which it lives— and they are sustained across generations by diverse cultural transmissions, hardly any of which, including slang and jokes, even purport to have a scientific basis. Stereotypes, then, are not the products of bad science, but are social constructions that perform central functions in maintaining society's conception of itself.

On this understanding, it is easy to see that the anti-gay stereotypes surrounding gender identification are chiefly means of reinforcing still powerful gender roles in society. If, as this stereotype presumes (and condemns), one is free to choose one's social roles independently of gender, many guiding social divisions, both domestic and commercial, might be threatened. The socially gender-linked distinctions would blur between breadwinner and homemaker, protector and protected, boss and secretary, doctor and nurse, priest and nun, hero and whore, saint and siren, lord and helpmate, and God and his world. The accusations "fag" and "dyke" (which recent philology has indeed shown to be rooted in slang referring to gender-bending, especially cross-dressing)[5] exist in significant part to keep women in their place and to prevent men from breaking ranks and ceding away theirs.

The stereotypes of gays as child molesters, sex-crazed maniacs, and civilization destroyers function to displace (socially irresolvable) problems from their actual source to a foreign (and so, it is thought, manageable) one. Thus, the stereotype of child molester functions to give the family unit a false sheen of absolute innocence. It keeps the unit from being examined too closely for incest, child abuse, wife-battering, and the terrorism of constant threats. The stereotype teaches that the problems of the family are not internal to it, but external.

Because this stereotype has this central social function, it could not be dislodged even by empirical studies, paralleling Hooker's efforts, that showed heterosexuals to be child molesters to a far greater extent than the actual occurrence of heterosexuals in the general population.[6] But one need not even be aware of such debunking empirical studies in order to see the same cultural forces at work in the social belief that gays are molesters as in its belief that they are crazy. For one can see them now in society's and the media's treatment of current reports of violence, especially domestic violence. When a mother kills her child or a father rapes his daughter—regular Section B fare even in major urban papers—this is never taken by reporters, columnists, or pundits as evidence that there is something wrong with heterosexuality or with traditional families. These issues are not even raised.

But when a homosexual child molestation is reported it is taken as confirming evidence of the way homosexuals are. One never hears of heterosexual murders, but one regularly reads of "homosexual" ones. Compare the social treatment of Richard Speck's sexually motivated mass murder in 1966 of Chicago nurses with that of John Wayne Gacy's serial murders of Chicago youths. Gacy was in the culture's mind taken as symbolic of gay men in general. To prevent the possibility that The Family was viewed as anything but an innocent victim in this affair, the mainstream press knowingly failed to mention that most of Gacy's adolescent victims were homeless hustlers, even though this was made obvious at his trial.[7] That knowledge would be too much for the six o'clock news and for cherished beliefs.

The stereotype of gays as sex-crazed maniacs functions socially to keep individuals' sexuality contained. For this stereotype makes it look as though the problem of how to address one's considerable sexual drives can and should be answered with repression, for it gives the impression that the cyclone of dangerous psychic forces is *out there* where the fags are, not within one's own breast. With the decline of the stereotype of the black man as raping pillaging marauder (found in such works as *Birth of a Nation, Gone with the Wind,* and *Soul on Ice*), the stereotype of gay men as sex-crazed maniacs has become more aggravated. The stereotype of the sex-crazed threat seems one that society desperately needs to have somewhere in its sexual cosmology.

For the repressed homosexual, this stereotype has an especially powerful allure—by hating it consciously, he subconsciously appears to save himself from himself, at least as long as the ruse does not exhaust the considerable psychic energies required to maintain it, or until, like ultraconservative Congressmen Robert E. Bauman (R-Md.) and Jon C. Hinson (R-Miss.), he is caught importuning hustlers or gentlemen in washrooms.[8] If, as Freud and some of his followers thought, everyone feels an urge for sex partners of both genders, then the fear of gays works to show us that we have not "met the enemy and he is us."[9]

By directly invoking sex acts, this second set of stereotypes is the more severe and serious of the two—one never hears child-molester jokes. These stereotypes are aimed chiefly against men, as in turn stereotypically the more sexed of the genders. They are particularly divisive for they create a very strong division between those conceived as "us" and those conceived as "them." This divide is not so strong in the case of the stereotype of gay men as effeminate. For women (and so the woman-like) after all do have their place. Nonstrident, nonuppity useful ones can even be part of "us," indeed, belong, like "our children," to "us." Thus, in many cultures with overweening gender-identified social roles (like prisons, truckstops, the armed forces, Latin America, and the Islamic world) only passive partners in male couplings are derided as homosexual.[10]

Because "the facts" largely do not matter when it comes to the generation and maintenance of stereotypes, the effects of scientific and academic research and of enlightenment generally will be, at best, slight and gradual in the changing fortunes of gays. If this account of stereotypes holds, society has been profoundly immoral. For its treatment of gays is a grand scale rationalization and moral sleight-of-hand. The problem is not that society's usual standards of evidence and procedure in coming to judgments of social policy have been misapplied to gays, rather when it comes to gays, the standards themselves have simply been ruled out of court and disregarded in favor of mechanisms that encourage unexamined fear and hatred.

Partly because lots of people suppose they do not know a gay person and partly through their willful ignorance of society's workings, people are largely unaware of the many ways in which gays are subject to discrimination in consequence of widespread fear and hatred. Contributing to this social ignorance of discrimination is the difficulty for gay people, as an invisible minority, even to complain of discrimination. For if one is gay, to register a complaint would suddenly target one as a stigmatized person, and so, in the absence of any protections against discrimination, would in turn invite additional discrimination.

Further, many people, especially those who are persistently downtrodden and so lack a firm sense of self to begin with, tend either to blame themselves for their troubles or to view their troubles as a matter of bad luck or as the result of an innocent mistake by others—as anything but an injustice indicating something wrong with society. Alfred Dreyfus went to his grave believing his imprisonment for treason and his degradation from the French military, in which he was the highest ranking Jewish officer, had all just been a sort of clerical error, merely requiring recomputation, rather than what it was—lightning striking a promontory from out of a storm of national bigotry.[11] The recognition of injustice requires doing something to rectify wrong; the recognition of systematic injustices requires doing something about the system, and most people, especially the already beleaguered, simply are not up to the former, let alone the latter.

For a number of reasons, then, discrimination against gays, like rape, goes seriously underreported. What do they experience? First, gays are subject to violence and harassment based simply on their perceived status rather than because of any actions they have performed. A[n] . . . extensive study by the National Gay and Lesbian Task Force found that over 90 percent of gays and lesbians had been victimized in some form on the basis of their sexual orientation.[12] More than one in five gay men and nearly one in ten lesbians had been punched, hit, or kicked; a quarter of all gays had had objects thrown at them; a third had been chased; a third had been sexually harassed and 14 percent had been spit on—all just for being perceived to be gay.

The most extreme form of anti-gay violence is queerbashing—where groups of young men target another man who they suppose is gay and beat and kick him unconscious and sometimes to death amid a torrent of taunts and slurs. Such seemingly random but in reality socially encouraged violence has the same social origin and function as lynchings of blacks—to keep a whole stigmatized group in line. As with lynchings . . . the police and courts have routinely averted their eyes, giving their implicit approval to the practice.

Few such cases with gay victims reach the courts. Those that do are marked by inequitable procedures and results. Frequently judges will describe queerbashers as "just All-American Boys." In 1984, a District of Columbia judge handed suspended sentences to queerbashers whose victim had been stalked, beaten, stripped at knife point, slashed, kicked, threatened with castration, and pissed on, because the judge thought the bashers were good boys at heart—after all they went to a religious prep school.[13]

In the summer of 1984, three teenagers hurled a gay man to his death from a bridge in Bangor, Maine. Though the youths could have been tried as adults and normally would have been, given the extreme violence of their crime, they were tried rather as children and . . . [were to] be back on the streets again automatically when they turn[ed] twenty-one.[14]

Further, police and juries simply discount testimony from gays.[15] They typically construe assaults on and murders of gays as "justified" self-defense—the killer need only claim his act was a panicked response to a sexual overture.[16] Alternatively, when guilt seems patent, juries will accept highly implausible insanity or other "diminished capacity" defenses. In 1981 a former New York City Transit Authority policeman, later claiming he was just doing the work of God, machine-gunned down nine people, killing two, in two Greenwich Village gay bars. His jury found him innocent due to mental illness.[17] The best known example of a successful "diminished capacity" defense is Dan White's voluntary manslaughter conviction for the 1978 assassination of openly gay San Francisco city councilman Harvey Milk—Hostess Twinkies, his lawyer successfully argued, made him do it.[18]

These inequitable procedures and results collectively show that the life and liberty of gays, like those of blacks, simply count for less than the life and liberty of members of the dominant culture. . . .

NOTES

1. "Public Fears—And Sympathies," *Newsweek*, August 12, 1985, p. 23.

2. Alfred C. Kinsey, et al., *Sexual Behavior in the Human Male* (Philadelphia: Saunders, 1948), pp. 650–51. On the somewhat lower incidences of lesbianism, see Alfred C. Kinsey, et al., *Sexual Behavior in the Human Female* (Philadelphia: Saunders, 1953), pp. 472–75.

3. Evelyn Hooker, "The Adjustment of the Male Overt Homosexual," *Journal of Projective Techniques* (1957) 21:18–31, reprinted in Hendrik M. Ruitenbeck, ed., *The Problem of Homosexuality*, pp. 141–61, epigram quote from p. 149 (New York: Dutton, 1963).

4. See Ronald Bayer, *Homosexuality and American Psychiatry* (New York: Basic Books, 1981).

5. See Wayne Dynes, *Homolexis: A Historical and Cultural Lexicon of Homosexuality* (New York: Gay Academic Union, Gai Saber Monograph No. 4, 1985), s.v. dyke, faggot.

6. For studies showing that gay men are no more likely—indeed, are less likely—than heterosexuals to be child molesters and that the most widespread and persistent sexual abusers of children are the children's fathers, stepfathers or mother's boyfriends, see Vincent De Francis, *Protecting the Child Victim of Sex Crimes Committed by Adults* (Denver: The American Humane Association, 1969), pp. vii, 38, 69–70; A. Nicholas Groth, "Adult Sexual Orientation and Attraction to Underage Persons," *Archives of Sexual Behavior* (1978) 7:175–81; Mary J. Spencer, "Sexual Abuse of Boys," *Pediatrics* (July 1986) 78(1):133–38.

7. See Lawrence Mass, "Sanity in Chicago: The Trial of John Wayne Gacy and American Psychiatry," *Christopher Street* [New York] (June 1980) 4(7):26. See also Terry Sullivan, *Killer Clown* (New York: Grosset & Dunlap), 1983, pp. 219–25, 315–16; Tim Cahill, *Buried Dreams* (Toronto: Bantam Books, 1986), pp. 318, 352–53, 368–69.

8. For Robert Bauman's account of his undoing, see his autobiography, *The Gentleman from Maryland* (New York: Arbor House, 1986).

9. On Freud, see Timothy F. Murphy, "Freud Reconsidered: Bisexuality, Homosexuality, and Moral Judgment," *Journal of Homosexuality* (1984) 9(2–3):65–77.

10. On prisons, see Wayne Wooden and Jay Parker, *Men Behind Bars: Sexual Exploitation in Prison* (New York: Plenum, 1982). On the armed forces, see George Chauncey Jr., "Christian Brotherhood or Sexual Perversion? Homosexual Identities and the Construction of Sexual Boundaries in the World War One Era," *Journal of Social History* (1985) 19: 189–211.

11. See Jean-Denis Bredin, *The Affair: The Case of Alfred Dreyfus*, trans. Jeffrey Mehlman (1983; New York: George Braziller, 1986), pp. 486–96.

12. National Gay and Lesbian Task Force, *Anti-Gay/Lesbian Victimization* (New York: National Gay and Lesbian Task Force, 1984). See also "Anti-Gay Violence," Subcommittee on Criminal Justice, Committee on the Judiciary, House of Representatives, 99th Congress, 2nd Session, October 9, 1986, serial no. 132.

13. "Two St. John's Students Given Probation in Assault on Gay," *The Washington Post*, May 15, 1984, p. I.
  The 1980 Mariel boatlift, which included thousands of gays escaping Cuban internment camps, inspired U.S. Federal District Judge A. Andrew Hauk in open court to comment of a Mexican illegal alien caught while visiting his resident alien daughter: "And he isn't even a fag like all these faggots we're letting in." *The Advocate* [Los Angeles], November 27, 1980, no. 306, p. 15. Cf. "Gay Refugees Tell of Torture, Oppression in Cuba," *The Advocate*, August 21, 1980, no. 299, pp. 15–16.

14. See *The New York Times*, September 17, 1984, p. D17, and October 6, 1984, p. 6.

15. John D'Emilio writes of the trial of seven police officers caught in a gay bar shakedown racket: "The defense lawyer cast aspersions on the credibility of the prosecution witnesses . . . and deplored a legal system in which 'the most notorious homosexual may testify against a policeman.' Persuaded by this line of argument, the jury acquitted all of the defendants." *Sexual Politics, Sexual Communities: The Making of a Homosexual Minority in the United States, 1940–1970* (Chicago: University of Chicago Press, 1983), p. 183.

16. See for discussion and examples, Pat Califia, "'Justifiable' Homicide?" *The Advocate*, May 12, 1983, no. 367, p. 12; and Robert G. Bagnall, et al., "Burdens on Gay Litigants and Bias in the Court System: Homosexual Panic, Child Custody, and Anonymous Parties," *Harvard Civil Rights–Civil Liberties Law Review* (1984) 19:498–515.

17. *The New York Times*, July 25, 1981, p. 27, and July 26, 1981, p. 25.

18. See Randy Shilts, *The Mayor of Castro Street: The Life and Times of Harvey Milk* (New York: St. Martin's, 1982), pp. 308–25.

3

WHITE LIES

Maurice Berger

On the left-hand side of the two-page advertisement in *The New York Times Magazine* is a regal head shot of a polo pony framed against a bright-blue background. His neck is long and muscular. Bound in the leather straps of the bridle, his head is a deep mahogany, with a strip of white running down the snout. His mane is closely cropped. His ears are small and rigid. His eyes glisten like black marbles. His nostrils flare. His closed mouth appears almost to be grinning.

On the right-hand side of this advertisement (for Ralph Lauren Polo shirts) is a human counterpart to the majestic horse. The man is strikingly beautiful. His head looks to the left, a perfect pendant to the right-facing horse. His skin is a deep mahogany. His elegant, shaved pate has just a hint of black stubble. His small ears curve upward and slightly away from his head. His eyes are dark and dramatic. His nostrils appear to be slightly flared; white light bounces off the bridge of his nose. His full, luscious lips seem almost to be breaking into a smile. His bright-blue shirt nearly blends into the background, giving the effect of a head and neck that graphically float, naked and powerful, against a sea of blue.

It is strange to see a black man representing a company that made its mark appealing to the American middle-class fascination with WASP wealth and taste — even if the man is Tyson Beckford, the first African American male supermodel. Beckford has been the designer's "Polo man" since March 1995, which suggests, in part, that Lauren is reaching out to prospective black customers. But juxtaposing a picture of a black man to one of an animal — the model is not wearing polo gear and is not even in the same space as the horse, suggesting that the two, rather than interacting, are being compared to each other — is an unfortunate ploy. Intentionally or otherwise, the ad replays a long-standing racist fantasy about black people: no matter how beautiful, smart, or talented, they are in some ways always exotic and animal-like.

This fantasy allows white people to feel superior to black people who they suspect may be more beautiful, more talented, or better endowed than they are. It may explain why black models are rarely seen on the cover of fashion and women's and men's magazines and why images of violent black men and irresponsible black mothers abound in the media. Positive images of black men often center on their physicality or athleticism: "Athletes, more than rappers, are more like national heroes," says Beckford's agent, Bethann Hardison. "But also, when it comes down to black men's bodies, historically it's been about how strong and well defined they are—that's what's had value. It's the same old story." The press release for a recent show of menswear by the designer John Bartlett, unusual in that it featured six black models, celebrated the special prowess of black men: "They just have a certain natural masculinity to them," Bartlett observes.

The association between blackness and innate physicality, masculinity, or naturalness often relegates black men to a less-than-human status in the media. In 1988, for example, TV sportscaster Jimmy "the Greek" Snyder offered this on-air explanation of black athletic gifts: "[T]he slave owner would breed his big black with his big black woman so that he could have a big black kid. . . . The black is a better athlete to begin with because he's been bred to be that way because of his thigh size and his big size. [Blacks can] jump higher and run faster." (Snyder was later fired by CBS Sports.)

Like Lauren's vision of the black man as polo pony, such stereotypes deny the intellectual and human dimension of blackness just as surely as they systematically ascribe to black people bestial traits that are rarely applied to whites (the Marlboro Man, after all, is riding *on* his majestic horse). Sometimes this belittling of blackness is more subtle, though by no means free of the prejudices of racial biology. In 1994, for example, golfer Jack Nicklaus told an interviewer that black men have "different muscles that react in different ways" and thus were anatomically unsuited to play golf. (A few years later, of course, Tiger Woods won the U.S. Open, dispelling Nicklaus's racist assumption forever.) Nicklaus's and Snyder's views of black athleticism both see athletic aptitude as inborn, physical, and even genetic; such traits as intelligence, skill, perseverance, and dedication do not come into play.

Black male models present a problem for the fashion industry, argues Hilton Als, where they "still tend to generate lurid fantasies of subway 'gangstas,' and many American designers aren't sure that black men can *sell*." Lauren has found a way out of this problem: transformed into a metaphorical satyr—half man, half horse— Beckford is freed from the specificity of contemporary black masculinity, thus making him more accessible to the white reader. This effect is also achieved, as John Hoberman points out in *Darwin's Athletes: How Sport Has Damaged Black America and Preserved the Myth of Race,* by dissolving ethnic blackness into a genteel and nonviolent "sporting world that is exclusively and impeccably white: golfing, fishing, tennis, rowing, sailing, and polo—the sports of dynamic imperial males unwinding from the rigors of colonial administration."

Yet Lauren's "Polo man" is only allowed to join this world as the counterpart to one of its beautiful, imperial animals. A handsome model, black or white, can help lure the consumer into the fantasy that buying a particular garment will grant him access to the garment's aura of beauty. The risk, however, is that the consumer may also feel competitive with or even threatened by another man's attractiveness. The very presence of black models, then, challenges the often unconscious desires of white men to see themselves as superior to black men. To some extent, Lauren neutralizes these competitive feelings by inviting us to see mirrored in the face of his mahogany "Polo man" the features of an animal prized for its physical endowments.

Too often, white people acknowledge a particular strength in a black colleague, sports figure, politician, or entertainer but dilute their recognition with the same kind of ambivalence implicit in the Lauren ad. In a study of the racial attitudes of sports reporters, for example, *Boston Globe* writer Derek Jackson analyzed the coverage of five National Collegiate Athletic Association basketball games and seven National Football League play-off games during a single season. More than three-quarters of the adjectives used to describe white football players referred to their brains, while just under two-thirds of the adjectives used for black players referred to their brawn. In basketball, the ratio was 63 percent brains for white players, 77 percent brawn for black players.

Cultural and social institutions controlled by white people have been slow to reward black accomplishment not because African Americans don't excel but because such rewards declare that a black person may, in fact, be more talented, more intelligent, or more beautiful than his white peers. One need look no further than the film industry to see white people's indifference to black people's excellence. Although African Americans buy movie tickets in the disproportionate numbers (they make up 12 percent of the population but 25 percent of movie patrons), black people in Hollywood rarely achieve crossover superstar status, or are thought capable of carrying a movie, or receive such markers of success as Academy Award nominations. The 1997 Oscars were a case in point: all twenty acting nominees were white and a number of their performances were less than outstanding; overlooked were the extraordinary and critically acclaimed work of black actors Djimon Hounsou in *Amistad*; Samuel L. Jackson, Debbi Morgan, and Lynn Whitfield in *Eve's Bayou*; and Pam Grier in *Jackie Brown*. The argument, advanced by several white critics, that these films were weak and thus placed their actors at a disadvantage for Oscar nominations is specious: *Eve's Bayou* was widely praised by critics (though the film apparently did not reach white audiences) and Grier's and Hounsou's white co-stars, Robert Forster and Anthony Hopkins, were nominated. In the end, most black men in Hollywood—from Denzel Washington to James Earl Jones—remain character actors: "In other words, they are *safe*," observes actress Ellen Holly in an op-ed piece in *The New York Times* on the obstacles faced by black actors in the film industry. "They may be doing some of the most riveting work in film . . . but none is breaking the sexual taboos that keep a black man from becoming a high-wattage star."

Mainstream American culture's avoidance of black talent and excellence suggests one of the greatest deficiencies of whiteness: its inability to celebrate and learn from the strengths and accomplishments of black people. Too often, white people live by the rules of self-protection, competitiveness, and self-aggrandizement—rules which tell us that black men may be no more handsome or intelligent than the polo ponies on which their rich white brothers ride.

4

AM I THIN ENOUGH YET?

Sharlene Hesse-Biber

"Ever since I was ten years old, I was just a very vain person. I always wanted to be the thinnest, the prettiest. 'Cause I thought, if I look like this, then I'm going to have so many boyfriends, and guys are going to be so in love with me, and I'll be taken care of for the rest of my life. I'll never have to work, you know?"

— *DELIA, COLLEGE SENIOR*

What's Wrong with This Picture?

Pretty, vivacious, and petite, Delia was a picture of fashionable perfection when she first walked into my office. Her tight blue jeans and fringed Western shirt showed off her thin, 5-ft frame; her black cowboy boots and silver earrings completed a presentation that said, "Look at me!"

The perfect picture had a serious price. Delia had come to talk about her "problem." She is bulimic. In secret, she regularly binges on large amounts of food, then forces herself to vomit. It has become a powerful habit, one that she is afraid to break because it so efficiently maintains her thin body. For Delia, as for so many others, being thin is everything.

"I mean, how many bumper stickers have you seen that say 'No Fat Chicks,' you know? Guys don't like fat girls. Guys like little girls. I guess because it makes them feel bigger and, you know, they want somebody who looks pretty. Pretty to me is you have to be thin and you have to have like good facial features. It's both. My final affirmation of myself is how many guys look at me when I go into a bar. How many guys pick up on me. What my boyfriend thinks about me."

Delia's Story

Delia is the eldest child, and only girl, in a wealthy Southern family. Her father is a successful dentist and her mother has never worked outside the home. They fought a lot when she was young—her father was an alcoholic—and they eventually divorced. According to Delia, both parents doted on her.

"I've never been deprived of anything in my entire life. I was spoiled, I guess, because I've never felt any pressure from my parents to do anything. My Dad would say, 'Whatever you want to do, if you want to go to Europe, if you want to go to law school, if you don't want to do anything . . . whatever you want to do, just be happy.' No pressure."

He was unconcerned about her weight, she said, but emphasized how important it was to be pretty. Delia quickly noticed this message everywhere, especially in the media.

"I am so affected by *Glamour* magazine and *Vogue* and all that, because that's a line of work I want to get into. I'm looking at all these beautiful women. They're thin. I want to be just as beautiful. I want to be just as thin. Because that is what guys like."

When I asked what her mother wanted for her, she recited, "To be nice and pretty and sweet and thin and popular and smart and successful and have everything that I could ever want and just to be happy." "Sweet and pretty and thin" meant that from the age of ten she was enrolled in a health club, and learned to count calories. Her mom, who at 45 is "beautiful, gorgeous, thin," gave her instructions on how to eat.

"'Only eat small amounts. Eat a thousand calories a day; don't overeat.' My mom was never critical like, 'You're fat.' But one time, I went on a camping trip and I gained four pounds and she said, 'You've got to lose weight.' I mean, she watched what I ate. Like if I was going to get a piece of cake she would be, 'Don't eat that.'"

At age 13 she started her secret bingeing and vomiting. "When I first threw up I thought, well, it's so easy," she told me. "I can eat and not get the calories and not gain weight. And I was modeling at the time, and I wanted to look like the girls in the magazines."

Delia's preoccupation with thinness intensified when she entered high school. She wanted to be a cheerleader, and she was tiny enough to make it. "When I was sixteen I just got into this image thing, like tiny, thin . . . I started working out more. I was Joe Healthy Thin Exercise Queen and I'd just fight eating because I was working out all the time, you know? And so I'm going to aerobics two or three times a day sometimes, eating only salad and a bagel, and like, no fat. I just got caught up in this circle."

College in New England brought a new set of social pressures. She couldn't go running every day because of the cold. She hated the school gym, stopped working out, and gained four pounds her freshman year. Her greatest stress at college had nothing to do with academics. "The most stressful thing for me is whether I'm going to eat that day, and what am I going to eat," she told me, "more than getting good grades."

After freshman year Delia became a cheerleader again. "Going in, I know I weighed like 93 or 94 pounds, which to me was this enormous hang-up, because I'd never weighed more than 90 pounds in my entire life. And I was really freaked out. I knew people were going to be looking at me in the crowd and I'm like, I've got to lose this weight. So I would just not eat, work out all the time. I loved being on the squad, but my partner was a real jerk. He would never work out, and when we would do lifts he'd always be, 'Delia, go run. Go run, you're too heavy.' I hadn't been eating that day. I had already run seven or eight miles and he told me to run again. And I was surrounded by girls who were all so concerned about their weight, and it was just really this horrible situation."

College life also confirmed another issue for Delia, a cultural message from her earliest childhood. She did *not* want to be a breadwinner. She put it this way, "When I was eight I wanted to be President of the United States. As I grew older and got to college I was like, wow, it's hard for women. I mean, I don't care what people say. If they say the society's liberated, they're wrong. It's still really hard for women. It's like they look through a glass window [*sic*]. They're vice presidents, but they aren't the president. And I just figured, God, how much easier would it be for me to get married to somebody I know is going to make a lot of money and just be taken care of . . . I want somebody else to be the millionaire." . . .

Economic and career achievement is a primary definition of success for men. (Of course, men can also exhibit some self-destructive behaviors in pursuit of this success, such as workaholism or substance abuse.) Delia's upbringing and environment defined success for her in a different way. She was not interested in having a job that earned $150,000 a year, but in marrying the guy who did. She learned to use any tool she could to stay thin, to look good, and to have a shot at her goal.

No wonder she was reluctant to give up her behavior. She was terrified of losing the important benefits of her membership in the Cult of Thinness. She knew she was hurting psychologically and physically, but, in the final analysis, being counted among "the chosen" justified the pain.

"God forbid anybody else gets stuck in this trap. But I'm already there, and I don't really see myself getting out, because I'm just so obsessed with how I look. I get personal satisfaction from looking thin, and receiving attention from guys."

I told Delia about women who have suggested other ways of coping with weight issues. There are even those who advocate fat liberation, or who suggest that fat is beautiful. She was emphatic about these solutions.

"Bullshit. They live in la-la land . . . I can hold onto my boyfriend because he doesn't need to look anywhere else. The bottom line is that appearance counts. And you can sit here and go, 'I feel good about myself twenty pounds heavier,' but who is the guy going to date?"

A Woman's Sense of Worth

Delia's devotion to the rituals of beauty work involved a great deal of time and energy. She weighed herself three times a day. She paid attention to what she put in her mouth; when she had too much, she knew she must get rid of it. She had to act and look a certain way, buy the right clothes, the right makeup. She also watched out for other women who might jeopardize her chances as they vied for the rewards of the system.

A woman's sense of worth in our culture is still greatly determined by her ability to attract a man. Social status is largely a function of income and occupation. Women's access to these resources is generally indirect, through marriage.[1] Even a woman with a successful and lucrative career may fear that her success comes at the expense of her femininity. . . .

Cultural messages on the rewards of thinness and the punishments of obesity are everywhere. Most women accept society's standards of beauty as "the way things are," even though these standards may undermine self-image, self-esteem, or physical well-being. Weight concerns or even obsessions are so common among women and girls that they escape notice. Dieting is not considered abnormal behavior, even among women who are not overweight. But only a thin line separates "normal" dieting from an eating disorder.[2] . . .

Profiting from Women's Bodies

Because women feel their bodies fail the beauty test, American industry benefits enormously, continually nurturing feminine insecurities. Ruling patriarchal interests, like corporate culture, the traditional family, the government, and the media also benefit. If women are so busy trying to control their bodies through dieting, excessive exercise, and self-improvement activities, they lose control over other important aspects of selfhood that might challenge the status quo.[3] In the words of one critic, "A secretary who bench-presses 150 pounds is still stuck in a dead-end job; a housewife who runs the marathon is still financially dependent on her husband."[4]

In creating women's concept of the ideal body image, the cultural mirror is more influential than the mirror reflecting peer group attitudes. Research has shown that women overestimate how thin a body their male and female peers desire. In a recent study using body silhouettes, college students of both sexes were asked to indicate an ideal female figure, the one that they believed most attractive to the same-sex peer and other-sex peer. Not only did the women select a thinner silhouette than the men,[5] but when asked to choose a *personal* ideal, rather than a peer ideal, the women selected an even skinnier model.

Advertisements and Beauty Advice: Buy, Try, Comply

Capitalism and patriarchy most often use the media to project the culturally desirable body to women. These images are everywhere—on TV, in the movies, on billboards, in print. Women's magazines, with their glossy pages of advertising, advertorials, and beauty advice, hold up an especially devious mirror. They offer "help" to women, while presenting a standard nearly impossible to attain. As one college student named Nancy noted in our interviews,

The advertisement showed me exactly what I should be, not what I was. I wasn't tall, I wasn't blonde, I wasn't skinny. I didn't have thin thighs, I didn't have a flat stomach. I am short, have brown curly hair, short legs. They did offer me solutions like dyeing my hair or a workout or the use of this cream to take away cellulite. . . .

Not everyone is taken in, of course. One student I interviewed dismissed the images she saw in the advertising pages of magazines as "constructed people."

I just stopped buying women's magazines. They are all telling you how to dress, how to look, what to wear, the type of clothes. And I think they are just ridiculous. . . . You can take the most gorgeous model and make her look terrible. Just like you can take a person who is not that way and make them look beautiful. You can use airbrushing and many other techniques. These are not really people. They are constructed people.

Computer-enhanced photography has advanced far beyond the techniques that merely airbrushed blemishes, added highlights to hair, and lengthened the legs with a camera angle. The September 1994 issue of *Mirabella* featured as a cover model "an extraordinary image of great American beauty." According to the magazine, the photographer "hints that she's something of a split personality . . . it wasn't easy getting her together. Maybe her identity has something to do with the microchip floating through space, next to that gorgeous face . . . true American beauty is a combination of elements from all over the world." In other words, the photo is a computerized composite. It is interesting that *Mirabella's* "melting pot" American beauty has white skin and predominantly Caucasian features, with just a hint of other ethnicities.

There are a number of industries that help to promote image, weight, and body obsession, especially among women. If we examine the American food and weight loss industries, we'll understand how their corporate practices and advertising campaigns perpetuate the American woman's dissatisfaction with her looks.

The American Food Industry: Fatten Up and Slim Down

. . . It is not uncommon for the average American to have a diet cola in one hand and high-fat fries and a burger in the other. Food and weight loss are inescapably a key part of the culture of the 1990's. The media bombard us with images of every imaginable type of food — snack foods, fast foods, gourmet foods, health foods, and junk foods. Most of these messages target children, who are very impressionable, and women, who make the purchasing decisions for themselves and their families. At the same time women are subjected to an onslaught of articles, books, videos, tapes, and TV talk shows devoted to dieting and the maintenance of sleek and supple figures. The conflicting images of pleasurable consumption and an ever leaner body type give us a food consciousness loaded with tension and ambivalence.

Social psychologist Brett Silverstein explains that the food industry, like all industries under capitalism, is always striving to maximize profit, growth, concentration, and control. It does so at the expense of the food consumer. "[It] promotes snacking so that consumers will have more than three opportunities a day to consume food, replaces free water with purchased soft drinks, presents desserts as the ultimate reward, and bombards women and children with artificially glamorized images of highly processed foods."[6]

Diet foods are an especially profitable segment of the business. . . .

In 1983, the food industry came up with a brilliant marketing concept, and introduced 91 new "lite" fat-reduced or calorie-reduced foods.[7] The success of lite products has been phenomenal. The consumer equated "lightness" with health. The food industry seemed to equate it with their own expenses—lite foods have lower production costs than "regular" lines, but they are often priced higher. . . .

The Diet and Weight-Loss Industry: We'll Show You the Way

. . . Increasingly, American women are told that they can have the right body if only they consume more and more products. They can change the color of their eyes with tinted contacts, they can have a tanned skin by using self-tanning lotion. They can buy cellulite control cream, spot firming cream, even contouring shower and bath firming gel to get rid of the "dimpled" look. One diet capsule on the market is supposed to be the "fat cure." It is called Anorex-eck, evoking the sometimes fatal eating disorder known as anorexia. It promises to "eliminate the cause of fat formation . . . so quickly and so effectively you will know from the very start why it has taken more than 15 years of research . . . to finally bring you . . . an ultimate cure for fat!"[8] . . .

There are currently more than 17,000 different diet plans, products, and programs from which to choose.[9] Typically, these plans are geared to the female market. They are loaded with promises of quick weight loss and delicious low-calorie meals. . . .

Many of these programs produce food products that they encourage the dieter to buy. The Jenny Craig member receives a set of pre-packaged meals that cost about $10 per day. (It allows for some outside food as well.) Some diet companies are concerned with the problem of gaining weight back and have developed "maintenance" products. Maintenance programs are often expensive and their long-term outcomes are unproven. What *can* be proven are bigger profits and longer dependence on their programs.

The Dis-eased Body: Medicalizing Women's Body Issues

The therapeutic and medical communities tend to categorize women's eating and weight problems as a disease.[10] In this view, behavior like self-starvation or compulsive eating is often called an addiction. An addiction model of behavior assumes that the cause and the cure of the problem lies within the individual. Such an emphasis fails to examine the larger mirrors that society holds up to the individual.[11]

. . . While a disease model lessens the burden of guilt and shame and may free people to work on change, it also has political significance. According to feminist theorist Bette S. Tallen, "The reality of oppression is replaced with the metaphor of addiction." It places the problem's cause within a biological realm, away from outside social forces.[12] Issues such as poverty, lack of education and opportunity, racial and gender inequality remain unexamined. More important, a disease-oriented model of addiction, involving treatment by the health care system, results in profits for the medical-industrial complex. Addiction, Tallen notes, suggests a solution that is personal—"Get treatment!"—rather than political—"Smash patriarchy!" It replaces the feminist view, that the personal is political, with the attitude of "therapism," that the "political is personal."[13] One of Bette Tallen's students told her that she had learned a lot from reading *Women Who Love Too Much* after her divorce from a man who had beaten her. Tallen suggested that "perhaps the best book to read would not be about women who love too much but about men who hit too much."[14]

The idea that overweight is a disease, and overeating represents an addiction, reinforces the dis-ease that American women feel about their bodies. The capitalist and patriarchal mirror held before them supports and maintains their obsession and insecurity. . . .

Women continue to follow the standards of the ideal thin body because of how they are rewarded by being in the right body. Thinness gives women access to a number of important resources: feelings of power, self-confidence, even femininity; male attention or protection; and the social and economic benefits that can follow. . . .

NOTES

1. Pauline B. Bart, "Emotional and Social Status of the Older Woman," in *No Longer Young: The Older Woman in America. Proceedings of the 26th Annual Conference on Aging,* ed. Pauline Bart et al. (Ann Arbor: University of Michigan Institute of Gerontology, 1975), pp. 3–21; Daniel Bar-Tal and Leonard Saxe, "Physical Attractiveness and Its Relationship to Sex-Role Stereotyping," *Sex Roles* 2 (1976): 123–133; Peter Blumstein and Pepper W. Schwartz, *American Couples: Money, Work and Sex* (New York: Willian Morrow, 1983); Glen H. Elder, "Appearance and Education in Marriage Mobility," *American Sociological Review* 34 (1969): 519–533; Susan Sontag, "The Double Standard of Aging," *Saturday Review* (September, 1972), pp. 29–38.

2. J. Polivy and C. P. Herman, "Dieting and Binging: A Causal Analysis," *American Psychologist* 40 (1985):193–201.

3. Ilana Attie and J. Brooks-Gunn, "Weight Concerns as Chronic Stressors in Women," in *Gender and Stress*, eds. Rosalind K. Barnett, Lois Biener, and Grace Baruch (New York: Free Press, 1987), pp. 218–252.

4. Katha Pollitt, "The Politically Correct Body," *Mother Jones* (May 1982): 67. I don't want to disparage the positive benefits of exercising and the positive self-image that can

come from feeling good about one's body. This positive image can spill over into other areas of one's life, enhancing, for example, one's self-esteem, or job prospects.

5. See Lawrence D. Cohn and Nancy E. Adler, "Female and Male Perceptions of Ideal Body Shapes: Distorted Views Among Caucasian College Students," *Psychology of Women Quarterly* 16 (1992): 69–79; A. Fallon and P. Rozin, "Sex Differences in Perceptions of Desirable Body Shape," *Journal of Abnormal Psychology* 94 (1985): 102–105.

6. Brett Silverstein, *Fed Up!* (Boston: South End Press, 1984), pp. 4, 47, 110. Individuals may be affected in many different ways, from paying too much (in 1978, concentration within the industry led to the overcharging of consumers by $12 to $14 billion [p. 47]) to the ingestion of unhealthy substances.

7. Warren J. Belasco, "'Lite' Economics: Less Food, More Profit," *Radical History Review* 28–30 (1984): 254–278; Hillel Schwartz, *Never Satisfied* (New York: Free Press, 1986), p. 241.

8. Advertised in *Parade* magazine (December 30, 1984).

9. Deralee Scanlon, *Diets That Work* (Chicago: Contemporary Books, 1991), p. 1.

10. See Stanton Peele, *Diseasing of America: Addiction Treatment Out of Control* (Lexington, MA: D.C. Heath and Co., 1989).

11. There are a few recovery books that point to the larger issues of the addiction model. Anne Wilson Schaef's book, *When Society Becomes an Addict*, looks at the wider institutions of society that perpetuate addiction. She notes that society operates on a scarcity model. This is the "Addictive System." This model assumes that there is never enough of anything to go around and we need to get what we can. Schaef sees society as made up of three systems: A White Male System (the Addictive System), A Reactive Female System (one where women respond passively to men by being subject to their will), and the Emerging Female System (a system where women lead with caring and sensitivity). Society needs to move in the direction of the Emerging Female System in order to end addiction. Another important book is Stanton Peele's *Love and Addiction*. Another book by Stanton Peele, *The Diseasing of America: How the Addiction Industry Captured Our Soul* (Lexington, MA: Lexington Books, 1989), stresses the importance of social change in societal institutions and advocates changing the given distribution of resources and power within the society as a way to overcome the problem of addiction. See Anne Wilson Schaef, *When Society Becomes an Addict* (New York: Harper & Row, 1987), and Stanton Peele, *Love and Addiction* (New York: New American Library, 1975).

12. Bette S. Tallen, "Twelve Step Programs: A Lesbian Feminist Critique," *NWSA Journal* 2 (1990): 396.

13. Tallen, "Twelve Step Programs: A Lesbian Feminist Critique," 404–405.

14. Tallen, "Twelve Step Programs: A Lesbian Feminist Critique," 405.

5

ADVERTISING AT THE EDGE OF THE APOCALYPSE

Sut Jhally

In this article I wish to make a simple claim: 20th century advertising is the most powerful and sustained system of propaganda in human history and its cumulative cultural effects, unless quickly checked, will be responsible for destroying the world as we know it. As it achieves this it will be responsible for the deaths of hundreds of thousands of non-western peoples and will prevent the peoples of the world from achieving true happiness. **Simply stated, our survival as a species is dependent upon minimizing the threat from advertising and the commercial culture that has spawned it.** I am stating my claims boldly at the outset so there can be no doubt as to what is at stake in our debates about the media and culture as we enter the new millennium.

Colonizing Culture

Karl Marx, the pre-eminent analyst of 19th century industrial capitalism, wrote in 1867, in the very opening lines of *Capital* that: "The wealth of societies in which the capitalist mode of production prevails appears as an 'immense collection of commodities'" (Marx 1976, p. 125). In seeking to initially distinguish his object of analysis from preceding societies, Marx referred to the way the society showed itself on a surface level and highlighted a *quantitative* dimension—the number of objects that humans interacted with in everyday life.

Indeed, no other society in history has been able to match the immense productive output of industrial capitalism. This feature colors the way in which the society presents itself—the way it *appears*. Objects are everywhere in capitalism. In this sense, capitalism is truly a revolutionary society, dramatically altering the very landscape of social life, in a way no other form of social organization had been able to achieve in such a short period of time. . . .

It is not enough of course to only produce the "immense collection of commodities"—they must also be sold, so that further investment in production is feasible. Once produced commodities must go through the circuit of distribution, exchange and consumption, so that profit can be returned to the owners of capital and value can be "realized" again in a money form. If the circuit is not completed the system would collapse into stagnation and depression. Capitalism therefore has to ensure that sale of commodities on *pain of death*. In that sense the problem of capitalism is not mass production (which has been solved) but is instead the *problem of consumption*. That is why from the early years of this century it is more accurate to use the label "the consumer culture" to describe the western industrial market societies.

So central is consumption to its survival and growth that at the end of the 19th century industrial capitalism invented a unique new institution — the advertising industry — to ensure that the "immense accumulation of commodities" is converted back into a money form. The function of this new industry would be to recruit the best creative talent of the society and to create a culture in which desire and identity would be fused with commodities — to make the dead world of things come alive with human and social possibilities. . . . And indeed there has never been a propaganda effort to match the effort of advertising in the 20th century. More thought, effort, creativity, time, and attention to detail has gone into the selling of the immense collection of commodities than any other campaign in human history to change public consciousness. One indication of this is simply the amount of money that has been exponentially expended on this effort. Today, in the United States alone, over $175 billion a year is spent to sell us things. This concentration of effort is unprecedented.

It should not be surprising that something this central and with so much being expended on it should become an important presence in social life. Indeed, commercial interests intent on maximizing the consumption of the immense collection of commodities have colonized more and more of the spaces of our culture. For instance, almost the entire media system (television and print) has been developed as a delivery system for marketers — its prime function is to produce audiences for sale to advertisers. Both the advertisements it carries, as well as the editorial matter that acts as a support for it, celebrate the consumer society. The movie system, at one time outside the direct influence of the broader marketing system, is now fully integrated into it through the strategies of licensing, tie-ins and product placements. The prime function of many Hollywood films today is to aid in the selling of the immense collection of commodities. As public funds are drained from the non-commercial cultural sector, art galleries, museums and symphonies bid for corporate sponsorship. Even those institutions thought to be outside of the market are being sucked in. High schools now sell the sides of their buses, the spaces of their hallways and the classroom time of their students to hawkers of candy bars, soft drinks and jeans. In New York City, sponsors are being sought for public playgrounds. In the contemporary world everything is sponsored by someone. The latest plans of Space Marketing Inc. call for rockets to deliver mile-wide Mylar billboards to compete with the sun and the moon for the attention of the earth's population.

For too long debate has been concentrated around the issue of whether ad campaigns create demand for a particular product. If you are Pepsi Cola, or Ford, or Anheuser Busch, then it may be the right question for your interests. But, if you are interested in the social power of advertising—the impact of advertising on society—then that is the wrong question.

The right question would ask about the *cultural* role of advertising, not its marketing role. Culture is the place and space where a society tells stories about itself, where values are articulated and expressed, where notions of good and evil, of morality and immorality, are defined. In our culture it is the stories of advertising that dominate the spaces that mediate this function. If human beings are essentially a storytelling species, then to study advertising is to examine the central storytelling mechanism of our society. The correct question to ask from this perspective, is not whether particular ads sell the products they are hawking, but what are the consistent stories that advertising spins as a whole about what is important in the world, about how to behave, about what is good and bad. Indeed, it is to ask what values does advertising consistently push.

Happiness

Every society has to tell a story about happiness, about how individuals can satisfy themselves and feel both subjectively and objectively good. The cultural system of advertising gives a very specific answer to that question for our society. *The way to happiness and satisfaction is through the consumption of objects through the marketplace.* Commodities will make us happy (Leiss 1976, p. 4). In one very important sense, that is the consistent and explicit message of every single message within the system of market communication.

Neither the fact of advertising's colonization of the horizons of imagination or the pushing of a story about the centrality of goods to human satisfaction should surprise us. The immense collection of goods has to be consumed (and even more goods produced) and the story that is used to ensure this function is to equate goods with happiness. Insiders to the system has recognized this obvious fact for many years. Retail analyst Victor Liebow said, just after the second world war:

> Our enormously productive economy . . . demands that we make consumption our way of life, that we convert the buying and the selling of goods into rituals, that we seek our spiritual satisfaction, our ego satisfaction in commodities. . . . We need things consumed, burned up, worn out, replaced, and discarded at an ever increasing rate. (in Durning 1991, p. 153)

So economic growth is justified not simply on the basis that it will provide employment (after all a host of alternative non-productive activities could also provide that) but because it will give us access to more things that will make us happy. This rationale for the existing system of ever increasing production is told by advertising in the most compelling form possible. In fact it is this story, that human satisfaction is intimately connected to the provisions of the market, to economic growth, that is the major motivating force for social change as we start the 21st century.

The social upheavals of eastern Europe were pushed by this vision. As Gloria Steinhem described the East German transformation: "First we have a revolution then we go shopping" (in Ehrenreich 1990, p. 46). The attractions of this vision in the Third World are not difficult to discern. When your reality is empty stomachs and empty shelves, no wonder the marketplace appears as the panacea for your problems. When your reality is hunger and despair it should not be surprising that the seductive images of desire and abundance emanating from the advertising system should be so influential in thinking about social and economic policy. Indeed not only happiness but political freedom itself is made possible by access to the immense collection of commodities. These are very powerful stories that equate happiness and freedom with consumption—and advertising is the main propaganda arm of this view.

The question that we need to pose at this stage (that is almost never asked) is, "Is it true?" Does happiness come from material things? Do we get happier as a society as we get richer, as our standard of living increases, as we have more access to the immense collection of objects? Obviously these are complex issues, but the general answer to these questions is "no." (See Leiss et al. 1990, Chapter 10 for a fuller discussion of these issues.)

In a series of surveys conducted in the United States starting in 1945 (labeled "the happiness surveys") researchers sought to examine the link between material wealth and subjective happiness, and concluded that, when examined both cross-culturally as well as historically in one society, there is a very *weak* correlation. Why should this be so?

When we examine this process more closely the conclusions appear to be less surprising than our intuitive perspective might suggest. In another series of surveys (the "quality of life surveys") people were asked about the kinds of things that are important to them—about what would constitute a good quality of life. The findings of this line of research indicate that if the elements of satisfaction were to be divided up into social values (love, family, friends) and material values (economic security and success) the former outranks the latter in terms of importance. What people say they really want out of life is: autonomy and control of life; good self-esteem; warm family relationships; tension-free leisure time; close and intimate friends; as well as romance and love. This is not to say that material values are not important. They form a necessary component of a good qualify of life. But above a certain level of poverty and comfort, material things stop giving us the kind of satisfaction that the magical world of advertising insists they can deliver.

These conclusions point to one of the great ironies of the market system. The market is good at providing those things that can be bought and sold and it pushed us—via advertising—in that direction. But the real sources of happiness—social relationships—are outside the capability of the marketplace to provide. The marketplace cannot provide love, it cannot provide real friendships, it cannot provide sociability. It can provide other material things and services—but they are not what makes us happy.

The advertising industry has known this since at least the 1920s and in fact has stopped trying to sell us things based on their material qualities alone. If we examine the advertising of the end of the 19th and first years of the 20th century, we would see that advertising talked a lot about the properties of commodities—what they did, how well they did it, etc. But starting in the 1920s advertising shifts to talking about the relationship of objects to the social life of people. It starts to connect commodities (the things they have to sell) with the powerful images of a deeply desired social life that people say they want.

No wonder then that advertising is so attractive to us, so powerful, so seductive. What it offers us are images of the real sources of human happiness—family life, romance and love, sexuality and pleasure, friendship and sociability, leisure and relaxation, independence and control of life. That is why advertising is so powerful, that is what is real about it. The cruel illusion of advertising however is in the way that it links those qualities to a place that by definition cannot provide it—the market and the immense collection of commodities. The falsity of advertising is not in the appeals it makes (which are very real) but in the answers it provides. We want love and friendship and sexuality—and advertising points the way to it through objects.

To reject or criticize advertising as false and manipulative misses the point. Ad executive Jerry Goodis puts it this way: "Advertising doesn't mirror how people are acting but how they are dreaming" (in Nelson 1983). It taps into our real emotions and repackages them back to us connected to the world of things. What advertising really reflects in that sense is the dream life of the culture. Even saying this however simplifies a deeper process because advertisers do more than mirror our dream life—they help to create it. They translate our desires (for love, for family, for friendship, for adventure, for sex) into our dreams. Advertising is like a fantasy factory, taking our desire for human social contact and reconceiving it, reconceptualizing it, connecting it with the world of commodities and then translating it into a form that can be communicated.

The great irony is that as advertising does this it draws us further way from what really has the capacity to satisfy us (meaningful human contact and relationships) to what does not (material things). In that sense advertising reduces our capacity to become happy by pushing us, cajoling us, to carry on in the direction of things. If we really wanted to create a world that reflected our desires then the consumer culture would not be it. It would look very different—a society that stressed and built the institutions that would foster social relationships, rather then endless material accumulation.

Advertising's role in channeling us in these fruitless directions is profound. In one sense, its function is analogous to the drug pusher on the street corner. As we try and break our addiction to things it is there, constantly offering us another "hit."

By persistently pushing the idea of the good life being connected to products, and by colonizing every nook and cranny of the culture where alternative ideas could be raised, advertising is an important part of the creation of what Tibor Scitovsky (1976) calls "the joyless economy." The great political challenge that emerges from this analysis is how to connect our real desires to a truly human world, rather than the dead world of the "immense collection of commodities."

"There Is No Such Thing as 'Society'"

A culture dominated by commercial messages that tells individuals that the way to happiness is through consuming objects bought in the marketplace gives a very particular answer to the question of "what is society?"—what is it that binds us together in some kind of collective way, what concerns or interests do we share? In fact, Margaret Thatcher, the former conservative British Prime Minister, gave the most succinct answer to this question from the viewpoint of the market. In perhaps her most (in)famous quote she announced: "There is no such thing as 'society.' There are just individuals and their families." According to Mrs. Thatcher, there is nothing solid we can call society—no group values, no collective interests— society is just a bunch of individuals acting on their own.

Indeed this is precisely how advertising talks to us. It addresses us not as members of society talking about collective issues, but as *individuals*. It talks about our individual needs and desires. It does not talk about those things we have to negotiate collectively, such as poverty, healthcare, housing and the homeless, the environment, etc.

The market appeals to the worst in us (greed, selfishness) and discourages what is the best about us (compassion, caring, and generosity).

Again this should not surprise us. In those societies where the marketplace dominates then what will be stressed is what the marketplace can deliver—and advertising is the main voice of the marketplace—so discussions of collective issues are pushed to the margins of the culture. They are not there in the center of the main system of communication that exists in the society. It is no accident that politically the market vision associated with neo-conservatives has come to dominate at exactly that time when advertising has been pushing the same values into every available space in the culture. The widespread disillusionment with "government" (and hence with thinking about issues in a collective manner) has found extremely fertile ground in the fields of commercial culture.

Unfortunately, we are now in a situation, both globally and domestically, where solutions to pressing nuclear and environmental problems will have to take a *collective* form. The marketplace cannot deal with the problems that face us at the turn of the millennium. For example it cannot deal with the threat of nuclear extermination that is still with us in the post-Cold War age. It cannot deal with global warming, the erosion of the ozone layer, or the depletion of our nonrenewable resources. The effects of the way we do "business" are no longer localized, they are now global, and we will have to have international and collective ways of dealing with them. Individual action will not be enough. As the environmentalist slogan puts it "we *all* live downstream now."

Domestically, how do we find a way to tackle issues such as the nightmares of our inner cities, the ravages of poverty, the neglect of healthcare for the most vulnerable section of the population? How can we find a way to talk realistically and passionately of such problems within a culture where the central message is "don't worry, be happy." As Barbara Ehrenreich says:

> Television commercials offer solutions to hundreds of problems we didn't even know we had—from 'morning mouth' to shampoo build-up—but nowhere in the consumer culture do we find anyone offering us such mundane necessities as affordable health insurance, childcare, housing, or higher education. The flip side of the consumer spectacle . . . is the starved and impoverished public sector. We have Teenage Mutant Ninja Turtles, but no way to feed and educate the one-fifth of American children who are growing up in poverty. We have dozens of varieties of breakfast cereal, and no help for the hungry. (Ehrenreich 1990, p. 47)

In that sense, advertising systematically relegates discussion of key societal issues to the peripheries of the culture and talks in powerful ways instead of individual desire, fantasy, pleasure and comfort.

The End of the World as We Know It

The consumer vision that is pushed by advertising and which is conquering the world is based fundamentally, as I argued before, on a notion of *economic growth*. Growth requires resources (both raw materials and energy) and there is a broad consensus among environmental scholars that the earth cannot sustain past levels of expansion based upon resource-intensive modes of economic activity, especially as more and more nations struggle to join the feeding trough.

The environmental crisis is complex and multilayered, cutting across both production and consumption issues. For instance just in terms of resource depletion, we know that we are rapidly exhausting what the earth can offer and that if the present growth and consumption trends continue unchecked, the limits to growth on the planet will be reached sometime within the next century. Industrial production uses up resources and energy at a rate that had never before even been imagined. Since 1950 the world's population has used up more of the earth's resources than all the generations that came before (Durning 1991, p. 157). In 50 years we have matched the use of thousands of years. The west and especially Americans have used the most of these resources so we have a special responsibility for the approaching crisis. In another hundred years we will have exhausted the planet.

But even more than that, we will have done irreparable damage to the environment on which we depend for everything.

Imagining a Different Future

Over a 100 years ago, Marx observed that there were two directions that capitalism could take: towards a democratic "socialism" or towards a brutal "barbarism." Both long-term and recent evidence would seem to indicate that the latter is where we are headed, unless alternative values quickly come to the fore.

Many people thought that the environmental crisis would be the linchpin for the lessening of international tensions as we recognized our interdependence and our collective security and future. But as the Persian Gulf War made clear, the New World Order will be based upon a struggle for scarce resources. Before the propaganda rationale shifted to the "struggle for freedom and democracy," George Bush reminded the American people that the troops were being dispatched to the Gulf to protect the resources that make possible "our way of life." An automobile culture and commodity-based culture such as ours is reliant upon sources of cheap oil. And if the cost of that is 100,000 dead Iraqis, well so be it. In such a scenario the peoples of the Third World will be seen as enemies who are making unreasonable claims on "our" resources. The future and the Third World can wait. Our commercial dominated cultural discourse reminds us powerfully every day, we need *ours* and we need it *now*. In that sense the Gulf War is a preview of what is to come. As the world runs out of resources, the most powerful military sources will use that might to ensure access.

The destructive aspects of capitalism (its short-term nature, its denial of collective values, its stress on the material life) are starting to be recognized by some people who have made their fortunes through the market. The billionaire turned philanthropist George Soros (1997) talks about what he calls "the capitalist threat"—and culturally speaking, advertising is the main voice of that threat. To the extent that it pushes us towards material things for satisfaction and away from the construction of social relationships, it pushes us down the road to increased economic production that is driving the coming environmental catastrophe. To the extent that it talks about our individual and private needs, it pushes discussion about collective issues to the margins. To the extent that it talks about the present only, it makes thinking about the future difficult. To the extent that it does all these things, then advertising becomes one of the major obstacles to our survival as a species.

BIBLIOGRAPHY

Ehrenreich, Barbara (1990). "Laden with Lard." ZETA, July/Aug.

Durning, Alan (1991). "Asking How Much Is Enough" in Lester Brown et al., *State of the World 1991*. Norton, New York.

Leiss, William (1976). *The Limits to Satisfaction*. Marion Boyars, London.

Leiss, William, Stephen Kline, and Sut Jhally (1990). *Social Communication in Advertising* (second edition). Routledge, New York.

Marx, Karl (1976). *Capital* (Vol. 1), trans. by B. Brewster. Penguin, London.

Nelson, Joyce (1983). "As the Brain Tunes Out, the TV Admen Tune In." *Globe and Mail.*

Scitovsky, Tibor (1976). *The Joyless Economy.* Oxford University Press, New York.

Soros, George (1997). "The Capitalist Threat" in *The Atlantic Monthly,* February.

Some of the ideas in this chapter have been presented by myself before in "Commercial Culture, Collective Values and the Future" (*Texas Law Review,* Vol. 71, No. 4, 1993) and the videotape *Advertising and the End of the World* (Media Education Foundation, Northampton, MA, 1998).

6

THE PLUTOCRATIC CULTURE
INSTITUTIONS, VALUES, AND IDEOLOGIES

Michael Parenti

American Plutocracy

American capitalism represents more than just an economic system; it is an entire cultural and social order, a plutocracy—that is, a system of rule by and for the rich—for the most part. Most universities and colleges, publishing houses, mass circulation magazines, newspapers, television and radio stations, professional sports teams, foundations, churches, private museums, charity organizations, and hospitals are organized as corporations, ruled by boards of trustees (or directors or regents) composed overwhelmingly of affluent businesspeople. These boards exercise final judgment over all institutional matters.[1]

Consider the university: institutions of higher education are public or private corporations (e.g., the Harvard Corporation, the Yale Corporation) run by boards of trustees with authority over all matters of capital funding and budget; curriculum, scholarships, and tuition; hiring, firing, and promotion of faculty and staff; degree awards; student fees; and so on. Most of the tasks related to these activities have been delegated to administrators, but the power can be easily recalled by the trustees, and in times of controversy it usually is. These trustees are granted legal

From *Democracy for the Few,* 5th ed., by Michael Parenti, 1988. Reprinted with permission of Wadsworth, a division of Thomson Learning, www.thomsonrights.com.

control of the property of the institution, not because they have claim to any academic experience but because as successful businesspeople they supposedly have proven themselves to be the responsible leaders of the community.[2]

This, then, is a feature of real significance in any understanding of political power in America: *almost all the social institutions existing in this society, along with the immense material and vocational resources they possess, are under plutocratic control, ruled by nonelected, self-selected, self-perpetuating groups of affluent corporate representatives who are answerable to no one but themselves.*

The rest of us make our way through these institutions as employees and clients. These institutions shape many of our everyday experiences and much of our social consciousness; yet we have no vote, no portion of the ownership, and no legal decision-making power within them. The power they exercise over us is hierarchical and nondemocratic.

The existing social order and culture are not independent of the business system. Nor are social institutions independent of each other, being controlled by the more active members of the business class in what amounts to a system of interlocking and often interchanging directorates. We can point to more than one business leader who not only presides over a bank or corporation but has served as a cabinet member in Washington, is a regent of a large university, a trustee of a civic art center, and at one time or another a member of the board of a major newspaper, foundation, church, or television network.

Through this institutional control, the business elites are able to exercise a good deal of influence over the flow of mainstream ideas and over the actions of broad constituencies. The ruling ideas, as Karl Marx once said, are the ideas of the ruling class. Those who control the material production of society are also able to control the mental production. What exactly are the dominant values of our society and how are they propagated?

Socialization into Orthodoxy

The power of business does not stand naked before the public; it is enshrouded in a mystique of its own making. The agencies of ruling class culture, namely the media, the schools, the politicians, and others, associate the capitalist system with the symbols of patriotism, democracy, prosperity, and progress. Criticisms of the system are equated with un-Americanism. Capitalism is treated as an inherent part of democracy, although, in truth, capitalism also flourishes under the most brutally repressive regimes, and capitalist interests have supported the overthrow of democracies in Chile, Guatemala, and other Third World countries and the installment of right-wing dictators who make their lands safe for corporate investments. Capitalism is presented as the sole alternative to "communist tyranny." The private enterprise system, it is taught, creates equality of opportunity, rewards those who show ability and initiative, relegates the parasitic and slothful to the bottom of the ladder, provides a national prosperity that is the envy of other lands, and safeguards (through unspecified means) personal liberties and political freedom.

Among the institutions of plutocratic culture, our educational system looms as one of the more influential purveyors of dominant values. From the earliest school years, children are taught to compete individually rather than work cooperatively for common goals and mutual benefit. Grade-school students are fed stories of their nation's exploits that might be more valued for their inspirational nationalism than for their historical accuracy. Students are instructed to believe in America's global virtue and moral superiority and to fear and hate the Great Red Menace. They are taught to hold a rather uncritical view of American politico-economic institutions. One nationwide survey of 12,000 children (grades two to eight) found that most youngsters believe "the government and its representatives are wise, benevolent and infallible, that whatever the government does is for the best."

Teachers concentrate on the formal aspects of representative government and accord little attention to the influences that wealthy, powerful groups exercise over political life.[3] Teachers in primary and secondary schools who wish to introduce radical critiques of American politico-economic institutions do so often at the risk of jeopardizing their careers. High-school students who attempt to sponsor unpopular speakers and explore dissident views in student newspapers have frequently been overruled by administrators and threatened with disciplinary action.[4]

School texts at the elementary, high-school, and even college levels seldom give but passing mention to the history of labor struggle and the role of American corporations in the exploitation and maldevelopment of the Third World. Almost nothing is said of the struggles of indentured servants, of Latino, Chinese, and European immigrant labor, and of small farmers. The history of resistance to slavery, racism, and U.S. expansionist wars is largely untaught in American schools at any level.[5] One learns that the Soviet Union is to blame for all cold-war tensions. Teaching about the "evils of communism" is required by law in many state education curricula, although little of any informational value is taught about the actual social realities of existing socialist societies.[6]

Schools are inundated with millions of dollars worth of printed materials, films, and tapes provided by the Pentagon and the giant corporations at no cost, to promote a glorified view of the military and to argue for tax subsidies to business and deregulation of industry. Pro-business propaganda on nutrition (boosting commercial junk foods), nuclear power, environmental issues, and the wonders of free enterprise are also widely distributed in schools and communities.[7]

Colleges and graduate and professional schools offer a more sophisticated extension of this same orthodox socialization. Over the last decade, conservative think tanks and academic centers have proliferated, along with conservative journals, conferences, and endowed chairs, all funded by tens of millions of dollars from corporations and right-wing foundations.[8] College faculty, and even students, have been subjected to discriminatory treatment because of their dissenting views and political activities, suffering negative evaluations and loss of scholarships, research grants, and jobs. While sometimes portrayed as being above worldly partisan interests, the average American university performs a wide range of services—from advanced research to specialized personnel training and recruitment—which are essential to military and corporate interests. The "neutral" university also has a direct investment link to the corporate structure in the form of a substantial stock portfolio.[9]

Socialization into the orthodox values of American culture is achieved not only by indoctrination but also by economic sanctions designed to punish the dissident critics and reward the political conformists. This is true of the training and advancement of lawyers, doctors, journalists, engineers, managers, bureaucrats, and teachers. To get along in one's career, one learns to go along with things as they are and avoid the espousal of views that conflict with the dominant economic interests of one's profession, institution, and society.[10]

Another agent of political socialization is the government itself. Government officials prevent leaks of potentially embarrassing information but these same officials flood the public and the media with press releases and planted information supporting the viewpoints of government, industry, and the military. Hardly a day passes without the president or some White House official feeding us reassuring pronouncements about the economy and alarming assertions about communist threats from abroad.

Although we are often admonished to "think for ourselves," we might wonder if our socialization process allows us to do so. Ideological orthodoxy so permeates the plutocratic culture, masquerading as "pluralism," "democracy," and the "open society," that it is often not felt as indoctrination. The worst forms of tyranny are those so subtle, so deeply ingrained, so thoroughly controlling as not even to be consciously experienced. So, there are Americans who conform unswervingly to the capitalist orthodoxy, afraid to entertain contrary notions for fear of jeopardizing their jobs, but who think they are "free."

In a capitalist society, one is bombarded with inducements to maintain a lifestyle that promotes the plutocratic culture. Each year business spends billions to get people to consume as much as they can—and sometimes more than they can afford. Mass advertising offers not only commodities but a whole way of life, teaching us that the piling up of possessions is a life goal, a measure of one's accomplishment and proof of one's worth. As Philip Green noted, American capitalists spend billions of dollars in advertising to persuade us to expend all our incomes upon ourselves and our families: "Of the last hundred TV commercials any of us saw, it would be miraculous if more than one or two (or any) advocated devoting a significant portion of one's own economic resources to a public purpose."[11]

In the plutocratic culture, the emphasis is on self-absorption: "do your own thing" and "look out for number one." We are taught to seek more possessions and more privacy: a private home, private car, private vacation place; and we often feel alienated and lonely when we get them. Born of a market economy, the capitalist culture is essentially a market culture, one that minimizes cooperative efforts and human interdependence and keeps us busily competing as workers and consumers. The ability or desire to work collectively with others is much retarded.[12]

We are admonished to "get ahead." Ahead of whom and what? Of others and of one's present material status. This kind of "individualism" is not to be mistaken for the freedom to choose deviant political and economic practices. Each person is expected to operate "individually" but in more or less similar ways and similar directions. Everyone competes against everyone else but for the same things. "Individualism" in the United States refers to *privatization* and the absence of social forms of ownership, consumption, and recreation. You are individualist in that you are expected to get what you can for yourself and not be too troubled by the problems faced by others. This attitude, considered inhuman in some societies, is labeled approvingly as "ambition" in our own and is treated as a quality of great social value.

Whether or not this "individualism" allows one to have control over one's own life is another story. The decisions about the quality of the food we eat, the goods we buy, the air we breathe, the prices we pay, the wages we earn, the way work tasks are divided, the opinions fed to us by the media—the controlling decisions concerning the realities of our lives—are usually made by people other than ourselves.

People who want to maintain or further their positions within the social hierarchy become committed to the hierarchy's preservation. They fear that they might be overtaken by those below, making all their toil and sacrifice count for naught.[13] The plutocratic culture teaches us that proximity to the poor is to be shunned, while wealth is something to be pursued and admired. Hence the road upward should be kept open, free of artificial impediments imposed by the government on those who can advance, while the road behind should not be provided with special conveyances for those who wish to catch up.

The insecurities of capitalism propagate a scarcity psychology even among affluent people. There is always more to get, and more to lose. The highly paid professional feels the pressure of "moreness," as does the lowly paid blue-collar worker. Economically deprived groups are seen as a threat because they want more, and more for the have-nots might mean less for the haves. The scarcity psychology, then, leaves some people with the feeling that the poor and the racial minorities (potential competitors) should be kept in their place.

Those possessed by a scarcity psychology will sometimes convince themselves of the inferiority of deprived groups. Unfortunately, the racism, sexism, and class bigotry thus activated militate against working people's understanding of their common interests and leave some of them inclined to exclude categories of people from competing for the desired things in life. So, bigots can convince themselves that the hardships endured by victimized minority groups are due to the groups' deficiencies. "Those people don't *want* to better themselves," say the bigots, who then become quite hostile when deprived groups take actions intended to better their lot.

Small hate groups like the American Nazi party and the Ku Klux Klan try to redirect the anger that working Americans might feel toward the financial class, by targeting irrelevant foes such as Blacks, Latinos, Jews, women, trade unionists, and radicals. The religious right, with organizations like the Moral Majority and various television preachers, often well-financed by moneyed persons and accorded generous publicity and media access, attempt to direct legitimate class grievances toward noneconomic issues such as school prayer, abortion, pornography, and gay rights, while warning us of the imminent dangers of communism and "secular humanism."[14]

. . . A special word should be said about *class* bigotry, which, along with racism and sexism, is one of the widely held forms of prejudice in American society and the least challenged. In movies, on television, in school textbooks, and in popular fiction, the world is portrayed as a predominantly White upper-middle-class place. Working-class people are often presented as villainous characters or as uncouth, unintelligent, and generally undesirable persons.

The message we get is that material success is a measure of one's worth; thus the poor are not worth much and society's resources should not be squandered on them. If rich and poor get pretty much what they deserve, then it is self-evident that the poor are not very deserving.[15] As the American humorist Will Rogers once said: "It's no disgrace to be poor, but it might as well be."

It would be easy to fault Americans, who manifest these competitive, acquisitive traits, as people who lack some proper measure of humanity. But most such attitudes evolve as products of plutocratic class dominance. The emphasis placed on getting ahead and making money is not the outcome of some genetic flaw in the American character. Americans have their doubts about the rat race, and many who are able to, seek an alternative life-style, consuming less and working in less demanding jobs. But the economy does not always allow such a choice. With wage cutbacks, inflation, and growing tax burdens, most people must keep running on the treadmill just to stay in the same place. In a society where money is the overriding determinant of one's life chances, the competitive drive for material success is not merely a symptom of greed but a factor in one's very survival. Rather than grasping for fanciful luxuries, most Americans are still struggling to provide for basic necessities. If they need more money than was essential in earlier days, this is largely because essentials cost so much more.

Because human services are based on ability to pay, money becomes a matter of life and death. To have a low or modest income is to run a higher risk of illness, insufficient medical care, and job exploitation, and to have a lesser opportunity for education, leisure, travel, and comfort. The desire to "make it," even at the expense of others, is not merely a wrong-headed attitude but a reflection of the material conditions of capitalist society wherein no one is ever really economically secure except the super-rich.

NOTES

1. My book *Power and the Powerless* (New York: St. Martin's Press, 1978) has a more detailed discussion of business power within social and cultural institutions.

2. Ibid., pp. 156–63; also David N. Smith, *Who Rules the Universities?* (New York: Monthly Review Press, 1974). Businesspeople who are trustees generally have no administrative or scholarly experience in higher education. They are more transient than the students, faculty, and staff, usually visiting the campus from out-of-town for monthly board

meetings. They take none of the financial risks; their decisions are covered by insurance paid out of the university budget. On most fiduciary and technical problems, they rely on consultants, and accountants. The reason businesspeople are trustees, we might conclude, is that they are there to exercise a class control function—which they do.

3. A Carnegie Institute three-year study reported in the *New York Times*, September 23, 1970.

4. Commission of Inquiry into High School Journalism, *Captive Voices: High School Journalism in America* (New York: Schocken Books, 1974). A survey of 500 high school newspapers found censorship to be widespread; see *Washington Post*, December 30, 1981. For an overall analysis of American schools, see Samuel Bowles and Herbert Gintis, *Schooling in Capitalist America* (New York: Basic Books, 1976).

5. Philip Meranto, Oneida Meranto, Matthew Lippman, *Guarding the Ivory Tower, Repression and Rebellion in Higher Education* (Denver: Lucha Publications, 1985); Frances FitzGerald, *America Revised* (New York: Random House, 1980).

6. For instance, Florida has no minimum math, science, or language requirements for a high school diploma, but it does require every student to complete a thirty-hour course called "Americanism vs. Communism." The Florida law dictates: "No teacher or textual material assigned in this course shall present Communism as preferable to the system of constitutional government and the free-enterprise, competitive economy indigenous to the U.S." *New York Times*, May 4, 1983.

7. Sheila Harty, *Hucksters in the Classroom: A Review of Industry Propaganda in Schools* (Washington, D.C.: Center for Study of Responsive Law, 1979); Betty Medsger, "The 'Free' Propaganda That Floods the Schools," *Progressive*, December 1976, p. 42.

8. Peter Stone, "Businesses Widen Role in Conservatives 'War of Ideas,'" *Washington Post*, May 12, 1985.

9. Meranto et al., *Guarding the Ivory Tower.*

10. For studies of ideological orthodoxy and political repression in the United States, see William Preston, Jr., *Aliens and Dissenters* (Cambridge, Mass.: Harvard University Press, 1963); William Appleman Williams, *The Great Evasion* (Chicago: Quadrangle Books, 1964); Michael Parenti, *The Anti-Communist Impulse* (New York: Random House, 1969); Sidney Fine, *Laissez-Faire and the General-Welfare State* (Ann Arbor: University of Michigan Press, 1964); Meranto, *Guarding the Ivory Tower.*

11. Philip Green, "Two Cheers for the State," *Nation*, April 14, 1979, p. 399.

12. Philip Slater, *The Pursuit of Loneliness* (Boston: Beacon Press, 1970), p. 7; also Robert Bellah et al., *Habits of the Heart, Individualism and Commitment in American Life* (New York: Harper and Row, 1985).

13. According to one study, the higher their income and education, the less people believe that all groups should have equal political power. Low-income people and Blacks were the firmest supporters of equality; see William Form and Joan Rytina, "Ideological Beliefs on the Distribution of Power in the United States," *American Sociological Review*, 34 (February 1969), pp. 19–31.

14. Flo Conway and Jim Siegelman, *Holy Terror: The Fundamentalist War on America's Freedom of Religion, Politics and Our Private Lives* (New York: Dell, 1986).

15. James T. Patterson, *America's Struggle Against Poverty* (Cambridge, Mass.: Harvard University Press, 1981); Janet M. Fitchen, *Poverty in Rural America* (Boulder, Colo.: Westview, 1981). These books discuss the low esteem in which the poor are held, often by the poor themselves. See also Sidney Lens, "Blaming the Victims, 'Social Darwinism' Is Still the Name of the Game," *Progressive*, August 1980, pp. 27–28; and William Ryan, *Blaming the Victim* (New York: Random House, 1972).

MEDIA MAGIC
Making Class Invisible

Gregory Mantsios

Of the various social and cultural forces in our society, the mass media is arguably the most influential in molding public consciousness. Americans spend an average twenty-eight hours per week watching television. They also spend an undetermined number of hours reading periodicals, listening to the radio, and going to the movies. Unlike other cultural and socializing institutions, ownership and control of the mass media is highly concentrated. Twenty-three corporations own more than one-half of all the daily newspapers, magazines, movie studios, and radio and television outlets in the United States.[1] The number of media companies is shrinking and their control of the industry is expanding. And a relatively small number of media outlets is producing and packaging the majority of news and entertainment programs. For the most part, our media is national in nature and single-minded (profit-oriented) in purpose. This media plays a key role in defining our cultural tastes, helping us locate ourselves in history, establishing our national identity, and ascertaining the range of national and social possibilities. In this essay, we will examine the way the mass media shapes how people think about each other and about the nature of our society.

The United States is the most highly stratified society in the industrialized world. Class distinctions operate in virtually every aspect of our lives, determining the nature of our work, the quality of our schooling, and the health and safety of our loved ones. Yet remarkably, we, as a nation, retain illusions about living in an egalitarian society. We maintain these illusions, in large part, because the media hides gross inequities from public view. In those instances when inequities are revealed, we are provided with messages that obscure the nature of class realities and blame the victims of class-dominated society for their own plight. Let's briefly examine what the news media, in particular, tells us about class.

About the Poor

The news media provides meager coverage of poor people and poverty. The coverage it does provide is often distorted and misleading.

The Poor Do Not Exist

For the most part, the news media ignores the poor. Unnoticed are forty million poor people in the nation—a number that equals the entire population of Maine, Vermont, New Hampshire, Connecticut, Rhode Island, New Jersey, and New York combined. Perhaps even more alarming is that the rate of poverty is increasing twice as fast as the population growth in the United States. Ordinarily, even a calamity of much smaller proportion (e.g., flooding in the Midwest) would garner a great deal of coverage and hype from a media usually eager to declare a crisis, yet less than one in five hundred articles in the *New York Times* and one in one thousand articles listed in the *Readers Guide to Periodic Literature* are on poverty. With remarkably little attention to them, the poor and their problems are hidden from most Americans.

When the media does turn its attention to the poor, it offers a series of contradictory messages and portrayals.

The Poor Are Faceless

Each year the Census Bureau releases a new report on poverty in our society and its results are duly reported in the media. At best, however, this coverage emphasizes annual fluctuations (showing how the numbers differ from previous years) and ongoing debates over the validity of the numbers (some argue the number should be lower, most that the number should be higher). Coverage like this desensitizes us to the poor by reducing poverty to a number. It ignores the human tragedy of poverty—the suffering, indignities, and misery endured by millions of children and adults. Instead, the poor become statistics rather than people.

The Poor Are Undeserving

When the media does put a face on the poor, it is not likely to be a pretty one. The media will provide us with sensational stories about welfare cheats, drug addicts, and greedy panhandlers (almost always urban and Black). Compare these images and the emotions evoked by them with the media's treatment of middle-class (usually white) "tax evaders," celebrities who have a "chemical dependency," or wealthy businesspeople who use unscrupulous means to "make a profit." While the behavior of the more affluent offenders is considered an "impropriety" and a deviation from the norm, the behavior of the poor is considered repugnant, indicative of the poor in general, and worthy of our indignation and resentment.

The Poor Are an Eyesore

When the media does cover the poor, they are often presented through the eyes of the middle class. For example, sometimes the media includes a story about community resistance to a homeless shelter or storekeeper annoyance with panhandlers.

Rather than focusing on the plight of the poor, these stories are about middle-class opposition to the poor. Such stories tell us that the poor are an inconvenience and an irritation.

The Poor Have Only Themselves to Blame

In another example of media coverage, we are told that the poor live in a personal and cultural cycle of poverty that hopelessly imprisons them. They routinely center on the Black urban population and focus on perceived personality or cultural traits that doom the poor. While the women in these stories typically exhibit an "attitude" that leads to trouble or a promiscuity that leads to single motherhood, the men possess a need for immediate gratification that leads to drug abuse or an unquenchable greed that leads to the pursuit of fast money. The images that are seared into our mind are sexist, racist, and classist. Census figures reveal that most of the poor are white, not Black or Hispanic, that they live in rural or suburban areas, not urban centers, and hold jobs at least part of the year.[2] Yet, in a fashion that is often framed in an understanding and sympathetic tone, we are told that the poor have inflicted poverty on themselves.

The Poor Are Down on Their Luck

During the Christmas season, the news media sometimes provides us with accounts of poor individuals or families (usually white) who are down on their luck. These stories are often linked to stories about soup kitchens or other charitable activities and sometimes call for charitable contributions. These "Yule time" stories are as much about the affluent as they are about the poor: they tell us that the affluent in our society are a kind, understanding, giving people—which we are not.* The series of unfortunate circumstances that have led to impoverishment are presumed to be a temporary condition that will improve with time and a change in luck.

Despite appearances, the messages provided by the media are not entirely disparate. With each variation, the media informs us what poverty is not (i.e., systemic and indicative of American society) by informing us what it is. The media tells us that poverty is either an aberration of the American way of life (it doesn't exist, it's just another number, it's unfortunate but temporary) or an end product of the poor

---

*American households with incomes of less than $10,000 give an average of 5.5 percent of their earning to charity or to a religious organization, while those making more than $100,000 a year give only 2.9 percent. After changes in the 1986 tax code reduced the benefits of charitable giving, taxpayers earning $500,000 or more slashed their average donation by nearly one-third. Furthermore, many of these acts of benevolence do not help the needy. Rather than provide funding to social service agencies that aid the poor, the voluntary contributions of the wealthy go to places and institutions that entertain, inspire, cure, or educate wealthy Americans—art museums, opera houses, theaters, orchestras, ballet companies, private hospitals, and elite universities. (Robert Reich, "Secession of the Successful," *New York Times Magazine*, February 17, 1991, p. 43.)

themselves (they are a nuisance, do not deserve better, and have brought their predicament upon themselves).

By suggesting that the poor have brought poverty upon themselves, the media is engaging in what William Ryan has called "blaming the victim."[3] The media identifies in what ways the poor are different as a consequence of deprivation, then defines those differences as the cause of poverty itself. Whether blatantly hostile or cloaked in sympathy, the message is that there is something fundamentally wrong with the victims—their hormones, psychological makeup, family environment, community, race, or some combination of these—that accounts for their plight and their failure to lift themselves out of poverty.

But poverty in the United States is systemic. It is a direct result of economic and political policies that deprive people of jobs, adequate wages, or legitimate support. It is neither natural nor inevitable: there is enough wealth in our nation to eliminate poverty if we chose to redistribute existing wealth or income. The plight of the poor is reason enough to make the elimination of poverty the nation's first priority. But poverty also impacts dramatically on the nonpoor. It has a dampening effect on wages in general (by maintaining a reserve army of unemployed and underemployed anxious for any job at any wage) and breeds crime and violence (by maintaining conditions that invite private gain by illegal means and rebellion-like behavior, not entirely unlike the urban riots of the 1960s). Given the extent of poverty in the nation and the impact it has on us all, the media must spin considerable magic to keep the poor and the issue of poverty and its root causes out of the public consciousness.

About Everyone Else

Both the broadcast and the print news media strive to develop a strong sense of "we-ness" in their audience. They seek to speak to and for an audience that is both affluent and like-minded. The media's solidarity with affluence, that is, with the middle and upper class, varies little from one medium to another. Benjamin DeMott points out, for example, that the *New York Times* understands affluence to be intelligence, taste, public spirit, responsibility, and a readiness to rule and "conceives itself as spokesperson for a readership awash in these qualities."[4] Of course, the flip side to creating a sense of "we," or "us," is establishing a perception of the "other." The other relates back to the faceless, amoral, undeserving, and inferior "underclass." Thus, the world according to the news media is divided between the "underclass" and everyone else. Again the messages are often contradictory.

The Wealthy Are Us

Much of the information provided to us by the news media focuses attention on the concerns of a very wealthy and privileged class of people. Although the concerns of a small fraction of the populace, they are presented as though they were the concerns of everyone. For example, while relatively few people actually own stock, the news media devotes an inordinate amount of broadcast time and print space to business news and stock market quotations. Not only do business reports cater to a particular narrow clientele, so do the fashion pages (with $2,000 dresses), wedding announcements, and the obituaries. Even weather and sports news often have a class bias. An all news radio station in New York City, for example, provides regular national ski reports. International news, trade agreements, and domestic policies issues are also reported in terms of their impact on business climate and the business community. Besides being of practical value to the wealthy, such coverage has considerable ideological value. Its message: the concerns of the wealthy are the concerns of us all.

The Wealthy (as a Class) Do Not Exist

While preoccupied with the concerns of the wealthy, the media fails to notice the way in which the rich as a class of people create and shape domestic and foreign policy. Presented as an aggregate of individuals, the wealthy appear without special interests, interconnections, or unity in purpose. Out of public view are the class interests of the wealthy, the interlocking business links, the concerted actions to preserve their class privileges and business interests (by running for public office, supporting political candidates, lobbying, etc.). Corporate lobbying is ignored, taken for granted, or assumed to be in the public interest. (Compare this with the media's portrayal of the "strong arm of labor" in attempting to defeat trade legislation that is harmful to the interests of working people.) It is estimated that two-thirds of the U.S. Senate is composed of millionaires.[5] Having such a preponderance of millionaires in the Senate, however, is perceived to be neither unusual nor antidemocratic; these millionaire senators are assumed to be serving "our" collective interests in governing.

The Wealthy Are Fascinating and Benevolent

The broadcast and print media regularly provide hype for individuals who have achieved "super" success. These stories are usually about celebrities and superstars from the sports and entertainment world. Society pages and gossip columns serve to keep the social elite informed of each others' doings, allow the rest of us to gawk at their excesses, and help to keep the American dream alive. The print media is also fond of feature stories on corporate empire builders. These stories provide an occasional "insider's" view of the private and corporate life of industrialists by suggesting a rags to riches account of corporate success. These stories tell us that corporate success is a series of smart moves, shrewd acquisitions, timely mergers, and well thought out executive suite shuffles. By painting the upper class in a positive light, innocent of any wrongdoing (labor leaders and union organizations usually get the opposite treatment), the media assures us that wealth and power are benevolent. One person's capital accumulation is presumed to be good for all. The elite, then, are portrayed as investment wizards, people of special talent and skill, whom even their victims (workers and consumers) can admire.

The Wealthy Include a Few Bad Apples

On rare occasions, the media will mock selected individuals for their personality flaws. Real estate investor Donald Trump and New York Yankees owner George Steinbrenner, for example, are admonished by the media for deliberately seeking publicity (a very un-upper class thing to do); hotel owner Leona Helmsley was caricatured for her personal cruelties; and junk bond broker Michael Milkin was condemned because he had the audacity to rob the rich. Michael Parenti points out that by treating business wrongdoings as isolated deviations from the socially beneficial system of "responsible capitalism," the media overlooks the features of the system that produce such abuses and the regularity with which they occur. Rather than portraying them as predictable and frequent outcomes of corporate power and the business system, the media treats abuses as if they were isolated and atypical. Presented as an occasional aberration, these incidents serve not to challenge, but to legitimate, the system.[6]

The Middle Class Is Us

By ignoring the poor and blurring the lines between the working people and the upper class, the news media creates a universal middle class. From this perspective, the size of one's income becomes largely irrelevant: what matters is that most of "us" share an intellectual and moral superiority over the disadvantaged. As *Time* magazine once concluded, "Middle America is a state of mind."[7] "We are all middle class," we are told, "and we all share the same concerns": job security, inflation, tax burdens, world peace, the cost of food and housing, health care, clean air and water, and the safety of our streets. While the concerns of the wealthy are quite distinct from those of the middle class (e.g., the wealthy worry about investments, not jobs), the media convinces us that "we [the affluent] are all in this together."

The Middle Class Is a Victim

For the media, "we" the affluent not only stand apart from the "other"—the poor, the working class, the minorities, and their problems—"we" are also victimized by the poor (who drive up the costs of maintaining the welfare roles), minorities (who commit crimes against us), and workers (who are greedy and drive companies out and prices up). Ignored are the subsidies to the rich, the crimes of corporate America, and the policies that wreak havoc on the economic well-being of middle America. Media magic convinces us to fear, more than anything else, being victimized by those less affluent than ourselves.

The Middle Class Is Not a Working Class

The news media clearly distinguishes the middle class (employees) from the working class (i.e., blue collar workers) who are portrayed, at best, as irrelevant, outmoded, and a dying breed. Furthermore, the media will tell us that the hardships faced by blue collar workers are inevitable (due to progress), a result of bad luck (chance circumstances in a particular industry), or a product of their own doing (they priced themselves out of a job). Given the media's presentation of reality, it is hard to believe that manual, supervised, unskilled, and semiskilled workers actually represent more than 50 percent of the adult working population.[8] The working class, instead, is relegated by the media to "the other."

In short, the news media either lionizes the wealthy or treats their interests and those of the middle class as one in the same. But the upper class and the middle class do not share the same interests or worries. Members of the upper class worry about stock dividends (not employment), they profit from inflation and global militarism, their children attend exclusive private schools, they eat and live in a royal fashion, they call on (or are called upon by) personal physicians, they have few consumer problems, they can escape whenever they want from environmental pollution, and they live on streets and travel to other areas under the protection of private police forces.*[9]

The wealthy are not only a class with distinct life-styles and interests, they are a ruling class. They receive a disproportionate share of the country's yearly income, own a disproportionate amount of the country's wealth, and contribute a disproportionate number of their members to governmental bodies and decision-making groups—all traits that William Domhoff, in his classic work *Who Rules America*, defined as characteristic of a governing class.[10]

This governing class maintains and manages our political and economic structures in such a way that these structures continue to yield an amazing proportion of our wealth to a minuscule upper class. While the media is not above referring to ruling classes in other countries (we hear, for example, references to Japan's ruling elite),[11] its treatment of the news proceeds as though there were no such ruling class in the United States.

Furthermore, the news media inverts reality so that those who are working class and middle class learn to fear, resent, and blame those below, rather than those above, them in the class structure. We learn to resent welfare, which accounts for only two cents out of every dollar in the federal budget (approximately $10 billion) and provides financial relief for the needy,** but learn little about the $11 billion the federal government spends on individuals with incomes in excess of $100,000 (not needy),[12] or the $17 billion in farm subsidies, or the $214 billion (twenty times the cost of welfare) in interest payments to financial institutions.

---

*The number of private security guards in the United States now exceeds the number of public police officers. (Robert Reich, "Secession of the Successful," *New York Times Magazine*, February 17, 1991, p. 42.)

**A total of $20 billion is spent on welfare when you include all state funding. But the average state funding also comes to only two cents per state dollar.

Middle-class whites learn to fear African Americans and Latinos, but most violent crime occurs within poor and minority communities and is neither interracial* nor interclass. As horrid as such crime is, it should not mask the destruction and violence perpetrated by corporate America. In spite of the fact that 14,000 innocent people are killed on the job each year, 100,000 die prematurely, 400,000 become seriously ill, and 6 million are injured from work-related accidents and diseases, most Americans fear government regulation more than they do unsafe working conditions.

Through the media, middle-class—and even working-class—Americans learn to blame blue collar workers and their unions for declining purchasing power and economic security. But while workers who managed to keep their jobs and their unions struggled to keep up with inflation, the top 1 percent of American families saw their average incomes soar 80 percent in the last decade.[13] Much of the wealth at the top was accumulated as stockholders and corporate executives moved their companies abroad to employ cheaper labor (56 cents per hour in El Salvador) and avoid paying taxes in the United States. Corporate America is a world made up of ruthless bosses, massive layoffs, favoritism and nepotism, health and safety violations, pension plan losses, union busting, tax evasions, unfair competition, and price gouging, as well as fast buck deals, financial speculation, and corporate wheeling and dealing that serve the interests of the corporate elite, but are generally wasteful and destructive to workers and the economy in general.

It is no wonder Americans cannot think straight about class. The mass media are neither objective, balanced, independent, nor neutral. Those who own and direct the mass media are themselves part of the upper class, and neither they nor the ruling class in general have to conspire to manipulate public opinion. Their interest is in preserving the status quo, and their view of society as fair and equitable comes naturally to them. But their ideology dominates our society and justifies what is in reality a perverse social order—one that perpetuates unprecedented elite privilege and power on the one hand and widespread deprivation on the other. A mass media that did not have its own class interests in preserving the status quo would acknowledge that inordinate wealth and power undermines democracy and that a "free market" economy can ravage a people and their communities.

NOTES

1. Martin Lee and Norman Solomon, *Unreliable Sources*, Lyle Stuart (New York, 1990), p. 71. See also Ben Bagdikian, *The Media Monopoly*, Beacon Press (Boston, 1990).

*In 92 percent of the murders nationwide the assailant and the victim are of the same race (46 percent are white/white, 46 percent are black/black), 5.6 percent are black on white, and 2.4 percent are white on black. (FBI and Bureau of Justic Statistics, 1985–1986, quoted in Raymond S. Franklin, *Shadows of Race and Class*, University of Minnesota Press, Minneapolis, 1991, p. 108.)

2. Department of Commerce, Bureau of the Census, "Poverty in the United States: 1992," *Current Population Reports, Consumer Income*, Series P60–185, pp. xi, xv, 1.

3. William Ryan, *Blaming the Victim*, Vintage (New York, 1971).

4. Benjamin Demott, *The Imperial Middle*, William Morrow (New York, 1990), p. 123.

5. Fred Barnes, "The Zillionaires Club," *The New Republic*, January 29, 1990, p. 24.

6. Michael Parenti, *Inventing Reality*, St. Martin's Press (New York, 1986), p. 109.

7. *Time*, January 5, 1979, p. 10.

8. Vincent Navarro, "The Middle Class—A Useful Myth," *The Nation*, March 23, 1992, p. 1.

9. Charles Anderson, *The Political Economy of Social Class*, Prentice Hall (Englewood Cliffs, N.J., 1974), p. 137.

10. William Domhoff, *Who Rules America*, Prentice Hall (Englewood Cliffs, N.J., 1967), p. 5.

11. Lee and Solomon, *Unreliable Sources*, p. 179.

12. *Newsweek*, August 10, 1992, p. 57.

13. *Business Week*, June 8, 1992, p. 86.

8

Still Separate, Still Unequal
America's Educational Apartheid

Jonathan Kozol

Many Americans who live far from our major cities and who have no firsthand knowledge of the realities to be found in urban public schools seem to have the rather vague and general impression that the great extremes of racial isolation that were matters of grave national significance some thirty-five or forty years ago have gradually but steadily diminished in more recent years. The truth, unhappily, is that the trend, for well over a decade now, has been precisely the reverse. Schools that were already deeply segregated twenty-five or thirty years ago are no less segregated now, while thousands of other schools around the country that had been integrated either voluntarily or by the force of law have since been rapidly resegregating. . . .

"There are expensive children and there are cheap children," writes Marina Warner, an essayist and novelist who has written many books for children, "just as there are expensive women and cheap women." The governmentally administered diminishment in value of the children of the poor begins even before the age of five or six, when they begin their years of formal education in the public schools. It starts during their infant and toddler years, when hundreds of thousands of children of the very poor in much of the United States are locked out of the opportunity for preschool education for no reason but the accident of birth and budgetary choices of the government, while children of the privileged are often given veritable feasts of rich developmental early education.

In New York City, for example, affluent parents pay surprisingly large sums of money to enroll their youngsters, beginning at the age of two or three, in extraordinary early-education programs that give them social competence and rudimentary pedagogic skills unknown to children of the same age in the city's poorer neighborhoods. The most exclusive of the private preschools in New York, which are known to those who can afford them as "Baby Ivies," cost as much as $24,000 for a full-day program. Competition for admission to these pre-K schools is so extreme that private counselors are frequently retained, at fees as high as $300 an hour, to guide the parents through the application process.

At the opposite extreme along the economic spectrum in New York are thousands of children who receive no preschool opportunity at all. Exactly how many thousands are denied this opportunity in New York City and in other major cities is almost impossible to know. Numbers that originate in governmental agencies in many states are incomplete and imprecise and do not always differentiate with clarity between authentic pre-K programs that have educative and developmental substance and those less expensive child-care arrangements that do not. But even where states do compile numbers that refer specifically to educative preschool programs, it is difficult to know how many of the children who are served are of low income, since admissions to some of the state-supported programs aren't determined by low income or they are determined by a complicated set of factors of which poverty is only one.

There are remarkable exceptions to this pattern in some sections of the nation. In Milwaukee, for example, virtually every four-year-old is now enrolled in a preliminary kindergarten program, which amounts to a full year of preschool education, prior to a second kindergarten year for five-year-olds. More commonly in urban neighborhoods, large numbers of low-income children are denied these opportunities and come into their kindergarten year without the minimal social skills that children need in order to participate in class activities and without even such very modest early-learning skills as knowing how to hold a crayon or a pencil, identify perhaps a couple of shapes and colors, or recognize that printed pages go from left to right.

Three years later, in third grade, these children are introduced to what are known as "high-stakes tests," which in many urban systems now determine whether students can or cannot be promoted. Children who have been in programs like those offered by the "Baby Ivies" since the age of two have, by now, received the benefits of six or seven years of education, nearly twice as many as the children who have been denied these opportunities; yet all are required to take, and will be measured by, the same examinations. Which of these children will receive the highest scores? The ones who spent the years from two to four in lovely little Montessori programs and in other pastel-painted settings in which tender and attentive and well-trained instructors read to them from beautiful storybooks and introduced them very gently for the first time to the world of numbers and the shapes of letters, and the sizes and varieties of solid objects, and perhaps taught them to sort things into groups or to arrange them in a sequence, or to do those many other interesting things that early childhood specialists refer to as prenumeracy skills? Or the ones who spent those years at home in front of a TV or sitting by the window of a slum apartment gazing down into the street? There is something deeply hypocritical about a society that holds an eight-year-old inner-city child "accountable" for her performance on a high-stakes standardized exam but does not hold the high officials of our government accountable for robbing her of what they gave their own kids six or seven years earlier.

Perhaps in order to deflect these recognitions, or to soften them somewhat, many people, even while they do nor doubt the benefit of making very large investments in the education of their own children, somehow—paradoxical as it may seem—appear to be attracted to the argument that money may not really matter that much at all. No matter with what regularity such doubts about the worth of spending money on a child's education are advanced, it is obvious that those who have the money, and who spend it lavishly to benefit their own kids, do not do it for no reason. Yet shockingly large numbers of well-educated and sophisticated people whom I talk with nowadays dismiss such challenges with a surprising ease. "Is the answer really to throw money into these dysfunctional and failing schools?" I'm often asked. "Don't we have some better ways to make them 'work'?" The question is posed in a variety of forms. "Yes, of course, it's not a perfectly fair system as it stands. But money alone is surely not the sole response. The values of the parents and the kids themselves must have a role in this as well you know, housing, health conditions, social factors." "Other factors"—a term of overall reprieve one often hears—"have got to be considered, too." These latter points are obviously true but always seem to have the odd effect of substituting things we know we cannot change in the short run for obvious solutions like cutting class size and constructing new school buildings or providing universal preschool that we actually could put in place right now if we were so inclined.

Frequently these arguments are posed as questions that do not invite an answer because the answer seems to be decided in advance. "Can you really buy your way to better education for these children?" "Do we know enough to be quite sure that we will see an actual return on the investment that we make?" "Is it even clear that this is the right starting point to get to where we'd like to go? It doesn't always seem to work, as I am sure that you already know," or similar questions that somehow assume I will agree with those who ask them.

Some people who ask these questions, although they live in wealthy districts where the schools are funded at high levels, don't even send their children to these public schools but choose instead to send them to expensive private day schools. At some of the well-known private prep schools in the New York City area, tuition and associated costs are typically more than $20,000 a year. During their children's teenage years, they sometimes send them off to very fine New England schools like Andover or Exeter or Groton, where tuition, boarding, and additional expenses rise to move than $30,000. Often a family has two teenage children in these schools at the same time, so they may be spending more than $60,000 on their children's education every year. Yet here I am one night, a guest within their home, and dinner has been served and we are having coffee now; and this entirely likeable, and generally sensible, and beautifully refined and thoughtful person looks me in the eyes and asks me whether you can really buy your way to better education for the children of the poor.

As racial isolation deepens and the inequalities of education finance remain unabated and take on new and more innovative forms, the principals of many inner-city schools are making choices that few principals in public schools that serve white children in the mainstream of the nation ever need to contemplate. Many have been dedicating vast amounts of time and effort to create an architecture of adaptive strategies that promise incremental gains within the limits inequality allows.

New vocabularies of stentorian determination, new systems of incentive, and new modes of castigation, which are termed "rewards and sanctions," have emerged. Curriculum materials that are alleged to be aligned with governmentally established goals and standards and particularly suited to what are regarded as "the special needs and learning styles" of low-income urban children have been introduced. Relentless emphasis on raising test scores, rigid policies of nonpromotion and nongraduation, a new empiricism and the imposition of unusually detailed lists of named and numbered "outcomes" for each isolated parcel of instruction, an oftentimes fanatical insistence upon uniformity of teachers in their management of time, an openly conceded emulation of the rigorous approaches of the military and a frequent use of terminology that comes out of the world of industry and commerce—these are just a few of the familiar aspects of these new adaptive strategies.

Although generically described as "school reform," most of these practices and policies are targeted primarily at poor children of color; and although most educators speak of these agendas in broad language that sounds applicable to all, it is understood that they are valued chiefly as responses to perceived catastrophe in deeply segregated and unequal schools.

"If you do what I tell you to do, how I tell you to do it, when I tell you to do it, you'll get it right," said a determined South Bronx principal observed by a reporter for the *New York Times*. She was laying out a memorizing rule for math to an assembly of her students. "If you don't, you'll get it wrong." This is the voice, this is the tone, this is the rhythm and didactic certitude one hears today in inner-city schools that have embraced a pedagogy of direct command and absolute control. "Taking their inspiration from the ideas of B. F. Skinner . . . ," says the *Times*, proponents of scripted rote-and-drill curricula articulate their aim as the establishment of "faultless communication" between "the teacher, who is the stimulus," and "the students, who respond."

The introduction of Skinnerian approaches (which are commonly employed in penal institutions and drug-rehabilitation programs), as a way of altering the attitudes and learning styles of black and Hispanic children, is provocative, and it has stirred some outcries from respected scholars. To actually go into a school where you know some of the children very, very well and see the way that these approaches can affect their daily lives and thinking processes is even more provocative.

On a chilly November day four years ago in the South Bronx, I entered P.S. 65, a school I had been visiting since 1993. There had been major changes since I'd been there last. Silent lunches had been instituted in the cafeteria, and on days when children misbehaved, silent recess had been introduced as well. On those days the students were obliged to sit in rows and maintain perfect silence on the floor of a small indoor room instead of going out to play. The words SUCCESS FOR ALL, the brand name of a scripted curriculum—better known by its acronym, SFA—were prominently posted at the top of the main stairway and, as I would later find, in almost every room. Also frequently displayed within the halls and classrooms were a number of administrative memos that were worded with unusual didactic absoluteness. "Authentic Writing," read a document called "Principles of Learning" that was posted in the corridor close to the principal's office, "is driven by curriculum and instruction." I didn't know what this expression meant. Like many other undefined and arbitrary phrases posted in the school, it seemed to be a dictum that invited no interrogation.

I entered the fourth grade of a teacher I will call Mr. Endicott, a man in his mid-thirties who had arrived here without training as a teacher, one of about a dozen teachers in the building who were sent into this school after a single summer of short-order preparation. Now in his second year, he had developed a considerable sense of confidence and held the class under a tight control.

As I found a place to sit in a far corner of the room, the teacher and his young assistant, who was in her first year as a teacher, were beginning a math lesson about building airport runways, a lesson that provided children with an opportunity for measuring perimeters. On the wall behind the teacher, in large letters, was written: "Portfolio Protocols: 1. You are responsible for the selection of [your] work that enters your portfolio. 2. As your skills become more sophisticated this year, you will want to revise, amend, supplement, and possibly replace items in your portfolio to reflect your intellectual growth." On the left side of the room: "Performance Standards Mathematics Curriculum: M-5 Problem Solving and Reasoning. M-6 Mathematical Skills and Tools . . ."

My attention was distracted by some whispering among the children sitting to the right of me. The teacher's response to this distraction was immediate: his arm shot out and up in a diagonal in front of him, his hand straight up, his fingers flat.

The young co-teacher did this, too. When they saw their teachers do this, all the children in the classroom did it, too.

"Zero noise," the teacher said, but this instruction proved to be unneeded. The strange salute the class and teachers gave each other, which turned out to be one of a number of such silent signals teachers in the school were trained to use, and children to obey, had done the job of silencing the class.

"Active listening!" said Mr. Endicott. "Heads up! Tractor beams!" which meant, "Every eye on me."

On the front wall of the classroom, in handwritten words that must have taken Mr. Endicott long hours to transcribe, was a list of terms that could be used to praise or criticize a student's work in mathematics. At Level Four, the highest of four levels of success, a child's "problem-solving strategies" could be described, according to this list, as "systematic, complete, efficient, and possibly elegant," while the student's capability to draw conclusions from the work she had completed could be termed "insightful" or "comprehensive." At Level Two, the child's capability to draw conclusions was to be described as "logically unsound"; at Level One, "not present." Approximately 50 separate categories of proficiency, or lack of such, were detailed in this wall-sized tabulation.

A well-educated man, Mr. Endicott later spoke to me about the form of classroom management that he was using as an adaptation from a model of industrial efficiency. "It's a kind of 'Taylorism' in the classroom," he explained, referring to a set of theories about the management of factory employees introduced by Frederick Taylor in the early 1900s. "Primitive utilitarianism" is another term he used when we met some months later to discuss these management techniques with other teachers from the school. His reservations were, however, not apparent in the classroom. Within the terms of what he had been asked to do, he had, indeed, become a master of control. It is one of the few classrooms I had visited up to that time in which almost nothing even hinting at spontaneous emotion in the children or the teacher surfaced while I was there.

The teacher gave the "zero noise" salute again when someone whispered to another child at his table. "In two minutes you will have a chance to talk and share this with your partner." Communication between children in the class was not prohibited but was afforded time slots and, remarkably enough, was formalized in an expression that I found included in a memo that was posted on the wall beside the door: "An opportunity . . . to engage in Accountable Talk."

Even the teacher's words of praise were framed in terms consistent with the lists that had been posted on the wall. "That's a Level Four suggestion," said the teacher when a child made an observation other teachers might have praised as simply "pretty good" or "interesting" or "mature." There was, it seemed, a formal name for every cognitive event within this school: "Authentic Writing," "Active Listening," "Accountable Talk." The ardor to assign all items of instruction or behavior a specific name was unsettling me. The adjectives had the odd effect of hyping every item of endeavor. "Authentic Writing" was, it seemed, a more important act than what the children in a writing class in any ordinary school might try to do.

"Accountable Talk" was some thing more self-conscious and significant than merely useful conversation.

Since that day at P.S. 65, I have visited nine other schools in six different cities where the same Skinnerian curriculum is used. The signs on the walls, the silent signals, the curious salute, the same insistent naming of all cognitive particulars, became familiar as I went from one school to the next.

"Meaningful Sentences," began one of the many listings of proficiencies expected of the children in the fourth grade of an inner-city elementary school in Hartford (90 percent black, 10 percent Hispanic) that I visited a short time later. "Noteworthy Questions," "Active Listening," and other designations like these had been posted elsewhere in the room. Here, too, the teacher gave the kids her outstretched arm, with hand held up, to reestablish order when they grew a little noisy, but I noticed that she tried to soften the effect of this by opening her fingers and bending her elbow slightly so it did not look quite as forbidding as the gesture Mr. Endicott had used. A warm and interesting woman, she later told me she disliked the regimen intensely.

Over her desk, I read a "Mission Statement," which established the priorities and values for the school. Among the missions of the school, according to the printed statement, which was posted also in some other classrooms of the school, was "to develop productive citizens" who have the skills that will be needed "for successful global competition," a message that was reinforced by other posters in the room. Over the heads of a group of children at their desks, a sign anointed them BEST WORKERS OF 2002.

Another signal now was given by the teacher, this one not for silence but in order to achieve some other form of class behavior, which I could not quite identify. The students gave exactly the same signal in response. Whatever the function of this signal, it was done as I had seen it done in the South Bronx and would see it done in other schools in months to come. Suddenly, with a seeming surge of restlessness and irritation—with herself, as it appeared, and with her own effective use of all the tricks that she had learned—she turned to me and said, "I can do this with my dog."

"There's something crystal clear about a number," says a top adviser to the U.S. Senate committee that has jurisdiction over public education, a point of view that is reinforced repeatedly in statements coming from the office of the U.S. education secretary and the White House. "I want to change the face of reading instruction across the United States from an art to a science," said an assistant to Rod Paige, the former education secretary, in the winter of 2002. This is a popular position among advocates for rigidly sequential systems of instruction, but the longing to turn art into science doesn't stop with reading methodologies alone. In many schools it now extends to almost every aspect of the operation of the school and of the lives that children lead within it. In some schools even such ordinary acts as children filing to lunch or recess in the hallways or the stairwells are subjected to the same determined emphasis upon empirical precision.

"Rubric For Filing" is the printed heading of a lengthy list of numbered categories by which teachers are supposed to grade their students on the way they march along the corridors in another inner-city district I have visited. Someone, in this instance, did a lot of work to fit the filing proficiencies of children into no more and no less than thirty-two specific slots:

"Line leader confidently leads the class. . . . Line is straight. . . . Spacing is right. . . . The class is stepping together. . . . Everyone shows pride, their shoulders high . . . no slumping," according to the strict criteria for filing at Level Four.

"Line is straight, but one or two people [are] not quite in line," according to the box for Level Three. "Line leader leads the class," and "almost everyone shows pride."

"Several are slumping. . . . Little pride is showing," says the box for Level Two. "Spacing is uneven. . . . Some are talking and whispering."

"Line leader is paying no attention," says the box for Level One. "Heads are turning every way. . . . Hands are touching. . . . The line is not straight. . . . There is no pride."

The teacher who handed me this document believed at first that it was written as a joke by someone who had simply come to be fed up with all the numbers and accounting rituals that clutter up the day in many overregulated schools. Alas, it turned out that it was no joke but had been printed in a handbook of instructions for the teachers in the city where she taught.

In some inner-city districts, even the most pleasant and old-fashioned class activities of elementary schools have now been overtaken by these ordering requirements. A student teacher in California, for example, wanted to bring a pumpkin to her class on Halloween but knew it had no ascertainable connection to the California standards. She therefore had developed what she called "The Multi-Modal Pumpkin Unit" to teach science (seeds), arithmetic (the size and shape of pumpkins, I believe—this detail wasn't clear), and certain items she adapted out of language arts, in order to position "pumpkins" in a frame of state proficiencies. Even with her multi-modal pumpkin, as her faculty adviser told me, she was still afraid she would be criticized because she knew the pumpkin would not really help her children to achieve expected goals on state exams.

Why, I asked a group of educators at a seminar in Sacramento, was a teacher being placed in a position where she'd need to do preposterous curricular gymnastics to enjoy a bit of seasonal amusement with her kids on Halloween? How much injury to state-determined "purpose" would it do to let the children of poor people have a pumpkin party once a year for no other reason than because it's something fun that other children get to do on autumn days in public schools across most of America?

"Forcing an absurdity on teachers does teach something," said an African-American professor. "It teaches acquiescence. It breaks down the will to thumb your nose at pointless protocols to call absurdity 'absurd.'" Writing out the standards with the proper numbers on the chalkboard has a similar effect, he said; and doing this is "terribly important" to the principals in many of these schools. "You *have* to post the standards, and the way you know the children know the standards is by asking them to *state* the standards. And they do it—and you want to be quite certain that they do it if you want to keep on working at that school."

In speaking of the drill-based program in effect at P.S. 65, Mr. Endicott told me he tended to be sympathetic to the school administrators, more so at least than the other teachers I had talked with seemed to be. He said he believed his principal had little choice about the implementation of this program, which had been mandated for all elementary schools in New York City that had had rock-bottom academic records over a long period of time. "This puts me into a dilemma," he went on, "because I love the kids at P.S. 65." And even while, he said, "I know that my teaching SFA is a charade . . . if I don't do it I won't be permitted to teach these children."

Mr. Endicott, like all but two of the new recruits at P.S. 65—there were about fifteen in all—was a white person, as were the principal and most of the administrators at the school. As a result, most of these neophyte instructors had had little or no prior contact with the children of an inner-city neighborhood; but, like the others I met, and despite the distancing between the children and their teachers that resulted from the scripted method of instruction, he had developed close attachments to his students and did not want to abandon them. At the same time, the class- and race-specific implementation of this program obviously troubled him. "There's an expression now," he said. "The rich get richer, and the poor get SFA." He said he was still trying to figure out his "professional ethics" on the problem that this posed for him.

White children made up "only about one percent" of students in the New York City schools in which this scripted teaching system was imposed,[1] according to the *New York Times*, which also said that "the prepackaged lessons" were intended "to ensure that all teachers—even novices or the most inept"—would be able to teach reading. As seemingly pragmatic and hardheaded as such arguments may be, they are desperation strategies that come out of the acceptance of inequity. If we did not have a deeply segregated system in which more experienced instructors teach the children of the privileged and the least experienced are sent to teach the children of minorities, these practices would not be needed and could not be so convincingly defended. They are confections of apartheid, and no matter by what arguments of urgency or practicality they have been justified, they cannot fail to further deepen the divisions of society.

There is no misery index for the children of apartheid education. There ought to be; we measure almost everything else that happens to them in their schools. Do kids who go to schools like these enjoy the days they spend in them? Is school, for most of them, a happy place to be? You do not find the answers to these questions in reports about achievement levels, scientific methods of accountability, or structural revisions in the modes of governance. Documents like these don't speak of happiness. You have to go back to the schools themselves to find an answer to these questions. You have to sit down in the little chairs in first and second grade, or on the reading rug with kindergarten kids, and listen to the things they actually say to one another and the dialogue between them and their teachers. You have to go down to the basement with the children when it's time for lunch and to the playground with them, if they have a playground, when it's time for recess, if they still have recess at their school. You have to walk into the children's bathrooms in these buildings. You have to do what children do and breathe the air the children breathe. I don't think that there is any other way to find out what the lives that children lead in school are really like.

High school students, when I first meet them, are often more reluctant than the younger children to open up and express their personal concerns; but hesitation on the part of students did not prove to be a problem when I visited a tenth-grade class at Fremont High School in Los Angeles. The students were told that I was a writer, and they took no time in getting down to matters that were on their minds.

"Can we talk about the bathrooms?" asked a soft-spoken student named Mireya.

In almost any classroom there are certain students who, by the force of their directness or the unusual sophistication of their way of speaking, tend to capture your attention from the start. Mireya later spoke insightfully about some of the serious academic problems that were common in the school, but her observations on the physical and personal embarrassments she and her schoolmates had to undergo cut to the heart of questions of essential dignity that kids in squalid schools like this one have to deal with all over the nation.

Fremont High School, as court papers filed in a lawsuit against the state of California document, has fifteen fewer bathrooms than the law requires. Of the limited number of bathrooms that are working in the school, "only one or two . . . are open and unlocked for girls to use." Long lines of girls are "waiting to use the bathrooms," which are generally "unclean" and "lack basic supplies," including toilet paper. Some of the classrooms, as court papers also document, "do not have air conditioning," so that students, who attend school on a three-track schedule that runs year-round, "become red-faced and unable to concentrate" during "the extreme heat of summer." The school's maintenance records report that rats were found in eleven classrooms. Rat droppings were found "in the bins and drawers" of the high school's kitchen, and school records note that "hamburger buns" were being "eaten off [the] bread-delivery rack."

No matter how many tawdry details like these I've read in legal briefs or depositions through the years, I'm always shocked again to learn how often these unsanitary physical conditions are permitted to continue in the schools that serve our poorest students—even after they have been vividly described in the media. But hearing of these conditions in Mireya's words was even more unsettling, in part because this student seemed so fragile and because the need even to speak of these indignities in front of me and all the other students was an additional indignity.

"The problem is this," she carefully explained. "You're not allowed to use the bathroom during lunch, which is a thirty-minute period. The only time that you're allowed to use it is between your classes." But "this is a huge building," she went on. "It has long corridors. If you have one class at one end of the building and your next class happens to be way down at the other end, you don't have time to use the bathroom and still get to class before it starts. So you go to your class and then you ask permission from your teacher to go to the bathroom and the teacher tells you, 'No. You had your chance between the periods . . .'

"I feel embarrassed when I have to stand there and explain it to a teacher."

"This is the question," said a wiry-looking boy named Edward, leaning forward in his chair. "Students are not animals, but even animals need to relieve themselves sometimes. We're here for eight hours. What do they think we're supposed to do?"

"It humiliates you," said Mireya, who went on to make the interesting statement that "the school provides solutions that don't actually work," and this idea was taken up by several other students in describing course requirements within the school. A tall black student, for example, told me that she hoped to be a social worker or a doctor but was programmed into "Sewing Class" this year. She also had to take another course, called "Life Skills," which she told me was a very basic course—"a retarded class," to use her words—that "teaches things like the six continents," which she said she'd learned in elementary school.

When I asked her why she had to take these courses, she replied that she'd been told they were required, which as I later learned was not exactly so. What was required was that high school students take two courses in an area of study called "The Technical Arts," and which the Los Angeles Board of Education terms "Applied Technology." At schools that served the middle class or upper-middle class, this requirement was likely to be met by courses that had academic substance and, perhaps, some relevance to college preparation. At Beverly Hills High School, for example, the technical-arts requirement could be fulfilled by taking subjects like residential architecture, the designing of commercial structures, broadcast journalism, advanced computer graphics, a sophisticated course in furniture design, carving and sculpture, or an honors course in engineering research and design. At Fremont High, in contrast, this requirement was far more often met by courses that were basically vocational and also obviously keyed to low-paying levels of employment.

Mireya, for example, who had plans to go to college, told me that she had to take a sewing class last year and now was told she'd been assigned to take a class in hair-dressing as well. When I asked her teacher why Mireya could not skip these subjects and enroll in classes that would help her to pursue her college aspirations, she replied, "It isn't a question of what students want. It's what the school may have available. If all the other elective classes that a student wants to take are full, she has to take one of these classes if she wants to graduate."

A very small girl named Obie, who had big blue-tinted glasses tilted up across her hair, interrupted then to tell me with a kind of wild gusto that she'd taken hair-dressing twice! When I expressed surprised that this was possible, she said there were two levels of hairdressing offered here at Fremont High. "One is in hair-styling," she said. "The other is in braiding."

Mireya stared hard at this student for a moment and then suddenly began to cry. "I don't want to take hairdressing. I did not need sewing either. I knew how to sew. My mother is a seamstress in a factory. I'm trying to go to college. I don't need to sew to go to college. My mother sews. I hoped for something else."

"What would you rather take?" I asked.

"I wanted to take an AP class," she answered.

Mireya's sudden tears elicited a strong reaction from one of the boys who had been silent up till now: a thin, dark-eyed student named Fortino, who had long hair down to his shoulders. He suddenly turned directly to Mireya and spoke into the silence that followed her last words.

"Listen to me," he said. "The owners of the sewing factories need laborers. Correct?"

"I guess they do," Mireya said.

"It's not going to be their own kids. Right?" "Why not?" another student said.

"So they can grow beyond themselves," Mireya answered quietly. "But we remain the same."

"You're ghetto," said Fortino, "so we send you to the factory." He saw low in his desk chair, leaning on one elbow, his voice and dark eyes loaded with a cynical intelligence. "You're ghetto—so you sew!"

"There are higher positions than these," said a student named Samantha.

"You're ghetto," said Fortino unrelentingly. "So sew!"

Admittedly, the economic needs of a society are bound to be reflected to some rational degree within the policies and purposes of public schools. But, even so, there must be *something* more to life as it is lived by six-year-olds or by teenagers, for that matter, than concerns about "successful global competition." Childhood is not merely basic training for utilitarian adulthood. It should have some claims upon our mercy, not for its future value to the economic interests of competitive societies but for its present value as a perishable piece of life itself.

Very few people who are not involved with inner-city schools have any real idea of the extremes to which the mercantile distortion of the purposes and character of education have been taken or how unabashedly proponents of these practices are willing to defend them. The head of a Chicago school, for instance, who was criticized by some for emphasizing rote instruction that, his critics said, was turning children into "robots," found no reason to dispute the charge. "Did you ever stop to think that these robots will never burglarize your home?" he asked, and "will never snatch your pocketbooks. . . . These robots are going to be producing taxes."

Corporate leaders, when they speak of education, sometimes pay lip-service to the notion of "good critical and analytic skills," but it is reasonable to ask whether they have in mind the critical analysis of *their* priorities. In principle, perhaps some do; but, if so, this is not a principle that seems to have been honored widely in the schools I have been visiting. In all the various business-driven inner-city classrooms that I have observed in the past five years, plastered as they are with corporation brand names and managerial vocabularies, I have yet to see the two words "labor unions." Is this an oversight? How is that possible? Teaches and principals themselves, who are almost always members of a union, seem to be so beaten down that they rarely even question this omission.

It is not at all unusual these days to come into an urban school in which the principal prefers to call himself or herself "building CEO" or "building manager." In some of the same schools teachers are described as "classroom managers."[2] I have never been in a suburban district in which principals were asked to view themselves or teachers in this way. These terminologies remind us of how wide the distance has become between two very separate worlds of education.

It has been more than a decade now since drill-based literacy methods like Success For All began to proliferate in our urban schools. It has been three and a half years since the systems of assessment that determine the effectiveness of these and similar practices were codified in the federal legislation, No Child Left Behind, that President Bush signed into law in 2002. Since the enactment of this bill, the number of standardized exams children must take has more than doubled. It will probably increase again after the year 2006, when standardized tests, which are now required in grades three through eight, may be required in Head Start programs and, as President Bush has now proposed, in ninth, tenth, and eleventh grades as well.

The elements of strict accountability, in short, are solidly in place; and in many states where the present federal policies are simply reinforcements of accountability requirements that were established long before the passage of the federal law, the same regimen has been in place since 1995 or even earlier. The "tests-and-standards" partisans have had things very much their way for an extended period of time, and those who were convinced that they had ascertained "what works" in schools that serve minorities and children of the poor have had ample opportunity to prove that they were right.

What, then, it is reasonable to ask, are the results?

The achievement gap between black and white children, which narrowed for three decades up until the late years of the 1980s—the period in which school segregation steadily decreased—started to widen once more in the early 1990s when the federal courts began the process of resegregation by dismantling the mandates of the *Brown* decision. From that point on, the gap continued to widen or remained essentially unchanged; and while recently there has been a modest narrowing of the gap in reading scores for fourth-grade children, the gap in secondary school remains as wide as ever.

The media inevitably celebrate the periodic upticks that a set of scores may seem to indicate in one year or another in achievement levels of black and Hispanic children in their elementary schools. But if these upticks were not merely temporary "testing gains" achieved by test-prep regimens and were instead authentic education gains, they would carry over into middle school and high school. Children who know how to read—and read with comprehension—do not suddenly become nonreaders and hopelessly disabled writers when they enter secondary school. False gains evaporate; real gains endure. Yet hundreds of thousands of the inner-city children who have made what many districts claim to be dramatic gains in elementary school, and whose principals and teachers have adjusted almost every aspect of their school days and school calendars, forfeiting recess, canceling or cutting back on all the so-called frills (art, music, even social sciences) in order to comply with state demands, those students, now in secondary school, are sitting in subject-matter classes where they cannot comprehend the texts and cannot set down their ideas in the kind of sentences expected of most fourth- and fifth-grade students in the suburbs. Students in this painful situation, not surprisingly, tend to be most likely to drop out of school.

In 48 percent of high schools in the nation's 100 largest districts, which are those in which the highest concentrations of black and Hispanic students tend to be enrolled, less than half the entering ninth-graders graduate in four years. Nationwide, from 1993 to 2002, the number of high schools graduating less than half their ninth-grade class in four years has increased by 75 percent. In the 94 percent of districts in New York State where white children make up the majority, nearly 80 percent of students graduate from high school in four years. In the 6 percent of districts where black and Hispanic students make up the majority, only 40 percent do so. There are 120 high schools in New York, enrolling nearly 200,000 minority students, where less than 60 percent of entering ninth-graders even make it to twelfth grade.

The promulgation of new and expanded inventories of "what works," no matter the enthusiasm with which they're elaborated, is not going to change this. The use of hortatory slogans chanted by the students in our segregated schools is not going to change this. Desperate historical revisionism that romanticizes the segregation of an older order (this is a common theme of many separatists today) is not going to change this. Skinnerian instructional approaches, which decapitate a child's capability for critical reflection, are not going to change this. Posters about "global competition" will certainly not change this. Turning six-year-olds into examination soldiers and denying eight-year-olds their time for play at recess will not change this.

"I went to Washington to challenge the soft bigotry of low expectations," said President Bush in his campaign for reelection in September 2004. "It's working. It's making a difference." Here we have one of those deadly lies that by sheer repetition is at length accepted by surprisingly large numbers of Americans. But it is not the truth; and it is not an innocent misstatement of the facts. It is a devious appeasement of the heartache of the parents of the black and brown and poor, and if it is not forcefully resisted it will lead us further in a very dangerous direction.

Whether the issue is inequity alone or deepening resegregation or the labyrinthine intertwining of the two, it is well past the time for us to start the work that it will take to change this. If it takes people marching in the streets and other forms of adamant disruption of the governing civilities, if it takes more than litigation, more than legislation, and much more than resolutions introduced by members of Congress, these are prices we should be prepared to pay. "We do not have the things you have," Alliyah told me when she wrote to ask if I would come and visit her school in the South Bronx. "Can you help us?" America owes that little girl and millions like her a more honorable answer than they have received.

NOTES

1. SFA has since been discontinued in the New York City public schools, though it is still being used in 1,300 U.S. schools, serving as many as 650,000 children. Similar scripted systems are used in schools (overwhelmingly minority in population) serving several million children.

2. A school I visited three years ago in Columbus, Ohio, was littered with "Help Wanted" signs. Starting in kindergarten, children in the school were being asked to think about the jobs that they might choose when they grew up. In one classroom there was a poster that displayed the names of several retail stores: J. C. Penney, Wal-Mart, Kmart, Sears, and a few others. "It's like working in a store," a classroom aide explained. "The children are learning to pretend they're cashiers." At another school in the same district, children were encouraged to apply for jobs in their classrooms. Among the job positions open to the children in this school, there was an "Absence Manager" and a "Behavior Chart Manager," a "Form Collector Manager," a "Paper Passer Outer Manager," a "Paper Collecting Manager," a "Paper Returning Manager," an "Exit Ticket Manager," even a "Learning Manager," a "Reading Corner Manager," and a "Score Keeper Manager." I asked the principal if there was a special reason why those two words "management" and "manager" kept popping up throughout the school. "We want every child to be working as a manager while he or she is in this school," the principal explained. "We want to make them understand that, in this country, companies will give you opportunities to work, to prove yourself, no matter what you've done." I wasn't sure what she meant by "no matter what you've done," and asked her if she could explain it. "Even if you have a felony arrest," she said, "we want you to understand that you can be a manager someday."

9

SEX AND RACE
The Analogy of Social Control

William Chafe

. . . Analogies should not be limited to issues of substance alone, nor is their purpose to prove that two categories or objects are exactly identical. According to the dictionary, an analogy is "a relation of likeness . . . consisting in the resemblance not of the things themselves but of two or more attributes, circumstances or effects." Within this context, the purpose of an analogy is to illuminate a process or relationship which might be less discernible if only one or the other side of the comparison were viewed in isolation. What, then, if we look at sex and race as examples of how social control is exercised in America, with the primary emphasis on what the analogy tells us about the modes of control emanating from the dominant culture? . . . What if the nature of the analogy is not in the *substance* of the material existence which women and blacks have experienced but in the *forms* by which others have kept them in "their place" and prevented them from challenging the status quo?

The virtues of such an approach are many. First, it provides greater flexibility in exploring how the experience of one group can inform the study of another. Second, it has the potential of developing insights into the larger processes by which the status quo is perpetuated from generation to generation. In this sense, it can teach us about the operation of society as a whole and the way in which variables like sex and race have been made central to the division of responsibilities and power within the society. If the forms of social control used with blacks and women resemble each other in "two or more attributes, circumstances, or effects," then it may be possible to learn something both about the two groups and how the status quo has been maintained over time. The best way to pursue this, in turn, is through looking closely at the process of social control as it has operated on one group, and then comparing it with the process and experience of the second group.

In his brilliant autobiographical novel *Black Boy*, Richard Wright describes what it was like to grow up black in the Jim Crow South. Using his family, the church, his classmates, his jobs, and his fantasies as stage-pieces for his story, Wright plays out the themes of hunger, fear, and determination which permeated his young life. Above all, he provides a searing account of how white Southerners successfully controlled the lives and aspirations of blacks. A series of concentric circles of social control operated in devastating fashion to limit young blacks to two life options—conformity to the white system, or exile.*

The outermost circle of control, of course, consisted of physical intimidation. When Richard asked his mother why black men did not fight white men, she responded, "The white men have guns and the black men don't." Physical force, and ultimately the threat of death, served as a constant reminder that whites held complete power over black lives. Richard saw that power manifested repeatedly. When his Uncle Hoskins dared to start his own saloon and act independently of the white power structure, he was lynched. The brother of one of Richard's schoolmates suffered a similar fate, allegedly for fooling with a white prostitute. When Richard worked for a clothing store, he frequently saw the white manager browbeat or physically attack black customers who had not paid their bills on time. When one woman came out of the store in a torn dress and bleeding, the manager said, "That's what we do to niggers when they don't pay their bills."[1]

The result was pervasive fear, anchored in the knowledge that whites could unleash vicious and irrational attacks without warning. Race consciousness could be traced, at least in part, to the tension which existed between anger at whites for attacking blacks without reason, and fear that wanton violence could strike again at any time, unannounced and unrestrained. "The things that influenced my conduct as a Negro," Richard wrote, "did not have to happen to me directly; I needed but to hear of them to feel their full effects in the deepest layers of my consciousness. Indeed the white brutality that I had not seen was a more effective control of my behavior than that which I knew . . . as long as it remained something terrible and yet remote, something whose horror and blood might descend upon me at any moment, I was compelled to give my entire imagination over to it, an act which blocked the springs of thought and feelings in me."[2]

The second circle of control rested in white domination of the economic status of black people. If a young black did not act the part of "happy nigger" convincingly, the employer would fire him. Repeatedly, Richard was threatened with the loss of work because he did not keep his anger and independence from being communicated to his white superiors. "Why don't you laugh and talk like the other niggers?" one employer asked. "Well, sir, there is nothing much to say or smile about," Richard said. "I don't like your looks nigger. Now git!" the boss ordered. Only a limited number of economic roles were open to blacks, and if they were

---

*Despite the problems created by using a novel for purposes of historical analysis, the interior perspective that is offered outweighs the limitation of "subjectiveness." Wright has been criticized for being overly harsh and elitist in his judgment of his black peers. His depiction of the conditions blacks had to cope with, on the other hand, corresponds well with the historical record. In the cases of both women and blacks, novels provide a vividness of detail and personal experience necessary to understand the larger processes at work in the society, but for the most part unavailable in conventional historical sources. (For amplification of Wright's experience with Jim Crow, see Selection 2, in Part I of this book.)

not played according to the rules, the job would be lost. A scarce supply of work, together with the demand that it be carried out in a deferential manner, provided a powerful guarantee that blacks would not get out of line.[3]

Significantly, the highest status jobs in the black community—teachers, ministers, civil servants—all depended ultimately upon acting in ways that pleased the white power structure.* One did not get the position at the post office or in the school system without being "safe"—the kind of person who would not make trouble. The fundamental precondition for success in the black community, therefore, was acting in ways that would not upset the status quo. When Richard tried to improve his own occupational chances and learn the optical trade, the white men who were supposed to teach him asked: "What are you trying to do, get smart, nigger?"[4]

The third circle of control consisted of the psychological power of whites to define and limit the reach of black aspirations. The sense people have of who they are and what they might become is tied intimately to the expectations communicated to them by others. The verbal cues, the discouragement or encouragement of authority figures, the picture of reality transmitted by friends or teachers—all of these help to shape how people think of themselves and their life chances. Stated in another way, human beings can envision careers as doctors and lawyers or a life of equality with others only to the extent that someone holds forth these ideals as viable possibilities.

Within this realm of social psychology, white Southerners exerted a pervasive and insidious control upon blacks. When Richard took his first job in a white household, he was given a bowl of molasses with mold on it for breakfast, even as his employers ate bacon and eggs. The woman he worked for asked what grade he was in, and when he replied the seventh, she asked, "Then why are you going to school?" When he further answered, "Well, I want to be a writer," she responded: "You'll never be a writer . . . who on earth put such ideas into your nigger head?" By her response, the woman attempted to undercut whatever sense of possibility Richard or other young blacks might have entertained for such a career. In effect, the woman had defined from a white perspective the outer boundaries of a black person's reality. As Richard noted, "She had assumed that she knew my place in life, what I felt, what I ought to be, and I resented it with all my heart . . . perhaps I would never be a writer; but I did not want her to say so." In his own time Richard Wright was able to defy the limits set upon his life by white people. But for the overwhelming majority of his fellow blacks, the ability of whites to intimidate them psychologically diminished the chance that they would be able to aspire realistically to a life other than that assigned them within a white racist social structure.[5]

---

*There is an important distinction, of course, between jobs which were tied to white support and those with an indigenous base in the black community. Black doctors, morticians, and barbers, for example, looked to the black community itself for their financial survival; hence they could be relatively free of white domination. On the other hand, the number of such independent positions was small. Although many people would include ministers in such a category, the visibility of the ministerial role created pressure from blacks concerned with the stability and safety of their churches for ministers to avoid a radical protest position. That started to change during the civil rights movement.

The most devastating control of all, however, was that exercised by the black community itself out of self-defense. In the face of a world managed at every level by white power, it became an urgent necessity that black people train each other to adapt in order to survive. Thus the most profound and effective socialization toward accepting the racial status quo came from Richard's own family and peer group. It was Richard's mother who slapped him into silence "out of her own fear" when he asked why they had not fought back after Uncle Hoskins's lynching. To even ask the question posed a threat to safety. Similarly, it was Richard's Uncle Tom who insisted that Richard learn, almost by instinct, how to be accommodating. If Richard did not learn, the uncle said, he would never amount to anything and would end up on the gallows. Indeed, Richard would survive only if somebody broke his spirit and set the "proper" example.[6]

The instances of social control from within the black community abound in Wright's *Black Boy*. It was not only the white employer, but almost every black he knew, who opposed Richard's writing aspirations. "From no quarter," he recalled, "with the exception of the Negro newspaper editor, had there come a single encouraging word . . . I felt that I had committed a crime. Had I been aware of the full extent to which I was pushing against the current of my environment, I would have been frightened altogether out of my attempts at writing." The principal of his school urged vehemently that Richard give a graduation speech written by the principal rather than by Richard himself so that the proper tone of accommodation could be struck; the reward for going along was a possible teaching job. Griggs, Richard's best friend, was perhaps the most articulate in demanding that Richard control his instincts. "You're black and you don't act a damn bit like it." When Richard replied, "Oh Christ, I can't be a slave," Griggs responded with the ultimate lesson of reality: "But you've got to eat . . . when you are in front of white people, think before you act, think before you speak . . . you may think I'm an Uncle Tom, but I'm not. I hate these white people, hate them with all my heart. But I can't show it; if I did, they'd kill me." No matter where he went or whom he talked to in his own community, Richard found, not support for his protest, but the warning that he must behave externally in the manner white people expected. Whatever the hope of ultimate freedom, survival was the immediate necessity. One could not fight another day if one was not alive.[7]

Paradoxically, even the outlets for resistance within the system provided a means of reinforcing it. There were many ways of expressing unhappiness with one's lot, and all essential to let off steam. The gang on the corner constantly verbalized resentment and anger against the white oppressor. Yet the very fact that the anger had to be limited to words and out of the earshot of whites meant that in practical terms it was ineffectual. Humor was another form of resistance. Richard and his friends joked that, if they ate enough black-eyed peas and buttermilk, they would defeat their white enemies in a race riot with "poison gas." But the end of the joke was an acknowledgment that the only way in reality to cope with the "mean" white folks was to leave.[8]

Indeed, the most practical form of resistance—petty theft—almost seemed a ploy by white people to perpetuate the system. Just as modern-day department store owners tolerate a certain degree of employee theft as a means of making the workers think they are getting away with something so they will not demand higher wages, so white employers of black people appear to have intentionally closed their eyes to a great deal of minor stealing. By giving blacks a small sense of triumph, white employers were able to tie them even more closely into the system, and prevent them from contemplating outright defiance. As Wright observed:[9]

> No Negroes in my environment had ever thought of organizing . . . and petitioning their white employers for higher wages. . . . They knew that the whites would have retaliated with swift brutality. So, pretending to conform to the laws of the whites, grinning, bowing, they let their fingers stick to what they could touch. And the whites seemed to like it.

> But I, who stole nothing, who wanted to look them straight in the face, who wanted to talk and act like a man, inspired fear in them. The southern whites would rather have had Negroes who stole work for them than Negroes who knew, however dimly, the worth of their own humanity. Hence, whites placed a premium upon black deceit; they encouraged irresponsibility, and their rewards were bestowed upon us blacks in the degree that we could make them feel safe and superior.

From a white point of view, a minor exercise of indirect and devious power by blacks was a small price to pay for maintaining control over the entire system. Thus, whites held the power to define black people's options, even to the point of controlling their modes of resistance.*

The result of all this was a system that functioned smoothly, with barely a trace of overt protest or dissension. Everyone seemed outwardly content with their place. At a very early age, Wright observed, "the white boys and the black boys began to play our traditional racial roles as though we had been born to them, as though it was in our blood, as though we were guided by instinct." For most people, the impact of a pervasive system of social control was total: resignation, a lowering of aspirations, a recognition of the bleakness of the future and the hopelessness of trying to achieve major change. In Wright's images life was like a train on a track; once headed in a given direction, there was little possibility of changing one's course.[10]

Wright himself, of course, was the exception. "Somewhere in the dead of the southern night," he observed, "my life had switched onto the wrong track, and without my knowing it, the locomotive of my heart was rushing down a dangerously steep slope, heading for a collision, heedless of the warning red lights that blinked all about me, the sirens and the bells and the screams that filled the air." Wright

---

*It is important to remember that there existed a life in the black community less susceptible to white interference on a daily basis. Black churches, lodges, and family networks provided room for individual self-expression and supplied emotional reinforcement and sustenance. In this connection it is no accident that black institutions are strongest in the South where, until recently, the vast majority of blacks resided. On the other hand, the freedom which did exist came to a quick end wherever blacks attempted to enter activities, occupations, or areas of aspiration involving whites; or defined as white-controlled. Thus even the realm where freedom existed was partially a reflection of white control.

had chosen the road of exile, of acute self-consciousness and alienation. For most blacks of his era, though, the warning red lights, the sirens, the bells, and the screams produced at least outward conformity to the status quo. In the face of forms of social control which effectively circumscribed one's entire life, there seemed no other choice.[11]

Obviously, women have not experienced overtly and directly the same kind of consistent physical intimidation that served so effectively to deter the black people of Richard Wright's childhood from resisting their condition. On the other hand, it seems clear that the physical strength and alleged dominance of men have been an important instrument of controlling women's freedom of action. The traditional image of the male as "protector" owes a great deal to the notion that women cannot defend themselves and that men must therefore take charge of their lives physically. The same notion of male strength has historically been responsible for restricting jobs involving heavy labor to men. Nor is the fear with which women view the potential of being struck or raped by a male lover, husband, or attacker an insignificant reality in determining the extent to which women historically have accepted the dominance of the men in their lives. Richard Wright observed that "the things that influenced my conduct . . . did not have to happen to me directly; I needed but to hear of them to feel their full effects. . . ." Similarly, women who have grown up with the image of powerful and potentially violent men need not have experienced a direct attack to share a sense of fear and intimidation. "Strength," the psychologist Jerome Kagan has observed, "is a metaphor for power." Thus, despite the substantive difference in the way women and blacks have been treated, the form of social control represented by physical strength has operated similarly for both groups.[12]

An even stronger case can be made for the way in which economic controls have succeeded in keeping blacks and women in their place. In 1898 Charlotte Perkins Gilman argued in *Women and Economics* that the root of women's subjection was their economic dependency on men. As long as women were denied the opportunity to earn their own living, she argued, there could never be equality between the sexes. The fact that women had to please their mates, both sexually and through other services, to ensure their survival made honest communication and mutual respect impossible. The prospect of a "present" from a generous husband, or a new car or clothes, frequently served to smooth over conflict, while the implicit threat of withholding such favors could be used to discourage carrying conflict too far.[13]

In fact, the issue of women not controlling their own money has long been one of the most painful and humiliating indexes of inequality between the sexes, especially in the middle class. Since money symbolizes power, having to ask others for it signifies subservience and an inferior status. Carol Kennicott, the heroine of Sinclair Lewis's *Main Street*, recognized the problem. After begging prettily for her household expenses early in her marriage, she started to demand her own separate funds. "What was a magnificent spectacle of generosity to you," she told her husband, "was a humiliation to me. You *gave* me money—gave it to your mistress if she was complaisant." Beth Phail, a character in Marge Piercy's novel *Small Changes*, experienced the same conflict with her husband, who was immediately threatened by the idea of her economic autonomy. Indeed, few examples of psychological control seem more pointed than those represented in husbands' treating their wives as not mature enough to handle their own money.[14]

Even the women who held jobs reflected the pattern by which economic power was used to control women's freedom of action. Almost all women workers were concentrated in a few occupations delineated as "woman's" work. As secretaries, waitresses, cooks, and domestic workers, women on the job conformed to the "service" image of their sex. Significantly, the highest status jobs available— nurses and teachers—tended to reinforce a traditional image of women and the status quo between the sexes, just as the highest jobs available within the black community—teachers and civil servants—reinforced a pattern of accommodation with the existing white power structure. Any woman who chose a "man's job" automatically risked a loss of approval, if not total hostility. For most, the option simply did not exist.

Even those in the most prestigious positions illustrated how money could be used as an instrument of social control. If they were to succeed in raising funds, college administrators in black and women's schools frequently found that they had to shape their programs in conformity to social values that buttressed the status quo. Booker T. Washington represented the most outstanding example of this phenomenon. Repeatedly he was forced to appease white racist presumptions in order to get another donation for Tuskegee. As the funnel through which all white philanthropic aid to blacks was channeled, Washington had to ensure that no money would be spent in a way which might challenge the political values of his contributors, even though privately he fought those political values. But Washington was not alone. During the 1830's Mary Lyons, head of Mt. Holyoke Seminary, agreed not to attend trustee meetings lest she offend male sensibilities, and Mary Alice Baldwin, the very effective leader of the Women's College of Duke University, felt it necessary to pay homage to the conservative tradition of "the Southern lady" as the price for sustaining support of women's education at Duke.[15]

In all of these instances, economic controls functioned in parallel ways to limit the freedom of women and blacks. If a group is assigned a "place," there are few more effective ways of keeping it there than economic dependency. Not only must the group in question conform to the expectations of the dominant class in order to get money to live; those who would do otherwise are discouraged by the fact that no economic incentives exist to reward those who challenge the status quo. The absence of financial support for those who dare to deviate from prescribed norms has served well to perpetuate the status quo in the condition of both women and blacks. "I don't want to be a slave," Richard Wright observed. "But you have to eat," Griggs replied.

The strongest parallel, however, consists of the way in which blacks and women have been given the psychological message that they should be happy with their "place." In both instances, this form of control has effectively limited aspiration to non-conventional roles. Although Beth Phail of *Small Changes* wanted to go to college and law school, her family insisted that her highest aspiration should be marriage and homemaking. A woman should not expect a career. Similarly, when Carol Kennicott told her college boyfriend, "I want to do something with my life," he responded eagerly: "What's better than making a comfy home and bringing up some cute kids . . . ?" The small town atmosphere of Gopher Prairie simply reinforced the pressure to conform. Carol was expected to be a charming hostess, a dutiful wife, and a good homemaker, but not a career woman. Thus, as Sinclair Lewis observed, she was a "woman with a working brain and no work." The messages Carol received from her surroundings were not designed to give her high self-esteem. Her husband called her "an extravagant little rabbit," and his poker partners, she noted, simply expected her "to wait on them like a servant."[16]

Although Carol's personality was atypical, her social experience was not. When high school girls entertained the possibility of a career, they were encouraged to be nurses, not doctors. The qualities that received the most praise were those traditionally associated with being a "lady," not an assertive individual ready to face the world. Significantly, both women and blacks were the victims of two devices designed to discourage non-conformity. Those who sought to protest their status, for example, were subjected to ridicule and caricature. The black protestor was almost certain to be identified with subversive activity, just as the women's rights advocate was viewed as unsexed and a saboteur of the family. (Ordinary blacks and females were subject to a gentler form of humor, no less insidious, as in the characters of Amos 'n Andy's "King Fish" or Lucille Ball's "Lucy.") In addition, it was not uncommon for blacks to be set against blacks and women against women in a competition which served primarily the interests of the dominant group. According to Judith Bardwick and Elizabeth Donavan, girls are socialized to use oblique forms of aggression largely directed at other females, while men's aggression is overt. The stereotype of women doing devious battle over an attractive man is an ingrained part of our folk tradition. Nor is the "divide and conquer" strategy a stranger to the history of black people, as when white workers sowed seeds of suspicion between Richard Wright and another black worker in order to make them fight each other for the entertainment of whites.[17]

In both cases the psychological form of social control has operated in a similar fashion. The aspirations, horizons, and self-images of blacks and women have been defined by others in a limiting and constrictive way. More often than not, the result historically has been an acceptance of society's perception of one's role. The prospect of becoming an architect, an engineer, or a carpenter is not easy to sustain in an environment where the very idea is dismissed as foolish or unnatural. Instead of encouragement to aspire to new horizons of achievement, the message transmitted to blacks and women has been the importance of finding satisfaction with the status quo.

But in the case of women, as with blacks, the most effective instrument of continued control has been internal pressure from the group itself. From generation to generation, mothers teach daughters to please men, providing the instruction that prepares the new generation to assume the roles of mothers and housewives. Just as blacks teach each other how to cope with "whitey" and survive within the system, women school each other in how to win a man, how to appear charming, where to "play a role" in order to avoid alienating a potential husband. When Beth in *Small Changes* rebelled against her husband and fought the idea of tying herself down with a child, it was the other women in her family who urged her to submit and at least give the *appearance* of accepting the role expected of her.[18]

In fact, dissembling in order to conform to social preconceptions has been a frequent theme of women's socialization. As Mirra Komarovsky has demonstrated, college women in the 1940's were taught to hide their real ability in order to make their male friends feel superior. "My mother thinks that it is very nice to be smart in college," one of Komarovsky's students noted, "but only if it doesn't take too much effort. She always tells me not to be too intellectual on dates, to be clever in a light sort of way." It is not difficult to imagine one woman saying to another as Griggs said to Richard Wright, "When you are around white people [men] you have to act the part that they expect you to act." Even if deception was the goal, however, the underlying fact was that members of the "oppressed" group acted as accomplices in perpetuating the status quo.[19]

Basic to the entire system, of course, has been the extent to which a clearly defined role was "woven into the texture of things." For blacks the crucial moment might come as soon as they developed an awareness of whites. In the case of women, it more likely took place at puberty when the need to begin pleasing potential husbands was emphasized.

The core of this process has been the use of a visible, physical characteristic as the basis for assigning to each group a network of duties, responsibilities, and attributes. It is the physical foundation for discriminatory treatment which makes the process of social control on sex and race distinctive from that which has applied to other oppressed groups. Class, for example, comes closest to sex and race as a source of massive social inequity and injustice. Yet in an American context, class has been difficult to isolate as an organizing principle. Because class is not associated with a visible physical characteristic and many working class people persist in identifying with a middle-class life-style, class is not a category easy to identify in terms of physical or psychological control. (The very tendency to abjure class consciousness in favor of a social mobility ethic, of course, is its own form of psychological control.) Ethnicity too has frequently served as a basis for oppression, but the ease with which members of most ethnic minorities have been able to "pass" into the dominant culture has made the structure of social control in those cases both porous and complicated. Thus although in almost every instance invidious treatment has involved the use of some form of physical, economic, psychological, or internal controls, the combinations have been different and the exceptions frequent.

The analogy of sex and race is distinctive, therefore, precisely to the extent that it highlights in pure form the process of social control which has operated to maintain the existing structure of American society. While many have been victimized by the same types of control, only in the case of sex and race—where physical attributes are ineradicable—have these controls functioned systematically and clearly to define from birth the possibilities to which members of a group might aspire. Perhaps for that reason sex and race have been cornerstones of the social system, and the source of values and attitudes which have both reinforced the power of the dominant class and provided a weapon for dividing potential opposition.

NOTES

1. Richard Wright, *Black Boy* (New York, 1937), pp. 48, 52, 150, 157. Quotations used by permission of the publishers Harper and Row, New York.

2. Wright, pp. 65, 150–51.

3. Wright, p. 159.

4. Wright, p. 164.

5. Wright, pp. 127–29.

6. Wright, pp. 139–40.

7. Wright, pp. 147, 153–55, 160–61.

8. Wright, pp. 68–71, 200.

9. Wright, p. 175.

10. Wright, p. 72.

11. Wright, p. 148.

12. Wright, pp. 150–51; Susan Brownmiller, *Against Our Will* (New York, 1975); Jerome Kagan and H. A. Moss, *Birth to Maturity* (New York, 1962).

13. Carl Degler, "Introduction," *The History of Women* (Oxford, 1975).

14. Sinclair Lewis, *Main Street* (New York, 1920), pp. 74, 167; Marge Piercy, *Small Changes* (Greenwich, Conn., 1972), p. 33.

15. Louis P. Harlan, *Booker T. Washington 1856–1901* (New York, 1972); Ralph Ellison, *Invisible Man* (New York, 1952); Eleanor Flexner, *Century of Struggle* (Cambridge, Mass., 1959), p. 33; and Dara DeHaven, "On Educating Women—The Co-ordinate Ideal at Trinity and Duke University," Master's thesis, Duke University, 1974.

16. Piercy, *Small Changes*, pp. 19–20, 29, 40–41; Lewis, *Main Street*, pp. 14–15, 86, 283.

17. Judith Bardwick and Elizabeth Donovan, "Ambivalence: The Socialization of Women" in *Women in Sexist Society: Studies in Power and Powerlessness*, eds. Barbara Moran and Vivian Gornick (New York, 1971); Wright, *Black Boy*, pp. 207–13.

18. Piercy, *Small Changes*, pp. 31, 34, 316–17.

19. Piercy, pp. 30–31, 34, 39; Mirra Komarovsky, "Cultural Contradictions and Sex Roles," *American Journal of Sociology* 52 (November 1946).

10

MASKED RACISM
Reflections on the Prison Industrial Complex

Angela Davis

Imprisonment has become the response of first resort to far too many of the social problems that burden people who are ensconced in poverty. These problems often are veiled by being conveniently grouped together under the category "crime" and by the automatic attribution of criminal behavior to people of color. Homelessness, unemployment, drug addiction, mental illness, and illiteracy are only a few of the problems that disappear from public view when the human beings contending with them are relegated to cages.

Prisons thus perform a feat of magic. Or rather the people who continually vote in new prison bonds and tacitly assent to a proliferating network of prisons and jails have been tricked into believing in the magic of imprisonment. But prisons do not disappear problems, they disappear human beings. And the practice of disappearing vast numbers of people from poor, immigrant, and racially marginalized communities has literally become big business.

The seeming effortlessness of magic always conceals an enormous amount of behind-the-scenes work. When prisons disappear human beings in order to convey the illusion of solving social problems, penal infrastructures must be created to accommodate a rapidly swelling population of caged people. Goods and services must be provided to keep imprisoned populations alive. Sometimes these populations must be kept busy and at other times—particularly in repressive super-maximum prisons and in INS detention centers—they must be deprived of virtually all meaningful activity. Vast numbers of handcuffed and shackled people are moved across state borders as they are transferred from one state or federal prison to another.

All this work, which used to be the primary province of government, is now also performed by private corporations, whose links to government in the field of what is euphemistically called "corrections" resonate dangerously with the military industrial complex. The dividends that accrue from investment in the punishment industry, like those that accrue from investment in weapons production, only amount to social destruction. Taking into account the structural similarities and profitability of business–government linkages in the realms of military production

From *Colorlines* (Fall, 1998).

and public punishment, the expanding penal system can now be characterized as a "prison industrial complex."

The Color of Imprisonment

Almost two million people are currently locked up in the immense network of U.S. prisons and jails. More than 70 percent of the imprisoned population are people of color. It is rarely acknowledged that the fastest growing group of prisoners are black women and that Native American prisoners are the largest group per capita. Approximately five million people—including those on probation and parole—are directly under the surveillance of the criminal justice system.

Three decades ago, the imprisoned population was approximately one-eighth its current size. While women still constitute a relatively small percentage of people behind bars, today the number of incarcerated women in California alone is almost twice what the nationwide women's prison population was in 1970. According to Elliott Currie, "[t]he prison has become a looming presence in our society to an extent unparalleled in our history—or that of any other industrial democracy. Short of major wars, mass incarceration has been the most thoroughly implemented government social program of our time."

To deliver up bodies destined for profitable punishment, the political economy of prisons relies on racialized assumptions of criminality—such as images of black welfare mothers reproducing criminal children—and on racist practices in arrest, conviction, and sentencing patterns. Colored bodies constitute the main human raw material in this vast experiment to disappear the major social problems of our time. Once the aura of magic is stripped away from the imprisonment solution, what is revealed is racism, class bias, and the parasitic seduction of capitalist profit. The prison industrial system materially and morally impoverishes its inhabitants and devours the social wealth needed to address the very problems that have led to spiraling numbers of prisoners.

As prisons take up more and more space on the social landscape, other government programs that have previously sought to respond to social needs—such as Temporary Assistance to Needy Families—are being squeezed out of existence. The deterioration of public education, including prioritizing discipline and security over learning in public schools located in poor communities, is directly related to the prison "solution."

Profiting from Prisoners

As prisons proliferate in U.S. society, private capital has become enmeshed in the punishment industry. And precisely because of their profit potential, prisons are becoming increasingly important to the U.S. economy. If the notion of punishment as a source of potentially stupendous profits is disturbing by itself, then the strategic dependence on racist structures and ideologies to render mass punishment palatable and profitable is even more troubling.

Prison privatization is the most obvious instance of capital's current movement toward the prison industry. While government-run prisons are often in gross violation of international human rights standards, private prisons are even less accountable. In March of this year, the Corrections Corporation of America (CCA), the largest U.S. private prison company, claimed 54,944 beds in 68 facilities under contract or development in the U.S., Puerto Rico, the United Kingdom, and Australia. Following the global trend of subjecting more women to public punishment, CCA recently opened a women's prison outside Melbourne. The company recently identified California as its "new frontier."

Wackenhut Corrections Corporation (WCC), the second largest U.S. prison company, claimed contracts and awards to manage 46 facilities in North America, U.K., and Australia. It boasts a total of 30,424 beds as well as contracts for prisoner health care services, transportation, and security.

Currently, the stocks of both CCA and WCC are doing extremely well. Between 1996 and 1997, CCA's revenues increased by 58 percent, from $293 million to $462 million. Its net profit grew from $30.9 million to $53.9 million. WCC raised its revenues from $138 million in 1996 to $210 million in 1997. Unlike public correctional facilities, the vast profits of these private facilities rely on the employment of non-union labor.

The Prison Industrial Complex

But private prison companies are only the most visible component of the increasing corporatization of punishment. Government contracts to build prisons have bolstered the construction industry. The architectural community has identified prison design as a major new niche. Technology developed for the military by companies like Westinghouse are being marketed for use in law enforcement and punishment.

Moreover, corporations that appear to be far removed from the business of punishment are intimately involved in the expansion of the prison industrial complex. Prison construction bonds are one of the many sources of profitable investment for leading financiers such as Merrill Lynch. MCI charges prisoners and their families outrageous prices for the precious telephone calls which are often the only contact prisoners have with the free world.

Many corporations whose products we consume on a daily basis have learned that prison labor power can be as profitable as third world labor power exploited by U.S.-based global corporations. Both relegate formerly unionized workers to joblessness and many even wind up in prison. Some of the companies that use prison labor are IBM, Motorola, Compaq, Texas Instruments, Honeywell, Microsoft, and Boeing. But it is not only the hi-tech industries that reap the profits of prison labor. Nordstrom department stores sell jeans that are marketed as "Prison Blues," as well as t-shirts and jackets made in Oregon prisons. The advertising slogan for these clothes is "made on the inside to be worn on the outside." Maryland prisoners inspect glass bottles and jars used by Revlon and Pierre Cardin, and schools throughout the world buy graduation caps and gowns made by South Carolina prisoners.

"For private business," write Eve Goldberg and Linda Evans (a political prisoner inside the Federal Correctional Institution at Dublin, California) "prison labor is like a pot of gold. No strikes. No union organizing. No health benefits, unemployment insurance, or workers' compensation to pay. No language barriers, as in foreign countries. New leviathan prisons are being built on thousands of eerie acres of factories inside the walls. Prisoners do data entry for Chevron, make telephone reservations for TWA, raise hogs, shovel manure, make circuit boards, limousines, waterbeds, and lingerie for Victoria's Secret—all at a fraction of the cost of 'free labor.' "

Devouring the Social Wealth

Although prison labor—which ultimately is compensated at a rate far below the minimum wage—is hugely profitable for the private companies that use it, the penal system as a whole does not produce wealth. It devours the social wealth that could be used to subsidize housing for the homeless, to ameliorate public education for poor and racially marginalized communities, to open free drug rehabilitation programs for people who wish to kick their habits, to create a national health care system, to expand programs to combat HIV, to eradicate domestic abuse— and, in the process, to create well-paying jobs for the unemployed.

Since 1984 more than twenty new prisons have opened in California, while only one new campus was added to the California State University system and none to the University of California system. In 1996–97, higher education received only 8.7 percent of the State's General Fund while corrections received 9.6 percent. Now that affirmative action has been declared illegal in California, it is obvious that education is increasingly reserved for certain people, while prisons are reserved for others. Five times as many black men are presently in prison as in four year colleges and universities. This new segregation has dangerous implications for the entire country.

By segregating people labeled as criminals, prison simultaneously fortifies and conceals the structural racism of the U.S. economy. Claims of low unemployment rates—even in black communities—make sense only if one assumes that the vast numbers of people in prison have really disappeared and thus have no legitimate claims to jobs. The numbers of black and Latino men currently incarcerated amount to two percent of the male labor force. According to criminologist David Downes, "[t]reating incarceration as a type of hidden unemployment may raise the jobless rate for men by about one-third, to 8 percent. The effect on the black labor force is greater still, raising the [black] male unemployment rate from 11 percent to 19 percent."

Hidden Agenda

Mass incarceration is not a solution to unemployment, nor is it a solution to the vast array of social problems that are hidden away in a rapidly growing network of prisons and jails. However, the great majority of people have been tricked into believing in the efficacy of imprisonment, even though the historical record clearly demonstrates that prisons do not work. Racism has undermined our ability to create a popular critical discourse to contest the ideological trickery that posits imprisonment as key to public safety. The focus of state policy is rapidly shifting from social welfare to social control.

Black, Latino, Native American, and many Asian youth are portrayed as the purveyors of violence, traffickers of drugs, and as envious of commodities that they have no right to possess. Young black and Latina women are represented as sexually promiscuous and as indiscriminately propagating babies and poverty. Criminality and deviance are racialized. Surveillance is thus focused on communities of color, immigrants, the unemployed, the undereducated, the homeless, and in general on those who have a diminishing claim to social resources. Their claim to social resources continues to diminish in large part because law enforcement and penal measures increasingly devour these resources. The prison industrial complex has thus created a vicious cycle of punishment which only further impoverishes those whose impoverishment is supposedly "solved" by imprisonment.

Therefore, as the emphasis of government policy shifts from social welfare to crime control, racism sinks more deeply into the economic and ideological structures of U.S. society. Meanwhile, conservative crusaders against affirmative action and bilingual education proclaim the end of racism, while their opponents suggest that racism's remnants can be dispelled through dialogue and conversation. But conversations about "race relations" will hardly dismantle a prison industrial complex that thrives on and nourishes the racism hidden within the deep structures of our society.

The emergence of a U.S. prison industrial complex within a context of cascading conservatism marks a new historical moment, whose dangers are unprecedented. But so are its opportunities. Considering the impressive number of grassroots projects that continue to resist the expansion of the punishment industry, it ought to be possible to bring these efforts together to create radical and nationally visible movements that can legitimize anti-capitalist critiques of the prison industrial complex. It ought to be possible to build movements in defense of prisoners' human rights and movements that persuasively argue that what we need is not new prisons, but new health care, housing, education, drug programs, jobs, and education. To safeguard a democratic future, it is possible and necessary to weave together the many and increasing strands of resistance to the prison industrial complex into a powerful movement for social transformation.

11

BLAMING THE VICTIM

William Ryan

Twenty years ago, Zero Mostel used to do a sketch in which he impersonated a Dixiecrat Senator conducting an investigation of the origins of World War II. At the climax of the sketch, the Senator boomed out, in an excruciating mixture of triumph and suspicion, "What was Pearl Harbor *doing* in the Pacific?" This is an extreme example of Blaming the Victim.

Twenty years ago, we could laugh at Zero Mostel's caricature. In recent years, however, the same process has been going on every day in the arena of social problems, public health, anti-poverty programs, and social welfare. A philosopher might analyze this process and prove that, technically, it is comic. But it is hardly ever funny.

Consider some victims. One is the miseducated child in the slum school. He is blamed for his own miseducation. He is said to contain within himself the causes of his inability to read and write well. The shorthand phrase is "cultural deprivation," which, to those in the know, conveys what they allege to be inside information: that the poor child carries a scanty pack of cultural baggage as he enters school. He doesn't know about books and magazines and newspapers, they say. (No books in the home; the mother fails to subscribe to *Readers' Digest.*) They say that if he talks at all—an unlikely event since slum parents don't talk to their children— he certainly doesn't talk correctly. (Lower-class dialect spoken here, or even—God forbid!—Southern Negro.) *(Ici on parle nigra.)* If you can manage to get him to sit in a chair, they say, he squirms and looks out the window. (Impulse-ridden, these kids, motoric rather than verbal.) In a word he is "disadvantaged" and "socially deprived," they say, and this, of course, accounts for his failure (*his* failure, they say) to learn much in school.

Note the similarity to the logic of Zero Mostel's Dixiecrat Senator. What is the culturally deprived child *doing* in the school? What is wrong with the victim? In pursuing this logic, no one remembers to ask questions about the collapsing buildings and torn textbooks, the frightened, insensitive teachers, the six additional desks in the room, the blustering, frightened principals, the relentless segregation, the callous administrator, the irrelevant curriculum, the bigoted or cowardly members of the school board, the insulting history book, the stingy taxpayers, the fairy-tale readers, or the self-serving faculty of the local teachers' college. We are encouraged to confine our attention to the child and to dwell on all his alleged defects. Cultural deprivation becomes an omnibus explanation for the educational disaster area known as the inner-city school. This is Blaming the Victim.

Pointing to the supposedly deviant Negro family as the "fundamental weakness of the Negro community" is another way to blame the victim. Like "cultural deprivation," "Negro family" has become a shorthand phrase with stereotyped connotations of matriarchy, fatherlessness, and pervasive illegitimacy. Growing up in the "crumbling" Negro family is supposed to account for most of the racial evils in America. Insiders have the word, of course, and know that this phrase is supposed to evoke images of growing up with a long-absent or never-present father (replaced from time to time perhaps by a series of transient lovers) and with bossy women ruling the roost, so that the children are irreparably damaged. This refers particularly to the poor, bewildered male children, whose psyches are fatally wounded and who are never, alas, to learn the trick of becoming upright, downright, forthright all-American boys. Is it any wonder the Negroes cannot achieve equality? From such families! And, again, by focusing our attention on the Negro family as the apparent *cause* of racial inequality, our eye is diverted. Racism, discrimination, segregation, and the powerlessness of the ghetto are subtly, but thoroughly, downgraded in importance.

The generic process of Blaming the Victim is applied to almost every American problem. The miserable health care of the poor is explained away on the grounds that the victim has poor motivation and lacks health information. The problems of slum housing are traced to the characteristics of tenants who are labeled as "Southern rural migrants" not yet "acculturated" to life in the big city. The "multiproblem" poor, it is claimed, suffer the psychological effects of impoverishment, the "culture of poverty," and the deviant value system of the lower classes; consequently, though unwittingly, they cause their own troubles. From such a viewpoint, the obvious fact that poverty is primarily an absence of money is easily overlooked or set aside.

The growing number of families receiving welfare are fallaciously linked together with the increased number of illegitimate children as twin results of promiscuity and sexual abandon among members of the lower orders. Every important social problem—crime, mental illness, civil disorder, unemployment—has been analyzed within the framework of the victim-blaming ideology. . . .

I have been listening to the victim-blamers and pondering their thought processes for a number of years. That process is often very subtle. Victim-blaming is cloaked in kindness and concern, and bears all the trappings and statistical furbelows of scientism; it is obscured by a perfumed haze of humanitarianism. In observing the process of Blaming the Victim, one tends to be confused and disoriented because those who practice this art display a deep concern for the victims that is quite genuine. In this way, the new ideology is very different from the open prejudice and reactionary tactics of the old days. Its adherents include sympathetic social scientists with social consciences in good working order, and liberal politicians with a genuine commitment to reform. They are very careful to dissociate themselves from vulgar Calvinism or crude racism; they indignantly condemn any notions of innate wickedness or genetic defect. "The Negro is *not born* inferior," they shout apoplectically. "Force of circumstance," they explain in reasonable tones, "has *made* him inferior." And they dismiss with self-righteous contempt any claims that the poor man in America is plainly unworthy or shiftless or enamored of idleness. No, they say, he is "caught in the cycle of poverty." He is trained to be poor by his culture and his family life, endowed by his environment (perhaps by his ignorant mother's outdated style of toilet training) with those unfortunately unpleasant characteristics that make him ineligible for a passport into the affluent society.

Blaming the Victim is, of course, quite different from old-fashioned conservative ideologies. The latter simply dismissed victims as inferior, genetically defective, or morally unfit; the emphasis is on the intrinsic, even hereditary, defect. The former shifts its emphasis to the environmental causation. The old-fashioned conservative could hold firmly to the belief that the oppressed and the victimized were born that way—"that way" being defective or inadequate in character or ability. The new ideology attributes defect and inadequacy to the malignant nature of poverty, injustice, slum life, and racial difficulties. The stigma that marks the victim and accounts for his victimization is an acquired stigma, a stigma of social, rather than genetic, origin. But the stigma, the defect, the fatal difference—though derived in the past from environmental forces—is still located *within* the victim, inside his skin. With such an elegant formulation, the humanitarian can have it both ways. He can, all at the same time, concentrate his charitable interest on the defects of the victim, condemn the vague social and environmental stresses that produced the defect (some time ago), and ignore the continuing effect of victimizing social forces (right now). It is a brilliant ideology for justifying a perverse form of social action designed to change, not society, as one might expect, but rather society's victim.

As a result, there is a terrifying sameness in the programs that arise from this kind of analysis. In education, we have programs of "compensatory education" to build up the skills and attitudes of the ghetto child, rather than structural changes in the schools. In race relations, we have social engineers who think up ways of "strengthening" the Negro family, rather than methods of eradicating racism. In health care, we develop new programs to provide health information (to correct the supposed ignorance of the poor) and to reach out and discover cases of untreated illness and disability (to compensate for their supposed unwillingness to seek treatment). Meanwhile, the gross inequities of our medical care delivery systems are left completely unchanged. As we might expect, the logical outcome of analyzing social problems in terms of the deficiencies of the victim is the development of programs aimed at correcting those deficiencies. The formula for action becomes extraordinarily simple: change the victim.

All of this happens so smoothly that it seems downright rational. First, identify a social problem. Second, study those affected by the problem and discover in what ways they are different from the rest of us as a consequence of deprivation and injustice. Third, define the differences as the cause of the social problem itself. Finally, of course, assign a government bureaucrat to invent a humanitarian action program to correct the differences.

Now no one in his right mind would quarrel with the assertion that social problems are present in abundance and are readily identifiable. God knows it is true that when hundreds of thousands of poor children drop out of school—or even graduate from school—they are barely literate. After spending some ten thousand hours in the company of professional educators, these children appear to have learned very little. The fact of failure in their education is undisputed. And the racial situation in America is usually acknowledged to be a number one item on the nation's agenda. Despite years of marches, commissions, judicial decisions, and endless legislative remedies, we are confronted with unchanging or even widening racial differences in achievement. In addition, despite our assertions that Americans get the best health care in the world, the poor stubbornly remain unhealthy. They lose more work because of illness, have more carious teeth, lose more babies as a result of both miscarriage and infant death, and die considerably younger than the well-to-do.

The problems are there, and there in great quantities. They make us uneasy. Added together, these disturbing signs reflect inequality and a puzzlingly high level of unalleviated distress in America totally inconsistent with our proclaimed ideals and our enormous wealth. This thread—this rope—of inconsistency stands out so visibly in the fabric of American life, that it is jarring to the eye. And this must be explained, to the satisfaction of our conscience as well as our patriotism. Blaming the Victim is an ideal, almost painless, evasion.

The second step in applying this explanation is to look sympathetically at those who "have" the problem in question, to separate them out and define them in some way as a special group, a group that is *different* from the population in general. This is a crucial and essential step in the process, for that difference is in itself hampering and maladaptive. The Different Ones are seen as less competent, less skilled, less knowing—in short, less human. The ancient Greeks deduced from a single characteristic, a difference in language, that the barbarians—that is, the "babblers" who spoke a strange tongue—were wild, uncivilized, dangerous, rapacious, uneducated, lawless, and, indeed, scarcely more than animals. Automatically labeling strangers as savages, weird and inhuman creatures (thus explaining difference by exaggerating difference) not infrequently justifies mistreatment, enslavement, or even extermination of the Different Ones.

Blaming the Victim depends on a very similar process of identification (carried out, to be sure, in the most kindly, philanthropic, and intellectual manner) whereby the victim of social problems is identified as strange, different—in other words, as a barbarian, a savage. Discovering savages, then, is an essential component of, and prerequisite to, Blaming the Victim, and the art of Savage Discovery is a core skill that must be acquired by all aspiring Victim Blamers. They must learn how to demonstrate that the poor, the black, the ill, the jobless, the slum tenants, are different and strange. They must learn to conduct or interpret the research that shows how "these people" think in different forms, act in different patterns, cling to different values, seek different goals, and learn different truths. Which is to say that they are strangers, barbarians, savages. This is how the distressed and disinherited are redefined in order to make it possible for us to look at society's problems and to attribute their causation to the individuals affected. . . .

Blaming the Victim can take its place in a long series of American ideologies that have rationalized cruelty and injustice.

Slavery, for example, was justified—even praised—on the basis of a complex ideology that showed quite conclusively how useful slavery was to society and how uplifting it was for the slaves.[1] Eminent physicians could be relied upon to provide the biological justification for slavery since after all, they said, the slaves were a separate species—as, for example, cattle are a separate species. No one in his right mind would dream of freeing the cows and fighting to abolish the ownership of cattle. In the view of the average American of 1825, it was important to preserve slavery, not simply because it was in accord with his own group interests (he was not fully aware of that), but because reason and logic showed clearly to the reasonable and intelligent man that slavery was good. In order to persuade a good and moral man to *do* evil, then, it is not necessary first to persuade him to *become* evil. It is only necessary to teach him that he is doing good. No one, in the words of a legendary newspaperman, thinks of himself as a son of a bitch.

In late-nineteenth-century America there flowered another ideology of injustice that seemed rational and just to the decent, progressive person. But Richard Hofstadter's analysis of the phenomenon of Social Darwinism[2] shows clearly its functional role in the preservation of the *status quo*. One can scarcely imagine a better fit than the one between this ideology and the purposes and actions of the robber barons, who descended like piranha fish on the America of this era and picked its bones clean. Their extraordinarily unethical operations netted them not only hundreds of millions of dollars but also, perversely, the adoration of the nation. Behavior that would be, in any more rational land (including today's America), more than enough to have landed them all in jail, was praised as the very model of a captain of modern industry. And the philosophy that justified their thievery was such that John D. Rockefeller could actually stand up and preach it in church. Listen as he speaks in, of all places, Sunday school: "The growth of a large business is merely a survival of the fittest. . . . The American Beauty rose can be produced in the splendor and fragrance which bring cheer to its beholder only by sacrificing the early buds which grow up around it. This is not an evil tendency in business. It is merely the working-out of a law of nature and a law of God."[3]

This was the core of the gospel, adapted analogically from Darwin's writings on evolution. Herbert Spencer and, later, William Graham Sumner and other beginners in the social sciences considered Darwin's work to be directly applicable to social processes: ultimately as a guarantee that life was progressing toward perfection but, in the short run, as a justification for an absolutely uncontrolled laissez-faire economic system. The central concepts of "survival of the fittest," "natural selection," and "gradualism" were exalted in Rockefeller's preaching to the status of laws of God and Nature. Not only did this ideology justify the criminal rapacity of those who rose to the top of the industrial heap, defining them automatically as naturally superior (this was bad enough), but at the same time it also required that those at the bottom of the heap be labeled as patently *unfit*—a label based solely on their position in society. According to the law of natural selection, they should be, in Spencer's judgment, eliminated. "The whole effort of nature is to get rid of such, to clear the world of them and make room for better."

For a generation, Social Darwinism was the orthodox doctrine in the social sciences, such as they were at that time. Opponents of this ideology were shut out of respectable intellectual life. The philosophy that enabled John D. Rockefeller to justify himself self-righteously in front of a class of Sunday school children was not the product of an academic quack or a marginal crackpot philosopher. It came directly from the lectures and books of leading intellectual figures of the time, occupants of professorial chairs at Harvard and Yale. Such is the power of an ideology that so neatly fits the needs of the dominant interests of society.

If one is to think about ideologies in America in 1970, one must be prepared to consider the possibility that a body of ideas that might seem almost self-evident is, in fact, highly distorted and highly selective; one must allow that the inclusion of a specific formulation in every freshman sociology text does not guarantee that the particular formulation represents abstract Truth rather than group interest. It is important not to delude ourselves into thinking that ideological monstrosities were constructed by monsters. They were not; they are not. They are developed through a process that shows every sign of being valid scholarship, complete with tables of numbers, copious footnotes, and scientific terminology. Ideologies are quite often academically and socially respectable and in many instances hold positions of exclusive validity, so that disagreement is considered unrespectable or radical and risks being labeled as irresponsible, unenlightened, or trashy.

Blaming the Victim holds such a position. It is central in the mainstream of contemporary American social thought, and its ideas pervade our most crucial assumptions so thoroughly that they are hardly noticed. Moreover, the fruits of this ideology appear to be fraught with altruism and humanitarianism, so it is hard to believe that it has principally functioned to block social change.

A major pharmaceutical manufacturer, as an act of humanitarian concern, has distributed copies of a large poster warning, "LEAD PAINT CAN KILL!" The poster, featuring a photograph of the face of a charming little girl, goes on to explain that if children *eat* lead paint, it can poison them, they can develop serious symptoms, suffer permanent brain damage, even die. The health department of a major American city has put out a coloring book that provides the same information. While the poster urges parents to prevent their children from eating paint, the coloring book is more vivid. It labels as neglectful and thoughtless the mother who does not keep her infant under constant surveillance to keep it from eating paint chips.

Now, no one would argue against the idea that it is important to spread knowledge about the danger of eating paint in order that parents might act to forestall their children from doing so. But to campaign against lead paint *only* in these terms is destructive and misleading and, in a sense, an effective way to support and agree with slum landlords—who define the problem of lead poisoning in precisely these terms.

This is an example of applying an exceptionalistic solution to a universalistic problem. It is not accurate to say that lead poisoning results from the actions of individual neglectful mothers. Rather, lead poisoning is a social phenomenon supported by a number of social mechanisms, one of the most tragic by-products of the systematic toleration of slum housing. In New Haven, which has the highest reported rate of lead poisoning in the country, several small children have died and many others have incurred irreparable brain damage as a result of eating peeling paint. In several cases, when the landlord failed to make repairs, poisonings have occurred time and again through a succession of tenancies. And the major reason for the landlord's neglect of this problem was that the city agency responsible for enforcing the housing code did nothing to make him correct this dangerous condition.

The cause of the poisoning is the lead in the paint on the walls of the apartment in which the children live. The presence of the lead is illegal. To use lead paint in a residence is illegal; to permit lead paint to be exposed in a residence is illegal. It is not only illegal, it is potentially criminal since the housing code does provide for criminal penalties. The general problem of lead poisoning, then, is more accurately analyzed as the result of a systematic program of lawbreaking by one interest group in the community, with the toleration and encouragement of the public authority charged with enforcing that law. To ignore these continued and repeated law violations, to ignore the fact that the supposed law enforcer actually cooperates in lawbreaking, and then to load a burden of guilt on the mother of a dead or dangerously ill child is an egregious distortion of reality. And to do so *under the guise* of public-spirited and humanitarian service to the community is intolerable.

But this is how Blaming the Victim works. The righteous humanitarian concern displayed by the drug company, with its poster, and the health department, with its coloring book, is a genuine concern, and this is a typical feature of Blaming the Victim. Also typical is the swerving away from the central target that requires systematic change and, instead, focusing in on the individual affected. The ultimate effect is always to distract attention from the basic causes and to leave the primary social injustice untouched. And, most telling, the proposed remedy for the problem is, of course, to work on the victim himself. Prescriptions for cure, as written by the Savage Discovery set, are invariably conceived to revamp and revise the victim, never to change the surrounding circumstances. They want to change his attitudes, alter his values, fill up his cultural deficits, energize his apathetic soul, cure his character defects, train him and polish him and woo him from his savage ways.

Isn't all of this more subtle and sophisticated than such old-fashioned ideologies as Social Darwinism? Doesn't the change from brutal ideas about survival of the fit (and the expiration of the unfit) to kindly concern about characterological defects (brought about by stigmas of social origin) seem like a substantial step forward? Hardly. It is only a substitution of terms. The old, reactionary exceptionalistic formulations are replaced by new progressive, humanitarian exceptionalistic formulations. In education, the outmoded and unacceptable concept of racial or class differences in basic inherited intellectual ability simply gives way to the new notion of cultural deprivation: there is very little functional difference between these two ideas. In taking a look at the phenomenon of poverty, the old concept of unfitness or idleness or laziness is replaced by the newfangled theory of the culture of poverty. In race relations, plain Negro inferiority—which was good enough for old-fashioned conservatives—is pushed aside by fancy conceits about the crumbling Negro family. With regard to illegitimacy, we are not so crass as to concern ourselves with immorality and vice, as in the old days; we settle benignly on the explanation of the "lower-class pattern of sexual behavior," which no one condemns as evil, but which is, in fact, simply a variation of the old explanatory idea. Mental illness is no longer defined as the result of hereditary taint or congenital character flaw; now we have new causal hypotheses regarding the ego-damaging emotional experiences that are supposed to be the inevitable consequence of the deplorable child-rearing practices of the poor.

In each case, of course, we are persuaded to ignore the obvious: the continued blatant discrimination against the Negro, the gross deprivation of contraceptive and adoption services to the poor, the heavy stresses endemic in the life of the poor. And almost all our make-believe liberal programs aimed at correcting our urban problems are off target; they are designed either to change the poor man or to cool him out.

We come finally to the question, Why? It is much easier to understand the process of Blaming the Victim as a way of thinking than it is to understand the motivation for it. Why do Victim Blamers, who are usually good people, blame the victim? The development and application of this ideology, and of all the mythologies associated with Savage Discovery, are readily exposed by careful analysis as hostile acts—one is almost tempted to say acts of war—directed against the disadvantaged, the distressed, the disinherited. It is class warfare in reverse. Yet those who are most fascinated and enchanted by this ideology tend to be progressive, humanitarian, and, in the best sense of the word, charitable persons. They would usually define themselves as moderates or liberals. Why do they pursue this dreadful war against the poor and the oppressed?

Put briefly, the answer can be formulated best in psychological terms—or, at least, I, as a psychologist, am more comfortable with such a formulation. The highly charged psychological problem confronting this hypothetical progressive, charitable person I am talking about is that of reconciling his own self-interest with the promptings of his humanitarian impulses. This psychological process of reconciliation is not worked out in a logical, rational, conscious way; it is a process that takes place far below the level of sharp consciousness, and the solution—Blaming the Victim—is arrived at subconsciously as a compromise that apparently satisfies both his self-interest and his charitable concerns. Let me elaborate.

First, the question of self-interest or, more accurately, class interest. The typical Victim Blamer is a middle-class person who is doing reasonably well in a material way; he has a good job, a good income, a good house, a good car. Basically, he likes the social system pretty much the way it is, at least in broad outline. He likes the two-party political system, though he may be highly skilled in finding a thousand minor flaws in its functioning. He heartily approves of the profit motive as the propelling engine of the economic system despite his awareness that there are abuses of that system, negative side effects, and substantial residual inequalities.

On the other hand, he is acutely aware of poverty, racial discrimination, exploitation, and deprivation, and, moreover, he wants to do something concrete to ameliorate the condition of the poor, the black, and the disadvantaged. This is not an extraneous concern; it is central to his value system to insist on the worth of the individual, the equality of men, and the importance of justice.

What is to be done, then? What intellectual position can he take, and what line of action can he follow that will satisfy both of these important motivations? He quickly and self-consciously rejects two obvious alternatives, which he defines as "extremes." He cannot side with an openly reactionary, repressive position that accepts continued oppression and exploitation as the price of a privileged position for his own class. This is incompatible with his own morality and his basic political principles. He finds the extreme conservative position repugnant.

He is, if anything, more allergic to radicals, however, than he is to reactionaries. He rejects the "extreme" solution of radical social change, and this makes sense since such radical social change threatens his own well-being. A more equitable distribution of income might mean that he would have less—a smaller or older house, with fewer yews or no rhododendrons in the yard, a less enjoyable job, or, at the least, a somewhat smaller salary. If black children and poor children were, in fact, reasonably educated and began to get high S.A.T. scores, they would be competing with *his* children for the scarce places in the entering classes of Harvard, Columbia, Bennington, and Antioch.

So our potential Victim Blamers are in a dilemma. In the words of an old Yiddish proverb, they are trying to dance at two weddings. They are old friends of both brides and fond of both kinds of dancing, and they want to accept both invitations. They cannot bring themselves to attack the system that has been so good to them, but they want so badly to be helpful to the victims of racism and economic injustice.

Their solution is a brilliant compromise. They turn their attention to the victim in his post-victimized state. They want to bind up wounds, inject penicillin, administer morphine, and evacuate the wounded for rehabilitation. They explain what's wrong with the victim in terms of social experiences *in the past*, experiences that have left wounds, defects, paralysis, and disability. And they take the cure of these wounds and the reduction of these disabilities as the first order of business. They want to make the victims less vulnerable, send them back into battle with better weapons, thicker armor, a higher level of morale.

In order to do so effectively, of course, they must analyze the victims carefully, dispassionately, objectively, scientifically, empathetically, mathematically, and hardheadedly, to see what made them so vulnerable in the first place.

What weapons, now, might they have lacked when they went into battle? Job skills? Education?

What armor was lacking that might have warded off their wounds? Better values? Habits of thrift and foresight?

And what might have ravaged their morale? Apathy? Ignorance? Deviant lower-class cultural patterns?

This is the solution of the dilemma, the solution of Blaming the Victim. And those who buy this solution with a sigh of relief are inevitably blinding themselves to the basic causes of the problems being addressed. They are, most crucially, rejecting the possibility of blaming, not the victims, but themselves. They are all unconsciously passing judgments on themselves and bringing in a unanimous verdict of Not Guilty.

If one comes to believe that the culture of poverty produces persons *fated* to be poor, who can find any fault with our corporation-dominated economy? And if the Negro family produces young men *incapable* of achieving equality, let's deal with that first before we go on to the task of changing the pervasive racism that informs and shapes and distorts our every social institution. And if unsatisfactory resolution of one's Oedipus complex accounts for all emotional distress and mental disorder, then by all means let us attend to that and postpone worrying about the pounding day-to-day stresses of life on the bottom rungs that drive so many to drink, dope, and madness.

That is the ideology of Blaming the Victim, the cunning Art of Savage Discovery. The tragic, frightening truth is that it is a mythology that is winning over the best people of our time, the very people who must resist this ideological temptation if we are to achieve nonviolent change in America.

NOTES

1. For a good review of this general ideology, see I. A. Newby, *Jim Crow's Defense* (Baton Rouge: Louisiana State University Press, 1965).

2. Richard Hofstadter, *Social Darwinism in American Thought* (revised ed.; Boston: Beacon Press, 1955).

3. William J. Ghent, *Our Benevolent Feudalism* (New York: The Macmillan Co., 1902), p. 29.

Suggestions for Further Reading

Cole, David. *No Equal Justice: Race and Class in the American Criminal Justice System.* New York: The New Press, 1999.

Fraser, Steve, and Gary Gerstle. *Ruling America: A History of Wealth and Power in a Democracy.* Cambridge: Harvard University Press, 2005.

Goings, Kenneth W. *Mammy and Uncle Mose: Black Collectibles and American Stereotyping.* Bloomington: Indiana University Press, 1994.

Harding, S., and M. B. Hintikka. *Discovering Reality: Feminist Perspectives on Epistemology, Metaphysics, Methodology, and Philosophy of Science,* 2nd ed. New York: Springer, 2007.

Harvey, David. *Spaces of Global Capitalism: A Theory of Uneven Geographical Development.* New York: Verso, 2006.

Holtzman, Linda. *Media Messages: What Film, Television, and Popular Music Teach Us about Race, Class, Gender, and Sexual Orientation.* Armonk, NY: M. E. Sharp, 2000.

hooks, bell. *Teaching to Transgress: Education as the Practice of Freedom.* New York: Routledge, 1994.

Kuttner, Robert. *Obama's Challenge: America's Economic Crisis and the Power of a Transformative Presidency.* White River Jct., VT: Chelsea Green Publishing, 2008.

Lewis, Amanda E. *Race in the Schoolyard.* New Brunswick, NJ: Rutgers University Press, 2003.

Loewen, James. *Lies My Teacher Told Me,* Rev. ed. New York: New Press, 2008.

Madrick, Jeff. *The Case of Big Government.* Princeton, NJ: Princeton University Press, 2008.

Mazzocco, Dennis W. *Networks of Power: Corporate TV's Threat to Democracy.* Boston: South End Press, 1999.

Orenstein, Peggy. *School Girls.* New York: Doubleday, 1994.

Parenti, Michael. *Inventing Reality,* 2nd ed. New York: St. Martin's Press, 1992.

Sadker, Myra, and David Sadker. *Failing at Fairness: How America's Schools Cheat Girls.* New York: Scribners, 1994.

Schor, Juliet B., *Born to Buy: The Commercialized Child and the New Consumer Culture.* New York: Scribners, 2004.

Silliman, Jane, and Anannya Bhattacharjee. *Policing the National Body: Race, Gender, and Criminalization.* Boston: South End Press, 2002.

Smith, Andrea. *Conquest: Sexual Violence and American Indian Genocide.* Cambridge: South End Press, 2005.

Spender, D. *Man Made Language,* 2nd ed. Boston: Routledge and Kegan Paul, 1985.

Thompson, Becky W. *A Hunger So Wide and So Deep,* 2nd ed. Minneapolis: University of Minnesota Press, 1996.

Yates, Michael D. *More Unequal: Aspects of Class in the United States.* New York: Monthly Review Press, 2007.

PART IX

Social Change: Revisioning the Future and Making a Difference

A n adequate understanding of the nature and causes of race, class, and gender oppression is a critical first step toward moving beyond them. Solutions to problems are generated, at least in part, by the way we pose them. That is why so much of this book is devoted to defining and analyzing the nature of these systems of oppression. Only when we appreciate the subtle and complex factors that operate together to create a society in which wealth, privilege, and opportunity are unequally divided will we be able to formulate viable proposals for bringing about social change.

What, then, have the selections in this book told us about racism, sexism, heterosexism, and class divisions? First, that there is no single cause. Eliminating these forms of oppression will involve changes at the personal, social, political, and economic levels. It will require us to think differently about ourselves and others and see the world through new lenses and using new categories. We will have to learn to pay close attention to our attitudes and behavior and ask what values and what kinds of relationships are being created and maintained, both consciously and unconsciously, by them. We will have to reevaluate virtually every institution in society and critically appraise the ways in which those institutions, intentionally or unintentionally, privilege some and disadvantage others in the course of what we take to be their normal course of operations. As we identify the ways in which our society reproduces the forms of inequality and privilege that we have been studying, we will have to act to change them. In short, we must scrutinize every aspect of economic, political, and social life with a view to asking whose interests are served and whose are denied when the world is organized in this way.

In Selection 1, poet and writer Audre Lorde suggests that we will need to begin by redefining and rethinking the meaning of difference. While acknowledging that real differences of race, age, and sexuality exist, Lorde argues that it is not these differences in themselves that separate us as much as it is our refusal to acknowledge them and the role they play in shaping our relationships and social institutions. Denying or distorting those differences keeps us apart but embracing these differences can provide a new starting point from which to work together to reconstruct our world.

In Selection 2, bell hooks joins Audre Lorde in urging us to rethink difference. At the same time, she continues another of the major projects of this book, understanding the ways in which sex, race, and class function as interlocking, mutually supportive systems of domination. While acknowledging past failures of much feminist theory to adequately address issues of race, sexism, and class, hooks argues that a revisioned feminism can provide the most comprehensive perspective from which to challenge all forms of oppression and domination. This is true, she maintains, because sexism is the form of oppression we confront daily: "Sexism directly shapes and determines relations of power in our private lives, in familiar social spaces, in that most intimate context—home—and in that most intimate sphere of relations—family." hooks envisions a process of education and consciousness-raising whereby women from diverse backgrounds come together in small groups to talk about feminism and to learn from each other, but she calls on men as well to commit themselves to overthrowing patriarchal domination.

Cooper Thompson picks up the challenge in Selection 3. A new vision of society will require new choices and options for men as well as women. In his essay, Thompson is profoundly critical of the ways in which boys are socialized to believe that violence is an acceptable, "even desirable," way to establish their manhood and to negotiate differences. He believes that this socialization leads to both misogyny and homophobia and makes it difficult for men to form warm and loving friendships with members of both sexes. Because the social costs of prevailing conceptions of masculinity are so high, Thompson urges us to develop a new vision of manhood, one that allows boys to claim many of the qualities previously defined as "feminine." Thompson concludes with a warning: "The survival of our society may rest on the degree to which we are able to teach men to cherish life."

Confronted by the enormity of the work to be done, many of us feel overwhelmed and disheartened when we think about how we can act to bring about change. But significant and lasting change in our society will only come about when each of us assumes responsibility for making a difference. In Selection 4, Andrea Ayvazian suggests that one way to overcome a sense of immobilization and despair is to become an ally of those who are oppressed. According to Ayvazian, "an ally is a member of a dominant group in our society who works to dismantle any form of oppression from which she or he receives the benefit." By acting consciously and deliberately to challenge oppression and to make privilege visible, allies provide role models for us all and demonstrate ways in which each of us can act as powerful agents of change.

The next three articles, all new to this section, provide concrete examples of people working together to bring about change. Their stories are interesting and inspiring and make it clear that thinking creatively about how to change our system is an exciting and important way to make a real difference.

In Selection 8, "Rethinking Volunteerism in America," Gavin Leonard cautions us that seeking to provide help to oppressed or disadvantaged groups is not without some serious pitfalls and urges us to function as allies offering our solidarity rather than as disengaged individuals who merely provide charity. Charity, according to Leonard, amounts to providing help without regard for the individual's or group's own sense of what they need or the form in which they wish to receive it, so charity can often appear to be patronizing or condescending. Solidarity, on the other hand, involves working with people to arrive at an understanding of what kind of help would be useful to them and what kinds of ends are desirable. It takes time and commitment. If you are involved in a service-learning experience at your institution or plan to be, I think you will find the points in this essay particularly worth thinking about.

This part of the book and our study ends with a plea from William Rivers Pitt (written as a Thanksgiving op-ed), who asks us to "Here. Now. Do Something."

1

AGE, RACE, CLASS, AND SEX
Women Redefining Difference

Audre Lorde

Much of Western European history conditions us to see human differences in simplistic oppression to each other: dominant/subordinate, good/bad, up/down, supe-
rior/inferior. In a society where the good is defined in terms of profit rather than
in terms of human need, there must always be some group of people who, through
systematized oppression, can be made to feel surplus, to occupy the place of the
dehumanized inferior. Within this society, that group is made up of Black and
Third World people, working-class people, older people, and women.

As a forty-nine-year-old Black lesbian feminist socialist mother of two, including one boy, and a member of an interracial couple, I usually find myself a part of
some group defined as other, deviant, inferior, or just plain wrong. Traditionally,
in american society, it is the members of oppressed, objectified groups who are expected to stretch out and bridge the gap between the actualities of our lives and
the consciousness of our oppressor. For in order to survive, those of us for whom
oppression is as american as apple pie have always had to be watchers, to become
familiar with the language and manners of the oppressor, even sometimes adopting them for some illusion of protection. Whenever the need for some pretense of
communication arises, those who profit from our oppression call upon us to share
our knowledge with them. In other words, it is the responsibility of the oppressed
to teach the oppressors their mistakes. I am responsible for educating teachers who
dismiss my children's culture in school. Black and Third World people are expected to educate white people as to our humanity. Women are expected to educate men. Lesbians and gay men are expected to educate the heterosexual world.
The oppressors maintain their position and evade responsibility for their own actions. There is a constant drain of energy which might be better used in redefining ourselves and devising realistic scenarios for altering the present and
constructing the future.

Paper delivered at the Copeland Colloquium, Amherst College, April 1980. Reprinted with
permission from *Sister Outsider* by Audre Lorde. Copyright 1984 by Audre Lorde, The Crossing
Press, a division of Ten Speed Press, Berkeley, CA. www.tenspeed.com

Institutionalized rejection of difference is an absolute necessity in a profit economy which needs outsiders as surplus people. As members of such an economy, we have *all* been programmed to respond to the human differences between us with fear and loathing and to handle that difference in one of three ways: ignore it, and if that is not possible, copy it if we think it is dominant, or destroy it if we think it is subordinate. But we have no patterns for relating across our human differences as equals. As a result, those differences have been misnamed and misused in the service of separation and confusion.

Certainly there are very real differences between us of race, age, and sex. But it is not those differences between us that are separating us. It is rather our refusal to recognize those differences, and to examine the distortions which result from our misnaming them and their effects upon human behavior and expectation.

Racism, the belief in the inherent superiority of one race over all others and thereby the right to dominance. Sexism, the belief in the inherent superiority of one sex over the other and thereby the right to dominance. Ageism. Heterosexism. Elitism, Classism.

It is a lifetime pursuit for each one of us to extract these distortions from our living at the same time as we recognize, reclaim, and define those differences upon which they are imposed. For we have all been raised in a society where those distortions were endemic within our living. Too often, we pour the energy needed for recognizing and exploring difference into pretending those differences are insurmountable barriers, or that they do not exist at all. This results in a voluntary isolation, or false and treacherous connections. Either way, we do not develop tools for using human difference as a springboard for creative change within our lives. We speak not of human difference, but of human deviance.

Somewhere, on the edge of consciousness, there is what I call a *mythical norm*, which each one of us within our hearts knows "that is not me." In america, this norm is usually defined as white, thin, male, young, heterosexual, christian, and financially secure. It is with this mythical norm that the trappings of power reside within society. Those of us who stand outside that power often identify one way in which we are different, and we assume that to be the primary cause of all oppression, forgetting other distortions around difference, some of which we ourselves may be practicing. By and large within the women's movement today, white women focus upon their oppression as women and ignore differences of race, sexual preference, class, and age. There is a pretense to a homogeneity of experience covered by the word *sisterhood* that does not in fact exist.

Unacknowledged class differences rob women of each others' energy and creative insight. Recently a women's magazine collective made the decision for one issue to print only prose, saying poetry was a less "rigorous" or "serious" art form. Yet even the form our creativity takes is often a class issue. Of all the art forms, poetry is the most economical. It is the one which is the most secret, which requires the least physical labor, the least material, and the one which can be done between shifts, in the hospital pantry, on the subway, and on scraps of surplus paper. Over the last few years, writing a novel on tight finances, I came to appreciate the enormous differences in the material demands between poetry and prose. As we reclaim our literature, poetry has been the major voice of poor, working class, and Colored women. A room of one's own may be a necessity for writing prose, but so are reams of paper, a typewriter, and plenty of time. The actual requirements to produce the visual arts also help determine, along class lines, whose art is whose. In this day of inflated prices for material, who are our sculptors, our painters, our photographers? When we speak of broadly based women's culture, we need to be aware of the effect of class and economic differences on the supplies available for producing art.

As we move toward creating a society within which we can each flourish, ageism is another distortion of relationship which interferes with our vision. By ignoring the past, we are encouraged to repeat its mistakes. The "generation gap" is an important social tool for any repressive society. If the younger members of a community view the older members as contemptible or suspect or excess, they will never be able to join hands and examine the living memories of the community, nor ask the all important question, "Why?" This gives rise to a historical amnesia that keeps us working to invent the wheel every time we have to go to the store for bread.

We find ourselves having to repeat and relearn the same old lessons over and over that our mothers did because we do not pass on what we have learned, or because we are unable to listen. For instance, how many times has this all been said before? For another, who would have believed that once again our daughters are allowing their bodies to be hampered and purgatoried by girdles and high heels and hobble skirts?

Ignoring the differences of race between women and the implications of those differences presents the most serious threat to the mobilization of women's joint power.

As white women ignore their built-in privilege of whiteness and define woman in terms of their own experience alone, then women of Color become "other," the outsider whose experience and tradition is too "alien" to comprehend. An example of this is the signal absence of the experience of women of Color as a resource for women's studies courses. The literature of women of Color is seldom included in women's literature courses and almost never in other literature courses, nor in women's studies as a whole. All too often, the excuse given is that the literatures of women of Color can only be taught by Colored women, or that they are too difficult to understand, or that classes cannot "get into" them because they come out of experiences that are "too different." I have heard this argument presented by white women of otherwise quite clear intelligence, women who seem to have no trouble at all teaching and reviewing work that comes out of the vastly different experiences of Shakespeare, Molière, Dostoyefsky, and Aristophanes. Surely there must be some other explanation.

This is a very complex question, but I believe one of the reasons white women have such difficulty reading Black women's work is because of their reluctance to see Black women as women and different from themselves. To examine Black women's literature effectively requires that we be seen as whole people in our actual complexities—as individuals, as women, as human—rather than as one of those problematic but familiar stereotypes provided in this society in place of genuine images of Black women. And I believe this holds true for the literatures of other women of Color who are not Black.

The literatures of all women of Color recreate the textures of our lives, and many white women are heavily invested in ignoring the real differences. For as long as any difference between us means one of us must be inferior, then the recognition of any difference must be fraught with guilt. To allow women of Color to step out of stereotypes is too guilt provoking, for it threatens the complacency of those women who view oppression only in terms of sex.

Refusing to recognize difference makes it impossible to see the different problems and pitfalls facing us as women.

Thus, in a patriarchal power system where whiteskin privilege is a major prop, the entrapments used to neutralize Black women and white women are not the same. For example, it is easy for Black women to be used by the power structure against Black men, not because they are men, but because they are Black. Therefore, for Black women, it is necessary at all times to separate the needs of the oppressor from our own legitimate conflicts within our communities. This same problem does not exist for white women. Black women and men have shared racist oppression and still share it, although in different ways. Out of that shared oppression we have developed joint defenses and joint vulnerabilities to each other that are not duplicated in the white community, with the exception of the relationship between Jewish women and Jewish men.

On the other hand, white women face the pitfall of being seduced into joining the oppressor under the pretense of sharing power. This possibility does not exist in the same way for women of Color. The tokenism that is sometimes extended to us is not an invitation to join power; our racial "otherness" is a visible reality that makes that quite clear. For white women there is a wider range of pretended choices and rewards for identifying with patriarchal power and its tools.

Today, with the defeat of ERA, the tightening economy, and increased conservatism, it is easier once again for white women to believe the dangerous fantasy that if you are good enough, pretty enough, sweet enough, quiet enough, teach the children to behave, hate the right people, and marry the right men, then you will be allowed to co-exist with patriarchy in the relative peace, at least until a man needs your job or the neighborhood rapist happens along. And true, unless one lives and loves in the trenches it is difficult to remember that the war against dehumanization is ceaseless.

But Black women and our children know the fabric of our lives is stitched with violence and with hatred, that there is no rest. We do not deal with it only on the picket lines, or in dark midnight alleys, or in the places where we dare to verbalize our resistance. For us, increasingly, violence weaves through the daily tissues of our living—in the supermarket, in the classroom, in the elevator, in the clinic and the schoolyard, from the plumber, the baker, the saleswoman, the bus driver, the bank teller, the waitress who does not serve us.

Some problems we share as women, some we do not. You fear your children will grow up to join the patriarchy and testify against you, we fear our children will be dragged from a car and shot down in the street, and you will turn your backs upon the reasons they are dying.

The threat of difference has been no less blinding to people of Color. Those of us who are Black must see that the reality of our lives and our struggle does not make us immune to the errors of ignoring and misnaming difference. Within Black communities where racism is a living reality, differences among us often seem dangerous and suspect. The need for unity is often misnamed as a need for homogeneity, and a Black feminist vision mistaken for betrayal of our common interests as a people. Because of the continuous battle against racial erasure that Black women and Black men share, some Black women still refuse to recognize that we are also oppressed as women, and that sexual hostility against Black women is practiced not only by the white racist society, but implemented within our Black communities as well. It is a disease striking the heart of Black nationhood, and silence will not make it disappear. Exacerbated by racism and the pressures of powerlessness, violence against Black women and children often becomes a standard within tour communities, one by which manliness can be measured. But these woman-hating acts are rarely discussed as crimes against Black women.

As a group, women of Color are the lowest paid wage earners in america. We are the primary targets of abortion and sterilization abuse, here and abroad. In certain parts of Africa, small girls are still being sewed shut between their legs to keep them docile and for men's pleasure. This is known as female circumcision, and it is not a cultural affair as the late Jomo Kenyatta insisted, it is a crime against Black women.

Black women's literature is full of the pain of frequent assault, not only by a racist patriarchy, but also by Black men. Yet the necessity for and history of shared battle have made us, Black women, particularly vulnerable to the false accusation that anti-sexist is anti-Black. Meanwhile, womanhating as a recourse of the powerless is sapping strength from Black communities, and our very lives. Rape is on the increase, reported and unreported, and rape is not aggressive sexuality, it is sexualized aggression. As Kalamu ya Salaam, a Black male writer, points out, "As long as male domination exists, rape will exist. Only women revolting and men made conscious of their responsibility to fight sexism can collectively stop rape."[1]

Differences between ourselves as Black women are also being misnamed and used to separate us from one another. As a Black lesbian feminist comfortable with the many different ingredients of my identity, and a woman committed to racial and sexual freedom from oppression, I find I am constantly being encouraged to pluck out some one aspect of myself and present this as the meaningful whole, eclipsing or denying the other parts of self. But this is a destructive and fragmenting way to live. My fullest concentration of energy is available to me only when I integrate all the parts of who I am, openly, allowing power from particular sources of my living to flow back and forth freely through all my different selves, without the restrictions of externally imposed definition. Only then can I bring myself and my energies as a whole to the service of those struggles which I embrace as part of my living.

A fear of lesbians, or of being accused of being a lesbian, has led many Black women into testifying against themselves. It has led some of us into destructive alliances, and others into despair and isolation. In the white women's communities, heterosexism is sometimes a result of identifying with the white patriarchy, a rejection of that interdependence between women-identified women which allows the self to be, rather than to be used in the service of men. Sometimes it reflects a diehard belief in the protective coloration of heterosexual relationships, sometimes a self-hate which all women have to fight against, taught us from birth.

Although elements of these attitudes exist for all women, there are particular resonances of heterosexism and homophobia among Black women. Despite the fact that woman-bonding has a long and honorable history in the African and African-american communities, and despite the knowledge and accomplishments of many strong and creative women-identified Black women in the political, social and cultural fields, heterosexual Black women often tend to ignore or discount the existence and work of Black lesbians. Part of this attitude has come from an understandable terror of Black male attack within the close confines of Black society, where the punishment for any female self-assertion is still to be accused of being a lesbian and therefore unworthy of the attention or support of the scarce Black male. But part of this need to misname and ignore Black lesbians comes from a very real fear that openly women-identified Black women who are no longer dependent upon men for their self-definition may well reorder our whole concept of social relationships.

Black women who once insisted that lesbianism was a white woman's problem now insist that Black lesbians are a threat to Black nationhood, are consorting with the enemy, are basically un-Black. These accusations, coming from the very women to whom we look for deep and real understanding, have served to keep many Black lesbians in hiding, caught between the racism of white women and the homophobia of their sisters. Often, their work has been ignored, trivialized, or misnamed, as with the work of Angelina Grimke, Alice Dunbar-Nelson, Lorraine Hansberry. Yet women-bonded women have always been some part of the power of Black communities, from our unmarried aunts to the amazons of Dahomey.

And it is certainly not Black lesbians who are assaulting women and raping children and grandmothers on the streets of our communities.

Across this country, as in Boston during the spring of 1979 following the unsolved murders of twelve Black women, Black lesbians are spearheading movements against violence against Black women.

What are the particular details within each of our lives that can be scrutinized and altered to help bring about change? How do we redefine difference for all women? It is not our differences which separate women, but our reluctance to recognize those differences and to deal effectively with the distortions which have resulted from the ignoring and misnaming of those differences.

As a tool of social control, women have been encouraged to recognize only one area of human difference as legitimate, those differences which exist between women and men. And we have learned to deal across those differences with the urgency of all oppressed subordinates. All of us have had to learn to live or work or coexist with men, from our fathers on. We have recognized and negotiated these differences, even when this recognition only continued the old dominant/subordinate mode of human relationship, where the oppressed must recognize the masters' difference in order to survive.

But our future survival is predicated upon our ability to relate within equality. As women, we must root our internalized patterns of oppression within ourselves if we are to move beyond the most superficial aspects of social change. Now we must recognize differences among women who are our equals, neither inferior nor superior, and devise ways to use each others' difference to enrich our visions and our joint struggles.

The future of our earth may depend upon the ability of all women to identify and develop new definitions of power and new patterns of relating across difference. The old definitions have not served us, nor the earth that supports us. The old patterns, no matter how cleverly rearranged to imitate progress, still condemn us to cosmetically altered repetitions of the same old exchanges, the same old guilt, hatred, recrimination, lamentation, and suspicion.

For we have, built into all of us, old blueprints of expectation and response, old structures of oppression, and these must be altered at the same time as we alter the living conditions which are a result of those structures. For the master's tools will never dismantle the master's house.

As Paulo Freire shows so well in *The Pedagogy of the Oppressed*,[2] the true focus of revolutionary change is never merely the oppressive situations which we seek to escape, but that piece of the oppressor which is planted deep within each of us, and which knows only the oppressor's tactics, the oppressors' relationships.

Change means growth, and growth can be painful. But we sharpen self-definition by exposing the self in work and struggle together with those whom we define as different from ourselves, although sharing the same goals. For Black and white, old and young, lesbian and heterosexual women alike, this can mean new paths to our survival.

We have chosen each other
and the edge of each others battles
the war is the same
if we lose
someday women's blood will congeal
upon a dead planet

if we win
there is no telling
we seek beyond history
for a new and more possible meaning.[3]

NOTES

1. From "Rape: A Radical Analysis, An African-American Perspective" by Kalamu ya Salaam in *Black Books Bulletin*, vol. 6, no. 4 (1980).
2. Seabury Press, New York, 1970.
3. From "Outlines," unpublished poem.

2

FEMINISM
A Transformational Politic

bell hooks

We live in a world in crisis—a world governed by politics of domination, one in which the belief in a notion of superior and inferior, and its concomitant ideology—that the superior should rule over the inferior—affects the lives of all people everywhere, whether poor or privileged, literate or illiterate. Systematic dehumanization, worldwide famine, ecological devastation, industrial contamination, and the possibility of nuclear destruction are realities which remind us daily that we are in crisis. Contemporary feminist thinkers often cite sexual politics as the origin of this crisis. They point to the insistence on difference as that factor which becomes the occasion for separation and domination and suggest that differentiation of status between females and males globally is an indication that patriarchal domination of the planet is the root of the problem. Such an assumption has fostered the notion that elimination of sexist oppression would necessarily lead to the eradication of all forms of domination. It is an argument that has led influential Western white women to feel that feminist movement should be *the* central political agenda for females globally. Ideologically, thinking in this direction enables Western women, especially privileged white women, to suggest that racism and class exploitation are merely the offspring of the parent system: patriarchy. Within feminist movement in the West, this has led to the assumption that resisting patriarchal domination is a more legitimate feminist action than resisting racism and other forms of domination. Such thinking prevails despite radical critiques made by black women and other women of color who question this proposition. To speculate that an oppositional division between men and women existed in early human communities is to impose on the past, on these non-white groups, a world view that fits all too neatly within contemporary feminist paradigms that name man as the enemy and woman as the victim.

Clearly, differentiation between strong and weak, powerful and powerless, has been a central defining aspect of gender globally, carrying with it the assumption that men should have greater authority than women, and should rule over them. As significant and important as this fact is, it should not obscure the reality that women can and do participate in politics of domination, as perpetrators as well as victims—that we dominate, that we are dominated. If focus on patriarchal domination masks this reality or becomes the means by which women deflect attention from the real conditions and circumstances of our lives, then women cooperate in suppressing and promoting false consciousness, inhibiting our capacity to assume responsibility for transforming ourselves and society.

Thinking speculatively about early human social arrangement, about women and men struggling to survive in small communities, it is likely that the parent–child relationship with its very real imposed survival structure of dependency, of strong and weak, of powerful and powerless, was a site for the construction of a paradigm of domination. While this circumstance of dependency is not necessarily one that leads to domination, it lends itself to the enactment of a social drama wherein domination could easily occur as a means of exercising and maintaining control. This speculation does not place women outside the practice of domination, in the exclusive role of victim. It centrally names women as agents of domination, as potential theoreticians, and creators of a paradigm for social relationships wherein those groups of individuals designated as "strong" exercise power both benevolently and coercively over those designated as "weak."

Emphasizing paradigms of domination that call attention to woman's capacity to dominate is one way to deconstruct and challenge the simplistic notion that man is the enemy, woman the victim; the notion that men have always been the oppressors. Such thinking enables us to examine our role as women in the perpetuation and maintenance of systems of domination. To understand domination, we must understand that our capacity as women and men to be either dominated or dominating is a point of connection, of commonality. Even though I speak from the particular experience of living as a black woman in the United States, a white-supremacist, capitalist, patriarchal society, where small numbers of white men (and honorary "white men") constitute ruling groups, I understand that in many places in the world oppressed and oppressor share the same color. I understand that right here in this room, oppressed and oppressor share the same gender. Right now as I speak, a man who is himself victimized, wounded, hurt by racism and class exploitation is actively dominating a woman in his life—that even as I speak, women who are ourselves exploited, victimized, are dominating children. It is necessary for us to remember, as we think critically about domination, that we all have the capacity to act in ways that oppress, dominate, wound (whether or not that power is institutionalized). It is necessary to remember that it is first the potential oppressor within that we must resist—the potential victim within that we must rescue—otherwise we cannot hope for an end to domination, for liberation.

This knowledge seems especially important at this historical moment when black women and other women of color have worked to create awareness of the ways in which racism empowers white women to act as exploiters and oppressors. Increasingly this fact is considered a reason we should not support feminist struggle even though sexism and sexist oppression is a real issue in our lives as black women (see, for example, Vivian Gordon's *Black Women, Feminism, Black Liberation: Which Way?*). It becomes necessary for us to speak continually about the convictions that inform our continued advocacy of feminist struggle. By calling attention to interlocking systems of domination—sex, race, and class—black women and many other groups of women acknowledge the diversity and complexity of female experience, of our relationship to power and domination. The intent is not to dissuade people of color from becoming engaged in feminist movement. Feminist struggle to end patriarchal domination should be of primary importance to women and men globally not because it is the foundation of all other oppressive structure but because it is that form of domination we are most likely to encounter in an ongoing way in everyday life.

Unlike other forms of domination, sexism directly shapes and determines relations of power in our private lives, in familiar social spaces, in that most intimate context—home—and in that most intimate sphere of relations—family. Usually, it is within the family that we witness coercive domination and learn to accept it, whether it be domination of parent over child, or male over female. Even though family relations may be, and most often are, informed by acceptance of a politic of domination, they are simultaneously relations of care and connection. It is this convergence of two contradictory impulses—the urge to promote growth and the urge to inhibit growth—that provides a practical setting for feminist critique, resistance, and transformation.

Growing up in a black, working-class, father-dominated household, I experienced coercive adult male authority as more immediately threatening, as more likely to cause immediate pain than racist oppression or class exploitation. It was equally clear that experiencing exploitation and oppression in the home made one feel all the more powerless when encountering dominating forces outside the home. This is true for many people. If we are unable to resist and end domination in relations where there is care, it seems totally unimaginable that we can resist and end it in other institutionalized relations of power. If we cannot convince the mothers and/or fathers who care not to humiliate and degrade us, how can we imagine convincing or resisting an employer, a lover, a stranger who systematically humiliates and degrades?

Feminist effort to end patriarchal domination should be of primary concern precisely because it insists on the eradication of exploitation and oppression in the family context and in all other intimate relationships. It is that political movement which most radically addresses the person—the personal—citing the need for transformation of self, of relationships, so that we might be better able to act in a revolutionary manner, challenging and resisting domination, transforming the world outside the self. Strategically, feminist movement should be a central component of all other liberation struggles because it challenges each of us to alter our person, our personal engagement (either as victims or perpetrators or both) in a system of domination.

Feminism, as liberation struggle, must exist apart from and as a part of the larger struggle to eradicate domination in all its forms. We must understand that patriarchal domination shares an ideological foundation with racism and other forms of group oppression, that there is no hope that it can be eradicated while these systems remain intact. This knowledge should consistently inform the direction of feminist theory and practice. Unfortunately, racism and class elitism among women has frequently led to the suppression and distortion of this connection so that it is now necessary for feminist thinkers to critique and revise much feminist theory and the direction of feminist movement. This effort at revision is perhaps most evident in the current widespread acknowledgement that sexism, racism, and class exploitation constitute interlocking systems of domination—that sex, race, and class, and not sex alone, determine the nature of any female's identity, status, and circumstance, the degree to which she will or will not be dominated, the extent to which she will have the power to dominate.

While acknowledgement of the complex nature of woman's status (which has been most impressed upon everyone's consciousness by radical women of color) is a significant corrective, it is only a starting point. It provides a frame of reference which must serve as the basis for thoroughly altering and revising feminist theory and practice. It challenges and calls us to re-think popular assumptions about the nature of feminism that have had the deepest impact on a large majority of women, on mass consciousness. It radically calls into question the notion of a fundamentally common female experience which has been seen as the prerequisite for our coming together, for political unity. Recognition of the inter-connectedness of sex, race, and class highlights the diversity of experience, compelling redefinition of the terms of unity. If women do not share "common oppression," what then can serve as a basis for our coming together?

Unlike many feminist comrades, I believe women and men must share a common understanding—a basic knowledge of what feminism is—if it is ever to be a powerful mass-based political movement. In *Feminist Theory: From Margin to Center*, I suggest that defining feminism broadly as "a movement to end sexism and sexist oppression" would enable us to have a common political goal. We would then have a basis on which to build solidarity. Multiple and contradictory definitions of feminism create confusion and undermine the effort to construct feminist movement so that it addresses everyone. Sharing a common goal does not imply that women and men will not have radically divergent perspectives on how that goal might be reached. Because each individual starts the process of engagement in feminist struggle at a unique level of awareness, very real differences in experience, perspective, and knowledge make developing varied strategies for participation and transformation a necessary agenda.

Feminist thinkers engaged in radically revisioning central tenets of feminist thought must continually emphasize the importance of sex, race, and class as factors which *together* determine the social construction of femaleness, as it has been so deeply ingrained in the consciousness of many women active in feminist movement that gender is the sole factor determining destiny. However, the work of education for critical consciousness (usually called consciousness-raising) cannot end there. Much feminist consciousness-raising has in the past focused on identifying the particular ways men oppress and exploit women. Using the paradigm of sex, race, and class means that the focus does not begin with men and what they do to women, but rather with women working to identify both individually and collectively the specific character of our social identity.

Imagine a group of women from diverse backgrounds coming together to talk about feminism. First they concentrate on working out their status in terms of sex, race, and class using this as the standpoint from which they begin discussing patriarchy or their particular relations with individual men. Within the old frame of reference, a discussion might consist solely of talk about their experiences as victims in relationship to male oppressors. Two women—one poor, the other quite wealthy—might describe the process by which they have suffered physical abuse by male partners and find certain commonalities which might serve as a basis for bonding. Yet if these same two women engaged in a discussion of class, not only would the social construction and expression of femaleness differ, so too would their ideas about how to confront and change their circumstances. Broadening the discussion to include an analysis of race and class would expose many additional differences even as commonalities emerged.

Clearly the process of bonding would be more complex, yet this broader discussion might enable the sharing of perspectives and strategies for change that would enrich rather than diminish our understanding of gender. While feminists have increasingly given "lip service" to the idea of diversity, we have not developed strategies of communication and inclusion that allow for the successful enactment of this feminist vision.

Small groups are no longer the central place for feminist consciousness-raising. Much feminist education for critical consciousness takes place in Women's Studies classes or at conferences which focus on gender. Books are a primary source of education, which means that already masses of people who do not read have no access. The separation of grassroots ways of sharing feminist thinking across kitchen tables from the spheres where much of that thinking is generated, the academy, undermines feminist movement. It would further feminist movement if new feminist thinking could be once again shared in small group contexts, integrating critical analysis with discussion of personal experience. It would be useful to promote anew the small group setting as an arena for education for critical consciousness, so that women and men might come together in neighborhoods and communities to discuss feminist concerns.

Small groups remain an important place for education for critical consciousness for several reasons. An especially important aspect of the small group setting is the emphasis on communicating feminist thinking, feminist theory, in a manner that can be easily understood. In small groups, individuals do not need to be equally literate or literate at all because the information is primarily shared through conversation, in dialogue which is necessarily a liberatory expression. (Literacy should be a goal for feminists even as we ensure that it not become a requirement for participation in feminist education.) Reforming small groups would subvert the appropriation of feminist thinking by a select group of academic women and men, usually white, usually from privileged class backgrounds.

Small groups of people coming together to engage in feminist discussion, in dialectical struggle make a space where the "personal is political" as a starting point for education for critical consciousness can be extended to include politicization of the self that focusses on creating understanding of the ways sex, race, and class together determine our individual lot and our collective experience. It would further feminist movement if many well known feminist thinkers would participate in small groups, critically re-examining ways their works might be changed by incorporating broader perspectives. All efforts at self-transformation challenge us to engage in ongoing, critical self-examination and reflection about feminist practice, about how we live in the world. This individual commitment, when coupled with engagement in collective discussion, provides a space for critical feedback which strengthens our efforts to change and make ourselves new. It is in this commitment to feminist principles in our words and deeds that the hope of feminist revolution lies.

Working collectively to confront difference, to expand our awareness of sex, race, and class as interlocking systems of domination, of the ways we reinforce and perpetuate these structures, is the context to which we learn the true meaning of solidarity. It is this work that must be the foundation of feminist movement. Without it, we cannot effectively resist patriarchal domination; without it, we remain estranged and alienated from one another. Fear of painful confrontation often leads women and men active in feminist movement to avoid rigorous critical encounter, yet if we cannot engage dialectically in a committed, rigorous, humanizing manner, we cannot hope to change the world. True politicization—coming to critical consciousness—is a difficult, "trying" process, one that demands that we give up set ways of thinking and being, that we shift our paradigms, that we open ourselves to the unknown, the unfamiliar. Undergoing this process, we learn what it means to struggle and in this effort we experience the dignity and integrity of being that comes with revolutionary change. If we do not change our consciousness, we cannot change our actions or demand change from others.

Our renewed commitment to a rigorous process of education for critical consciousness will determine the shape and direction of future feminist movement.

Until new perspectives are created, we cannot be living symbols of the power of feminist thinking. Given the privileged lot of many leading feminist thinkers, both in terms of status, class, and race, it is harder these days to convince women of the primacy of this process of politicization. More and more, we seem to form select interest groups composed of individuals who share similar perspectives. This limits our capacity to engage in critical discussion. It is difficult to involve women in new processes of feminist politicization because so many of us think that identifying men as the enemy, resisting male domination, gaining equal access to power and privilege is the end of feminist movement. Not only is it not the end, it is not even the place we want revitalized feminist movement to begin. We want to begin as women seriously addressing ourselves, not solely in relation to men, but in relation to an entire structure of domination of which patriarchy is one part. While the struggle to eradicate sexism and sexist oppression is and should be the primary thrust of feminist movement, to prepare ourselves politically for this effort we must first learn how to be in solidarity, how to struggle with one another.

Only when we confront the realities of sex, race, and class, the ways they divide us, make us different, stand us in opposition, and work to reconcile and resolve these issues will we be able to participate in the making of feminist revolution, in the transformation of the world. Feminism, as Charlotte Bunch emphasizes again and again in *Passionate Politics*, is a transformational politics, a struggle against domination wherein the effort is to change ourselves as well as structures. Speaking about the struggle to confront difference, Bunch asserts:

> A crucial point of the process is understanding that reality does not look the same from different people's perspective. it is not surprising that one way feminists have come to understand about differences has been through the love of a person from another culture or race. It takes persistence and motivation—which love often engenders—to get beyond one's ethnocentric assumptions and really learn about other perspectives. In this process and while seeking to eliminate oppression, we also discover new possibilities and insights that come from the experience and survival of other peoples.

Embedded in the commitment to feminist revolution is the challenge to love. Love can be and is an important source of empowerment when we struggle to confront issues of sex, race, and class. Working together to identify and face our differences—to face the ways we dominate and are dominated—to change our actions, we need a mediating force that can sustain us so that we are not broken in this process, so that we do not despair.

Not enough feminist work has focussed on documenting and sharing ways individuals confront differences constructively and successfully. Women and men need to know what is on the other side of the pain experienced in politicization. We need detailed accounts of the ways our lives are fuller and richer as we change and grow politically, as we learn to live each moment as committed feminists, as comrades working to end domination. In reconceptualizing and reformulating strategies for future feminist movement, we need to concentrate on the politiciza-

tion of love, not just in the context of talking about victimization in intimate relationships, but in a critical discussion where love can be understood as a powerful
force that challenges and resists domination. As we work to be loving, to create a
culture that celebrates life, that makes love possible, we move against dehumanization, against domination. In *Pedagogy of the Oppressed*, Paulo Freire evokes this
power of love, declaring:

> I am more and more convinced that true revolutionaries must perceive the revolu-
> tion, because of its creative and liberating nature, as an act of love. For me, the revo-
> lution, which is not possible without a theory of revolution—and therefore science—is
> not irreconcilable with love . . . The distortion imposed on the word "love" by the
> capitalist world cannot prevent the revolution from being essentially loving in charac-
> ter, nor can it prevent the revolutionaries from affirming their love of life.

That aspect of feminist revolution that calls women to love womanness, that calls
men to resist dehumanizing concepts of masculinity, is an essential part of our
struggle. It is the process by which we move from seeing ourselves as objects to acting as subjects. When women and men understand that working to eradicate patriarchal domination is a struggle rooted in the longing to make a world where
everyone can live fully and freely, then we know our work to be a gesture of love.
Let us draw upon that love to heighten our awareness, deepen our compassion, in-
tensify our courage, and strengthen our commitment.

3

A NEW VISION OF MASCULINITY

Cooper Thompson

I was once asked by a teacher in a suburban high school to give a guest presentation on male roles. She hoped that I might help her deal with four boys who exercised extraordinary control over the other boys in the class. Using ridicule and
their status as physically imposing athletes, these four wrestlers had succeeded in
stifling the participation of the other boys, who were reluctant to make comments
in class discussions.

As a class we talked about the ways in which boys got status in that school and
how they got put down by others. I was told that the most humiliating put-down
was being called a "fag." The list of behaviors which could elicit ridicule filled two

From Franklin Abbot and Cooper Thompson, *New Men, New Minds.* Copyright © 1987 by Cooper
Thompson. Reprinted by permission of the author.

large chalkboards, and it was detailed and comprehensive; I got the sense that a boy in this school had to conform to rigid, narrow standards of masculinity to avoid being called a fag. I, too, felt this pressure and became very conscious of my mannerisms in front of the group. Partly from exasperation, I decided to test the seriousness of these assertions. Since one of the four boys had some streaks of pink in his shirt, and since he had told me that wearing pink was grounds for being called a fag, I told him that I thought he was a fag. Instead of laughing, he said, "I'm going to kill you."

Such is the stereotypic definition of strength that is associated with masculinity. But it is a very limited definition of strength, one based on dominance and control and acquired through the humiliation and degradation of others.

Contrast this with a view of strength offered by Pam McAllister in her introduction to *Reweaving the Web of Life*:

> The "Strength" card in my Tarot deck depicts, not a warrior going off to battle with his armor and his mighty sword, but a woman stroking a lion. The woman has not slain the lion nor maced it, not netted it, nor has she put on it a muzzle or a leash. And though the lion clearly has teeth and long sharp claws, the woman is not hiding, nor has she sought a protector, nor has she grown muscles. She doesn't appear to be talking to the lion nor flattering it, nor tossing it fresh meat to distract its hungry jaws.
>
> The woman on the "Strength" card wears a flowing white dress and a garland of flowers. With one hand she cups the lion's jaws, with the other she caresses its nose. The lion on the card has big yellow eyes and a long red tongue curling out of its mouth. One paw is lifted and the mane falls in thick red curls across its broad torso. The woman. The lion. Together they depict strength.

This image of strength stands in direct contrast to the strength embodied in the actions of the four wrestlers. The collective strength of the woman and the lion is a strength unknown in a system of traditional male values. Other human qualities are equally foreign to a traditional conception of masculinity. In workshops I've offered on the male role stereotype, teachers and other school personnel easily generate lists of attitudes and behaviors which boys typically seem to not learn. Included in this list are being supportive and nurturant, accepting one's vulnerability and being able to ask for help, valuing women and "women's work," understanding and expressing emotions (except for anger), the ability to empathize with and empower other people, and learning to resolve conflict in nonagressive, noncompetitive ways.

Learning Violence

All of this should come as no surprise. Traditional definitions of masculinity include attributes such as independence, pride, resiliency, self-control, and physical strength. This is precisely the image of the Marlboro man, and to some extent, these are desirable attributes for boys and girls. But masculinity goes beyond these qualities to stress competitiveness, toughness, aggressiveness, and power. In this context, threats to one's status, however small, cannot be avoided or taken lightly. If a boy is called a fag, it means that he is perceived as weak or timid—and therefore not masculine enough for his peers. There is enormous pressure for him to fight back. Not being tough at these moments only proves the allegation.

Violence is learned not just as a way for boys to defend allegations that they are feminized, but as an effective, appropriate way for them to normally behave. In "The Civic Advocacy of Violence" [M., Spring 1982] Wayne Ewing clearly states:

> I used to think that we simply tolerated and permitted male abusiveness in our society. I have now come to understand rather, that we advocate physical violence. Violence is presented as effective. Violence is taught as the normal, appropriate and necessary behavior of power and control. Analyses which interweave advocacy of male violence with "SuperBowl Culture" have never been refuted. Civic expectations—translated into professionalism, financial commitments, city planning for recreational space, the raising of male children for competitive sport, the corporate ethics of business ownership of athletic teams, profiteering on entertainment—all result in the monument of the National Football League, symbol and reality at once of the advocacy of violence.

Ultimately, violence is the tool which maintains what I believe are the two most critical socializing forces in a boy's life: *homophobia*, the hatred of gay men (who are stereotyped as feminine) or those men believed to be gay, as well as the fear of being perceived as gay; and *misognyn*, the hatred of women. The two forces are targeted at different classes of victims, but they are really just the flip sides of the same coin. Homophobia is the hatred of feminine qualities in men while misogyny is the hatred of feminine qualities in women. The boy who is called a fag is the target of other boys' homophobia as well as the victim of his own homophobia. While the overt message is the absolute need to avoid being feminized, the implication is that females—and all that they traditionally represent—are contemptible. The United States Marines have a philosophy which conveniently combines homophobia and misogyny in the belief that "When you want to create a group of male killers, you kill 'the woman' in them."

The pressures of homophobia and misogyny in boys' lives have been poignantly demonstrated to me each time that I have repeated a simple yet provocative activity with students. I ask them to answer the question, "If you woke up tomorrow and discovered that you were the opposite sex from the one you are now, how would you and your life be different?" Girls consistently indicate that there are clear advantages to being a boy—from increased independence and career opportunities to decreased risks of physical and sexual assault—and eagerly answer the question. But boys often express disgust at this possibility and even refuse sometimes to answer the question. In her reports of a broad-based survey using this question, Alice Baumgartner reports the following responses are typical of boys: "If I were a girl,

I'd be stupid and weak as a string"; "I would have to wear makeup, cook, be a mother, and yuckky stuff like that"; "I would have to hate snakes. Everything would be miserable"; "If I were a girl, I'd kill myself."

The Costs of Masculinity

The costs associated with a traditional view of masculinity are enormous, and the damage occurs at both personal and societal levels. The belief that a boy should be tough (aggressive, competitive, and daring) can create emotional pain for him. While a few boys experience short-term success for their toughness, there is little security in the long run. Instead, it leads to a series of challenges which few, if any, boys ultimately win. There is no security in being at the top when so many other boys are competing for the same status. Toughness also leads to increased chances of stress, physical injury, and even early death. It is considered manly to take extreme physical risks and voluntarily engage in combative, hostile activities.

The flip side of toughness—nurturance—is not a quality perceived as masculine and thus not valued. Because of this boys and men experience a greater emotional distance from other people and few opportunities to participate in meaningful interpersonal relationships. Studies consistently show that fathers spend very small amounts of time interacting with their children. In addition, men report that they seldom have intimate relationships with other men, reflecting their homophobia. They are afraid of getting too close and don't know how to take down the walls that they have built between themselves.

As boys grow older and accept adult roles, the larger social costs of masculinity clearly emerge. Most women experience male resistance to an expansion of women's roles; one of the assumptions of traditional masculinity is the belief that women should be subordinate to men. The consequence is that men are often not willing to accept females as equal, competent partners in personal and professional settings. Whether the setting is a sexual relationship, the family, the streets, or the battlefield, men are continuously engaged in efforts to dominate. Statistics on child abuse consistently indicate that the vast majority of abusers are men, and that there is no "typical" abuser. Rape may be the fastest growing crime in the United States. And it is men, regardless of nationality, who provoke and sustain war. In short, traditional masculinity is life threatening.

New Socialization for Boys

Masculinity, like many other human traits, is determined by both biological and environmental factors. While some believe that biological factors are significant in shaping some masculine behavior, there is undeniable evidence that cultural and environmental factors are strong enough to override biological impulses. What is it, then, that we should be teaching boys about being a man in a modern world?

- Boys must learn to accept their vulnerability, learn to express a range of emotions such as fear and sadness, and learn to ask for help and support in appropriate situations.
- Boys must learn to be gentle, nurturant, cooperative and communicative, and in particular, learn nonviolent means of resolving conflicts.
- Boys must learn to accept those attitudes and behaviors which have traditionally been labeled feminine as necessary for full human development—thereby reducing homophobia and misogyny. This is tantamount to teaching boys to love other boys and girls.

Certain qualities like courage, physical strength, and independence, which are traditionally associated with masculinity, are indeed positive qualities for males, provided that they are not manifested in obsessive ways nor used to exploit or dominate others. It is not necessary to completely disregard or unlearn what is traditionally called masculine. I believe, however, that the three areas above are crucial for developing a broader view of masculinity, one which is healthier for all life.

These three areas are equally crucial for reducing aggressive, violent behavior among boys and men. Males must learn to cherish life for the sake of their *own* wholeness as human beings, not just *for* their children, friends, and lovers. If males were more nurturant, they would be less likely to hurt those they love.

Leonard Eron, writing in the *American Psychologist*, puts the issue of unlearning aggression and learning nurturance in clear-cut terms:

> Socialization is crucial in determining levels of aggression. No matter how aggression is measured or observed, as a group males always score higher than females. But this is not true for all girls. There are some girls who seem to have been socialized like boys who are just as aggressive as boys. Just as some females can learn to be aggressive, so males can learn *not* to be aggressive. If we want to reduce the level of aggression in society, we should also discourage boys from aggression very early on in life and reward them too for others' behaviors; in other words, we should socialize boys more like girls, and they should be encouraged to develop socially positive qualities such as tenderness, cooperation, and aesthetic appreciation. The level of individual aggression in society will be reduced only when male adolescents and young adults, as a result of socialization, subscribe to the same standards of behavior as have been traditionally encouraged for women.

Where will this change in socialization occur? In his first few years, most of a boy's learning about masculinity comes from the influences of parents, siblings and images of masculinity such as those found on television. Massive efforts will be needed to make changes here. But at older ages, school curriculum and the school environment provide powerful reinforcing images of traditional masculinity. This reinforcement occurs through a variety of channels, including curriculum content, role modeling, and extracurricular activities, especially competitive sports.

School athletics are a microcosm of the socialization of male values. While participation in competitive activities can be enjoyable and healthy, it too easily becomes a lesson in the need for toughness, invulnerability, and dominance. Athletes learn to ignore their own injuries and pain and instead try to injure and inflict pain on others in their attempts to win, regardless of the cost to themselves or their opponents. Yet the lessons learned in athletics are believed to be vital for full and complete masculine development, and as a model for problem-solving in other areas of life.

In addition to encouraging traditional male values, schools provide too few experiences in nurturance, cooperation, negotiation, nonviolent conflict resolution, and strategies for empathizing with and empowering others. Schools should become places where boys have the opportunity to learn these skills; clearly, they won't learn them on the street, from peers, or on television.

Setting New Examples

Despite the pressures on men to display their masculinity in traditional ways, there are examples of men and boys who are changing. "Fathering" is one example of a positive change. In recent years, there has been a popular emphasis on child-care activities, with men becoming more involved in providing care to children, both professionally and as fathers. This is a clear shift from the more traditional view that child rearing should be delegated to women and is not an appropriate activity for men.

For all of the male resistance it has generated, the Women's Liberation Movement has at least provided a stimulus for some men to accept women as equal partners in most areas of life. These are the men who have chosen to learn and grow from women's experiences and together with women are creating new norms for relationships. Popular literature and research on male sex roles is expanding, reflecting a wider interest in masculinity. Weekly news magazines such as *Time* and *Newsweek* have run major stories on the "new masculinity," suggesting that positive changes are taking place in the home and in the workplace. Small groups of men scattered around the country have organized against pornography, battering, and sexual assault. Finally there is the National Organization for Changing Men which has a pro-feminist, pro-gay, pro–"new man" agenda, and its ranks are slowly growing.

In schools where I have worked with teachers, they report that years of efforts to enhance educational opportunities for girls have also had some positive effects on boys. The boys seem more tolerant of girls' participation in coed sports activities and in traditionally male shops and courses. They seem to have a greater respect for the accomplishments of women through women's contributions to literature and history. Among elementary school aged males, the expression of vulnerable feelings is gaining acceptance. In general, however, there has been far too little attention paid to redirecting male role development.

Boys Will Be Boys

I think back to the four wrestlers and the stifling culture of masculinity in which they live. If schools were to radically alter this culture and substitute for it a new vision of masculinity, what would that look like? In this environment, boys would express a full range of behaviors and emotions without fear of being chastised. They would be permitted and encouraged to cry, to be afraid, to show joy, and to express love in a gentle fashion. Extreme concern for career goals would be replaced by a consideration of one's need for recreation, health, and meaningful work. Older boys would be encouraged to tutor and play with younger students. Moreover, boys would receive as much recognition for artistic talents as they do for athletics, and, in general, they would value leisure-time, recreational activities as highly as competitive sports.

In a system where maleness and femaleness were equally valued, boys might no longer feel that they have to "prove" themselves to other boys; they would simply accept the worth of each person and value those differences. Boys would realize that it is permissible to admit failure. In addition, they would seek out opportunities to learn from girls and women. Emotional support would be commonplace, and it would no longer be seen as just the role of the female to provide the support. Relationships between boys and girls would no longer be based on limited roles, but instead would become expressions of two individuals learning from and supporting one another. Relationships between boys would reflect their care for one another rather than their mutual fear and distrust.

Aggressive styles of resolving conflicts would be the exception rather than the norm. Girls would feel welcome in activities dominated by boys, knowing that they were safe from the threat of being sexually harassed. Boys would no longer boast of beating up another boy or of how much they "got off" of a girl the night before. In fact, the boys would be as outraged as the girls at rape or other violent crimes in the community. Finally, boys would become active in efforts to stop nuclear proliferation and all other forms of military violence, following the examples set by activist women.

The development of a new conception of masculinity based on this vision is an ambitious task, but one which is essential for the health and safety of both men and women. The survival of our society may rest on the degree to which we are able to teach men to cherish life.

4

INTERRUPTING THE CYCLE
OF OPPRESSION
The Role of Allies as Agents of Change

Andrea Ayvazian

Many of us feel overwhelmed when we consider the many forms of systemic oppression that are so pervasive in American society today. We become immobilized, uncertain about what actions we can take to interrupt the cycles of oppression and violence that intrude on our everyday lives. One way to overcome this sense of immobilization is to assume the role of an ally. Learning about this role—one that each and every one of us is capable of assuming—can offer us new ways of behaving and a new source of hope.

Through the years, experience has taught us that isolated and episodic actions—even dramatic, media-grabbing events—rarely produce more than a temporary blip on the screen. What does seem to create real and lasting change is highly-motivated individuals—usually only a handful at first—who are so clear and consistent on an issue that they serve as a heartbeat in a community, steadily sending out waves that touch and change those in their path. These change agents or allies have such a powerful impact because their actions embody the values they profess: their behavior and beliefs are congruent.

What Is an Ally?

An ally is a member of a dominant group in our society who works to dismantle any form of oppression from which she or he receives the benefit. Allied behavior means taking personal responsibility for the changes we know are needed in our society, and so often ignore or leave to others to deal with. Allied behavior is intentional, overt, consistent activity that challenges prevailing patterns of oppresion, makes privileges that are so often invisible visible, and facilitates the empowerment of persons targeted by oppression.

From *Fellowship* (January–February 1995). Reprinted with the permission of Rev. Dr. Andrea Ayvazian, Dean of Religious Life, Mount Holyoke College, South Hadley, MA 01075.

I use the term "oppression" to describe the combination of prejudice plus access to social, political, and economic power on the part of a dominant group. Racism, a core component of oppression, has been defined by David Wellman as a system of advantage based on race. Wellman's definition can be altered slightly to describe every other form of oppression. Hence we can say that sexism is a system of advantage based on gender, that heterosexism is a system of advantge based on sexual orientation, and so on. In each form of oppression there is a dominant group—the one that receives the unearned advantage, benefit, or privilege—and a targeted group— the one that is denied that advantage, benefit, or privilege. We know the litany of dominants: white people, males, Christians, heterosexuals, able-bodied people, those in their middle years, and those who are middle or upper class.

We also know that everyone has multiple social identities. We are all dominant and targeted simultaneously. I, for instance, am simultaneously dominant as a white person and targeted as a woman. A white able-bodied man may be dominant in those categories, but targeted as a Jew or Muslim or as a gay person. Some people are, at some point in their lives, entirely dominant; but if they are, they won't be forever. Even a white, able-bodied, heterosexual, Christian male will literally grow out of his total dominance if he reaches old age.

When we consider the different manifestations of systematic oppression and find ourselves in any of the categories where we are dominant—and therefore receive the unearned advantages that accrue to that position of advantage—we have the potential to be remarkably powerful agents of change as allies. Allies are whites who identify as anti-racists, men who work to dismantle sexism, able-bodied people who are active in the disability rights movement, Christians who combat anti-Semitism and other forms of religious prejudice. Allied behavior usually involves talking to other dominants about their behavior: whites confronting other whites on issues of racism, men organizing with other men to combat sexism, and so on. Allied behavior is clear action aimed at dismantling the oppression of others in areas where you yourself benefit—it is proactive, intentional, and often involves taking a risk.

To tether these principles to everyday reality, just think of the group Parents, Families and Friends of Lesbians and Gays (PFLAG) as the perfect example of allied behavior. PFLAG is an organization of (mainly) heterosexuals who organize support groups and engage in advocacy and education among other heterosexuals around issues of gay and lesbian liberation. PFLAG speakers can be heard in houses of worship, schools, and civic organizations discussing their own commitment to securing gay and lesbian civil rights. Because they are heterosexuals speaking (usually) to other heterosexuals, they often have a significant impact.

The anti-racism trainer Kenneth Jones, an African-American, refers to allied behavior as "being at my back." He has said to me, "Andrea, I know you are at my back on the issue of race equity—you're talking to white people who cannot hear me on this topic, you're out there raising these issues repeatedly, you're organizing with other whites to stand up to racism. And I'm at your back. I'm raising issues of gender equity with men, I am talking to men who cannot hear you, I've made a commitment to combat sexism."

Available to each one of us in the categories where we are dominant is the proud and honorable role of ally: the opportunity to raise hell with others like us and to interrupt the cycle of oppression. Because of our very privilege, we have the potential to stir up good trouble, to challenge the status quo, and to inspire real and lasting change. William Stickland, an aide to Jesse Jackson, once said: "When a critical mass of white people join together, rise up, and shout a thunderous 'No' to racism, we will actually alter the course of history."

Reducing Violence

When I ponder the tremendous change a national network of allies can make in this country, I think not only of issues of equity and empowerment, but also of how our work could lead to diminishing levels of violence in our society. Let us consider for a moment the critical connection between oppression and violence on one hand, and the potential role of allied behavior in combating violence on the other.

A major source of violence in our society is the persistent inequity between dominant and targeted groups. Recall that oppression is kept in place by two factors:

1. Ideology, or the propagation of doctrines that purport to legitimize inequality; and
2. Violence (or the threat of violence) by the dominant group against the targeted group.

The violence associated with each form of systemic oppression noticeably decreases when allies (or dominants) rise up and shout a thunderous "No" to the perpetuation of these inequities. Because members of the dominant group are conferred with considerable social power and privilege, they carry significant authority when confronting perpetrators of violence in their own group—when whites deter other whites from using violence against people of color, when heterosexuals act to prevent gay bashing, and so on.

Research studies have confirmed what observers and allies have been saying for years: that when a woman is the victim of ongoing, violent domestic abuse, it makes no difference to her chances of survival if she has counseling, takes out a restraining order, or learns to fight back. According to the studies, the only factor that statistically increases a woman's chances of survival is if the victimizer himself is exposed to direct and ongoing anti-battering intervention.

These studies have inspired the creation of model mentoring programs in places like Quincy, Massachusetts, Duluth, Minnesota, and New York City—programs in which men prone to violence against women work with other men through a series of organized interventions. The success of these programs has demonstrated that it is actually possible to interrupt and stop the cycle of violence among batterers. In 1992, for instance, the model program in Quincy helped cut the incidence of domestic homicide to zero. The Batterers Anonymous groups, in which men who are former perpetrators work with men who are current batterers, have also had remarkable success in breaking the habit of violence. These groups are allied behavior made manifest; their success in reducing the incidence of violence against women is now statistically proven.

In our society, oppression and violence are woven together: one leads to the other, one justifies the other. Furthermore, members of the dominant group who are not perpetrators of violence often collude, through their silence and inactivity, with those who are. Allied behavior is an effective way of interrupting the cycle of violence by breaking the silence that reinforces the cycle, and by promoting a new set of behavior through modeling and mentoring.

Providing Positive Role Models

Not only does allied behavior contribute to an increase in equity and a decrease in violence, but allies provide positive role models that are sorely needed by today's young people. The role of ally offers young people who are white, male, and in other dominant categories a positive, proactive, and proud identity. Rather than feeling guilty, shameful, and immobilized as the "oppressor," whites and other dominants can assume the important and useful role of social change agent. There have been proud allies and change agents throughout the history of this nation, and there are many alive today who can inspire us with their important work.

I often speak in high school classes and assemblies, and in recent years I have taken to doing a little informal survey from the podium. I ask the students if they can name a famous living white racist. Can they? Yes. They often name David Duke—he ran for President in their lifetime—or they sometimes name Senator Jesse Helms; and when I was in the midwest, they named Marge Schott, the owner of the Cincinnati Reds. It does not take long before a hand shoots up, or someone just calls out one of those names.

Following that little exercise, I ask the students, "Can you name a famous living white anti-racist (or civil rights worker, or someone who fights racism)?" Can they? Not very often. Sometimes there is a whisper or two, but generally the room is very quiet. So, recently, I have been saying: forget the famous part. Just name for me any white person you know in your community, or someone you have heard of, who has taken a stand against racism. Can they? Sometimes. Occasionally someone says "my mom," or "my dad." I have also heard "my rabbi, my teacher, my minister." But not often enough.

I believe that it is difficult for young people to grow up and become something they have never heard of. It is hard for a girl to grow up and become a commercial airline pilot if it has never occurred to her that woman can and do fly jet planes. Similarly, it is hard for young people to grow up and fight racism if they have never met anyone who does.

And there *are* many remarkable role models whom we can claim with pride, and model ourselves after. People like Laura Haviland, who was a conductor on the Underground Railroad and performed unbelievably brave acts while the slave-catchers were right on her trail; Virginia Foster Durr, a southern belle raised with great wealth and privilege who, as an adult, tirelessly drove black workers to and from their jobs during the Montgomery bus boycott; the Rev. James Reeb, who went south during the Mississippi Freedom Summer of 1964 to organize and march; Hodding Carter, Jr., editor and publisher of a newspaper in the Mississippi Delta who used his paper to battle for racial equity and who took considerable heat for his actions. And more: the Grimke sisters, Lucretia Mott, William Lloyd Garrison, John Brown, Viola Liuzzo.

There are also many contemporary anti-racists like Morris Dees, who gave up a lucrative law practice to start the Southern Poverty Law Center and Klan Watch in Alabama and bring white supremacists to trial; Anne Braden, active for decades in the civil rights struggle in Kentucky; Rev. Joseph Barndt, working within the religious community to make individual churches and entire denominations proclaim themselves as anti-racist institutions. And Peggy McIntosh, Judith Katz, and Myles Horton. And so many others. Why don't our young people know these names? If young people knew more about these dedicated allies, perhaps they would be inspired to engage in more anti-racist activities themselves.

Choosing Our Own Roles

We also need to consider our role as allies. In our own communities, would young people, if asked the same questions, call out our names as anti-racists? In areas where we are dominant, is our struggle for equity and justice evident? When we think about our potential role as allies, we need to recall a Quaker expression: "Let your life be your teaching." The Quakers understand that our words carry only so much weight, that it is our actions, our daily behaviors, that tell the true story.

In my own life I struggle with what actions to take, how to make my beliefs and my behaviors congruent. One small step that has had interesting repercussions over the last decade is the fact that my partner (who is male) and I have chosen not to be legally married until gay and lesbian couples can be married and receive the same benefits and legal protection that married heterosexual couples enjoy. A small step, but it has allowed us to talk with folks at the YMCA about their definition of "family" when deciding who qualifies for their "family plan"; to challenge people at Amtrak about why some "family units" receive discounts when traveling together and others do not; and to raise questions in the religious community about who can receive formal sanction for their loving unions and who cannot. These are not earth-shattering steps in the larger picture, but we believe that small steps taken by thousands of people will eventually change the character of our communities.

When we stop colluding and speak out about the unearned privileges we enjoy as members of a dominant group—privileges we have been taught for so long to deny or ignore—we have the potential to undergo and inspire stunning transformation. Consider the words of Gandhi: "As human beings, our greatness lies not so much in being able to remake the world, as in being able to remake ourselves."

In my own community, I have been impressed by the efforts of three middle-aged males who have remade themselves into staunch allies for women. Steven Botkin established the Men's Resource Center in Amherst, Massachusetts twelve years ago and put a commitment to eliminating sexism in its very first mission statement. Another Amherst resident, Michael Burkart, travels nationwide and works with top executives in Fortune 500 companies on the issue of gender equity in their corporations. And Geoff Lobenstine, a social worker who identifies as an anti-sexist male, brings these issues to his work in Holyoke, Massachusetts.

Charlie Parker once said this about music: "Music is your own experience, your thoughts, your wisdom. If you don't live it, it won't come out of your horn." I think the same is true about us in our role as allies—it is our own experience, our thoughts, our wisdon. If we don't live it, it won't come out of our horn.

Preparing for the Long Haul

Now I would be the first to admit that personally and professionally the role of ally is often exhausting. I know that it involves challenges—being an ally is difficult work, and it can often be lonely. We must remember to take care of ourselves along this journey, to sustain our energy and our zest for those ongoing challenges.

We must also remember that it is hard to go it alone: allies need allies. As with any other struggle in our lives, we need supportive people around us to help us to persevere. Other allies will help us take the small, daily steps that will, in time, alter the character of our communities. We know that allied behavior usually consists of small steps and unglamorous work. As Mother Teresa once said: "I don't do any great things. I do small things with great love."

Finally two additional points about us in our role as allies: First, we don't always see the results of our efforts. Sometimes we do, but often we touch and even change lives without ever knowing it. Consequently, we cannot measure our success in quantitative terms. Like waves upon the shore, we are altering the landscape—but exactly how, may be hard to discern.

Doubts inevitably creep up about our effectiveness, about our approach, about the positions we assume or the actions we take. But we move forward, along with the doubts, the uncertaintly, and often the lack of visible results. In our office, we have a famous William James quote on the wall to sustain us: "I will act as though what I do makes a difference." And, speaking personally, although my faith gets rattled, I try to act as though what I do does make a difference.

Second, there is no such thing as a perfect ally. Perfection is not our goal. When I asked my colleague Kenneth Jones what stood out for him as the most important characteristic of a strong ally, he said simply: "being consistently conscious." He didn't say "never stumbling," or "never making mistakes." He said:

"being consistently conscious." And so we do our best: taking risks, being smart, making errors, feeling foolish, doing what we believe is right, based on our best judgment at the time. We are imperfect, but we are steady. We are courageous but not faultless. As Lani Guinier said: "It is better to be vaguely right than precisely wrong." If we obsess about looking good instead of doing good, we will get caught in a spiral of ineffective action. Let's not get side-tracked or defeated because we are trying to be perfect.

And so we move ahead, pushing ourselves forward on our growing edge. We know that although none of us are beginners in dealing with issues of oppression and empowerment, none of us are experts either. These issues are too complex, too painful, and too pervasive for us to achieve a state of clarity and closure once and for all. The best we can hope for is to strive each day to be our strongest and clearest selves, transforming the world one individual at a time, one family at a time, one community at a time. May we summon the wisdom to be devoted allies today. May we walk the walk, living as though equity, justice and freedom for all have already arrived.

Like most activists, I carry a dream inside me. As I travel nationwide for my work, I can actually see signs of it becoming true. The dream is that we will create in this country a nonviolent army of allies that will challenge and break the cycle of oppression and usher in a new era of liberation, empowerment, and equity for persons historically targeted by systemic oppression. Within each individual is the potential to effect enormous change. May we move foward, claiming with pride our identities as allies, interrupting the cycle of oppression, and modeling a new way of behaving and believing.

5

ORGANIZING THE FIELDS

Kirk Nielsen

He wasn't exactly hoeing, but it was a very tough row. One day in 1993, not long after he migrated from southern Mexico to southwestern Florida to work in tomato fields, a seventeen-year-old Mexican kid named Lucas Benitez stood up for a breather. He was outside the town of Immokalee on a crew that was jamming wood

Reprinted by permission of *The Progressive*, 409 E. Main Street, Madison, WI 53703.

stakes into rows of soil to hold up tomato plants. He finished his row ahead of the others, and stopped to wait for them before launching into another set of rows. A field boss drove over in his pickup truck and ordered the teenager to resume staking.

"I always learned from my parents that one has to be respected for his work, and no matter if it's the most humble work that exists, you shouldn't let yourself be humiliated," Benitez says in Spanish. So he told the boss that he was merely resting for a minute while the others caught up. The boss got off the pickup truck and took a swing at him. Benitez dodged the blow, then squared off, clutching a tomato stake, prepared to fight. "I weighed 120 pounds and the boss weighed a little over 200," Benitez notes. The boss backed off. But when Benitez arrived the next morning to take the bus to the fields, the boss told him he had no job.

"This happened to various workers," Benitez says. "But many didn't report it, many didn't say anything. They just kept quiet, tolerating it."

That seventeen-year-old couldn't have known that more than a decade later his instincts for justice would land him at a table with executives from fast food empires. But the kid knew something was wrong, and found other farmworkers who were equally ready to rumble. They formed the Southwest Florida Farmworker Project. Soon they joined forces with Greg Asbed, a gringo from Florida Rural Legal Services, and changed their name to the Coalition of Immokalee Workers.

An actual beating in 1996 became the tipping point. A Guatemalan worker named Edgar arrived at the coalition's office, his shirt bloodstained and his nose "entirely deformed," Benitez recalls. "Edgar's only mistake was to want to drink some water." The coalition helped him file a complaint with the police, as other abused workers had previously done. But this time, coalition members decided to take some new steps. One night about 500 workers chanting "No more abuses!" marched to the residence of the contractor whose field bosses had assaulted Edgar.

The demonstration was only the first surprise for the contractor. Another awaited him the next morning at the vast parking lot where workers board buses bound for the fields. "When the boss came to this parking lot, nobody got in his bus," Benitez remembers. "When he started to say, 'Here, I have work,' the workers said, 'No, because people get hit there. So we're not going with you.' His whole work season was ruined."

Other contractors took heed and reined in the thuggery. "The bosses saw that the community was changing," Benitez says.

Those who didn't see it would eventually feel the coalition's sting, particularly the ones running a slave labor operation in Lake Placid, an isolated citrus grove region about sixty miles north of Immokalee. Members had heard rumors of the racket in 2000 and decided to send Romeo Ramirez, a coalition co-founder, to take an orange-picking job there. Three fellow harvesters promptly corroborated the rumors. The trio had arrived from Mexico via a human smuggling outfit and fell immediately into debt because the contractors had covered the transportation bill. The contractors—two gun-toting brothers named Juan and Ramiro Ramos—barred the new migrants from quitting until they cleared their debt. That was virtually impossible because the workers earned little more than subsistence wages. And they were in the middle of rural Florida.

Coalition members managed to plan a rescue mission with the three trapped workers over the phone. On an April evening in 2001, Benitez parked a car on the highway near an apartment building that served as a workers' dormitory. He then raised the hood, the sign that it was their rescue vehicle. A fourth worker had decided to join the three enslaved Mexicans, and they all ran to the car, leaving all their belongings behind. Benitez sped off with them.

Two years later, a judge sentenced the Ramoses to twelve years in prison, and a cousin of theirs to ten, for conspiracy, extortion, and illegal firearms possession. Coalition members have helped federal agencies prosecute a number of other slavery operations that have led to similarly long prison terms. In the latest case, five men pleaded guilty in September to running an enslavement scheme that included beating farmworkers and locking them in trucks. The defendants face sentences of ten to thirty-five years.

Ramirez, who won the Robert F. Kennedy Human Rights Award in 2003, along with Benitez and coalition member Julia Gabriel, is reticent about his personal role, preferring to give credit to the coalition as a whole.

Brutality notwithstanding, the bulk of the coalition's work has focused on simply winning decent pay for Florida's farmworkers. At first, it took the traditional approach, staging marches, holding strikes, and launching hunger strikes, trying to shame growers into paying more than the thirty-five cents per thirty-two-pound plastic bucket that tomato pickers were receiving in the late 1990s. At that rate, after working furiously for eight hours and picking literally a ton of tomatoes, one might take home a mere $20. Federal minimum wage and overtime pay laws don't apply to farmworkers, and the National Labor Relations Act exempts employers from having to negotiate with them. So in Florida, which lacks protections farmworkers enjoy in California and other states, tomato pickers are at the mercy of farm owners.

Coalition members believe their protests in the late 1990s helped spur incremental pay increases, but they concluded that strikes were an unrealistic tactic for the Immokalee farmworker community.

"People can stop working a week, maybe," Benitez says. "But after a week it's very difficult to do it, because we don't have any kind of strike support like some unions have." Tomato farm owners could easily weather short strikes and ignore marches. The workers needed another form of leverage to extract a living wage.

The idea to boycott fast food corporations arose in 2001 at one of the coalition's regular Wednesday night community meetings. Virgilio, an Oaxacan in his twenties, came up with it. "He said, 'You know what? We've done so many actions here against the farmers. We know that the buyers have a lot of power. Why don't we do something that's called a boycott, so that people stop buying?'" Benitez recalls. "We said, 'That's a good idea. Why *don't* we do it?'"

They chose Taco Bell for their first target and, since there were no Taco Bell restaurants in Immokalee, they drove to one on Highway 41 in Fort Myers. Total number of protesters: about fifteen. "Looking back on it now, it was something crazy. Such a small group of workers determined to confront such a big corporation like Taco Bell," Benitez says. "It was commitment more than anything. We have a mathematical equation, which is 'C plus C equals C.' Consciousness plus Commitment equals Change."

They also sent a letter to Taco Bell headquarters in Irvine, California, describing their working conditions and asking the company to help improve them. But a year passed without a reply. They sent another letter. A second year passed. Meanwhile, the boycott was gaining momentum, as a growing alliance of student and church groups across the United States joined the cause.

In March 2005, after four years of protests and spates of media reports on the appalling conditions in which the tomatoes in your burritos are produced, Taco Bell executives relented. They signed an agreement with the coalition under which Taco Bell pays 1.5 cents more per pound of Florida tomatoes. One cent goes to farmworkers, the other half-cent to tomato farmers to administer the new regimen. The additional cent means that a harvester who fills 100 thirty-two-pound buckets can now earn about $75 per day. But many growers still pay only half that much.

After two more years of grassroots organizing, boycott threats, and the intervention of Jimmy Carter, McDonald's executives signed a similar agreement with the coalition in 2007. In a remarkable turnaround, Burger King's chiefs capitulated only this past May, calling on tomato growers to be more socially responsible, but not before admitting that the Miami-based chain had hired a firm to spy on coalition members and student activists.

These historic agreements also commit the signatories to codes of conduct aimed at providing farmworkers the freedom from abuse that other American workers enjoy. An incident last fall at a farm that supplies tomatoes to Yum Brands, Taco Bell's parent company, provided the last big test. Tomato harvesters take their filled buckets to a truck and hand them to a supervisor called a *dumpeador*—a dumper—who deposits them into the back of a truck. In exchange, the worker receives a ticket to cash in at the end of the day. First, the dumpeador didn't want to give a harvester his ticket. The next time around, the *dumpeador* threw the empty bucket into the worker's face.

"It hit the worker in the nose," Benitez says. "The worker came to us. We communicated with Yum. Yum communicated with the grower's human resources office. The next day, the dumper who had done that had been fired from the company."

Since the Burger King accord, the coalition has aimed its Fair Food Campaign at tomato-consuming companies that are presumably more progressive. Whole Foods Market signed in September, saying the agreement was in line with the company's "core values."

But Chipotle, whose slogan is "Food with Integrity," has resisted. The Denver-based company's initial response was to eschew Florida tomatoes rather than pay an extra penny per pound. But, accusing the company of "Chipocrisy," the coalition wants Chipotle to join the fight.

Benitez doesn't understand why the company wouldn't bestow as much respect on tomato pickers as it does on free-range cattle. "They obligate ranchers to ensure the cows roam free, eating grass," Benitez observes. "The way that they demand that ranchers do that kind of thing, they can do the same with tomato producers."

6

SOLIDARITY AT THE LIQUOR STORE?
A New Project in Chicago Aims to Change Race Relations

Miriam Y. Cintron

Not many people consider the liquor store a place for racial solidarity, but that's the hope of Rami Nashashibi.

Nashashibi, who was born in Jordan and has lived in Chicago since the early 1990s, is the executive director of the Inner-City Muslim Action Network, better known by its acronym of IMAN. He's hoping his organization's new project, Muslim Run, will improve relations between Black residents in Chicago and the Muslim families who run liquor stores and other businesses in Black neighborhoods.

Since the 1970s and '80s, these stores have proliferated throughout predominantly Black communities in cities like Chicago, Detroit and Cleveland. Today, Muslim-owned businesses in Black communities have come to include fast-food restaurants, wireless phone outlets and tax agencies. But the Muslim-owned food and liquor stores are often a site of conflict between the business owners and Black residents. The stores are perceived as a source of major problems in poor neighborhoods because they may be dilapidated and poorly lit, and some are a source of liquor for minors, a haven for illegal drug transactions and a hangout spot for gang bangers, Nashashibi explained.

In Chicago, various community initiatives have sprung up over the years seeking to deny permits to store owners, not just because of moral concerns, but also because of how the community viewed these places.

Nashashibi's group is beginning by gathering information. This spring, the group completed a survey of 27 storeowners and 51 residents in conjunction with the Applied Research Center in the city's Englewood neighborhood.

Some of the more striking conclusions drawn from the survey: While 70 percent of surveyed store owners felt their businesses "have a positive impact on the community," only 18 percent of residents felt the same; and while more than half the residents surveyed felt there needed to be more grocery stores in the area, 72 percent also said that too many of the existing stores were Muslim-owned.

IMAN plans to put together focus groups around the issues raised in the surveys and facilitate conversation between both sides, establishing trust and allowing a deeper understanding of where each side is coming from. "People still rely on the most cursory stereotypical information about each other even with intense weekly contact," Nashashibi explained.

According to the survey, for Blacks, the only contact most had with a person outside their race was with store owners. Similarly, store owners have their most intense experiences with people outside their racial group while at work. IMAN wants to galvanize something positive out of the frequent contact between these two racial groups.

Other goals include improving the stores' appearances and encouraging changing the business practices of the owners, specifically to stop selling alcohol. Beginning in the 1960s, saying a business was Black-owned was about more than just the name on the lease, Nashashibi said. It signified a set of principles pioneered by Black Muslims about giving back to the community.

"We want to stimulate that sense within the Muslim community," Nashashibi explained, "and challenge Muslim store owners to implement the higher principles and ideals of their faith in their businesses."

7

UPLOAD REAL CHANGE

Roberto Lovato

While crisscrossing cracked streets to knock on the rickety doors of rundown row houses in Philadelphia's 14th Ward, Liza Sabater also found herself crossing the overlapping lines of political and technological history late last spring as she canvassed for Barack Obama's campaign.

"I got to spend some time with these Puerto Rican mechanics—guys most people wouldn't expect to have Internet access," said Sabater, an Afro-Puerto Rican

Reprinted with permission of *ColorLines Magazine*.

technologist who blogs at culturekitchen and The Daily Gotham. "But there—among the wrenches and jacks—were their cell phones and handheld devices they use to surf the Web."

Sabater, who helps nonprofits use technology to further their missions, canvassed in Philadelphia with her two sons and coordinated work in the 14th Ward with three Latino volunteers from the Obama campaign. She saw in the mechanics' mobile devices proof of her belief that "the 'digital divide' is a crock when we realize that laptops and desktops aren't the only ways to access the Web." But was the Obama campaign reaching these mechanics on their cells?

As they write future narratives of Obama's astounding rise, historians will likely foreground how skillfully the "change" candidate maneuvered around the racial, geopolitical and economic terrain of our crises-ridden time. Lost in the background of most of these narratives will be how Obama, the former community organizer, took what he learned about mobilizing working- and middle-class residents on Chicago's South Side and combined it with the stuff that actually wins elections: money, organizing and technology.

Obama's campaign for the White House deployed in unparalleled ways Web. 2.0 tools—the set of technological developments that turned the World Wide Web into the ubiquitous, mobile, wireless and interactive Web we use today. As this issue of *ColorLines* went to production in late August, Obama's Web site, Mybarackobama.com, was as interactive as any online social networking site. More than 10 million people had signed up at the site, and the campaign had raised millions of dollars. The Web site was the centerpiece of an online and offline political strategy that defeated the Clintons—one of the most powerful Democratic political dynasties—and, in the process, Obama took community organizing to new territory as he redefined the practice of electoral politics in the United States. Whatever the election results, Obama's campaign demonstrated that it's possible—and necessary—to go online and move people to action offline.

Sabater, who was born in New York's El Barrio neighborhood and raised in Mayaguez, Puerto Rico, was one of the many who responded to the campaign's appeal. She is still fascinated by how Obama's team fused state-of-the-art media and technology with the community organizing that the candidate learned in poor communities. Yet while she thinks community-based organizations can learn from the online organizing methods innovated by the Obama campaign, she also sees reason for concern in the cracked streets of Philadelphia. Sabater noted, for example, that although her fellow Obama campaign volunteers were by definition "Latinos," it was a poor decision on the part of the campaign to send three middle-class Chicanos from the west coast to a predominantly working-class, Spanish-speaking, Puerto Rican neighborhood.

"When my colleagues told me 'we don't speak Spanish' and couldn't interact with the people, I saw the interface problem," said Sabater, adding, "I saw the disconnect between the online and offline strategies, both of which are focused on middle-class people. Nobody's reaching out and targeting these working-class communities of color with technology. They don't think that the mechanics and maids use technology or vote." The Obama campaign fell through the cultural cracks in the street, while members in the community fell through the technological cracks of the campaign's Web strategy.

"The [Obama] campaign created a fantastic interface for people to join the campaign," Sabater said. "But it didn't do as well in reaching people who don't have laptops and whose technology is primarily their cell phones. There's an age and class and race gap."

Sabater saw these gaps while trolling the same streets canvassed in a previous era by W.E.B. Du Bois, who went door-to-door documenting how railroad tracks in Jim Crow Philadelphia served as a wood-and-steel color line dividing poor, politically disenfranchised Black neighborhoods from wealthier white neighborhoods where electoral participation was encouraged and expected.

Today, Sabater and others concerned with poor communities must prepare for similar but perhaps more nuanced racial, political and economic divisions in the city of brotherly love and other urban areas. If left to the folks who ran the Obama campaign, equity and freedom may well depend on which side of the silicon and fiber optic tracks a person lives on. If activists take to heart the lessons of this last presidential campaign, though, we might just see what political changes can happen among poor people when we combine media and technology with street-level political organizing beyond elections.

Anyone dealing with what are traditionally defined as "racial" or "social justice" issues (housing, labor, criminal justice, immigration, LGBT, women's issues, etc.) will have to figure out the "interface" problems identified by Sabater and others like U.C. Berkeley's danah boyd. A digital anthropologist, boyd caused considerable controversy when she wrote a paper in 2007 positing that MySpace was more working-class than Facebook, which she says tends to cater to older, more elite social networkers.

Whether we deploy MySpace or Facebook, those of us committed to pursuing the possibility of bottom-up democracy in the digital age will also have to confront the same kinds of issues Benjamin Franklin identified in Philadelphia. Back when newspapers began their long reign as the defining medium of politics, Franklin wrote: "Those who govern, having much business on their hands, do not generally like to take the trouble of considering and carrying into execution new projects. The best public measures are therefore seldom adopted from previous wisdom, but forced by the occasion." But one definitive difference between Franklin's age and ours is the degree to which our economy, our government and politics, and even our culture are for better and for worse being fundamentally reconfigured by media and digital technology.

The need to deploy media and technology as a force on those who govern is a daily concern for Chris Rabb, a Philadelphia resident, entrepreneur and founder of the popular political blog Afro-Netizen. Of particular concern to Rabb is the urgent need for Black, Latino and other communities to use media to flatten the deeply entrenched political pyramids built by the large national Black and Latino nonprofits born in the waning decades of the industrial age in the United States.

Many of these nonprofits, he says, center power in Washington, D.C., at the expense of the majority of Blacks and Latinos who are far from the Beltway.

"Hierarchies in Black and brown communities are as bad as in any other community," said Rabb, who also consults with nonprofit organizations about how to make media and technology a component of their core strategy. "There's so little power that people hold on to power as long as they can. Blacks are the most urban, overwhelmingly Democrat-leaning community in the country, but we have the least democracy. Black politicians last forever, and lots of our [nonprofit] organizations tend to be run by people who stay there for life."

Rabb thinks the stunning accomplishments of the Obama campaign mirror the ways in which technology gives communities the capacity to self-organize on a scale never before seen.

"We need to study the Obama movement," he asserted. "They weren't the first to use the media in this way, but he came along at that precise moment when the technology had matured, when the audience of media users had reached critical mass."

To illustrate his point, Rabb mentions the Jena 6 movement, which, he said, used media and technology to alter the game of "ethnic" politics. Initially ignored by the mainstream media and major civil rights organizations, as well as by traditional leaders, bloggers concerned about the Jena 6 case, like Color of Change's James Rucker and Rabb, took their case directly to the community by using the Web.

By combining Web 2.0 tools—blogs, MySpace, and other social networking sites and interactive Web sites—with traditional media like radio and newspapers, the more youthful organizers of the Jena 6 movement made it politically impossible for mainstream Black leaders like Al Sharpton, Jesse Jackson and NAACP leaders to ignore the cause. The tech-savvy organizers gathered hundreds of thousands of signatures, raised hundreds of thousands of dollars on the Web, and in the process, they informed, engaged and activated constituents. Similar media and generational dynamics can be found in the immigrant rights movement.

Policy people at the National Council of La Raza, the National Immigration Forum and the majority of large Latino and immigrant rights organizations were in the throes of defensiveness before the onslaught of the Sensenbrenner immigration bill, which sought to criminalize the undocumented. One jaded policy analyst told me at that time that the Republicans "are going to push Sensenbrenner through—and there's nothing we can do." Apparently, someone forgot to communicate the analyst's resignation to the local and regional grassroots groups who used media and technology to organize the largest simultaneous mass mobilizations in U.S. history in 2006.

Like those organizing the movement in support of the Jena 6, the local and regional networks at the core of the immigrant rights movement also deployed a number of media tools to bypass the lethargic hierarchies of the larger Washington-based groups. Many in the media focused their coverage on better-funded and (mainstream) media-savvy groups in the Beltway who rallied behind different versions of the McCain-Kennedy immigration bill, which, in its "bipartisan tradeoff" combined legalization with some of the most punitive immigration proposals in U.S. history. Left out of this coverage was the galaxy of organizations opposed to McCain-Kennedy.

In the face of such a limiting of the political debate around immigration, local and regional activists combined old-school media with a big "M" (television, radio, bullhorns and butcher paper) with new-school media with a small "m" (MySpace, text messaging, cell phones, radio, video and YouTube). Suddenly, mainstream media outlets were forced to cover the political messages that Latino teens were sending with their cell phones in the suburbs of Washington, D.C., and in rural Oregon.

While the mainstream media's immigration coverage remains in its default position of focusing on the larger, better-funded national immigrant groups in Washington, activists like Sabater are combining online and offline organizing to influence the political process around and coverage of immigration and other issues that strongly impact Latinos. Sabater joined other bloggers to form the Sanctuary, a bloggers' hub that combines information-sharing with offline activism. Members of the Sanctuary developed a survey of the presidential candidates and received coverage by CNN and other media outlets who usually interview only the National Council of La Raza and other large Latino organizations when it comes to "Latino issues." At a time when political theorists like Manuel Castells tell us that "media is the space of politics," the old rules just don't apply, and that can be good news for poor communities of all colors.

Regardless of the election outcome, Rabb, Sabater and others see valuable lessons in how the Obama campaign positioned itself to benefit from the epic self-organizing movement enabled by Web 2.0. It's especially critical for activists (and everyone else, for that matter) to learn how the Obama campaign used its Web site, Mybarackobama.com. More than 10 million people signed up at the site, and 1.5 million of those donated money. At the site, the campaign provided volunteers and organizers with campaign literature, virtual meeting spaces and other resources. Even viewers who might have been skeptical of Obama as a candidate or those not interested in electoral politics couldn't help but be a bit curious. At every turn, the site insisted on interactivity. In August, a huge banner on the site stated: "Who will be Barack's VP? Be the First to Know. Sign Up Now." Below it was the "make a difference" banner with ways to volunteer and find local events, and then, of course, there was the "Obama Map"—where a few clicks and the inputting of zip codes got Americans tuned in to groups supporting Obama in their neighborhoods. Indeed, by the time Obama's party gave him the official nomination in August, journalists and historians were already pointing out how the multimedia-genic Obama fit as well with the media of his time as did Kennedy at the dawn of the age of television.

"The next step of activism is for grassroots groups to connect online and offline organizing like Obama did, but targeting working-class people," said Sabater. "And the first step is for us to learn how our communities use their media and to engage them on their own terms."

Rabb agreed. "The big question is whether activists for social justice can make the leap from what an organizer candidate did in the presidential cycle to the kind of organizing needed at a time when media and technology are so central to the work of government and power," he said.

Rabb believes that groups who are organizing communities need to prioritize breaking down the barriers that separate media from their programmatic work. "It's the very nature of organizing to want to reach audiences on race, class, immigration and other issues" he said, adding, "People have to get with the fact that media's not replacing but complementing and enhancing their ability to do more with less, to achieve better and greater outcomes."

8

RETHINKING VOLUNTEERISM IN AMERICA

Gavin Leonard

About a year ago, an old friend of mine asked me if our old Mennonite church youth group—the one we both attended and he was now leading—could come down to Cincinnati's Over-the-Rhine neighborhood to do some volunteer work. I work for an organization that develops and maintains affordable housing in this city's poorest neighborhood. My friend thought it would be a good opportunity for the youth from the small suburban town Bluffton, Ohio, to see what is going on in the inner city.

I had been working with volunteers for about seven years now and lately, I had been thinking a lot about the two types of distinct volunteerism approaches: "charity" versus "solidarity." As I see it, charity means coming in and helping somebody, with little or no regard for what that person or group of people wants or how they want to get it. There's an assumption made that anything a volunteer does is helpful. It's a top-down process.

Solidarity, on the other hand, is about working with that somebody to identify what it is that the people who are being helped need and want, along with how they want to get it. Solidarity assumes equality or at least recognition of a volunteer's privilege that leads to working more collaboratively and with respect. Solidarity is based on an idea that social inequalities exist in a context that one needs to take time to understand. Working in solidarity requires patience.

The lines between charity and solidarity are never clearly down, and I'd say the chances that somebody is going to say they're all about charity, are pretty slim. But, given the opportunity to take a bird's eye view of an organization or individuals' interaction in a volunteer setting, I think it's possible to see the distinction.

I talked through some of these issues with my friend and expressed my desire for this group of volunteers to intentionally be in solidarity with people that they are trying to help. Theoretically, I saw the chance to develop a process that would start far before the group came to Over-the-Rhine and would continue long after.

With deeper knowledge of the situation they were entering, how they relate to it, and how that relates to national policies, I feel like the opportunity could exist for a truly long-term positive change. In my work locally, the best volunteers have been the people who came to the organization through a charity-minded group, and then stayed connected by themselves in various ways. People who read our newsletter, stop by just to check in, read books or materials we suggest—these are the folks who add real capacity and value in a model of solidarity.

Volunteers who are aware of their shortcomings, vulnerabilities, and stereotypes, and who are willing to confront them head on, make a lasting difference. There is a recognizable feeling of authenticity and truth that emerges as we begin to notice our own problems and issues while we are working with others to address their needs.

In contrast, my vision of a charity-minded volunteer is one where the experience is a single, short-term event. I've seen more than a few individuals take in difficult and complicated explanations of serious social issues and then within minutes walk away joking about this or that. I'm not saying people need to pour their lives into the organization they are supporting for that day or two—but a concerted effort to extend these conversations into peoples' everyday lives would be valuable in creating real, longer-term change.

I talked to my friend about the differences I saw between charity and solidarity and I was hopeful we could do more than just your typical weekend-charity outing to the hood. I suggested that the youth group participate in a process that led up to the trip to Cincinnati, and then spend significant time talking about it afterward. I suggested an essay that tackles some of these issues—a review of *Sweet Charity*, a book by Janet Poppendieck—as a starting point for discussion. It seemed to me that setting up structured conversations and background in the months prior to a visit would lead to an experience with considerably more depth and impact.

I heard back a little while later that my friend couldn't commit to a process; he just didn't have the time. He was passing it on to the new youth group leader, along with copies of our correspondence. The next time I heard from the new leader, it was to say that the youth did not have time to do something like this, and they were sorry, but they wouldn't be able to make it.

To say I was disappointed would be an understatement. I really had hoped that the group would be interested in engaging at this level. It's the kind of thing I really only felt safe asking of a church that I had attended for many years and I don't feel it was unreasonable.

Realistically, it's hard work. Working in solidarity takes a commitment and ability to listen and learn that often raises very tough issues that most of us would rather not deal with: racism, sexism, classism, homophobia, and other socially divisive realities can't be ignored once you really start to pay attention.

I wrote back expressing my feelings and decided that this was a fight I'd have to fight another day. As a leader on the non-profit side that works with volunteers, I'd like to share a level of responsibility here. I really need to work harder to carve out space and time to engage with potential volunteers in a way that not only suggests, but also supports a process of working towards solidarity. I also feel that the supervisors and community service liaisons at churches, schools, and universities need to carve out similar time and energy. At the end of the day, the full burden of moving such a process needs to be shared.

Engaging in a Better Way

My involvement as a volunteer has been fairly extensive for my age and I've spent a lot of time and thought on what it should look like. What I've come to believe is that we need to be very intentional, forthcoming, and thoughtful about how we engage in the communities we want to help.

Sweet Charity by Poppendieck is a well-researched look into the unintended consequences of charity work. It shows how volunteers are often just playing out their own guilt and working to achieve a level of personal fulfillment. It shows that charity often views the poor as sub-human and if and when this benevolent mentality is not checked it has the potential to actually hurt, not help, the people who are supposed to be gaining something. We often ignore the systemic problems that are actually causing the holes we seek to plug. I think she's right to question this process, and it's something that all of us should take a hard look at in the current context of the growing wealth disparity and increasing reliance on charities.

Charity often comes across as patronizing and disingenuous. Corporations often spend nearly the amount of money advertising the fact they made a contribution to a non-profit as the amount of the contribution itself. And it's truly shocking how few of the volunteers I interface with actually ask a heartfelt question.

Solidarity takes more time. To think about and learn about a person is difficult. Not to mention that poverty is depressing.

Still, without professing to have the whole thing figured out, I'd like to make four suggestions for working towards a better way of engaging as volunteers:

1. **Learn about the organization.** Spend some time learning about the organization you'll be going to work with before you start the job. Don't create more work for it—do your research independently and then ask questions.

2. **Learn about the larger issues.** Look for resources that focus on the systemic issues that create the conditions you'd like to see eradicated. That way you can join the dialogue on how to eliminate the problem itself, not just its symptoms. Ask thoughtful questions of the leader or liaison.
3. **Express your appreciation.** Recognizing that volunteer work is often much more beneficial to you—whether as an opportunity for personal fulfillment, or a way to see a place you might not otherwise have access to, or simply as a way to pay off your parking ticket—saying "thanks" is something far too few people do.
4. **Find small ways to engage after leaving.** Sign up for an email list, a newsletter, stop by once in a while. If all of us take baby steps towards becoming more engaged as active citizens, we'll be on the right track.

Leaders of non-profits should work to maintain an up-to-date resource list for volunteers, and leaders at institutions bringing volunteers could establish a checklist that they discuss with volunteers covering ways to stay engaged before, during, and after the brief engagement.

So, how do we actually implement these types of steps and conversations so that we are moving in a positive way towards solidarity?

Volunteerism in America is a complicated web of individuals, groups, and institutions that are all shaping how we view people that are not like us. I think it is high time we make a concerted effort to share the responsibility and move towards a long-term solidarity model for volunteerism that is respectful, dignified, and purposeful. Charity will only get us so far.

HERE. NOW. DO SOMETHING.

William Rivers Pitt

So we come to it in the end, the great battle of our time, in which many things shall pass away. But at least there is no longer need for hiding. We will ride the straight way and the open road and with all our speed. The muster shall begin at once.

—THEODEN, LORD OF THE MARK

Reprinted by permission of the author.

There's an old man who lives down the street from my house. I made a point to introduce myself to him roundabout last September, after he put a No War sign up in his front yard. About a week before Bush showed up here for a GOP fundraiser, he put up a second sign describing the date, time and location of Bush's arrival. Under this information was a single word: PROTEST! His hand was twisted with arthritis when I shook it, but he still used it to drive those signs into the ground.

Every couple of months, some friends and I make a trip to the Kinko's copy shop. We run off about 500 flyers, crafted that day, which outline a number of issues and facts the mainstream media doesn't bother with anymore. The flyers break down data on the PATRIOT Act, the push for war in Iraq, the unmentionable questions surrounding 9/11, and Bush connections to corporate crime. We take these and station ourselves in well-traveled parts of the city. We hand them out with a smile. We have never gone home with extras, and often people come back for two or three copies to share with friends. Through internet networking, the flyers we create wind up getting handed out on streetcorners all across the country. People leave them at bus stops, libraries, doctor's offices and in supermarkets.

Last week I went back in time for a while. It had been 10 years since I'd heard the Grateful Dead live in concert, eight years since the band played a note. Walking down Canal Street towards the Fleet Center, The Other Ones, a band comprised of all the surviving Grateful Dead members, was in town for a show. I could almost see the old Boston Garden in the distance, through the crowds that hadn't changed a lick in almost 4,000 days.

After the concert was over (spectacular, in case you were wondering) I made my way outside towards the train. I was waylaid by a young woman handing out flyers which argued against war in Iraq. Her brother works the crowd, as well, along with several others. They had volunteered with a group called Peace Action.

There is an email making the rounds nowadays carrying an article by a right-wing radio personality named Chuck Baldwin. The article was originally sent out on an email list called The Republican, and is entitled "Bush Government Out of Control."

Mr. Baldwin laments the passage of the Homeland Security legislation and the establishment of the outrageously Orwellian "Total Information Awareness" database. This database, run by convicted felon John Poindexter of Iran/Contra fame, will collect personal data on your purchases—including guns—along with school grades, websites visited and trips taken. In one paragraph, Mr. Baldwin asks a powerful question: "Does that mean one must leave the Republican Party in order to fight for liberty? Maybe so."

Leaders never lead, unless the people lead them. Leaders, left to their own devices, will follow the call of the folks writing the checks. For too long in this country, the people have abdicated their basic responsibility—to rule. In the absence of the people's leadership, our elected officials have begun listening to the corporations and the well-funded interest groups instead. The result is the mess we are in. This is without question a bipartisan problem that affects both parties. Look no further than the fact that the vast majority of newly registered voters sign up as Independent.

Maybe it has gone too far to be fixed. Between the PATRIOT Act and this new Homeland Security Department, there is very little substance left to the founding documents and principles that once were the people's sword and shield. The media has become an adjunct mouthpiece for the corporations that own the outlets, and the politicians who receive the corporate donations and thus dutifully toe the line shout into this echo chamber and drown out all dissent. Those few elected officials who do stand against the nation we are devolving into see their voices disappear in the wake of parroted noise. Sometimes, those who speak out wind up dead.

So. If leaders no longer lead, and if the information font has become unutterably corrupted, what is left? Demonstrably, the instinct to go tharn in the road, hoping those onrushing headlights will swerve at the last moment, has become predominant among most Americans. We have reached a point, however, where inaction is not only inadvisable, but worthy of the charge of treason.

Do something.

You do not have to be rich or powerful or well-connected to erect a sign in your yard. You do not have to be a salesperson to hand out informational leaflets at a bus stop. You do not have to be young to volunteer with an organization. You do not have to be liberal to know that something is badly, badly out of joint.

Do something. Do anything.

At the end of the day, it does not matter what you do. A sign in your yard, a button in the lapel of your coat, an email sent around to friends, will have a small but salutary effect. It will make others in the country who feel isolated in their fear that something has gone terribly wrong understand that they are not alone. Big storms gather around small particles.

Think on this as you give thanks for what you've got. The moment is here, now, upon us all. Even the smallest effort can and will make a difference. On a large enough scale, it could change the face of the world. Be thankful for that, as well, and do something with it.

Suggestions for Further Reading

Colby, Anne, and William Damon. *Some Do Care: Contemporary Lives of Moral Commitment*. New York: Free Press, 1992.

Dees, Morris. *A Season of Justice: A Lawyer's Own Story of Victory Over America's Hate Groups*. New York: Touchstone Books, 1991.

Eisenstein, Zillah R. *The Color of Gender: Reimagining Democracy*. Berkeley: University of California Press, 1994.

Featherstone, Liza. *Selling Women Short: The Landmark Battle for Women's Rights at Wal-Mart*. New York: Basic Books, 2004.

Kivel, Paul. *Uprooting Racism: How White People Can Work for Racial Justice*. New York: New Society Publishers, 1996.

Marable, Manning. *The Great Wells of Democracy: The Meaning of Race in American Life*. New York: Basic Civitas Books, 2003.

Reddy, Maureen T. *Everyday Acts against Racism*. Seattle: Seal Press, 1996.

Spring, Joel. *Deculturalization and the Struggle for Equality: A Brief History of the Education of Dominated Cultures in the U.S.*, 6th ed. New York: McGraw-Hill, 2009.

Stoltenberg, Jon. *The End of Manhood: A Book for Men of Conscience*. New York: Dutton, 1993.

Thompson, Becky. *A Promise and a Way of Life: White Antiracist Activism*. Minneapolis: University of Minnesota Press, 2001.

INDEX